The Big Book of Hints

from Heloise®

The Big Book of Hints

from Heloise®

A Perigee Book

HELOISE is a federally registered trademark licensed exclusively to Heloise, Inc.

A Perigee Book
Published by The Berkley Publishing Group
A division of Penguin Putnam Inc.
375 Hudson Street
New York, New York 10014

Perigee special sales edition: March 2002

Perigee special sales edition ISBN: 0-399-52831-8

Visit our website at www.penguinputnam.com

The Library of Congress has catalogued the Perigee edition
of *All-New Hints from Heloise*® as follows:

Heloise.
    All-new hints from Heloise
       p.   cm.
    "A Perigee original."
    ISBN 0-399-51510-1
    1. Home economics.   I. Title.
    TX158.H43   1992   88-33651 CIP
    640 .2—dc19

The Library of Congress has catalogued the Perigee edition
of *Heloise*® *from A to Z* as follows:

Heloise.
    Heloise from A to Z
       p.   cm.
    ISBN 0-399-51750-2 (trade paperback : alk. paper)
    1. Home economics.   I. Title.
    TX158.H434   1992   91-43955 CIP
    640—dc20

Printed in the United States of America
10 9 8 7 6 5 4 3 2

ACKNOWLEDGMENTS

What would I do without my everfaithful research editor, Marcy Meffert, who smooths out the lumps and bumps for me; my King Features editors Merry Clark, who gives me guidance and laughs, and Sandy Klink, who keeps me within the borders; and Roger Scholl of The Putnam Publishing Group, who has been patient and gentle when giving me directions!

If you have a hint you would like to share with me, don't hesitate to write to me at the address below. However, because of the volume of mail I receive, not every letter can be answered personally.

Heloise
P.O. Box 795000
San Antonio, TX 78279

—Heloise

To Mr. Thurston Twigg-Smith, President and Publisher, and Mr. Buck Buchwach, Executive Editor of the *Honolulu Advertiser,* who over 30 years ago gave my mother, the original Heloise, a chance to start her column. Also to my dear, wonderful father, Mike Cruse, who told her she could do it, gave her emotional and business support, and to this day helps me run the office.

Thank you, gentlemen.

—Heloise

CONTENTS

All-New Hints from Heloise

INTRODUCTION   23

CHAPTER 1.   SAVING TIME IN THE
             KITCHEN   29
FAMILY KITCHENS   29

APPLIANCES   30
Appliance Life Expectancies   31

DISH-WASHING   32
Dishwasher Efficiency   32
Getting Sparkling Clean Dishes and Glassware   33
Cleaning Your Dishwasher   34
Trouble-Shooting   35
Washing Dishes by Hand   36

REFRIGERATOR AND FREEZER CARE 37
Cleaning and Defrosting Refrigerators and Freezers 37
Storing Food in the Refrigerator 38

CLEANING KITCHEN RANGES 39
Continuous-Cleaning and Self-Cleaning Ovens 39
Cleaning Standard Ovens 41
Cleaning Range Tops 41

MICROWAVE OVENS 42
Microwave Oven Utensils 43

GARBAGE DISPOSALS 45
Disposal Odors 45

APPLIANCES 47

KITCHEN CLEANING TIPS 49
Countertops 49
Chopping-Block Countertops 49
Tile Countertops 49
Kitchen Sinks 50
Pots and Pans 51
Cast-Iron Cookware 51
Non-Stick Pans 53
Enamelware 53
Glass Cookware 54
Cleaning Silver 54
Cleaning Tin 55
Cleaning Copper and Brass 55

HOME PEST CONTROL 56
Roach Extermination Formula 56
Weevil Extermination 57

COFFEE AND TEA BEVERAGES 59
Coffee 59
Tea 60

LEFTOVERS 62
Being Creative with Leftovers 62
Keeping Track of Stored Leftovers 63

CONTENTS _____ *11*

COOKING AND CLEANUP 63
Cooking Tips 64
Microwave Oven Cooking Tips 65
Using Spices and Herbs 65
Cleanup 67

UTENSILS 67

CHAPTER 2. SAVING SUPERMARKET DOLLARS 70

SAVING TIME AND $$$ BY PLANNING AHEAD 70
Menus and Shopping Lists 71
Coupons 71
Coupon Holders 72

SHOPPING TRIPS 73
Buying Produce 75
Buying Fruits and Berries 76
Buying Vegetables 79
Buying Staples 81

STORING 82
Cereals, Flour, Grains 82
Spices 83
Canned Goods 83
Fresh Vegetables 84
Eggs 85
Cheeses 86
Meat, Poultry, Seafood 86
Temperature Danger Zone 87
Storage Limits for Keeping Food 87
Refreezing 90
Special-Care Foods 91
Champagne and Wine 91

CHAPTER 3. IN AND AROUND THE HOUSE 95

BATHROOMS 96
Cleaning Tiles and Bathroom Fixtures 97
Cleaning the Toilet Bowl 99

Cleaning the Bathtub   100
Shower Cleaning   101
Mirrors   102

**CLEANING AND ORGANIZING BEDROOMS
AND LIVING AREAS**   103
Organizing and Cleaning Bedrooms   103
General Cleaning   105

GENERAL CLEANING AND REPAIRING TIPS   106
Picking Up Clutter   106
Knickknacks   106
Lamps   106
Cleaning Oil Paintings and Frames   107
Dusting and Polishing Wood Furniture   107
Repairing Furniture   109
Refinishing Furniture   111
Carpet Care   112
Upholstered Furniture   114
Dry-Mopping, Sweeping, Scrubbing, and/or Waxing Non-Carpeted
  Floors   115
Wood Floor Care   116
Squeaky Floors   117
Care of Vinyl Floors   118
Draperies and Blinds   120
Cobwebs and Other Fuzzy Dust   120
Walls and Woodwork   121
Wall Coverings   121
Heavy Metal Cleaning   122
Decorating Tips   123
Hang-Ups   123
Decorating Windows   126
Wallpaper Decorating Tips   126
Extraordinary Decorating with Ordinary Things   127
Storage Space to End Clutter   127

CHAPTER 4.   HOME MAINTENANCE   129
PLUMBING   130
Drippy and Noisy Faucets   130
Clogged Drains   131
Plumbing Repairs   132
Noisy Pipes   132

Frozen Pipes 133
Toilet Tank and Bowl 133
Septic Tanks 134
Water Heaters 134
Water Purifiers 135

USING TOOLS 135
Hammering Safely 135
Using Screwdrivers 135

WINDOW REPAIRS 136
Window Screens 136

REPAIRING DOORS 137

REPAIRING WALLS 137
Patching Walls 137

PAINTING OUTSIDE AND INSIDE THE HOUSE 138
When to Paint 138
Color Selection 139
Preparing the Surface for Paint 140
Using a Ladder Safely 141
Dripless Painting 142
Cleaning Up 142
After the Job Is Over 144
Storing Paint 144
Painting Cupboards and Cabinets 145
Spray Painting 145

DO'S AND DON'TS FOR HOME SECURITY 146
Fire Safety 148

WASHING WINDOWS AND LARGE OBJECTS 150
Windows 150
Your House 150
Polishing Large Appliances 150
Car Washing and Maintenance 151

GARAGES 152
Parking Your Car in the Garage 152
Greasy Garage Floors 153
Storing Things in the Garage 153

THE FINAL WORD ON MAINTENANCE 154

CHAPTER 5. PLANTS AND YARD CARE 155

HOUSE PLANTS   155
Planting Pits and Seeds   155
A Medicinal Plant   156
Plant Cuttings   157
Watering Your Plants   157
Watering Plants When You're on Vacation   158
Drainage Tips   159
Plant Pest Control   159
TLC (Tender, Loving Care) for Plants   160
Indoor Vegetable Gardens   161
Storing Garden Pesticides   162

OUTSIDE THE HOUSE   163
Digging into Gardening   163
Getting Gardening Help   164
Shrubs and Other Plants   165
Composting   165
Garden Beds   166
Planting an Herb Garden   167
Planting from Seeds   168
Growing Fruits and Vegetables   169
Getting Rid of Plant Pests Without Strong Insecticides   170
Lawn Care   171
Watering   172
Gardening Equipment   173
Garden Walls and Fences   174
Stepping Stones, Walkways, Driveways   175
Snow Shoveling and Ice Removal   175
Outdoor Lighting   176

SWIMMING POOLS   176
Pool Safety   177
Keeping the Pool Clean   178
Mowing the Grass Near the Pool   178
Pool Cleaning   178
Keeping the House Clean and Your Sanity When You Have a
  Pool   178
Wading Pools for Small Children   179
Other Uses for Small Plastic Wading Pools   179

CHAPTER 6. CHILDREN 181

BABIES 181
Bringing Baby Home 182
Feeding Baby 183
Breast-Feeding 185
Giving Baby Solid Foods 186
Feeding Toddlers and Young Children 187
High Chair Helps 188
Bath Time 189
Baby's Laundry 191
Little Tips for Little People Care 192
In a Pinch 193
Teething Pain 193

KEEPING KIDS SAFE 194
Safety for Kids' Sake 194
Toy Safety 194
Poisonous Plants 195
General Safety Tips 196
Safety When Kids Help Around the House 197

SPECIAL CHILDREN'S CARE 197
Caring for a Sick Child 197
Getting Dressed 199

HAVING FUN WITH CHILDREN 200
Birthday Parties 201
Playing with Kids 202
Traveling With Children 203
General Tips for Traveling with Children 204
Hiring Someone for Child Care in Your Home 205
Dealing with Older Children 206
Allowances 207
Grandparenting 208
Families Are Forever 208

CHAPTER 7. CLOTHING CARE 210

STAIN REMOVAL 211
Pesky Stains 213

LAUNDRY TIPS   217
Putting Away the Laundry   218
Trouble-Shooting Washers   219
Trouble-Shooting Dryers   220
Laundromats   220
Several Ironing Tips   221
Ironing Travel Hints   224
How to Iron a Shirt or Blouse   224
How to Iron a Skirt   225
How to Iron Pants   225
Ironing Boards   226
Dry Cleaning   226

QUICK CLOTHING REPAIRS   227

SEWING   228
Using Patterns   230
Storing Sewing Supplies   231

CLOSETS   232
Closet Cleaning   232
Donate Your Discards   233
Ending Closet Clutter   234
Storing Infrequently Worn or Seasonal Garments   235

CLOTHES SHOPPING   236

CHAPTER 8. PERSONAL TIPS   239

ORGANIZING YOURSELF   239
Letter Writing   241
Bill Paying   242

KEEPING YOURSELF HEALTHY   244
Exercising   244
Eating Right   245
Cholesterol in Our Diets   246
Quality Protein Combinations   247
Salt   248
Sugar   248
Fiber   249
Beverages   249

If You Need to Lose Weight 249
Your Skin 251
If You Still Smoke 252
Having a Healthy Smile—Dental Health 254
Those Sneezy, Wheezy Days with Allergies 255

THE EYES HAVE IT 256
Sunglasses 257
Eyeglasses 257
Contact Lenses 258
Choosing the Right Type of Contact Lens 259
The Taco Test for Determining If Lenses Are Backward 259

MAKE YOURSELF COMFORTABLE 259

FIRST AID FOR POISONING 261
Syrup of Ipecac and Epsom Salts 261
The Poison Control Center Number 261
Common Potentially Poisonous Household Products 261

CHAPTER 9. WORKING COUPLES 263

WORKING COUPLES 263
Taking Self Time 264

DINING IN AND OUT BUT ON THE RUN 265
Eating Out 265
Eating at Home 266

A PLACE TO LIVE 266

MONEY MATTERS 267
Managing the Budget 268
Saving Tips 268

SETTING UP A HOME OFFICE 268
Finding Office Space 269
Home Office Hours 269
Tax Breaks for Home Business Offices 269
Office Furniture and Equipment 270

PERSONAL COMPUTERS   271
General Computer Use Tips   271
Power Surge Protectors   272
Transporting Disks   273
Working, Writing, Editing, Saving, Moving Copy Around   274
Buying a Computer   276
Learning How to Use It and Getting Rid of Computer Phobia   276
Dealing with the Glare of Computer Screens   277
Computing in Comfort   277
Speaking Computerese   278
Computers as Household Helpers   280
Printers   281

**CHAPTER 10.   REC-TECH: TELEVISION, STEREOS,
                CAMERAS, AND MORE**   283

TODAY'S TECHNOLOGY   283
General Tips   283
Television   285
Home Satellite Television   286
Video Cassettes and Recorders   287
Videotape Care   289
Caring for Your VCR   289
Portable VCRs/Camcorders   290
Videotaping Tips   290
Audio Cassette Tapes   292
Storing Audio Cassette Tapes   293

PUTTING IT ON TAPE   293
Cassette-Taping Tips   293

MUSICAL NOTES   296
Compact Discs   296
Compact Disc Players   297
Record Players/Turntables   298
Records   299
Speakers   301
Headsets and Stereo Headphones   302
Audio-Video Furniture   302
When the TV Tube Plays Its Last Picture Show   303

Cameras   303
Carrying Around Audio/Video Equipment   305
Rec-Tech Information Source   306

HELP TECH   306
Answering Machines   306
Telephone Installation   308
Cordless Phones   309
Multi-Function Phones   309
Car Phones   310
Intercom Systems   310
TV Shopping Channels and Offers   311

COMFORT TECH   312
Air-Conditioning   312
Programmable Thermostats   314
Ceiling Fans   314
Humidifiers   314
Dehumidifiers   315
Heaters   316
Electric Blankets   317

CHAPTER 11. PETS   318

CHOOSING A PET   318

GENERAL PET FIRST-AID AND HEALTH TIPS   320
Pet Dental Care   322
Fleas   323

TRAVELING WITH YOUR PET   325
Legal Requirements for Transporting Pets   326
How to Select a Pet Carrier   326
When Your Pet Is a Car Passenger   326

BIRDS   327

CATS   328
Disciplining a Cat   328
Cat Toys   329
Cat Scratchers   329

Cat Health   330
Neutering and Spaying   330
Cat Litter Boxes   331
Cat Carriers   332

DOGS   332
Bringing a Puppy Home   332
Housebreaking a Puppy   332
Heartworm Medication   334
Feeding Your Dog   334
General Dog Care Tips   334

TROPICAL FISH   335
Choosing Tropical Fish   335
Maintaining Aquariums   337
Aquarium Equipment   338
Fish Nutrition   339

GERBILS, HAMSTERS, GUINEA PIGS   339

WILD ANIMALS   341

LOSS OF A PET   341

CHAPTER 12.   ENTERTAINING   343

HAVING FUN AT YOUR OWN PARTY   343
Food Planning   346
Using Your Freezer for Parties   347
The "Good China, Crystal, and Linens"   348

TABLEWARE   349
Storing China, Crystal, Serving Pieces   349
Tableware Tricks   350
Heating Plates   352

LINENS   353
Table Setting   353
Linen Laundering   353
Repairing Linens   354
Storing Linens   354
Miscellaneous Tips   355

BRIDAL/GROOM SHOWERS AND WEDDINGS   357
Shower Memories   359

BABY SHOWERS   361
Other Help for Mom   362

LONG-DISTANCE BRIDAL AND BABY SHOWERS   362

LONG-DISTANCE BIRTHDAY PARTY   362

GENERAL PARTY TIPS   363
Organizing a Co-Hosted Party   363
Where's the Party?   364
Traffic Flow   364
Breaking the Ice   364

CHAPTER 13.   LEAVING THE HOME BEHIND   367

PLANNING YOUR TRIP   368
Buying Airline Tickets   368
Dealing with Travel Agents   369
How to Complain About Poor Travel Service   369
Lost Luggage   370
Vacation Information Sources   371
Travel for Handicapped People   371
Deciding on Vacation Ideas   371
Finding a Place to Stay   372
Cruises   372
Boating   373
Traveling by Car   374
Renting a Car   376
Calculating Expenses of Car Travel   376
Eating Out While on Vacation   377
Tipping   377
While You Are Gone   379

GETTING PACKED   379
Carry-On Luggage or Checked Luggage   379
Travel Wardrobes   380
Men's Wardrobes Need Coordinating Too   381

General Tips on Selecting Travel Clothes 381
How to Pack 382
Don't Forget Your Comfies 384
Packing the Essentials 385
Travel Checklist 385
Crushed Clothing 386
Other Hints 387
When You Travel Outside the United States 388

CAMPING AND HIKING 389
Hiking 389
What to Wear 389
Trudging On 390
Insects—Unwelcome Outdoor Companions 390
Hiking with Pets 391
Sleeping Bags 391
Disposable and Homemade Camping Aids 391
Eating in the Wilderness 393
Camping with Children 394

APPENDIX: THE HELOISE SURVIVAL KIT 396

INDEX 397

Heloise from A to Z 415

Acknowledgments
Preface 421
A to Z 425
Spots and Stains 810
Odors 832

INTRODUCTION

When the "Hints from Heloise" newspaper column began thirty years ago, one mention of using cocoa butter to help heal a minor burn or using boric acid to rid your house of roaches caused a "run" on these items in drugstores. The reader reaction is the same today. Every time I mention using white iodine to strengthen fingernails, my pharmacist asks me to please let him know about it ahead of time, because he just can't keep it on the shelves. So, although the column has spanned several decades, Heloise fans are still as loyal and numerous as ever, if not more so!

The fan of thirty years ago was a "housewife," but today's fan is anyone, young or old, male or female, whose life-style demands saving time, money, and energy.

When my mother began this column thirty years ago, one of her carpet cleaning hints came from the Orient, where she lived with my military-career father. Some of her Chinese friends showed her how they cleaned their carpets by rubbing them with the cut side of cabbages which had been chopped in half. Yes, it works, but you need a ton of cabbages!

As the Heloise fans grew to the millions, Mother's kitchen cupboards became famous, for they had been rendered nearly paintless from testing so many readers' cleaning solution hints. My jeans and sneakers were always game for testing reader hints; most worked but some were disasters!

I grew up with Heloise hints, as did most of America, and this is certain: Although the times, the hints, and the fans may have changed, the need for hints is greater than ever before. The sources of information for hints have evolved, so I have to consult with experts in a wide range of fields, major manufacturers, government agencies, and consumer information services.

For example, I can't suggest rubbing carpets with cabbages anymore. While most people had wool carpets thirty years ago, today's carpets are into second and third generations of improved man-made fibers and blends of fibers, and each has its own peculiarities.

I don't test cleaning hints on my cupboards. With the vast selection of paints, varnishes, and other finishes used today, my only recourse, if I'm to provide valid Heloise hints, is to call a paint and varnish research facility or a professional association to find out what cleaning preparation will work on which surface.

Just as the way we keep house has changed, the keepers of houses have changed. People who used to run vacuum cleaners and mixers are using microwave ovens and computers. Instead of just watching our television sets, we tape and view movies with our VCRs.

Throughout this new Heloise hints book, you'll find that tips on dealing with the new products and technology that are a part of our homes and life-styles have been included, along with some of the classic Heloise helps readers have enjoyed for thirty years.

Our homes are filled with hi-tech electronics that help us live well if we use them efficiently, but hi-tech has to help us instead of making our lives more complicated.

Perhaps computers are the most prominent of the new hi-tech electronics in American homes. Adults who didn't learn about computers in school have been pushed into the computer age by their jobs. Many adults learn about computers from their children, who view them as ordinary classroom equipment, on the same level with the pencils and Big Chief tablets their parents used in "the olden days." Most of us who work on computers don't care about their inner workings; we just want to know how we can get the most use from them. We don't need information overload—when you ask somebody for the time, you don't want an explanation of how a watch works. I've attempted to include a wide variety of advice and suggestions on how you can use your home computer, if you own one, to help in the organizing and running of daily life—from grocery lists and menu planning to record keeping and more.

In fact, the "Hints from Heloise" column and this book are produced on computers and the copy is circulated via modem to computers in three cities: San Antonio, where I have my office; New Orleans, where my research editor, Marcy Meffert, lives; and New York, where my King Features editors, Merry Clark and Sandy Klink, work. We will share what we've learned about juggling computer data later in the book.

As we approach the 1990s, over 55 percent of today's women work outside as well as in their homes. For these women, time is more valuable than money. They aren't likely to recycle such things as egg cartons, aluminum foil, and other containers, nor do many of them sew or spend most of their time cooking or cleaning. (I should note that when the Heloise column began, aluminum foil was a new, wonderful household aid!) Today's busy part-time homemakers haven't the time, energy, or desire to do the "extraordinary" tasks accomplished by full-time homemakers.

Whether or not we personally approve of these changes, we can't escape reality; changes have occurred and are here to stay. Women are making choices, and whether we are full-time or part-time homemakers we must respect those choices. Also, we have to recognize that for those who work outside the home, household chores are often shared with spouses, children, roommates, and hired help.

While those who stay home may seem to have the time to do it all, they need help too. A big Heloise hug to the unsung heroes who also contribute their time and energy outside the home, volunteering time to their communities and getting paid in thank-you certificates and plaques instead of money.

Whether they work for money or thank-yous, working women need help, and not all of them are getting it. *Working Mother* magazine (February 1988 issue) reported on a survey that revealed that few of the 2,811 women interviewed got regular help from spouses or children. Of these women, 77 percent prepared dinner and 64 percent cleaned up afterwards without help. Only 17 percent of husbands, 6 percent of eldest daughters, and 5 percent of eldest sons cleaned up after dinner as a regular chore. Of these women, 92 percent did laundry regularly and only 25 percent had children or husbands who regularly did laundry. Some children are being recruited for housework; this magazine survey revealed that eight-year-olds were using microwave ovens and vacuum cleaners and eleven- and twelve-year-olds were using washers and dryers. A Johnson's Wax survey of 1,409 households revealed that women still do about 84 percent of the housecleaning and that women, ages twenty-five to forty-four, spend about 6.8 hours a week on housework, while men spend only 2.4 hours a week doing housework.

You don't need any more numbers to see why so many women feel tired, overworked, and underappreciated. Getting rid of that tired, worn-out excuse "I don't know how" is the best way to get help and therefore have more time "to smell the daisies."

Which brings me to the reason for writing this new Heloise hints book. In addition to tips on how to do things better, more quickly, and more economically, you'll find that some of the information in this book is very basic, such as how to iron or what exactly to do when cleaning a room.

I'm hoping that whoever is in charge of running the household—and not all the in-charge people are women—will be able to use this book when writing notes to household helpers—for example, "Please start [the laundry, supper, cleaning the bathrooms, etc.]. See page _____ in *All-New Hints from Heloise.*" The pages to use for a particular job can be paper-clipped and the specific way of doing a chore can be highlighted so that the helper knows exactly what to do.

I hope the in-charge person will make a copy of the stain removal section, then thumbtack it to the wall above the washer so that all members of the household can get their own stains out before the stains have set. A copy of the room cleaning steps can be tacked on a bedroom door.

Now, we all know that not everyone lives in the so-called nuclear family with two parents and 1.7 or 2.5 children, a dog, two cats, and a bowl of fish or cage of gerbils. Many men and women are choosing to remain single or marry much later in life. *Over 50* magazine, for example, reports that twenty-two million people over fifty live alone by choice. This book will help people who are on their own for the first time, whether they are students, formerly married people, or others who have been previously uninvolved with the responsibilities of caring for themselves.

The housekeeping priorities for people who don't live in a nuclear family differ from those who do. Moreover, as a result of changing priorities, lifestyles have changed. People whose moms slaved for hours in the kitchen to entertain guests are likely to serve some store-bought deli treat—before they go out to a restaurant dinner. The emphasis in entertaining has shifted to one of expediency and convenience.

"Priority" is a major buzzword today. In a sense, my hints have always been about priorities. Do you want to spend your time cleaning the bathroom tiles with a toothbrush? Or would you rather visit a friend or read a book? You make the choice; you set your own priorities.

"Clean" to some people means uncluttered; to others, it's totally and antiseptically spotless and shining. To still others, "clean" is a four-letter word, something to be avoided whenever possible.

When I travel throughout the country, people often teach me new words. For example, in the northeastern part of the United States, some people use a very descriptive word for the kind of frantic cleanup that goes on in a house between the time you see someone walking toward your door and the time that person rings your doorbell. The word is "scurryfunge." In some areas they "red up the house," meaning "ready up the house for company."

Most of us don't feel the need to present an aura of super cleanliness to anyone anymore. Much of the time, we're just too tired to "scurry," but every now and then we do "funge," whether we "red up the house" for company or just for ourselves.

Doing a funge may be a constructive solution when we've had a really bad, problem-filled week and need to vent our frustrations upon something. Dirt bashing is always a good way to work off some steam (which, by the way, cleans and presses things well).

The point is that we spend less time cleaning and more time in other areas of our so-often busy lives. Cleaning can be done as it is needed, and each person's level of what is "clean" is different. One benefit of my new book is that everyone can take exactly what he or she needs—and skip what doesn't fit into today's busy schedule.

I know my mother would like this book and the new "into the 1990s" approach I've begun to take in the "Hints from Heloise" column, because she was always looking for ways to make all chores easier and life more pleasant.

I just know she is up there on a cloud of nylon net smiling, because angels' wings really are made of nylon net!

CHAPTER 1

Saving Time in the Kitchen

Family Kitchens

The kitchen has been called "the heart of the home" because for most families it's the center for nourishment of both soul and body.

Some of the best communication between friends and family occurs when people work together on meal preparation and even on cleanup, neither of which is a chore when it's shared.

People who remember the days before dishwashers remember that washing and drying dishes was an opportunity for the "washer" and the "dryer" to talk, maybe not about important things, but to make the kind of small talk that binds people together.

Have you ever noticed at parties that a lot of the fun and real getting-to-know-people goes on in the kitchen?

When we designed our home, we designed the kitchen to have the traffic pattern of people flow and to be large enough so that we could entertain in the kitchen. Even the center island is larger than normal—it's about 5 feet by 6 feet and 41 to 42 inches high, which makes it leaning height—so I can put out chips and dip, and people are comfortable in the kitchen.

How many children do their homework at the kitchen table while one of their parents fixes dinner? And how many kitchen tables have been the scene of such happy family memories as coloring Easter eggs, making Christmas cookies, and the best unifier of families, a daily meal together in which events of everyone's day are shared?

Many people, including me, have desks or work areas in their kitchens to make household planning and management convenient, and it sure seems more pleasant. A lot of people also use their kitchen tables as home offices. I'm known to do some of my best work right here.

Whatever goes on in your kitchen, I know that the hints gathered for this chapter will help you to spend less time on chores and more time on pleasant kitchen activities.

Appliances

They slice, dice, chop, stir, wash, dry, clean, cool, heat; and, like the human helpers in our lives, appliances need some TLC (tender, loving care).

We keep our human helpers going by saying "please" and "thank you" and "You sure did a good job." We keep our appliances going with maintenance. And, just as some humans need more encouragement than others, some appliances need more pleases and thank-yous than others.

The most important tip I can give you about all appliances is to read the booklet that comes with each appliance.

Manufacturers spend a lot of money researching and developing their products and they provide printed materials with them so that you will know how to properly use and trouble-shoot these products. You paid for the research and development and the resulting booklets when you paid for the appliance, so you might as well get your money's worth by at least glancing through the instruction and help booklets.

• Put appliance instruction booklets, guarantees, and warranties in a three-ring binder or accordion folder, or assign one special drawer in the kitchen for them. Keep the instruction booklets, guarantees, and warranties for all of your appliances in one place so that you can get them easily.

In the following table, I've listed the appliance; then the average number of years it can be expected to function; and then, in parentheses, the low and high numbers of years the appliance functions. These life expectancies are based on the first owner's length of use time and don't necessarily mean that the appliance is worn out.

• If your brand of appliance has not lasted as long as the average, you may want to buy a different brand the next time. And, naturally, if your brand has lasted longer than the average, you'll surely want to buy the same brand next time.

• If your appliance conks out at an age that is near the maximum, it may be more economical to buy a new one than to have it repaired—most likely over and over again, until you've spent enough money to have bought a new appliance.

Here are, according to appliance, the average, minimum, and maximum life expectancies (in years):

APPLIANCE LIFE EXPECTANCIES

Appliance	Average	Minimum	Maximum
Air conditioner (room)	11	8	14
Blanket (electric)	8	7	10
Can opener (electric)	7	5	10
Charcoal grill (outdoor)	6	3	9
Clock (electric)	8	5	10
Clothes washer	12	9	14
Compact hi-fi system	6	5	7
Corn popper	5	4	7
Desk calculator	7	5	10
Dishwasher	11	8	14
Dryer			
Electric clothes dryer	13	11	16
Gas clothes dryer	14	12	16
Electric fan	16	11	22
Fax machine	8	7	10
Floor polisher	11	4	13
Furnace			
Electric furnace	18	15	22
Gas furnace	16	13	20
Garbage disposal	10	7	12
Hair dryer	4	2	6
Home-security alarm system	14	10	17
Humidifier	8	6	11
Ice-cream maker (electric)	9	7	10
Iron	9	6	12
Lawn mower (power)	8	5	10
Microwave oven	11	10	14

Appliance	Average	Minimum	Maximum
Percolator (electric)	6	5	9
Personal computer	6	5	10
Range			
Electric range	15	13	19
Gas range	15	11	18
Refrigerator	13	11	18
Shaver (electric)	4	3	5
Smoke detector	10	8	15
Styling comb (electric)	4	3	5
Telephone answering machine	5	3	5
Television (color)	8	6	10
Television (projection)	7	5	7
Toaster	8	5	9
Toothbrush (electric)	3	1	3
Trash compactor	10	8	13
Typewriter (electric)	8	7	9
Vacuum cleaner	11	4	12
Videocassette recorder	7	6	8
Waffle iron	10	5	11
Water heater			
Electric water heater	12	8	17
Gas water heater	10	5	13
Snow thrower	10	6	12

Dish-Washing

Dishwasher Efficiency

• To get maximum dishwasher efficiency, start by choosing the right detergent. Shake the box of powdered detergent; if you can't hear the granules rattling inside, don't buy it. Lumpy dishwasher detergent won't dissolve well enough to do its job.

• Find a better place to store detergent than under the kitchen sink, where it's moist and warm—it is the worst place to store powdered dishwasher detergent.

• If you find that the larger box of the powdered dishwasher detergent does get lumpy, you might want to consider buying smaller boxes, because you'll use them up more quickly and they won't go bad.

Getting Sparkling Clean Dishes and Glassware

If you follow the directions in the booklet that came with your dishwasher and you still get enough film and water spots to feel like you're in a TV detergent commercial, it's probably because the water isn't hot enough.

Some machines have built-in "boosters" that heat the water when it's in the machine; if yours does not have a booster, here are some tips:

• To test if your hot water is hot enough to dissolve dishwasher detergent and help your dishwasher do its job, run hot water in your sink until it's the hottest it can get. Then, fill a tall glass and put a tablespoon of dishwasher detergent in. If the detergent dissolves before it gets to the bottom, the water is hot enough.

• DO let the water run from the faucet until it's hot before you run the dishwasher. Keep the water heater setting at 120 degrees Fahrenheit. If the heater is set for 140 to 160 degrees, the water is too hot; children and even adults have been scalded by hot bath water, often with serious consequences.

• DON'T run the dishwasher while the washing machine is running and during or after baths unless you have more than one water heater. (Running the dishwasher—clothes washer too—during baths in homes with limited water pressure can be harmful to the health of relationships. Nobody wants cold water to suddenly spew out on a shampoo-lathered head! Also, fluctuating hot water flows can burn if the hapless bather adjusts the shower to the hot water flow during the washer's fill cycle.)

• DO try different detergents. Some people may get better results with the new, thick liquid dishwasher detergents. Also, different brands of detergent seem to work better in one part of the country than another because of variances in water hardness. The one Mom used when you were home may not work in the city you live in. Use your coupons to try the smallest size of a new brand to see which works best in your area.

• If you have softened water, don't forget to use less than the full recommended amount of detergent. Using too much detergent can etch your glasses, causing them to look cloudy and "dirty," and nothing will make them clear again.

• Glasses will also become etched from improper loading or overloading of the dishwasher, a blocked filter, a spray arm that doesn't move as it should, or any other situation that prevents water from adequate washing and rinsing. If the proper water action is blocked, detergent will remain on the glassware too long and will not rinse off completely, thereby etching your glassware. I wash and dry my best crystal by hand. It takes only a few seconds to do this.

• However, if your glasses are cloudy because of hard water buildup, soak them in warm vinegar, then try to wash off the cloudy part. (Read on to find the two-step method for cleaning the dishwasher and its contents.)

• If you have an older-model dishwasher, you may need to rinse the dishes well before loading them.

• Starchy foods such as rice seem to cause the most trouble if you don't rinse dishes before loading the dishwasher. Also, dishwasher efficiency depends upon how long you've let food dry on the dishes.

• DO check your dishwasher filter regularly (if your model has one) and keep it clean. The cleaner the filter, the cleaner the dishes. If the filter is dirty, food particles will recirculate over your clean dishes.

• Also, check the bottom of the dishwasher door if you have a front-loading dishwasher. Use a wadded paper towel or thick sponge to protect your hands when you wipe this area because some dishwasher doors have sharp bottom edges. And, I've found broken glass and even a missing spoon!

You will be surprised at the gunk (mostly hardened fats and oils) that accumulates here. It is more likely to accumulate when the dishwater isn't hot enough and can ultimately damage the seal in some washers.

• If you rinse all of your dishes before loading, you'll surely have family members confused about whether dishes in the dishwasher are clean or dirty. One good signal is to put one cup right side up when you load the dishwasher. This cup will get filled with water during the cycle and you'll know that the dishwasher has been run.

• Some people like to put magnets on the front with little notes that say, "Wash me" or "I'm washed." Some of the new models have green lights that glow if the dishwasher has gone through its cycle.

Cleaning Your Dishwasher

Wait! Don't skip this section because you think this is a useless chore or a chore to totally avoid.

Often the reason your dishwasher won't clean properly is that it needs a cleaning beyond its own self-washing. Also, sometimes a real ogre of a landlord who's determined to keep your apartment damage deposit will have one less point to pick on if you put a sparkle on the appliances. Sparkling appliances help sell your house, too.

• Dishwasher stains can be removed by wetting the stains and sprinkling instant powdered orange breakfast drink or powdered lemon drink on them. The citric acid removes the stain. Let it stand for at least one hour.

Then, wipe a bit off to see if the stain has disappeared. If it has, load the dishwasher; add the dishwasher detergent, and let it run through the cycle.

• An easy way to clean the entire dishwasher, if it looks generally grungy, is to put citric acid or powdered orange or lemon drink in the detergent cup and let the washer run through its normal cycle.

• Here's a two-step method to get the dishwasher and its contents clean and sparkling.

CAUTION: Never combine the bleach and vinegar for a one-step process. It's dangerous! Also, DO NOT put gold-trimmed dishes, glassware, or silverware in the dishwasher when you use this process, because it damages such trim and objects.

Step one: Pour one cup of bleach into a bowl and set the bowl on the bottom rack of the dishwasher. Run it through the "wash" cycle only. Do not dry. If your dishwasher can't be stopped after a cycle, then punch the "cancel drain" button.

Step two: Fill the bowl again, this time with one cup of vinegar. Let the dishwasher run through the entire cycle this time.

Your dishes will be sparkling clean, and the discolorations, film, and mineral buildup on the interior of your dishwasher should have disappeared; if not, repeat steps one and two.

Trouble-Shooting

• Before you call a repairman to fix an improperly working dishwasher, check the following:

Has the circuit breaker tripped or a fuse blown?

Is the water hot enough? Check the temperature on your water heater.

Make sure the filter-strainer is clean.

Washing Dishes by Hand

Some things just don't go into the dishwasher. Also, not everyone has a dishwasher that operates on electricity. Some "dishwashers" are run by human energy.

• Dip washed dishes in a vinegar water bath to rinse them clean.

• To help protect your fine crystal, line the sink with a thick dish towel or washcloth. Be sure to wear rubber gloves, because you can rinse glasses with hotter water that way, which means they dry faster.

• If you spray glass baking dishes with oven cleaner, let them stand for about 30 minutes; you'll get the burned-on grease off and have sparkling clean dishes again. This is especially important if the glass dishes are used with silver holders, where burned-on gunk looks doubly bad.

• Soak dishes and pans with dried egg or milk in cold water: Hot water actually cooks these foods onto their containers and makes cleaning more work.

• Soak gunky dishes in hot, soapy water as you are preparing a meal for family or guests and you won't have as much scraping to do during the final cleanup. Just fill the sink with water and then add utensils, pots, and dishes as you finish with them.

• CAUTION: Never drop knives into a sink full of dishwater, because you might cut your hand while you're groping around for dishes.

• If you have lost something in the dishwater, use a drinking glass to peer through the suds to see what's in the bottom of the sink.

• If you break a glass, let the water drain out and use a paper towel to retrieve it so you don't cut your hand.

• Have an extra sink strainer handy to accommodate the extra dishes you use when you have company. If you have people drying dishes as you wash, you can put one strainer on each side of the sink and ease the traffic congestion in the kitchen. (With two strainers, you can also give the more fragile pieces to the more careful dish dryers, especially if you have children helping you!)

• Make a spare strainer and avoid clutter in your cupboards: Cover several layers of newspaper with a clean towel; the newspaper will absorb the dripping water and keep it from flowing across your countertops.

• If you are washing stacks of dishes, put the whole stack into the dishwater at one time so that the bottom ones soak while you swish off the top ones. This is much easier than putting a stack of dishes beside the sink and putting dishes one at a time into the dishwater for washing.

Refrigerator and Freezer Care

Sometimes we take our appliances for granted, but can you imagine life now without a refrigerator or freezer?

Like our other appliances, refrigerators and freezers have lives of their own. And, if we are to keep them in good shape, we have to take time to properly care for them.

Cleaning and Defrosting Refrigerators and Freezers

• CAUTION: Be sure you unplug the refrigerator before doing any major cleaning.

• When junk and lint collect under the refrigerator, simply attach an old stocking or nylon net to the end of a yardstick or broom handle with a rubber band. Carefully slip it under the refrigerator and move the stick from side to side. If you don't do this regularly, get ready for a shock the first time a repair person moves your appliance from its usual spot. Accumulated dust and dirt can interfere with the air circulation around, and therefore the self-cooling system of, the coils and motor; you can also use your vacuum cleaner to pull the dust off from the bottom front of the refrigerator coils.

• DO pull out the refrigerator/freezer at least three or four times a year so that you can scrub the floor and vacuum the condenser coils at the back and bottom of the appliance. More expensive refrigerators may have the back coils enclosed within their walls, but they still need cleaning underneath.

• DON'T forget the inside of the refrigerator and freezer. The best time to clean the interior is the day the trash is being picked up and before you go grocery shopping.

• When you wash and rinse frost-free or automatic-defrost refrigerator parts, you can use hot, sudsy water and hot rinse water on metal and porcelain parts, but since plastic and glass can crack from sudden changes in temperature, use lukewarm water for washing and rinsing these parts.

• Don't use strong-scented detergents for washing plastic refrigerator/freezer parts, because they may retain the odors.

- Defrost refrigerators or freezing compartments when frost buildup is about one-fourth inch thick. Cooling efficiency decreases when frost buildup is greater than a quarter of an inch, and energy use increases because the engine runs more.

- Keep the food you've removed from the freezer in a cooler or in a laundry basket lined with newspapers. Cover the laundry basket with more newspapers and put ice cubes on top. Or line your kitchen sink with newspapers. Place the frozen food there and top it with newspapers to help insulate it.

- CAUTION: Never poke at ice with an ice pick, because you could puncture the coils.

- Also, if you use one of those electric defrosters, be careful to keep it away from plastic meat trays or the freezer door, because the heat can melt plastics.

- Wipe out the freezer with detergent, borax, or baking soda solution, then rinse and wipe dry. Then set the controls and plug it in again. (You unplugged the fridge/freezer for defrosting, right?)

- Prevent frost buildup by not overloading refrigerators and by opening the door as seldom as possible, especially in hot weather.

- Covering all cooked foods and liquids not only prevents spills and transfer of odors to other foods but helps prevent humidity buildup.

- Door gaskets that are clean last longer. Always wipe the door gasket with borax or baking soda solution only. Strong detergents or bleach can cause deterioration and result in a bad seal.

- Test your refrigerator door seals by closing the door over a piece of paper or a dollar bill so that it's half in and half out of the appliance. If you can pull the paper or bill out easily, the seal may need replacing, or the latch, if there is one, may need adjusting.

- The painted metal exterior of refrigerators and freezers should be cleaned with mild detergent or appliance polish only. Strong spray-on–wipe-off cleaners tend to ultimately remove the paint from metal.

Storing Food in the Refrigerator

- I like to save various sizes of jars and buy clear plastic containers on sale to use for storing my leftovers; it helps everyone see what's there. I try to keep them in the front and always on the same shelf so that I can have easy access to them and they don't get lost when somebody does the refrigerator shuffle. (The refrigerator shuffle is a dance some people do during the TV commercial go-get-a-snack break.)

• I've developed a system of keeping certain things in the door shelves, and using certain shelves like assigned parking spaces for specific foods. For example, the dairy products, such as milk, yogurt, and cheese, are kept on the top shelf, leftovers are kept on the second shelf, and so on.

• If you find food way in the back of the refrigerator that's grown "hairy and green" and has left a terrible odor in the refrigerator, you can freshen the fridge by washing it with a mixture of one tablespoon of baking soda to the wash water. For a wonderful aroma add some lemon extract or a teaspoon of vanilla in clean water, then wipe the interior thoroughly.

• Always keep baking soda or a cup of fresh charcoal in the back of the refrigerator to keep it smelling fresh and clean. When you move and expect to have your refrigerator/freezer closed up for several days on a van or in storage, tossing in a handful of baking soda, charcoal, or unused ground coffee in a cloth bag (or knotted knee-high or pantyhose leg) will prevent your being greeted by a musty odor the first time you open your appliance. (This is a favorite among military families, whose appliances are frequently in storage while they go to new stateside or overseas duty stations.)

Cleaning Kitchen Ranges

Continuous-Cleaning and Self-Cleaning Ovens

Let's face it, if 10 is the highest rating on your Fun Things to Do Chart, cleaning the oven is rated at best a −93, but somebody's gotta do it.

However, this most dreaded chore has been made much less horrible and even bearable by "continuous-cleaning" and "self-cleaning" ovens. Whether you have either of these or a standard oven, like it or not, your oven has to be cleaned, if only to prevent oven grease fires or the unpleasantness of filling your oven and house with smoke and spoiling the flavor of whatever you're cooking. Also, if the oven and its thermostat are covered with baked-on grease, the thermostat may not accurately determine the oven's temperature.

Many people are confused by the difference between continuous-cleaning and self-cleaning ovens.

• A self-cleaning oven provides for the removal of soil during a separate high-heat cycle. This means you have to set the cycle for cleaning when needed.

• A continuous-cleaning oven gradually reduces oven soil on a specially treated surface to a "presentable" clean condition during normal baking or broiling operations. Each time you cook, the oven burns off dirt and grease. You'll need to clean up large spills to keep the oven looking good.

• NEVER use any kind of cleaning aid in a continuous-cleaning or self-cleaning oven. The finish will be removed. Once that happens, the oven will no longer clean itself. Do all wiping up with ordinary detergent and water or window cleaner.

• In self-cleaning ovens, use a plain water-dampened sponge or paper towel to wipe up the ash that remains in the bottom after the cleaning process has finished.

• If you choose to clean the oven racks in a self-cleaning oven cycle, be prepared to have them become discolored and dull finished. If the appearance of the oven racks is of no importance to you, you can clean them in the oven. Some stove booklets instruct you to wipe the sides of the racks and the grooves in which the racks slide with salad oil after cleaning so that the racks will slide more easily without scratching the oven walls.

• The racks will not come clean in some ovens. To clean them, take them outside, if possible, put them in a large heavy-duty plastic trash bag and spray them with an oven cleaner or ammonia. Then, close it tight. You can clean your racks in the bathtub with this method, but make doubly sure the bag is sealed tightly.

No matter where you do the cleaning, keep the racks in the bag overnight. The next day spray them off with a hose and use a steel wool pad to get any hard-to-remove grease spots off. Rinse in the sink or tub with hot water.

CAUTION: ALWAYS turn on the vent and/or open a window to protect yourself from fumes and ALWAYS keep children and pets away from such cleaning projects!

• Many people try to experiment with cleaning other greasy kitchen things in the oven during the self-cleaning cycle. Remember that these ovens get as high as 500 degrees Fahrenheit and sustain that temperature for more than an hour. A friend of mine tried to clean greasy barbecue grill lava briquets during the cycle. The result was an oven full of flaming grease to contend with. Fortunately for her, the rush of air into the oven when she opened the oven door (to spray the fire with a kitchen extinguisher) put the fire out.

• When you are dealing with extreme temperatures and strong chemicals, follow the directions given for them to the letter and don't get too creative. You may get results you haven't bargained for!

Cleaning Standard Ovens

Manufacturers recommend cleaning this type of oven with a commercial oven cleaner. You must be very careful using these, because most of them contain lye and nitrogen compounds, which can cause burns.

• When you use oven cleaners, be sure to wear rubber gloves and have plenty of circulating fresh air. The fumes are dangerous to inhale; keep children and pets away from the area. To be on the safe side, protect yourself by wearing a face mask or at least eyeglasses.

• Don't spray near any electrical connections, heating elements, or the thermostat.

• Try not to spray on an unprotected hot (because of being lit) oven light bulb; the bulb may shatter.

• If your oven isn't too grimy, try baking soda. Sprinkle some on a damp cloth and scrub.

• The best advice is to clean up any spill as it happens. It is easier to clean one layer of gunk than several old, hard-as-asphalt layers.

• You can get most of the burned food off if you pour some salt on the spill; allow the oven to cool; wipe clean.

• To prevent further spillovers when baking "bubbly" things, put a sheet of heavy aluminum foil or a cookie sheet in the bottom of the oven. If you have an electric oven, you must place the aluminum foil under the heating coils. Cover food when possible and cook at the lowest temperature to prevent splattering.

Cleaning Range Tops

Keeping range-top burners and reflectors clean makes them reflect heat more efficiently, saving energy.

• Sponge range-top surfaces with hot water and let dry. Stainless-steel surfaces should be towel-dried to prevent water spots. Harsh scouring powders will scratch chrome, so use metal polishes made especially for chromium and soft metals when you need to do serious cleaning (more than a wipe-up).

• To keep the stainless steel surface really sparkling and shiny, clean it with a window cleaner or full-strength vinegar, or with a dab of ammonia on a sponge. Or, to really cheat, put a little cooking oil on a paper towel and wipe over all surfaces, then polish.

• Electric coil units are self-cleaning; they burn off spills when turned on high heat. But turn on the vents and open windows when you do this, even if it's just for a few minutes.

• Gas burners, drip trays, burner rims, and other removable parts of the range top can be soaked in strong detergent solutions such as one half to one cup of laundry or dishwasher detergent added to a gallon of hot water and dissolved. Rinse well after soaking and dry with a towel.

• CAUTION: Gas burners must be drained and dried before you replace them so that residual water will not divert the flow of gas.

• To thoroughly dry the gas burner, use a hand-held hair dryer on high to get to any places you can't reach so that you remove all moisture.

Microwave Ovens

Isn't it great that in this world of hurry, rush, and hurry again, it no longer takes hours to prepare meals?

While microwave ovens don't completely replace conventional ovens and range tops, they certainly make life easier.

• Cooking times vary according to the wattage. For example, the lower the wattage, the more slowly the food cooks. If you're not sure of your microwave oven's wattage, here's a simple test.

Put ice in a two-cup measure and add one cup of water. Stir for about two minutes or until the ice stops melting and the water is very cold. (Your objective is to have extremely icy, the coldest possible, water without actually using ice itself.) Remove the ice and put the cold water into a one-cup microwave-safe glass measure. Put it in the microwave oven uncovered, on the high setting, until the water begins to boil.

If your oven has 600 to 700 wattage, the water will boil in less than 3 ½ minutes. If it takes 3 ½ to 4 ½ minutes to boil, the wattage output is 500 to 600 watts. If it takes longer than 4 ½ minutes, the wattage output is less than 500 watts.

• Use the temperature and time for the meal you're preparing suggested in the cookbook that comes with your microwave oven. The manufacturers know what they are talking about. They have tested and tested these recipes to get the right times and temperatures for specific food portions—why not use their research?

Microwave Oven Utensils

Many wonderful microwave-safe glass, plastic, and ceramic dishes and utensils are made specifically for the microwave oven, and using paper plates and towels diverts even more kitchen time to personal "put your feet up and rest" time, because it eliminates cleanup.

Some people think that any container that is not metal may safely be used in the microwave oven, but this is not true.

For example, if, when you heat water in a mug for tea or instant coffee, the handle becomes too hot to hold, the mug is probably not recommended for a microwave oven. You can boil water, as I do, in a microwave-safe glass measuring cup. The handle doesn't get hot even when the water is still bubble-boiling in the measuring cup.

• Here's a test from the Association of Home Appliance Manufacturers to determine if a dish is microwave-safe:

Place a glass measuring cup of water next to the empty dish to be tested. (Never metal or gold-trimmed dishes!) Heat on full power for one minute, then check the temperature of the dish.

If the dish is cool and the water very warm, the dish can be used. If the dish is slightly warm, it can be used for short-term cooking only. If the dish is hot and the water is cool, do not use the dish. A hot dish means that the utensil is absorbing the rays instead of permitting them to pass through, as they should for safe cooking.

• Certain plastic containers and dishes cannot be used. For example, the foam trays on which meat is sold at the store and fast food containers will melt at high temperatures.

• Never use dishes with gold or silver trim or trademark signatures on the bottom (metallic); it may cause arcing (sparks) and discoloring, and the dishes may break.

Arcing occurs when an electric current flows from the microwave wall to the metal in the oven. It causes a popping sound and a light flash that could damage the microwave oven.

• Some instruction booklets say that you should NEVER use glass jars, not even canning jars, which withstand high temperatures, because they can break due to microwave action on the curved edge at the top of the jar. I have not had this happen, but perhaps it's better to be safe than sorry, as the old saying goes, and to use another container for heating things.

• CAUTION: If you heat babies' bottles in the microwave oven, always shake the bottle after heating to mix well. You must always test a few drops on the inside of your wrist to feel the temperature. The bottle may feel only warm on the outside, but the milk on the inside may be scalding hot.

• ALWAYS remove all lids carefully by first tilting them with the open side AWAY from your face; escaping steam burns skin. Position your hands so that they are not burned by steam or spillovers. Be especially cautious when you've put plastic wrap over a dish or container; always open the wrap so that steam escapes away from your face or, for that matter, away from anyone who is watching you cook.

• When you boil water for cocoa, tea, or instant coffee in the cup from which you'll drink it, be aware that stirring or dropping in a tea bag can cause the water to bubble over the edge of the cup if the microwaves are still active in the water. The water is less likely to bubble over if you wait a few seconds before making your beverage.

• Be careful not to run the microwave oven with the tea bag in it. I know of one case where the metal staple in the teabag ruined the microwave oven.

• Always place larger, thicker pieces of food to the outside of the container and smaller, thinner pieces toward the center. Using round plates and baking dishes will make you do this automatically.

• When placing several dishes in a microwave oven at the same time, place one dish in the center and all the other dishes around it.

• If your microwave oven doesn't have a built-in rotator, be sure to rotate and stir the food often, or buy one when you find a sale. Rotating the food is often the key to successful cooking.

• Cover the dish with a microwave-safe lid or plastic wrap; it can help promote even cooking by trapping the heat and steam inside.

• As you do with other appliances, it's important to wipe up spills when they occur. The microwave oven surface is easy to clean. If soil doesn't just wipe off, try heating a bowl of water, so that the steam will soften the spills, then wipe clean. Wipe around the door seal, door surface, or frame frequently to maintain a good seal.

• If your microwave oven needs a serious cleaning, put two tablespoons of either lemon juice or baking soda in a cup of water in a microwave-safe four-cup bowl. Let the mixture boil in the microwave oven for about five minutes so that steam condenses on the inside walls of the oven. Then wipe off the walls, inside of the door, and door seals.

I love my microwave oven and experiment with different dishes all the time. I'm sure you will too.

Garbage Disposals

If you own a garbage disposal, you know how they speed cleanup. Here are some tips on keeping that disposal grinding and flushing away for many years.

• ALWAYS run lots of water while using it and for a few seconds after use. This is the most important instruction for using a disposal. My husband, who is a plumbing contractor, has told me that if the garbage disposal ever backs up, it's my fault because I always forget to run a lot of extra water. If you don't run enough water when using your disposal, food waste will back up into the disposal and damage the unit, not to mention clog the plumbing.

Disposal Odors

• Sometimes odors can occur; I call them bad breath in the kitchen. Here's how you can sweeten the disposal.

Fill an ice tray with water with one-half cup of white vinegar added; then freeze. (Don't use that tray for your drinks; mark it.) Put the vinegared ice cubes down the garbage disposal about once a week; they will freshen it and clean the disposal and clean off the blades as well.

CAUTION: Be sure your disposal is of a good, sturdy quality if you do this. The less expensive brands may not have the capability of chopping up the ice cubes.

• You can also grind orange and lemon rinds to get rid of odors, which is a real time-saver because you were probably going to grind them up just to get rid of them!

• Check the garbage disposal gasket (the rubber piece that fits in the drain hole). If you can remove it, take it out and clean it thoroughly. If not, put on rubber gloves, be sure the disposal has no chance of being turned on, stick your hand down the disposal, and scrub underneath. That will help eliminate a lot of the bad odor.

• If you add other foods when you are grinding up tough, stringy stuff, you won't be as likely to get a garbage jam in the disposal. However, under no circumstances do you put artichoke leaves, asparagus, or very stringy vegetables or food down the garbage disposal. You're only asking for trouble.

• NEVER use hot water while using the disposal, just cold water and plenty of it so that you'll flush the waste all the way down and prevent odors from coming back to haunt your kitchen.

• NEVER use drain cleaners in the disposal, because they may damage it.

• Occasionally, flush the disposal drain by filling up your sink with water and then draining the sink with the disposal running.

CAUTIONS:

• NEVER put your hand or any non-grindable object down the disposal while it is running. Keep the cover on it at all times until ready to use.

• DON'T position your head directly over the disposal when you turn it on. If a knife or spoon or any utensil has fallen into the disposal without your knowledge, turning the disposal on could turn the utensil into a dangerous projectile when the disposal force shoots it out of the opening.

• To unjam a garbage disposal: Look carefully at the disposal. There's usually a red restart button. Press it and then turn the garbage disposal on, and many times this will do the trick. You may have to try this once or twice. If this does not work, place a broom handle or a very sturdy stick into the disposal and turn it counterclockwise to try to unjam the motor. Pull the stick out, run water, flip the switch, and see if that does it.

Appliances

Often the problems we have with appliances result from misuse or lack of cleaning. Here are some hints for best appliance use and care:

• Some appliances such as electric fry pans or roasters may not heat properly when plugged into extension cords. Try plugging such appliances directly into the wall socket.

• CAUTION: Always unplug appliances for cleaning or servicing. Never immerse a whole appliance, and never immerse the electrial components, in water unless the manufacturer specifically states you can do so.

• Coffee percolator stems can get clogged, effecting the ability to perk and affecting the coffee taste. Clean the stem with a small round brush. You can also make a super long cotton swab by wetting the end of a wooden shish-kebab stick and twisting it in a wad of cotton to clean the inside of the stem.

• To avoid coffee grounds from getting into the percolator stem while you fill the basket with coffee, hold your finger over the stem.

• Off-tasting coffee in a drip coffee maker can mean there is too much hard-water mineral deposit accumulating in the brew chamber. To clean a drip coffee maker, run the fullest measure the pot allows of white vinegar through the cycle, followed by a cycle or two of the fullest measure of fresh water. (Some coffee maker brands have you run the vinegar through twice, or have you unplug the coffee maker to make the vinegar work longer. Check your manual for instructions.)

• To avoid wasting vinegar that has been used to clean a coffee maker, collect the filtered vinegar in a coffee pot after it has run through and store it in an empty jar. The vinegar can be used again in cleaning the coffee maker a couple of times. (You can also use the stored vinegar to clean and "sweeten" drains, etc.)

• Avoid having to clean your coffee maker by brewing your coffee with distilled water. This will make for better coffee, too.

• If the tray in the bottom of your toaster is covered with crumbs, the thermostat won't work properly to give your toast the shade of brown you want. Also, crumbs at the bottom of the toaster can catch fire. Usually there is a latch on the bottom of the toaster that pops the tray open so that you can clean it.

• To catch drippings and crumbs in a toaster oven, place a piece of aluminum foil on the bottom of the "catch" tray. (Check the manufacturer's instructions first, however.)

• Quick-clean your blender or food processor by half-filling it with water and adding a drop or two of liquid dishwashing detergent; run it a few seconds, rinse, and let dry.

• If you have a hand-held European-style blender, fill a deep bowl or large glass with water and a dash of liquid detergent, cover, whirr it a few moments, rinse, and let dry.

• Blenders operate best if only two-thirds full. A blender that is too full may not operate at all.

• Never attempt to slice or grate hard frozen cheese or other frozen foods with your food processor or slicer. The processor blades are likely to break.

• Electric can openers need clean cutters to work well. Clean the blade with a scouring pad or scrubber. Or you can use an old toothbrush. Clean blades not only help your opener work more efficiently, they are more sanitary as well.

• Waffle-iron grids can accumulate burned-on grease. To clean metal grids place an ammonia-soaked paper towel or napkin between them, and leave it overnight. Then clean with steel wool. If you have non-stick grids, follow manufacturer's instructions.

• New or recently cleaned grids can stick. Before using them, grease with unsalted fat and preheat thoroughly before pouring on batter.

• If your vacuum cleaner has lost suction, check to see if the bag is too full or if objects are caught in the intake mechanism.

• Use a seam-ripper or a single-edged razor blade to cut across the hairs and threads that get wound around a vacuum cleaner's or carpet sweeper's rotating brush.

Kitchen Cleaning Tips

Countertops

• Never use abrasive cleansers on plastic laminated tops; they scratch and eventually remove the finish. If stains occur, squeeze fresh lemon juice over them; allow the juice to soak about 45 minutes. Then sprinkle baking soda over the lemon juice and rub with a soft cloth.

• A solution of mild dish-washing liquid and water does the daily cleanup job. Just wash, rinse with clear water, and your countertop should look good for a long, long time.

• You can also clean countertops by pouring club soda on the counter and wiping up the soda with a soft cloth. Then rinse with warm water and wipe dry. You can finish the job on dull-finished countertops by polishing the countertops with a plastic laminate cleaner, which gives them a low luster.

• Shiny-finish countertops will stay shiny if you apply lemon oil about once a week and wipe dry. It not only cleans but preserves the finish.

Chopping-Block Countertops

• Tiny knife cuts are natural wear for these tops, because they are made to be cutting surfaces. They must be scrubbed with soap and water. Small crevices can harbor bacteria, so occasionally you may want to disinfect the counter or chopping block with a mild bleach solution (two to three tablespoons of bleach to a quart of water). Rinse well always, and then rejuvenate the surface with a thin coat of mineral oil; let it soak for a half an hour and buff.

• A baking soda scrub will also clean chopping blocks and will also remove stains and some light burn marks. Rinse, then rub with oil as above.

Tile Countertops

Although a lot of people think that the grout between tiles will stain and always look dirty, tile is really easy to keep clean.

• Grout is no problem at all if you seal it with a grout sealer, found in tile stores. Follow the directions on the box. You may have to repeat the process once a year.

• The grout between kitchen tiles can start to look very grungy. You can make a mild bleach solution—two tablespoons to a quart of water—and dab at just the grouting with a cotton swab to bleach out the grout.

• Wash tiles with dish-washing liquid and water or vinegar and water when the they look grimy. You get best results if you scrub tiles with a nylon brush or nylon net. Just wash, rinse, and then step back to admire your handiwork. Then take a break; you deserve it for making your tiles look so great!

• For a quick fix, you can use typewriter correction fluid, which comes in a variety of colors in addition to white. This also works in the bathroom.

• If you've always wanted hand-painted wall tiles, such as those in decorator shops, but can't afford to rip out your old tiles and replace them, try putting decals on your tiles. You can either make a border of decal tiles or make your own design by alternating decal tiles with plain tiles. When you change colors (and then the decals on the tiles), you can buy a decal remover kit where decals are sold.

I have also used decals on bathroom walls. They can be applied to glossy or semi-glossy paint. Three butterflies were applied so that they looked as if they were fluttering across the bathroom toward the window.

• If you have artistic talent or artistic friends, you can use acrylic paints or waterproof markers to draw murals or decorations on your walls. Just be sure the drawing is done with waterproof materials, or you'll have some really "drippy" designs when you wipe off the walls!

I took several colored waterproof markers and drew wispy willow trees on my bathroom walls rather than repainting the whole thing. When I get tired of this, I'll simply spray it with a sealer and paint over it.

Kitchen Sinks

• Stainless-steel sinks should never be cleaned with abrasive cleaners, which will scratch the surface; you'll never be able to get the sink to look good again.

• If you feel you must use a powdered cleanser, be sure to rub WITH the grain of the stainless steel rather than in circles or in the opposite direction.

• To clean stainless steel sinks, use baking soda; even some liquid cleansers may scratch surfaces. ALWAYS read those labels! Just sprinkle some baking soda in the sink and scrub with a damp cloth. Vinegar is great for removing water spots and attacking gunk buildup.

• Wipe the sink dry after each use. To keep the sink shiny or for a hurry-up sparkle, wipe it with a little oil or vinegar on a soft, clean cloth.

• White and light-colored porcelain sinks sometimes need a good whitening treatment to get rid of accumulated stains. Try pouring liquid bleach into the bottom (enough to cover the bottom), then fill the sink with cold water. Let it soak for at least one-half hour. Tell your family what's going on and watch out for children or pets, especially sneaky cats who drink from sinks, so that they won't be accidentally harmed by the bleach.

• Never use any kind of bleach on colored porcelain sinks, because it fades the colors. Clean colored porcelain sinks with mild liquid detergents, baking soda, or vinegar.

• CAUTION: Powdered abrasive cleansers and mild liquid cleansers can still be abrasive enough to wear off the glaze of your kitchen or bathroom sink. This is very important to remember, because once the glaze is gone, your sink will never be shiny again and it will be harder and harder to keep clean.

Pots and Pans

• Aluminum pans can be kept shiny by filling them to the brim with water, adding two tablespoons of cream of tartar, then letting the water boil. The shine comes back in a few minutes.

• To clean a stained aluminum pot "automatically," try cooking tomato sauce in it. The acid brings back the aluminum shine and gets rid of most dark stains. If you have no plans to cook with tomato sauce, you can also clean aluminum pots by adding two tablespoons of white vinegar to boiling water.

• DO NOT use any type of ammonia or bleach-based cleaner on aluminum; it will cause pitting.

Cast-Iron Cookware

Most serious cooks say that cast iron is the best cookware you can use. It may take a little more work to take care of cast iron, but it's worth it. I have several cast-iron pots and skillets that have been passed on to me from my mother. They are more than 60 years old but still cook better than any other skillets I've used.

• Most new cast-iron skillets have been seasoned, but in case you've bought one that has not, here's what to do.

First wash it with sudsy water, then rinse with hot water and dry well. Slather on a thick layer of unsalted vegetable shortening over the inside and outside of both the pot and lid. Cover the pot with the lid, set it on a cookie sheet, and bake it in an oven at 250 degrees Fahrenheit for 1 ½ hours. Swab the grease around occasionally with a dry cloth or paper towel to keep the surface of the pot evenly coated.

After baking the pot allow it to cool, then wipe out any excess grease. Buff to a sheen with a dry, clean cloth or paper towel.

• If you have an old cast-iron skillet that has become rusty, all you need to do is reseason it. First remove all the rust by using a scouring pad, then wash and dry. Season as described above.

• You can season and reseason a cast-iron skillet by using it to deep fry. You'll be boiling the oil into it.

• Never let the skillet soak in soapy water. As soon as you have finished using it and it has cooled, wash it quickly in soap and hot water, using a mild dish-washing liquid, or run lots of hot water on it and scrub with a nylon net scrubber.

• If food particles have become baked on, remove with a nylon scrubber. Never use a harsh cleanser or metal scouring pads, which will scratch the surface.

• Rinse the pan after washing, then place it on the burner on medium high for a few seconds to dry it. Don't keep it on the burner long; if it starts smoking, the seasoning will be removed.

• Rub the pan with a light coating of vegetable oil when it is completely dry and before storing. Place a heavy grocery bag (or paper plate or coffee filters) above and below the pan if you're stacking it in a cupboard.

• Every now and then, you need to clean the grease that gets burned onto your iron skillet and sticks to the bottom and sides like asphalt on a road. Many people simply put the iron skillet into the fire of a barbecue grill after they've finished cooking so that the grease just burns off as the coals burn down and go out. The skillet needs to stay in the hot fire for about an hour.

CAUTION: Don't touch the skillet until you are absolutely sure it has burned off and cooled. And don't try to cool it with cold water; it will crack the iron. After it's cool, reseason the skillet as noted in this section.

It really doesn't take that long to season an iron skillet. Seasoning should be done at least once a year so that your skillet can last you a lifetime and beyond—consider how many of us have inherited iron skillets from our mothers and grandmothers.

• If you haven't been lucky enough to inherit a good cast-iron skillet, buy one at an antique store, flea market, or garage sale, where you can find one that has been cooked in and seasoned for years and years.

Non-Stick Pans

• Never use metal utensils on non-stick surfaces of pots, pans, and other cooking equipment, because they scratch easily. Even when the tags say you can use metal utensils, it's still better to use plastic or wood to save the surfaces from scars.

• Non-stick surfaces are very easy to keep clean; just soak them in hot, sudsy water and clean with a nylon scrubber. DON'T ever use abrasive cleaners, and especially don't use steel wool.

• If you have a heavily soiled or discolored non-stick pan, just fill the pan with water and add two tablespoons of bleach or dishwasher detergent. Simmer the solution in the pan to loosen the crusty stuff.

• CAUTION: DO be very careful not to let non-stick pots and pans burn dry. The fumes can contain a poison that is especially hazardous to babies and small animals, and deadly to pet birds.

• As with anything else, if you take care of your non-stick cookware, it will last a long time.

Enamelware

• Enamelware is usually made with a metal base; the outside and inside may be coated with porcelain enamel, or the outside may have an epoxy enamel, acrylic enamel, or polyurethane finish. This cookware washes well in the dishwasher, but must never be scoured with powders or steel wool. Porcelain enamels may be scratch-resistant, but you shouldn't use any abrasives until you check the manufacturer's directions carefully. Soak pans with burned-on food in water and then scrub with nylon scrubbers.

Glass Cookware

• Commercial cleaners are available for ceramic and glass cookware and ceramic tops on ranges.

• You can get burned-on foods off by soaking the cookware in hot, sudsy water. If you've burned starchy or sugary foods, try adding baking soda to the soak; scrub with more baking soda and a nylon scrubber.

• Burned-on grease can be removed with ammonia.

• Coffee and tea stains will come out if soaked in a solution of two tablespoons liquid chlorine bleach per cup of water or two tablespoons automatic dishwasher detergent to a pot of warm water.

• Mineral deposits on range-top cookware will come off if you boil full-strength vinegar in the pot for about 15 minutes. (Pour this used vinegar down your kitchen drain to clean and sweeten it.)

• CAUTION: Never scrub glass cookware with a highly abrasive cleanser or a steel wool pad, because it can eventually weaken the glass to the point where it will crack if used at too high a temperature.

Cleaning Silver

Sterling silver cries out to be used instead of being hidden in drawers. The tiny scratches that occur naturally when it's used produce what is called the "patina."

• Wash silver in hot, sudsy water, rinse, and buff dry with a soft cloth.

• Sterling silver, except for knives with cemented handles, can be washed in dishwashers.

• Silver plate, which is normally treated just like sterling, should not be washed in the dishwasher.

• Silver gets tarnished faster when it is exposed to eggs, salad dressing, and other foods that contain sulfur. Salt will corrode silver. Infrequently used items can be wrapped in silver cloth (cloth treated with silver nitrate), plastic bags, or plastic wrap. Do not wrap silver with rubber bands—the rubber can discolor the silver.

• Many commercial polishes are available.

   CAUTION: Using quick-dip cleaners can eventually permanently damage your silver.

• The following cleaning method is quick but not for all silver pieces and should be used only occasionally.

   Place aluminum foil in the bottom of a cooking pot. (Aluminum pots may get darkened if used for this process.) Add enough water to cover the silver pieces. For each quart of water, add one teaspoon of salt and one teaspoon of baking soda. Bring solution to boil. Add silver. Boil two to three minutes or until the tarnish is removed. Remove silver, rinse, and buff dry with a soft cloth.
   The quick and easy way that I do this is to put a piece of aluminum foil at the bottom of the kitchen sink, fill the sink with hot, hot tap water, and then do the rest of the procedure.
   CAUTION: The above method leaves a dull white luster and removes the dark accents in design crevices, which is usually not desirable. It may also soften the cement of hollow-handled flatware.

Cleaning Tin

Most tin utensils are solid tin. Tin-plated iron items will rust if the plating is worn away by polish. Because unpolished tin absorbs heat better than polished, most tinware is not polished.

• Remove rust by rubbing with 0000 steel wool that has been dipped in mineral or vegetable oil.

   For more on cleaning and polishing metal surfaces, see Chapter 3, "In and Around the House."

Cleaning Copper and Brass

Tarnish can be removed with commercial cleaners or with some of the home-made cleaners listed below. Those made with lemon juice or vinegar will give copper and brass a bright finish; the oil and rottenstone cleaner will give these metals a soft luster.

• Saturate a sponge or cloth with vinegar or lemon juice; sprinkle salt on the sponge; and then rub metal, rinse, and dry.

• Rub metal with a paste made by adding flour to the salt and vinegar or lemon juice; rinse; and dry.

• Make a thin paste from rottenstone (an abrasive powder available at hardware stores) and an oil such as cooking or salad oil. Wipe off excess oil after rubbing; polish with a clean cloth.

Home Pest Control

Roach Extermination Formula

• Whenever my roach recipe is published I get an avalanche of mail from people who forgot to clip it from their newspapers. So here it is—you'll never have to clip it again.

It doesn't matter where you live—hot climate or cold—you're bound to find roaches. They are difficult to eliminate, but you can keep control of them using the following boric acid formula. I have found it does a great job, and my readers agree.

ROACH EXTERMINATION FORMULA

¼ cup shortening or bacon drippings
⅛ cup sugar
 8 ounces powdered boric acid
½ cup flour
½ small onion, chopped (optional)
   Enough water to form a soft dough

Mix the shortening and sugar together until they form a creamy mixture. Mix together the boric acid, flour, and onion and add to the sugar and shortening.

Blend well, then add water to form a soft dough. Shape the mixture into small balls or just drop a small amount of it into an opened small plastic sandwich bag.

The mixture will stay soft for a longer period of time if placed in bags. When they harden it's time to replace them.

Variation

I prefer to make a dry mixture that is easy to apply.

Mix powdered boric acid with an equal or larger amount of flour, cornmeal, or sugar. For example: 4 ounces of boric acid mixed with 4 to 8 ounces of sugar, flour, or cornmeal.

Place the boric acid balls or the powdered mixture throughout the house. Put them under your kitchen and bathroom sinks, near the pipes; under the dishwasher, refrigerator, and stove; where you store paper grocery bags and paper goods. Remove your wall plates and sprinkle the mixture behind the outlets. Put some in the garage. Place some under your deck. Put some under your water heater and in the closet.

In short, sprinkle this powder or place dough balls in the out-of-the-way places where roaches like to hide. After they walk through it, they groom themselves and become poisoned.

• When we built our house, I had this formula mixed in large batches and put in between the walls.

• You can buy small quantities of powdered boric acid (4, 8, or 12 ounces) at drugstores, pharmacies, or grocery stores. To buy larger quantities (50 pounds or more), look in the telephone book Yellow Pages under "Chemical Distributors," some of which sell boric acid. (Most commercial products for killing roaches contain boric acid.)

CAUTION: Keep the mixture away from small children and pets. Boric acid can be poisonous if ingested in sufficient quantities. It can cause diarrhea, cramps, and vomiting.

• If your child or pet does swallow some, immediately call your local poison control center for instructions.

• Why not write down the phone number of the poison control center in your area right now! Or, if you have a programmable phone, designate a poison control center button, just as you've programmed a 911 or other emergency button. Teach children to use the emergency numbers (use pictures to identify the numbers for very young children), but make sure they understand that emergency numbers are not for play; emergency phone operators answering joke calls are being taken away from real emergency calls, and children should be taught the seriousness of calling these numbers.

Weevil Extermination

Weevils don't cause as much worry as roaches, but they are just as unwanted in the kitchen.

It's best to keep them from becoming established in your cupboards. As noted in the food storage section (Chapter 2), storing flour, cornmeal, grits, and other grains in jars or sealed plastic bags or containers prevents weevils from migrating from one food package to another.

• Putting newly bought starchy foods into the freezer for at least 7 days or just storing such foods in the freezer or refrigerator is one way to control weevils, because freezing kills larvae.

Here are some old wives' tales that work.

• Sticking in a few dried bay leaves into the flour, cornmeal, and so forth, containers helps repel weevils, and I've found that putting a few sticks of unwrapped spearmint gum on cupboard shelves or sprinkling black pepper where staples are kept discourages weevils, roaches, and other bugs.

• Once weevils have taken up residency in your cupboards, you'll have to take some pretty drastic measures to get rid of them. I've learned that there are 18 different species of weevils, each having its own food preference. Some parts of the country have flying as well as crawly insect invaders, with the corresponding different species.

• Here's how to get rid of weevils and other cabinet invaders. (Warning: This process is a chore if ever there was one!)

First, take everything out of your cabinets and destroy every visibly infested box or bag. You may feel that this is wasteful, but in the long run it's cheaper than continually throwing out infested food.

Be sure to check every single box of staples, including flour, meals, cereals, dried fruits, spices, dry pet food, pasta products, dry beans, peas, etc.

Next, take the boxes in which you have not seen any weevils and put them into the freezer for four days at zero-degree temperature or in an oven at 150 to 160 degrees Fahrenheit for 30 minutes. DO NOT SKIP THIS STEP. Freezing or heating will destroy the weevil eggs, which you cannot see and which will hatch and reinfest your cupboards if they are not destroyed.

The third step is to scrub shelves with hot, sudsy water using a stiff bristled brush and paying special attention to cracks, crevices, and undersides of shelves, where weevils or eggs are likely to be hidden, ready to reinfest everything after you've cleaned up.

Before returning anything to your cabinets, spray shelves, crevices, and cabinet walls with an insecticide that says it kills weevils or whatever unwelcome insects have established a village in your cabinets. Allow cabinet doors to remain closed for three to four hours. The alternative to spraying cabinets is to close up the kitchen, cover all food, get children and pets out of the house, and use a fogger type of insecticide according to directions given on the can.

After doing all of the above, put everything into sealable glass jars before returning foods to the shelves. Glass or clear plastic containers will allow you to see if foods are reinfested and prevent weevils from migrating to other parts of the cabinets.

• My best advice is to buy small quantities of staples—enough for a few weeks—and get into the habit of freezing them before using. Open each food package when you get home from the store and return any infested items (with sales slip) without delay.

• I understand that the small brown "German" roaches often lay their eggs in the grocery store brown paper sack stacks and when they hatch, the babies feed on the glue used in manufacturing paper sacks. Therefore, wherever you store stacks of brown paper grocery sacks, you are likely to have roach infestation.

• See section on gardening and the storage of insecticides (page 162).

I can't emphasize this enough: ALWAYS store chemicals where children and pets can't get to them, and when you throw away used containers of chemicals, bag them carefully so that children and pets can't get at them. We want to avoid tragedies!

Coffee and Tea Beverages

Coffee

Grinding your own coffee beans and creating your own special "house blends" is fun. Freezing coffee (whole beans or ground) in a well-sealed container or zipper bag is a great way to preserve flavor. Also, you can keep various kinds of coffee in the freezer and have different blends every day. I like to mix blends of decaffeinated and caffeinated coffees for a milder brew.

• Try adding about one-fourth to one-half teaspoon of instant coffee to spaghetti sauce. It gives the sauce a nice, less acid flavor and adds a bit of brown color to the bright red tomato sauce that makes it look more homemade-cooked-for-hours.

• If you don't feel like reheating leftover coffee in the microwave oven, make yourself a glass of iced coffee from your morning pot's leftovers for a tasty coffee break during the day. I like iced coffee as a treat with a dash of cinnamon or nutmeg.

• If you like café au lait (coffee with boiled milk), you can make it instantly by heating milk in a microwave-safe mug in the microwave oven and then pouring hot coffee into the boiled milk. It's not the famous Café du Monde of New Orleans, but it's a pretty good substitute. Canned skim milk makes especially good quickie no-pans-to-wash café au lait, and saves a few fat calories too.

Tea

• Tea bags hold dried tea leaves but do not protect the flavor unless individually wrapped and sealed in plastic or foil. Tea is considered a fragrant herb, and whether you buy loose tea or tea bags, tea should be stored in a container with a tightly fitting lid.

• When you buy tea, the number of tea bags per pound tells you how strong the tea is. Most teas are sold with 200 bags to the pound; if you usually get one to two cups per bag from such a tea, then you may get four cups per bag from a tea that has 150 bags per pound and may need two bags for one cup if the tea has more than 200 bags per pound.

• When you use tea bags in a teapot, take the paper tags off to avoid having them drop into the pot and adding a paper taste to the tea. You can also keep the tags out of the tea by tying or looping the strings to the teapot or cup handle. You may be able to clip the tag to the rim or handle of your cup with a spring clothespin.

• Tea concentrate for a large crowd can be prepared ahead of time. Here's how to make 40 to 50 cups of tea.

1. Bring 1 ½ quarts fresh, cold water to a rapid boil.
2. Remove water from heat and immediately add one-fourth pound loose tea. Stir to immerse leaves and then cover. (Double this recipe for 80 to 90 cups.)
3. Let stand five minutes. Strain into a teapot until ready to use.
4. To serve this concentrate as hot tea, bring out a pot of boiling fresh water, right from the boiling kettle, pour about two tablespoons of tea concentrate into each cup, and fill up with hot water. The strength of the tea depends upon the water-tea ratio.

If you are using this concentrate for iced tea, add 50 percent more tea to allow for melting ice—that is, use six tea bags or six teaspoons of tea for four glasses of iced tea.

• Use leftover hot tea for iced tea, or freeze "tea cubes" to cool your next cup of hot tea or glass of iced tea.

• If you make a pitcher of iced tea and the tea becomes cloudy, add a small amount of boiling water and stir, and the tea will clear up. Some teas are sold especially for iced tea and these teas are less likely to get cloudy.

• Sun tea is not only an energy saver (yours and electrical power). It tastes better too, and can be made with any kind of tea.

1. Put the appropriate number of tea bags (about the same number of bags for the amount of water as for hot tea) into a glass container (quart or gallon).
2. Fill with fresh cool water and put the container on a sunny patio or doorstep where it will be safe from curious pets and children. Depending upon the weather, you'll have tea by noon or certainly 4 P.M. tea time.
3. Pour over ice and add flavorings of choice.

• If you are in a hurry, make "sun tea" in your microwave oven by boiling water in a glass jar or pitcher, then tossing in the appropriate number of tea bags and letting the tea steep on the kitchen counter for a couple of hours until it reaches the right strength. I once tried to speed this process along by simmering the tea bags in the pitcher in the microwave oven, but it was a mess because the bags broke and I had to strain the tea to use it. So, better let the tea steep naturally.

• You can boil water in the cup in the microwave oven for tea or coffee in three to four minutes, then add instant coffee or a tea bag for one-cup ease.

• CAUTION: If you add the tea bag or stir the instant coffee with a spoon immediately (within a second or two) after removing the cup from the microwave oven, the water is likely to bubble over because of the microwaves' action in the cup. Wait a few seconds before adding more action to the cup, and put the cup where spillovers won't burn you.

• When you are buying herb teas, read the labels to be sure what sorts of ingredients have been combined. You don't want to drink herbs you're allergic to. Also, some of the properties of certain herb tea ingredients may have effects you haven't bargained for, especially if you drink excessive amounts.

For example, many herb teas contain caffeine, which you may be trying to avoid. Some contain chicory and other herbs that are mild laxatives and that could cause distress if you drank too much. Some herbs (tonka beans, sweet clover, and other plants) are coumarins (substances that prevent blood clotting) and could be dangerous to some people when consumed in excess (several pots daily).

Leftovers

Leftovers are great time and money savers. They can be popped into the microwave or conventional oven whenever you need a quick meal and cooking is the farthest thing from your mind.

Don't hesitate to serve the same foods two days in a row. If it's a nutritious meal on Monday, it will be a nutritious meal on Tuesday, and may even taste better. If your family rebels, there are ways to disguise almost any food. When you look into your refrigerator, don't think of the food as leftovers; think of it as the beginning of your next meal—build around it and consider it a bonus.

Being Creative with Leftovers

• One of the ways to disguise leftovers is to add some fresh ingredients or spices. The leftover stew that's enough for only two might become a hearty soup, enough for four, if fresh or canned stewed tomatoes, some frozen or canned mixed vegetables, and noodles or rice are added. Some casseroles, stews, and pot roasts actually taste better the next day, after their flavors have blended. Texas chili is always better the second and third day.

• You can make a hot dish using accumulated leftover vegetables. A combination of vegetables and macaroni, and that last wiener or slice of meat, can be put into a pan with a can of beef vegetable soup. If you are using a lot of leftovers, you may want to add a bouillon cube to flavor the soup and possibly corn starch to thicken the sauce.

I once read in a French cookbook that just about anything you add water to will taste better if you add bouillon instead. Many types and flavors of bouillon are available. Some of the gourmet department liquid bouillons also add color to stews and soups.

• To save time, you can prepare your own TV dinners by cooking extra portions and then freezing them. You can freeze individual portions in plastic zipper-type freezer bags or on ready-to-heat-and-eat-from plates. Keep three-sectioned heavy paper plates on hand or heavy plastic plates, found on sale, to freeze leftover portions to be reheated in the microwave oven. Fill each plate with one serving, place it in a freezer-safe plastic bag, and freeze. Aluminum plates can be used for leftovers that will be reheated in conventional ovens.

• Try freezing larger amounts of leftovers in a plastic-lined bowl. When the food is frozen, remove the contents from the bowl and put them in a freezer-safe bag. This way you haven't lost a bowl to the freezer, and this also helps save valuable freezer space.

• Using the plastic bag or foil and this idea, you can also freeze casseroles in the same casserole in which they will be heated so that the block of food will fit into its proper cooking container. Always date everything you put into your freezer; it's so easy to lose track of time.

Keeping Track of Stored Leftovers

You should date all leftovers in the refrigerator so you won't end up throwing them away because you don't know how long they have been stored. Tape an 8" × 11" sheet of fairly stiff plastic to the inside of a cupboard door. Cut little squares from a roll of masking tape and stick them on the plastic. When you need a date sticker, remove one of the squares and write the date on it (i.e., 5 for the fifth of that month or 25 for the twenty-fifth—there will really be no need for a month on refrigerator leftovers because, we hope, you won't have anything left over for that long). When the dish used is empty, replace the date sticker on the heavy plastic to be reused; it's all marked and ready for the next leftover!

• Always put leftovers on the top shelf or in the same area of your refrigerator. Even consider marking the area "Leftovers." This way, they'll never be over-looked or forgotten. One of my favorite hints is to put them in glass jars so that I can see what I have to work with when I'm holding a "combination-of-leftovers gourmet event."

Cooking and Cleanup

It can't be said too often: We need to have help from the people we live with, and we need to take shortcuts when we can. Otherwise, we won't have time and energy left to enjoy the people and events in our lives that make us happy.

• Here's a good thawing tip to help teenagers and other cooks' assistants to remember to take items out of the freezer for dinner: Tape a memo sheet on the door and write down the item to be taken out. This easy reminder will prevent dinner delays while you quick-thaw something for dinner. Or, take the meat out of the freezer the night before and let it thaw in the refrigerator during the day so that it will be ready when you are ready to cook.

• If you have little ones who seem to demand most of your time in the late afternoon instead of the morning, try cooking that night's meal in the morning, when you have more time and may be in the kitchen anyway.

• Most of our days begin and end in the kitchen anyway, so if you take a few minutes the night before to plan what you'll have the next evening, it will take only a little while the next morning to put it all together. Be sure to refrigerate the dinner preparations properly so that you can reheat them safely when dinnertime rolls around.

Cooking Tips

• Cook ground meat thoroughly. This is very important because it's handled so often in the preparation and packaging process that it can quickly develop bacteria. Do not eat raw ground meat.

Steak tartare is the exception to this rule, but you should eat it only if you can be certain that the meat has been freshly ground and properly handled before it was served. You have to decide if you trust the chef or friend who serves it in a restaurant or at home.

• Never put cooked meat, chicken, or seafood on a platter that you have used for uncooked meat, chicken, or seafood unless the platter has been carefully washed. Bacteria from raw meat can be transferred to the cooked meat.

• Plastic cutting boards are safer than wooden cutting boards because they aren't likely to harbor bacteria from foods. If you use a wooden cutting board, clean the board with a mixture of two teaspoons of chlorine bleach and one teaspoon of vinegar to a gallon of water. Reseason the wooden board by rubbing it with mineral oil. If you use salad oil for reseasoning, it's likely to become rancid and you won't be able to use the board anymore. (This same process applies also to unfinished wooden utensils and salad bowls.)

• Onions: If you put onions into the freezer 15 minutes before use or into the fridge the day before, you'll reduce the spray of onion oils that vaporize when you cut them, and your eyes won't cry.

• Garlic: If you like fresh garlic or garlic-flavored oil, try this. Buy fresh garlic, peel all of the cloves at one time, then immerse them in light sesame or safflower oil in a glass jar. The oil seals the garlic from the air, and some sources say it will keep without refrigeration up to six weeks. I still think it's better to keep it in the fridge. If the cloves turn pale brown, the flavor is being lost. The bonus here is that you not only have garlic ready to use, but you have garlic-flavored oil for cooking or salads. Just keep replacing the oil you take from the jar.

• Sour cream substitute: The texture and flavor is not exactly the same, but if you need a substitute for sour cream in a pinch, combine six ounces of cottage cheese with one teaspoon of lemon juice in a food processor or blender until it's smooth. Plain, unflavored yogurt can also substitute for sour cream in many recipes.

Microwave Oven Cooking Tips

• To adapt your recipes to microwave cooking, find a similar dish in the cookbook that came with your microwave oven to determine cooking time, dish size, and proportions of ingredients to use.

• Adding a large amount of liquid to a dish lengthens the cooking time, so you need to reduce the amount of liquid to about half that used in a conventional recipe. Also, if the container is sealed in plastic wrap, very little liquid will evaporate.

• Since you will be using less liquid, reduce the amount of salt in your recipe.

• Because alcohol flavors are very unstable in microwave cooking, you will need to increase the proportion of wine in cooking liquids to get the flavor you want.

• Garlic cooks out very quickly, so increase the amount you use.

• Dried herbs and pepper flavors will be intensified, so reduce the amount of these ingredients. However, you need to increase the amount of fresh herbs.

Using Spices and Herbs

You can be creative with spices and herbs. It doesn't take much time to toss in a pinch of this and a few leaves of that to put a bit of zip into otherwise plain food. For quick flavors try adding the following:

• One-fourth teaspoon of allspice to simmering chicken or turkey stock to get the wonderful fragrance of cinnamon, cloves, and nutmeg.

• Allspice to cream soups or a pinch sprinkled over citrus fruits.

• Basil to tofu or tempeh marinades.

• A pinch of basil to peas, green beans, eggplant, zucchini, macaroni. And sprinkle it on cut tomatoes or cucumbers.

• One medium bay leaf to a six-serving recipe of soup, chicken or meat stew, spaghetti sauce, venison.

• A dash of cayenne to Hungarian goulash or anything else you want to bite you back!

• Garlic rubbed on pork, sprinkled with caraway seed and brown sugar before roasting.

• Chili powder to perk up sloppy joes, eggs, or cottage cheese.

• Dried chives on cottage cheese or on your cream-cheese sandwich. Also on your baked potato, omelet, and cucumber or lettuce salad. Chives are good when combined with any herbs.

• One teaspoon celery seed to one cup French dressing.

• Chervil to potato salad.

• A dash of cinnamon in dark wild-game gravies.

• A pinch of cloves to sweet potatoes or sliced buttered carrots.

• Cumin to potatoes, rice, and bread.

• Curry powder to egg salad and to barbecue sauce for grilled chicken or salmon, and to beef pot pies.

• Cardamom to curries, and acorn or butternut squash; also, a pinch into baked custard.

• Cayenne into coleslaw.

• Cilantro into scrambled eggs.

• Dill into salads, sour cream, cottage cheese, and omelets, and on salmon.

• A pinch of fennel into coleslaw and cooked cauliflower.

• Ginger into kale or collard greens, carrots, beets, and tomato soups, and with miso.

• Marjoram into soups, salads, and tofu or tempeh stir-fries.

• Mint to cold steamed squash, cauliflower, and potato or bean salad.

• Mustard powder into coleslaw, potato or bean salad, vegetable soups, and cream sauces.

• A pinch of crumbled rosemary to mashed potatoes.

• Tarragon into lentil or split-pea soup.

• Thyme into omelets, tomato dishes, and lentil or split-pea soup.

Cleanup

• To clean up more easily when cooking spaghetti, macaroni and cheese, scalloped potatoes, or meat loaf, line the baking dish with aluminum foil (but only if you're cooking in the regular oven, not in the microwave oven!). After dinner remove the foil, and there's no more fretting over scrubbing an encrusted food dish. If there are leftovers, wrap the aluminum foil over the food, label it, and place in the freezer.

• When a pot is layered with thick scorched or caramelized food, try boiling a mixture of one tablespoon of baking soda per cup of water in the pot to lift that mess off.

For more cleanup tips, see Chapter 12, "Entertaining."

Utensils

• If you keep cooking utensils in a kitchen drawer, you can identify them more easily by turning the handles to the back of the drawer. This way you can find the tool you want.

• To make chopped eggs easily, after slicing them in an egg slicer place the slices crosswise and slice again. You can also use the egg slicer for slicing fresh mushrooms. Placed stem up, two or three small ones can be sliced at a time. The slices are thicker than those produced by a food processor and are more uniform.

• When the edges of plastic utensils get a bit rough or burred, file them down with a fresh emery board. You can cut away the rough edges of rubber and plastic scrapers with good kitchen shears. You save on having to purchase new spatulas and turners, and prevent scratching those expensive non-stick-surface pans.

• Some of the best kitchen shears I know are blunt-ended surgical shears, available in medical supplies stores. You have to be careful where you put your fingers when you are working because they are extremely sharp, but you'll also be able to disjoint a chicken (raw or cooked) faster than with a knife. These shears can also make quick snips in the fatty edges of steaks and chops, even after they are already in the pan and starting to curl up (because you forgot to snip).

Of course, you already knew that the fatty edges of steaks and chops must be snipped in two or three places before frying and broiling to prevent their curling up into a difficult-to-serve cup-o-chop or steak cup. One might argue that when the meat curls up into a cup it holds sauces better, but if it's curled up, it won't brown and cook properly.

• Another all-purpose tool that you can buy at medical supplies stores is forceps. These pointy-nosed, handle-locking medical "pliers" (actually a doctor's version of needle-nosed pliers) will retrieve things from small openings (drawstrings from pajamas, drape cords from the rods, bobby pins or jewel stones from crevices); will hold small objects for placement (jewel stones, decals) when they are being glued; and help in a variety of crafts. They clamp on to things you'd usually use tweezers to grasp and hold them until you release the handles. They also can be used to fix jewelry clasps and bezels.

• Spaghetti grabbers, sold in most kitchen utensils departments, are terrific multi-use utensils. They are either ten-fingered plastic "hands" on a handle or wooden utensils that have several pegs on a broad flat "spoon" end of the handle. Both are handy, but the plastic grabbers are the most versatile because they'll grab just about any food in the kitchen that has to be manipulated while it's in hot water or oil. (CAUTION: Extremely hot oil might melt the plastic grabbers.) Use a spaghetti grabber to:

1. Stir/separate cooking noodles and then lift pasta out of the pot.
2. Remove the bouquet garni (bag of spices) from soups and stews before serving.
3. Remove the meat/chicken/turkey hunks from soup for deboning and then to return the boned meat to the pot without splashing.
4. Remove vegetables from the pot-roast pan and arrange them on the platter.
5. Pull one batch of boiling anything out of the water when you intend to reuse the boil for more batches, as when you are boiling fresh shrimp.
6. Pull out the soft potatoes and leave the undone ones in the pot for more cooking when you are boiling potatoes for salad.
7. Break up tuna fish and stir it into pasta salad without totally smashing ingredients.
8. Fish soaking utensils out of hot, sudsy water, especially if you think you've tossed a knife into it.

And on and on, whenever you need an extra hand that doesn't mind a dip in hot water or oil so that you can pull just about anything out of bubbling hot liquid and put any lumpies into liquid without splashing.

And if nobody is looking, you can use it to scratch that unreachable place between your shoulder blades!

• Spring (colored metal, wood, plastic) clothespins are helpful everywhere in the house. They hold skirts on hangers, notes on curtains, mail to mailboxes, and in the kitchen they pinch bags shut, hold coupons and recipe cards together, clip a recipe to a nearby object so it's easily read, clip a dish towel to your blouse when you need an apron and are in too much of a hurry to get one, clip a towel around a child's neck for an instant bib, and . . . need I say more? Keep a bunch in the kitchen clipped to any convenient object.

• Use a tea or spice ball to hold the bouquet garni of spices when you make soup or stew—nobody will ever bite into a stray whole pepper ball, and you won't have to fish around with your spaghetti grabber for those bay leaves that lurk in the murky depths of pots.

• If you have long hair that gets in your way while you are busily cooking or cleaning in the kitchen, cut four to six one-inch slashes (like an asterisk) across the center of a plastic lid (nut, baking powder, chip can) and poke your hair through it for a ponytail. It's not glamorous but will do until you are finished with your work and can put yourself together again in your usual gorgeous style. This idea could help at the beach when your hair is wet and blowing in the wind.

• For a cute holder in which to store your small kitchen utensils, cover a coffee can (large size) or other similar container with leftover wallpaper. If you haven't cut up the lid for a ponytail holder, you can put it on the bottom of the can to protect it from wet counter spills.

CHAPTER 2

Saving Supermarket Dollars

Saving money at the supermarket goes beyond using coupons, shopping the specials, and knowing how to pick out the best from the display. In addition to saving money, shopping efficiently also saves time. And, if you store your food, cook it, and use up leftovers efficiently, you get the utmost for the time and money you spend at the supermarket.

Saving Time and $$$ by Planning Ahead

We all hate to sit down and write lists, but I have found that planning ahead, making lists, and taking a little time to organize really does save time, not to mention money, in the long run.

Even the busiest person needs to sit down and sip a cup of tea or coffee once in a while, and if you're the kind of person who needs an excuse to take a break, use list-making time as your excuse! You may even find that by getting organized you'll have saved enough time to have a bona fide, pleasant, uplifting "fun break."

We all feel happier when we are running our homes and schedules instead of having our homes and schedules run us.

Menus and Shopping Lists

• Meal planning doesn't have to be a boring chore. If you make separate index cards for each dinner you prepare for a few months, menu planning becomes a simple matter of pulling out enough index cards for the number of meals you'll be shopping for; your food shopping list is always ready-made!

• If you are lucky enough to have a family computer, you can keep all sorts of menu files that can be called up and printed whenever you're ready to shop. It really saves time to keep a master shopping checklist to print out which will remind you to check for those things you usually forget. You can keep track of what you buy and then revise your list and run off a supply of lists every three months or so.

• Another ready-made grocery list is the sale page from your newspaper. Just check off on the ad page the items you need, and jot down items that aren't in the ad. Grocery ads help you plan menus around things that are on sale, which saves money!

• Save time and money by planning weekly menus before you shop. Shopping for one week eliminates those short but time-consuming treks to the store; menus not only discourage expensive impulse buying, they also eliminate having to make that daily decision of what to fix for dinner.

• Save time by going to the store early Saturday morning before it becomes crowded or shop at any time you've noticed is unpopular at your store, such as during sports events or popular TV shows. Waiting in long lines at the checkout counter is just one more tedious thing that can be avoided if you plan ahead.

• While bargain shopping is a good practice, time is money and a full day of bargain shopping and wasting gas in an attempt to save a dollar or two is usually not a bargain at all.

Coupons

• When making a shopping list, place a "C" next to items that have a coupon to be redeemed, to make couponing easier for you.

• Or, if you are shopping with a roommate, spouse, or child, make two lists—one for coupon items and one for regular shopping. Have one person go off with the coupons and a separate cart; then both of you can meet at the checkout counter in half the usual shopping time. Reading the coupon requirements is not only fun for kids, but it teaches them how to be aware of details. If you're having a child do the coupon hunt, always offer an incentive by making sure that some of the coupons are for favorite cereals and other goodies.

• When grocery stores accept double coupons, check the newspaper section to see how many coupons will be useful to you. If there are a lot, you can save money by buying another copy of the paper.

• I keep a few coupons for items I frequently use and need in my purse at all times. The money they save really does add up.

• Keep a box handy when you read newspapers or magazines. When you see coupons, tear out the entire page and put it in the box. When your children are bored or watching television, they can cut them out.

• Go through your coupons every other month and pull out those due to expire in the next two months, then clip these together and put them in front of the others. If there's no expiration date, write the word "none" across the coupon. Also, when you clip a coupon out of a newspaper or magazine, you can underline the expiration date or mark it with a highlighter pen. This helps to organize coupons and helps the cashier find the expiration date, saving the cashier's time and yours.

Coupon Holders

Keep all of your coupons in one place instead of scattered around the house. There are many different ways to organize them.

• One way that works well is to arrange your coupon file in the order of the supermarket's aisles. I use an accordion-style canceled check file to avoid the bulk of a recipe file box.

• A spare napkin holder can keep coupons in one place and can also hold your shopping list.

• An old checkbook cover is also a handy holder.

• Those little wallets that traveler's checks come in are good coupon holders. Holes can be punched at the end of each coupon so that you can fasten them to the metal brads. And they fold up nice and snug.

• You can hold a legal-size envelope on the refrigerator with a magnet, then write your grocery list on the envelope and place coupons to be redeemed inside it. Don't waste money on a new envelope; it can be recycled from "junk mail." You might as well get some use from it!

• A plastic recipe box is large enough to handle hundreds of coupons. Use the index card dividers to separate food groups.

• You can also keep coupons in a large metal or plastic lunch box, using file box dividers to separate coupons into groups. The lunch box fits into the seat portion of the shopping cart and makes handling coupons easy.

• You can use a clothespin to hold coupons you plan to redeem; this will leave your hands free for shopping.

• When clipping coupons, why not take some of the money you save and give it to a charity or perhaps to a friend who is struggling?

• Take extra coupons to work to share with your fellow workers.

• Tuck coupons for baby products in with baby shower gifts.

• Treat yourself. Keep track of the money you save couponing and then spend it when you're on vacation, use it for gifts to yourself or others, or spend it on something you want but don't need.

Shopping Trips

If you organize your shopping trips, you'll save time as well as money and gas. For example, you can buy several weeks' worth of supplies on double-coupon days or when your favorite brands are on sale.

Most of us use certain products more frequently than others. It helps to know how much of a product you use over a period of time so that you can stock up without overstocking when there's a sale.

• Date such products as they are put to use, so that you'll know how long it takes to use them up. For example, if you find that you use about six tubes of toothpaste and eleven bottles of shampoo in one year, you can safely buy those amounts of toothpaste and shampoo.

I don't date food items that I will consume in short periods of time, but I do date such items as a large jar of jelly, aluminum foil, instant and regular coffee, salt, and pepper.

• When I run errands all day, I put a plastic laundry basket in the trunk of the car and put my packages in the basket. Small bags don't get lost, and you can carry in the basket with all the bags in one trip when you get home.

• Put an inexpensive foam cooler in the car, and you can put frozen foods in it when you grocery shop. Then you don't have to worry if you need to make extra stops en route home and you won't have to pass up a good buy on milk or meat; and ice cream will be in better shape too.

• If you keep transparent tape in the glove compartment of your car, on shopping days you can attach a piece of tape to the top of your shopping list when you leave your car and then stick the exposed half of the tape onto the middle of the grocery cart handle. Your list will be easy to read; it won't get lost and you'll have both hands free to shop. Don't forget to remove it from the cart when you're through!

• If you have friends who meet for a weekly card game, tennis, or whatever, do your shopping together on that day and take turns driving. One car going for weekly groceries sure beats several when it comes to saving gas, and you have the added bonus of pleasant company. You and your friends also can buy in bulk and then split for extra economy.

• Another tip to make shopping more pleasant is to remember that the shopping carts that work, the ones that don't have wheels with minds of their own, are the carts left in the parking lot by previous shoppers! Take one with you when you enter the store and make dozens of store employees happy at the same time.

• Higher-priced items in the store are usually placed at eye level; you'll save money if you look up, down, and sideways at all the brands of the product you want.

• Always compare weights and volume, not just the size of the package. A box or jar may be bigger but still contain the same contents. Also, the giant economy size may not cost less per ounce, pound, etc. Many people carry small calculators to avoid supermarket math, and some stores have price per ounce or piece actually posted on the shelf.

• When you have bought several six-packs of canned soft drinks encased in the popular plastic rings, it saves room in the shopping cart if you place the six-pack with three cans on each side of the grocery cart's edge, letting them hang by the plastic holder. They'll hang there securely and take up little cart space.

• Always purchase meat and poultry last and refrigerate them as soon as possible when you get home.

• To save time in the grocery checkout line, place meat packages in clear plastic bags (from produce section) so that their price labels show through the unprinted side of the bag. The clerk can see clearly the price and code and can ring up items more quickly, without the other groceries getting messy.

Buying Produce

Anyone who gardens knows how to buy produce, because watching things grow teaches you to observe what's old and what's fresh.

For example, broccoli with little yellow flowers trying to poke through the green heads is older than broccoli that has no flowers. The same goes for asparagus, which also "flowers" when it's mature.

• You can tell how long asparagus, lettuce, and other vegetables that have obvious cut ends have been in the store just by looking at the cut end. Is it a fresh cut or is it brown and, in the case of asparagus, somewhat dry?

• When you see delicate leaves on the ends of carrots or radishes, you know they didn't just get off the turnip truck yesterday; they are sprouting and, therefore, old.

• The rule of thumb is don't press your thumb into produce, because such bruising causes a lot of waste and spoilage that the rest of us shoppers end up paying for.

Other shopping rules are:

• Buy in season (grocery ads and specials will indicate this).

• Buy the best quality you can afford but avoid overpriced out-of-season foods.

• Don't buy too-ripe or too-green produce because, in most cases, flavor will never reach its peak.

• Be wary of oversize fruits, which may not taste as good as they look (except for Bing cherries and blueberries, where bigger is better).

Some of the following information on buying fruits and vegetables is from my own experience, but I checked with the experts too. Some of the information is from a book called *Buying Produce* by Jack Murdich (Hearst Books, New York, 1986), who is an experienced produce buyer, and some of it is from the U.S. Department of Agriculture.

Buying Fruits and Berries

Many fruits and berries used to be luxury foods, available only if you grew them in your own backyard or lived in areas of the country where they were grown. Otherwise, if they were available at all, the costs were prohibitive.

The kiwi is a good example. Not only were these fuzzy brown, yummy fruits rare in markets, they were so expensive that few people would even try them. One small kiwi (and all are relatively small for the price) used to cost more than $1 each. Now that kiwis are grown commercially and shipped throughout the U.S., they can even be found as "specials" priced reasonably for just about anyone's fruit salad.

It takes time and trial and error to learn how to select the best of those fruits, berries and melons that are relatively new to supermarket displays. Here are tips to help you:

• Gooseberries: These look like green grapes and can be eaten raw, but are usually made into jam or pies and are seldom seen in stores.

• Guavas: Available from December to February, guavas are light green or yellow. They are plum-shaped; the flesh is white to dark pink. Unless tree ripened, they are tart. They are usually made into jelly.

• Kiwis (or kiwifruit): Available from May through November when grown in California, and from November through May when imported from New Zealand. Buy fairly firm kiwis and ripen them at room temperature for about a week. A kiwi that is about as soft as a ripe plum is ready to eat. Tip: If a kiwi is in this stage at the store, it may be bruised and ready to deteriorate.

Some people like to sprinkle kiwi, after it's been peeled and sliced into rounds, with lime juice and eat it as is; others use it for chocolate fondue, and it is also glazed for topping pastries. If you like yogurt, then kiwi and any kind of berries or vanilla-flavored low-fat yogurt is a tasty and fairly low-calorie dessert.

- Kumquats: They peak from December to May, are very tart, and contain a lot of seeds. Few people like to eat them raw, and they are usually used for marmalade. Buy firm, orange fruit and store it in the fridge. Don't buy green kumquats; they won't ripen to an acceptable flavor.

- Loquats: They peak from mid-March to May and are usually too expensive to be more than just a "taste" item. They look like small, fuzzy apricots and have three or four pits.

- Lychees (lychee nuts): You are not likely to find these in regular supermarkets because they're very expensive. They are about as big as a golf ball and have a rough, tough inedible skin which fades from strawberry color to dusty pink after it is picked. The light green flesh surrounds an inedible nut. The edible part of one lychee is about the same as two or three grapes. Both fresh and dried lychees are sold in Oriental communities as gifts.

- Mangoes: In season from January through September, they peak in May, June, and July. Ranging in size from a few ounces to four pounds, several types of mangoes are available in the United States. Some mangoes are fibrous and stringy, but three types are recommended: the Haden (yellow-skinned with a red cheek when ripe); the Kent (large, green-skinned, with reddish cheek); and the Keitt (large, green, with or without red cheek). Flat, kidney-shaped mangoes are usually fibrous and sour.

   Tree-ripened mangoes are the sweetest, and imported mangoes are usually ready to eat when bought at the market. Florida mangoes are picked hard and need a week at room temperature to ripen. Buy unbruised fruit. You can peel and slice mangoes and serve them alone or in fruit salad.

- Papayas: In season year-round, papayas are usually light green when harvested; they ripen to a golden yellow. The flesh is yellow or orange-pink.

   Buy firm, pale green or pale yellow fruit and ripen it at room temperature. It's better not to refrigerate papayas.

- Passion fruit: About as big as an egg. Its inedible skin is usually purple but can be red and gold; the flesh is yellow. I used to pluck them from the trees in Hawaii when I was a child and eat them until I was stuffed.

- Persimmons: Domestic persimmons are available from October to January; Chilean ones are sold in the spring. Ripe persimmons look like shiny, acorn-shaped, deep orange tomatoes.

Eating an unripened persimmon can cause you to pucker more than you'll ever know or want to remember. The old wives' tale about freezing unripe persimmons so that they will be ripe and edible when they thaw is true. Buy firm, colorful persimmons and ripen them for several days at room temperature. When the skin is shriveled (blistered skin is not yet ripe) and has lost its color, the fruit can be eaten. The skin can be eaten if you wish.

• Pineapples: Available year-round, pineapples are jetted in from Hawaii or shipped from Latin America. Generally, Hawaiian pineapples are the sweetest and juiciest, because Latin American pineapples are picked while too green to have reached their full sugar content. The tags will tell you where the pineapples have been grown. Buy the largest pineapple in the display that is firm and shows some color.

• Pomegranates: Although some have yellow skin, most commercially grown pomegranates have red, leathery skin. The flesh is made up of juicy red kernel clusters, and each kernel has a seed that is optionally edible. They peak in October and November and need no refrigeration, although fridge storage will help them last longer.

It's interesting to know that the Egyptians used pomegranate juice for ink and dyeing fabric—a warning not to dribble any of the juice on your clothing!

• Prickly pears: These are the fruit of the cactus and are not actually pears, although they are more or less pear-shaped. Although most are deep red, some are pale yellow, orange, or pink. Buy large fruit, ripen at room temperature, then refrigerate.

You have to be determined to eat prickly pear because its skin is covered with barbs and the pulp has lots of seeds, which are edible but very hard to chew. Most prickly pear in the market has been singed to remove the barbs. To eat it, cut off the top and bottom and then cut it from end to end so that you can peel off the inedible skin. You will be rewarded by a tasty, juicy fruit.

• Star fruit (carambolas): Relatively new to our markets, star fruit peak from September to January. They look like five-pointed starfish and most come from Hawaii and the Caribbean islands, although some are grown in the United States. The deeper the yellow color of the fruit's waxy-looking edible skin, the less tart the fruit. They can be eaten raw, used in jams and jellies, and included in fruit punches.

• Watermelons: They peak from June through August. The way to select all watermelons is the same: The only way to be certain of a watermelon's ripeness is to cut a plug or to buy one that is cut in half or quarters. Sometimes, melons that have been displayed in very hot sun at roadside stands will be sun damaged—almost mushy, as if cooked. (This is also true of tomatoes.) Ask to have the watermelon plugged so you can see what's inside.

Buying Vegetables

It's no secret that I love vegetables and only rarely eat meat. Veggies—raw, steamed, stir-fried—please the eye as well as the palate, and, as medical research is showing, the fiber from vegetables and grains may be our best ally against numerous diseases, including cancer of the colon, a disease almost unknown in parts of the world where people eat an abundance of fruits, vegetables, and grain and very little meat. Dietary fiber intake is becoming important in the control of diabetes as well. Plus, if you are trying to lose weight, veggies fill you up without filling you with lots of calories, unless you smother them in sauces or butter.

Modern farming and shipping give us a variety of vegetables throughout the year, and like fruit, many vegetables and herbs which we can buy at any supermarket were almost unknown or totally unknown by our grandmothers and even our mothers.

Combinations of vegetables are available in the frozen-food sections, but fresh vegetables are becoming more popular because they are so readily available and priced so reasonably these days.

Here are some tips to help you get your money's worth when you buy vegetables, which, until recently, were not always available in supermarkets.

Unless otherwise noted the vegetables listed are available year-round and should be kept refrigerated.

• Anise (sweet fennel): Usually out of season in hot weather, anise has fernlike green foliage that looks a bit like fresh dill weed. The greens can be chopped and used for seasoning. Buy fresh, green foliage and crisp-looking bulbs for a sweet licorice flavor.

• Avocados: Most avocados used to be sold very firm and took a long while to ripen; now many are ready to use when bought, but because they are so ripe they are often bruised at the market.

To quick-ripen avocados in half the natural time, put the avocado into a brown paper bag with a tomato and then put the bag in the warmest part of the house. The natural ethylene gas from the avocado and tomato plus warmth is what speeds up ripening.

To test for ripeness, put the avocado in the palm of your hand. A Florida avocado is ready to serve if it yields to slight pressure. Let a California avocado ripen one more day after this test. Florida avocados are usually twice as big as California ones and have a lower calorie count. California avocados have a more nutlike flavor and a richer, creamier flesh. According to some avocado fans, the difference between California and Florida avocados is like that between ice cream and ice milk, with the Florida product being the ice milk.

Cut avocados turn dark when exposed to air. Sprinkle the surface with fresh lemon or lime juice and use as soon as possible. If you only use a half avocado, leave the pit in the unused half. Here in Texas, we put the pit into avocado dip when we refrigerate it to prevent darkening.

Avocados don't ripen in the fridge, and refrigeration will make the flesh turn black. You can freeze pureed but not whole or cut avocados.

• Broccoli: Broccoli should be firm, green, and not yellow or budded with yellow flowers. Some broccoli has a slightly purple cast to the buds and this is a mark of quality.

• Celeriac (knob celery): Used as a cooked vegetable or raw in salads, celeriac is usually sold in bunches with three knobs and green tops attached. Larger knobs tend to be woody; buy smaller ones. If the greens are fresh, they can be used for soup. It's easy to peel after cooking. If served raw, you'll need to sprinkle it with lemon juice because it discolors when cut.

• Kale: A curly-leafed member of the cabbage family, kale tastes much like cabbage when it's cooked. Buy crisp, dark green or slightly blue leaves. Wilted, limp, or yellow leaves are old. When you see pink, purple, or white-hearted kale, it's ornamental and usually too expensive to eat.

• Kohlrabi: This looks like pale green beets but grow above the ground. Buy kohlrabi that is the same size as beets to avoid getting a woody, overmature one. It should look crisp; if the leaves are wilted/yellow, don't buy it. The leaves, if green and fresh, can be cooked like spinach. Kohlrabi is served cooked or raw.

• Mustard greens: Although these are popular in the South, they aren't often eaten in the rest of the United States. Buy dark or light green leaves, which may have a bronze cast. If limp and yellow, they are old; don't buy them. They are wonderful when cooked and seasoned the old-fashioned way, which is to cook the living heck out of them after adding salt, pepper, bacon drippings, or bits of ham.

Chinese mustard greens have white stems, green leaves, and a slightly bitter flavor. They are usually stir-fried or used in soups.

• Okra: This native African vegetable is like the little girl in the nursery rhyme: When she was good, she was very, very good, but when she was bad, she was horrid. When okra is overcooked it is really horrid—it's gluey and slimy.

Buy velvety, small (less than 2½ inches—bigger ones are woody and stringy) pods, then bake, boil, or fry them in various ways. Okra is popular in Cajun dishes, and in the South it's often fried after being rolled in cornmeal. If you cook it in water, especially in an aluminum pot, add lemon juice to prevent discoloration of the okra and the pot.

Chinese okra *(sing gwa)* is dark green and about an inch in diameter and about 12 inches long. It is often used with seafood dishes.

• Peppers: Either sweet or hot, peppers come in many sizes, shapes and colors. Immature peppers are green; mature peppers can be red, yellow and purple. Generally speaking, the redder the pepper, the sweeter the flavor and shorter the storage time. To tell the difference between hot and sweet peppers, you need to know their names. For example, chili, jalapeño, cayenne, pulla and serrano are hot peppers. Bell and California Wonders are sweet peppers.

HINT: Wear rubber gloves when handling hot peppers; they can really irritate your skin. Some people say it's the seeds that are hot, and some say it's the veins in serrano peppers that are hottest. Whatever's the hottest, wear rubber gloves (the thickest possible) to protect your hands. And don't ever rub your eyes!

• Swiss chard: Sold in bunches, chard should have crisp green leaves, not wilted ones that are turning yellow. Popular for cooking, even when over-cooked, Swiss chard will keep its texture and color and won't get dull and slimy like spinach. Bok choy is an Oriental type of Swiss chard.

Buying Staples

When you are buying canned goods and other products, the cheapest may not be the best buy. With so many brands of everything on the market, the best buy depends upon your personal taste and the way you'll use the product. Generic canned vegetables may be just fine for adding to soups or stews, but may not be tasty and attractive when served as a separate course at dinner.

The basic guidelines for quality of brands of any product are these: national name brands; private labels/house brands; economy brands; and generics, or "no-names."

• National name brands: These are usually the most expensive; if they have been around for several years, they are bound to have good quality because competition is so keen that national name-brand products that aren't as good as their competition aren't likely to survive.

• Private labels/house brands: The prices of these are 10 to 20 percent lower than national brands; the quality is comparable, although the taste—for example, of soups—may not be the same as that of a national brand. However, many store brands are produced by national manufacturers for the large chains.

• Economy brands: These are sold at about 25 percent less than national brands; they are a type of house brand and are generally a bit lower in quality than national or house brands. Supermarket chains usually have their own house and economy brands.

• Generics: Often with yellow, white, or other plain labels and plain black letters designating contents, these products can be production overages from processing plants but are more likely to be lower-quality fruits, vegetables, and so on or end runs in the production line. The quality can vary greatly from one purchase to another; the price will always be well below that of the other labels. I certainly think these are good buys for things like paper plates, napkins, bubble bath for the kids, and anything where quality isn't important and saving money is.

Storing

Food costs too much to waste it by improper storage, but waste isn't the only reason you should store food properly. The Centers for Disease Control (CDC) estimates that as many as four million people get bacterial infections that cause diarrhea, fever, and vomiting, and as many as two thousand people die annually from common food poisoning. Most salmonella poisoning is traced to contaminated meat, poultry, eggs, or milk, but the bacteria can also be harbored in other foods that come in contact with contaminated water or foodstuff. For information on salmonella and other food poisoning, you can call the U.S. Department of Agriculture's hot line, 1-800-535-4555. Put your tax dollars to good use.

Generally, you should keep foods in cool, dry places, and avoid overloading your refrigerator (which prevents it from cooling food properly). The temperature in the refrigerator should be 42 to 44 degrees Fahrenheit in its warmest part and 40 degrees or less in its coldest part (other than the freezer).

Cereals, Flour, Grains

• When I buy raw cereals, flour, rice, and certain packaged foods, I put them into glass jars to prevent bug traffic from one food to the other. I save the cooking instructions and put them into the jar or tape them on the outside. Big ol' gallon pickle jars are my favorites.

• If you put foodstuffs made from grain, especially flour and cornmeal, into the freezer for at least 7 days after bringing them home, any visible or invisible infestations will be destroyed and you won't have to share your groceries with uninvited crawling creature "guests."

• The FDA recommends storing cornmeal in the refrigerator, especially in the summer.

Spices

• Spices and most canned and packaged foods should be stored in a cool, dry place and not above the stove. Because heat rises, the shelves above the stove are pretty warm when the stove is in use and, if you have a gas stove with a pilot light, the heat will be constant. Spices especially will lose their flavor if stored near heat. Like other foods, color and odor changes indicate loss of quality. For best use, buy the smallest quantity.
  The FDA and cooking experts say that keeping spices and herbs frozen or refrigerated is the best way to preserve flavor.

• The next-best way is in a cool, dry, dark cupboard, where most of us keep them.

• You can keep track of the age of spices by marking the date of purchase on a strip of masking tape and sticking it to the bottom of the container.

• If you grow your own herbs for drying or if you like to make your own spice mixtures, you can use clean, dry baby food jars to store them.

• If you're short on cupboard space, nail or glue the jar lids to the underside of a shelf so that you can just unscrew jars from their lids when you use spices.

Canned Goods

• If you are on a low-fat diet, keep unopened cans of soup or chili in the refrigerator. After the food is sufficiently chilled, you can easily skim off the congealed fat, then heat as usual. You'll never miss the fat and the flavor will be as good as before.

• Canned goods should be kept in a dry, cool room with a temperature of about 70 degrees Fahrenheit. Never store canned goods near steam pipes, furnaces, kitchen ranges, or in the garage, because both freezing and too much heat will affect the quality of canned goods.

Nonacid canned foods are safe in the above conditions for two to three years, with some vegetables such as potatoes keeping as long as five years. Acid foods, such as tomatoes and all fruits, are safe for about 18 months.

• If you see rust or discoloration on a can at the seam or anywhere else or if a can bulges at either end, throw out the can without opening it and certainly without handling or tasting it. Consider any discolored or off-odor food to be spoiled and poisonous; discard it and make sure children and pets can't get at it.

• CAUTION: Whenever you are in doubt about the age of canned foods or they even hint at being spoiled, it always makes sense to be cautious and throw them out. No amount of money saved is worth taking a chance of making yourself sick.

In fact, never taste-test any type of questionable food, whether it's canned, home-cooked, carry-out, or even fresh from the market. Always throw out foods that you suspect may be spoiled. When in doubt, throw it out!

• Dispose of spoiled or questionable foods carefully. Seal them in containers. If possible, flush spoiled foods down the disposal or toilet to keep them away from pets who might raid your garbage. To prevent garbage jamming in the pipe of your garbage disposal, be sure to always run lots of water when you turn it on. Let the water run a few seconds after turning it off to thoroughly flush out the pipes.

Fresh Vegetables

• Eating fresh vegetables as soon as possible ensures getting maximum food value from them. Vegetables should be stored in the refrigerator; most refrigerators have crisper drawers for this purpose. (See storage times listed elsewhere in this chapter.)

• However, if you have a garden or access to large quantities of certain vegetables, you may want to freeze the surplus. Except for green peppers or onions for seasoning, most vegetables need to be blanched (put in boiling water for several minutes) before freezing to prevent deterioration.

• Tomatoes have a high water content and tend to collapse when thawing, thus losing their juice. A lot of people freeze surplus garden tomatoes anyway. They are easy to peel (hold under running water for a minute or so and the peel comes off) and then easy to pop, still frozen, into soups, stews, and sauces.

• Potatoes need to be cooked before freezing.

• Lettuce, cabbage, onions, celery, and carrot sticks will lose crispness and get limp and tough, and therefore can't be eaten raw if frozen, but are fine for soups, stews, and casseroles.

The U.S. Department of Agriculture (USDA) has many fine booklets on canning, preserving, and freezing that can be obtained by calling the USDA's local office or your local Cooperative Extension Agent. Look in the government section (blue in some cities, but not all) of your phone book under the federal government listings for the USDA or under your state listings for your local county Cooperative Extension Agent.

Eggs

• The American Egg Board tells us that fresh eggs can be stored in their cartons in the refrigerator as long as five weeks and that the store carton is the best container for storage. Contrary to what we would think, the shell is porous; it does allow odors to penetrate.

The reason the store carton is the best container is that if you take the eggs out of the carton and put them in the egg holder in the door, every time you open and close the door the eggs are subject to temperature variation and to movement, which causes them to spoil more quickly.

• Eggs can be stored eight to ten days if hard-cooked in shells, and two to four days for egg whites in a covered container or egg yolks covered with water.

• Eggs cannot be frozen in their shells, but raw whole eggs, whites, and yolks and hard-cooked yolks can be frozen. Follow the directions below.

Egg whites should be sealed tightly in a freezer container that is labeled with the number of whites and the date.

To freeze whole eggs or yolks, add either ⅛ teaspoon salt or 1½ teaspoon sugar or corn syrup for each four yolks or two whole eggs. In addition to the date and number of yolks or whole eggs, note whether you've added salt or sugar to the eggs so that you'll know if they can be used for main dishes.

Thaw frozen eggs overnight in the refrigerator or under cool running water. Yolks and whole eggs should be used as soon as they're thawed; thawed whites will have better volume when beaten if they are kept at room temperature for about 30 minutes.

Cheeses

• Store cheeses in the refrigerator. Some American cheeses will crumble if frozen, which is fine if you plan to use them in a sauce or as a salad topping, but not so fine if you want slices.

• Sliced cheeses can be refrigerated in their original film wrappers. You can wrap cheese with waxed paper or plastic and then with foil before refrigerating it. Processed cheese, cheese food, and spreads sold in sealed jars or packages keep without refrigeration but must be refrigerated after you open the containers.

• Cheeses are classified as very hard (for grating), hard, semisoft, soft, and also as ripened or unripened cheeses.

Very hard cheeses include Asiago old, Parmesan, Romano, sapsago, and Spalen. Hard cheeses include cheddar, granular or stirred curd, Caciocavallo, Swiss, Emmentaler, and Gruyère. Among the semisoft cheeses are brick, Muenster, Limburger, Port du Salut, Trappist, Roquefort, Gorgonzola, blue, Stilton, and Wensleydale. Soft cheeses include Bel Paese, Brie, Camembert, cooked, hand, and Neufchâtel (as made in France). The above cheeses are all ripened cheeses.

Among the unripened cheeses are these soft cheeses: cottage, pot, baker's, cream, Neufchâtel (as made in the United States), mysost, primost, and fresh ricotta.

• Generally, ripened cheeses keep longer than unripened cheeses, and you can buy enough to last for several weeks. Most soft unripened cheeses are perishable, so it's best to buy only as much as you'll use in a short time.

Meat, Poultry, Seafood

• Take a tip from the fish market: Store all seafood on ice in the refrigerator. If you put fish, shrimp, and other seafood on ice in a colander, and then put the colander in a water-catching pan or dish, the seafood won't get waterlogged by soaking in melted ice if it has to wait several hours before going to pot or pan.

• Use fresh seafood the day you buy it. When you have to freeze it, freeze it as soon as possible IMMERSED IN WATER, in sealed containers, to best preserve flavor. Clean milk cartons or zippered plastic bags are good containers for fish.

• If you buy fresh shrimp to freeze in the raw stage at home, remove the heads from the shrimp before freezing. Fat in shrimp heads will become rancid even in the freezer and spoil the taste of shrimp. You can also freeze cooked and shelled shrimp for use as hors d'oeuvres.

• Many people like to soak thawed frozen fish in milk for several hours before cooking, because milk tends to take away any "fishy" taste (or "gamey" taste from game fish) that may have developed. Blot the milk from the fish and prepare as planned. You can thaw frozen shrimp in salted cold water.

• Refrigerate unfrozen raw meat, poultry, and fish; keep commercially frozen stuffed poultry in the freezer until you cook it. Cold cuts should be refrigerated promptly and never kept for more than two or three hours in the temperature danger zone (see FDA recommendations below).

Temperature Danger Zone

Bacteria grow and toxins are produced when food is not cooled and refrigerated properly. The U.S. Department of Agriculture tells us to keep hot foods hot (above 165 degrees Fahrenheit) and cold foods cold (below 40). The danger zone for food is between 40 and 140 degrees, the temperature range in which bacteria grow rapidly. Food that has been kept in the temperature danger zone for more than two or three hours may not be safe to eat. This includes food that is kept in the oven at danger zone temperatures.

Either serve food after cooking or refrigerate it promptly. You can refrigerate hot foods if they will not raise the refrigerator temperature above 45 degrees F. Letting foods cool down to room temperature before refrigerating them is no longer recommended. This old wives' tale is a hangover from the days of iceboxes when hot foods would melt the ice chunk. If you place the hot food on the coldest shelf of your refrigerator, it will cool down quickly. Give the dish some air space to help it cool down faster and make sure you don't put the hot dish next to butter, margarine, jelled cranberries, or anything else that will be easily affected by the heat.

Storage Limits for Keeping Food

If foods are properly handled before purchase and stored in the average, properly working refrigerator, the following times are the storage limits suggested by the U.S. Food and Drug Administration's "FDA Consumer" and various U.S. Department of Agriculture publications and *Good Housekeeping* magazine.

• Apples and cherries: Store without washing in a crisper or moisture-resistant wrap. Apples keep about one month; citrus fruits, two weeks; most other fruit, five days, except pineapple, which keeps about two days. Canned and cooked fruits (in covered container) keep one week; unopened canned fruit keep one year; dried fruit, six months.

• Baby foods (covered, in original can or jar): Two to three days.

• Bananas: Should not be refrigerated.

• Beef, fresh: Variety meats such as heart and liver, one to two days in the refrigerator; ground beef, one to two days; chops, steaks, three to five days; sausages, one to two days; roasts, three to five days.

   Frozen beef: Variety meats, one to two months; and sausage, one to two months; ground beef, three to four months; chops, six to nine months; steaks, six to twelve months; roasts, six to twelve months.

• Berries and cherries (in crisper or moisture-proof wrapping): Three days.

• Bread: Commercially frozen, baked bread can be frozen for three months; for unbaked bread, check label.

• Butter (margarine): In the refrigerator, one to two weeks; freeze nine months.

• Casseroles, stews: Three to four days in the refrigerator; freeze cooked meat dishes, two to three months; and cooked pastry dishes, four to six months.

• Cheeses: Opened cream cheese, two weeks; cottage cheese, ten to thirty days; opened Swiss, brick, processed, three to four weeks.

• Chicken (Poultry): Refrigerate two to three days; freeze for nine to twelve months. Chicken livers will keep one to two days in the refrigerator, three months frozen.

• Custards, custard sauces, cream-filled pies or cakes (on coldest shelf): Two to three days.

• Fish: Fresh fish, shellfish (all wrapped loosely) are best if kept only twenty-four hours in the refrigerator. Cooked fish and shellfish (covered or wrapped), canned fish and shellfish (opened, covered), one day.

• Fruit juices (in covered container): Three to four days.

• Gravy: Can be kept one to two days in the refrigerator and can be kept frozen up to one month.

• Ice cream (sherbert): One month in the freezer.

• Ketchup: Unopened, twelve months on the shelf; refrigerate after opening.

• Lettuce: Unwashed, head lettuce keeps five to seven days in the refrigerator crisper; washed and drained, three to five days.

• Lunch meats: Can be refrigerated three to five days. (Always look at the date on the package.)

• Mayonnaise, salad dressing: Unopened on the shelf, two to three months; in the refrigerator after opening, six to eight weeks.

• Meats: Generally, processed or cured meats (such as sliced ham) keep one week in the refrigerator, one to two months in freezer. Bacon and franks will keep three to five days in fridge; bacon keeps one month in the freezer; franks, one to two months. Ground meat (loosely wrapped) is best kept only twenty-four hours in the refrigerator; fresh poultry (wrapped loosely) can be kept one to two days.

• Milk: Keeps about five days in the refrigerator. Cream in carton keeps one week; one week for evaporated milk (in opened can). (Always check the date on the carton when buying milk or cream.)

• Pasta: Dried pasta has a shelf life of two years.

• Peanut butter: Best kept refrigerated. Keeps 6 months unopened; two months after opening.

• Pork: Fresh, three to five days for chops, one to two days for ground; three to five days for roasts. Frozen, three to four months for ground; three to four months for chops; four to eight months for roasts.

• Potatoes: Store in cool, dry place but not in the refrigerator.

• Rice, white: Up to two years if kept in a tightly closed container, in a cool, dry place; brown, one year.

• Soups: Can be refrigerated for one to two days; freeze for one to four months.

• Sugar: Granulated sugar keeps two years in a tightly closed container. Brown sugar keeps four months.

• Vegetables: Store-bought frozen vegetables can be kept up to eight months in the freezer; fresh vegetables, from one to seven days in the refrigerator.

Root vegetables (carrots, rutabagas, etc.) keep up to two weeks in the refrigerator.
Fresh vegetables, salad greens (in crisper or moisture-proof wrapping) keep up to five days.
Leftover vegetables (in covered container) and canned vegetables (in original can or other covered container) keep three days in the refrigerator.

Refreezing

Generally, if a food is safe to eat and is only partially thawed, it's safe to refreeze it, but any food which has an off-odor or color should be discarded.

• Foods that have partially thawed, that still contain ice crystals and have been held no longer than one or two days at refrigerator temperatures can be refrozen, but you should use all refrozen foods as soon as possible.

• Refrozen foods will never have the same quality as fresh or never-thawed frozen foods. They lose texture, appearance, and flavor, and may also lose food value. Ice cream and uncooked baked goods, especially, will deteriorate in texture and taste if refrozen. Most of my sources recommend discarding thawed ice cream.

• If you've thawed meat, fish, and poultry in the refrigerator, you can refreeze them within 24 hours of defrosting. However, stews, casseroles, and other combination dishes that have been thawed should not be refrozen.

• If you have a power failure which accidentally thaws foods over a period of days, you can refreeze foods only if they still have ice crystals in them. The exceptions are fruit and juice concentrates.

• If food has thawed completely (either by accident or by choice of the cook), or has warmed to room temperature and been kept at room temperature for more than two hours, throw it out.

Fruit and juice concentrates will ferment if they are spoiled by thawing and being kept at room temperatures. Always discard any fruit with an "off" flavor.

Special-Care Foods

• Eggs and any uncooked or cooked foods containing eggs should be refrigerated.

• Creams, custards, meringue pies, and foods with custard fillings—including cakes, cream puffs, and eclairs—should not be kept at room temperature. Cool slightly and then refrigerate. If such foods are taken on picnics, keep them in a cooler. Salads and sandwiches made with salad dressings containing eggs or milk products and little vinegar or other acids also need refrigeration.

• Caviar, that extra-elegant treat, needs special care because it is highly perishable. It should be removed from the refrigerator 15 minutes before eating and the lid should be removed only at the last moment. Unopened, a container of fresh caviar may be stored in the refrigerator for up to four weeks. Serve caviar in its original container placed in a bed of ice. If the caviar is oversalted, serve it with chopped hard-cooked egg; if it is fishy, serve it with chopped onion; if it is somewhat sour, serve with lemon juice.

By the way, here's some information to use when you play trivia board games: The caviar names such as Beluga, Sevruga, Osetrova, and Sterlet tell you which sturgeons produced it. Caviar tins are labeled with the name of the district where the fish was caught. "Malosol" means that the caviar is only slightly salted. It comes from the Russian words *malo* ("little") and *soleny*, ("salted").

Champagne and Wine

If you buy caviar, you'll probably buy champagne to enjoy with it (although some people like vodka with caviar). In France, all sparkling wine labeled "Champagne" can come, by law, only from the Champagne region. American vintners are not prevented from calling their sparkling wines "champagne." German sparkling wine is *Sekt*, and in Italy it's *spumante*.

• Champagne is ready to drink when you buy it and need not be saved for aging.

• Champagne should not be opened so that it shoots out of the bottle like Old Faithful geyser in Yellowstone National Park, unless, of course, you are a ballplayer celebrating a World Series win.

The best way to open a bottle of champagne is to put a napkin or handkerchief between your hand and the bottle. (This protects your hand if the bottle breaks and keeps the heat of your hand from the narrowest point on the bottle and therefore the point of most pressure from the bubbly inside.)

Remove the foil, then the wiring, keeping the bottle pointed away from yourself and not at anyone else. (The cork can pop out once the wiring is off. This is especially true for a bottle that has been jostled en route to opening.)

As you hold the cork in one hand, twist the bottle gently away from the cork with the hand protected by the napkin. If the cork doesn't ease out, you'll have to carefully push it away from the bottle with your thumb. Sometimes running warm water over just the neck of the bottle will help. If you keep the bottle at a 45-degree angle during this procedure, more of the champagne's surface will be exposed to the atmosphere and therefore the champagne will be less likely to have pressure built up at the bottle neck and will be more likely to remain in the bottle until you can pour it and enjoy.

• While we're on the subject of champagne, here's some champagne measure language for you to use when you play guessing board games and which will help you shop when you have a party.

A half-pint (1–2 glasses) is called a split
⅛ gallon (2–3 glasses) is a pint
¼ gallon (5 glasses) is a quart (a bottle)
2 quarts (10 glasses) is a magnum
4 quarts (21 glasses) is a jeroboam
6 quarts (31 glasses) is a rehoboam
8 quarts (41 glasses) is a methuselah
12 quarts (62 glasses) is a salmanasar
16 quarts (83 glasses) is a balthazar
20 quarts (104 glasses) is a nebuchadnezzar

• If you are buying champagne for the future, it's better to buy bottles of less than a magnum size. They last longer. Keep dated records of where and when you bought champagne and wine, then record any comments after you open and taste it.

Champagne is meant to be drunk within a short period of time. Therefore, do not buy champagne to keep and store away for five or ten years at a time. And most important, do not store the champagne in the refrigerator. (Purists think that champagne can absorb odors from other foods in the refrigerator over a long period of time. In addition, the cork, in cold temperatures, will eventually shrink, allowing the bubbles to escape and the wine to go flat.) Store it in a cool, dark place on its side. Then put it in the refrigerator or in a bucket of ice water two hours before serving.

• Wine that is capped instead of corked is wine that is ready to drink when you buy it; enjoy!

• Whether your taste is for sparkling or still (nonbubbly) wines, proper storage of wine will preserve the flavors you've spent your hard-earned money to buy.

• Remember that wine that doesn't require aging or that you will drink soon can be stored standing up for a short time, but wine that is to be aged should be stored lying down to keep the cork damp so that no air can reach the wine. You can set notched boards at right angles to your storage shelves to let bottles lie on their sides without clanging into each other.

• Accordion-type wooden wine racks can be installed in any type of cabinet or bookcase to hold wine bottles on their sides and in the dark, as nature demands.

• If you buy a case of wine, the case can be placed on its side in a cool basement for storage. Wine boxes (cases) can be inserted into cabinets to hold stored wine bottles on their sides.

To make your own wine "rack":

• Construct a concrete-block "student" bookcase by layering blocks with sturdy boards and then stacking wine bottles, which have been inserted into mailing tubes, on the shelves.

• Or stack clay tubular drain tiles against a cool cellar wall to hold wine bottles. The tiles can be supported on the sides of this "wine rack" if they are placed wall to wall or within a bookcase or other sturdy frame.

• Or fit two sturdy pieces of wood, which have been fitted with grooves so that they are joined diagonally to form an X, into a square cabinet and then insert wine bottles in the spaces.

• Most oenophiles (wine experts) agree that the ideal temperature for a wine cellar should be 55 to 60 degrees Fahrenheit, with 45 to 70 degrees as the outer limits. Keeping the temperature constant is even more important than the exact temperature.

• Humidity prevents the corks from drying out and allowing the wine to evaporate or spoil. Too much humidity, however, will allow fungus to grow. The best humidity level is 75 percent.

• Remember that wine can "breathe" through the cork, and therefore cellar odors can be absorbed by the wine.

• Wine rests better in the dark, and it doesn't like vibrations, especially if it is an aged wine. Keep your stored wine away from laundry machines or other vibrating equipment.

• If you are moving during very hot or very cold weather, you will need to insulate the wines. My sources advise me that when you are moving at any time, wrap the wine bottles in about a one-inch thickness of newspapers for shipping; once they are moved, let the bottles rest undisturbed for at least a month before they are opened.

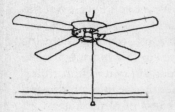

CHAPTER 3

In and Around the House

Sometimes we top-clean and sometimes we get an uncontrollable urge to clean up every speck, spot, and smudge in the house.

Although we may do a thorough type of cleaning only at Christmas, Easter, or when we are moving out of a house or apartment, we do need to top-clean often. For most people, that means at least once a week. We all know that if you keep things reasonably clean, you don't need to do serious cleaning as often. For example, a carpet that's vacuumed frequently won't develop dirty traffic paths that need shampooing as quickly as one that is seldom vacuumed. Bathroom fixtures that are cleaned frequently don't accumulate excessive hard water deposits and stains. And, of course, clean things (any things) last longer.

You can prevent unnecessary cleaning if you get rid of clutter as a habit, if you organize proper storage systems and places, and if you can get the people you live with to cooperate and help. You can reduce the amount of dirt in the house by confining eating and messy projects to easily cleaned areas, by wiping up spills as soon as possible, and by controlling household pests. (I don't mean people here!)

If you are among the millions of Americans who live alone, you can't delegate cleaning chores unless you hire someone. If you are one of the almost thirty million working couples in the United States or one of the many families with children under eighteen in which both parents work, you have even less time to clean.

Few people can keep up the pace of working at two jobs—home and outside the home—forever. Many people have developed systems for more equitable sharing of housework. For example, working couples alternate chores each Saturday or Sunday—one person cleans, the other does the week's laundry and grocery shops; the next week they trade jobs, and so on.

Many families either rotate certain chores from person to person or use the "job jar" system, in which different jobs are written on pieces of paper and drawn on a certain day so that the "winner" gets a chore by chance.

Whatever system is used, I know that this book can help. The page number on which the appropriate cleaning tip is printed could be written on the job jar assignment note. Parents who leave notes designating certain chores to be done by children after school can also note the page on which appropriate instructions for that chore are given. Favorite cleaning hints can be marked with a highlighter pen so that the chore person of the day can find them easily.

It's often difficult to get a system going, especially when everyone is used to "good ol' mom" (or whoever is the usual family cleaner) doing everything. However, if everyone pitches in, everything gets done faster and everyone, including "good ol' mom" or "good ol' whoever," gets a bit more self time. (Self time is when you read a book, call a friend, exercise, meditate, or do anything else that gives you pleasure and renews your spirit.)

Rewards work, no doubt about it. After a housework session, whether it's a top cleaning or a serious and even under-the-rug cleaning, all the workers deserve something special—a movie, dinner out, a picnic, anything that's fun, and the reward system applies whether you live alone, as a couple, or in a family.

Who knows, when you get more people into the cleaning act, you may develop better ways of getting jobs done, which, of course, you'll want to send to my Heloise's column so that others can benefit too.

Whenever you are cleaning, always follow directions on products. Read labels before buying products appropriate to the type of cleaning you will do. Many cleaning products are poisonous or flammable or both. Store them away from kitchen ranges, radiators, or furnaces, and ALWAYS store cleaning products out of the reach of small children, never under the kitchen sink.

Bathrooms

Cleaning the bathroom is a terrible chore to most people. But think about this: The bathroom is usually the smallest room of the house, so there is really less total area to clean, whether you measure it in cubic feet or square feet of surfaces. Isn't that a nice thought?

We have to accept the fact that no matter how spotless we make them, bathrooms don't stay pristine clean unless locked shut. But there are ways of making this chore less tedious, and some of them are listed below.

Cleaning Tiles and Bathroom Fixtures

• One of the easiest ways I know to quick-clean a bathroom, especially one with tile walls and floor, is to get a bunch of paper towels and a spray bottle of commercial window cleaner or the homemade one described below.

• Make your own all-purpose cleaner and shiner (mix and store in an empty plastic quart bottle) by adding two tablespoons of vinegar or two tablespoons of sudsy ammonia and filling the bottle with water. Be sure to label this clearly as your homemade cleaner so it doesn't get used for other purposes.

Clean from the top down, changing paper towels as you go and saving all the wet ones to do the floor. Do mirrors, sink area, wall tiles, the outside and rim of the bathtub, toilet tank and seat, and finally the floor. (Most plastic and painted wood toilet seats and many wall paints can be cleaned with liquid window cleaner. Test an inconspicuous place first to make sure.)

• Wash the floor with the used towels and more sprays of cleaner, wiping it with dry towels as you back out of the room to avoid putting footprints on the wet floor. It helps if you get dust and hairs off the floor first, but it's not absolutely necessary.

Close the shower curtain to cover the tub, throw a rug over the heavy traffic patch of the floor, and you have a shiny, clean bathroom. (Clean the tub or shower stall some other day, when you aren't in such a rush.)

• You can make your own ceramic-tile cleaner from common household ingredients. Mix one-fourth cup baking soda, one-half cup white vinegar, and one cup ammonia in a bucket.

Add one gallon of warm water and stir until the baking soda dissolves. Apply with a sponge or scrub brush. You'll need to mix a fresh batch for each cleaning, because this is not a "keeper."
CAUTION: Wear rubber gloves, because this is a bit unkind to your skin and nails.

• A variation of the cleaner above, which can be used for serious scrubbing or heavy-duty grout cleaning, is the following paste made from three cups baking soda and one cup warm water. In a medium-size bowl, mix to a smooth paste and then scrub it into the grout with a damp sponge or toothbrush. Rinse thoroughly afterward. Always mix a fresh batch for each cleaning.

• Cleaning things with baking soda really makes your fingernails white. This is a good cleaning job to do after you've done some craft or project that stains the undersides of your fingernails or have been digging in the garden without wearing gloves. You can clean two messes with one paste! Follow up with hand lotion.

• Here's another quickie cleaner for tiles and shower doors. Spray tiles or glass shower doors liberally with any brand of pre-wash spray. Wait a few minutes, then rub the scum away with a damp sponge. (If you use a petroleum or oil-based pre-wash spray, be sure to rinse or wash out the bottom of the tub or shower stall carefully, as it can be slippery.)

Rinse the area thoroughly and dry with a towel.

• Do family members leave squished-out toothpaste all over the sink? Take a wet sponge or dirty washcloth and use the toothpaste to clean the sink and fixtures. Rinse the sink and toss the washcloth into the laundry.

• You can remove most mildew from the grout between tiles by rubbing it with an old toothbrush or nail brush dipped in laundry bleach. (Don't use abrasive powders or steel wool pads, because they'll scratch the tile.)

Rinse with clear water after cleaning.

• You can also remove mildew from the grouting between tiles by dabbing a toothbrush in powdered cleanser, wetting it, and scrubbing it in between the tiles, then letting it sit for a few moments before rinsing off.

• If some brown spots remain no matter what you do, you can camouflage stained grout with a white fingernail pencil or white typewriter correction fluid.

• To keep tiles and shower doors looking shiny, spray them with your favorite furniture spray and shine with a soft cloth or paper towels.

Of course, the tiles must be clean before you use this, or you'll just end up with a mucky mess. And again, be sure that the floor of the tub or shower is completely clean, as it can be slippery.

Cleaning the Toilet Bowl

Almost everyone who moves around from apartment to apartment, house to house, will occasionally find a bathroom that has escaped not only regular real cleaning, but also minimal care! If you find yourself in an apartment or house that was previously inhabited by someone with toilet-cleanophobia (the fear of cleaning toilets), the first tip in this section may help.

• Sprinkle one-fourth cup sodium bisulfate (sodium acid sulfate from hardware store or drugstore) into a wet toilet bowl for a single scrubbing and flushing.

   CAUTION: Wear rubber gloves. Also, don't use this acid with chlorine bleach, because the resulting fumes are toxic.
   Let it stand for 15 minutes; then scrub and flush as usual.

• In some parts of the United States, the only way to completely avoid rust-stained toilet bowls is to not have toilet bowls, and who could live with that!

   Rust stains under a toilet bowl rim will sometimes yield to chlorine bleach, but be sure to protect your hands with rubber gloves, even when you use a long-handled brush, because even splashes of bleach can hurt your skin. This is true also for strong commercial preparations for toilet bowl cleaning.
   The best way is to get a good commercial rust remover made specifically for porcelain. Be sure to read the directions carefully.
   CAUTION: Never combine bleach with toilet bowl cleaners; the mix can release toxic gases.

• If all else fails, gently rub off truly stubborn rust stains with extra-fine steel wool or with wet-dry sandpaper (available at hardware stores).

• Cola that has gone flat can be poured into the toilet bowl. If left to soak for an hour, the drink will clean the bowl.

   (Sort of a scary thought, isn't it? Makes you wonder what cola does to your body's plumbing!)

• A quick way to remove a lot of stains in the toilet is to drop in several denture cleaner tablets, let them foam and bubble, scrub and brush, and flush away.

• CAUTION: Chemical toilet bowl cleaners, commercial or homemade, should never be used to clean the bathtub or sink, because the chemicals will etch and ruin their finishes.

Once the glaze finish is removed from sinks and bathtubs, they will stain gray even with normal daily use and be difficult to brighten with ordinary cleaning.

Certain epoxy finishes or reglazing can be applied by professionals or by using finishing kits available at some hardware stores. This is a major project, and prevention is a better idea.

If you haven't been lucky enough to prevent the glaze from being removed from your tub, reglazing is a good alternative. Look in the Yellow Pages under "Bathtub Refinishers" or "Bathtub Reglazers." Be sure to ask to see references, or talk to references, and ask how long they have been in the business and if the people you called were happy with the job. Once this has been done, you must be sure never, ever to use abrasive cleansers on that finish, or it will simply be a waste of your money.

Cleaning the Bathtub

• You can enjoy your bath without leaving a tub ring if you add water-softener bath crystals or bubble bath to the water. If you are out of anything fancy, try a capful of mild liquid dish-washing detergent in the bathwater. Of course, this is if you have no allergies, and this is not preferable for young children.

• Rub away ring-around-the-tub with an old nylon stocking rolled into a ball. Old pantyhose can become a nonscratch scrub pad for cleaning sink and tub. You can also use old skin-cleaning pads once they become too worn and abrasive for your skin.

• A nylon-net ball or pad will scrub away rings without the aid of any cleaner.

• If you have to deal with a stubborn bathtub ring, try covering it with a paste of cream of tartar and hydrogen peroxide. When the paste dries, wipe it off along with the ring.

• To get rid of bathtub rust stains, try rubbing them with a paste of borax powder and lemon juice. If the stain persists, use a dry-cleaning solution. (You will also find commercial preparations for this chore; follow directions exactly.)

• You can clean a rubber or vinyl bathtub mat by tossing it into the washer with bath towels. The terry cloth scrubs the mat, and all come out clean at the same time.

• A quick way to clean the bath mat is to spray it with a foamy spray bathroom cleaner, let it sit a few moments, scrub, and rinse with very hot water.

Shower Cleaning

Shower enclosures are a chore to keep clean. If you can teach the people who live and shower in your house to wipe down the shower walls and glass doors with a rubber window wand wiper or the towel they've just used while they're still standing in the tub, you can stretch the intervals between vigorous, thorough cleanings.

Eventually, some cleaning has to be done, but it can be less of a chore if you use the following tips.

• When the walls need a thorough cleaning, run the shower water at its hottest temperature so the steam will loosen the dirt before you start to scrub on it.

CAUTION: Don't stay in the tub for this.

• To clean in a jiffy, without even getting your hands wet, use a sponge mop dipped into a mixture of one-half cup vinegar, one cup clear ammonia, and one-quarter cup baking soda in one gallon of warm water. (Yes, yes, vinegar, ammonia, baking soda, and aren't they great?)

After cleaning, rinse with clear water.

• Never use harsh abrasive powders or steel-wool pads, because they'll scratch porcelain tile or fiberglass.

• To get mineral deposits off a shower head, remove it, take it apart, and soak in vinegar. Then brush deposits loose with an old toothbrush. Clean the holes by poking them with a wire, pin, toothpick, or ice pick.

• If the shower head cannot be removed, take a plastic sandwich bag, fill it with vinegar, wrap it around the shower head, and attach it tightly with a thick rubber band. Let it sit overnight. Proceed with the cleaning.

• Lemon oil furniture polish will remove water spots on metal frames around shower doors and enclosures.

• Glass shower doors will sparkle again if you clean them once a week with a sponge dipped in white vinegar. This is a good tip; regular cleaning of any part of the bathroom will help you avoid having to use strong chemicals and lots of energy (yours) to clean it.

My favorite way is to spray with pre-wash spray, let it sit a few moments, and simply wipe away with a sponge. Use a handful of nylon net or a plastic scrubby to really get at the grungy stuff, and then rinse it all down the drain.

• You can wash plastic shower curtains in the washer. Wash them with towels to get some automatic scrubbing action.

Put them in the washing machine with one-half cup detergent and one-half cup baking soda, along with two large bath towels.

Add a cup of vinegar to the rinse cycle, then hang the curtains up immediately after washing and let them air dry.

• You can get wrinkles out of the plastic shower curtain and soften it at the same time by tossing it into the dryer with the towels for a few minutes.

A shower curtain doesn't need to go through the whole drying cycle; some will all but melt! Just let it spin for two, three, or four minutes, depending upon the heat of your dryer, then remove it from the dryer and hang immediately.

• When you clean a plastic shower curtain, you can keep it soft and flexible by adding a few drops of mineral oil to the rinse water.

Mirrors

Some people keep full-length mirrors in their bathrooms as reminders to stay on their diets. There's nothing like finding out where all those calories go after they leave your lips. But whatever size mirror you have, a shiny one makes the whole room look clean.

• To make your bathroom mirror sparkle, try polishing it with a cloth dipped in a borax-and-water solution or in denatured alcohol. Wipe dry to shine with a lint-free cloth, newspapers, paper toweling, or an old nylon stocking.

• Rubbing alcohol will wipe away that dull hair spray haze from a mirror.

• This is one of my favorite hints. For a quick swipe, to make the bathroom sparkle, dab a little rubbing alcohol or even vinegar on a facial tissue, wipe the mirror, and it will sparkle and shine.

• Bathroom mirrors won't steam up if you run an inch of cold water in the bathtub before you add the hot water.

• If you need to defog a bathroom mirror in a jiffy, try "spraying" it with hot air from your hand-held dryer.

• To help prevent the mirror from getting foggy, wipe it with an anti-fog product that is sold for automobiles. Or, if you have a medicine cabinet where the mirrors slide over each other, close them so that one mirror is covered while you're taking a shower. Then, when you're ready to use the mirror, simply slide the door back and there's an unfogged mirror to use.

• This glass-cleaning solution is good for cleaning mirrors in any room. Mix two cups water with one cup isopropyl rubbing alcohol (70 percent) and one tablespoon household ammonia. Pour into a clean pump-spray bottle.

Cleaning and Organizing Bedrooms and Living Areas

When you get ready to do a serious deep cleaning of the entire house, you will sabotage your whole effort if you take the clutter from one room and distribute it to the others. What gets picked up should get put where it belongs and, if it doesn't belong anywhere, it should be given to a charity or thrown out.

• Work in one room at a time and don't switch to another until the first room is finished, even if it takes several days. Seeing progress in one room will give you a greater sense of accomplishment than having several half-finished, mostly torn-up rooms.

• If the first room's work has taken most of the day, don't start another when you're already tired. Wait until morning, when you're more likely to be in the mood to clean thoroughly.

• Remember, it's easier to do a little each day. Get rid of papers and junk as they accumulate, and vacuum and dust daily if you can.

• If you clean your living room daily, you'll always have one clean and orderly refuge from clutter. One clean room prevents your feeling overwhelmed by a whole house in need of attention. And, you'll have someplace to sit comfortably if a friend drops over for a coffee-chat break.

Organizing and Cleaning Bedrooms

• Organize your dresser drawers. Shoe boxes that fit inside drawers make great dividers for underwear, stockings, and jewelry. Divide to conquer is the motto for drawer organizing. To organize your closets, see Chapter 7, which deals with cleaning out closets and clothing management.

• Keep a hall tree handy in the bedroom or walk-in closet for airing clothing that doesn't get washed after each wearing. A hall tree is a good "guest closet" too.

• To make your bed easily, attach two safety pins on the underside of the bedspread—one on each side at the end of the mattress to indicate its width. Feel for the pin, and line it up with the edge to save yourself from walking back and forth, from one side of the bed to the other, lining up the spread.

You can line up sheets the same way, except instead of using safety pins, sew a couple of colored stitches on each side. This saves a lot of steps if you have a king-size bed.

• Unless you are one of those sleepers who completely pulls apart the bedding each night or you have a bed partner who does it, you can make your bed before you even get out of it, like I do.

When you're ready to get out of bed, sit in the middle of the bed and pull up the sheets, blanket, spread, and so on, then smooth out any folds, then slide out the side. Then finish off the head of the bed in whatever way you keep it.

If you just use a quilt or coverlet, instead of a bedspread and blanket, and let the pillows show, all you have to do is fold the top of the top sheet over the edge of the quilt before you slide out and the bed is made.

• Having one side of the bed close to a wall is a problem when you're making the bed. If you have a lightweight spread, you can pin weights (nuts and bolts) to the underside of the spread's edge. Then the spread will slide right down into place on the wall side.

• A lace or cut-work tablecloth spread over a colored sheet can be a pretty guest-room spread and a way to store and to get more use from the tablecloth.

• If you have the space in your closet, keeping your bedding in the bedroom where it's used saves you steps at bed-changing time.

• And a way to really save space is to put the bedspread or extra blankets on hangers and hang them at the very back of the closet.

• If you're short on bedding storage space, keep guest-room beds made up and toss a fabric softener sheet or a mildly scented bar of soap under the blanket to keep the linens fresh smelling.

• If you have a daybed with a pull-out twin bed underneath and only one guest, have the guest sleep on the pull-out bed instead of the top one. Then, instead of having to arrange pillows and spreads on the daybed every day, you can just slide the bottom bed into its usual place each morning.

• Store extra pillows on beds and sofas. Cover them with zippered corduroy or other room color coordinating pillowcases.

• If you make your bed with sheets still warm from the dryer, they will "iron" themselves on the bed, and you'll save time by not having to fold them up and put them away.

• Although we've always been taught to rotate sheets and towels in our linen closets to keep them fresh, if you don't live in a damp climate and your house is always air-conditioned or heated, you may not have to do this at all. In fact, it may make more sense to use only one set at a time.

You can just use the same color-coordinated sheets and towels over and over right from the dryer, without ever having to fold and put them away, until they are worn out, and then you can choose a new color scheme without having a closet cluttered with half-worn-out things that don't match your rooms anymore.

This is one of my father's favorite hints. It is his way of solving the how-do-you-fold-the-fitted-sheet problem—he doesn't.

Also, rotating your sets of sheets and towels means that all of these items will last longer but will wear out at the same time. It's really easier on the budget to replace only one set at a time.

General Cleaning

Adopt a routine or a sequence of cleaning steps such as the sequence shown below, which works well for cleaning just about any room in the house. When you use the same routine over and over, it becomes so automatic that you can think about something else while you're doing it. Some people like to "plug in" to their radio or cassette earphones while they clean. Music with a beat helps beat the cleaning blues. Here's a top-to-bottom routine to try.

1. Pick up all papers, magazines, or any other clutter that doesn't have to be there.
2. Dust knickknacks, paintings, lamps, and so on.
3. Dust or polish all wood furniture.
4. Vacuum floors, carpets, and upholstered furniture.
5. Dry mop, sweep, or scrub non-carpeted floors.

6. Do any heavy cleaning chores such as window cleaning, silver/brass polishing, miscellaneous repairs, and so on.

7. Close the door and go on to another room. Closing the door keeps dirt and dust from getting back into clean rooms and gives you the satisfaction of having finished something.

8. If you pick up items that need to go to another part of the house, don't leave that room. Put them outside the door and then remove them all at once. Don't let yourself get sidetracked.

General Cleaning and Repairing Tips

I've tried to arrange these tips in the order of the cleaning routine suggested above, so that the quick-clean tips are first and the deep, serious, grungicide hints follow.

Picking Up Clutter

• Drag around a plastic or paper garbage bag or wastebasket as you clean, so that you won't have far to go to throw away clutter.

• Make up a cleaning kit. Use a box, plastic carrier with a handle, or bucket to tote all of your cleaning supplies around so that you won't be running back and forth for rags, furniture wax, window cleaner, vacuum bags, and so forth.

Knickknacks

• You can wash most knickknacks in less time than it takes to dust them if you swish them in water containing a touch of liquid detergent. Then, rinse and drain on a towel. If you want to make sure every crevice is dry, use a hand-held hair dryer to blow away moisture.

• To wash fragile objects without breaking them, put them on a towel-covered tray in the sink and spray them first with window cleaner and then with water. Let them air dry on a towel.

• To keep your phone clean and germ free, wipe it with an alcohol-soaked paper towel often. Most of us don't think about cleaning a phone, but it does need a wipe every now and then. I know mine does.

Lamps

• Clean lamp shades and see how much more light your lamp will give off. Don't forget to clean the bulb too! You can dust them with a new, soft paintbrush or your vacuum cleaner dusting brush.

- If you need to go beyond dusting, you can wash some lamp shades. Check the instructions that came on their labels. (You did save the labels in your household file, didn't you?)

When lamp shades aren't glued to their frames, gently wash them in the bathtub with warm water and a spray hose. Dry them quickly after washing so the frames won't rust. An electric fan or hair dryer can speed the drying process.

Cleaning Oil Paintings and Frames

Valuable oil paintings should be cleaned by experts. It's too risky to use home remedies on such things. And, according to most experts, it's better to under-clean than overclean (which could severely damage paintings).

The simple inexpensive oil paintings that most of us have in our homes may be cleaned as follows. (You must decide values of paintings to be cleaned at home.)

- The surface of most paintings gathers household dust, which can be removed with a soft brush. Never use a rag or a feather duster. Threads from the rag or feathers can get caught in any tiny lifted areas in the oil paint or cracked ridges, causing damage to the painting. A camel or badger hairbrush is best; use a gentle back-and-forth motion. A vacuum brush attachment is too coarse and will scratch a varnished painting.

- To clean a deeply carved picture frame, use an empty clean, dry, plastic squeeze bottle; pump the bottle like small bellows to blow dust from tiny crevices. (This works when you are cleaning 35-mm slides, too.) Of course, one of my most favorite and the easiest way is to use your hand-held hair dryer on blow, with cold air only.

- To make a tarnished gilt frame gleam again, wipe it with a turpentine-dampened rag. Chipped gilt frames can be repaired with touch-up kits available at some hardware stores.

Dusting and Polishing Wood Furniture

Most of the time we need only to dust furniture with a feather duster or a soft dirt-collecting cloth. Some people wax and oil their furniture regularly. Others wax or oil only when they feel a need to work off excess energy. Many of the tips in this section will help you put a shine on your furniture without ruining most of your fingernails and getting yourself too tired to appreciate the results of your work.

The good news and excuse for not waxing and polishing too often is that using too much oil on furniture eventually darkens it, because dirt and oil form a film on the surface. I once used a commercial furniture cleaner on a very old piece of furniture bought at an auction and was amazed to find very elaborate light fruitwood-colored veneer designs underneath what I thought was a plain, dark walnut finish.

In all cases, when you are planning to wax or oil furniture, remember that the finish on the furniture determines which method you will use. Generally, high luster furniture needs a liquid polish or paste wax, which dries to high shine. Low luster or satin finish furniture needs a greaseless cream polish or wax that protects without shine. Natural oil-finished furniture needs to be reoiled with the type of oil originally used by the manufacturer (or boiled linseed oil). Most manufacturers say it's not good to switch back and forth with different products, using wax one time, oil the next, and some other polish later.

• To dust furniture with a double-barreled approach, dampen two old cotton gloves or socks with furniture polish, slip them on, and then dust with both hands.

• To remove sticky residue that collects on wooden furniture and around the handles of varnished kitchen cupboards, use a good furniture cleaner. You can find one in hardware stores and some larger grocery stores, usually in the furniture refinishing or housewares department.

While you are there, buy some fine (0000) steel wool. Do not use any that is coarser; make sure the package has at least four zeroes. This will remove any residue that the cleaner leaves behind. Be careful to rub the wood very gently, with the grain, and only until the buildup is removed. Don't rub excessively or you will scratch the finish.

After cleaning, apply a good furniture polish and buff to a shine.

• Furniture polish recipe: Here's a tried-and-true recipe for furniture polish that doesn't create an oily/waxy buildup and doesn't put a high, glossy shine on wood, just a nice, deep glow.

Mix together one-third cup vinegar, one-third cup turpentine, and one-third cup boiled linseed oil, which is available at most paint stores. DO NOT attempt to boil your own linseed oil; the oil is highly flammable.

CAUTION: ALWAYS label the container clearly. DO NOT use this polish on plastic or laminated furniture.

To use this polish, moisten a soft cloth with it and rub over your furniture, going back over it with a clean cloth.

• Most water rings on wood tables can be removed easily if you get to them right away. Immediately moisten a cloth, dip it into cigar ashes (some people claim cigarette ashes work well too), and rub the milky spot gently. You can also mix mayonnaise or vegetable oil in with the ashes.

If no one in your house is a smoker (and we sincerely hope they aren't), using mayonnaise or vegetable oil and a dry cloth first just might do the trick.

• Paste shoe polish covers small scratches, marks, or discolorations on furniture, cabinets, or wood paneling. Use dark brown on dark wood, tan on lighter wood. It works like magic and leaves a nice glow.

• If you sprinkle a little cornstarch on furniture after you've polished it, and then rub it to a high gloss, you'll find that the cornstarch absorbs excess oil and leaves a glistening, fingerprint-free surface.

• To avoid leaving fingerprints while polishing furniture, wear cotton gloves. They'll protect your hands from the polish, too.

• If you keep ashtrays in your house, give them a wipe with the cloth you've used for waxing furniture; it makes them easier to clean. Please note that I said, "If you keep ashtrays in your house," because many people have put ashtrays to better use—to hold paper clips, soap, jewelry, or pot plants—because they've quit smoking and have non-smoking homes.

• Got paper stuck to a polished table? Saturate the paper with cooking oil and let it sit awhile, and it will peel right off.

• You can hide mini-scratches on finished wood by rubbing walnut or pecan meat over them.

• Leftover tea makes a good cleaning agent for varnished furniture.

Repairing Furniture

Most of us can do simple repairs on most furniture ourselves. Really valuable antiques are best repaired by professionals. Check with a few of the best antiques stores in your town to find out where they send their work. Ask to see samples of repaired furniture before you release your valuable pieces to a repair shop and then agree beforehand what will be done—repairs, replacement of parts or hardware, reupholstery, refinishing wood, or just cleaning and polishing it. Some people like to totally refinish antique or old pieces, and others feel that the antique value is destroyed when anything beyond serious cleaning and functional repairs is done.

Here are a few tips on repairing the "dings" that show up in our furniture from daily use.

• Dents in wood furniture can be "ironed" out—really, they can. If you have a dent (where wood fibers are not actually cut, just bent), set your electric iron on medium heat and get a damp cloth.

Place the cloth on the dent, then hold the iron on it until the cloth begins to dry. Repeat the process (redampen the cloth each time) until the dent is raised.

• If you have a pesky cabinet or dresser knob that keeps coming loose, dip the screw end into clear fingernail polish or shellac, then return the knob to the hole. When the polish or shellac hardens, the screw will be set and the knob will be tight. (And your aggravation will be gone!)

• When your chair wobbles because one leg is shorter than the others, you can lengthen the short leg by molding a piece of wood putty in the shape of the chair leg tip. After the putty dries, sand and stain it to match the leg and glue it in place. No more wobble-rocking!

• When wooden drawers stick, you can make them glide better if you rub the contact surfaces with a bar of soap or an old candle stub.

Just remember that you've unstuck the drawer the next time you open it; otherwise, you'll pull with your usual "darn this stuck drawer" force and end up with everything dumped on the floor for an unplanned drawer-cleaning session.

• You can tighten loose furniture leg casters by wrapping the caster stems with rubber bands before reinserting them.

• When you are repairing furniture or putting together unassembled new items fitted with dowels, most of the glue gets pushed into the bottom of the hole and the rest of it squishes out of the rim when you insert the dowel into its hole.

This happens because the dowel is exactly the size of the hole, and the result is that the joint may not hold as well as it should. If you cut a few grooves into the dowel, the glue will distribute itself along the dowel surface into the grooves and you'll get a better bond.

• Wicker furniture can be kept from getting wobbly by lightly misting old wicker pieces with water, using a plant mister every now and then. You can tighten wobbly wicker furniture by washing it outdoors (or in the shower if it will fit) with hot, soapy water; then, rinse with a hose and let it air dry. The water treatment will shrink and tighten the wood and cane.

• If you need to dismantle a piece of furniture to repair it, number/label the parts with strips of masking tape so that you can put them all together again.

Use this tip for furniture that disassembles-assembles for moving. It's hard enough to get your life back in order when you move without adding extra confusion to the chaos.

• Here's an old-fashioned but effective way to unwarp a table leaf or other board, using water and hot summer sun. Thoroughly water a sunny, grassy area; place the board concave side down on the wet grass. As the dry side of the board absorbs moisture from the grass, the moist (convex) side will get dried out by the sun and usually, in no more than a day, the board will un-warp itself.

Refinishing Furniture

To see a Cinderella develop from an Ugly Duckling is a very rewarding experience. You can find many new products on the market for deep cleaning and refinishing old, pre-owned (sounds better than "used") furniture nowadays, all of which save time and energy. You can also find excellent-quality unfinished furniture to stain in colors of your choice and to blend in with furniture you already own.

• Keep dust circulation to a minimum by switching off the central heating system in your house before you begin refinishing and varnishing furniture indoors. However, you must always keep your work space well ventilated and with a constant temperature over 70 degrees Fahrenheit. Cooler temperatures prevent finishes and glues from working properly.

• Many furniture strippers and stains will dissolve ordinary rubber gloves; buy heavy-duty gloves to protect your skin and fingernails.

• Wear cloth work/garden gloves when sanding or steel-wooling raw wood to prevent putting your fingerprints on the wood. Oils in your skin can make marks that show up when you wipe on the stain.

• Old socks and cotton knit underwear make great wiping cloths for stain. Inside-out terry sports socks absorb well for wiping off stain, and fuzzy nylon men's crew socks make good applicators for some stains and sealers.

Carpet Care

• When you vacuum, take slow, overlapping strokes (at least seven strokes) to really clean out embedded dirt particles.

• If you have a pet and the resulting problems with fleas in your carpets, your vacuum cleaner is your best ally in the battle against these pests. Always vacuum thoroughly after applying flea killers. Some people toss a few mothballs into the vacuum cleaner bag to kill the bugs that get evicted from their homes in the carpet.

• You can't vacuum well if the bag is full; check the vacuum cleaner bag often. If the bag must be emptied, you can prevent dust clouds from polluting your home if you empty the vacuum cleaner bag into a large plastic garbage bag. Hold the mouth of the bag shut as you dump the dust inside it. If your vacuum cleaner uses disposable bags, keep them handy in your cleaning tote.

• Shedding is common in new carpeting, as loose fibers left over from the manufacturing process rise to the surface. Don't panic!

• Static electricity in some carpet fibers plagues us mostly in the winter months when humidity is low in the home. The commercial anti-static sprays made especially for fabrics and carpets found in supermarkets are effective. Running a humidifier can help. (It's also good for your skin and lungs if very dry air causes you to have dry skin or breathing problems.)

• You can use a steam iron to remove indentations caused by furniture legs. Hold the iron above the indentation, but don't let it touch the carpeting. Let the steam penetrate the area. The fibers should spring back to normal. You may have to repeat the steaming for stubborn dents. Use a brush to fluff up the pile after steaming.

• A quick-fix way to do this is to place a single ice cube in the indentation. As it slowly melts, the moisture will go into the fibers and plump them up.

• It's a good idea to keep drapes closed on sunny days. Overexposure to the sun will fade some carpet fibers.

• Carpeting that has not been tacked down properly will wrinkle, especially on humid summer days. Winter heating removes the extra moisture, so the rug usually lies flat. The only way to eliminate this seasonal wrinkle is to have the carpet restretched.

CARPET STAINS AND REPAIRS

While many of the stain removal tips in Chapter 7, "Clothing Care," can also be used when removing spots and stains from carpets, you need to take a few extra steps when you are working with them.

• After using the appropriate solution for the spot or stain, it's important to rinse the area. With clothing, of course, you can just hold the garment under running water or immerse it. With carpets, after you rinse the area with clear water to remove all detergents or other stain removers, you have to blot up as much of the moisture as you can to prevent rings from forming around the area you worked on.

Here's how: Place an old white towel or wads of white paper towels (use white to prevent any possible color bleeding) over the wet area, then walk around on the towels, reversing them so the dry sides are touching the carpet. Keep doing this until the area feels mostly dry.
Then place another dry white towel on the area and weigh it down (with bricks, a heavy book wrapped in foil or plastic wrap to protect it from moisture, or a stack of magazines) so that it will help draw out any remaining moisture. Leave the weighted towel on the area overnight. In the morning or whenever the carpet is dry, fluff up the nap with your fingers, a brush, or the vacuum cleaner.

• Clean all spills immediately. Set stains will be difficult to remove, especially those from beverages that contain sugar and from pet urine. (See Chapter 7.)

• Mysterious returning spots: A mysterious stain that keeps reappearing could be from an oily substance that was not totally removed or cleaned well. It could also be coming up from the foam or back of the carpet.

Sometimes products used to clean the carpet can be at fault if they leave a sticky film that attracts dirt and lint.

• Bleach spots: You can recolor small bleach spots with this home remedy. Mix food coloring or clothing dye with water to make the correct shade and apply. The color can be reapplied as it fades. Because wet fibers appear darker in color than they really are, you'll have to allow the retouched area to dry before you can tell if the color is a match. Don't toss out the mix; you may have to reapply the color.

• A color crayon can be used in a pinch. Color the spot, then cover with wax paper and iron on low setting. This can be reapplied if it fades.

• Musty-smelling carpets: A musty smell is usually a sign that the carpet or padding is damp. If it cannot be taken outside to dry in the sunlight, dry it with a fan, or if it's a small area, use a hair dryer on a low setting.

• If the odor remains after the carpet is completely dry, there may be mildew on the back. Try sprinkling some baking soda underneath (if the carpet is not tacked down) and on top. Wait a day, then vacuum.

• If you are so unfortunate as to have a carpeted room get flooded, you'll have to remove the foam padding and allow it to dry before you can get the carpet to dry.

If the flooding is very bad, please take the time to remove the entire carpet and all of the padding and allow to dry thoroughly before replacing. If you try to do it halfway, and think you can get away with it naturally drying on the floor, you're asking for trouble, because the backing and the padding will eventually mildew.

• Repairing cigarette burns: Cut out the burned section of fibers. Using cuticle scissors helps. Gather some strands and fuzz from an out-of-the-way spot, and glue them in the hole with fabric glue. Place a piece of wax paper over this repair, put a book on top, and allow it to dry thoroughly for at least 24 hours.

• If the burn is large and deep you may have to call a professional to reweave the area. Burn holes in furniture upholstery can also be rewoven by professionals.

Upholstered Furniture

• To remove cat or dog hair from upholstery, rub a rubber glove over the upholstery; the hair will roll into a neat pile with each glove stroke. You can minimize the amount of shedding by brushing your pets regularly. Some cats love the attention, others protest, but it's worth a try. I even know some cats and dogs that love to be vacuumed!

- Upholstered furniture sold after 1970 usually has a letter code somewhere on its tag that tells which cleaning or spot-removal methods are safe for the fabric.

  The code is as follows:

  W—Use water and cleaning agents or foam mixed with water.
  S—Use no water. Use dry-cleaning solvents.
  W-S—Use either water-based or dry-cleaning solvents.
  X—Don't use liquid or foam cleaning agents. Soil can be removed by brushing or vacuuming only.

- Upholstered leather furniture should never be cleaned with oils or furniture polishes; these may make the leather sticky. Clean leather chairs or tabletops by rubbing with a lather of warm water and castile or saddle soap. Wipe with a clean cloth and buff dry with a soft cloth.

- Vinyl furniture can be cleaned with a solution of warm water and mild detergent. Rub to loosen soil, rinse, dry with towel. Commercial vinyl cleaners are available and best used for greasy or stubborn stains. Vinyl fabrics can be waxed with milk paste wax such as automobile wax.

- The most-often-asked-about stain to remove from vinyl or leather furniture is ballpoint pen ink. Simply use a cotton swab and dip it in a little rubbing alcohol, then gently dab at the stain. Some people use hair spray on the cotton swab, but you must be careful because that does leave lacquer. After removing the ballpoint ink, wipe with a damp sponge and recondition the leather or vinyl.

Dry-Mopping, Sweeping, Scrubbing, and/or Waxing Non-Carpeted Floors

- To prevent scratching the floor when moving heavy furniture across uncarpeted areas, slip scraps of old carpeting, facedown, under all furniture legs.

- If a newly cleaned floor continues to be sticky or tacky after more than 20 or 30 minutes of drying, or if the polish layer powders, flakes, or scratches easily, it may be due to old polish that was not removed, cleaner residue not well rinsed off, too much polish, or not allowing enough time between polish applications.

  The solution is to clean the floor thoroughly, removing all polish, and then to reapply polish according to directions on the container.

• Buildup of soil between polish layers can cause white or light-colored vinyl floors to yellow. Removing all of the polish and starting over can help. Exposure to strong sunlight or being covered with a rug with a rubber backing or furniture also can yellow such floors. Sometimes, such yellowing is permanent.

• In a fix and don't have a dustpan when you're sweeping the floor? Just take a paper plate, cut it in half (and a really easy hint is to moisten the edge), set it on the floor, and there you go—a disposable dustpan.

Wood Floor Care

Hardwood floors are prized for their beauty and durability; if you have them, you are lucky indeed. Generally speaking, water is wood's enemy and should not be used to clean wood floors unless the manufacturer's instructions say it's okay. Normally, wood floors are cleaned with solvents such as turpentine, nontoxic dry-cleaning fluids, or liquid or paste spirit-solvent waxes.

• The best thing you can do for wood floors is to sweep or dry mop as often as possible. The culprit is ground-in dirt, so the more you sweep it, the better it will look.

• Zap your mop with a little spray wax before dusting wood floors and you'll keep them shiny-clean with only a few minutes of effort each day.

• CAUTION: When spraying wax on mops or furniture, don't let wax "puddles" accumulate on the floor. You'll have the equivalent of slippery and dangerous ice patches, which people won't see but which they will find the hard way—by falling on them.

• Very old and dull wood floors may need to be sanded and finished. You can refinish them yourself; many new easy-to-use products are available at hardware stores.

• Never use liquid wax made for vinyl flooring on wood floors. It tends to darken wood. Use paste wax or liquid waxes specifically for wood instead.

• Always read the directions on the wax container. Some products will specify that you have to remove all other finishes first, and you may not be up to that chore. Other products, such as paste waxes, may require machine buffing, and if you don't have a buffer, you'll have to rent one for waxing day.

• Sanding floors by hand causes so much friction that you can get friction burns on your fingertips even through work gloves. Some people have even sanded the skin right off their hands. If you are determined to sand by hand, apply masking tape to all fingertips and put on gloves to save your skin.

• If you get small slivers from steel wool or some types of soft wood in your fingers, instead of poking around in your skin with tweezers, try spreading a film of white school glue over the sliver areas. Let the glue dry, then peel it off. This method works eight out of ten times.

• Don't let sanded wood set any longer than 12 hours before you apply the stain or finish. Raw sanded wood absorbs moisture, which could affect the way it absorbs stain colors and/or the adhesion of the finish.

• Instead of using a rag to apply paste wax to floors when you wax them by hand, slip a glove-style potholder or working glove over your hand to get a better grip and to protect your skin. The gloves are more durable and easier to clean than your skin.

• You can hand buff a floor to a beautiful shine with a pad made by inserting a folded old bath towel into an old nylon stocking. The wax buffs to a shine faster than you'd think could be done by hand. The stocking will get snagged and you'll have to change it frequently, so gather up a bunch of old ones.

• Dancing chair legs (or actually chair feet) often mar hardwood floors. Try applying self-adhesive-backed moleskin to the bottoms of chair legs to help them glide smoothly across the floor without making marks.

• If furniture feet have dented your floors, you may be able to fill the dents with clear nail polish or shellac. Since they are clear, the floor color will show through and the dents will be less noticeable.

(Now remember, this is a Heloise home-style hint, but it sure does work in a pinch and will alleviate some of the aggravation from staring at that dent day after day after day.)

Squeaky Floors

• Whether or not you want to silence a squeaky hardwood floor probably is determined by the ages of your children. While the pitter-patter of little feet added to squeaky boards can drive a parent a bit balmy, such squeaks can be a parenting aid when you have older children. Many teens have inadvertently announced their late-night arrivals with squeaky floorboards.

Here's the tip for whoever will benefit from it: Try sprinkling talcum powder over the "musical areas" for a dry lubricant. Sweep the talc back and forth until it filters down between the cracks and you'll probably get blessedly quiet floorboards.

• If the squeaky wood floor is under tile or carpet, you might be able to eliminate the squeak without removing the floor covering. It's sometimes possible to reset loose boards by pounding the loose nails back into place. Place a block of scrap wood over the squeaky area to protect the flooring and then pound with a hammer.

Care of Vinyl Floors

Vinyl flooring is usually referred to as "resilient flooring," in contrast to "hard-surface" flooring such as wood, stone, concrete, marble, terrazzo, and ceramic tile. Linoleum, asphalt, rubber, and cork flooring is no longer manufactured, but some people still have these materials in their homes. Most of these materials, except wood and cork, can be cleaned with water or mild detergent or household cleaners as described below.

• When floors are only slightly soiled, just sweep or vacuum, then damp-mop with a clean sponge mop and warm water, pressing hard enough to loosen surface dirt.

• When you wet-mop, attack small areas at a time, and be sure to rinse the mop frequently in the bucket of clean water; otherwise you are just smearing dirt around the floor instead of cleaning it up. Change the water when it's dirty, which may be several times for a large room.

• Really dirty floors need to be washed with a no-rinse cleaner or a general-purpose liquid detergent. Flooring manufacturers warn against washing with soap, dish-washing liquid, or gritty powders or cleansers.

• REMEMBER: When you scrub asphalt tile floors with water, wring out the cloth or sponge well to avoid soaking the floor with excess water. Excess water can seep into the seams and loosen the adhesives that hold the flooring. We want to destroy dirt, not our decor.

• Always follow the directions on the no-rinse cleaners. For most of them, you apply them with a sponge mop and just wipe them up.

• When using the detergents recommended for your type of floor, prepare the bucket of detergent and water according to label instructions. Use two buckets: one for detergent solution and one for your rinse water.

Scrub the floor as follows:

1. Dip the sponge mop into the bucket.
2. Don't squeeze or wring the mop out before you spread the cleaning solution over a small area.
3. Wait for a minute for the detergent action to loosen the dirt. The detergent is supposed to work for you, not you for your detergent.
4. Scrub the area with the mop, then wipe up the liquid.
5. Rinse well, being sure not to leave any detergent on the floor. Be sure to change rinse water often.

• Always rinse floors with clean water, even when the directions for the floor cleaner say you don't have to.

Flooring manufacturers tell me that the reason no-wax floors get dull is that they are not rinsed properly after detergents and floor cleaners are used on them, or the incorrect floor cleaner is used on a no-wax floor. It's very important to check with the manufacturer of the no-wax floor that is in your home to be sure you're using the proper cleaning agent, if any agent is to be used at all on it.

If you don't thoroughly rinse no-wax floors, a shine-hiding, sticky film builds up and traps dirt. The more often you wash without rinsing, the more film buildup you get.

• When your floor dries after rinsing and still has a dull film, try mopping again with a solution of one cup or so of white vinegar to a bucket of water. (Yes, I know, where there's Heloise and a bucket of water, there's a cup or so of vinegar. But, believe me, when it comes to shine, vinegar does it.)

• If your highly waxed floor gets dull between washings, mop it with a solution of one cup of fabric softener in one-half pail of water.

• Before you put a new coat of wax on your linoleum or tile floors, you'll need to remove the old wax to get good results for your efforts. If you mop with a solution of three parts of water to one part of rubbing alcohol, the floor will be clean and ready for new wax.

• If you're all fired up to wax your floors and find out that you have no commercial wax, don't quit when you're "on a roll." You can "wax" a floor with a solution of two tablespoons furniture polish and one-half cup vinegar added to a bucket of warm water.

• A long-handled paint roller can be used to apply wax to floors when you don't have an official waxer. Rollers work fast and reach under furniture for you.

• You can hand buff your newly waxed floor and get your muscle-toning exercise at the same time. Just wrap a bath towel around each foot and "skate" around the floor. And of course, be very careful while you're skating so that you don't fall.

• Shoe heel scuff marks on resilient flooring can be removed by rubbing them with a pencil eraser or fine, dry steel wool. Crayon marks come off when rubbed with a damp rag containing toothpaste or silver polish.

• If you drop a raw egg on the floor and don't have an eager dog to clean it up for you, sprinkle the egg glob with salt, let it sit for 12 to 20 minutes, and then sweep it up with a broom.

• You can patch a gouge in resilient flooring if you grate a flooring scrap with a food grater, mix the grated flooring with clear nail polish, and then plug the gouge. This tip is not for dents, just gouges or holes.

Draperies and Blinds

• You can toss most drapes or curtains into the dryer for a few minutes on air setting to remove dust.

• An aerosol spray made for cleaning crystal chandeliers will clean painted metal blinds. With the blinds in a semi-closed position, spray and then wipe off the dirt droplets with paper towels or terry towel rags. Liquid window cleaner and our homemade cleaner will also work, but you'll have to totally wipe each slat instead of just wiping droplets.

Cobwebs and Other Fuzzy Dust

• Vacuum moldings, air-conditioning/heating vents, and corners of walls to get rid of fuzzy dust and any cobwebs that may be on the ceiling.
  If your vacuum extensions aren't long enough, you may be able to reach corners with a broom, mop, or fishing pole covered by an old pillowcase, T-shirt, or nylon net.

• Unreachable cobwebs can sometimes be "caught" if you wrap a racquetball or tennis ball in a dust rag and then toss it up into the cobweb corner.

CAUTION: Don't get too enthusiastic when tossing the ball or you'll "score" costly knickknack-breaking rebounds.

Walls and Woodwork

• Dust walls before washing and wash from the bottom up so that drips won't make their marks. Clean small areas at a time, then rinse and dry, before moving to another area.

• Wash most painted surfaces with soap or mild detergent and water, or mild commercial household cleaners.

• You can soften soap waters and rinse waters by adding one tablespoon of borax or a commercial water softener per quart of water.

Wall Coverings

Since there are so many types of wall coverings—paper, plastic, fabric, resin coated or impregnated materials—you need to get the manufacturer's care directions when you have the walls covered.

• If you don't know what your wall covering should be cleaned with, always test cleaners on an inconspicuous place before proceeding. Colors can bleed, papers can come off the wall, and who knows what else can happen if you use the wrong cleaner!

• Most washable coverings can be gently washed with mild detergent and cool water. Work from the bottom up, using as little water as possible. Work on small areas and overlap as you wash. Rinse with clear water and blot dry.

• Many nonwashable wall coverings can be cleaned when rubbed gently with art gum eraser, fresh white bread, or doughy wallpaper cleaners (available at hardware stores). If you use the doughy cleaner, knead and turn it often so that you are using clean surfaces on the wall. (I knew there had to be some good use for white bread.)

• Spot-clean wallpaper before spots set. Blot grease spots with paper towels or facial tissue while you press lightly a warm iron over the towels or tissue.

• A paste of nonflammable dry-cleaning solvent and absorbent powder (fuller's earth, talcum, cornstarch) can be applied to a stain, allowed to dry, then brushed off.

• Crayon can sometimes be sponged off with dry-cleaning solvent. Pencil marks and smudges can sometimes be removed with art gum or pencil erasers. Always rub gently.

• Ink may be removed by bleach, or commercial ink remover may work on wallpaper, but either one may also remove the color of the wallpaper; test first.

Heavy Metal Cleaning

Many ornamental metal objects are lacquered and should not be cleaned with any commercial or homemade cleaners, which may remove the lacquer. Always check the tags of ornamental metal objects to find out how they should be cleaned. After noting what the item is on the tag, store the tag in your household file for reference. Don't depend upon memory.

BRASS AND COPPER

Tarnish can be removed with commercial cleaners or with some of the homemade cleaners listed below. Those made with lemon juice or vinegar will give copper and brass a bright finish, and the oil and rottenstone cleaner will give these metals a soft luster.

• Saturate a sponge or cloth with vinegar or lemon juice, sprinkle salt on the sponge, and then lightly rub, rinse, and dry.

• Rub with a paste made by adding flour to the salt and vinegar or lemon juice, rinse, and dry.

• Make a thin paste from rottenstone (an abrasive powder available at hardware stores) and an oil such as cooking or salad oil. Wipe off excess oil after rubbing, polish with a clean cloth.

• Brass fireplace tools can be buffed with fine emery cloth, which is available at hardware stores.

CHROMIUM

• Most of the time, chromium plating on small appliances, faucet handles, and so forth can be cleaned with sudsy water and buffed dry.

• If suds aren't enough, rub with baking soda that has been sprinkled on a damp sponge or cloth, or wipe with vinegar; buff dry. Use commercial cleaners for really stubborn gunk.

PEWTER

• Rub with a paste made by mixing denatured alcohol and whiting (an abrasive powder available in hardware stores). After the paste dries, wash, rinse, and buff with a soft cloth.

• To get a duller finish on pewter, make a paste with rottenstone and oil, rub, rinse, buff dry.

• Corrosion can be removed by gently rubbing with fine (0000) steel wool dipped in oil.

Decorating Tips

I like to visit people whose knickknacks are personal treasures (which has nothing to do with price) instead of just decorator dust catchers. I have many things in my home that are heirlooms, gifts, or just things that entertain me every time I look at them. For example, I have a butler at my door—a mannequin dressed in full tuxedo. Everyone who visits me has fun "talking" to my "butler."

Not everyone will have a "butler," but we all accumulate certain treasures that we are fond of and that give our homes a personal look rather than a magazine photo layout look.

• To give a room a focal point, group photographs or any other souvenirs and personal collections in one place rather than scattering them about the house. Then you'll have one large, memorable, attractive display.

• If you tend to collect things made from a single specific material—such as shell, brass, wood, copper, porcelain, or whatever—you'll find that when you group your collection, everything will "match" no matter what color, size, or shape it is.

Hang-Ups

• Quilting is an American art, and quilts are as appropriate for wall hangings as European tapestries. Attach wooden rings to a quilt and hang it from a wide, wooden rod.

• Frame anything that appeals to you, such as an old map, family documents (Grandpa's citizenship papers), children's artwork, a nice piece of print paper or fabric, needlework art.

• Oil paintings usually are not matted or covered with glass. Etchings and delicate flower prints are usually covered with glass and put into lightweight frames.

• When preparing to move, as you take down wall hangings and pictures, remove the nails or hooks from the walls at the same time and tape them to the back of each object. Then, when you're ready to rehang them at the new place, you won't need to look for hooks or nails.

• Tabs from aluminum cans make great hangers for lightweight pictures. Drive a nail or tack through the rivet into the picture frame, then bend the tab to the desired shape. This won't hold heavy pictures, but works well on lightweight pictures and wall plaques.

• If you're hanging a picture from a molding but you don't like the looks of the exposed picture wire, substitute nylon fishing line. The transparent nylon is almost invisible and your picture can star on its own.

• Giving an inexpensive, glossy picture the texture of an oil painting is easier than most of us would think. Purchase some nylon net and cut it to overlap the picture; tape the corners to keep the net flat and taut. Brush shellac on lightly, let it set for a couple of seconds, then carefully remove the net and let the picture dry. After it dries, it will have the texture of canvas and look like an oil painting.

• Picture hanging can be frustrating if you simply try to "eyeball" the right spot to put the hook. Some people measure with tape and yardstick and still don't get the picture where they want it. You can place a picture exactly where you want it the first time by following this method.

Cut a sheet of paper to the exact size of the frame. Position the pattern on the picture's back side and pull up taut the picture's hanging wire so that you will see an inverted V. Mark the "V" point on the pattern and poke a hole through that marked point.

After you determine where you'll put the picture, place the pattern on the wall, and use the V point hole to make a pencil mark showing exactly where the nail should go. The picture will hang precisely where you want it.

• If the picture isn't too heavy, another time-saving method is to hold the picture itself by its wire and decide where you want it positioned. Wet a fingertip and press it on the wall to mark the wire's inverted V point. The fingerprint mark will stay wet long enough for you to drive a nail and hook on target.

• Take the guesswork out of arranging several pictures on the wall; do it like a pro. Spread out a large sheet of wrapping paper or several taped-together newspapers on the floor and experiment with frame positions.

When you decide on a pleasing grouping, outline the frames on the paper, tape the paper to the wall, and drive hooks through the paper into the wall. Then remove the paper and hang the pictures.

• Group pictures of similar subjects, colors, frames, or sizes. When putting a grouping over a large piece of furniture such as a sofa, it's usually better to keep the bottom line even. But no rules are permanently nailed to any wall; use an arrangement that pleases you.

• Sometimes a picture that was positioned correctly has a mind of its own and won't hang straight. Give it some gentle guidance by wrapping masking tape around the wire on both sides of the hook so the wire can't slip. Or install parallel nails and hooks a short distance apart: two hooks are better than one for keeping pictures in their places.

• Squares of double-faced tape affixed to the frame's two lower back corners also will keep pictures from roving.

• Don't lose a perfect picture grouping when you repaint a room. If you insert toothpicks in the hook holes and paint right over them, when the paint dries, you can remove the toothpicks and rehang your pictures.

• And a quick, easy way to remember the grouping is to take a photo of your picture arrangement.

• To prevent a plaster wall from crumbling when driving a nail or hook into it, first form an X over the nail spot with two strips of masking tape or transparent tape.

• Make small rooms look larger and brighter by installing mirrors on one wall to create double width with reflections of opposite walls. This works whether you are installing mirror tiles or hanging a mirror collection.

• Hang mirrors to reflect you but not the sun, because some mirror backings are adversely affected by direct sunlight.

• When hanging a mirror with screws that go through mounting holes in the glass, don't tighten the screws all the way. Leave enough play so the mirror won't crack if the wall shifts.

Decorating Windows

• Hanging plants can substitute for curtains on windows. (And talk about no-iron, drip-dry!)

• An Indian print bedspread can become an instant drapery. Hang it full width across a window, then pick up a bottom corner to open the "drapery" diagonally across half the window, and secure with a tieback.

• For an airy, summery window, try stretching gauze or chiffon between two dowels, and hang them inside the window frame.

• Glue fabric to cheap window shades, finish the edges with braid or fringe, and you won't need curtains. In bedrooms, an inexpensive way to achieve a coordinated look is to buy extra matching sheets to use as window dressings, table covers, and even as throws over chairs.

   If your fabric is rather heavy, the roller springs won't work well and you may have to keep the shade at half mast all the time, so plan the pattern accordingly.

• Colorful printed bed sheets can be made into curtains for any room in the house. They can also be stapled to walls for a fabric "wallpaper" look.

• "Frame" a window with bookshelves, either built-in or freestanding. You can top "store-bought" shelves with a board if they are as tall as the window and thereby add an extra shelf across the top of the window. You'll be adding storage space and avoiding curtain maintenance at the same time.

Wallpaper Decorating Tips

• When you are selecting wallpaper, remember that if it has one or more of the dominant colors already in the room, the wallpaper will tie everything together.

• If you have a large room and want it to appear smaller and cozier, choose a wallpaper with a large, bold pattern. Don't, however, use it in a small room, because bold patterns will "close in on you" and make the room look small and crowded.

• A mural-pattern wallpaper makes a small room appear larger.

• You can raise or lower ceilings with wallpaper. A high ceiling seems lower if the walls are papered with a bold pattern. A low ceiling seems higher if the walls are papered with a small print or a texture.

Extraordinary Decorating with Ordinary Things

• Children's room too small? Add a miniature hammock to a corner in a child's room to make a bed for all those stuffed animals.

• A nonworking fireplace, primed and freshened with paint, makes a cozy niche for an aquarium or flower/plant arrangements.

• Need an instant centerpiece? A branch cut from any blossoming tree or bush makes an unusual centerpiece on a dining or coffee table. Greenery of any kind can be used; just add something appropriate for the season, such as artificial red holly berries or peppers or Easter eggs.

• Just about anything that holds water can be a vase. Display flowers in a crystal ice bucket, fluted champagne glasses, mugs, cocktail pitchers.

• You don't have to throw away a favorite crystal water glass or pitcher when it gets a chipped lip; use it to hold fresh or artificial flowers. Silk flowers can be arranged in favorite containers that don't hold water.

• Buy gourds in the fall at the supermarket. Use them for a month or so in an arrangement, then put them someplace warm and dry for a while. The gourds become very light as they dry, and the colors mute beautifully with age.

• Garlic braids or dry hot peppers threaded on a long string make a kitchen decor cook!

(And the garlic, according to legend, keeps away vampires. I've never seen a vampire in a kitchen that has garlic hanging in it! Of course, I've never seen a vampire in a kitchen without garlic either.)

Storage Space to End Clutter

• Put old bookcases into closets for ready-made shelving. You can paint them to match or leave them as they are.

• Install shelves over the commode in the bathroom to hold towels and miscellaneous bathroom accessories.

• Use pegboards to hang up utility items such as tools, pots and pans, sewing supplies, or anything else that fits on a hook or peg.

• Check out the notions departments of variety stores to find ways of hanging up ironing boards, irons, and other household aids with various "over-the-door" devices.

• Shoe bags can be used in many rooms and not only for shoes. They'll hold sewing supplies, crafts tools, kitchen utensils, and anything else that fits.

• Two nails or pegs can hold brooms, rakes, shovels, and other garden tools on the garage wall so that they are out of tripping range.

• The best tip is to use every nook and cranny in your home for storage—just add a bit of imagination and innovation!

CHAPTER 4

Home Maintenance

Maintenance and making minor repairs prevent major problems and budget-breaking bills.

However, not everyone can fix plumbing or do carpentry and painting, and many people can't do any "fix-it" activity beyond picking up the phone to call in a home service person. And sometimes, having the pros fix what you have broken while trying to fix it yourself costs more than it would have to call for professional service in the first place.

However, many people can do simple repairs, and just about everyone can do preventive maintenance. The maintenance and simple repairs tips in this chapter will help even an "all thumbs" person to make household helpers last longer so that you get your money's worth from them.

Here are two important and very basic tips.

• When you build a house, build on additions, buy an already built one, or rent a house, find out which pipes are gas and which are water; the location of all buried pipes; the location of electrical or other cables; the location of all fuse boxes; which outlets are 220V (for air conditioners and stoves) and which are 110V. If the house is in an area that still has septic tanks, know the location of the tank and its lateral drains.

Knowing these things will prevent the digging up of phone cables when you are landscaping and will help you know when something is wrong. For example, a constant pool of water in one part of the yard could mean a broken pipe or a malfunctioning septic tank.

If you have to hire someone to fix buried plumbing or wiring, think about the extra labor costs for paying a professional person to walk around looking for pipes and connections or guessing at where they ought to be. That time and money is best spent actually fixing whatever is broken.

• Many adult education courses are available through city colleges and school districts to help you learn about home maintenance and automobile repairs. Such courses are useful even if you don't plan to do major projects yourself, because they help you deal with the service people you hire.

Plumbing

• Here's a simple plumbing tip that can save all sorts of mess: Teach everyone in the house where the main cutoff valve is and how to use it, as well as the various sink, toilet, and washer cutoffs so that all family members, housekeepers, and baby-sitters know how to to stop a flood before they are up to their ankles in water.

Drippy and Noisy Faucets

• You don't have to turn faucet handles off until they feel tight. Just turn until the water goes off. Any further turning compresses the gaskets, which will make the faucets leak.

• If you have a drippy faucet disrupting your sleep in the middle of the night, tie a two-foot-long piece of string around the faucet so that the drips can go down the string from the nozzle into the drain without making any noise. If you don't have string, wet a small towel or washcloth and drape or wrap it around the faucet any old way that makes it catch the drips silently.

• If your faucet squeals (a sound as penetrating as a fingernail on a blackboard), the stem's metal threads and the faucet's threads are grinding against each other. Take the handle and stem off, then coat both sets of threads with petroleum jelly, and you won't have goose bumps every time the faucet is turned. And the handle will be easier to turn, too.

• Faucet aerators need cleaning. Unscrew the aerator, take the screen out, and rinse it. If it is totally clogged with mineral deposits and hard water buildup, you can soak the aereator screen in vinegar to remove that, and then put the entire mechanism back together.

Clogged Drains

While it seems that drains get clogged at the most inconvenient times, the fact is that drains warn us ahead of time. The problem is that we tend to ignore a "slow" drain until it's too late. It's so easy to ignore unseen gunk, isn't it? Prevention is the best idea.

• If you have a completely clogged drain, try a "plumber's friend."

• DO NOT use drain cleaners in completely clogged drains; if the plumber's friend doesn't do the job, call the plumber!

• Plungers get better suction if their rubber caps are covered with water. To keep from spattering the walls, yourself, the sink countertop, and just about anything in a radius of five feet when you are "plunging" a small sink, make a tent from a bath towel over your arm, the plunger, and the splatters.

• Some sinks and all tubs have overflow openings. If you plug this opening when you use the plunger, you'll get better suction and force.

• If the plumber's helper doesn't unclog the clog, you can try dislodging it with a straightened wire coat hanger, bent at one end to form a small hook. However, the best advice at this point may be to call a plumber.

• If the drain is only slightly clogged, it can sometimes be cleaned by flushing boiling water down into it. A solution of one pound of washing soda in three gallons of boiling water can be poured down the drain.

• Commercial drain cleaners can also be used. However, commercial drain cleaners should always be used with caution, because some may damage drain pipes and the finish around the drain.

• If you have young children and don't like to keep drain cleaners around the house, buy only the amount of drain cleaner needed to do all of the drains in your house at one session and then put the cleaner in the drains as soon as you get your groceries into the house. By the time you've put them away, you can flush all the cleaner away and throw away the container.

• CAUTION: Always be careful when disposing of containers with chemicals; wrap them so that children and pets can't get at them.

• To help prevent clogged drains, use the following procedure once a month. Make a home-style noncorrosive drain cleaner by mixing one cup baking soda, one cup table salt, and one-quarter cup cream of tartar in a small bowl. Stir thoroughly. Store this cleaner in a clean, covered jar. (You will have 2 ¼ cups of drain cleaner.) CAUTION: Label the container so that this white powder isn't mistaken for food, and don't store it where food is stored.

To use this drain cleaner, you need to pour one-fourth cup of it into a drain, then immediately add one cup of boiling water. Wait 10 seconds, then flush with cold water for at least 20 seconds.

• To keep kitchen and bathroom drains clear of hair and clogged grease, try this weekly: Pour one cup baking soda into the drain, followed by one cup vinegar. As the soda and vinegar foam, flush the drain with very hot water.

• When floor drains, such as those in shower stalls and basements, are clogged and the clog isn't close to the opening, try to unclog the drain with water pressure from a garden hose. With the hose attached to a faucet, feed it into the drain as deeply as it will go; close up the open spaces around the hose by tightly jamming rags into the opening. Then turn on the water full blast for a few minutes.

Plumbing Repairs

• Wrenches can really mess up chrome-plated plumbing fixtures. Wrap the fixture with a double layer of plastic electrical tape before attacking it with tools.

Noisy Pipes

Isn't it awful when your plumbing "sings"? Sometimes it's the water pressure that makes pipes screech and whine and sometimes vibrate and bang against the walls in extreme cases.

• If the water pressure in your house is at or higher than 70 to 80 pounds per square inch, you may have to install a pressure-reducing valve to silence your protesting pipes. To measure the average water pressure in your home, you need to attach a pressure gauge to the cold-water faucet nearest the main shutoff valve. Since you probably don't own such a device, if this problem is annoying enough, you may want to call a plumber to fix it.

Or you can wait until the next time you have a plumbing repair and tell the plumber about the water pressure problem, but say that you want this checked when you make the appointment. "By the way, will you check . . ." is not a good way to get things done. The plumber may have a tight schedule and have only enough time to fix whatever it is you called about in the first place.

• If a noisy water pipe is banging against a wall, try wedging a wood block between the pipe and the wall. If you are handy, you can clamp the pipe to the block for more stability.

Frozen Pipes

Protection of pipes in cold weather is a must, and the amount of protection can range from foam pipe wraps, which you buy in the hardware store, to covering pipes with straw when you live in rural areas. The idea is to protect pipes from the cold wind and temperatures so that they don't burst.

• Some people let faucets dribble to keep the water flowing and less likely to freeze, but in some areas, where water pressure is low, having everyone's water running, even at a dribble, can hamper fire fighting with inadequate water pressure. Find out what is the appropriate way to protect pipes from freezing in your community by calling a county Cooperative Extension Agent or watching for the TV and newspaper stories that are inevitable when a freeze is predicted.

• To thaw a frozen pipe, heat the pipe starting at the tap end. If you start in the middle, steam from melting ice can burst the pipe. Open the tap so that melting ice and steam can run off.

• In a pinch, you can use a hair dryer to thaw frozen pipes.

Toilet Tank and Bowl

If you've ever had a faulty toilet (or septic tank) cause an overflow, it's an experience you'll never forget, despite wanting desperately never to think about it again.

• Don't flush a clogged toilet if there is only a little water in it. Flushing will cause it to overflow. Get out the old plumber's helper, and if there isn't enough water to cover the rubber cup, get water from some other source and pour it over the plunger cup to make the suction better. Some people poke an unbent hanger down the commode, but if you do this, it may scratch the bowl and then the scratches will stain. A real plumber's "snake" from the hardware store is probably better to use. If the plumber's helper or snake don't work, call the plumber. The clog may be farther down into the drain and need to be "rooted" out with a motorized device.

• If you aren't getting enough water from the tank to flush the bowl clean, check the tank's water level. If the water level in the tank isn't within 1 ½ inches of the top of the overflow tube, you need to bend the float arm UP slightly so that more water will be allowed to enter the tank.

• Conserve water by placing a sealed or foil-covered brick in the toilet tank so that less water is needed to activate the flush mechanism. Be sure to place the brick so that it does not interfere with the flushing mechanism.

• You also can place an upright glass jar (quart or pint mayo size will do) into the tank. The jar will remain filled with water when the tank is flushed, saving a pint or quart each flush. The weight of the water will keep the jar in place.

• Many automatic toilet bowl cleaners that you drop into the tank contain strong bleach, which ultimately "eats up" the soft parts of the flush mechanism. Read labels before you buy!

Septic Tanks

• If you live in an area that has septic tanks, you might want to flush down something to keep its chemical activity going. Here's a septic tank activator recipe. Mix two envelopes of active dry yeast with a pound of brown sugar in a large bowl. Add four cups of warm water. Stir until completely blended. Allow the mixture to rest in a warm place for 10 to 20 minutes until foamy and increased in volume. Flush down the toilet. Commercial activators can also be bought at hardware stores.

Water Heaters

• If you live in a hard-water area, you need to drain your water heater monthly to get rid of the mineral deposits that collect on the bottom and that eventually prevent the heater from functioning properly.

Directions should have come with your water heater, or ask the plumber who installed it.

• If you've been away for an extended time, you can prevent possible explosions by opening all hot-water taps for a few minutes after reentering your house to release any possible hydrogen gas that may have built up in the water heater.

Water Purifiers

• If you have a water purification system, change the filters periodically. Follow the recommendations of the manufacturer.

• When you have a purifier with a holding tank, run the tank for several minutes if you've been away so that the tank will be refilled with fresh water.

Using Tools

Hammering Safely

• If you have to pound in a nail at a level that is below your knees, face away from the wall, standing or crouching near the nail. Pound in the nail by hammering toward the rear.

• If a nail is too short to hold, press it through a piece of cardboard or index card. Hold the paper in one hand and the hammer in the other. Tear away the cardboard before you pound the last taps or tap the last pounds, whichever sounds right to you. The cardboard will protect the wall from "hits and misses" too.

• You can also place the nail between the teeth of a comb to hold it while you're hammering.

• Use a nail punch for the final hammer drives to prevent "scars" on the surface from "hits and misses."

• When you have to drive a nail into a crevice, use a nail punch set to get the nail all the way in.

Using Screwdrivers

• Screwdrivers come in different sizes. Using the right size will keep the screw head from being damaged.

- If you make a small hole with a nail first, it is easier to screw in a screw.

- If you soap or wax screw threads, the screw will go in more easily.

Window Repairs

Oh come on, don't say, "I don't do windows." Unless we hire other people to do them we all have to do windows once in a while or we miss all the sunshine. For many of us, doing windows is a major project even if it's just to clean them. Some of the tips below go beyond the mere cleaning level but are simple repairs that can be done with simple tools.

- When the window gets stuck, get a block of wood and place it on the spot before you tap (not pound) the window sash with a hammer. If you hit the sash directly with the hammer, it will dent.

- To remove cracked glass from a window without cutting yourself and having dangerous pieces of glass to clean up, crisscross both sides of the broken pane with many strips of masking tape before you tap it out with a hammer. The tape will hold most of the pieces together safely.

Window Screens

- Repair a small tear in wire screening by pushing the wire strands back into place with an ice pick. If you can't completely close up the hole, sparingly brush clear nail polish or shellac across the remaining opening. After the sealer dries, reapply until the pinhole is invisibly sealed. Blot up any drips of sealer that run down the screen to make this a neat job.

- A clean cut or tear in a window screen can be stitched together if you use a long needle and strong nylon thread, fishing line, or fine wire. As you zigzag-stitch back and forth across the cut, don't pull the thread or wire too tightly, because this will pucker the patch. After you are finished with the mend, apply clear nail polish to keep the thread or wire from pulling loose.

- If the screen has a large hole, cut a patch from a screening scrap of the same type of screening, then zigzag the patch into place. Apply clear nail polish to the stitching to reinforce it.

- You can heat-fuse a patch when you have to repair fiberglass screening. Just lay a fiberglass patch over the tear or hole and carefully run a hot iron around the patch edges. You'll need to put some foil over the screen and patch to keep the iron from touching it directly.

• Aluminum screens tend to pit, but you can prevent this kind of damage if you clean them with kerosene. Just dip a rag in the kerosene and rub both sides of the screen and frames; wipe off excess. This treatment is also a rust inhibitor for older screens.

CAUTION: This is an outside job and kerosene is flammable. DON'T light anything up while you are doing this and do it outdoors, where you'll have plenty of ventilation. ALWAYS work with and store flammables in a cool place. It's best to buy only what you'll need for one job so that you won't have to store it at all.

Repairing Doors

• Take the squeak out of door hinges by lubricating the pin with petroleum jelly. Unlike oil, petroleum jelly won't drip on the floor.

• When you need to polish door hardware (on furniture as well as entryway doors), cut a cardboard shield so that it fits around the metal parts and then hold the shield in place with masking tape while you work on the hardware.

• Sliding door safety: Many people already do this, but it bears repeating. Apply a decal on sliding glass doors at eye level so that nobody will mistake a closed door for an open one. I even have one down at eye level on the special door for my schnauzer.

• People have been known to walk into lightweight screens too, so you might want to put a decal or sew a zigzag of colored yarn on the screen.

• For door locks that seem to stick, try some graphite in the lock before calling the lock repair service. Often that will clear up the problem immediately.

Repairing Walls

Patching Walls

• Quick-patch nail holes in white walls with white toothpaste or with moistened crushed aspirin and push it into the hole.

• After patching nail holes in colored walls, use a dab of watercolor paints if you don't have leftover paint. You'll be amazed at how closely you can match colors with water paint.

• You can also cover over the patch on colored walls by using color-coordinated typewriter correction fluid.

• If you have leftover paint, touch up small spots with cotton swabs instead of a brush. You don't waste paint and you don't have a brush to clean.

• To patch larger holes, use joint compound, available in any hardware store. You can use an upside-down lid or a bathroom plunger for a mini-hod (a hod is a trough used by masons to carry mortar), in which you can mix the compound and hold it while you are doing the repair. Hold on to the lid's knob or the plunger's handle with one hand and trowel away with the other. (When you've finished, make sure you rinse out the lid before any residue hardens.)

• If you add a tablespoon of white vinegar (I know, vinegar again!) to the water when you are mixing patching plaster, the compound won't dry so quickly and you'll be able to work more slowly.

• When you are filling wide cracks in plaster, it's best to fill from the inside out, pressing fresh plaster in with a putty knife or a trowel.

• A beer can opener makes cutting loose plaster out of a wall before patching a large crack a snap. You can use the pointed end of the opener to undercut and widen the opening.

• When a screw hole in the wall has worn grooves, stuff the hole with a cotton ball soaked in white glue, let it dry for 24 hours, and then put the new screw into the hole securely with a screwdriver.

Painting Outside and Inside the House

If you've had the advantage of learning to paint by watching a pro or at least a semi-pro, you can probably paint with a minimum of smears, drips, and mess-ups.

Unfortunately, most of us learn how to paint by trial and error . . . and mostly error. Ultimately we learn how to prepare a surface before we paint, which part or area of anything to paint first, and how to clean up instead of having to throw away our painting clothes and paint equipment. The tips below will help both novices and semi-pro painters to do it all better, more easily, and ultimately more cheaply.

When to Paint

Spring is the ideal time to paint a house's exterior. Do it as soon as the weather turns warm enough, but before the temperature gets too hot. When the heat is blistering, paint dries too quickly and leaves marks where strokes were overlapped.

Spring usually puts us in the mood to redecorate anyway. When flowers start blooming and nature renews itself, we want to make our whole environment fresh and new.

Before you rush out to the paint store, do a little planning so that you'll have some idea about the color you want and the equipment you'll need when you go to the paint store.

Get advice from the salesperson in the paint department. Some paints and varnishes are better applied with man-made bristle brushes and others are better with natural bristles. Edges of brushes are made feathered or blunt, and each bristle tip works best with specific types of paint or varnish. Also, a variety of rollers and paint pads is also available. Using the correct implement to spread the paint will ensure the best results.

Information printed on the paint or varnish can will tell you what sort of applicator to use and give you general instructions about painting. Always check the label to find out if the paint or varnish you are buying is appropriate for the surface you want to cover—wood, stucco, masonry, or metal. Certain paints are better for certain wear areas, such as porch paints for walk-on surfaces, enamels for woodwork, flat for walls, and so forth.

Color Selection

Cosmetic application of paint to your house is like applying eye shadow, blusher, and contour makeup to your face. It hides the bad and accents the good.

• Take a photograph of the outside of your house, then look it over and determine what you don't like about it. Study the photograph to see if your house looks top heavy, small, or dumpy.

• If your house is small and you want it to look larger, paint the trim, walls, and shutters a light color. If you are reroofing, add a light-color roof.

• If your house looks too narrow and tall, paint the upper story a darker shade than the lower story.

• To make a house look less dumpy and awkward, use a dark color on the roof and the side walls. The dark color outlines and limits the shape of the house against the landscape and sky and helps in making it look less chunky or short.

• To help minimize unattractive trim, paint it the same color as the house, and it will be less conspicuous.

Preparing the Surface for Paint

If the surface is properly prepared, your paint job will look better and last longer.

• Water stains on the ceiling: You can't paint over water stains or mildew on walls or ceilings. You'll need to pretreat the spot by either applying a commercial spray product from paint or hardware stores or you can apply shellac, let it dry, and then paint over the area.

• Paint does not adhere well to dirty surfaces. If paint is applied to dirty surfaces it is likely to peel, crack, or blister off the walls. First, scrape off all loose, peeling paint. Then scrub the surface well with a detergent solution and a broom or long-handled brush. Rinse well. You can use a garden hose to wash down exterior walls.

• Mildew is a problem in shady areas on house exteriors. Mildew looks like fuzzy patches of black dirt. If your house has mildew, wash it with a mixture of one quart of bleach to every gallon of non-ammonia detergent solution. After cleaning, let surfaces dry thoroughly before painting. CAUTION: Please be careful with the bleach and don't let it get on something that it could whiten or streak. You might want to drape plastic drop cloths over the shrubbery and flower beds; if you are using bleach, remove any fabric awnings and lawn furniture cushions from the splash areas.

• Be sure to wait for dew to dry before painting. Paint will not bind on a surface that is wet from morning dew or on a prime coat that is not thoroughly dry. And without proper bonding, paint will peel.

• Wrinkling occurs when too much paint is applied or when the paint is too thick. You can correct wrinkling easily by sanding the surface and brushing on paint of a lighter consistency. See the paint can for thinning directions.

• Don't try using a flame to soften alligatored paint. The flame can shoot into a crack and ignite the sheathing.

• It's not always necessary to remove the old paint when you are preparing old wood surfaces for paint. Seal all knots with thinned shellac and sand when dry. If the knot is loose, tighten it with wood caulking. After the caulking has dried, coat the spot with shellac and then sand the area smooth.

• Revolving disc sanders shouldn't be used to remove paint from wood siding, because they tend to gouge the surface.

• When painting the outside of your house, drape newspapers over the tops of doors and then close them. You won't paint the doors shut.

• To avoid marring a paint job when leaning a ladder against clapboard siding, cover the top ends of the ladder with heavy woolen socks. The paint will remain unblemished.

• Windowpanes intimidate even the most ambitious home improvement buffs. Believe me, you can paint the wooden strips around windowpanes without getting paint on the glass and having to endure a pain-in-the-neck cleanup job. Cut newspapers into long one-inch strips, then dip each strip in clear water. Gently pull the strips between your thumb and forefinger to get some of the water out and then stick the strips onto the windowpanes up close to the woodwork.

Because the strips dry out, you can do only two panes at a time, but if you don't have to painstakingly dab at narrow wood strips, you can really lay that paint on fast. Lift the paper strips off after you paint and wipe remaining water off the glass with a paper towel wrapped around the tip of your finger.

• Also, smearing petroleum jelly on the windowpane itself will make it easy to remove any paint that happens to drip onto the glass.

• Or you can use masking tape to tape around the window frame on the glass, but be sure to remove it as soon as the paint dries so that the goo doesn't adhere to the glass.

Using a Ladder Safely

• To safely position a ladder so that it won't fall forward or backward, the distance from the ladder's base to the wall or tree should be one fourth of the ladder's extended length.

• If you are going to work on a ladder in front of a closed door, lock the door so that you won't be knocked over if someone inadvertently tries to open it.

• Paint cans tumbling and splashing around on your kids and pets or anyone beneath your ladder is funny only in cartoons. Here's how to avoid paint showers when kids and pets might just nudge your ladder while you are working.

Securely tack the lid from a two- or three-pound coffee or shortening can to the bucket shelf of your ladder with the rim facing up. After filling the can with as much paint as you think is safe, set it into the plastic lid. The grip will hold well enough to hold the paint can against most wobblings. You can even move the ladder with paint in place if you're reasonably careful. Of course, nothing will help if you and the ladder tip over; better keep the kids and pets out of the way.

Dripless Painting

There is so much information about paint (how to thin it, how to get it off clothing, etc.) on the paint can label that it is really a good idea to keep the can from being covered with drips. That's why you shouldn't wipe your paintbrush against the lip of the paint can. The lip will soon fill up with paint, which will dribble down the side and cover all the information.

• If you stretch a strong rubber band around the can lengthwise and use it to wipe your brush, you'll keep all the drips inside the can, where they belong.

• Or, using an ice pick, punch holes in the rim of the paint can, and the paint will drip through the holes back into the can.

• You can pour as much paint as you'll use into a coffee can or other container. Keep the remainder covered, if you are working outside and want to keep dirt, leaves, and insects out of your main paint supply.

• Painting rain gutters is easy, but down spouts can be tricky. To protect the downspout's interior against rust, drop a string with a weight on it down through the spout and tie a sponge to the string's bottom end. The sponge should be large enough so that it must be compressed to fit inside the spout.

Using plenty of paint, soak the sponge and then pull on the string to squeeze the sponge up through the spout. The paint will spread evenly from bottom to top as the sponge goes up.

Cleaning Up

• As soon as you finish painting, and before paint has a chance to dry and clog the nozzles of spray paint cans, pop the nozzles into a small glass jar and cover them with lacquer thinner.

• You don't have to completely clean up your paint roller, brushes, and pan between coats. After you apply the first coat, store your roller, brushes, edger, and other equipment into the paint tray and then put the whole thing into a plastic bag. Leftover paint and the applicators will stay pliable and fresh until you are ready to start the second coat a few hours later or the next day. Wrapped in foil or plastic, paintbrushes can be stored for a longer period of time.

• If you line your paint tray with a plastic bag before pouring in your paint, cleanup is no chore. After you've finished, you can toss used rags, paper towels, or disposable paint applicators into the tray, then turn the plastic bag clean side out as you remove it from the tray. You'll have messy rags wrapped up and a clean tray.

• You can also press a sheet of aluminum foil onto the tray before pouring the paint into it, and when you're finished, wrap up your paint rags and so on in the foil when you discard it.

• Soaking a new oil paintbrush in linseed oil for a day before it's used will make the brush last longer and easier to clean.

• Also, adding a capful of fabric softener to a quart of water and then soaking the paintbrushes in it will do the same trick.

• If you clean paintbrushes by just poking them into a can of solvent or turpentine and letting them soak, you'll find that the bristles get squash-bent tips. But if you take an empty coffee can with a plastic lid and suspend the brushes from the plastic lid so that the bristles don't rest on the bottom of the can, you'll be able to reuse those brushes.

You need to make two slits in the center of the plastic lid to form an X, then push the brush handle up through the X and replace the lid, which will protect the brushes and prevent the solvent from evaporating.

• If you pour the solvent for cleaning your paintbrushes into a heavy-duty clear plastic bag and then put the brushes into the bag, you can work the solvent into the bristles throughout the plastic without messing up your hands.

• To clean a paint roller, you start by rolling it as dry as possible, first on the newly painted surface and then on several sheets of newspaper. Then remove the roller from its support and clean it with water, solvent, or whatever is suggested for the type of paint you've used.

• You can reuse the paint thinner left over from cleaning brushes. Here's how: Pour paint thinner into an empty coffee can. Then, after you've cleaned your brushes in it, cover the can tightly, put it in a safe place out of the reach of children or pets, and let it rest for several days. Paint from the brushes will settle to the bottom as sediment. Drain off the "clean" thinner into another can and store for reuse.

• After cleaning your brush, give it a final rinse in water containing fabric softener; it will stay soft as new.

• Paste type of paint removers remove paint spots from brick.

• If you get oil-base paint on your work clothes, pour a little turpentine on the spot and rub it with a soft toothbrush. Then wet a bar of body soap and rub this into the spot, brushing gently with a toothbrush. After you have washed the garment with your regular detergent, the spot should be gone.

CAUTION: Turpentine is flammable. ALWAYS do this away from any flames and in a well-ventilated place. (See Chapter 7 for more on removing paint from clothing.)

After the Job Is Over

• If you write the amount, brand, and color of paint you used for a room on the back of a light-switch plate in that room, you'll always have a handy reminder of how much and what kind of paint to buy when you repaint.

Storing Paint

• You can keep paint in an opened can from drying out if you make a pattern from the lid from wax paper. (Don't use plastic wrap.) Lay the wax paper directly on the paint, then put the lid on. The paper really will keep the either oil-base or water-base paints fresh for months! The paper is easy to remove and can be reused if you wish.

• If, for some reason (such as losing the lid), you can't store paint in its original can, you can store it in a gallon-size plastic milk jug.

Be sure to label the jug with a marker, noting the color, number, and store where you bought it. When you need to touch up, shake the jug well, pour a dab or two of paint into a throw-away margarine tub, and touch up the spot.

• If you mark the label on the can with the level of remaining paint before you seal the lid for storage, you'll know how much is left inside without having to open the can the next time you want to use it. You can use a marker or just dab a paint-level mark with your paintbrush.

• If you mark the label with the room in which the paint was used, reordering the paint for touch-ups is easy.

• A partly used can of paint can be stored upside down to keep a "skin" from forming on the paint surface. But, before you turn that can upside down, be sure the lid is tight or you'll not have any paint to store because it will be flowing all over the work surface.

• If you have leftover paint that has lumps or shreds of paint skin, strain it through window screening to delump or unlump it before use.

• Also, to unlump paint, use an old pair of pantyhose stretched across the can.

• If you stir a drop of black paint into it, white paint won't yellow.

Painting Cupboards and Cabinets

• When you're painting cabinets, paint the insides first, then the tops, bottoms, and sides of doors before you paint the door fronts. This keeps you from having to reach over already painted areas and smearing the paint and yourself.

• You won't have drips on drawer fronts if you remove the drawers and paint the fronts when the surface is "faceup."

• It's always best to take off hardware before painting, but if you can't, coat the hardware with petroleum jelly before painting. Paint splats will wipe right off.

• You can wrap doorknobs with aluminum foil or enclose them in plastic sandwich bags to protect them from paint smears.

Spray Painting

Spray painting is quick and there are no brushes to clean, but if you aren't careful, you'll have a worse mess to clean up than a few brushes, rollers, and a tray. To help prevent unsightly spray paint mess in garages, on lawns, in car ports, and in driveways when painting, try the following.

• When spray painting small items, place them inside a large cardboard box. Spray the exposed surfaces, then turn the items to expose other surfaces for painting.

Spray painting in a box helps to eliminate ugly spots on grass or concrete, and it also keeps the paint mist from "attacking" shoes and clothing.

• If you've bought everything for painting but the plastic paint tarps, old plastic tablecloths, plastic shower curtains, and even old draperies or furniture throws make good substitute paint tarps. Fabric won't protect anything from liquid paint spills, but it will protect surfaces from spray paint mist.

• Some people need to protect themselves as much as they need to protect the environment when they spray paint. If you have allergies, you may be bothered by the fumes from spray paints and varnishes. Wear a surgical mask to keep the paint fumes and mist out of your nose, bronchial tubes, and lungs.

This may be a good idea even if you're not allergic to paint. I know people who wear surgical masks when they mow their lawns or spray insecticides in their gardens. I think your health is always more important than appearances or the few dimes it costs you to buy protective masks and goggles.

• Also, this is the perfect time to wear your old glasses, so that when you're painting ceilings, paint doesn't splatter in your eye.

Do's and Don'ts for Home Security

• Don't leave spare keys in the traditional places: in mailboxes, under door-mats, under pot plants, and so forth. Find a secret way of concealing the extra key, such as putting it in a film canister, or a small can, or wrapping it in a wad of foil and then burying it in a special place in the garden where it can easily be dug up when you've forgotten your keys.

• Don't leave notes for repair people or family members on the door where anyone can read that you will be home at a specific time.

• Unless you have an answering machine, adjust your telephone ring to its lowest volume if you plan to be away from home for a day or longer. Prowlers know a home is empty if the phone rings unanswered.

• Use timers to switch lights, radios, and TV sets on and off when you're not at home, so that your house appears to be occupied at all times.

• When you go on a trip, don't cancel your mail and newspapers; you'll just be letting a lot of strangers know you'll be gone and for how long. It's better to have a neighbor take in your mail, newspapers, and any flyers left on your door, so that your house looks occupied.

• If for some reason your plans to be away from home have been publicized, as through announcements of a funeral or wedding, hire a house sitter or have a friend stay in your house while the event is going on. Burglars often use newspaper announcements that tell who will be where and how long to schedule their "working hours."

• A barking dog is the best prowler alarm and burglar deterrent. Even a small yappy dog is an effective announcer of people presence.

• Have a locksmith reset all of the lock tumblers when you move into a new house, or buy new locks. Nobody knows how many sets of keys are with how many people!

• If you don't already have them, install double cylinder locks that need to be opened with a key from the inside and outside. Then, if a thief breaks a pane of glass in your door to get in, he's still have to fiddle around with a lock instead of just a knob.

• When door hinges are set on the outside of your house, all a burglar has to do is knock out the pins from the hinges and the door will come off for easy entry. It's best to reset hinges inside.

• Burglars can easily break glass panels set beside doors and then reach around to open the door from the inside. If you have such doors, put up a grille over the panel to fortify them. Use double-cylinder locks to prevent thieves from breaking in.

• Burglar-proof your glass patio doors by buying adjustable safety bars at hardware stores or by cutting a pipe, metal bar, or broom handle exactly to the measurement of the inside bottom track of the door so that you can wedge it in on the track when you want to bar the door.

• If your sliding door is installed so that you can't drop a broom handle in, simply drill a hole through both sliding doors and then insert a bolt or a nail to keep the doors from sliding.

• If you think that someone can enter your house through your attached garage, a C clamp can provide extra security. If your garage door lifts on a track, the door cannot be opened if you tighten the C clamp on the track next to the roller.

• Prowlers can't tell that you are gone because your car is not in your garage if you cover your garage windows with a frost plastic decorative paper or spray with a can of frost.

Fire Safety

Here are some do's and don'ts to protect your home from fire.

• This is the number one, most important, tip: Never spend more than 30 seconds fighting a fire. If the fire can't be extinguished, warn others and get out of the house. Go to a neighbor's house to phone the fire department.

• Hold family fire drills on a regular basis and make sure that everyone knows what to do in case of fire. Make double sure that everyone can actually get out of the house according to the plans you have made.

• Have a designated meeting place where all family members will congregate for a "head count" to make sure everyone did get out of the house.

• Keep combustible materials away from the furnace, which can give off flames or sparks at times, and keep them away from all pilot lights, such as on the hot water heater.

• Don't keep lawn mowers that contain gasoline in unventilated rooms with hot-water heaters. Here in Texas, where I live, we have one or two explosions/fires each year because of the intense heat that builds up in such dangerous conditions.

• Don't run extension cords under the rugs. They can wear, fray, bend to expose wire, be bitten by pets, and then short out to cause a fire. The U.S. Consumer Product Safety Commission has been conducting a study of the causes of appliance cord failures, because such failures result annually in about 5,500 home fires, 70 deaths, and more than 200 injuries. Check your appliance cords and extension cords for the beginning signs of wear, then get them repaired or replace them before they are totally worn. Your life is worth more than any repair bill or extension cord cost.

• Buy a fire extinguisher and make sure to check its effectiveness date regularly. Also, keep baking soda on hand for extinguishing small emergency kitchen fires.

• Don't install a gas cooktop near windows where curtains can blow into the flames or where wind could extinguish the cooking flames. If you already have such an installation, keep that window closed, don't have curtains over the stove, or vent the drafts by installing draft guards, which you can buy in hardware stores or through some catalogs.

- Install smoke detectors in your home with just a screwdriver and the set of instructions that comes in the box.

In fact, install smoke detectors on each floor of your home, usually in the hallway near each separate sleeping area.

- Don't mount a smoke detector too close to areas such as the kitchen, where smoke and steam from cooking will activate the alarm; in a bathroom, where shower steam may activate it; or in the garage, where combustion products from the car's engine can set it off.

When you buy your smoke detectors, you will get instructions for proper placement and for checking the batteries to make sure they are still working. CAUTION: If the batteries are dead, you are not protected.

- More people are overcome by smoke and inhalation of chemicals produced by burning textiles and other parts of the building than are burned by fire. If you have to go down a smoke-filled hall, crawl on the floor and put a wet cloth over your nose and mouth to serve as a filter.

- If you are in a room and suspect there is fire outside it because of smoke or an actual alarm, touch the door before opening it. If it is hot, DON'T open it. The fire is likely to rush—more likely, explode—into the room before you can get the door closed again.

Heat rises, so the top of the door will warm up first. If the door feels cool but you see smoke curling in at the bottom, the area on the other side is filled to the floor with smoke, and you must find another way out. Smoke rises and fills a room or a hallway from the top down. If you are on the first floor, get out through the window and don't worry about breaking it or pushing out the screen. If you have to break a window, put a blanket over yourself or find a way to protect yourself from cuts.

- The universal signal to fire fighters when you are in a multi-story building is to hang a sheet out of a window to say, "Somebody's in here; come get me."

- CAUTION: Before you open any windows, if you are in a hotel or apartment, take wet sheets, blankets, towels, and stuff them around the door. Opening the windows can cause the heat and smoke from the hall to explode into the room.

Washing Windows and Large Objects

Windows

Sometimes, when you think it's foggy outside, it's really grime on your windows. Eventually it will get so bad you can't use the excuse that you are trying to filter out the sun's rays to keep your furniture from fading.

• My best window-washing hint is that when you dry windows, dry them on the outside from right to left, and on the inside, dry with the strokes up and down. That way, if there's a streak, you can tell whether it's on the inside or the outside of the window.

• Second, the best and cheapest thing to use when drying windows is newspapers. You don't need to use paper towels or cloths that have lint on them. There seems to be something in the printer's ink that makes windows shine and sparkle, and it hasn't cost you an extra penny.

• Always wash and dry windows on an average day, not on an extremely hot, sunny day, because the washing solution will dry too quickly and you'll end up with lots of streaks.

Your House

• Try hosing down your house. You won't get the windows perfectly clean, but you will get some of the daily dust off and the bonus is that you'll get a lot of cobwebs off the rest of the house. Do this on a hot day in your swimsuit and cool off at the same time. Get the children into the act and you'll end up with a day the whole family remembers! (Let the children use water pistols and you control the hose—claim parent privilege!)

• If you have textured aluminum siding on your house, the texture will gather dirt, but this accumulation is easily removed by attaching a car-washing brush to your hose and just brush rinsing the house about every six months or so, depending upon how much rain and dust your climate abuses your house with. You don't really need any soap or detergent. Water will usually do the job.

Polishing Large Appliances

• You can wax large appliances with appliance or car wax to make them shine. Wax will "erase" fine line scratches nicely if you are selling the appliance.

Car Washing and Maintenance

• Dirt, pollen, bird droppings, road gunk, and salt (in winter climates) accumulate on our cars and make them look years older. Not removing the mess ultimately damages the paint surface, and even if you don't care about how your car usually looks, the dealer will certainly care when you try to trade it in for a new model.

• After you wash your car at home, wipe down the car with old terry towels instead of just letting it dry. The chlorine in city water will leave droplet marks if you don't towel dry your car.

• The pros use soaps on cars with zero pH factor. The pH factor is the amount of acidity or alkalinity in a solution: high pH signifies high acid; low pH signifies a very alkaline solution. Both are bad for your car finish.

• Detergents are not the best cleaning agent for a car. If you use detergent to wash your car, mix only a small amount in a large bucket.

• Use only clean rags on your car. It takes only a bit of grit to scratch a line across the finish. Use plastic or nylon net scrubbers to get stuck-on soil off the car. Terry cloth is better than chamois for washing and good for drying too.

• A good heavy-duty paste wax will last six months or more and will give the finish better protection than liquid waxes, as a rule.

• If you don't have a sealed battery, check to make sure your battery has water in it; water evaporates especially fast during intense summer heat. Water is cheap, a new battery is not!

• If the battery terminals are heavily corroded, the quickest and easiest way to solve the problem is to pour a can or bottle of carbonated soft drink over them; it will eat away all the corrosion.

• Or, you can mix one or two tablespoons baking soda with water and pour over battery terminals, and again, it will bubble away the corrosion.

• After removing the connection to the terminal, and cleaning it well, rub a little petroleum jelly around the post and the inside of the terminal, and then reattach. This will help prevent the corrosion, which is the major cause of not being able to recharge the battery.

• Carry duct tape in your car for emergencies. You can patch belts and make many minor repairs with it that will last long enough to get to a garage and help.

Garages

• An unpainted garage door can swell and warp and then be hard to open. Let the door dry out when you have dry weather for a few days, and then paint all surfaces, including the edges, to seal the wood so that it won't absorb moisture.

• If you have an automatic garage door opener, you may find that your garage door mysteriously opens and closes when you haven't meant it to. It's possible that someone else has an opener set on the same frequency as yours. If you can't reset the frequency or have it done, be sure to unplug the opener mechanism when you are at home, especially at night, or when you are on vacation to ensure keeping your garage door closed.

Parking Your Car in the Garage

Even if you know that your new car is the same size or just an inch or so wider or longer than your old one, parking it in the garage is a test of your depth perception. Here are a few tips on parking without nicking or denting either car or garage.

• Paint bright or luminous stripes, or stick on reflector or brightly colored tape on the rear garage wall to help you aim the car down the center.

• Stick reflector tape on anything that seems to be in your way at night, if you don't have good lighting in the garage.

• If knowing when you should stop is a problem, hang a ball on a string from the garage ceiling so that it touches the windshield at about eye level when you have the car in the right place. If you hang the ball in the center of your parking space, you can use it for a centering guide as well as a stop sign. Bright colors and a piece of reflector tape will help you see your guide.

• Old inner tubes cut in pieces can be used to pad anything that you tend to brush against with your car or touch when you open the car door, such as support studs, framing, or even the nearest walls. Other padding materials include carpet scraps, old rubber mats, and foam rubber.

• If you like to back into the garage, an old tire hung at bumper height can be a wall-protecting, dent-preventing stopper.

Greasy Garage Floors

• Grease and oil spots are unsightly in a garage, but the real problem is that people step in them and bring the gunk into the house. An old cookie sheet or cake pan filled with cat litter or sand and placed at the drip site will collect leaking grease or oil. If you don't have cat litter or sand handy, use a piece of corrugated cardboard to fit the cookie sheet and change it as necessary.

• Staple heavy-duty aluminum foil to a piece of corrugated cardboard for a disposable drip pad.

• Clean up oil and grease spots by applying paint thinner, then covering them with cat litter, dry cement, or sand, and letting the absorbant remain on the spot overnight. Sweep up the absorbent material and repeat the process if you have to.

• Other absorbent materials include baking soda and cornmeal. Just sprinkle on and sweep off, repeating the process until you've got a clean-enough garage floor.

• If the absorbents don't work, try dousing the spot with full-strength laundry bleach and wiping up the excess with rags or paper towels. CAUTION: Wear protective gloves when you're using bleach or other strong chemicals.

• If you still can't get rid of the stain and it bothers you, paint a wide black stripe the width of the space between your car tires and use the stripe as a centering aid.

Storing Things in the Garage

Garages tend to get dumped in, and stuff just accumulates in them. In climates where people don't have basements, garages have to serve as combination basement/garage storage areas, and you really can get an accumulation of jumbled-up "junque." ("Junque" is plain old junk you don't admit to being junk.)

• If you're handy, you can use up all that air space in the top half of your garage by building storage shelves on side and back walls. If you're not, peg boards and ready-made shelving are for you.

• Save floor space by hanging garden tools, sports gear, bikes (on special heavy-duty hooks for that purpose), or anything else that will hang up.

• If you're not afraid that your family will overload them, you can install deep shelves in the back end of the garage so that your car hood will be under them.

• Lay a platform or shelving across ceiling joists in the garage, on which to store seldom used or seasonal items, such as storm windows and window screens.

• Take a tip from your city's parking lots. Paint "parking area" lines on the garage floor to designate spaces for bikes, the lawn mower, or other large objects, so that these "targets" have their own spaces and you'll be less likely to hit them with the car when you're pulling into the garage. (Isn't it annoying to have to get out of the car to move a bike or lawn mower a couple of inches so that you can drive in? Especially if you've had a bad day!)

The Final Word on Maintenance

Take time to relax and to enjoy the people in your life. You only get one chance at savoring each day. Once the day is over, it's over. Don't miss opportunities!

I get a lot of letters from women who feel guilty about not having homes as spotless as their mothers had. I tell them that nobody ever died from a little bit of dust. Most of us just don't have the same life-styles our mothers had, and we don't have the time to keep house as they did.

I've never heard a eulogy in which the person was praised for having a perfectly clean house, car, office, whatever. People are remembered for a sense of humor, kindness to others, community service, and other achievements that affect the well-being of others.

CHAPTER 5

Plants and Yard Care

House Plants

This is my favorite subject. I'm a whiz at growing avocado plants. Some of mine are so tall they touch the ceiling. They're really beautiful and so much fun to grow.

Have you ever thought about making an indoor garden of plants from fruits and vegetables bought at your local food market? The advantage is that you have the fun and satisfaction of seeing things grow without putting out a lot of money. And, if pits and seeds don't grow, not to worry, they were free!

Planting Pits and Seeds

• Usually, I allow three to four days for the pit or seed to dry. Plant it in three parts potting soil and one part vermiculite—fat, rounded end down at least an inch into the soil.

Place in a window (but not in harsh sunlight); a plant light also works well. Be sure to keep the soil damp but not soaked. You should see the beginning of the sprouts in three to four weeks. I always plant several seeds, since some won't sprout.

• Start avocado plants by putting three toothpicks into the seed at about the middle. (If the seed were the earth, you'd put toothpicks at its equator.) Put water in a glass and put the avocado fat side down into the glass. The toothpicks will hold it up so the water level is covering only half the seed. Be sure to change the water often, as it tends to get algae.

It doesn't take long for it to sprout. When there are enough roots, put it into the soil mixture described above.

I'm especially proud of one of my avocado trees. It's seven years old and twelve feet high. It grows in my home beautifully.

• Mango seeds are easily grown. Lay each pit flat on top of potting soil, then push it down into the soil. Keep it damp and somewhere where it will remain warm. These take about a month to germinate. They will sprout a root and then the seedling.

• Date palms grow nicely too. Start with unpasteurized dates. Plant the pits and keep the pot moist and warm. Wait (as usual). Date pits, like most palm seeds, are slow to germinate. So be patient.

• To grow a coconut palm you need an unhusked coconut. Place it on top of sandy soil in a wide-diameter pot. Keep the pot warm, damp, and in good light. The shoot will emerge from one end of the husk. It usually takes about three years to grow a three-foot tree.

• You could add a finishing touch to your indoor garden by sprouting fresh unroasted coffee beans. Roasted beans won't germinate. I've had some very good luck, but be prepared for some failures, because coffee beans are a bit temperamental. Do you suppose it's too much caffeine?

A Medicinal Plant

The aloe vera plant is pretty and practical because it's excellent first aid for minor burns. Aloe vera jelly soothes the pain and aids healing. Apply the jellylike fluid in the lance-shaped leaves immediately to minor dry burns, scalds, and cuts and scrapes.

Just pick a leaf, break it open, and squeeze on the jelly. Each leaf contains quite a lot of fluid, so when the break in the leaf looks dry, just peel back the outer skin of the leaf and you'll get more fluid. A bad burn may require several applications. Serious burns should be seen by a physician as soon as possible.

Keep a plant in the kitchen, where most burns occur, or by the back door for those painful sunburns.

Plant Cuttings

Some plants will root in water, but it's obvious that water is not a plant's natural domain. In fact, roots that form under water have a different structure than roots formed in soil, so, when a water-started cutting is planted, it has to grow a whole new set of roots. It's better to start cuttings in soil.

• Here's a simple home method.

Place one to two inches of a very light potting soil and vermiculite in the bottom of a "zipper"-closing plastic sandwich or food storage bag. Moisten it thoroughly, but pour off any excess water.

Snip small, actively growing cuttings with a sharp knife or shears, cutting at an angle. Wet the cut ends and dip them into root hormone (available at nurseries and other places that sell plants). Trim off any leaves that cover the lower one to two inches of the cuttings and plant the tip into the soil.

Inflate the bag by sealing it almost across the top, then blow into the bag as you complete the seal. This keeps the plastic from touching the leaves.

Leave the bag in partial light, not full sun, until the cuttings have rooted. This may take from three days to three weeks, depending on the plant. Check to be sure the soil stays moist.

• You can put larger clippings in a pot filled with vermiculite and potting soil. Do the same as above, clip stems and wet the end, then dip into root hormone and put into soil.

Watering Your Plants

• If you own a freshwater fish tank, instead of throwing out the water when cleaning, use it to water the plants. It's a great fertilizer.

• If you have opened bottles of club soda left over, feed the contents to your house plants or outdoor plants. Flat soda is beneficial to green, growing things because of all the minerals in it.

• Cool the water left over from cooking spaghetti or potatoes and use to water your plants. They love the starch.

• After you boil eggs, use the cooled water on your house plants. Egg water is packed with growth-stimulating minerals. Diluted plain Jane coffee (no sugar or cream) is my Heloise home fertilizer, too.

• Melted snow contains minerals that make it good for watering your plants.

• If your house's rain gutters have a spout, you can collect rainwater for your plants by putting a large plastic garbage can under the drain spout. (I have a friend who used to use rainwater as a final rinse for her hair; she said it made her hair soft and shiny, though I haven't tested this hint.)

• Put your plant watering can under the shower before you step in. The first spray is enough for a dozen plants, and helps conserve water. Some people may think this is a silly hint, but I live in central Texas, where conserving water is a serious responsibility, especially if we are having a long, dry spell in the summer.

• Save the rinse water from dish-washing if you wash and rinse dishes by hand. Mist plants with it, as the soap film kills some pests such as mites and scale. This occasional misting won't hurt most plants (except for African violets).

• Use an old knitting needle or a pencil to test when your house plants need watering. If the needle or pencil eraser inserted into the soil comes out dry, get out your watering can.

• Group plants together rather than scattering them sparsely. When clustered, they create their own moist environment.

• During cold weather months, a room filled with house plants will benefit from the moisture provided by a portable vaporizer. So will you; vaporizers keep the air from getting so dry that some carpets produce almost enough electricity to light up the room, or so it seems. Isn't it unpleasant when your clothes cling to your body, every person you touch is "shocking," and worst of all, your skin feels like parchment and looks worse from winter dryness?

Watering Plants When You're on Vacation

• If you're planning a short vacation, try this. Put a big bucket of water in the bathtub and place the plants around it. Cut string in lengths long enough so that you can put one end into the soil and have enough string to reach from the plant to the water and down to the bottom of the bucket. The plants will "sip" enough water through the string to survive while you're gone.

Drainage Tips

• Every plant container should have drainage holes. If you're using a recycled one such as a plastic food tub, be sure to make holes. Trapped water causes root rot.

• Cracked walnut shells, broken pieces of clay pot, marbles, stones, or fruit pits can be used to provide drainage at the bottom of a house plant pot.

• For a lightweight drainage layer in the bottom of a hanging planter, use pieces of foam packing material.

• Set small potted plants on pebble trays filled with water. The moisture from pebble trays cuts down the plant's transpiration loss and you save water. This is especially true of African violets.

• Slip shower caps over the bottoms of hanging planters to catch the light drips when watering and remove after an hour or so.

Plant Pest Control

• A garlic clove planted beside your house plant will keep many types of pests away from it.

• When people take house plants outside for extra sun and then return them to their places indoors, they sometimes unwittingly bring bugs indoors too.

If you want to take plants outdoors, keep them isolated from other house plants for three to four weeks after you bring them back in. If you detect bugs on the plants, wipe the stems and leaves with a mild soap-and-water solution.

• If you think there may be root-damaging worms in the soil of your potted plants, place a slice of raw potato on the surface of each. The worms will crawl out to get at the potatoes, and you can capture and destroy them.

• When one of your house plants appears "sick," attach a pest strip, then cover the plant for a few days with a plastic bag. Keep the soil moist and don't seal the bag; it should fall loosely around the pot. Keep out of the sunlight.

By the time you remove the bag, the plant should have perked up nicely, because all of the pests will be on the strip.

• You can do a bug check by giving your plants a good soaking in the shower. The water will force many plant invaders to the top, because they'll be trying to escape drowning (a fate too good for such evil varmints) and you'll be able to see what's living beneath the soil surface. I once discovered that one of my ailing plants had millipedes in it.

I was glad that it was the only plant I'd put into the tub that day. The millipedes could have scurried over to healthy plants. Having lots of legs sure makes them move fast! Anyhow, knowing that it was millipedes made it easy for me to choose an insecticide to kill them. I'm happy to report that the millipede-infested palm tree got well and is still alive three feet and four years later.

• To get rid of plant lice on African violets, you'll need hair spray and a plastic bag big enough to hold the potted violet. Spray the hair spray into the plastic bag (never on the plant), then put the plant into the plastic bag, twist or tie it shut, and let the plant stay in the bag for a day.

TLC (Tender, Loving Care) for Plants

Home-style remedies:

• Unless they are fed regularly with fertilizer, potted plants, whether indoors or outdoors, can develop nutrient deficiencies they might not get if they were growing in an outdoor bed. The cure is commercial plant food, used according to directions.

• An ailing house plant can be treated with a tablespoon of castor oil dribbled on its soil, followed by a thorough watering.

• To make plant leaves shine, swab only the tops with a soft cloth dipped in glycerine. Unlike other gloss-producing substances, glycerine won't collect dust.

• Just like people, plants last longer if you don't let them go to seed. As blossoms begin to fade, it's best to cut them off, and that's where the plant-people analogy ends, because there's nothing to cut off with people. You just love them anyway, faded or not.

• If you pinch the tiny new shoots at the growing points, you'll encourage branching, which produces more growth for flowering. While most plants benefit from pinching, never pinch back palms; it's fatal to them.

Indoor Vegetable Gardens

If you have the space, you can grow vegetables indoors in artificial light.

• Lettuce does especially well when grown under fluorescent lights. Plant your lettuce garden in the basement, the attic, or anywhere the temperature stays between 65 and 70 degrees Fahrenheit during the day, and drops about ten degrees at night.

• Here's a novel but effective way to grow parsley in your kitchen or on your sun porch: Slice sponges in half and sprinkle them with parsley seeds. Arrange the sponges on dishes in a sunny location, keep them moist, and watch that parsley grow.

• Here's how you can grow your own sprouts in the kitchen.

Alfalfa and some other types of sprouts for your salads will grow on sponges just like the parsley will. The seeds are sold at health food and many upscale grocery stores.

Old jars, especially those from large-size instant tea, make good kitchen counter sprout growers. Use brown-tinted jars for mung beans (bean sprouts) and clear jars for other sprouts. (Mung bean seeds should be grown without sunlight to prevent them from producing green bean sprouts.)

Punch enough holes into the lids with a nail to allow you to drain the sprouts while the lid is on; it functions as a strainer. You can also make a strainer lid from the rims of two-piece canning jar lids and screening or cheesecloth. The cheesecloth, of course, is not reusable.

• Now, here's how you grow sprouts in jars.

Put in about an inch or so of mung bean, alfalfa, wheat, or whatever seeds into the bottom of the jar and let the seeds soak, covered with water, overnight or over a day, if you start in the morning.

Drain the soaking water. Allow the seeds to settle on the side of the jar; keep the jar on its side as the sprouts grow. Then irrigate the seeds/sprouts every day by pouring water on them and then draining them with the strainer lid on.

Let the sprouts grow until they are a size you like, then irrigate them one more time, drain, and put them into the refrigerator to stop growth, still in their jars, which can of course, stand upright.

• I have found that it's better to stop bean sprouts from growing more than two or three inches because they get leaves and too-long roots beyond that length. I stop most sprouts from growing when they show their first hints of wanting to leaf out.

• To get rid of the seed husks, especially on bean sprouts, before eating them, you can put them in a bowl or strainer and blast them with cold water at the greatest pressure you can get from your faucet. Then put the sprouts in a bowl filled with water, and swish them around so that most of the remaining hulls will float to the top or sink.

You can pick every single hull off if you want to, but I usually get bored with the process after the wash and dip and just leave the few remaining hulls in with the sprouts, which can then be eaten raw in salads or in sandwiches or, in the case of bean sprouts, used in Oriental dishes. Wheat and alfalfa sprouts are often baked in health breads. Once you get used to having fresh sprouts, you won't think growing them is an extra-effort chore at all.

Storing Garden Pesticides

Things that kill household and garden pests can also kill people. Always be careful with pesticides and ALWAYS keep them out of children's and pets' reach. Families with small children or people who live in neighborhoods with small children would probably be wise to store all poisonous chemicals in a padlocked cabinet or footlocker that is clearly marked POISON or DANGER.

• Manufacturers of pesticides are required to use signal words to call attention to how toxic certain products are to people. The signal words are:

DANGER—This means highly toxic. A taste to a teaspoonful can kill the average person.
WARNING—This means moderately toxic. A teaspoonful to a tablespoonful will kill the average person.
CAUTION—This means low toxicity; the product is comparatively danger free. It will take an ounce to more than a pint to kill the average person.

• The symptoms of pesticide poisoning include headache, giddiness, blurred vision, nausea, confusion, and diarrhea. If you have any of these symptoms after being around pesticides, see your physician and take along a container of the pesticide so that the physician can find out what chemicals are in it and treat you accordingly.

• When you use pesticides, carefully read the label twice to be sure that you use it on the pests it's recommended for and know what precautions to take when using it.

• Wear protective clothing and wash with soap and water after using pesticides. Don't smoke, eat, or drink until you have washed up.

• Never mix pesticides in an unventilated area, and don't use them on windy days. Keep children and pets away when you are treating an area and for a reasonable period of time afterward. Always read the prescribed times on the container.

• ALWAYS keep pesticides in their original containers. If the container is damaged and you have to put the pesticide in another container, don't use food, beverage, or medicine containers that might be mistaken for edibles. Mark containers clearly with DANGER and POISON in red, enclosing any labels that identify the contents.

• Clean up all spills from leaky containers. Put paper-bagged pesticides into heavy plastic bags for safer storage.

• When you dispose of pesticide containers, wrap them securely before putting them into a garbage can, where curious animals might get at them. Empty containers usually have some residual powders from the pesticide, which could harm anyone who gets in contact with the container.

• It's better to buy smaller amounts that get used up quickly and don't leave you with so many pesticides on your storage shelves.

Outside the House

Digging into Gardening

• The soil depends upon where you live, and different parts of a locale can have different soil conditions. If you are having topsoil trucked in, buy it only from a reputable garden firm; otherwise you'll be trucking in weeds or weed seeds in the soil that will make your garden life miserable for years to come.

• You can use an old window screen to sift topsoil before putting it into flower beds, but it would be difficult to sift the topsoil for an entire yard.

• If you want to keep your fingernails clean but think that using garden gloves is clumsy, before you go out to dig in the dirt, dig your nails into a bar of soap, or coat their undersides with nail whitening pencil. Your nails will wash clean easily.

• Before you start applying fertilizer to the soil, it's best to have a soil test so that you'll know what to add. You don't want to spend a lot of money on fertilizers that you don't need, and worse yet, if you don't know whether your soil is alkaline or acidic, you may actually add the wrong chemicals and make your soil less suitable for planting.

• Also, in many parts of the country, the soil has so much heavy clay in it that sand must be mixed with the soil to lighten it if anything is to grow well. In other parts of the country you need to mix sand and humus/compost in with the soil before planting.

• When you test your soil, you need to take at least a coffee can filled with soil to a local nursery or send the soil sample to your local county Cooperative Extension Service. To get directions on how to do this, look in the telephone book's section for United States Government, Agriculture, Department of— Extension Service and Home Economics Agents. You can label the container with an address label to make sure it stays properly identified.

Getting Gardening Help

The U.S. Department of Agriculture has booklets that will give you information about your area's gardening conditions, planting according to season, and just general good information. You can also get help with diseased plants from the USDA county extension horticulturists.

• A neighborhood garden center can be another resource. Neighborhood centers may have the advantage over large garden suppliers, because they often are aware of your particular neighborhood's gardening conditions and can help you select plants and control plant diseases.

• If you have just moved into a neighborhood, walk around to see just what grows well in the shady and sunny parts of your neighbors' yards before you go out to buy plants.

• If your city has a botanical center, it too can be a learning experience for you, because most centers will have displays of what grows locally as well as more exotic plants.

• Local county agents and gardening experts often write newspaper gardening columns, which can be good resources for information on planting and maintaining a garden, whether you grow flowers, fruits and vegetables, or just trees and grass.

• Local county Extension agents are more than happy to help you with any questions regarding gardening, landscaping, soil content, and so forth. Use your tax dollars, and give the agent a call.

Shrubs and Other Plants

• You can have fruit trees in a small yard. Plant dwarf fruit trees as a hedge or train them to grow against a trellis, wall, or fence. To make a fence from dwarf fruit trees, plant them only two feet apart and prune them three to four times during the summer. (The technical gardening name for such a fence is *espalier;* after pruning, such trees look like a main stem with many branch-arms going off to the sides.) Check with your nursery for your area's dwarf fruit tree varieties suitable for this use.

• Berry bushes also make good "edible" shrubs and hedges.

• Grass needs sun. If you don't plan to prune trees or shrubs to let the sun shine through, you'll have to plant ground cover plants under them, such as ivy, jasmine, or whatever is usually used for ground cover in your area.

• When you are planting bedding plants or ground cover plants, plant them close together to discourage and smother weeds that might want to poke through.

• You can also discourage weeds in flower beds by covering the soil with bark, compost, leaves, or whatever is usually used for mulch in your area. Mulch not only discourages weeds, it keeps the soil moist and decomposes as organic matter to enrich the soil. Leaves are free mulch!

Composting

Compost is a combination of manure, leaves, shredded grass clippings, and newspapers, which means it's one of the best recycling ideas around, especially when you consider the problems many cities are having as they use up available landfill sites!

It can also contain other organic matter, such as bark, humus, and peat moss. Soil can be added to help break down the compost materials. In some parts of the country, people can use organic garbage (fruit and vegetable peels, melon rinds, coffee grounds, and so forth) in their compost piles, but in other parts of the country, such as where I live, such organic matter tends to attract nematodes to the soil, thereby harming the plants. Consult local gardening resources for information on how best to garden in your area.

• You can use compost in its various stages to smother weeds and to conserve soil moisture and moderate its temperature. You don't have to wait until it's all decomposed.

• When you apply compost to your garden, you shouldn't pile it up near plant stems or tree trunks. If you do, stems and trunks may rot.

• Compost piles need to be turned frequently to keep them moist.

• Collect the bags of leaves and grass clippings and stacks of newspapers that your neighbors set out for trash pickup and then work these materials into the compost pile. This is recycling and saving money on fertilizer at the same time!

• You don't need a leaf shredder to shred compost materials if you have a motor-powered garden tiller. You can make a pile of leaves one or two feet high, and then run the power tiller through the pile to shred up the material so that it will compost more quickly.

• A power tiller helps you to mix compost into the soil before planting flower or vegetable beds; in some cities, such relatively expensive gardening aids can be rented.

Garden Beds

• If you don't have much space for a garden, organizing plants according to size lets you grow both flowers and veggies in the same bed. You can plant beans with sweet peas and tomatoes behind marigolds, put peppers in with petunias, and otherwise combine nature's bounty.

• Marigolds tend to repel mosquitoes, so they'll make your gardening more comfortable as well as pretty if you use them as a border around the garden plot.

• If you plant onions as a border around your garden, harvest the green ones to "thin" the row, then allow the remaining onions to mature to full-sized ones.

• Garlic can also be a border plant. Harvest the garlic chives for your salad by snipping off the green spikes; more will grow back.

• If you can, try to plant tall-growing plants on the north and northeast side of your garden so that, as they grow, they won't shade the rest of the bed.

• If you're planting a vegetable garden in the city or on a small lot, try to avoid shade from buildings and large trees. Large trees take soil nutrients and moisture away from your garden, besides blocking the sun. Remember that a tree's root system can reach way beyond the span of its branches.

• Veggies need at least six hours of direct sun each day, sometimes as much as eight to ten hours, so if you try to grow tomatoes, peppers, or eggplant in the shade, you'll get nice green shrubs but nothing to eat.

Planting an Herb Garden

• Here's my favorite tip for planting an herb garden: The best place to plant herbs is as close to your kitchen door as possible. Use pots and containers if that helps you grow them more conveniently to where you'll use them. If you have to walk through mud or other plants to get to the herbs, the chances are you won't use them at all, because it will be just too much mess and trouble.

• If you want to get the most pleasure from an herb garden, plant the herbs where they can be touched, picked, or brushed by people walking past them, because herbs don't release their fragrances until they are brushed or bruised.

• Thyme, marjoram, and parsley grow only a few inches high, so position them as borders where they won't be overshadowed by the other plants.

• Coriander, tarragon, and dill grow to about two feet high or more. These plants can be the center of a walk-around herb garden plot or be at the rear of a plot that is against a fence or wall. If you have shorter plants in front, you can easily reach the tall ones.

• If you grow rosemary and bay leaves in clay pots buried just beneath the surface of your garden's soil, you can easily move them indoors when the weather turns cold so that they will continue to provide flavor year-round. What a treat!

• Some herbs will really spread and try to take over an herb garden. Perennials like wild marjoram, tarragon, and mint will take up more space each season if you don't tell them where to stop. If you confine their roots with a buried section of stovepipe, they'll stay where you want them to.

• To get the best flavor from herbs, cut them just before they flower, when their oils are at peak. When cutting for storage, the best time to cut them is at mid-morning on a sunny day.

• Store them by freezing, drying, or in oil or vinegar. Use the oil and vinegar as preseasoned cooking ingredients.

• If you have refrigerator space, home-dried herbs, fruits, and vegetables keep better stored there.

• Some seasons, tomato plants go crazy and produce so much that you can't even give enough of them away. A food dryer can reduce buckets of tomatoes to quarts. Dried tomatoes can be crumpled and added with your dried herbs to flavor stews and soups, and they'll take much less space than canned or frozen ones.

Planting from Seeds

• When you're planting seeds in rows, use a broom handle to form the trenches. Place the broom handle on the line where you want the row, then step on it until it makes a groove about one-fourth inch deep in the soil and you'll have a straight trench with uniform depth.

• Some very tiny seeds need only be pressed into the soil surface. Check the seed packet for directions. When sowing such fine seeds on the surface of seedling trays, sift a light layer of sand or flour (use a strainer) over the soil surface so that you can see where the seeds are. The sand or flour also will keep the seeds undisturbed and from sticking to whatever you use to tamp them down.

• If you need to plant each seed in a separate hole, use a pencil, pen, or chopstick to poke holes in the soil, and mark it at the depth the seed needs to be planted so that the depths of the seeds are uniform.

• Here's a rule of green thumb for seeds: They need to be covered (sprinkled, not packed) with soil up to four times their smallest diameter. The next step is to moisten the soil, but not with a deluge or you'll wash the seeds away.

• When you are growing your own bedding plants, you can speed up seed germination by placing the seed trays on top of your refrigerator, where the temperature of 72 to 75 degrees Fahrenheit will encourage speedy growth. Or, place them on top of a TV set that is being used all day or on a dryer that is being used and cover lightly with a paper towel or light towel so that no draft disturbs the seeds.

• Always use fresh potting soil for starting your seeds and wash your hands between handling outdoor and indoor plants to prevent spreading plant diseases.

• When you are handling tiny seedlings to transplant them from trays to ground, don't pick them up by the stems. Stems are fragile and will break. Instead, let the plant fall out of the little plastic seedling tray into one hand; sometimes you need to gently squeeze the bottom of the little plastic tray and then transfer the plant to your other hand so that you can cup your palm and hold the plant by its roots. These baby plants need TLC.

• If you keep unused seeds in their packets and then put the packets in plastic bags, stored in the refrigerator, many of them will keep for years. If any don't keep, you won't have wasted any money because you'd have thrown out unused seeds anyhow!

Growing Fruits and Vegetables

• If you save bedding trays from season to season to use for sprouting your own seeds, wash them thoroughly before planting seeds so that your new crop will be free of plant diseases.

• You can use plastic-foam egg cartons for sprouting seeds. Just poke a small drain hole in the bottom of each cup and fill them with soil. Use the lid as a tray beneath this homemade planter. You'll be recycling the egg cartons for one more use before they're discarded.

• Sprout seeds or grow strawberries in an old gutter spout filled with soil. You can attach the spout to a fence if you are using it to grow strawberries or other short-rooted plants. Hanging plants from a fence solves the lack-of-sun problem in some yards and keeps weeds from getting in with the real plants.

• Corn takes up too much space in a small garden, but if you grow it in a washtub filled with soil, you can use your other garden space more productively. You'll get better results if you grow a small variety and, since it's not in the ground, you'll have to water it more often.

• Many herbs, flowers, and vegetables grow well in whiskey barrels, washtubs, and other containers, but remember that when you grow anything in a container, it needs to be fertilized and watered more often than plants grown in the ground. Don't forget to make drain holes in the bottom of the container that you are using.

• If you just don't know where some perennials (those that come back every year) will do well in your garden's shady and sunny areas, try planting them in containers so that you can move them around until you find the places where they'll have best growing conditions. Once you find out which beds they are happiest in, you can put them in the ground.

• You can also use movable containers when you are planning flower beds of perennials. Arrange the containers where you think you'll want those plants, and if they look right for that spot after they are fully grown and in bloom, you'll know where to plant them when it's time to put them into the ground.

Getting Rid of Plant Pests Without Strong Insecticides

A National Gardening Association survey published in the summer of 1988 revealed that insects "bugged" 33 percent of the gardens of people in the survey.

• For a healthy spring and summer garden, thoroughly clean out all garden junk in the fall. Get rid of vines, stalks, stems, or rotted fruits and vegetables.

• Pesty aphids, mealy bugs, cabbage worms, spider mites, and young scale can be removed from plants with a strong jet of water from your garden hose. You may not have to spray with pesticides.

• Chives resist both plant pests and virus diseases and can help the rest of your garden to do the same if you give it a "drink" of chive tea. Steep about one-half cup finely chopped chive leaves in one pint of boiling water (enough to cover the leaves). Let steep for 15 minutes and cool, then spray on your plants as a preventive treatment.

• Horseradish planted near potatoes will keep potato beetles away.

• Onions planted next to beets and carrots will keep bugs away.

• Planting basil near tomatoes keeps worms and flies away. Besides, it will be convenient when it's salad-picking time.

• Aphids and red spider mites will stay away if you use a rhubarb spray made by pouring two pints of boiling water over a pound of chopped rhubarb leaves. Let the mixture steep overnight; strain and add a tablespoon of detergent to the rhubarb "tea," then spray on vegetable plants. I knew there was a good use for rhubarb leaves!

CAUTION: Rhubarb leaves contain poisonous oxalic acid. DO NOT spray within a week of harvesting and keep children and pets away.

• When you first notice that insect pests are munching on your plants, you can either pick them or their eggs off by hand or brush them off into a jar coated with detergent.

• A mixture of one-half cup mild liquid dish-washing detergent to a pint of water can be used to spray both sides of plant leaves to kill insects. Wait an hour, then spray or hose down with clear water.

Lawn Care

The kind of lawn you plant—seed, plugs, sod—depends upon the growing conditions in your yard.

• When you lay sod, you'll get a smoother look if you stagger the joints of the rows of sod strips the way bricks are laid.

• Even the best-laid plans—and lawns—of gardeners and lawn layers produce some weeds. If you pull weeds in the early spring before the weeds have had a chance to flower and reseed themselves, you'll have a better chance of getting rid of those pesky things. Also, weeds grow faster than real grass, so if you have lots of them, you'll have to mow more often in the heat of summer.

• When you use chemical weed killers on your lawn and have children or pets playing on it, be especially cautious and read the labels. Many of these chemicals are extremely toxic. Some directions say that the chemicals for weed or flea killing must be allowed to dry or that some waiting period should be observed before children and pets can be allowed to play on the lawn again. Don't take any chances.

• In hot weather, it's usually better to set your lawn mower blades higher so that the longer grass shades and protects the roots.

• Your lawn still needs you in the fall. This is the best time to rake out summer's debris (clippings, dead leaves, etc.), which if allowed to remain on (and in) the lawn will keep water and air from the roots.

• Fall is the time to feed your lawn before winter's break from the growing season. Usually, people wait until leaves begin to fall and then apply a nitrogen-rich fertilizer. After applying fertilizer (with a spreader borrowed from a garden center if you don't own one) you need to give the soil a good soaking, down to a depth of three or four inches.

• You don't have to have a hole in your lawn beneath your roof's drain spout. Just put a large flat stone or garden step-stone beneath the drain spout, and rainwater will spread out instead of eroding the topsoil.

• One way to avoid all lawn care is to plant different kinds of ivy as ground cover instead of grass. You may have to cut it back once in a while, but you can give your mower to someone else and then sit on your patio and enjoy life.

Watering

Conserving water and making trees and plants resistant to drought conditions is common practice were I live, and recurring drought conditions in other parts of the country show that the need for water conservation and defensive gardening is important throughout the United States.

• Your garden needs its watering early in the morning so that leaves will dry quickly in the sun. When leaves stay wet all night after evening watering, spore and fungus diseases may get established.

• Because many plant diseases are encouraged by wet leaves, it's better to water toward the soil instead of at the leaves. However, don't cause a deluge that washes the soil away from the plant; water gently.

• If you don't want to stand and direct the hose to a specific area in your flower bed or to water certain shrubs or trees, bend a coat hanger into a V to hold the hose; you can poke the straightened-out hook end of the hanger into the ground.

• If you have potted plants on high ledges or hanging too high to reach, tie a bamboo cane (fishing pole) with twisties or string to the hose so that the cane and hose together are a rigid wand that reaches high up to the plants. Put an adjustable spray on the end of the hose so you don't wash away soil when you water the plants.

• When you water plants, soak the soil thoroughly when watering. A light sprinkling can cause roots to come to the surface and then get baked to death by the sun. The idea is to get roots to go down deep where they won't be subjected to summer heat.

• Many gardeners in hot climates actually train their plants (especially vegetables like tomatoes, squash, broccoli) to go deeply for water. Instead of watering directly on the plant, they make or buy soaker systems—hoses or pipes with holes in them that are placed between rows of plants or in garden beds and lawns, which keep water on the ground and prevent evaporation.

• You can easily make an inexpensive irrigation system by digging "watering holes" beside plants and between rows. Here's how it's done:

1. At the time of planting, dig holes about a foot deep, a foot or so from each plant or between plants.
2. Then, insert into the holes 32-ounce juice cans with tops and bottoms removed or similarly sized plastic pots (the kind larger bedding plants and house plants come in) with the bottoms cut out.

The cans or pots form walls that keep the holes from collapsing when you fill them with water from a hose. Watering this way soaks the ground beneath the plants and draws the roots downward.

• Special tubes for watering trees are available in garden stores that attach to the hose so that water is directed beneath the surface, thereby drawing roots downward, where they are protected.

• If the heat has wilted your potted patio plants (Say "potted patio plants" fast, three times in a row!), you can revive them by standing the pot in a watertight tray filled with moist gravel so that the humidity from the tray will perk up the plant. Mist the plant well with a mister, but be sure it's not in direct sunlight or this will only add to the wilted condition of the plant.

• If your potted plant is so totally dry that the roots and potting soil have pulled away from the pot sides, immerse the plant in its pot in water that is at least one inch above the top of the pot rim. Let the plant stay in the water for about 20 minutes until the bubbles stop rising to the surface and the roots and soil have absorbed enough water to swell up and fill the pot as before. Then remove and allow the plant to drain.

Gardening Equipment

• Long-handled garden tools can be stored in a metal garbage can. (Plastic garbage cans will work only if they are heavy enough not to tip over when the tools are inside.) Attach S hooks to the rim of the can for hanging smaller tools. Then you can tote the whole can to wherever you are working and have your tools handy.

• To store your garden hose, wrap the hose around a sturdy wooden coat hanger and hang it on a hook in the garage.

• Spring a leak? You can repair small holes or cracks in a rubber garden hose with rubber patches and adhesive tape.

1. Sand the surface around the hole lightly with fine sandpaper and sand the surface of the rubber patch, which you can cut from an old tube.
2. Apply contact cement to both sanded surfaces and wait until the cement is dry to the touch.
3. Press the patch over the hole very firmly and then wrap the patched area with rubber or vinyl electrical tape or duct tape. If you don't want to worry about repairing the hose, turn it into a soaker hose. Use an ice pick to punch holes along the length of the garden hose.

• Quick-patch small leaks in plastic hoses by just barely touching them with the tip of a hot ice pick. The idea is to melt the plastic so it self-seals the holes.

• Safety tip for sawing wood: When you use a chain saw, cut only wood that is smaller than the length of the guide bar; otherwise you are likely to have the saw kick back and be hard to control when the saw nose is buried in wood.

Garden Walls and Fences

• If you're having trouble with the neighborhood cats (or your own) using your well-worked vegetable garden soil as a comfy litter box and your baby plants as nap sites, try enclosing the beds with 4- to 5-foot wire fencing (sold in rolls at hardware stores) supported by steel fence posts. The posts need no cement and are just driven into the ground and have places on which to hook the fencing wire. While it's not really decorative, this type of fence is too flimsy for cats to leap up on and will keep cats out of your garden plot. (It's strong enough only for bird perching.)

• You can keep "varmints" and other animals from walking along wooden horizontal-slat fences by nailing carpet tacking strips on the top edge. (These strips are wood, about an inch wide, and have tiny carpet tacks pointed upward so that they hold carpeting in place when it's installed over wood floors.) The tacks are not big or sharp enough to actually hurt the animal, but they do make walking along the fence unpleasant enough to make the animals stay away.

• To paint wire or chain link fences or decorative ironwork quickly and without wasting spray paint, use a sponge to wipe on paint. This job will go very quickly if you have two people doing it. With one on either side of the fence, you dab sponges together and will paint both sides of the fence at one time without wasting paint. Rubber gloves are a must to protect your hands.

Stepping Stones, Walkways, Driveways

• Make your own "Hollywood Walk of the Stars," whether it's a cement sidewalk or a series of poured cement stepping stones: Have family members put their handprints, names, birth dates, or some other important dates in wet cement. We did just this when we built our home, and have names, initials, and date firmly etched in cement for posterity.

• If you use carpet remnants and strips of old carpet between garden rows, you won't have to step in mud when you pick your veggies and flowers. Either buy cheap remnants and pieces or use discarded old carpet for a "garden walkway."

• Old carpet can be used also for a greenhouse floor.

• If you have small cracks in your blacktop driveway, you can patch them with sand and liquid blacktop sealer. Fill the crack partway with sand and then pour the sealer into the crack. The sand will absorb the sealer, and you can repeat the process until the crack is filled and the surface is smooth.

Snow Shoveling and Ice Removal

• Before using your snow shovel, coat the front and back heavily with paste wax, and the snow will slide off fast and easy. The plus is that you won't be banging your shovel on the walk or driveway and bending the edge. If the snowfall catches you without paste wax, use an old candle or some canning wax—any wax works.

• Instead of trying to lift heavy, wet snow, move it with a metal garden rake—teeth up or teeth down—and you'll spare your back and arms a lot of lifting.

• A lightweight aluminum snow shovel is a good dustpan when you're cleaning off the patio or car port, and you can shovel leaves against the curb to clean gutters in front of your house, too.

• If you store some sand, rock salt, melting crystals, or any of the commercial products used to melt ice and snow in clean, dry plastic milk jugs, it's much easier to dispense the ice melters where you want them to be. Keep a jug handy beside the front or back door and in your car in case you get "iced in" one day.

• When you need to unstick a car from packed snow or ice, you can get traction if you keep a couple of coffee cans in the car filled with any kind of grit, such as cat litter, sand, small gravel.

• In a pinch you may even be able to get some traction for your auto tires from old bath towels, carpet scraps, or blankets stashed away in your trunk. Just place the towels behind or in front of the two driving wheels, depending upon whether you are going forward or backing up.

Outdoor Lighting

• If you live in a cold climate, you can avoid replacing burned-out hard-to-reach lightbulbs in the bitter cold if you replace them each year at end of the fall season and before the cold winds blow. You probably won't need to climb those ladders, trees, or poles until spring. If the bulbs you've removed are still good, save them for indoors or warm-weather outdoor use.

• Moisture often makes bulbs in outdoor fixtures stick when you try to remove them. Bulbs will unscrew more easily if you rub a light coat of petroleum jelly on their threads before you insert them. This also works on inside light fixtures that have a tendency to rust, as in damp basements or garages.

• Dim outdoor lighting in your yard or campsite brightens up if you place shiny, reflecting aluminum foil behind the lamp/light. If you need to enhance a flashlight's glow, wrap a collar of foil on the lighted end.

Swimming Pools

Few activities are as refreshing in the summer as jumping into a cool pool or sitting in spa bubbles, if your pool has this feature. Pools, unfortunately, do require maintenance, even if the newer ones are easier to care for than older models.

• You can have a pool in a small or narrow yard. Lap pools are popular in cities, where land is too expensive for expansive yards. A lap pool need be only about four feet deep, about four feet wide, and as long as you can get it. Often a lap pool's cement will be colored black or dark green, and when it's not being used for exercise swimming, it serves as a reflecting pool for nearby garden beds or other landscaping.

Pool Safety

• Always keep a rope, life ring, and/or your long-handled skimming net or pool brooms near the pool and in easy reach so that they can be used as a rescue pole in case a swimmer needs help.

• Take a tip from the public pools: Install a floating rope that shows where the deep part of your pool begins.

• Not all pool covers are safety devices that support weight, and small children and animals can drown even in a shallow puddle that forms in a pool cover. Don't take a chance.

• Children always need adult supervision when using a pool. Don't leave a child alone even for a moment to run into the house, whether it's to answer the phone or the front door. All it takes is a few seconds for a tragedy to happen.

• Swimming and first-aid/CPR lessons should be a must when a family installs a pool.

• Make family rules about how many and which children can be guests at the pool. To ensure the safety of all guests, you have the right and the obligation to ban those who won't follow your safety rules.

• The chemicals used to clean and sanitize pool water can be harmful when improperly used or stored. If mixed with other chemicals or elements, pool chemicals can cause explosions and fires.

• As with all chemicals, store out of the reach of children and in their original containers. Make sure that lids are tightly closed and do not stack different chemicals on top of one another.

• Never mix two chemicals together, and use a clean scoop for each chemical to avoid combining material from old and new containers.

• NEVER add chemicals to the water if swimmers are in the pool. And allow for the correct amount of time after adding chemicals for anyone to swim.

• Replace your test kit each year.

• Follow all safety rules regarding handling electrical switches, wires, and other equipment around water (including a portable phone).

• Never replace bulbs in underwater lights yourself; get an expert to do this.

Keeping the Pool Clean

• Have a foot rinse-off dishpan or tub near the pool to keep grass clippings and dirt out of the pool.

• This may be the biggest thing ever made from Heloise nylon net: If you sew, you can make a nylon net pool cover by sewing together strips of the net so that you can completely cover the pool. Hold this cover in place with gallon plastic jugs along the side of the pool filled with sand or water. If you have an above-the-ground pool, the cover can be clipped to the pool sides with spring clothespins. The advantage of nylon net is that it's so light, even with leaves on it, one person can handle it. This is an ideal, inexpensive way to make a cover for a hot tub/spa.

NOTE OF CAUTION: This pool cover is NOT a safety device and should not be considered to be such a thing. It WILL NOT SUPPORT THE WEIGHT of even a small child or animal. It is only a method of keeping leaves and bugs out of the pool.

Mowing the Grass Near the Pool

• It seems obvious, but if you're a new pool owner, you may not think of this: If you don't have a grass catcher on your lawn mower, be sure to "shoot" the cut grass away from the pool instead of into it, and, of course, vacuum the pool after or during, not before, a mowing session.

Pool Cleaning

• If you have an automatic pool vacuum sweeper, the kind that rolls around the bottom and sides all by itself, you'll find that an old knee-high stocking or pantyhose leg can be held on with a rubber band to serve as a disposable "vacuum cleaner bag" or liner for the mesh bag that comes with this wonderful pool aid. A few runs in the stocking won't matter, and the bonus is that you don't have to untangle bugs and bits of things from the vacuum bag mesh—just throw the whole thing out!

Keeping the House Clean and Your Sanity When You Have a Pool

If you install your pool as your house is being built, you can make provisions for clothes changing and bathroom going so that you don't have a parade of wet people through the house.

If you've added a pool to an existing home, you'll have to make some rules about drippy-wet traveling in the house or you'll begin to wonder why you ever wanted a pool.

• A small tent can be a temporary changing room during pool parties.

• A small garden "shack," such as those that come in kits, can be a pool house, and if you are willing to deal with it, you can install a camper's toilet in the garden shack.

• Make a path to the bathroom with inexpensive runner rugs and insist that all swimmers use it. Call it the "Yellow Brick Road" and yourself the "Wizard of Oz" or use some other catchy name to make this rule more acceptable.

• Have an outdoor hanging place (rack, clothesline, fence, lawn chair) for wet towels and bathing suits. If you have a large family or many swimmers, you can't keep up with washing so many towels each day. Even putting all the wet things in the dryer gets tedious by mid-summer.

Wading Pools for Small Children

• Molded pools and slides can be very slippery, but little feet can pitter and patter safely if you install bathtub appliqués or bathtub mats with suction cups at strategic places, such as the bottom of the pool and the step before the slide (a half of a mat may serve here, so you can install the other half in the foot rinse-off tub beside the pool).

• If the wading pool will fit into your child's sandbox, installing it inside the sandbox not only prevents a pool-size section of dead grass in your lawn where you've put the pool, but the sandbox seats on the sides are also pool seats.

• Put a stool or lawn chair beside your child's wading pool and soak your tired, aching feet while you supervise the play.

• At the end of the season, you can wash small, lightweight inflatable plastic pools in the washer—with some towels, just like you wash a shower curtain. If you wish, you can take it out before the spin cycle and just hang it on the line to dry.

Other Uses for Small Plastic Wading Pools

• Small children can sit in a small (empty of course!) plastic wading pool when they snack in front of the television set—no spills or goo on the carpet to clean up!

• A hard plastic wading pool with a pad on the bottom can be a handy playpen or bassinet for a very small baby, with supervision. (Especially at Grandma's house! It can be kept under a bed when baby's not visiting.)

• Since they are so easy to slide under a bed, outgrown rigid plastic wading pools can be used for toy bins, storage of craft items, plastic-bagged out-of-season clothing, or anything else that's lightweight and will fit under the bed.

Taking care of house plants or spending time in the yard and garden can not only provide beautiful scenery, but, for many people, me included, great pleasure from pruning, watering, and fussing. The results can be beautiful and eye-appealing, and many times the free plants you get from your cuttings can really add to the appearance of your yard or living area. If you just don't have a green thumb and can't be bothered with the care and feeding of another living thing, look around for some real-life-looking artificial plants. No fuss, no watering, no repotting, and when you get tired of them, just toss them in the garbage without guilt.

CHAPTER 6

Children

I'm just now experiencing motherhood as a stepmother to a thirteen-year-old boy. Like any other parent, I'm learning a lot.

Babies

They look so fragile—little fisted hands flailing about . . . tiny slit-eyes that open to stare in wonder at lights and moving things . . . wobbly, disproportionately large, bald or tousled-hair heads on too-frail necks. . . .

And their faces get so very red when they cry.

When it's your first baby, crying is scary because you are absolutely sure you must have done something wrong to cause it. That first night home ALONE with a new baby (and you feel alone no matter how many people are around to help you) is the scariest of all.

If you live through that first night, and generations of parents have survived it, you'll realize that your baby cries because the poor little thing can't talk.

Once you can tell a fuss cry from a hunger or discomfort cry, you are officially a parent. Baby tending becomes easier because you feel competent.

You'll also feel more competent if you aren't exhausted. Use your hospital or birthing center stay to rest. When you come home, focus on people, not the house; the dust will wait for you—use your energy to enjoy your baby and to share this pleasure with other people in your family.

If you are breast-feeding, you have the perfect excuse not to bother with household matters. You need your energy to feed and enjoy your baby. Babies grow up faster than you'll ever know. These moments won't happen again. Savor every single one.

If you're not breast-feeding, the advice is the same, except that other people can also feed the baby and more actively enjoy those precious first months in baby's life.

Feeding time, no matter who does it or how it's done, is a time to nourish souls as well as bodies. The person feeding the baby enjoys the cuddlings as much as the baby.

Make sure you have a comfortable chair and a place to put your feet up when you feed the baby. Always use feeding time to relax yourself. Babies are smart little creatures who seem to sense tenseness, and then respond with tension of their own. (If you don't believe this, next time you're on an airplane or in a restaurant listening to a crying baby, check out the person carrying that baby. More often than not, the tenser the carrier, the more fretful the baby.)

For most parents, first babies are the most awesome because that's when they are the most inexperienced, but all babies are wonders, and you can enjoy all of them more if you prepare for them.

Bringing Baby Home

• Hang a DO NOT DISTURB or BABY'S SLEEPING or MOM'S RESTING sign on your front door, warning solicitors and others that to ring your doorbell is a "no-no."

• If you own an answering machine, use it. Set the answering machine to answer any incoming calls on the first ring so as not to wake you or the baby during rest periods.

• An answering machine can also be a wonderful announcement maker. Record a message including the baby's time and date of birth, weight, length, and name, as well as "We are napping now and will call you back later."

• A new twist to the old passing out of cigars by proud fathers is to pass out pens with "It's a Girl" or "It's a Boy" printed on them. These make great keepsakes for loved ones and friends alike. Also, they can be given to women friends and nonsmokers.

Feeding Baby

• If you are bottle-feeding, always write the time and date that you opened the container of liquid formula (whether it is ready-to-feed or concentrate) on the can. For easy dating, keep a permanent black marker in a kitchen drawer or on the pantry shelf where you store the formula or even tied to a string attached to a drawer pull so it won't mysteriously walk out of the kitchen, for easy dating. Most formula should be used only up to 48 hours after opening (except for the powder form). This can be especially important when baby first comes home and is on a demand feeding schedule.

• If you stand them in a soft drink carton, those wobbly baby bottles won't tip over in the refrigerator.

• Try highlighting the ounce markers on baby's bottle with nail polish or a waterproof marker; you'll be able to read them in a dimly lit room and know if baby's at "burping time" and has consumed the usual amount for a feeding.

• Regulate the flow through the nipple by tightening the bottle collar for a slower flow and loosening the collar for a faster flow. Remember that too fast a flow might make some babies gulp their liquids and result in too many uncomfortable air bubbles in their tiny tummies.

• You can enlarge the holes in baby bottle nipples if you boil them for about five minutes, then allow to cool for about three minutes with toothpicks lodged in the holes. Or use a sterilized needle to enlarge the holes. If the opening is too large, just reboil the nipple and it will close up.

• If you store bottle nipples in a cool, dry place, they will last longer.

• An occasional brushing with a salt solution prevents baby bottle nipples from deteriorating.

• Whether or not you should heat baby's bottle in the microwave oven is controversial. Some authorities say that you should never warm a bottle in a microwave oven; the formula may be too hot, even though the bottle itself is cool to the touch. Also, excessive heat destroys vitamins.

• An old-fashioned yet safe way to heat a bottle is to put it in a pan or bowl and run hot tap water over it until the temperature is just right.

• If you warm baby's bottle in the microwave oven, here's how: To warm an eight-ounce bottle in a microwave oven, remove the nipple and put on high power for 10 to 25 seconds if the milk is at room temperature and for 25 to 45 seconds if it's cold from the refrigerator. Individual microwave ovens work differently, so times vary. Shake the bottle to mix well.

• CAUTION: Whatever way you heat the bottle, always shake the bottle after heating to mix well, and make it a habit to always test a few drops on the inside of your wrist to feel the temperature just before feeding baby.

• Some parents like to keep extra formula in the refrigerator to add to a too-warm bottle. You can also cool a too-hot bottle by placing it in a pan and running cold water over it for about 45 seconds; then, always retest.

• A baby fed in as upright a position as possible is less likely to suffer from trapped air bubbles. This position enables that stubborn bubble at the bottom of the stomach to rise more easily when baby is burped.

• It's not always necessary to pound baby's back to get those burps. Often massaging baby's back will bring up burps more gently.

• Some babies will burp as soon as they are placed on your shoulder or on their stomachs on your lap. Since many babies spit up when they burp, place a clean cloth diaper, towel, or other designated burp cloth on your shoulder or lap when feeding baby.

• One of the more effective ways of burping a baby is to have the baby seated on your lap and leaning forward supported by your hand, while you stroke or pat baby's back with your other hand. If your baby tends to spit up, hold a diaper under his chin with your supporting hand. This method works better with babies that are a month old or so, when their heads aren't totally wobbly.

• To rid the bottles of sour milk smell, fill them with warm water and add a teaspoon of baking soda. Shake well and let stand overnight. The next morning wash and sterilize as usual.

• You can boil the bottle nipples in a glass jar of water in your microwave oven. A teaspoonful of vinegar in the water will prevent any hard water deposits in the jar.

• Using bottle straws will help formula flow evenly no matter what position the bottle is in.

• When the time comes, baby can be weaned gradually from the bottle by letting him drink directly from the familiar container, but with the nipple removed or replaced by a soda straw.

Breast-Feeding

If you have decided to breast-feed, the main rule of thumb is to be comfortable and relaxed during feeding. Pick a favorite chair or area of your home and set up a feeding area with all the necessities you may need.

• A cushioned rocker, armchair, or sofa with low arms will help to make you comfortable while nursing.

• There is no rule that says you can't catch up on your reading while you are breast-feeding. If you are a tense person, reading may actually be relaxing and help you go with the flow, so to speak. Remember, being comfortable and relaxed is important for your flow of milk.

• If baby falls asleep while nursing at breast or bottle, take a tip from Mama Cat. No, I don't mean that you're supposed to lick the baby! But, if you gently stroke baby, especially on the cheeks and chin, you'll activate the baby's natural suckling mechanism so that feeding continues.

• Leakage of milk from the breasts can be absorbed by nursing pads, but even these will become soaked occasionally. To prepare yourself for such an occurrence in public, wear printed tops as much as possible. The stains from leakage will be less visible than if you are wearing a solid color. Also, print tops don't show baby-carrying wrinkles as much as solid colors do.

• If you run out of nursing pads, cut circles from one of baby's disposable diapers or panty liners to substitute for them.

• To ensure privacy when nursing away from home, place the baby on the lower corner of a receiving blanket instead of the middle as usual. Take the top triangular part of the blanket and place it over your shoulder when placing the baby to your breast. Baby won't smother and you can avoid the stares and curiosity of onlookers. You can also pin a small patch of self-gripping tape to the shoulder seam of your clothing, and sew a similar patch to the top corner of the "nursing" blanket for added security and privacy.

• While shopping in your local mall or clothing store, ask an attendant if you can use one of the dressing rooms to feed your baby privately and comfortably. It's more pleasant than the rest room.

Giving Baby Solid Foods

• Never feed baby directly from a jar that you intend to put back into the refrigerator half full. The enzymes in baby's saliva will be carried to the inside of the jar on the baby's spoon and will cause a breakdown of the food after feeding.

• Use an egg poacher to heat baby's food all at the same time. Each compartment will hold a different food item, and cleanup is easy.

• If you make your own baby food, you need to cover the blender blades with at least one inch of food to get lump-free baby puree.

• Blocks of baby food can be frozen in an ice cube tray, so you'll have variety in feedings without spoilage or waste. (Two cubes generally makes one three-ounce serving.)

• When a baby food jar lid just won't screw off, punch a small hole in the lid to break the vacuum seal, and the lid will twist right off.

• You can use cleaned, used baby food jars for many things, including a small, wet, traveling washcloth. Of course a plastic self-sealing bag works well too.

• Many babies fret when they are put to bed because the sheets are cold. If you put a heating pad in the crib or bassinet while baby is feeding, the bed will be as comfortably warm as your arms were, and baby may not even notice being returned to bed. And a quick way to warm sheets for baby and adult alike is to use your hand-held hair dryer.

• When traveling, take along a premixed feeding of one half dry cereal and one half powdered formula in a container. When you stop for lunch or dinner, just add hot water or formula, and the baby's food is heated and ready to eat. Add jar fruit or vegetables if desired. No waste, no fuss.

• If you are traveling cross-country, you may want to select a brand of bottled (non-fizz) water and then use it consistently for your baby's drinking or for mixing with powdered fruit, and so forth. Some babies are sensitive to the different mineral compositions of water in different locales and might have digestive disturbances from the changes. Check with your pediatrician.

• When baby proves to be a finicky eater, put his favorite food or fruit on the front part of the baby spoon and the dreaded vegetable/meat to the back.

When the fruit goes in, so does the vegetable/meat without the fuss. Sometimes they catch on to this trick a little too easily, but it's worth a try.

• Keep a felt-tipped marker handy to mark on the jar lid the date it was opened. This will ensure that baby eats only freshly opened foods. You will find that it takes no time at all for jars of foods to accumulate in the refrigerator, especially if you like to feed your baby a variety each day.

• If you use instant baby food, move the colored plastic lid to the bottom of the unopened can (thus exposing the lift tab), and you can easily tell which one is opened and which is not.

• When baby is ready for table foods, use a nut grinder to grind up table foods if you don't have a baby food mill.

• You can make your own baby foods by selecting fresh fruits and vegetables and steaming and pureeing them. Refrigerate or freeze small portions in covered ice cube trays; when frozen, pop out and put in a freezer-safe bag and clearly mark.

• Introduce new foods when the child is very hungry and therefore not too discerning about what it eats. As in all things you do with children, the "teachable moment" is the best time for any activity. It is always easier and more pleasant to lead and guide children; pushing them always takes more energy and gets more resistance. (If you don't believe this, ask any experienced parent, especially one who has survived teenhood!)

Feeding Toddlers and Young Children

• Awkward little fingers can hold on to a drinking cup more easily if you wrap several wide rubber bands or strips of tape around it.

• Finger foods are the key to self-feeding when toddlers get into "Me do it myself." When a toddler is learning to self-feed, sliced hot dogs, cooked carrots, potato hunks, or the non-fat oven-bake French fries found in the freezer section of the supermarket can be eaten by hand while you spoon-feed other foods. Finger foods can be put directly on the high chair tray; it eliminates the distraction of a plate.

• When you have picky eaters and children who don't have hearty appetites, think small. Make little meatloaves in muffin tins instead of serving a big slice; cut sandwiches into fourths; make "silver dollar"–size pancakes; cut fruit into slices or squares.

• Serve different bits of food in muffin tin compartments to make mealtime more interesting. One compartment will even hold a small drinking cup. Serving with a muffin tin is especially useful when a child is sick in bed.

• Try edible containers: An ice-cream cone will hold tuna, egg salad, cottage cheese, or yogurt.

• Serve messy sandwich salad fillings in pita bread, or cut pockets into unsliced buns to hold the fillings. Soft, sliced bread will fold over most fillings.

• Sloppy Joes will be less sloppy if you serve them this way: Cut a quarter-inch-thick layer from the top of an unsliced hamburger bun. Scoop out just enough bread to leave a "bowl" with "walls" to hold the sloppy Joe, then put the lid back on.

• Make breakfast more interesting with a cereal parfait: use one-half cup vanilla or fruited yogurt, 1⅓ cup dry cereal, and about a third of a sliced banana or equivalent with other soft fruit, such strawberries or peaches. Layer half of the yogurt, then the cereal, the remaining yogurt, and then top with fruit. Gosh, this even sounds good and healthy for adults.

Or make a breakfast banana split by peeling and splitting a banana and putting it into a dish for splits or a flat bowl; then sprinkle it with about a cup of dry cereal, and top with about a half-cup vanilla or fruit yogurt; garnish with a bit more of the dry cereal or some strawberries or grapes.
These aren't just for kids' breakfasts; have one yourself!

• Here's a recipe that's full of good stuff and could be a terrific snack or even a breakfast bread: Mix together two slightly beaten eggs, one-half cup chunky peanut butter, one-fourth cup honey, two-thirds cup nonfat dry milk powder; then add three cups dry cereal (I've not tested this with flakes, just "pebbles" type of cereals). Spread into a greased eight-inch pan. Bake for 20 minutes at 325 degrees Fahrenheit. Cool before serving and cut into six bars. The bars can be wrapped individually and stored in the fridge. For more flavor, you can spread these with jelly just before eating.

High Chair Helps

• Some babies are born wigglers. You can keep an overactive child's high chair from tipping by latching the chair to a wall with a childproof hook and eye.

• Tie a small child to the high chair with a large dish towel folded diagonally so that the bias part goes across the child's chest and the points are tied behind the chair back.

• NEVER leave a small child alone in a high chair, whether tied/belted in or not. Either is dangerous.

• If your baby keeps sliding down the seat of his high chair, place nonabrasive bathtub appliqués or a rubber sink or tub mat on the seat area of the chair. Baby's bottom will stay put.

• Try attaching a rubber-suction soap holder to baby's plate or bowl to keep it stuck to the tray when baby goes through that "drop and throw" stage.

• Attaching a towel bar to the back of a high chair will give you a nifty place to hang baby's bib and a washcloth, or even a half roll of paper towels.

• For quick cleanups when the high chair is a mess, and once baby self-feeds it will really be a mess, put it in the shower with a warm-water spray for a few minutes. Turn water off and wipe down, give it a quick rinse, and towel dry, and the high chair will look brand-new. (I would not suggest this for a wooden high chair.) I know one bachelor father who routinely takes the metal high chair to the car wash with him on Saturdays.

• If you spread a large plastic garbage bag, plastic tablecloth, or paint drop cloth beneath the high chair, you'll save a lot of floor cleaning and wiping.

The alternative is to have a perpetually hungry dog hovering under the chair. You may have to give the dog a bath if baby plays "Feed the doggie" and food lands on the dog instead of the floor, but no system is perfect!

Bath Time

Bath time can be a nice experience for both you and your baby. Just remember, one day without a bath is not a disgrace. If you skip a day because you are just too exhausted, nobody will come marching into your home and demand to erase your name from baby's birth certificate.

• Bath time shouldn't be a shock treatment. Always use warm body-temperature water, tested by dipping your elbow or wrist into it (your hands are used to greater temperature variances than your arm).

• Make sure the hot-water temperature on your hot-water heater is set at 120 degrees Fahrenheit or lower when you have small children in the house to prevent possible scalding during bath time. Again, always test baby's bath water first with your elbow as a safety precaution.

• Most babies hate having rough washcloths dragged across their faces. Make an envelope from the washcloth by folding it over your hand. With your hand wrapped in the washcloth, gently wipe baby's face with S motions. Many mothers prefer to wipe each of baby's eyes with a separate large cotton ball or at least one eye with each corner of the washcloth to prevent spreading bacteria from one eye to the other, if any might be present.

• Bath time is a good time to massage baby; the touch of your hands is important to an infant's emotional development. Besides, rubbing a soapy baby is fun; they smile and giggle and make you feel like you are one heck of a good parent.

• To keep soap or shampoo out of an infant's eyes, gently rub petroleum jelly on the eyelids and eyebrows. The jelly will make the shampoo run sideways rather than downward.

• An inexpensive plastic infant seat, with metal legs and cushions removed, will fit nicely into a sink or portable tub, providing a secure seat for baby.

   When bathing baby in the sink, make sure the faucet is completely out of the way. Babies have a way of grabbing and clutching things.

• A soapy baby won't be as slippery in the tub or sink if you line the tub with a towel or cloth diaper and if you wear a soft, cotton glove on one hand.

• You'll keep yourself dry even when baby splashes if you clip a towel around your neck like a bib. The bonus is that you have the towel ready to wrap around baby when the bath is finished.

• When baby graduates to the bathtub, put the metal legs back on the plastic infant seat and you will have a non-slip bath seat until baby can safely sit alone in a bathtub of water.

• Setting a clean plastic clothes basket in the tub will help you hold onto a small child during bath time. Put the basket into the tub, add water, and put the child into the basket.

• Non-slip cutouts on the bottom of your tub will give your toddler better footing in the bath and will give you better footing when you shower in the tub.

• If you let your toddler wear a small diving mask or eye goggles, bath time is fun, and you can rinse those shampoo suds off without tears!

• When toddlers reach the stage when they want to wash themselves, stuff an inside-out terry sock with small chunks of soap and fasten the open end or put soap pieces into a slit sponge. The toddler can scrub away without losing a slippery bar of soap in the bathwater, where it can be stepped on. Or, use a clean nylon stocking or the bottom part of a pair of pantyhose and drop a small soap sliver or two in, tie in knots, and give this to the baby to scrub with and to hold on to and play with.

• If you put baby powder into your hand before you apply it instead of just sprinkling it, it won't get into baby's face, and if you are powdering a toddler who is standing up, you won't get powder all over the bathroom.

Baby's Laundry

Did you ever imagine that one sweet little bundle could dirty so much laundry? Well, they can, and it won't get to be any less in the years to come.

• Cloth diapers can become a laundry problem if you neglect to rinse them, thus letting stains set in. Wash only about 18 diapers at a time, because overloading will not allow the diapers to get thoroughly clean. Wash diapers in hot, soapy water. You may add bleach if necessary daily or every two to three washings to remove stubborn stains. When using bleach, run diapers through a second, final rinse, adding one-half cup of vinegar to the water to be sure there is no soap or bleach residue left in the diapers. Note: Using fabric softener too often will cause the diapers to be less absorbent.

• When clothes are stained with formula and stains are left to set, they become permanent. No amount of bleach or magic formula will rémove them. This is why it is very important to try to remove the stain as soon as possible.

• To remove formula and other stains from baby's clothing, soak the clothes in an all-fabric bleach (also called non-chlorine bleach) that contains enzymes. Look for it on the shelves where laundry products are sold. Follow the directions on the back label for amounts to use. Use this type of all-fabric bleach on a daily basis and you will find the laundry will be cleaner. But always rinse well, so the bleach doesn't remain in baby's clothing.

• Diapers will be soft if you soak them as soon as you remove them in a solution of borax and water according to the directions on the box (about a handful or so of borax to a diaper pail of cold water). Always rinse off feces in the toilet bowl before soaking.

Soaked diapers (and milk-stained undershirts that have been soaking in borax water with them) can be dumped into the washer after you pour off any excess water from the pail into the toilet bowl. You don't have to wring out or even touch the diapers, the washer will do that for you.

Put the washer through a cold rinse cycle with a bit more borax, then wash through the heavy-duty cycle in the hottest water available with a mild detergent or soap.

With some washers, you need to add a second complete rinse to get all of the detergent out; some washers can be programmed for a second-rinse cycle. Most of the time you won't need fabric softener with this system and will have absorbent and odorless diapers.

• Using a diaper liner will help cut down on stains. You can purchase them or make your own, using soft, washable, and reusable material cut to fit. Or, for disposable diaper liners, cut to size handy disposable dishcloths.

• Keep an unwrapped bar of soap handy near baby's changing table. It makes a great pin cushion and the soap helps the pins slide easily through the cloth diaper.

• Disposable diapers have almost replaced washing diapers for people who can afford them. Of course, washing or worrying about getting them clean is not a problem with disposables, so I am all for them. The only drawback that I have heard about is that sometimes, one will have tabs that don't stick. You can use such a diaper if you secure it with duct or masking tape.

• The new diaper wipe cloths are wonderful as well. No more stacks of dirty, wet washcloths to deal with each day.

• Turn the baby wipes container upside down when not using to keep the top wipes moist. Store new containers of wipes this way too.

Little Tips for Little People Care

• When giving baby medicine, place the nipple part from baby's bottle in baby's mouth and administer the medicine with an eye dropper into the nipple. The medicine goes down easily as baby tries to nurse the nipple.

• Cut those scratchy tiny fingernails while baby is sleeping. You'll find blunt-end safety scissors at drugstores to make baby manicures easy.

• Hang blankets on a skirt hanger in the closet to save drawer space.

• Save labels from the baby food jars and diapers for special offers that will save you time, money, and energy when caring for baby.

• When baby outgrows the crib and starts sleeping in a bed, slide the crib mattress under the bed so at bedtime it can be pulled out to protect the child from any falls.

• Some children will roll back to the center of the bed if you place pillows or blanket rolls on the sides of the bed to serve as bumper guards.

In a Pinch

• If you're away from home and find you have no bathtub for baby, put a small plastic mesh laundry basket with holes in an adult-size bathtub. Place baby inside and wash away.

• If you run out of sheets for baby's bassinet, use standard-size pillowcases.

• For a bib, take a small child's old T-shirt and cut up the back, leaving the arm holes and neck opening intact. Slip over baby's head.

• Or use spring clothespins or those elastic clips that hold ironing board covers on the ironing board to fasten a washcloth or hand towel to baby's shirt for a quickie bib.

• Or use a sweater guard to hold a washcloth for a makeshift bib.

Teething Pain

• When your child is teething, soothe the pain and give him vitamin C with frozen orange sections. Baby will love both the coolness and the sweet taste. Frozen bananas are good too.

• Other teething biscuit substitutes are hardened bread, biscuits, or bagels.

• When some babies are teething they get so fretful that you may need a topical anesthetic for their gums if you or baby are to get any sleep. Check with your pediatrician before using such preparations, even if they are available without prescription.

Keeping Kids Safe

Safety for Kids' Sake

Accidents are the number one health hazard for all children. They kill more children than the five leading fatal diseases combined.

Falls, suffocation, poisonings, drownings, and burns cause more deaths to infants from birth to 12 months than all diseases combined. More than one-third of childhood deaths between the ages of 1 and 14 are caused by accidents.

And, in addition to being the greatest single cause of death of children under 15, accidents are the leading cause of permanent or temporary disabilities in children over 1 year old.

Three basic safety rules for infants are:

1. Never underestimate how fast babies develop physically and mentally; they can literally learn new tricks and movements while your back is turned.
2. Always expect the unexpected.
3. Never leave a baby alone unconfined by crib or playpen unless he or she is asleep, and in a confined, safe area.

Toy Safety

Babies are accustomed to receiving pleasure with their mouths. They examine new things with their mouths as much as with their eyes. This is a natural thing to do, and until the baby or toddler is old enough to understand "no" and actually understand why putting things in the mouth is a "no," adults must always be on guard against children swallowing small objects.

Even some 4-year-olds will swallow small objects, and many young children will poke small objects into their noses or ears for no reason other than to see if they will fit. Hospital emergency room personnel will testify to this!

Children need protection from their curiosity and natural tendencies. One mother told me that you can't trust a child under 18 to follow safety rules, and she's not sure if you can trust one over 18 either, because that's when the rules really get complicated.

• Toys should be too large to swallow, too tough to break, and have no sharp or hard edges.

• When a choking child can't clear the obstruction by himself, try putting his head facedown over your lap and gently pounding on his back. Get help by calling your local emergency number if this doesn't work.

- Very small infants enjoy watching and listening. A mobile firmly fastened above the crib will entertain a baby and stimulate development and response. All mobiles must be well out of baby's reach when he begins to grasp at things, which can occur when you least expect it.

- You can hang rattles, bells, music boxes, and other toys above or near the crib, but be sure baby can't grab them or strangle on the strings from which they are suspended.

- Teach other children in the family about baby's needs and make sure they understand which of their toys can and cannot be shared with baby.

- Show other children in the family how to hand a toy to baby; many a baby has been accidentally clouted with toys from siblings who were "only trying to be nice."

Poisonous Plants

That philodendron you chose so carefully for your low-light den, that hyacinth plant you bought to put spring into your living room, or the rhododendron and daffodils you planted just outside your front door could poison your child.

Third on the list of most-common human poisoning substances, plants poison thousands of children every year, and not all of the poisonous plants are out in the country or in forests; many are in our homes and backyards. Here are some plant protection tips.

- Curious children will taste almost anything and must be taught not to pick and eat anything, no matter how familiar it looks, without showing it to you first.

- It goes without saying that you have to watch creeping babies or toddlers like the proverbial hawk because they are the ones most likely to put things in their mouths. It's their natural tendency to do so as part of their "examining new things" process.

- You can get information about poisonous plants in books, from the Poison Control Center, and from your local county Cooperative Extension Agent, who will be familiar with plants that grow in your area.

- Check the tags on plants before you buy them; most tags show common names and scientific names. If you have very young children, it seems to me that it's simpler not to have such plants around. "Out of reach" is relative; who knows when a child will become a climber? If you have older children, they should be instructed not to taste.

• The two most dangerous common plants are certain types of mushrooms and oleander. Other common indoor and outdoor poisonous plants include:
  Poison Hemlock
  Stinkweed (all parts, especially the seeds)
  Hyacinth (the bulb)
  Wisteria (pods)
  Have the Poison Control Center number at hand. The best thing is to tape it directly on the phone or program it into a programmable phone.

• Keep syrup of ipecac (an emetic) in your medicine cabinet, but know when to use it. Vomiting may not always be the best solution to getting rid of something a child has swallowed. Get a good first-aid book; most drugstores have them, and frequently chain stores give away free pamphlets on first aid. Don't wait until you have an emergency to read the book or pamphlet; be prepared. The Boy Scout motto is a good one.

General Safety Tips

One of the best child safety laws to be passed in many states in the past few years is one that deals with disposing and storing used refrigerators and freezers. It's just so unfortunate that it took nationally publicized suffocations of children in discarded refrigerators to get people aware of this terrible danger. Always remove the doors of refrigerators that are not being used. Some people turn the fridge door-side to the wall, but I'm not sure that this is effective. The appliance could be moved for whatever reason and left available to the first child playing hide-and-seek.

• ALWAYS keep these items out of the reach of small children: matches, guns, knives, cosmetics, plants, bulbs, seeds, insecticides, all household chemicals, medicines, and breakable objects such as glass or china. Young children can't distinguish real guns from toys, edibles from non-edibles, and they will taste and touch just about anything out of curiosity. Most of us realize how important it is to keep things out of children's reach, but sometimes we get careless and it only takes a minute for a child to light up a match or lighter, cut a finger, or swallow a pretty pill.

• Remove the plastic spray nozzle from old aerosol cans when you discard them to prevent children from finding the cans and spraying chemicals into their own or others' eyes.

• Buy electric socket guards to keep little fingers, especially little drool-wet fingers, out of the sockets.

• You can buy plastic cupboard door guards, or if you have very young children, you can just roll up a magazine or newspaper and stuff it tightly through the cupboard hardware to make the cupboards stay securely shut. Another way is to use a bicycle lock to hook through the handles or even around knobs to keep little ones from opening doors and drawers.

• Identify your child's bicycle and your child at the same time. Either tape securely to the handlebars an index card showing name, address, and phone number or put that information on the bike with printed tape. With so many things to identify, buying a tape maker is a good investment. You could even color code each child's possessions.

Safety When Kids Help Around the House

A recent survey in the *Working Mother* magazine revealed that, in helping around the house, 8-year-olds are operating microwave ovens and vacuum cleaners and 11- to 12-year-olds are using clothes washers and dryers.
When children help:

• Instruct them on proper use of appliances and what to do in emergencies. Why not write out the instructions, maybe even take photos of the steps, and tape them above the washer or where the vacuum is stored, at eye level for the children?

• If children are allowed to cook, buy them cookbooks aimed specifically at children so that they can easily understand the directions.

• Teach children kitchen safety. So often we develop automatic safety habits and forget that novice cooks need to be instructed in such matters as using pot holders and cutting boards, in knife safety, and in what to do in case of burns.

Special Children's Care

Caring for a Sick Child

• Check out your drugstore's baby department. Many inexpensive medicine nipples and plastic spoons are available for medicine giving that don't dribble like a teaspoon and measure medicine more accurately too.

• ALWAYS give all of the medicine prescribed by the doctor, even after the child is feeling better. It's possible to feel better before all the "bugs" are out of the child's system. Old medicine leftovers should not be given to children (or taken by adults either), because chemical changes take place when medicines age that make them useless or even harmful.

• Keep a "barf" bag, bucket, or bowl under the bathroom sink or in some other convenient place. It can be placed bedside when sick children feel nauseated.

• If you have a child who tends to get carsick, a plastic bag inside a paper sack is a good emergency "barf bag." It's even more handy to have a few airline "accident bags" on hand if you are a frequent flyer and have access to them. These airline accident bags come in very handy for disposing of disposable diapers.

• Can't look into a child's throat? Try using a small lollipop for a tongue depressor. Sing the "ahh" with your child to get cooperation. Tell a young child you are trying to see the insides of her toes; she'll open her mouth to laugh.

• Many children balk at swallowing vitamins or other pills and tablets. If you can't get liquid forms, bury the pill in applesauce and see the pill go down the hatch! You may have to crush some tablets before mixing them with applesauce or other fruit puree.

• Sick-in-bed munchkins get bored even when they don't feel particularly energetic. Gather up books, coloring and drawing supplies, small toys, and games and then wrap them and label them with the time of day or order in which they can be opened. Your child will have something more fun to look forward to than just another spoonful of medicine.

• Read to a sick child. It's so hard to set aside reading time for children when TV is so distracting. Reading makes being sick an opportunity instead of just an unpleasant happening.

• Use an adjustable ironing board as a bedside sick table; it can be used to serve meals on—simply adjust the height to fit the little person. Also, to make it easier on the attendant adult, rather than running back and forth to serve food and drink, why not set up a little refreshment center? An ice bucket filled with ice, two or three bottles of fruit juice, a few plastic cups, and a plastic pitcher of water so that the bed-bound child can at least help himself to a glass of ice water or fruit juice whenever wanted.

Getting Dressed

• Trace paper patterns of clothing that already fits properly, and you can buy your child clothing without taking her along to the store.

• Zippers and snaps are easier to use than buttons when you are dressing a toddler. Anything that pulls on with elastic is even better.

• Putting shoes on a wiggly toddler is a test of stamina for both parent and child . . . unless you trap the child in a high chair so his little self stays put!

• Choosing what to wear gives children practice in decision making and encourages them to get dressed by themselves. But don't say, "What do you want to wear?" or you'll have a kid in swim trunks when you want to go to church. With very young or rebellious children, it's better to say, "Do you want to wear the blue shirt or the yellow one?" The child gets to make a decision, and you don't have to pretend you never saw that child before when you both appear in public.

• It's so basic that few people think about it: If you want your children to hang up their clothes, make sure they can reach the hanging place! The same goes for brushing teeth and combing hair; put the mirror where a child can see it!

• If you sew your children's clothing, it won't have labels to indicate which is the back and which is the front of the garment. Sew in a piece of ribbon or trim or decorative stitchery to indicate the back of garments. You can use matching tapes, ribbons, trim, or thread on garments that are to be worn together so that your child will match instead of mix.

• Mark one shoe with tape, marker, or whatever so that your child can tell the right from the left. Or mark the insides of each shoe.

• Keep shoelaces tied by dampening them before tying.

• The knees of jeans will last longer if you put iron-on patches inside the knees when they are new.

• You can make a "suddenly grown" child's winter jacket last to the end of the season by adding knitted cuffs to the jacket sleeves. Either buy ready-made knitted cuffs of matching or complementary colors at notion counters or use the ribbed ends of tube socks. As a bonus, the cuffs keep out cold air.

• Mitten clasps can hold more than mittens. They can hold a towel around a child's neck for an emergency apron or bib and they can be clipped to overall straps to keep them from slipping off tiny shoulders.

• Another way to keep those overall or skirt shoulder straps in place is to sew self-grip tabs where the straps cross.

• Fix that scuff hole in your child's rubber boots by using an inner tube repair kit from the hardware store.

• Identify your child's snow boots with colored tape or any other marking so that you will see the same boots you bought for that child come home every day. That boot pile at school has lots of similar boots, and most kids just grab and shove them on!

• If your child has a constant "slip of the tongue"—in his shoes, that is—cut two tiny parallel slits in the shoe's tongue, then pull the laces through the slots to tie as usual; the tongue won't slip down out of place. You can do this to adult sneakers too, if they don't already have tongue slits.

Having Fun with Children

Too often we spend so much time feeding and keeping children clean and safe that we forget to play with them. Children can be fun, they really can, and they grow up so fast—faster than we can keep track of. We don't want to be the kind of parent who pays attention to the children only when we tell them it's time to do something or when they need discipline . . . we don't want to be, but it's easy to slip into such a pattern unless you set aside time for play.

Working mothers are the ones who get the most "guilt trips," because they sometimes think that if they stayed home to bake cookies and be there with their children 24 hours a day, they'd have perfect children. They forget that children whose mothers stay at home can get into trouble at school or home too. Many studies have come out to show that just being at home with children doesn't always mean that you are spending time with them.

The term *latch-key children* adds to the guilt that working mothers feel. I wish we could come up with another, less grim-sounding name for these children. To me, they are "HUGS Kids"—"Heloise's Up-and-coming Go-getter Super Kids." I think they deserve hugs for learning to be independent and for being important family members and helpers. And, I think parents who teach their HUGS Kids to be self-sufficient deserve hugs too. Perhaps the bumper sticker that says "Have you hugged your kid today?" should be changed to "Have you hugged each other today?" Then, nobody would have a totally bad day, no matter what went wrong at work or at school. (Yes, kids have bad days too.)

Birthday Parties

When they have birthday parties for very young children, many parents make a rule that the number of guests equals the child's age. Huge numbers of toddlers or preschoolers often cause so much confusion that nobody has a good time, and until a child is three or more, the birthday celebration is mostly for the parents and relatives anyhow.

• Write the name, address, and time of the party in bright Magic Marker on balloons. Your invitation won't get tossed out before it's read, and the guest will have fun just anticipating the party.

• Action is the name of the game at a birthday party. Give everybody something to do. Let the guests decorate their own place mats and paper plates. Give each guest non-toxic felt-tip markers and cover the party table with shelf paper so the little artists will have plenty of room for their creativity. Even some older children will enjoy this.

• Very young children are seldom good losers, and a birthday party should be a happy occasion, not a series of tearful wails. Play games that let everyone play and win some sort of prize.

• If you have an undecorated frosted birthday cake ready and a big dish of sugar cookies, the birthday child can decorate the cake with jelly beans, candies, chocolate bits, and so on, and the rest of the kids can decorate the cookies, using instant frosting.

• If you poke each birthday candle into a small marshmallow, wax won't drip onto the frosting and discolor it.

• Have birthday cupcakes for very young children so that everyone has a candle to blow out. They are more easily eaten by small fry than cake slices anyway.

• Go to the max with easy cake eating. Make cupcakes in flat-bottomed ice-cream cones.

Fill the cones two-thirds full with batter and bake according to the timing for cupcakes. You can use different flavors of cake batter and colored cones, if you wish. Frost and/or decorate as usual.

• In a hurry with cupcakes for children's parties or school food donations? Place a marshmallow on top of cupcakes for a few minutes before they are to come out of the oven and they will be instantly frosted.

• Kindergarteners can make their own party hats if you provide old wallpaper samples, gift wrap, or newspaper comics, scissors, yarn for the ties, newspaper for making streamers, and a stapler. CAUTION: Supervise stapler use by small children; tiny fingers can fit under the stapler.

Playing with Kids

• Toddler artists love to squish and squeeze play clay into wondrous shapes. Here's a recipe you can mix up yourself: Mix in a plastic container that can be tightly sealed two cups of flour, one cup of salt, and just enough water to make the mixture rubbery and soft. Keep sealed to prevent drying out.

• You can make your own fingerpaints too. Mix one-fourth cup of cornstarch with 2 cups of cold water and boil the mixture till it thickens. Pour mixture into suitable-size containers and add harmless food coloring.

• Here's a recipe for fingerpaint or decorative play plaster: Mix two cups of soap flakes and two cups of liquid laundry starch in a large bowl. Blend with a wire whisk or an electric beater set at high speed until the mixture has the consistency of whipped cream. To color, add four to six drops of food coloring and beat the mixture again. Mix a fresh batch for each play period.

• For no apparent reason, paint containers and brush-dipping jars for water-coloring spill over when used by children. It's some sort of rule. You can avoid too many spills by cutting an opening in a sponge to fit the container and inserting it into the sponge, which will prevent tipping and absorb dribbles.

• Wrap crayons several times with masking tape, and enthusiastic little fingers won't snap them in two when creating colorful designs.

• Metal flip-top bandage containers hold crayons just like the original boxes did.

• Preserve the freshness of colors in valuable kid art by spraying the masterpieces with hair spray.

• When the princess or the prince needs crown jewels, make necklaces from dry macaroni (elbow, stars, whatever has holes) that has been dipped in water with a few drops of liquid food colors, drained, and dried. String with dental floss and a fat needle such as a needlepoint needle, which also has a larger hole for threading.

• You can make potato necklaces that end up looking like costume jewelry if you cut up potatoes into irregularly shaped pieces (the more angles the better) about one inch thick. Thread the potato pieces on dental floss, as with macaroni necklaces, so they are about twice as long as you want them to be. Allow them to dry in a food dehydrator, in the sun, just in a warm garage, anywhere where they can hang undisturbed for about a week, depending upon how humid your climate is. Each "bead" will dry to about half its original size, and the irregular shapes will become even more irregular. Knot the floss, spray paint (flat or enamel finish) the necklaces any color or use wood colored paint, and you have costume jewelry nobody will ever recognize as potatoes. (These turn out to be so attractive your children may want you to wear one to church, so be careful what you have them make.)

• Glue noodles of different shapes and sizes on the outside of orange juice cans, and leave them natural or spray paint them for pencil holder gifts children can make for adults.

• Toddlers have very short attention spans and lots of energy. They like to keep moving. Empty boxes are fun for them to sit in, push around, or pull.

• Toddlers love to pull things. Attach a string or rope to empty shoe boxes (one or two), a plastic or metal measuring cup, paper cup, paper towel tube, spool, wooden spoon, or anything else that can be tied up and pulled without making a noise that will drive you to aspirin.

• Make a "tunnel" by taking the ends out of a large cardboard box from the grocery store. Let an older child decorate the outside of the tunnel with crayons or paints, or by pasting paper shapes and comics to the "walls."

• Toddlers like to put things into other things. Give them a set of plastic measuring cups to stack and fit. Cut a hole in the top of an old shoe box big enough to allow the toddler to insert wooden spools, cardboard shapes, measuring spoons, or anything else that's safe to play with. The shoe box is fun because the toddler can take the lid off and be intrigued at what's found inside, then empty the stuff and start all over again.

It seems as though some of the favorite toys are those that are made from things at home, so just let your imagination run wild—it doesn't take much money.

Traveling with Children

The late humorist Robert Benchley has been quoted as saying that there are two ways to travel, "first class and with children."

Granted you can't take children everywhere, but it is possible to travel with children with a little bit of class, if you plan ahead.

General Tips for Traveling with Children

• Take some time to be alone with your children if you are at a large gathering of the clan so that you can talk about what is going on and who all those people are.

• Try taking along a tape recorder, and everyone gets to be a recording star. You can even make up new words to old songs and play them for grandparents when you arrive.

• Play such scenery games as finding or counting different state license plates, animals, vegetables, minerals, people—possibly in alphabetical order.

• Play mind games such as rhyming words, opposite-meaning words, and so on.

• Slates and magic slates are great substitutes for paper and pencils. An educational and always available game to play is count pennies, nickels, dimes, and quarters. But be careful—their little minds are very sharp, and you may not end up with any loose change.

• Read books. Bring along a picture album or pictures of people the children will be seeing and tell them who the people are and something about them. (Be careful—children often develop super memories when you make off-the-cuff remarks about Uncle Bob's frugal ways, Aunt Bessie's bad pies, or Cousin Hal's tippling.)

WHEN TRAVELING BY CAR

• Try to take rest stops every two hours or every 100 miles and try to have picnic lunches or light, nutritious snacks of fruit, raw veggies, or cheese and crackers.

• Pack surprise toys, pillows, blankets, clothing changes, and "wipes" or damp washcloths in plastic bags.

• Pack litter bags and have children take turns at "car litter patrol."

• When traveling by car, think about hanging a plastic shoe bag over the back of the front seat so the children can put all of their toys, loose games, and so on in the pockets. Or use a metal or plastic container with a lid to hold crayons, coloring books, and so forth; the children can use it as a lap tray too.

WHEN TRAVELING BY AIR

• When traveling by air, ask for a bulkhead seat so that you have more leg space for children.

• Ask for help from the flight attendants if you need it. Often they have coloring books, cards, and pilot's wings to give to children, which make the trip extra fun for kids.

• Relieve ear pressure on airplane takeoff and landing by having children suck on something (pacifier, bottle, hard candy, chewing gum) or have the children yawn or laugh with their mouths open to relieve the pressure.

Hiring Someone for Child Care in Your Home

Whether the sitter is being hired so that you can have a night out with your husband or friend or is being hired for daily child care while you are working, the person you hire must make your husband, yourself, and your children feel comfortable and secure.

• Check all references carefully. Call previous employers to find out exactly how well the sitter cared for other children.

• When you interview the sitter, don't be afraid to ask test questions such as "What do you do when the baby keeps crying or won't go to sleep?" You need to find out if the sitter's philosophy of child care is compatible with yours.

• For long-term daily child care, agree upon a trial period. Don't make permanent commitments until you are sure that the sitter and child are compatible.

• One of the worst guilt trips parents get is when their children cry when left behind with a sitter. Remember that at certain ages children are more apt to cry than at others. The game of peek-a-boo teaches very young children that when people disappear, they will return. Getting children ready to be left behind is an extended peek-a-boo game. You leave them for longer and longer periods until they can be left painlessly (for you and the child).

Also, you have to accept the fact that at some ages and stages children are more likely to object when left behind.

Here are some tips on conditioning children and leaving without agony.

• If the children are part of your leaving routine, they will be more likely to accept it. Have them help you find your coat or purse, have them help you carry something to the car; even make it a game of pushing you out the door.

• Arrange for the sitter to provide some distraction from your leaving, such as "Let's read a story" or getting out the crayons, blocks, games, or whatever.

• Exchange a big hug and kiss and say that when you touch the kiss-place, you will think about that child, and tell the child to think about Mom or Dad when touching the cheek or nose where you planted that big goodbye kiss.

• If nothing works and you are sure that the sitter is not an ogre, have a talk with the children (but not just as you are leaving) and ask them what would make leaving less upsetting. Most of the time, children just want to know that their feelings are important. Also, if their ideas are used, they have to prove that the ideas are valid.

• Call when you are going to be late so that everyone knows and nobody panics.

Dealing with Older Children

It's tough finding the right supervision for a child who is too old for a sitter and too young to stay alone.

Most child care experts say that children younger than 9 or 10 shouldn't be left alone on a regular basis, no matter how self-sufficient they seem to be. It's important to find some sort of supervised activity either at school or in community programs or with a home sitter. If you must leave older children alone, here are some ways to keep your children safe.

• Teach children what to do in case of emergencies such as injuries, fire, or crime. Rehearse first-aid methods, hold family fire drills, and always teach children not to open the door to strangers and not to let anyone who phones know that they are alone. Rehearse phone conversations with strangers and calling for emergency help with your children so that they know exactly what to say.

Use an answering machine and instruct the child to only pick up the phone and talk when it's someone he knows (parent, grandmother, relative, etc.).

• If more than one child is to be home without adult supervision, be sure to assign each child a responsibility and set up some structure for what activities will be allowed so that the children won't squabble.

• Make sure that children know the consequences of fighting, and follow through on whatever you and they agree will be the consequences. If you have two children who just can't get along, and this is not all that unusual, you'll just have to get a sitter.

• The best solution to problems is communication. Talk to your children about being left alone and find out what they think will make things better. Most children respond better to rules they have helped to formulate.

• Have a message center or leave cassette tapes with information on what the children are to do in your absence. Remind them of scout meetings, appointments, who will pick them up if they are going somewhere by car, and most important, which chores they can do to help the family and to help get supper on the table earlier.

• Many children feel better if you have a regular time for calling home to check if all is well. Some early teens may protest your calling, even when they really want you to call, because they think they should pretend to be totally self-sufficient.

• ALWAYS leave a phone number for where you can be reached.

• Consider a pet. A child who is greeted by an enthusiastic dog or an affectionate cat won't be lonely. Caring for the pet makes the child feel important and needed, and helps develop a sense of responsibility.

A child who is busily taking care of a pet—feeding, brushing, walking it—doesn't have time to be afraid of those "lions, tigers, and bears" that lurk between the walls and in the attics and basements of houses, waiting to scare little children!

Also, even a small, yappy dog will frighten away would-be intruders, imagined or real, and is definitely a better companion than the TV set or a battery-operated robot.

Allowances

My mail tells me that most parents do give their children allowances and that getting children to earn their allowances can become a family fuss.

• If you just can't afford to give the allowance your child asks for, try showing what happens to your checkbook balance after you pay bills. Few children realize what the cost of living is until shown in black (ink) and white or, in some cases, red (ink) and white.

• Children should make their own decisions on how the money is spent after they pay for fixed expenses; the child's birthday or when school starts or ends could be good times to make a yearly reassessment of how much money the child needs.

• Decide when the money will be paid. Weekly for very young children, biweekly or monthly for older teens. Payday should be on a specific day. Maybe on a parent's payday?

• Allowances should not be withheld as a form of punishment, nor should the child be given extra money between allowances.

• Chores are part of family living, and the child has to contribute to the family welfare. Each child should have some responsibilities, according to age and ability, and should not receive payment for doing what is expected of him. Adults don't get paid for brushing their teeth, dressing themselves, and making their own beds; it's part of daily living.

Grandparenting

Kids love to be read to by grandparents. This tip has been in my column and so well received that it bears repeating in this book. Grandparents (and parents too!) can read books and record them on cassette tapes for mailing to far-away grandchildren. Such phrases as "Turn the page" and "Rewind the tape" can be inserted at the proper times. The tapes can be mailed along with the books.

Hearing grandparents' voices helps erase some of the miles between them and their grandchildren in our very mobile society. Besides, it's fun for everyone!

• And, while that tape recorder is still plugged in, how about making a taped letter to Grandma or Grandpa?

• If you have a video camera and VCR, you can make videos and exchange them too. Everybody can be a TV star! (See more on taping in Chapter 10, "Rec-Tech.")

Families Are Forever

Perhaps the best way to close this chapter is to admit that we never really have enough time in the day to do everything, but it's important to set aside time to do the important things.

Family is an important thing. Friends come and go, jobs can give you burnout, money gets spent, and things get broken. Family lasts forever if you put your heart and soul into it, and take time to enjoy it, rather than just tend to serious matters. When you are rearing children, you only go down each road once with each child; enjoy the scenery and the company.

Working parents' time away from home doesn't have to split the family; it can hold the family together if each person in the family feels important to the well-being of everyone else.

Loving and caring are the keys, even when children are called "latch-key children" or, as I suggested earlier in this chapter, "HUGS Kids."

Hugs for everyone!

CHAPTER 7

Clothing Care

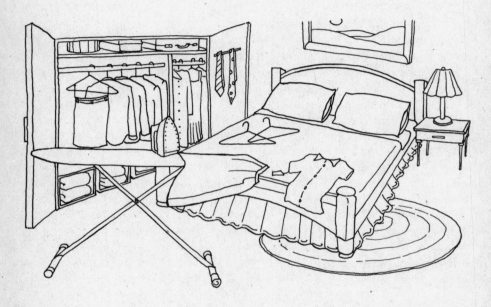

Sometimes I like to imagine what it was like to live in the biblical Garden of Eden, where all you had to do was toss away one set of fig leaves and pick another. Not only was clothing free, it was "one size fits all," and there were no colors to match, no crooked seams, no missing buttons, no stuck zippers, and, best of all, no cluttered closets or overflowing laundry baskets.

Nowadays, the price of quality and style is high. "One size fits all" usually means the garment fits almost nobody. Dye lots are such that even those of us who aren't colorblind have trouble making matches; even shades of black and white vex us. Fabrics are water-repellent, spot-resistant, breathable, washable, and, with the emphasis on "naturals," ironable. True "wash and wear" is rare.

You almost need to carry around a dictionary so that when you read labels, you know if you are capable of caring for that suit, dress, shirt, or blouse. We all have a few clothing items that should be declared as dependents on our income tax forms because they cost us so much in dry cleaning. And it isn't just women's clothing. Many men's shirts are so hard to iron the only way to get them really right is to send them to the laundry.

By the way, do you know why it usually costs more to have women's blouses/shirts laundered than men's? It's because men's shirts are standard shapes; they can be pressed quickly on a form. Women's blouses are of so many different designs that most have to be hand finished, which takes more time and, of course, costs more money.

There's a ray of sunshine in the men's/women's clothing enigma though. A few "better" (translated "more expensive") stores have begun to offer free hemming on higher-priced women's suit skirts, just as men's trousers have been hemmed as an automatic service with a sale. By no means are there enough of these stores, but a few are beginning to get enlightened. Unfortunately, some stores are becoming totally unenlightened and are charging men as well as women for hemming.

Frankly, I've always thought that hemming men's trousers is more difficult than hemming women's skirts; it might make more sense to charge for hemming pants and to do skirts for free. Women's skirt hems are shortened the same amount, front and back. Trousers are usually a bit longer (about one-fourth inch) in the back than in front and need to "break" a bit in the front. Just turning up a couple of inches on the bottom doesn't do it, especially since pant legs aren't usually straight up and down from hip to edge.

But this is not a chapter written to crusade for free hemming service; it's about clothing care. Taking care of your clothing means taking some time to read care labels, following the care instructions on those labels, and organizing your closets so that you don't have "pre-crushed" clothing everytime you want to get dressed.

Stain Removal

I think everyone has one blouse, shirt, dress, and so on, that seems to attract stains whenever it's worn. For some reason, when that bad-luck garment is worn, all ballpoint pens seem to be gooey and nonretractable, all chairs have strange stain makers deposited on them no matter where you sit, and, when you wear these spot grabbers to a restaurant, suddenly all waiters have accidents, all soup spoons have holes in them, and you're sure to fall victim to "flying lettuce" or "hyperactive noodles."

Naturally, the "flying lettuce" will have a vinegar and oil dressing and the "hyperactive noodles" will have a tomato sauce so that they will splat a superstain upon your hapless spot grabber. But then, who told you life would be stainless?

There is hope! Our friends at the International Fabricare Institute have sent me the following tips for the care and removal of stains from clothing, and I've found others that work. Here's some first aid for stain removal.

- Spills and stains should be treated immediately. The longer a spot remains, the more difficult it will be to remove.

- Blot up spills with clean, white, absorbent materials (towels, napkins, tissues, etc.).

- Do not overwet. Use small amounts of liquid and blot frequently. Always blot; do not rub or brush.

- Work from the outer edge of the spot toward the center to prevent rings.

- Remove a solid buildup of materials with a tablespoon, spatula, or edge of a dull knife.

- If you take your clothing to a dry cleaner, be sure to call attention to spots and stains, so that they can be pre-spotted. It helps if you can remember the cause of the stain, because the dry cleaner can more easily determine the appropriate remover to use.

- Never iron over a stain. The heat from the iron will set the stain, thus making it almost impossible to remove. A stained article shouldn't be placed in the dryer either.

- Always let your antiperspirant or deodorant dry completely before you get dressed. White stains will appear on clothing if it isn't allowed to dry completely and may permanently damage the material. (See "Pesky Stains," below, on how to remove this stain.)

- There are stains I call "mystery stains." They just appear after the clothing is washed, usually as brown or yellow spots.

These stains are most likely caused by any beverage that contains sugar, such as coffee, fruit juice, and tea. They are relatively easy to remove when they are fresh but become more difficult to remove as they age. They are almost impossible to remove when they have completely set.

- If the clothing is washable, spray the stain with a pre-wash stain remover spray, then wash it using a mild detergent. Repeat the process if the stain still remains.

- Never store clothing away unless it is clean. Although it looks clean, it still needs to be washed so mystery stains won't appear later.

Pesky Stains

• Baby formula: If formula stains are not removed after washing with detergent and bleach try this. Pour lemon juice on the stain and place it in the sunshine for as long as it takes. Sometimes it will work in as little as 15 minutes. If it doesn't get the stain completely out, repeat the process.

Or try this. For white, bleachable articles, place the following ingredients in an enamel, plastic, or stainless-steel container (no aluminum): one gallon hot water, one cup dishwasher detergent, and one-fourth cup liquid chlorine bleach; stir until dissolved. Put in the stained garments and let them soak for about 15 to 30 minutes. Rinse and wash as usual.

• Ballpoint pen ink: Pre-wash sprays will work on some ink stains, and I have found that aerosol hair spray works well too. Place some paper towels underneath the stain. Use some aerosol hair spray on a cloth and then keep blotting the stain and turn the cloth to clean the area until all the ink comes up and wash as usual.

Fingernail polish remover will remove ballpoint pen ink, but be sure it is safe for the fabric. (Test it on a part of the garment that isn't normally seen, such as a shirt or blouse tail.)

• Blood: Although blood stains are difficult to remove unless you get to them immediately, I have found that unseasoned meat tenderizer works well on fresh stains. Rinse with cold water first, then pour on some meat tenderizer. Let it stay on the stain for a few minutes and then wash the clothing as usual.

Try washing the stained article with a detergent containing enzymes, found on the supermarket shelf with all other detergents or bleaches. Enzyme detergents won't damage colored fabrics and work best on wine, coffee, tea, chocolate, and dairy stains.

You can also bleach the stained article with 3.5 percent hydrogen peroxide, but use caution, as this may bleach color also. Wash and rinse the article with cool water.

• Candle wax: Using the dull edge of a knife, scrape off as much of the hardened wax as possible. Place paper towels on either side of the wax-stained area of the fabric and iron on a low to medium setting; the wax will absorb into the towels. Change the towels often, as they become soiled.

If any stain remains, apply liquid detergent and water, and then rinse or wash as usual. Dry-cleaning fluid may be necessary to remove any dye from the wax.

• Catsup or chili sauce: Blot up as much of the stain as you can using a white cloth and cold water. Use an enzyme detergent as a pre-soak and launder as usual.

Hydrogen peroxide can be used on bleach-safe fabrics. Rinse with cold water after bleaching.

• Chewing gum: Apply an ice cube to the gum to harden it or place the garment in the freezer. Then scrape the gum off with the dull edge of a knife or spoon until all the gum is removed. Apply an enzyme detergent as a pre-wash spray to the back of the stain, rub in well, and wash as usual.

• Chocolate: Soak the garment for 30 minutes in cold water. Rub some detergent into the stain while still wet. Bleach will remove it, but use only with colorfast clothing.

• Cleaning-fluid rings: Sometimes these can be steamed out if the garment is held over a teakettle. CAUTION: Steam can burn; put the garment, not your hands, over the steam spout.

• Cosmetics: A bar of soap does a great job. Wet the stain and rub the soap into it. If the stain remains, use regular liquid detergent. Gently work it into the stain and then wash the garment as usual.

• Fingermarks on felt: Try rubbing the fingermarks with the finest sandpaper you can find. Rub gently with the felt's nap until the marks don't show.

• Fruit juices: Soak for about 30 minutes in cold water. Rub some detergent into the stain while it's still wet. Wash as usual. If this treatment doesn't work, apply hydrogen peroxide if the garment is bleach-safe, then rinse well.

• School glue: For school glue, apply some water and blot. Mix one teaspoon of a colorless, mild detergent or dish-washing liquid in a cup of lukewarm water and apply to the stain. Rinse with water and blot until dry.

• Grass: Apply an enzyme detergent and blot. Rinse with water or mix one tablespoon of clear household ammonia with one-half cup of water and apply to stain, then blot and rinse. Or mix one-third cup of white vinegar with two-thirds cup of water. Apply to stain and blot until dry. Wash as usual.

If the material is white and bleach-safe, use bleach according to bottle directions.

• Grease: A quick remedy for grease stains that occur when cooking is to apply some talcum powder or cornstarch to the stain. Apply just enough to cover the grease. You'll see the powder get thick as the grease is absorbed. Wipe it off and put fresh powder on, let stand awhile, and wipe it off again.

Place the stain facedown on paper towels and go over the back with full-strength liquid detergent or dry-cleaning solvent (don't mix these), using a clean, white cloth. Mechanics' hand cleaner may also be used to remove the spot. Launder as usual.

• Iron rust: Moisten the stain with water, apply lemon juice, and then rinse. You may have to repeat the treatment several times to get the stain out. CAUTION: It may be wise to test lemon juice on an inconspicuous place on the garment to make sure it won't bleach certain colors. Of course, if you can't wear the garment with the rust stain, it probably doesn't matter if it gets a bleach spot!

• Lipstick: Before washing, treat the stain with a pre-wash spray or rubbing alcohol and blot the spot with a clean, white cloth or paper towel. Keep applying the spray, always using a clean section on the cloth, or change the paper towel when you blot the spot.

You can also try wetting the article, then rubbing the stain with a bar of face soap. Wash as usual.

• Margarine or butter: Mix one teaspoonful of a colorless, mild detergent or dish-washing liquid in a cup of lukewarm water. Apply to stain and blot until dry. Mix one-third cup white vinegar with two-thirds cups of water; blot. Rinse with water and blot until dry. If all else fails, apply some dry-cleaning solvent and blot. Launder as usual.

• Mildew: Apply white vinegar or salt and lemon juice to the garment to kill the mildew. Then place the clothing in the sun. Wash as usual.

Bleach will kill mildew; follow directions on the bleach bottle.

• Milk: Soak article in warm water, using an enzyme detergent as a pre-soak product.

• Oil-base paint: A bit of turpentine or paint thinner can remove this if the fabric is color-safe; rinse well. Be sure to follow directions on the can of turpentine or thinner.

Rub with a detergent paste and wash as usual.

• Water-base paint: You will need to get to this stain as soon as possible; after this has set it cannot be removed.

Rinse the stain well in warm water and wash as usual.

• Perspiration: The International Fabricare Institute says that applying a large amount of deodorant and using cold "hard" water (high mineral, low alkaline water) when washing the garment can cause this problem.

Many deodorants and antiperspirants contain aluminum salts. When combined with laundry detergent and cold water, the salts cannot be easily dissolved and therefore remain on the fabric.

Before washing the garment, rinse the area with plain water, then wash with the rest of your laundry in either warm or hot water with good suds.

To remove fresh perspiration stains, apply diluted ammonia to the stains and rinse with water.

For old stains, try applying white vinegar and rinse with water.

• Scorch marks: Moisten the fabric, then place it in the sun. You may have to remoisten it several times. Persistent marks can be bleached with hydrogen peroxide if the fabric is bleach-safe; then rinse well.

• Pet urine stains on carpet: You'll get the best result if you get to the stain immediately.

Blot up as much liquid as possible with absorbent white paper towels. You will need to change the towels often, until no more moisture comes from the carpeting. Sponge a little white distilled vinegar on the stain to neutralize the urine. The vinegar also helps to stop discoloration of the carpet.

Blot the vinegar right away so it doesn't go through the carpet backing. Rinse by dabbing with water. Then mix two tablespoons of mild liquid dish-washing detergent to one cup of water. Apply this sparingly. Blot up any excess.

The final cleaning step is to rinse the stained area with clear water to remove all the detergent. Then, blot up as much of the wetness you can.

Place an old white towel over the wet area, then walk around on the towel. As it gets wet, change to a dry part of the towel. Keep doing this until the area seems pretty dry.

Place a dry towel over the area and weight it down. The towel will absorb any leftover moisture from the carpet and make it dry more quickly. Leave the towel on overnight. When it's dry in the morning, fluff up the carpet nap with your fingers.

• Urine stains on mattresses: Blot up as much as possible if the stain is still wet. Use upholstery shampoo on the stain and rub the spot from its outer edge to its center to avoid making it any larger. Spray with a dry fabric air freshener to prevent a musty or urine odor. If possible, put the mattress out in the sunshine to help air it. Note: Urine stains may cause permanent dye removal from fibers.

• Water on velvet: Hold the fabric over steam spouting from a teakettle for a few minutes; then shake off steam moisture until the garment is dry; then brush up the nap.

• Wine: First, blot up or rinse all liquid. Many have had luck pouring club soda on the stain, then rinsing in cool water. Many times the dye from wine is difficult to remove and sometimes impossible.

Try this: Mix one teaspoonful of a colorless, mild detergent or dish-washing liquid in a cup of lukewarm water; blot. Then mix one-third cup of white vinegar with two-thirds cup of water; blot. Then mix one tablespoon of clear household ammonia with one-half cup of water. Rinse thoroughly with water and blot until dry.

After treating the stain, launder as usual.

Laundry Tips

Following these simple guidelines will give you much brighter washes, even the first time.

You should know that not always getting bright-as-new clothing is not necessarily your fault. Manufacturers of white goods sometimes add brighteners to white fabric that wash out, partially with the first wash. This is especially true of cotton-synthetic blends. When the brightener washes out, a slight graying sometimes results.

• To get white clothing whitest, always use the hottest water safe for the fabric. If you have to use hard water, add water softener along with the detergent to increase the detergent's efficiency.

• If bleach is necessary, for maximum effectiveness add it after the load has washed for about five minutes. Never wash colored clothes with white ones, because color can easily transfer to the whites.

• Spot-treating and scrubbing the bottoms of socks, collars, and so on, before washing is always a good idea. An inexpensive way to scrub out stains is to wrap a bar of soap in nylon net, bunch it around the bar so it's rough, then tie a knot in the net or secure it with rubber bands.

• When you buy a new washing machine and are getting acquainted with unfamiliar automatic cycle changes, watch the dial closely to see where the last rinse cycle starts. Mark that spot with an arrow-shaped triangle of masking tape or red nail polish. This is the place you'll add your fabric softener. (Naturally, this is for machines without automatic softener dispensers.) Thereafter only a quick look at the dial will tell you if it is time to add softener. Mark each cycle (normal, permanent press, and gentle) the same way.

Do not overuse fabric softener, particularly on toweling. The overuse of fabric softener will cause the towels not to be absorbent.

• If your clothes come out wrinkled from the dryer, it may be that you are overloading the dryer and not allowing the clothes to tumble freely. So just wet a washcloth, hand towel, or whatever, wring it out well, and put it in the dryer with the clothes.

Let the clothes spin awhile longer, and they will be just as wrinkle free as can be.

• To remove dust and freshen drapes, valances, and quilts, put them into the dryer, turn the heat control to "air fluff," and add a fabric softener sheet.

They come out wrinkle-free and fresh-smelling.

• In the spring, save the lint you removed from the filter. Put it outside and watch the birds pick it up to use as nesting material. They'll have the softest nests in town!

• If you own a cat, be careful to check inside your dryer before you turn it on. Many a tabby, seeking a nice warm place to nap, has taken a spin in the dryer, with disastrous results. When you're in a hurry, you don't always check before you toss in a load and start the machine.

So, be careful. It's a good idea to close the dryer door in between taking clothes out and putting clothes into it. You won't have to change the light bulb so often either!

Putting Away the Laundry

• Save sorting and folding time by folding socks together as you take them out of the dryer or off the line.

The rest of the laundry seems to get folded faster, since there's no pile of socks to deal with.

• When folding clothes after washing and drying them, put fresh laundry under the existing stack (sheets, towels, handkerchiefs, underwear, etc.), so they will be rotated and the same ones won't be used all the time. Or place the fresh sheets on top and always grab off the bottom of the stack.

• Save space in a small linen closet by folding the towels, then rolling them.

• For a fresh scent, open bars of soap and put them between the sheets and towels in your linen closet and in your dresser drawers. Not only do the linens and clothes smell good, the soap lasts longer because it hardens.

• Used fabric softener sheets will also prevent musty smells wherever you store clothing or linen. Do not allow them to come in contact with silk.

• When children or adults in a household wear nearly the same size and/or have matching outfits, it's hard to tell which clothes belong to whom.

You can use a laundry pen to initial clothing in an inconspicuous place. Or, if there are several children whose clothing is unsortable, clothing can be color-coded. Assign a different color to each child and mark each one's cloth ing accordingly. A stitch of thread or dot of permanent ink marker in the child's assigned color on the neck or waist seam of undergarments and on the toe seam of socks ensures matching instead of mixing.

• Have your family help with the laundry. Tape-record detailed sorting in-structions as well as instructions on using the washer and dryer. They won't be able to use the time-worn excuse that they didn't know what to do. Or write down clear instructions of how to do these steps, from sorting, to washing, to drying, to folding/hanging, and tack or tape this up in the laundry room.

Trouble-Shooting Washers

These hints may save you a costly service call if your washer or dryer doesn't work. Sometimes it's as simple as a circuit breaker that has tripped, a loose plug, or a blown fuse.

Before you call the service agent, check the following:

1. Some washers will turn off automatically if the clothes aren't balanced. Rearrange them and push the button to start again.
2. There's a button under the lid of the washing machine that stops the machine action when the lid is raised. Check to see if the lid is closed tightly.

3. Is there a kink in any of the hoses or has the drain hose become disconnected from the machine?
4. Are the water faucets turned on?
5. Is the selector button pushed in all the way?
6. Is the plug connected? Has a fuse blown?

• To get rid of the residue left by detergents and minerals in hard water areas, fill the machine with hot water and pour in one quart of vinegar. (Yes, I know, vinegar again!) Run the machine through the entire cycle. The residue should vanish. Do this only occasionally, as overuse of vinegar can possibly hurt the inside of your washing machine.

Trouble-Shooting Dryers

Lint buildup will cause your dryer to take much longer to dry the clothing. Not only can this buildup damage the machine, but it will cost more money in electricity or gas to dry your clothes, and there is also the possibility of fire if the dryer overheats.

Here are a few tips for cleaning the filter.

• Use an old sponge-type fabric softener sheet to wipe off all the lint.

• A comb, hair-pick, pen, or pencil will remove the lint from the filter.

• Appliance service agents say that even though you "clean" the lint filter often to remove all the fuzz, a fine film forms on the filter that keeps air from circulating properly. You need to wash the filter with liquid dish-washing soap, a stiff brush, and warm water every so often. Let the water run through to remove every particle of lint.

• Here are some other trouble-shooting tips for your dryer:

1. Check the outside vent to make sure nothing is clogging it.
2. If it's a gas dryer, is the striker working properly and is the pilot light on?
3. Is the door closing tightly?
4. Has a fuse blown?

Laundromats

Here are some ideas to lighten your load if you do your wash in the Laundromat.

• Wear an apron or smock with two pockets, one for quarters and one for dimes. You can also buy a carpenter's apron at a hardware store and keep it always stocked with things you need at the Laundromat, such as change, sealable bags of detergent, tissues, and maybe a small box of raisins and a toy if you have to take children with you. Or use a heavy plastic self-sealing bag to carry laundry change in.

• Liquid detergent in the large containers is cheaper but not easy to carry. Save syrup or dish detergent bottles with the push-pull tops and use them—one for laundry detergent and the other for fabric softener.

• Powdered detergent can be pre-measured into reusable margarine tubs or sealable plastic bags so that you don't have to tote a heavy, giant-economy box of detergent with your laundry. Plastic rinsed-out yogurt cups work perfectly.

• An easy way to identify the washer and dryer you're using is to put a brightly colored magnet on it. It not only helps you, but others will know it's being used.

• Purchase three laundry baskets or bags; then, sort your clothes before washing. Or sort as you finish wearing them if you have the space. Put permanent press in one, white clothing in one, and colored clothing in the other.

When your family takes something off, they can learn to drop things directly into the proper basket. It's a great time saver, and you'll be teaching your children how to do their own laundry when they go away to school.

I'll bet the freshmen in any college can be identified by their pink socks, dyed by washing with "mixed loads." This tip, of course, helps whether you use the Laundromat or wash at home.

Several Ironing Tips

You can eliminate or at least make some garments easier to iron if you avoid overloading your dryer and if you avoid putting heavy items (large towels, sweatshirts, and jeans) in with much lighter items (made from nylon or polyester, or faux silk). Why crush one garment with another when enough air fluffing will save you energy?

Here are a few tips to remove starch buildup on your iron.

• Run your iron over a washcloth saturated with white vinegar. Place the cloth on a flat surface and run the warm iron over it several times, pressing gently. You'll see all the brown goop come off.

Now run the iron over a clean, damp cloth, to wipe off any remaining starch so that it will not mark the next garment you iron.

The secret is to clean the bottom of the iron frequently so that it doesn't get a major starch buildup.

• One way to clean a steel iron is to rub a small piece of very fine (0000) steel wool gently over the bottom of the iron.

CAUTION: Never use steel wool on a non-stick iron.

Wipe off the bottom of the iron with a clean, wet cloth and dry it well.

Turn the iron on a low setting and place a piece of wax paper on the ironing board. Run the iron over the wax paper several times. Then run the iron over an old towel or piece of cloth to remove any traces of wax. Your iron will be smooth and slick on the bottom.

• Remove the gunky buildup on a non-stick surface by spraying pre-wash spray onto a washcloth; then follow the above procedure.

• To keep your iron from clogging, use distilled water and drain it after each use. Distilled water prevents mineral buildup, the major cause of clogged irons.

• You'll find many excellent iron cleaners on the market that will remove any buildup on the bottom of an iron.

• If the manufacturer's care instructions don't advise against it, you can use white vinegar to clean the inside of your iron.

Fill the iron with vinegar. Let it steam for about five minutes, then let it rest a while. Empty the vinegar and rinse the iron well with water. Then heat it and run the bottom back and forth across a damp washcloth before using it to prevent mineral stains on your clothing.

• Iron detailed parts first so that you don't crush the rest of the garment getting at them after you have finished.

• I like to use sprays; I'm not sure if anyone mixes starch anymore, because it's so time consuming. You can choose a "fabric finish" spray to renew the "hand" or "body" of a garment or a "spray starch" to give a garment more body and stiffness.

• Some people sprinkle garments to dampen them before ironing, but if you use fabric finish, it dampens the garment and adds body at the same time.

• If you've sprinkled garments and then don't finish ironing them all in one spree, you can freeze or refrigerate the clothing in a plastic bag until you can iron again. If you just let damp clothing lie around, it will mildew or smell musty.

• Most of the time, blends of polyester and cotton will come out of the dryer either ready to wear or needing only a touch-up. Don't overload the dryer, and dry clothing of similar weight in each load. For example, if you wash a bunch of heavy towels in with cotton-polyester blouses or dress shirts and then dump the whole load into the dryer, the towels will smash up the shirts and require a longer drying time for the whole load, which ultimately means you'll have more creases to iron than if you put just the shirts and blouse into one dryer load and the towels in another.

Some of the crushed-look cottons really shouldn't be ironed or, at the most, should just be touched up with a steam iron. And whether or not you iron such things as jeans is a matter of taste and energy.

• Iron dark-colored fabrics and damp silks inside out or use a pressing cloth to prevent shine. Commercial press cloths are very good, but you can also use a cotton handkerchief or a linen dish towel if you don't have a commercial cloth.

• Iron embroidered areas from the inside. For extra depth, place them, embroidered side down, on a terry towel or soft (flour-sack fabric), folded dish towel for ironing.

• When ironing long dresses, large tablecloths, curtains, and so on, it's best to put a sheet on the floor under the ironing board so you don't dust the floor and iron at the same time. (I know it saves time to do two things at once, but this isn't one of those times when it's a good idea.) And don't forget to use the large, squared end of the ironing board for ironing these things.

• Use the temperature guide on your iron to determine which temperature goes with which fabrics. Since iron temperatures vary, test the iron on an inconspicuous spot when you are touching up delicate fabric that might melt from too much heat. Follow the temperature guide on the label or hang tag, too; that's what it's for!

• Dresses and blouses with puffy sleeves can be ironing headaches. A simple homemade sleeve roll can be made from a roll of toilet tissue covered with foil, then with terry cloth or any fabric that will withstand the heat of an iron.

• A half-used roll of paper towels, covered as suggested above, can also be used as a sleeve roll.

• A small pressing board to fit inside a pant leg, or whatever, can be made from an empty cardboard tube that fabric stores use to roll bolts of material on. Most stores throw them away, so you'll be able to pick one up. Pad it, then cover it with any desired fabric. This board can even be used as a seam board for pressing straight seams. Just stand it on its side by the sewing machine for easy access.

• A variety of pressing hams (firmly stuffed ham-shaped ironing aids especially useful for blouse/shirt and jacket shoulders and sleeve tops) and sleeve boards can be bought in sewing centers and variety stores to help you iron those parts of garments that don't lie flat on the ironing board.

Ironing Travel Hints

After a generation of drip-dry and no-iron, we've gone back to natural fabrics and, even if some of them are supposed to look "naturally crushed," many still need at least a touch-up. Here are a few travel tips, however, for when you don't have an iron handy.

• Many creases will hang out of garments if you hang them in the bathroom while someone is taking a hot shower; shower steam is a terrific travel "iron."

• I've also used a hot light bulb to "iron" garments in a hotel room.

Ironing is one of those household chores that can be delegated to teens and other members of the family, who can, at the very least, iron their own clothing and, at best, be kind to their parents and iron a few extras. Here's how to push the ol' iron over the clothes to make them wearable.

How to Iron a Shirt or Blouse

1. First iron the back of the collar, then the front of the collar. Some people like to iron the underside of the button and the button-hole facing next; some omit this step entirely.
      Some collars are cut so that they will curve around the neck smoothly. Iron these from their point toward the center, stopping short when the fabric shows a fold. While the collar is still warm, you can fold it along the seamed fold line where the collar and neck facing meet, and wrap it around your waist to curve it.
2. Iron the back and front of cuffs (also, pocket tabs if there are any; these should be unbuttoned).

3. Iron the backs and fronts of sleeves.

Some garments shouldn't have the crease that forms when you flatten the sleeve from underarm seam to shoulder line to iron it. You can buy a sleeve board to insert into the sleeve when you iron it.

4. Iron the shoulder parts—the yolk across the back, and the front yolk, if there is one.

With some garments and some ironing boards, you can do the whole shoulder area without moving the shirt, which is good. Wasted motions take up time that can be spent doing other things. When I was first learning to iron, I used to try different ways of arranging things on the ironing board so that I could iron as fast as possible. That tells you how much I like ironing, doesn't it?

5. Iron the two front sides or the front if it's one piece.

If the front parts are ironed before the back, the spray is less likely to dry out on one side while you do the back and cause one side of the front to look better than the other. The back isn't as important as the front.

6. Iron the back.

If the back has a pleat and it's important to you to have this pleat ironed, you can line up the pleat folds with the shirttail, and give them a good hard press, dampening them well and pressing dry the first time you wash the shirt. Often the lines will stay in the fabric through many launderings and be a guide for future ironings.

How to Iron a Skirt

1. Iron pocket flaps or facings, the undersides of button and button-hole facings (if the skirt opens down one side), and with certain machine-stitched hems, especially on heavy cotton or denim, iron the hem from the inside after spraying it with fabric finish to flatten it. This keeps the hem from rolling up.
2. Iron the body of the skirt.
3. Iron the waistband and, if needed, press the tops of pleats on a pleated skirt. If you are so unfortunate as to own a totally pleated skirt, you can line up the pleats and stick a non-rust straight pin at the hemline and into the ironing board to hold the pleats in place. (Bet you're sorry you bought it! And to make matters worse, dry cleaners charge by the pleat to press such garments!) And now you know why.

• If you have a gathered dirndl skirt and a bit of a "pooched out" tummy, lightly flatten the gathered areas when you iron the waistband so that they won't add more mid-section bulk.

How to Iron Pants

1. Iron pocket facings.
2. Insert the ironing board into the pants, one leg at a time, ironing the entire pant top and as far down on the leg as the ironing board will go.

3. To iron the pant-leg bottoms and put in the crease at the same time, match each pant leg seam to seam, and lay the pants across the ironing board. Tuck the pant leg closest to you under your chin so that you can work on the other leg without having the pants fall to the floor.

Starting at the hem, match the seams and iron sections until you have ironed the inside of the pant leg as far as the crotch. Turn the pants over, tuck the ironed leg under your chin, and repeat.

After both inside legs are ironed, the pants will lie flat across the ironing board so that you can iron the outsides of the legs.

• When pants have pleats at the top, the front crease needs to go from hem to the major pleat. If you use the system above, this usually happens automatically. Then all you have to do is insert the ironing board into each pant leg to touch up about an iron's width of the pleat.

• Some people like to do all this with the pants lying the length of the ironing board. It works if you have short-legged people in the house or a very long ironing board.

Ironing Boards

• If you find that you have to press hard or go over sections of clothing many times to get them ironed properly, you may need a new ironing board pad. Most of the time, we replace the cover only. We forget that we eventually iron the padding flat—too flat to be a cushion when we iron.

• You can put a piece of heavy-duty foil under the ironing board cover and over the pad so that heat is reflected to the undersides of garments, and then ironing is faster. Many of the silicone-type ironing board covers accomplish the same heat reflection.

Dry Cleaning

Professional dry cleaning is much more than just cleaning. It includes different operations performed by skilled people aimed at returning your wardrobe to that like-new appearance.

• Don't store clothing that needs dry cleaning. Any soil or stain left on a garment too long is sometimes impossible to remove without damaging the fabric. This is why it is very important to point out any stains to your dry cleaner when taking the garment in. This includes any that are light in color or invisible (soft drinks or white wine, for example). The heat from the drying process of dry cleaning can turn such stains brown or yellow.

• Frequent dry cleaning prolongs the life of a garment. Not only do stains set with age, making the garment unwearable, but ground-in dirt and soil act as an abrasive (like sandpaper), causing rapid wear of the fibers, and they can attract moths to wool garments.

• Protect your garments from perfumes and colognes, as well as deodorants and antiperspirants, by applying these items before dressing and allowing them to dry. Garments made of delicate fabrics, such as silk, can be seriously damaged by perfumes and hair sprays.

Remember, a good professional dry cleaner is the next most important thing to a good hairdresser. Be honest with them when you take in your garments and point out any stains; tell them anything that you have tried to use to remove the stain before bringing it in. They can work their miracle only if you help them. Many stains are impossible to remove regardless of what is attempted. So please remember that your dry cleaner is only human too.

Quick Clothing Repairs

• In an emergency, if your skirt hem becomes unstitched at an inconvenient time, don't be afraid to use the tried-and-true stapler. Staple from inside out to avoid snagging your stockings.

• Transparent or masking tape will hold on some fabrics. At least until you can get home to change.

• If you are near an iron, fusible tape will work to hold some fabrics. Fabric glue (sold at sewing centers) will work on others. Always test iron-on fusible tape or fabric glue on a seam to be sure you don't totally ruin the garment you're trying to quick-mend. They may "bleed through" on certain fabrics.

• The best way to mend holes in knit shirts is to iron lightweight fusible interfacing onto the wrong side of the shirt.

• Buttons with shanks can be pinned on with safety pins until you have time to sew them.

• When you need a heavy-duty repair for buttons that keep coming off certain garments, sew them on with thin nylon fishing line or dental floss. You have to cut it with scissors to remove the buttons. Hunting, work, and children's clothes and coats seem to be the chief offenders in the button-popping world.

• To extend a skirt waistband in an emergency, loop two rubber bands through the buttonhole (the official encyclopedia name for the loop knot that works here is "cow hitch," but somehow that sounds depressing when you find yourself in this situation!); next, loop the rubber bands over the button.

• If you sew, and want to make a more permanent waistband extender, take a piece of one-inch-wide elastic the length you need to extend the waistband. Sew a button on one end and put a buttonhole on the other. Put the button into the waistband buttonhole and put the elastic buttonhole over the skirt button.

Of course, if you use either of these extenders, you'll have to wear an overblouse. Also, you'll have to decide if you want to buy all new clothes or get rid of those extra waistline inches!

• Bargain garments can be personalized by replacing buttons or by adding trims and appliqués. Appliqués and trims can also hide small permanent stains or burn holes.

• If a burn hole is very small and the fabric texture allows, you can hide a burn hole by cutting a tiny piece of fabric from the seam allowance and gluing it in place (place a small piece of lighter-weight fabric underneath as backing), using fabric glue, fusible tape, or iron-on mending tape placed under the mend with stick-on side up. These mends won't hold well or have a satisfactory appearance with all fabrics, but are worth a try if you don't want to have the hole professionally mended. (With some fabric textures, frayed threads from the seam allowance can be glued instead of a small piece of fabric.)

Sewing

Sewing your own clothes enables you to be your own designer and save money at the same time. Knowing how to sew children's clothes is especially kind to a family budget.

Although I don't have the time to sew much, I appreciate the creativity that goes into making clothes and gifts and decorating homes with custom drapes, curtains, and upholstery. I've known people who have used their sewing talents to achieve rewarding and lucrative careers. There are plenty of non-sewing people around who are more than happy to pay for custom-fitted clothing and alterations.

Here are some sewing tips I think you can use, whether or not you make garments "from scratch."

- The whole skirt hem doesn't have to fall when one hemming thread breaks. When you're rehemming a skirt, knot the thread every few inches. The knots prevent the hem from opening up entirely if the thread breaks.

- Use transparent nylon thread for your sewing machine. You never have to change colors. It takes on the color of the material being used and is a much stronger thread.

- If you're sewing patches on your child's school or scout uniform pocket, slip a piece of cardboard into the pocket to keep from sewing the pocket to the shirt.

To position the patch properly, put it in place and then staple before sewing or use fabric glue to glue the patch in place; let glue dry and then sew it on.

Threading the sewing machine needle can be a challenge for some of us. Try these tips.

- Dampen the end of the thread with a bit of starch when you thread your sewing machine.

- Place a small piece of white paper behind the needle for better visibility. It works like a charm.

- For a fast spool change on your sewing machine (sometimes you want to change a color or type of thread), break the thread close to the spool already on the machine, then tie on the new color with a square knot and change the spools.

Gently pull the thread through all the tension stations and through the eye of your needle, and you're ready to continue sewing.

- One way to thread the bobbin without having to rethread the needle is to pull enough thread through the needle to start the bobbin, and place the bobbin on the bobbin-winding shaft. Then loosen the wheel and fill the bobbin as you normally would.

When the bobbin is full, remove it, tighten the wheel, and you're ready to start again. Be sure to adjust the thread tension on your machine so the thread does not break, both before and after filling the bobbin.

Using Patterns

Here are some hints for sewing clothes from patterns.

• Press the pattern before pinning it to the material. The pieces will lie flat on the material and give a much truer cut than when they are wrinkled from the pattern envelope.

• Lay the pattern out flat and measure it between seam lines. Compare your measurements to those of the pattern.

Check the following measurements: Length of body from waist to neck (bodice length), front and back; width of upper back from top of armhole seam; width across shoulder blades; armhole depth; sleeve length; width across abdomen; and skirt length. For pants, length of each leg and measurements of crotch.

• In order to avoid mistakes when altering a pattern, always make a duplicate of the pattern on a brown paper sack or newspaper and make alterations on this. Then mark the pattern itself.

• If you sew, you know that turning collars and cuffs properly is the key to a professional look. When turning the points of collars and cuffs, trim the seam close to the point as usual, then turn the collar right side out.

Thread a needle and make a rather large knot so it won't pull through the point. Place your needle as close as possible to the stitching of the collar point (place the needle on the interfaced side, being careful not to catch any material on either side).

Pull the thread through, and zip! A beautiful pointed collar. Cut the thread off the needle, close to the point of the collar. You will have no more "rounded" shirt collar points.

• When sewing, you'll have no more mess on the floor if you tape a plastic kitchen-size trash bag to the side of the sewing machine. As you cut and snip, drop the scraps into the bag. Cleanup is automatic.

• When sewing at the machine, use a magnet to pick up spilled pins and needles off the floor. You need to keep pins and needles away from children and pets for safety's sake, and using a magnet is so much less painful than "finding them" with your toes if you like to walk around the house shoeless.

• Use the dusting attachment on your vacuum cleaner to suck the lint and fuzz out of your sewing machine. (Remove the spool of thread, bobbin, and face plate first.)

It's amazing how much accumulates out of sight and can build up between working parts on your machine until the lint is like layers of felt.

• When you're ready to go shopping for parts for your sewing machine, write the name and model number on a small piece of paper and immediately put it in your wallet.

It's a waste of time to go shopping for a new belt, needles, or bobbins if you can't tell the clerk the name or model of the machine.

Storing Sewing Supplies

Organizing your sewing supplies really saves time, and, if you can find things quickly and easily, even mending can become less tedious. Here are some storing tips.

• After you have cut all the pieces out of a pattern, place them, the instructions, and all notions needed for that particular project in a plastic grocery bag that has handles. Drawstring hotel laundry bags are good storage bags too.

You can either hang each project on a hanger or lay it flat until you have time to complete the sewing. It's great if you tend to cut several projects at a time.

• You can store sewing machine bobbins in an empty prescription bottle that has been thoroughly washed. Colors are easy to find when the bobbins are stacked and kept together.

• To keep decorative lace and rickrack together, keep a plastic bag filled with empty thread spools with your sewing supplies. When you purchase lace or trimming, take it out of its package and wrap it around an empty spool, then secure it with a straight pin. You may also keep the trim on the original cards and then put leftovers on the empty spools. In either case, all the trimmings remain tangle free and ready to use on any outfit.

• A fishing-tackle box is the perfect organizer for storing sewing notions. It has compartments of different sizes, and the arrangement of the compartments is very suitable for scissors, needle threaders, buttons, and much, much more.

• To keep your spools of thread in view, drive headless nails at an angle into a peg board or on the right size of board for your needs.

Hang the board over your sewing machine and you will be able to select the color needed quickly and easily, without having to hunt for it.

• Use a bar of soap as a pin cushion. Keep the wrapper on and put the pins and needles in. Not only does it hold a lot of needles, but it makes them slide easily into fabric.

• Make your own travel mending kit. Wrap the small amounts of different-color threads left over from various sewing projects around a small, folded paper or a piece of cardboard. Add a needle threader and a small pair of scissors and you have your own travel sewing kit.

Closets

Closet cleaning may be a chore, but sometimes organizing one part of your life (in this case, it's your wardrobe) can lead to getting organized in other parts of your life.

If you don't believe me, think about the times when you are surrounded by the most household clutter. Is it when you feel as if the sun is shining just for you and the world is yours to dance on? Or is it when you feel as if the world is spinning so far out of orbit that you have lost your footing and are flying off into an outer space black hole?

The point is that when you feel in charge of your life and that everything is going your way, you can control clutter in your home and the rest of your life instead of having the clutter sneak up and control you.

Closet Cleaning

• Try to get rid of clothing that hasn't been worn in at least a year or two. I know we all say, "I'll wear that someday," and then we put it back into the closet to hang around for several more years.

• Start by taking all of your clothes out of the closet. (This is a good time to paint or clean the inside of the closet. It's also a good time to sew on loose buttons and do other repairs on clothes you want to keep.) As you put your clothes back into the closet, decide what you really want and really will wear again. Be ruthless. If you want to save the outfit you were wearing when you met that special person in your life, it's okay to be sentimental, but don't get carried away.

• Try this adaptation of the "A, B, and C" method of time management: Make three piles of clothing, A, B, C. The A clothing will definitely be kept. The B clothing might be kept. C clothing hasn't been worn for a year or so, for whatever reason, and won't go back into the closet. After putting the A pile back into the closet, go through the B pile again. If necessary, redivide the B items into A's and C's. Put the second group of A's back into your closet and make a mental note to yourself that these were almost discards. (The next time you clean your closets, if these same items are B's, they should immediately go into the C's for discarding.) Put all the C's together in large plastic bags and donate them to a non-profit group.

Donate Your Discards

• Knowing that your discards have value to somebody makes it easier to be objective when you sort the "Keeps" from the "Keep Nots." You will be helping yourself and somebody else at the same time. Battered women's shelters across the country, for example, always need women's and children's clothing, bedding, and towels, because their clients often come in with only the clothes they are wearing and obviously can't go home to get their possessions. This is where everything I "go through" is taken.

Pre-owned clothing is used by different organizations in different ways, depending upon its condition. Some organizations sell wearable clothing as fund-raising; others distribute it to needy people. Some organizations shred nonrepairable, nonwearable clothing, then sell it by the pound to rag dealers.

• Call the organization that will receive your discards to find out what it will do with them. Often, if an item is not sold during its allotted "rack life" of six weeks or so, donated items are passed on to individuals who use clothing and household items to help the homeless and others in need.

Many organizations, such as the St. Vincent de Paul Society and several other church and veterans' groups, operate thrift shops that use your donations to fund their operating costs and charitable causes. Some national organizations, such as the Salvation Army and Goodwill Industries, will repair donated items before resale, thus providing jobs for various people, including handicapped people. Such organizations will accept just about any kind of discards.

• Clothing that is too frayed and worn to be wearable can be given to groups that raise funds by selling to rag dealers.

There is no point in cleaning wearable clothing that is going to end up as rags. Conversely, it is not fair to give "almost rags" to a group that tries to maintain a presentable shop of nice, serviceable clothing. That's why it's best to call before you donate used clothing and other items. The bonus is you may find out that the organization will pick up items in your neighborhood. If the system is that you leave your donations on the porch to be picked up when the truck goes down your street, remember to clearly label what is to be picked up, with the name of the organization, or you may end up unintentionally donating lawn furniture, and so forth, that you wanted to keep!

Ending Closet Clutter

Need more hang-ups in your closets?

• Buy 18 inches of quarter-inch brass chain. Put one sturdy wood or metal hanger through the second or third link and hang it from the closet rod. Let the remainder of the chain dangle and put other hangers through the links as desired.

This is an excellent way to hang blouses, skirts, and children's clothes. You also can hang a chain in a soft garment bag so you get to use the wasted space at the bottom. Or just suspend a chain from the ceiling of your closet.

• Plastic milk crates sold in most department and variety stores can be stacked on their sides to form shelves or used to hold various items such as sweaters, shoes, and handbags, and then stacked on each other or on shelves in closets. When they're on shelves, you can just pull them out as you would drawers.

• Hang blouses and shirts in the closet according to color. Then when you're in a hurry, you can find what you need to match whatever you're wearing. And you may find, as a dear friend of mine did, that she had over thirty navy blue blouses because that was her favorite color. So now when she goes to shop, if she reaches for navy blue she closes her eyes and sees the vision of her closet and goes to another color.

• This hint helps young children who are learning to dress themselves and adults who are color-blind.

Put matching pants, shirts, socks, and even the underwear (for children) on one hanger. Getting dressed then becomes a matter of grabbing a clothing "ensemble" from the closet and putting it on. No more kids in "clown" outfits; no more beige shirts with gray suits and brown socks.

Children have parents to make "ensembles" for them. Color-blind adults need to get help from somebody who cares. Adult clothing could be numbered with laundry pens for identification and sorting, too. For example: Everything that goes with the blue suit is 1, the brown ensemble is 2, gray is 3, and so on. Of course, it's necessary to write up an index so that you don't forget and mix a 2 with a 3!

• This is a great idea for organizing children's dresser drawers. Put matching clothing in large zipper-type plastic bags and put them in the drawers. Children feel grown up selecting their own clothing, and it will all match.

• In regard to children's dresser drawers, you can help children and the sitter by labeling each drawer's front. Note the articles in each on an index card or stick-on note paper. It will save time and also a mess, since they won't have to dig through every drawer.

Storing Infrequently Worn or Seasonal Garments

• Wedding gown: After cleaning, wrap in unbleached muslin or acid-free white tissue paper, then wrap in blue tissue paper and store in a sealed box in a cool, dry place. It can last for many, many years and generations.

• Those under-the-bed boxes that are often on sale at variety stores are really convenient for storing your out-of-season clothing. They're out of the way, but still easy enough to get to when needed.

• Storing clothing in plastic garbage cans keeps it clean, off the menu of munching moths, and out of your way in your crowded closet. Lay the garbage can on its side. Start with your skirts. Roll them vertically, hem to the waistband, until you have a long, thin roll. Place the hem against the bottom of the can. If the waistband extends out of the can, that's all right.

Next fold blazers, lining side out, and roll them. Place hem side down on top of skirts. Continue with vests, slacks, dresses (fold from waist and roll).

By putting all hem ends down, the wider top portion of the can allows more room for bulk like shoulder padding in blazers. When the can is filled, stand it up and fold over skirt tops.

Place an inventory list on top of the clothes; drop in a few mothballs; if you want to, put the lid on; then seal. Store the can at the back of your closet until you need the contents again. If you store this can in an attic or dry basement, be sure to label it so that it doesn't accidentally get pitched out. You want to see your clothes again. Or place a round piece of plywood over the top of the trash can, throw a pretty tablecloth over it, and have a corner table.

It may sound unbelievable, but I got 17 skirts, 7 blazers, 4 vests, and 11 sweaters in one 30-gallon can.

• Don't ever store furs, leather, or leather-type garments in plastic bags; they need to breathe. If you need to keep them from gathering dust, cover them with old cotton pillowcases or sheets. You can also buy special "breathing" bags in notions departments for furs and leather; considering the price of such garments, a few dollars more for the proper storage bag doesn't seem like extravagance.

• Closets need to breathe too. To prevent musty odors in them, be sure they are well ventilated. Open the windows in the bedroom and open the closet doors a few hours each day.

• And NEVER put dirty clothes back into the closet. Not only will they cause odors and attract fabric-damaging insects, they won't be fresh and clean when you want them to be.

If you must hang a jacket back in the closet after wearing it and it may not be as fresh as you would like but it's still clean, turn the jacket inside out and hang it on a hanger outside the closet to allow it to breathe before putting it back into the closet.

• Always store your clothing out of direct sunlight and strong artificial light. Some of the brighter-colored fabrics and many silks can oxidize and fade.

Clothes Shopping

• Be sure to clean your closets before your next shopping trip so that you know what you have and won't buy things you don't need.

• Avoid emergency shopping whenever you can. It's a lot easier to select a special party dress or good suit that makes you look terrific if you aren't shopping for a party or job interview that's (Gasp!) tonight or tomorrow! And that's the best time to find the best bargains.

• Buy quality. Well-made clothing will fit, look, and wear better than poorly constructed clothing. Expect to pay for quality construction, but don't assume that all expensive clothing is carefully constructed. In moderate and more expensive clothing, check the following:

1. Seams should be flat and smooth. If the seams show signs of puckering when a garment is bought, they will only get worse after wear and laundering.
2. Patterns should be matched well at seams, collar, and armholes.
3. Buttonholes should be properly reinforced; buttons should be in proportion to the buttonholes and design of the garment.

4. Top stitching should be even; threads should not pull or pucker.
5. Shirt/blouse collars or cuffs that have stiff fusible interfacings should have the interfacings smoothly fused to the fabric. If they appear to be improperly fused in a new garment, they may pucker when the garment is washed, and no matter how you struggle to iron the collar or cuffs, they'll still look rumpled.
6. Trim should be sewn on properly and be of materials compatible with the garment. For example, nylon lace on a cotton blouse will surely melt at the heat you'll use to iron the cotton part of the blouse, but may be compatible with most polyester blouse fabrics. Trim such as beading should be sewn on instead of glued; glued trims don't stand up well to repeated washing or dry cleaning.
7. Check the care label to make sure that the garment can be cleaned by a process you can afford. With a few exceptions, clothing is required by the Federal Trade Commission to contain a permanent label with the care instructions. Manufacturers are required to specify only one care procedure, even when several are safe, and to warn consumers when certain garments will be damaged by certain cleaning methods.
8. Take special note of instructions for lined garments. Lining and garment fabrics may be incompatible. The result is that while the outside of the garment may be washable, the nondetachable lining must be dry cleaned.
9. Sizes vary. It's important to remember that different manufacturers and designers use different size standards. It's possible to wear size 8 or 10 in one label and still need size 12 in another label. On one particular shopping day I went from one store wearing a size 4 and 6 to three stores down, where I couldn't squeeze into even a 12. Let me tell you what that did for my psyche.

Sometimes this inconsistency in size standards makes you feel as if you have to go home and weigh yourself to make sure you haven't gained a size. Wouldn't it be wonderful if all the manufacturers would get together and decide upon standard size charts for men's, women's and children's clothing? I would think that the time saved by not having so many gifts returned to stores would make it worthwhile.
10. Check for motion. When trying on the garment, walk around and sit down in the clothing to be sure you can move and sit comfortably in it.
11. Consider when and how often you'll wear the garment. Fabrics should be compatible with your use of the garment. Obviously, fragile fabrics are better suited to special-occasion wear than they are for everyday workaday wear and the resulting frequent laundering or cleaning. Remember, very soft or loosely woven fabrics have a tendency to pill or ball up easily if subjected to a lot of friction, such as sit-fidgeting on that office chair. Certain fabrics (like rayon) lose their pleats quickly. Pleated fabrics can be expensive to dry clean, since most cleaners have cost-per-pleat rates. Lightweight wools and jerseys keep their shape and need little ironing. They make good traveling clothes.

• When you buy new clothes, note a description of the garment on the label and then save the tags in a file, envelope, shoe box, whatever, so that you can refer to them when you need to launder or dry-clean the garments.

• When shopping for a particular garment to match something that is in your closet, don't take a chance on guessing what color is right. Snip a very tiny piece of fabric from an inside seam and carry this with you to find a perfect match.

• When you are looking at a very expensive garment or even an inexpensive one, figure it on a cost-per-wearing basis. If you are going to buy the perfect smashing black dress, blue blazer, or winter coat, if you wear the garment for 4 to 5 years and wear it 10 to 20 times in a season, even if it's a very expensive garment, the cost per wearing breaks down to less than $10 per wearing to even $5 per wearing. However, if you are buying a nice little shell or tee to wear with shorts in the summertime and are going to wear it only three times or so, it isn't worth spending more than $50 dollars on.

CHAPTER 8

Personal Tips

Organizing Yourself

• Most of the well-organized people I know make lists. They use calendars, notebooks, bulletin boards, whatever works to keep track of the things they need to do. Writing it all down means never having to say, "I'm sorry, I forgot."

• Keep a small 3″ × 5″ memo book in your purse or pocket and write down whatever you need to remember. For example, if someone at a meeting asks you a question, you can call back with the answer if you have written the question and the person's phone number in the notebook. You can scribble the names of people you have just met or bits of information you might need in the future into the notebook, and then you won't forget names and facts.

Label these notebooks with the dates they were carried, such as June–December 1988, and then keep them so that you'll have all sorts of phone numbers and information handy when you need it.

• Spiral spelling test notebooks sold in school supplies sections are good for "To-Do" lists. They are about half the width of a secretary's notebook and are lined and numbered. If you have access to a heavy-duty paper cutter, you can cut a secretary's notebook in half lengthwise to make a To-Do list notebook.

• Instead of a memo book, you can buy a spiral pack of 3″ × 5″ index cards and use it like the memo book, but the advantage is that you can remove the cards from the spiral pack and file them in an index card file box.

• Believe me, if you have trouble remembering the names of people you meet at business functions, the little memo book is a wonderful aid. Writing down any information puts it more firmly into your brain's file cabinet, and if your brain is not recording that day, you can look up your notes anytime. I've even taken out my notebook in the rest room and written down the names of the people seated at my lunch table so that they will get engraved on a brain cell somewhere in my head.

• When you are given business cards at various functions, write down on the back of the card the function and the date and any other tips that identify the owner of the business card. Otherwise, you end up with a pile of business cards in a desk drawer that don't mean a thing to you.

• Keep track of birthdays and anniversaries by writing into your calendar all the important days at the beginning of the year. Then don't forget to check it at the beginning and middle of each month to make sure you'll get the card or gift bought in time.

• Some people buy greeting cards and address them in bunches every four months or so, then put the pack of cards into their bill-paying organizers (the accordion fold envelopes that have space for each month) so they are ready to go at the beginning of the month when the bills are paid. It's probably better to mail greetings early than not at all.

• One problem with paper is that you can accumulate so much of it that eventually you are buried in an avalanche of the stuff. Try to handle everything only once. Read your junk mail if it seems appealing, then throw it out. Read your bills and put them into whatever system you have for paying them. Read personal letters and answer them, or put them where they will get answered on your letter writing day.

• If you are constantly losing things right there in your own house, you have accumulated too much space-hogging, closet-cramming, shelf-sagging, aggravation-causing plain old and usually useless stuff. On a day when you are in a good mood to organize (or a bad mood that makes you want to throw things out), start tossing useless stuff into the trash or give it away to charity or anyone you know that might have a use for it. This applies to excess paper, books, magazines, clothing, whatever is your personal compulsion to collect.

Letter Writing

• If you don't have a postal scale and think your letter weighs more than one ounce, here's a "Rube Goldberg" scale to weigh envelopes that really works.

Balance a one-foot ruler on a pencil, in the middle, at the six-inch mark. Place the letter on the ruler, centered at nine inches, and a stack of five quarters (which weighs one ounce) centered at three inches. The quarters side will stay down if the letter is lighter than an ounce.

• You can write letters in secretary's notebooks whenever you are waiting someplace, such as at the beauty or barber shop, the doctor's office, in the car when you pick up children, and so forth. A tablet makes lap writing easy, and the people who care about you don't care if you have fancy stationery. When you are occupied, the waiting time seem shorter, and besides, you've used time that would otherwise be wasted. (Unless, of course, you're reading a good book—then the waiting time is never wasted!)

• If you do a lot of letter writing, you can keep track of who owes whom a letter if you make a list of those to whom you frequently write. Then, note the date you've received a letter from a person in black ink and the date you answered the letter in red ink. You can tell at a glance if you owe a letter.

• Use a highlighter pen to mark the parts of a letter that you need to answer or comment on.

• When you receive a letter, address an envelope to the sender immediately and put some stationery in it. Then you can take the envelope with you to places where you'll have waiting and letter writing time. Also, having the envelope stamped and addressed removes that stumbling block to writing for some people.

• Keep envelopes addressed to people you write to frequently so that you can insert newspaper clippings and cartoons that you think will interest that person. Then, when you are ready to write a letter, you'll have the clippings where they belong, ready to go.

• If you don't have time to write more than a short note, the clippings will show that at least you are often thinking about the recipient of your note.

• If your family is scattered throughout the country, put together a family newspaper, with each member contributing at least one article to it. Have one person in charge of gathering the information and getting it copied. Saving these newspapers in a scrapbook can provide a family history for generations to come.

• The newspaper could be compiled at Thanksgiving time, with everyone writing what they are thankful for in the past year, and then mailed so each member receives a copy at Christmas time to reflect upon as the new year approaches.

• If you and your siblings are all too involved with children, church, PTA, and work, keep a diary and send the information to each other at year's end. Knowing you are taking care of your letter writing at the same time is good incentive for keeping a diary, which is also a nice, sentimental family history. If you have a computer, keeping a diary on disk and making printouts is easy.

• Instead of writing, send pictures to small children, cut out of magazines and newspapers or hand drawn even if they are stick people.

• Don't forget to write children's names and addresses down when sending off for freebies or refunds. Children love to receive free things like that. Who doesn't?

Bill Paying

• Since paying your bills on time gets you lower rates, or at least avoids penalties for overdue payments, you need to have a bill paying system.
   Some people pay their bills as soon as they arrive; others pay on the first and fifteenth of the month.
   Some people throw their bills into a drawer and forget about them entirely. These people are called "the defendant" when they are summoned to small claims court!

• Keep track of when bills are to be paid by noting due days on a monthly or yearly calendar.

• One way to keep track of bills is to fill a three-ring notebook with pocket folders. Each month place all bills and receipts in designated pockets (car, insurance, house payments, utilities) and write the check number on the bill it was written for. You can also note interest paid, all income, and payments on the pocket folders so that at the end of the year at tax time you have all the information handy. After you have paid your taxes, you can tie up the notebook, clearly marked with what is inside and the year on it, and store it in a safe place.

• Another system would be to keep all unpaid bills in one folder, along with a list of each bill, the due date, and amount. As each bill is paid, it gets crossed off the list; the receipts, marked with check numbers and any other important information, are filed in folders designated for specific categories, such as utilities, house payments, and car.

• If you enter the phone number of the billing company into your check register, it will be handy if you have to call about a payment problem.

• Don't put messages on the outside of envelopes. Many businesses open envelopes with automated systems, so if you write messages on the outside of envelopes, they are not likely to be seen. Put messages on the bill or a separate piece of paper. Write address changes in bold letters or highlight them.

• Since automated envelope opening systems process as many as 40 or 45 letters per minute, coins or cash can actually fly out of the envelopes as they go through the opening machines. If you must send coins or cash through the mail, tape coins on the bill or a piece of paper with proper identification and write on the bill how much cash you have enclosed. Checks or money orders are, of course, much safer.

• When you send checks through the mail and wrap them in blank paper, it may slow up processing in automated systems. It's assumed that there is correspondence in the envelope, and therefore it is sent to a place other than where checks and bills go.

• If someone else is paying a bill for you, using their personal check, be sure YOUR name and account number are included for proper crediting.

• When you mail order or pay magazine subscriptions, put your code number, found on the mailing label, usually above your name, on your check for added identification.

• If your system is to do all of your letter writing, bill paying, and mail ordering in one session, you can make sure all the envelopes that need checks get them if you fold the sealing flap backward against the front of the envelope and write the required amount of money, if any, on the inside of the flap. Then, when you are finished, you can easily sort the envelopes and see which ones need checks and for how much.

• Make photocopies of all your credit cards. Put one copy in a safe place, such as a bank safety deposit box, keep one at home, and take one with you when you travel for quick reference in case you lose your wallet or have it stolen. (Obviously, you shouldn't keep the copy in your wallet!) Keeping a photocopy of all your credit cards and their numbers in your desk drawer is handy for catalog phone ordering and other bill paying.

I'm so organized I even have one of my major credit card numbers memorized, which means that I don't have to go searching for it when I find something in a mail-order catalog with an 800 number!

Keeping Yourself Healthy

Few of us can afford a personal live-in health counselor, and Mother usually gives up after you leave home, so here's a section designed to remind you that you need to take care of yourself.

Exercising

• Pick an activity and a time of day that suits you and your schedule so that you won't be tempted to skip your sessions.

• Don't exercise strenuously in hot, humid weather or within two hours after eating, because heat and digestion make heavy demands on your circulatory system. Combining these demands with exercise can be too much of an overload on your body.

• Don't wear rubberized or plastic clothing; these garments interfere with perspiration evaporation and can make your body temperature rise to dangerous levels.

• Generally, you should wear lighter clothes than the temperature would usually indicate, because exercise makes body heat. Wear light-colored clothing to reflect sun rays in the summer and dark clothing in winter.

• Warm-up and cool-down need to be a part of your exercise program so that your body gradually adjusts to starting and stopping activities.

Warm-up can be 5 to 10 minutes of walking, slow jogging, knee lifts, arm circles, or trunk rotations.

Cool-down can be 5 to 10 minutes of slow walking or low-level exercise combined with stretching.

• Walk instead of drive whenever you can. Walk up steps instead of taking the elevator. Park your car at the edge of the lot so that you will have a greater distance to walk to your destination.

• Get a dog and walk it. You can't ignore a dog that desperately needs to explore the neighborhood and inspect its trees and fire hydrants.

• Get a custom program designed by a personal trainer, join an exercise group, or get involved with a spa, community center, or YMCA or YWCA. If you develop an exercise program that you really like, you are less likely to get bored and quit.

• If you use exercise video tapes and find that jogging in place on your floor jars your joints too much, try doing the jogging phases of the tape on a mini-trampoline. A small, sturdy mini-trampoline can cost under $50, and they are often on sale. Or try low-impact aerobics.

• A medium-size adult who doesn't want to diet needs to walk more than 30 miles to burn up 3,500 calories (the equivalent of one pound of fat). If you walk one mile every day for 30 days, and don't eat any more or less food than you do in your regular diet, you can burn up one pound of fat.

• If you want to gain weight, you need to consume 100 calories a day beyond what your body needs, and then you will gain about 10 pounds in a year. However, if you want to take those 10 pounds off and keep them off, 30 minutes of moderate exercise daily will do the trick.

• Remember that exercise builds muscle tissue, which weighs more than fat, so if you are involved in a regular exercise program, your scale may not be the best way to determine if you are "fat." The ratio of body fat to muscle is the determining factor. Are your clothes tight or loose?

• When you are dieting, don't totally deny yourself the pleasure of eating your favorite foods. Just eat less of them and learn to view them as occasional treats instead of tempting, forbidden delicacies.

Eating Right

Eating right, according to the U.S. Departments of Agriculture and Health and Human Services, means eating a variety of foods; eating enough starch and fiber; drinking alcoholic beverages in moderation; maintaining your desirable weight; avoiding too much fat, saturated fat, and cholesterol; avoiding too much sugar; and avoiding too much sodium.

Here's some "food for thought" if you are planning to adopt healthier eating patterns.

• A healthy diet will include 20 to 30 grams of dietary fiber, have only 30 percent of its calories in fat, and contain a variety of vitamin- and mineral-rich fruits and vegetables.

• The typical American diet contains about 40 percent fat, despite the warning that a diet of 30 percent (or less) is healthier. It is sad that 540,000 people die each year in this country from cardiovascular disease, including heart attacks and strokes.

Cholesterol in Our Diets

The newest studies by the National Heart, Lung and Blood Institute say that cholesterol levels of 200 or below are desirable. People whose levels are 200 to 239 are considered borderline and require annual testing. People whose levels are 240 or more are considered high risk, and about 40 million Americans are in this category.

• The best way to reduce your cholesterol level is to reduce the animal fat in your diet. Meat, poultry, seafood, and dairy products contain cholesterol. Although there is no cholesterol in vegetables, fruits, cereals, and grains, these foods can contain certain saturated fats that stimulate the liver to produce cholesterol. Coconut, palm, and palm kernel oils have the same effect on your cholesterol level as animal fat and should be avoided. Read labels on packaged foods carefully to learn the fat source and content of products. You will be amazed!

• The American Heart Association recommends 300 mg (milligrams) a day as a healthy cholesterol intake.

Here's how to read labels according the Food and Drug Administration's food labeling regulations for defining cholesterol levels in food:

"Cholesterol Free" means one serving contains less than 2 mg of cholesterol.

"Low Cholesterol" means one serving contains less than 20 mg.

"Reduced Cholesterol" means one serving has at least 75 percent less cholesterol than the food it is replacing.

• Here are five ways to avoid excess fat, saturated, fats and cholesterol in your diet:

1. When choosing your protein sources, eat lean meat, fish, poultry, and dry beans and peas.
2. Trim the fat from meat and take the skin off poultry. Don't add fatty sauces.
3. Go easy on eating egg yolks and organ meats, and when you go to the dairy case, buy skim or low-fat milk and milk products.
4. Avoid fats and oils, especially those high in saturated fat, such as butter, cream, lard, hydrogenated (solid) shortenings and margarines, and foods with palm and coconut oils.
5. Get into the habit of broiling, baking, or boiling instead of frying, and limit fatty foods, such as those which are breaded and deep-fried.

A few simple changes like using skim milk instead of cream in your coffee or using a half of a pat of butter or margarine instead of a full pat are enough to make a difference in your diet. It only takes a little thought to eat as well as you can and help improve your life.

Quality Protein Combinations

Animal proteins are considered "high-quality proteins" and are readily available to the body when eaten. Plant protein sources are considered "lower-quality" proteins, because certain amino acids are either missing or not in sufficient quantities for the body's use. However, when high-quality protein foods are teamed with lower-quality protein foods, the foods are usable in the body. When you are following a vegetarian diet or combining lower- and high-quality proteins, you need to eat the food combinations at the same time so that the foods work as a team in the body.

• If you are combining animal proteins with grains, eat one of the following: a beef taco, milk with breakfast cereal, cheese pizza, a cheese sandwich, meat with Oriental vegetables and rice, milk with rice pudding, tuna with rice casserole, cheese with macaroni.

• If you are combining animal proteins with legumes, eat cheese with bean stew, chili con carne with beans, ham with split-pea soup.

• If you are combining animal proteins with seeds, eat meat with Oriental vegetables and nuts.

• If you follow a vegetarian diet (one with no animal proteins), you can get usable protein in your diet if you combine plant proteins with legumes and grains or legumes with seeds.

• Some combinations of plant proteins with legumes and grains are: baked beans with brown bread, blackeye peas with rice, beans with tortilla or cornbread (one of my favorites!), beans with barley soup, lima beans with corn (succotash), beans with pasta, peanut butter sandwich, refried beans with rice.

Salt

We need sodium in our diets for various body functions, but having certain medical problems such as cardiovascular disease, edema (swelling), hypertension, and kidney disease usually brings on a doctor's recommendation to lower salt intake. Here's how to read labels according the U.S. Food and Drug Administration's food labeling regulations:

"Sodium Free" means one serving has less than 5 mg of sodium.
"Very Low Sodium" means one serving has less than 35 mg of sodium.
"Low Sodium" means one serving has less than 140 mg of sodium.
"Reduced Sodium" means one serving has at least 75 percent less sodium than the food being replaced by this product.

• To decrease the amount of salt/sodium in your diet:

Flavor foods with herbs, spices, lemon juice.
Use garlic and onion powders instead of garlic and onion salts.

• "Heloisey"-style hints to help you reduce your salt intake:

1. Remove the salt shaker from the table.
2. Switch the tops on the salt shaker and the pepper shaker.
3. Combine half sodium substitute (i.e., salt substitute) and half salt.

Sugar

• To avoid eating too much sugar, eat fresh fruits or fruits processed with light or no syrup instead of "heavy" syrup, and avoid soft drinks, candies, cakes, and cookies.

• Sugar has many different names, but by any name the ingredient is the same—sugar. Some of sugar's aliases are sucrose, glucose, maltose, dextrose, lactose, fructose, syrup, and honey. Whether it's raw sugar, brown sugar, or white sugar, it's still sugar.

Keeping these names in mind, read the labels carefully; you will be absolutely shocked that some of the products you thought were all natural, with no sugar, actually do contain some form of sugar.

Fiber

• If you are on a weight-control or weight-loss diet, remember that starches and fiber have about half as many calories as fats, and fiber makes you feel full. High-fiber foods can also help reduce constipation, diverticular diseases, and some types of "irritable bowel syndrome."

Beverages

• Alcoholic beverages are high in calories but low in nutrition. To lose weight, try cutting out all alcohol for a month or two—you may be surprised at your weight loss.

• The National Institute on Alcohol Abuse and Alcoholism warns pregnant women not to use alcohol, because it can cause problems in pregnancy and birth defects in babies.

• NEVER DRINK AND DRIVE!

If You Need to Lose Weight

• Before eating anything, ask yourself if you really want it.

• Keep a food diary.

• Plan and set up a time schedule for meals and snacks.

• Buy a calorie book and record the calories in everything eaten.

• Measure all foods to check portion sizes.

• Drink at least one glass of water before eating. (If you are bored with water, add a slice of lemon, lime, or orange to it, or buy mineral waters as a treat.)

• Use smaller plates so smaller portions look larger. (This is especially true at buffets, where we tend to load up to fill the plate instead of taking just what we normally eat.)

• Divide servings in half, so you can have a second meal.

• Keep lower-calorie foods, like fruit and vegetables, for snacks in the most visible place in your fridge.

• Keep on hand only foods that require some preparation to make snacking a chore.

• Arrange home activities so that you don't pass through the kitchen so often.

• Find non-food ways to reward yourself. (New clothes when you get to a smaller size. A movie or other entertainment instead of an ice-cream cone.)

• Clear the table after each course.

• Throw leftover food away, give it away, or freeze it immediately. (This is especially helpful when you have a party and the leftovers are both extremely tempting and extremely high in calories!)

• Decide what you will order at the restaurant before you enter. (If you planned to order soup and salad, don't go batty when you see a "special" that will quadruple your calorie intake plans.)

• Share a serving with someone else. (Some restaurant pasta entrees are so large they serve two anyhow! Sometimes the pasta appetizer is enough for a meal.)

• Cook with a toothpick in your mouth. (But don't forget you have it there and then eat it! You need fiber, but not such large, pointy pieces!)

• Chew each bite thoroughly before swallowing. (Some people like to count bites and chew each bite a certain number of times.)

• Eat foods high in fiber. They require more chewing and make you feel fuller.

• Most sources say that you are considered "mildly obese" if you are a man with 25 percent body fat or a woman with 30 percent body fat, and are 20 to 40 percent over your ideal weight. For example, a medium-frame 5'4" woman, whose ideal eight is 127 to 141 pounds (according to the 1983 Metropolitan Height and Weight Tables), would be mildly obese if she were 25 to 55 pounds over that weight. Such a person can be treated for obesity by lay persons trained in weight control.

You are considered "moderately obese" if you are 40 to 100 percent over your ideal weight. That same 5'4" woman would be moderately obese if she were 56 to 140 pounds over her ideal weight. Such a person needs treatment by health professionals, and the treatment should include behavior modification, diet, and physical activity.

You are considered "severely obese" if you are more than 100 percent above your ideal weight. A severely obese 5'4" woman could weigh more than 140 pounds above her ideal weight. She should be under the care of a health professional, because medical complications almost always occur in such advanced obesity.

Your Skin

Dermatologists have been telling us for years that tanning causes skin cancer and wrinkles. They say that skin cancer cases have increased 1,200 percent since the 1930s, when tanning came into fashion.

In my *Heloise's Beauty Book,* I wrote that not all the "leathernecks" are in the U.S. Marine Corps; many of them are on the golf course and other places where necks get exposed to the sun regularly.

Here are a few kitchen remedies for skin conditions.

• Lemon juice is a safe skin bleach; apply to hands, elbows, knees, and so on, and leave it on for about 15 minutes. Wash and apply your favorite lotion.

• My favorite facial is the Heloise Honey Facial:

After I clean and steam my face, I apply honey and then leave it on for two or three minutes until it's sticky (some people like to leave it on for 10 minutes). Then I press in and snap out my fingers on my face—but gently! I always avoid the areas around my eyes, because that skin is more sensitive than the rest of the face. I remove the honey with a warm, wet towel or washcloth.

Honey cleans out pores, so they seem to shrink and you can more easily get blackheads out.

• Steaming your face before beginning a facial is a tip you'll get from most cosmetologists. But you don't need to rush out and buy a steamer. (A doctor told me that steamers tend to harbor bacteria and mold spores, so when you are steaming, you are also inhaling bacteria and mold spores—not a good idea, to say the least!)

Just pour hot water into a basin, tent a towel over your head, then hold your face over the water for about five minutes. You can also dip a washcloth into hot water and apply it to your face, dipping and redipping for about five minutes.

• You can use the washcloth technique while you are soaking in the tub. You can also give yourself a facial while you are soaking in the tub.

• Moisturize your skin after treatments. Moisturizers don't actually add anything to your skin; they trap the moisture in it so that it doesn't dry out, plumping up the skin cells.

The two heavy-duty, industrial-strength moisturizers are petroleum jelly and lanolin, and you'll find them in most commercial moisturizers. Other moisturizers are mineral oil, urea, stearic or lactic acid, and squalene (from shark liver oil). Urea, lactic acid, and squalene are also found in human skin and sweat. Lanolin is a very good moisturizing oil, but many dermatologists warn acne-prone people to avoid lanolin because it can cause blemishes to break out.

(And we all know when skin blemishes erupt: three minutes before your first date with someone you've drooled over for eons, on your wedding day, whenever you have an appointment with a professional photographer, and need I add more? Skin really is a mirror of our health and emotions.)

• Generally, you care for your skin by:

1. Cleaning it properly according to whether it's dry, oily, or combination skin.
2. Removing dead skin cells with washcloths, puffs, or scrubs.
3. Applying moisturizers immediately after washing to keep surface moisture from evaporating.
4. Replenishing moisture throughout the day. (I like to spritz my skin frequently with mineral water during the day.) I also wear sunscreen at all times to protect my skin from harmful rays.

• If your hands and feet get very dry and chapped, before bedtime apply olive oil or petroleum jelly, put on cotton gloves or socks for your feet, and your hands and feet will soften and be soothed overnight.

• If you have sore, red, rough, blemished, irritated skin, or if you notice any change in a mole or freckle or other skin condition changes, see a dermatologist.

If You Still Smoke

If you smoke, the U.S. Surgeon General, the American Cancer Society, the American Heart Association, the American Lung Association, and umpteen other health associations, plus the people who love you and Heloise all recommend that you quit.

• According to statistics, the number of smokers is declining overall. But the same statistics show that women are not giving up as easily. Most women are afraid to quit smoking because they are afraid that they will gain weight.

When you consider the way smoking causes wrinkles and all the wrinkle creams women buy, you'd think that women would want to quit more than they do. If you don't believe that smokers are more wrinkled, just look at someone who's over 40 and who's been smoking for 20 or more years and compare that person's face with a non-smoker's face.

As this is being written, the U.S. Surgeon General, C. Everett Koop, has declared that nicotine is as addicting as cocaine and heroin, and that most smokers kick the habit five times before they actually succeed. But you can't succeed at all if you don't try. Give yourself a break; break the habit.

Here are some tips from various sources to help you.

• You don't have to gain weight when you quit smoking. Try cutting 100 calories from your diet daily and exercising enough to burn about 50 calories. The exercise will help you feel less tense too.

• Many people crave sweets when they quit smoking. Try using artificial sweeteners and, to feel full, eat high-fiber breads and cereals.

• Talk to your doctor about prescribing nicotine gum. It's been very effective when follow-up care and behavior modification techniques are used.

• Pharmaceutical companies are researching slow-release adhesive patches, aerosol inhalers, nasal sprays, and other medications, such as antidepressants, to help ease smokers' withdrawal symptoms. The drug companies estimate that 85 percent of the 50 million smokers in this country want to quit but that it will be several years before their researched products will get to the marketplace.

• Hypnosis, according to some researchers, works about 15 percent of the time. Acupuncture has not been very effective, the research shows.

• Medical sources estimate that only about 25 percent of people can stop smoking without a program. The people who are most likely to quit and stay off tobacco are those who are quitting for themselves (to avoid health consequences, to save money), and those who are most likely to fail are those who are trying to please someone else or are personality types who must have instant results. You gotta want to do it! And you gotta keep at it!

• The American Cancer Society has a stop-smoking program that has helped many smokers to quit. The society is listed in the phone book. A call to them could be the most important call you ever make.

Having a Healthy Smile—Dental Health

• Brush and floss thoroughly at least once daily and after meals when you can.

• To make sure you are brushing and flossing properly, you can buy disclosing tablets at the drugstore. Chew these tablets after you brush, then rinse and spit out the excess. The plaque (gooey bacteria-laden substance that sticks to your teeth) that you have missed with your toothbrush will be bright red. This color isn't permanent, it's just a harmless vegetable dye. Brush again to remove the stain. Using disclosing tablets is especially effective with children when you are teaching them how to get into all the corners of the mouth.

• Here are the signs of tooth decay that should send you rushing to your dentist:

1. If a tooth is sensitive to heat, cold, and sweets.
2. If chewing causes pain.
3. If there is swelling or drainage at or below the gum line.
4. If you see a brown spot on a tooth.
5. If you have pain in the mouth or sinus trouble that doesn't go away.

• Tooth decay isn't the only way you lose permanent teeth. Did you know that three out of four people older than 35 have periodontal disease? Gum disease causes 70 percent of all tooth loss. And the real shocker is that more than half of all Americans older than age 18 have at least the early stages of gum disease; even 5- and 6-year-olds have it!

Here are the warning signs of periodontal (gum) disease:

1. Bleeding gums—if your gums bleed when you brush your teeth, it's not normal; you should see a dentist even if you don't feel pain.
2. Gums that are red, swollen, or tender.
3. Gums that have pulled away from the teeth.
4. Pus coming out from between the teeth and gums if you press your gums.
5. Loose or separating permanent teeth.
6. Your teeth fit together differently when you bite.
7. Your partial dentures or other dental appliances don't fit as they did previously.
8. Bad breath.

• Orthodontics isn't just for children anymore; adults can get their teeth straightened too, in many cases, and the old "metal mouth" look isn't always mandatory. Some people can have braces attached to the backs of the teeth.

Those Sneezy, Wheezy Days with Allergies

Those of us who suffer from allergies are the darlings of the advertising world. We consume antihistamines and decongestants, and nobody knows how many forests have been destroyed to produce the paper pulp for our nose tissues.
Here are some helps for allergy sufferers.

• See a doctor. Your allergist has a whole new battery of tests and medications to help you. Using some of the new inhalants before going where the pollen is will help a lot, and some of the new antihistamines, available by prescription, won't make you drowzy.

• Get rid of the allergens when you can. Cut your grass before it goes to pollination and seed; wear a mask when you mow the lawn to keep from inhaling the dust and pollen the mower is throwing into the air; find out when your town's peak pollen times are and stay indoors during those times; shower and shampoo immediately after working or playing outdoors to get pollen off your skin and out of your hair.

• When bedding is hung outside to air, pollen flying around in the air gets on it and is brought indoors with it to irritate you when you try to sleep in that "fresh" bed. Use a clothes dryer instead of hanging clothes and bedding outside.

• Often, people find out that they are allergic to feathers when they have a chance to sleep away from home on polyester-filled or foam rubber pillows.

• It's not uncommon to be allergic to dust mites, which live in carpets and furniture. Dry air (winter heat and summer air-conditioning) controls these mites.

• Occasionally, allergy-prone people will get some relief if the air-conditioning is not colder than 70 degrees.

• If you are sensitive to molds, you may be aggravating your allergies when you turn on your car air conditioner. Many car air conditioners are contaminated with mold spores, and most of them blast out at you when you turn on the air conditioner. If you run the air conditioner with the vent closed and your car windows open for a short time (better with you out of the car), you may get relief. You can have your air conditioner cleaned out at some car dealers and service centers.

• If you are allergic to molds, say goodbye to "real house plants," because molds grow in their soil and on their pots. If you replace your real plants with fake silk ones, don't forget to dust them, because you may be allergic to dust too.

• It's better to vacuum up dust and pollen and all the other stuff floating around and landing on the furniture if you have allergy sufferers in the house. A feather duster just throws the dust someplace else, where the poor allergy person can breathe it in just as well as if it were still on the tops of furniture!

• Yes, you can be allergic to pet dander, and yes, pets bring pollen into the house on their fur, but, like other animal lovers, I don't want to even think about getting rid of pets!

(However, if you have someone living in the house who becomes seriously ill with asthma or has other serious allergy problems from animals, you may have to consider that sad possibility.)

• If you have skin allergies, work with your allergist to find out if it's fabrics, metals (in jewelry), plants, or whatever, and then eliminate whatever you can. I know lots of people who are allergic to fabrics that contain even small percentages of wool, linen, or ramie, and many dyes can also irritate the allergy-prone skin.

The Eyes Have It

• Never share eye makeup and don't try on other people's glasses. These are ways to transmit eye diseases and infections. Some cosmetologists even say you should use a fresh cotton ball for each eye when you are removing eye makeup to avoid transferring bacteria from one eye to the other.

• Remove eye makeup by patting cleanser on closed eyelids and lashes; wipe lightly with a damp, natural sponge or soft cotton. Some of the new waterproof mascaras will come off with soap and water. You can remove eye makeup with mineral oil, petroleum jelly, or baby oil, all of which are less expensive than commercial preparations.

• Remember that nail polish ingredients can irritate eyes. When you are putting yourself together, wait until your nail polish is completely dry before you start on your face.

• Soothe tired eyes by covering them with two cold slices of cucumber or cold used tea bags while you take a 15-minute rest.

Sunglasses

So much is written about the need to protect your eyes from ultraviolet radiation that most of us know we need to protect our eyes. Eye doctors say that just about everybody needs protection in the summertime, and people who work outdoors may need protection no matter what season it is.

• Lenses should be labeled to say they meet American National Standards Institute Z80.3 standard, which means they block 95 percent of the radiation.

• Polarizing lenses cut the sun's glare, but some people find them distracting because they let you see stress patterns in some types of glass.

• Photochromic lenses darken in sunlight and lighten indoors, and although this is convenient, they may not clear completely indoors—a problem for people who have weak vision and need extra light.

• Here's a quick test for nonprescription sunglasses:

Hold the glasses at arm's length and look through them at both vertical and horizontal straight lines in the distance, such as window frames or the edges of a door.
Slowly move the lens back and forth across the line. If the line distorts, don't buy the glasses.
Also check for evenly applied color. If the lenses are darker at the top and shaded so that they are lighter at the bottom, be sure the shading is gradual.

Eyeglasses

• Getting tinted lenses in your glasses can cover a multitude of "sins," not to mention wrinkles.

• You can clean glass lenses with a drop of vinegar (Yes, vinegar again!), but don't use it on plastic lenses. Most glass or plastic lenses will come clean if you clean them with warm water and dry them with a lint-free cloth. Many instructions for glasses say not to use tissue on plastic lenses, because it causes fine scratches.

• Scratched eyeglass lenses are annoying. Try making a creamy paste of talcum powder and water in a small dish. Then rub the paste gently on both sides of the lenses and wipe it off. The talc will polish tiny scratches without making new ones.

• Avoid scratches by never putting your glasses down on their lenses. Either keep them in their case or set them so that they rest upside down on the glasses frame.

• If you are one of those unlucky souls who can't find your glasses without your glasses, try taping an eyeglass case to your nightstand or table beside your bed or wherever you take off your glasses, and get into the habit of putting them into it. Or nail a holder to the wall. I know people who have stepped on their glasses trying to find them, and I can't think of anything more inconvenient than broken glasses, can you?

Contact Lenses

Contact lenses are wonderful inventions, but a lot of my mail is about losing and finding them. It's almost as if contact lenses were made to be lost! Paying the extra money for lens insurance when you first buy your contact lenses can be a real money saver if you're the kind who loses them often.

Here are some tips that may work for hard and soft contact lens wearers.

• Try using a small spice or herb jar with a perforated plastic lid to wash lenses so that when you drain the water out, it goes through the perforations and the lenses do not. You can rinse in the same type of container. No more lenses down the drain.

• Put a towel or washcloth in the sink before you start to clean your lenses so that they don't get washed away.

• If your lens goes down the drain, you might be able to rescue it by wrapping absorbent cotton around the end of a long-handled screwdriver, wooden spoon, and so on, and then poking it as far down the drain as it will go. You might get lucky and the lens might stick to the cotton.

• If you drop a lens on the floor or on furniture, try covering the end of your vacuum cleaner nozzle with nylon net or pantyhose. You may be able to vacuum it up.

• Sometimes, if you shine a flashlight around where you think you dropped the lens, it will reflect the light and that tiny sparkle will guide you to your lens. You'll get better reflection sometimes if you place the flashlight on the floor and roll it instead of aiming the light at the floor from a standing position.

Choosing the Right Type of Contact Lens

• If you are very athletic, need extremely sharp vision for your job, do a lot of camping and traveling, and if you must have good vision the moment you wake up, extended-wear lenses may be for you. However, don't be overly optimistic about them. When the maximum time is given for keeping them in between cleanings, it means just that—maximum. You may have to remove your extended-wear lenses more often than the standard time. Ask your doctor for advice and then follow it to avoid irritation, infections, and damage to your precious eyes.

• In addition to the cost, your vision problem, lens prescription, life-style, and personality determine the type of contact lenses right for you. For example, impatient people do better with soft lenses, because they have the shortest adaptation period. Careful, reliable people will be able to deal with the extra care and frequent office visits required with extended-wear lenses.

Talk to your optometrist about the many different types of lenses before you make a choice.

The Taco Test for Determining If Lenses Are Backward

• When putting in your soft contact lens and it is on your index finger, you can make sure the lens isn't backward by bringing the edges together.
If the folded lens looks like a taco, you're holding it the right way. If it flares outward or looks like a bow tie, the lens is turned inside out.

Make Yourself Comfortable

Several of these tips are from the Arthritis Foundation and are designed to help those who suffer from this painful disease, but they can be used by any comfort seeker.

• Take the soft (pink or gray) foam rubber "tube" off a curler and put it on a pencil or pen for comfortable writing. This is such a good tip you may want to buy some curlers just for the foam, even if you never use them on your hair. They can also be put on nail files, toothbrushes, mascara wands, and eye pencils.

• Lengths of soft foam rubber insulator tubes normally used to cover outdoor pipes in the winter can be wrapped around rake, broom, mop, and vacuum cleaner handles and then held on with rubber bands or duct tape to make them easier to hold. These tubes are usually dark gray, in about four-foot lengths, and sold in hardware stores. They are slit for easy wrapping and can be cut with ordinary scissors.

• Put an adhesive bandage over the place rubbed by your scissors when you cut heavy fabric before it gets red and you get a blister.

• Tape a small piece of soft foam rubber on any finger or spot that gets abused, such as your thumb if you type a lot at a typewriter or computer.

• Save your fingernails and your temper—use a "church key" type of can opener to pry lids or poke holes in cardboard boxes.

• Quick-mend a split or torn fingernail with a drop of fast-drying glue. It'll hold until the damaged part of your fingernail grows out. If you need to strengthen the tear, glue on torn bits of white tissue paper—a smaller piece covered by a larger piece—and then file the paper to conform to your nail after the glue dries. Polish if you want to cover the mend.

• Hair tangled? Mix up some creme rinse in a "spritz bottle" and spritz those snarls before trying to comb them out.

• If you have arthritis or other hand problems, buy a plastic handle made for spray paint cans at the hardware store and use it on other household spray cans, such as cleaners, furniture polish, fabric finish, or hair spray.

• Wrapping wide rubber bands around doorknobs will give you a better grip on them. They can also be wrapped around jar lids for easier opening.

• Wrap duct or masking tape around a paring knife handle until it's fat enough for a good grip.

• No shaving cream? Don't scrape your skin; substitute creme rinse or shampoo. Apply them to wet skin.

• If you can't bend over to reach your legs when you are shaving them, tape your razor to a wooden dowel long enough to suit your needs.

• If you have to wear a soft cervical collar after a neck injury, you can keep it cleaner by wrapping it in knee-high stockings (or a pantyhose leg); they won't interfere with the self-gripping tape closure like a silk scarf will. And, since stockings come in different colors, you can coordinate them with what you wear.

Also, you can decorate the collar even more with a pin or silk flower. Anyone who's ever worn one for a long time knows how dreary you begin to feel, and decorating the collar actually lifts your spirits a bit.

First Aid for Poisoning

With so many chemical compounds stored in our homes, the danger of poisoning is very real, because many of them can have serious poisonous effects if they are consumed or inhaled, or if they come in contact with your skin.

Syrup of Ipecac and Epsom Salts

It's a good idea to keep syrup of ipecac, to induce vomiting, and epsom salts, which has laxative action, in your medicine cabinet for emergencies.

CAUTION: You shouldn't use either one unless you first check with the Poison Control Center or your doctor, because different poisons are dealt with differently. ALWAYS follow the directions given you for use of poison remedies.

The Poison Control Center Number

• If you have a programmable phone, put the Poison Control Center's number into it, and color the button red with a felt-tip marker.

• If you don't, put the number on a label and stick it on your phone. Each region has a different Poison Control number. Your region's Poison Control Center number may be listed inside the phone book cover or may be listed in the white or Yellow Pages. You can also get your region's toll-free number by calling the information number: 1-800-555-1212. Get the number today; don't wait until you have an emergency and are either sick or in a state of panic!

Teach children where the Poison Control Center phone number is and show them how to dial the number. Be sure to explain to them that it is not a game.

Common Potentially Poisonous Household Products

Here's a list of some common household products and the poisoning symptoms they can produce.

1. Cleaning products
   Ammonia, bleach, dish-washer soap, disinfectants, drain cleaners, toilet bowl cleaners—irritation or chemical burns in mouth and esophagus.
   Furniture polish—coughing, sleepiness.
   Laundry detergents and soaps—vomiting and/or diarrhea.

2. Garden and garage products
   Antifreeze—coma, blindness, convulsions, drunkenness.
   Fertilizers—vomiting or diarrhea.
   Gasoline, kerosene, turpentine, paint thinner, solvents, thinners, degreasers, charcoal lighter fluid—coughing, coma, burning irritation.
   Insecticides—headache, increased body secretions, vomiting, diarrhea, convulsions.
3. Personal products
   Nail polish remover—irritation and dryness inside mouth and esophagus.
   Perfumes, aftershaves, mouthwashes (if drunk), rubbing alcohol—incoordination, depression, coma, convulsions.
   Shampoo, soap, lotions—vomiting and/or diarrhea.

• Your medicine chest contains many wonderful health aids, but if taken to excess, your medicines can become poisons. Here are just a few of the common medicines and the poisoning symptoms they produce:

Antibiotics—allergic reactions, such as swelling, skin eruptions, breathing difficulties, shock.
Antihistamines—hallucinations, agitation, convulsions, coma, fever, depression.
Aspirin—fast breathing, ringing in ears, shock, sweating, fever, convulsions.
Camphor—convulsions, excitement, feeling warm, coma.
Cold preparations—hyperactivity, convulsions, coma.
Iron and vitamins with iron—bloody vomiting and diarrhea, shock, coma.
Oil of wintergreen—fast breathing, ringing in ears, shock, sweating, fever, convulsions.
Sleeping pills—convulsions, respiratory depression, coma.
Urine test tablets—chemical burns inside the mouth, throat, esophagus.

• ALWAYS KEEP ALL OF THE ABOVE SUBSTANCES AWAY FROM CHILDREN OR PETS. DISPOSE OF THEM SO THAT CHILDREN AND PETS CAN'T GET AT THEM WHEN THEY ARE IN THE GARBAGE.

• Never take medicine in the dark. Always turn on the light and read the container's label to avoid taking the wrong medicine or a poison by mistake!

• Dispose of old medicines by flushing them down the toilet.

CHAPTER 9

Working Couples

Working Couples

Something happened on our way from the 1960s to the 1990s. The percentage of women in the work force rose from 35.7 percent in 1960 to 55.8 percent in 1987.

By the 1970s the majority of wives were working outside the home either part time or full time, and the census figures of those years showed that only 7 percent of American families had a father who brought home the bacon, a mother who stayed home to fry it, two school-aged children who ate it, and a dog named Rover who got the leftovers.

Now, as we nudge the 1990s with another generation, many women don't expect to get married and live happily ever after by wearing an apron all day and baking pies, unless they are chefs in restaurants. Many men don't expect to be the only one in the family to bring home the "baco chips." (High-cholesterol fat/bacon is out, soy-protein "baco" substitute is in!) With or without children, the two-income family has become as "normal" as the "Leave It to Beaver" Cleaver family was in the 1950s.

Certainly the refrigerator door, bulletin board, or whatever is used as a message center is the core of a working couple's relationship, especially if their hours don't coincide. Keeping track of where everybody is becomes even more complicated when the couple has children.

Whether they are "yours, mine, or ours," according to many reports children are being nurtured by both parents instead of spending most of their time with their mothers.

When both people in a marriage travel in their work, they almost need to make appointments with each other to discuss important matters and just to make the kind of small talk that binds people together.

I know about this problem firsthand. I travel a lot, giving speeches and promoting my Heloise books and column, which is in five hundred newspapers. I have to keep in touch with my editors and readers so that I can produce a column with information they can relate to. I can't get a real feeling for what is going on with people across the country if I stay in my office. Reading my mail, of course, is a major contact with readers, but seeing them in person is very important.

In the middle of all this, I am a wife and a stepmother, which means I have to keep some sort of balance between my work and my personal life. My husband, David, also travels in his work, which means we have to make time so that all three of us can be together.

Taking Self Time

Like the other women in the United States who perform this double juggling act, I have to set priorities and then rearrange them every now and then. And, like the other jugglers, sometimes I have to let certain chores go so that I can have time with the people I love, and sometimes I have to allow for self time so that I can recharge my personal batteries and keep my enthusiasm going for everything I do.

One of my favorite ways of celebrating self time is to just take a day off, and, if possible, lounge around in bed catching up on my reading, watching TV, or whatever helps me escape. I even fix my meals on a tray and eat them in bed, as if I've been served by a personal maid and butler. Since I schedule this self time, I don't feel guilty about taking it. People who make lists can put self time on the list and then check it off just like the other completed "tasks."

Also, I don't think such self time is only for women; men need it too. Perhaps couples could trade off weekend self days, taking turns being the maid/butler for each other.

Or why not take selves time, and both take the day off together? And, if you don't want to lounge around, remember that not all vacations need to be out of town; anyone can play tourist wherever they live.

Dining In and Out but on the Run

Cooking from scratch was a matter of pride in Grandmother's day, but now even Grandmother takes shortcuts. A stroll through the supermarket shows you the many meals that need only be reheated or have one ingredient (such as meat or fish) added, and in 20 minutes you have dinner. I wonder if the idea of adding the chicken or shrimp (or whatever) was developed to keep us from feeling guilty about thawing or opening a can of something for dinner without adding any personal touch to it.

Eating Out

Here are a few tips on eating out that may help you lower your bill.

• To get a reservation at a very popular restaurant, try calling late in the day or shortly before you want to leave the house to see if there have been any cancellations or no-shows.

(Of course, if there haven't been any, you'll be looking for a place to eat without a reservation and will have to go to a less popular restaurant.)

• Ask the waiter if you and your companion can split a course. If the answer is no, decline to order it. But much of the time, rather than lose money, the waiter will probably agree.

• Consider going out to lunch instead of out to dinner. Often, lunch costs as much as 50 percent less. The portions are smaller, but with so many restaurants serving such large portions anyway, eating lunch out just means not having to ask for a "people bag."

• When you're eating out, here's one way to confirm restaurant coffee freshness: If cream swirls up brown, you have a freshly brewed cup of coffee; if it swirls up gray, the coffee has been on the burner too long. (I guess that if you don't put cream in your coffee, you probably can't confirm what your taste buds are telling you.)

• Does computing 15 percent for a tip tax your brain's math department? It's easier to do in small bites. Use your mental math to take 10 percent of the bill, then add one-half of that 10 percent for a total of 15 percent. For example: If your bill is $17 and some change, figure 10 percent of $17 is $1.70; then add half of that amount (.65) for a 15 percent tip of $2.35. Then, you can round the tip out to $2.50 if you wish. Or buy a "tip card," available in greeting card shops and some bookstores.

Eating at Home

Eating at home is still the least expensive way, and so many new products are on the market that in some cases cooking at home is "fast food."

To add to speedy preparation, the new foods are microwaveable and in single five-ounce portions for those who eat alone or for those who eat with people who don't share their tastes for certain foods. Single portions mean never having to eat someone else's favorite vegetable!

• Single-portion frozen desserts are diet aids. You can't have seconds because there aren't any, unless you like to eat piesickles!

• If you live alone and think it's too much trouble and mess to cook for one, consider cooking for yourself and a neighbor, as in "I'll make the casserole if you make the salad, and let's have dinner together." Couples can do the same, especially when you and your friends want to eat out but can't afford to do so. Potluck dinners aren't only for church get-togethers! Eating at someone else's house is eating out!

A Place to Live

An apartment lease is one of those standard-form legal documents that people may not read carefully enough to know the difference between landlord's and tenant's rights, which causes all sorts of trouble later on if terms of the lease are violated by either one.

• Most leases are drawn up by landlords, so if you are the tenant, remember whose side the lawyer was on. READ CAREFULLY! If you are the landlord, make sure your rules are in the lease.

• In addition to paying the first and last months' rents, you will be asked to pay a security deposit. Be sure to read what that deposit will cover. Nail holes in the wall may be a reason for not returning that security deposit.

• The lease will tell which repairs are made by the landlord and which by the tenant. If you are the tenant, keep all receipts for repairs or cleaning (such as carpet cleaning) in case you need them in small claims court for getting your security deposit back.

• Find out what a "clean" condition actually is, according to your lease, and when you move in, make note of all existing damage, soil, or stains.

• Take photos of furniture and carpeting when you move into a furnished apartment in case you need to show how worn they were when you moved in. Or even ask your landlord or apartment manager to stand in the photo with you. If you are the landlord, photos will show how new the furnishing were when the tenant moved in. Include a sign or newspaper with a date to prove when the photos were taken.

• Landlords and tenants need to agree on certain provisions, usually found in the lease's fine print and often not read by novice apartment renters. Here are some of them: Restrictions on children, pets, using an apartment for a home office, appropriate dress in the lobby/common areas, cooking on balconies, pot plants on windowsills, radio/TV antennas, storage and parking areas, the landlord's right to enter the apartment with or without notice whether or not the tenant is home, any additional services provided by the landlord, and, finally, conditions for eviction and terminating the lease.

• If you need to move before your lease is up, find out if the landlord will let you find another tenant to fill the apartment so that you won't be responsible for rent payments. Permission to sublet from the landlord does not release you from legal obligations to the landlord under the lease.

• You need permission to sublet if you want to rent part of your apartment to another person, or you can have the new person sign the original lease as an additional tenant, with the landlord's permission.

• If you are the landlord, be sure to tell your insurance agent if the apartment is furnished or unfurnished and then figure the additional insurance for a furnished apartment into the rent.

• If you are renting a furnished vacation cottage or home, you should store valuables and take photos of each room, major appliance or furniture pieces, and the exterior of the house, in case you have to make insurance claims because of damage or theft.

Money Matters

Because two-income families have more money to spend, they have a greater need to know how to manage their money. Standards of living tend to rise with income, so "rich" is relative. You go from having enough money for your "needs" to having enough money for your "wants."

Many couples get into financial trouble. This is especially true of couples who, instead of shared financial communication, have "his money" and "her money" arrangements, and don't ever get around to talking about how much "total money" they have.

Managing the Budget

• Money management experts believe that each partner should have some money that is separate from the family account that can be spent without mutual discussion and agreement.

• Couples planning to have a baby and have the wife stay home for a period of time to care for the baby might want to live on the husband's salary and save the wife's income as a nest egg for the extra expenses they'll have because of the baby.

Saving Tips

• If you have trouble saving, use payroll savings plans so that a certain amount of money gets saved with each paycheck.

• Make savings a fixed part of your budget instead of something you do with leftover money (there is no such thing for many people). Save a fixed amount, whether it's $20 or $200 per month, and put this money in an interest-bearing account so that compounded interest will make the account grow.

• Check out the different accounts offered by your bank to find out how much interest your savings will earn. Often you'll need to maintain a minimum balance of $500 to $2,500 or more to earn interest. Be realistic about the minimum balance that you can maintain.

Setting Up a Home Office

When you set up a home office, designing it to suit the one who uses it most of the time makes sense. If both "heads of household" work at home, it may be better to have "separate but equal" home offices if you have the space. Keeping a desk is such a personal thing that few people can share one. And it's always the messy ones who marry the neatophiles, isn't it? Although my main office is at one end of our house and David used to share an office off of that, he decided he needed his own space, because he said my secretaries' chatter was driving him crazy.

Finding Office Space

• Look around for nooks and crannies that will serve as an office if you don't have a separate room to use.

• If you don't have a separate room, do you have space for a fold-up, built-in desk so that you can confine your work and cover it up when you want to protect it from curious children and leaping cats?

• You can easily hide a corner-office mess from view with a three-panel screen.

• The dining-room table is a favorite working place because of the large working surface of the table. If your dining room isn't in the mainstream of traffic and if you seldom use it, the dining room may be a good office, but metal filing cabinets probably won't enhance its decor, and so you won't be able to keep everything you need in the same place.

Home Office Hours

• If you work at home in a home office, you have to develop a work schedule, even if it's a flexible one. It's too easy to procrastinate when you are your own boss and can take all the coffee breaks you want because the pot is there in the kitchen.

• Get a DO NOT DISTURB sign and have a place to hang it in your office; then make sure the rest of the family knows what it means. It's hard for a family to grasp the idea that someone who is still in the home is actually at a job, especially if that someone is Mom! Believe me, I know; I still haven't explained this to Zinfandel, the schnauzer, or Sheba, the keeshond. They just can't believe that I am really working.

Tax Breaks for Home Business Offices

According to a recent survey by the New York consulting firm of Link Resources, more than 11 million women are working from their homes with full- or part-time businesses.

• If you run your own business from your home, the IRS allows deductions only if you use your office exclusively and regularly for business, whether it's just a desk, a room, or a whole floor. The details can be found in IRS small business information booklets. Call your local IRS office to obtain them.

• Here's an important tip for people who use home office deductions: These deductions can become a liability if you are required to pay capital-gains tax on a fraction of the profit of a home sale equal to the proportion of household expenses you've deducted from your taxes. To avoid this, you need to convert the office back to personal use before the year of your house sale.

• Another important tip: Home-office deductions may flag your tax return for an audit, so it's best to consult a tax professional, keep extremely careful records, and follow the law to the letter.

Office Furniture and Equipment

• If you like the large surface of a dining-room table and have an extra room for an office, there's no rule that says only a desk can be a desk! A dining-room table from a used furniture store, with or without leaves, can be a desk. Remember when you used to study in the library at those large tables? You can have that atmosphere too. Just make sure your chair is the proper height for your desk/table.

• A prefinished hollow-core door mounted on two file cabinets, sawhorses, or concrete blocks can be a desk. You might need to use self-gripping fabric strips or dots or double-sided carpet tape to keep the door from sliding on metal file cabinets.

• Don't forget the old student bookcase of boards and brick stacks. You can buy prefinished boards for your brick-and-board bookshelves.

• Multicolored plastic "milk crates" can be used for files. You can even color-code what you store with these. Depending upon the casualness of your home decor, these crates can be part of the decoration because of their colors, or they can be stacked in a closet. Small plastic baskets from variety stores can hold "in" and "out" stuff.

• Use fiberboard cubes for bookcases and files, and to support a door/desk. These cubes, usually sold unassembled, are often on sale at hardware stores. When you paint fiberboard, you need to brush on a base coat. If you try to spray paint a first coat on fiberboard, you'll find that it absorbs paint like a sponge. It will take so many cans of paint to get a nice finish that you will wish you had bought a ready-made bookcase (or whatever) instead of trying to "do it yourself."

• These cubes also hold long-play record albums and are very sturdy when stacked on their sides.

• When you are selecting a chair to go with your desk, match the seat height to the desk for your comfort. If you will be spending long hours at the desk, your legs shouldn't dangle. If you know you are going to be spending a lot of time sitting on this chair at your desk or work station, it might just be worth the investment to buy a very good adjustable chair. It will save you many aches and pains in the long run.

• For comfort, the table for a typewriter or computer keyboard needs to be three to four inches lower than standard desk height. If you don't have a typing table or computer furniture of the ideal height, adjust your chair accordingly.

Personal Computers

Perhaps computers are the most prominent of the new hi-tech electronics in United States homes and offices. Adults who didn't learn about computers in school have been pushed into the computer age by their jobs. Many adults learn about computers from their children, who view them as ordinary classroom equipment, on the same level with the pencils and Big Chief tablets their parents used in "the olden days."

Computers are really a blessing for columnists like me who have lots of irons in the fire, or documents in memory, if we're going to speak "computerese" in this chapter.

The "Hints from Heloise" column is produced on computers and word processors, and my secretaries—Kelly Moravits, Ruth Rozelle, and Joyce Buffolino—and I marvel at how fast we can get our work out now. I don't know how we managed without them.

All the information used in my columns is checked and edited by me and by my staff and editors. Computers enable us to send copy via modem to each other and then to discuss the columns on the phone or on the modem "chat" mode within minutes. What used to take weeks takes only days, and sometimes only hours.

As with all new technology, there's a lot of information that's not in the manuals, many of which are hard to understand unless you have a doctorate in computer sciences (and maybe not then!).

General Computer Use Tips

A lot is learned by trial and error.

• For example, in my office, we learned that, if several people will be turning a computer on and off, a note on exactly how to do this should be taped on the computer or near it. We almost had a service call because we thought one of the computers was not working. Actually, someone had turned off the monitor and computer by using the individual switches instead of the power surge protector's main switch the way the person who usually works on that computer turns it off; then someone else saw the red button lighted up and switched off the power surge protector. The next morning, when the power surge protector was switched on, nothing happened.

We "entered" the instruction "use the power surge protector switch only" into the "memory" and then put notes by all the computers just in case somebody's brain got a "delete" command.

• We've also learned that when many people are working on the same document, it's hard to keep track of who has done what and when. That's why we put messages at the top of each document to serve as a history of that document, listing the different document names it has had, dates, and to whom it was sent by modem. The person working on the document notes the date she worked on it and a short description of what she did—just a phrase or word, nothing elaborate. I always note the date when I have seen and done the final editing of the material. This way, we all know what's going on and if the document we call up on the computer is the most recent one.

You can find commands in your software to mark the first page of notes so that it doesn't get printed when you print the document.

You can call up this information from your computer, but it's a time-saver if you can see everything you need to know about the previous work on a document when you call it up.

• Here's a hint on saving computer repairs from my computer consultant, David Kantor: It is better for your computer circuits to be turned on and left on for the day than turned on and off many times. Each time you turn on your computer you have a surge of power going through it, he explains, so the fewer turn-ons the better.

• If you need to leave your computer for a break, leave it on but dim the screen to black or turn off your monitor, because leaving documents on your screen for long periods of time can actually burn impressions into your screen.

Power Surge Protectors

• My researcher, Marcy Meffert, learned from a very expensive experience and from my computer consultant, David Kantor, that unless the bar of outlets into which you plug your computer equipment actually has "Power Surge Protector" printed right on it, it is really just a heavy-duty, multiple-outlet fancy extension cord. One stormy day in New Orleans, a power surge occurred while she was starting up her floppy disk-drive computer, and it badly (and expensively) damaged the disk drive. (She no longer boots up computers during storms, even with the power surge protector.)

• Many computer owners use computers in older homes in newly renovated city neighborhoods. If you are one of these people, you may want to have the power company check your main power lines. Often older homes (about 50 years old and more) have had numerous additions and changes in the electrical systems while retaining the same power lines run to the house when it was new and have had to supply only electricity for lightbulbs and MAYBE a refrigerator. The drain of microwave ovens, freezers, and other modern technology, including a computer, may be too much for such inadequate lines. The resulting frequent power surges and power outages can damage your computer or disk drives if they occur when you are using your computer.

• You may want to run a separate line for your computer if you have it on most of the day or night. Marcy, who lives in an older home, had numerous and very expensive problems with her computer and disk drives until she had new lines (more than twice the thickness of the old ones) installed by the power company to her fuse box; ultimately she had a separate line installed for her computer.

Transporting Disks

• My computer consultant says that although airport X rays and security gates may not damage your computer disks, it is safer NOT to let them go through the security system, because they CAN be damaged. Ask the attendant to hold the computer disks while you and your baggage go through security.

• Heat can damage disks. The temperature of the air in an automobile can be oven hot when the sun's rays beam in on car windows. Floppy disks kept in a car can warp or suffer other types of damage. You can help your disks keep cool by putting the disk caddy into an insulated box, such as a soft-drink cooler, while you are transporting them or by leaving them in the car for short periods. It's probably better if you just don't ever leave them in the car in the summer or in very warm climates.

• Store disks away from light and such heat sources as windowsills, hot desk lamps, and heating/cooling vents.

• Although some people put labels and indexing information on disk jackets, it's really more efficient to put the labels on the disks in case they get mixed up. Just remember never to write with ballpoint pen on a labeled disk, because it may damage the disk; use felt-tip markers.

Working, Writing, Editing, Saving, Moving Copy Around

• I have learned that keeping your fingers low to the keys with the palms of your hands almost touching the base of the keyboard makes typing faster, but everyone has to experiment to find the best way.

• Sometimes moving papers from one side of the computer to the other is all it takes to break the monotony and relieve neck strain of long hours at the computer.

• I like to use a clip stand to hold printed copy beside the computer.

• Having a telephone beside your computer is a must even if you don't have a modem; I have my phone on the wall beside my work station to keep it out of my way. With the phone beside the computer, I can phone various institutes and agencies to get information and then type it right into the computer as I get it. Also, I can call up documents when conferring with my editors so that I've got the copy we're discussing right there before me, where I can add notes and changes right away.

• Try keeping self-stick notes beside your computer so that you can stick them on the side of the monitor or nearby wall to remind you of copy changes, new names of documents, things to do, and anything else that pops up while you're working and don't want to interrupt your train of thought.

• Marcy found that because her new keyboard was more sensitive than the one on her first computer, she sometimes tapped the "enter" key accidentally whenever she was deleting to clean out her files and thereby deleted whatever document was listed first in the index.

Her previous work was on floppy disks only, so when she'd see the file delete, she'd forget about her new hard disk "bak" file and practically fall to the floor in a sobbing heap thinking she'd deleted hours of work. Now, to prevent panic, she keeps a fake document titled "1AAAA" in her files. All "1AAAA" says is "This is a fake document." If she accidentally deletes "1AAAA," she keeps her cool. Using the number 1 and four A's ensures the fake document of being first in the index.

• When you move paragraphs or sections around in a document, usually you save them by moving them to a glossary or under a certain document name on the disk and then call them up to insert them where you want them.

Most of the time, you will never need to see these document parts again and they will just clutter up your indexes and have to be "killed" or erased at some point.

• Here's a timesaving tip on how to avoid this clutter: If you always save temporary document parts under a certain name, such as "graph" or "thing" or another name that's never given to other documents you want to save, the computer will overwrite the previous document part saved under those names and you won't have lots of useless little bits and pieces taking up disk space and confusing you when you call up the index.

• When using certain software, you can delete parts of documents and save them elsewhere on the disk. The command to the computer is to delete from the cursor to the last word of the section you want to delete.

Since the last word of the section you are deleting and saving may have been used elsewhere in the document or in that section, the computer may delete to the wrong place. However, if you type your name at the end of the section to be deleted, you can tell the computer to delete as far as "Zelda" or "Helmut," which are words not likely to be used elsewhere in the text.

• To avoid having to read through all sorts of documents on the "doc" menu of a hard disk computer when she calls up whatever she's working on, Marcy usually considers any "doc" file document that has been worked on and sent to its destination as "finished" and "filed out of sight," so she deletes it from the "doc file." It's still on the "bak file" of her hard disk if she needs it for reference or rewriting.

• Like anyone else who is prudent, cautious, and scared to death losing hours of work (AGAIN!), each of us has learned to back up on a floppy disk any document that has been worked on during the day or has been designated as "finished," as an extra precaution.

• When working on floppy disk drive computers, you can provide back-up copies by making two copies of each document, each on a separate disk, just in case the "microchip monsters" decide to zap your circuits or damage the disk.

• Save time looking up small segments of miscellaneous information from your index by creating a "trivia" or "misc" file. Giving each small segment a separate index name soon clutters your index, and usually you forget what the names represent and waste time calling each one up to find out what it says.

• When you are typing in a correction, put in the correction before you delete even a single word, so if your mind hasn't "saved" the information, it's not gone to that big glossary in the sky (or wherever such info goes), never to be retrieved again.

Buying a Computer

• Get a company that services what it sells, offers training programs, has a good track record in your area, and has experienced consultants to help you select your software and hardware.

• With computers, you think about software first. You don't buy equipment and then find out what it can do. If you are familiar with certain softwares and know which ones you want to use, be certain the computer (or less expensive "clone" of a brand-name computer) that you select will operate the software that meets your needs.

This sounds elementary, but many people walk into shops, buy any Brand X computer, and then find that it doesn't do what they want it to do. For example, it's possible to bank by personal computer via modem, but you need a computer that has software enabling you to do such things.

• Some people may need only a word processor instead of a computer; others may want to do desktop publishing, which can't be done on all computers or with all printers. Still others may need desktop models that can fold up into a drawer, closet, or briefcase each day.

• If you have to keep your computer tucked away on shelves inside an armoire or closet instead of on a desk or table, you'll want one that has a lap keyboard so that you don't have to move all of your equipment out each time you need to use it.

• Make a list of what you want to do with your computer and printer, and where you'll use it, so the store consultant can help you make the best selection; and, like when you are making medical care decisions, get a second or third opinion. Read computer magazines if you can understand them.

Learning How to Use It and Getting Rid of Computer Phobia

• My best tip for getting rid of computer phobia is to play some games on your computer. Once you see that you can touch every one of the keys without creating a disaster or losing everything that's in it, you'll be more comfortable doing actual work on a computer.

• If you really are so certain that you'll lose your work, practice double caution for peace of mind: Make duplicate disks and always keep one of them out of the computer while you are working. You can't add or delete on a disk that's not even in a disk drive. You can also stick the little protector tabs that come with disks on the notch of your duplicate disk so that the "file" is "locked up."

• Computer training is available at many computer stores, and you can often hire a consultant to give you one-on-one lessons for an hourly rate. To get the most for your money when you hire such a consultant, schedule the training session for a time when you won't have any interruptions from telephones or visitors. Read the manual BEFORE the lessons and practice a few simple steps so that you'll know what questions to ask once you are "on the meter" and paying for time.

• Adult education classes are offered at many colleges and universities, but find out if the classes will work with the brand of computer you have bought, or sign up for an introductory course before you buy.

• Many large cities have computer clubs, some of which have sub-clubs for different computer brands. Club members train each other and share tips.

Dealing with the Glare of Computer Screens

• Tinted lenses in your eyeglasses can reduce glare. Use brown tints to reduce the glare of green text and blue-tinted lenses for amber text.

(If you have untinted plastic lenses, you can get them tinted to suit your computer needs. Also, you may be able to get the tint in your eyeglasses changed. See your optometry shop for advice on your type of lenses.)

• If your home office includes a computer, place the computer so that the screen is not getting a glare from windows or lights. You can buy glare-reducing screens for some computer monitors, and if you can't get a screen for your specific model, measure the screen, buy a glare-reducing screen that will cover the monitor's screen, and attach it with stick-on self-gripping fabric tape or dots.

Computing in Comfort

See the home office section in this chapter and then get tips from other computer owners on how they set up their equipment.

• Some work station arrangements cause people who wear bifocals to have to tilt their heads at an angle that allows them to read computer screens through the bottoms of their lenses, a position that's a real pain in the neck.

The solution is to get plain reading glasses made up with the prescription of the "bifocal bottoms." If you find optical chain specials of "Buy one, get one free" or reduced prices on second pairs of glasses, make that second pair your computer glasses.

• If your chair is a bit too high and/or your legs are a bit too short:

A phone book makes a good footstool, and the bonus is that you always know where it is!

Try wearing wooden clogs, wedgies, or some other thick-soled shoes when you work at the computer. You can "raise the floor" from one-half to one or more inches with shoes, and sometimes that's all you need! If you like to walk around barefoot or in socks for comfort, you can keep your "computer shoes" under the desk or worktable, ready for slipping your feet into when you sit down to work.

• Give yourself a break—literally. Take a break from your computer every now and then to walk around, stretch your legs, unkink your muscles, and refocus your eyes. Not only will you feel better, your work will go more smoothly if you don't push yourself into "lock" positions.

(It helps if you have a dog that just has to have a walk every few hours. Then you'll not only get a walk but some fresh air at the same time! The bonus is that you can tell the dog all about your work and get positive feedback every time.)

Speaking Computerese

It helps to know the language when you are in a foreign land, and for most of us the computer is a foreign territory. Here's a mini-dictionary of a few of the most basic terms to help you with the language of computer use.

BAUD: A baud is like "miles per hour" on your car. It's a measure of how fast data go through a port. A modem's measure is "baud rate," which means the higher the rate, the faster the information is transmitted.

CPU: Central Processing Unit, which means it's the computer without keyboard or monitor.

DATA BASE: This is really the "files"—the stored information. The categories in this file are called "fields," such as last names, phone numbers, address categories.

DOS: Disk operating system—this is the computer's "brain," and without a DOS you just have some silicon chips in a box.

DISKS: These are your computer "file cabinets."

Floppy disks: Not really floppy at all, these square 5¼" or 3½" diskettes have replaced the magnetic tape used with the first computers for data storage.

Hard disk: A hard disk can hold nearly 28 times as much data as one 5¼" floppy disk. Unlike floppy disks, which are inserted and removed from disk drives, the hard disk stays inside your computer.

MODEM: The name comes from what used to be an acronym for "modulator-demodulator," and what it really does is to let your computer talk to another computer via the phone lines.

MONOCHROME: A single-color monitor, mostly amber or green. A monitor that is like a color television set is an RGB monitor (red, green, blue monitor).

MOUSE: A type of "pencil" or "pointer" that lets you draw and edit on the screens of some computers.

PC: Stands for "personal computer," and it's a generic name, even if it was started by a well-known computer maker.

PC COMPATIBLE: Because IBM has been considered the standard computer, software designers made software that would run on IBM PCs, and this software is called PC compatible.

PORT: A computer name for "connection." You plug your printer into the appropriate "port."

Parallel port, serial port: A parallel port sends information through the cable by ranks, while a serial port sends it in a single file. Frankly, most of us aren't concerned about HOW information is sent. We only care about IF it's being sent. However, it's nice to know what your repair person is talking about if this term is used.

RAM and ROM: RAM means "random-access memory" and is the part of the computer's memory that YOU can use, as opposed to ROM, which is the "read-only memory" part of the computer's memory, which the COMPUTER uses to do its work.

SOFTWARE: These are the programs that are used by you and your computer to do whatever it is you bought the computer for. Without them, you might as well not have a computer at all.

SPREAD-SHEET PROGRAM: Helps you to put numbers together.

WORD PROCESSOR: This is the "typewriter" part of the computer, which helps you edit, move information around inside the document, and in some cases check spelling.

Computers as Household Helpers

You can make all sorts of forms to help you keep records easily. Here are just a few.

• Make a shopping list "form" that enables you (and everyone else in your house) to check off items you need, and magnetize it to your refrigerator door. You'll have a shopping list made out and ready to go when you are. Leave some blank lines to add seldom-bought items.

• Print a form on business envelopes to keep track of your trip expenses. (If you open the flaps of the envelopes, the envelopes will ride piggy-back on each other on the printer roller.) Take the envelope along with you on the trip and put all receipts in it, and then you'll be organized when you sit down to add it all up.

Here's a sample of what to print on your envelope.

Trip to: .... Date: ....
Purpose: ....
Expenses .... $ ....
Amount reimbursed .... $ ....
Amount to be declared on income tax as gain/loss .... $ ....

• Make a form to keep track of your calories or food units when your doctor or dietician gives you a diet.

• Special software advertised in health/nutrition magazines is available by mail that enables you to plan a diet for nutrition and calories. Such softwares have the calorie, fiber, fat, and nutritional content for as many as 1,500 different foods, and some even include analysis of fast foods from national restaurant chains so that you can calculate what you eat out as well as what you eat in.

• The repeat function used in making diet charts is also useful if you want to add short (just a paragraph or two), newsy notes to a mail-out like Christmas cards or birth announcements. Just fill a page with duplications of your short note, perhaps with a dotted line at the end of each duplication to serve as a cutting guide, and print. Cut the note strips apart and tuck one in each envelope.

• If you put your favorite recipes into the computer, all you have to do is print them out when someone asks you for them or if you are taking them to a potluck supper where recipes are requested.

• Collectors can make forms to use for recording dates of purchase, prices, appraisals, and any other information about the things they add to their collections.

• Menu forms and To-Do forms for entertaining and other "remembering" can be printed on computers.

• Letters to family members can be done on the computer. Just do a segment of general news and then add a personal message to each person receiving the letter at the top.

Note: If you always add the personal message at the top, you won't forget to change the name after "Dear ———."

• Here's a tip on a sticky subject: Computer games are fun for the whole family, but if you make a rule about no sticky foods being eaten while "playing computer," you won't have to clean off your computer after every family session. Liquid of any kind is a no-no!

Printers

• Some printers use either film or nylon ribbons. Since the film ribbons, which print more clearly and one time only, are more expensive than nylon ribbons, which print until you replace them, it saves money to use the nylon ribbons for first drafts and family letters and to use the more expensive film ribbons for final copies of reports and documents.

• You can also save older nylon ribbons and use them for first drafts and letters. Then, use new ribbons for final copies and other documents.

• A tractor feed, optional on some printers, helps to keep the paper from becoming slanted when you are printing long documents. If you don't have a tractor feed and if the weight of the printed pages drags on the paper feeder, making the pages of a long document crooked, it'll help to tear off your document every 20 or so pages.

• One of the problems with new technology is that we tend to look for complex solutions to simple problems.

For example, Marcy's printer feed appeared to be shredding the continuous-roll paper edges. After wasting time checking out the feed mechanism, she looked into the paper box itself, where she found tufts of cat hair. It seems that her paper-box-loving cat, Hexe, was sneaking into her office at night and nesting in the paper.

Now she guards it from cat attacks by putting it on a small stool that, with the added paper box height, just barely fits under the printer's table. Hexe still lurks around the stool but can't get into the box.

CHAPTER 10

Rec-Tech: Television, Stereos, Cameras, and More

Today's Technology

H i-tech has flipped our switches all over the country.
Even people who were around before the automatic pop-up toaster are using programmable microwave ovens and VCRs, and even some of our coffeepots have computer memories.

Let's face it, the American love for doing it fast has spurred hi-tech development onward to the point where half the homes in the United States have VCRs so that people can tape and view movies instead of merely watching TV. Hi-tech electronics is here to stay, and if we use it efficiently, it will help us instead of making our lives more complicated.

General Tips

• I know it's been said before, but it can't be said too often. Always keep the instruction books that come with your audio and video equipment in your household appliances file.

Each camera, and tape, record, and compact disc player has its own operating instructions, and whatever you did before and even some of the tips in this chapter may not work with your present equipment. Also, your booklets provide information about model and parts numbers when you need repairs, and have instructions for preparing the equipment for moving.

• If you don't understand the directions in the booklet that comes with your equipment, call the help phone number, which should be printed somewhere in the booklet, or call information (1-800-555-1212) to find out if the manufacturer has a toll-free consumer help number.

• Always keep all your equipment—cameras, tapes, records, and compact discs—away from direct sunlight, heat, and humidity. Never cover ventilation slots while the equipment is in use; trapped heat causes serious damage.

• Deliberate misuse can void the warranties of electronic equipment.

• Sometimes you can make substitute covers for your VCR and some other types of electronic equipment from various plastic bags, plastic by the yard, or, in some cases, a rectangular plastic dishpan. But most of the time, the covers sold for these appliances will fit better and do a better job of protecting the equipment from dust and moisture.

CAUTION: Always remove protective covers when using any electronic equipment to prevent heat damage!

• Before you make a service call for any electronic equipment that malfunctions, always check all switches, control knobs, and connections to make sure they are properly set. Seems obvious, but sometimes we get so wrapped up in what we are doing that we forget to the check the obvious and to perform all of the start-up steps.

• Always have any electronic equipment that has been dropped or exposed to water or moisture checked by a professional to ensure against electric shock or fire hazards.

• The Electronic Industries Association says plugging electronic equipment into a voltage surge suppressor is a good idea, because it will protect such rec-tech appliances as your VCR from power line surges. However, it doesn't protect against direct lightning strikes.

• When you have any electronic device repaired, have the service technician verify that the manufacturer's specified replacement parts have been used. Use of proper replacements prevents fire, shock, or other hazards. Also, ask the service technician to perform all safety checks noted in the service manual when the repair is completed.

• If you keep a service history on your equipment either in a notebook or on index cards, it will help you remember if and when you've cleaned your video or audiotape heads, the last time you had the stylus checked by an audio equipment dealer, when you've had any of your equipment professionally serviced, and so forth.

At the top of the page or note card, write the name of the equipment, the model and serial numbers, and installation or purchase date. Then record the dates you've cleaned it yourself or had it professionally serviced.

Make notes on professional services that include who did it, the type of service or repair, its cost, and your comments, such as "had to wait a week for parts, too expensive, find other service person."

If you cleaned the equipment yourself, note what cleaners you used, how you used them, and if you had any problems. Also note when you changed batteries and fuses.

Such maintenance records need not be elaborate, just short comments that will save you money in the long run and keep your equipment at its best performance.

• Here's a good shopping tip:

Sometimes, two heads are better than one. If you have a friend who is as confused about hi-tech equipment as you are, try researching together. One person could shop around gathering information from store brochures and sales people, and the other could gather consumer information magazines and other publications. Then, together, you can make a plus and minus chart of the benefits of different brands and help each other figure out what to buy.

You might even talk a salesperson into discounts, since you are buying two sets instead of one—asking for discounts is always worth a try, and you'd be surprised how often you'll get them. Think of the discount you'd get if your whole exercise class was buying!

Television

• Fuzzy television pictures don't always mean that something is wrong with your set. Before you call the service shop—and don't think this is silly—try cleaning your screen. And don't be too shocked at how much dirt a screen can collect! Wipe the screen with a damp, soft, clean cloth and then let it air dry.

- CAUTION: Never apply liquid or aerosol cleaners on the screen, and unplug the set before any cleaning.

- If you have a projection television set, do not touch or attempt to clean the screen; you may damage it beyond repair. Call a service professional.

- High winds or birds landing hard on an outdoor antenna can put it out of line. If you notice a change in reception, check to see if your antenna is bent or turned, or if its lead-in wires are worn or corroded. Installation and repairs of outdoor antennas should always be done by professionals.

- If a picture is bad on just one channel or if you get no picture at all on one channel; read your instruction book to see if your set has an Automatic Frequency Control (AFC) switch on the back. If so, turn that switch off. If the picture improves, readjust the fine tuning until you get a good picture. Be sure to turn the switch on again when you change channels!

- You can get interference (static noises and lines) from too many electrical appliances plugged into one outlet, a CB radio in the neighborhood, a nearby high-voltage tower, or, in some cases, from placing a VCR on top or beneath your TV even if there's a wood shelf in between.

- Projection TV sets often have a darker picture than your regular set. You may have to darken the room a bit to get better contrast.

- Does your TV schedule disappear? Punch a hole at the top, loop a string through the hole, then tape the other end of the string to the TV set each Sunday when the new schedule comes out.

- When you look through your weekly TV schedule, use a highlighter pen to mark the shows you want to see during the week so that you won't miss them.

Home Satellite Television

- Urban-area satellite dishes get more interference than rural ones. If you get interference, call the phone company to find out if you are between any phone relay stations. Television transmitters, Air Force radar facilities, and amateur radio transmitters may also cause interference. To minimize interference, you'll need upgraded and special equipment, such as a feed horn designed to minimize interference.

• Protect the dish from weather by installing it away from prevailing winds or providing some other sort of windbreak. If you decide to protect the dish by installing it in a pit, provide adequate drainage.

Video Cassettes and Recorders

• Never stack video tapes, TV schedule booklets, or anything else on the recorder. "Insulating" your recorder with stacked stuff keeps all the heat it generates inside and will ultimately cause deterioration and a service call. Your recorder and cable box need "breathing space" to keep their cool.

• Here are the four things to think about when buying a video tape recorder and some tips for enjoying it.

1. If all you use a video recorder for is playing rented movies, the most basic equipment is fine.
2. If you like to record TV shows for future viewing, look for models that are easy to set up ahead of time for automatic taping.
3. If you record a lot of programs and want to cut out the commercials, remote control is a must, and most models come with it now.
4. If you have invested in expensive video-cam equipment, you'll need a more elaborate type of recorder that allows you to edit and dub tapes.

• Many video shops have special prices for mid-week rentals, and mid-week is when you're more likely to get popular movies.

• Remember to reset the video tape machine clock if you've had a power outage.

• When taping a show, set the "on" time for five minutes earlier than the show's start time and five minutes past the show's scheduled end to make sure you don't miss anything.

• Identify the shows you've taped to save by clipping out the review from your newspaper's TV guide and then tape it onto the video tape cassette or its jacket with the clear plastic tape (¾" covers a review) that you can write on, and you'll know what the film/show is about and who starred in it.

These reviews fit nicely on the tape/jacket side, and if you are taping a series or several shows on one tape, you can usually get three to four reviews in a row on the wide edge. It doesn't matter if the transparent tape overlaps; you can write short notes or numbers on the tape if you need to identify parts 1, 2, 3.

• To avoid taping over a show that someone wanted to watch, stick self-stick notes on the tape jacket to record the date, show, and names of the people who want to watch it. As each watcher is finished, the name is checked off; the last watcher removes the note, which signals to everyone else in the house that the tape is free for recording again.

• To avoid taping over a "keeper" tape, use the "lockout tab" that's on all video tapes. When you remove the tab, the VCR is automatically "locked out" from recording on the tape. If you change your mind and decide not to keep the tape, you can put a small piece of adhesive tape over the lockout hole and record on it again.

• Have a family plan for keeping the remote control mechanism in a specific place; otherwise it will always be so "remote" that nobody can find it.

• Take a tip from fast-food restaurants, which keep their cash registers clean by covering them with plastic: Put your remote control mechanism into a zippered plastic bag, and the TV munchers can press all the buttons without making them icky.

• If you don't have a remote control mechanism with your older recorder, but have cable, you can rent remote control for cable.

• If you have an old-style plug-in remote control mechanism, tie bits of brightly colored ribbon on various places of the cord so people won't trip on it and dislodge it from the recorder.

• If you are an enthusiastic videophile and took a lot of home movies or collected movies before you bought a VCR, a tele-cine adapter, sold at many electronics stores, lets let you convert home movies or film slides to videotape. Commercial film companies can also do it.

• Many recorders allow you to record your favorite programs even if you are gone for a week. When you are learning how to program your VCR, do some practice programming to make sure you have mastered your VCR's system. Practicing when mistakes won't matter prevents losing the shows you want because of incorrect settings.

• Check the TV listings at the beginning of the week, set your VCR to tape the shows you want taped, and then let the VCR remember the taping sessions that are so easy to forget.

• Use a highlighter pen to mark the programs in your TV schedule so you can see at a glance what you've chosen to tape.

Videotape Care

• Keep videotapes away from any heat source to prolong tape life and preserve recorded material.

• Store recorded videotapes vertically to protect them from dust and dampness.

• Tapes should be fast-forwarded and rewound at least once a year.

• Always take up tape slack before playing. Wind the cassette hub with your finger until it's tight. You can run new tapes on fast forward before using to remove any slack unevenness.

• Never take tapes from cool to warm places just before playing them. If moisture condenses on the tape, it will stick to the video head.

• Beware: A tape left on top of a TV set can be erased when the TV is turned on due to the TV set's magnetic field. (Computer diskettes stored near telephones can lose information stored on them, because phones contain magnets too!)

Caring for Your VCR

• Many unnecessary service calls are made because of bad connections. If your VCR is connected to a defective cable converter box (which is, in turn, connected to the TV set), the VCR won't record properly even if it plays prerecorded tapes. Try connecting the VCR directly to the TV set. If it works properly, you'll know to call the cable company instead of your VCR repair service.

Tape heads get clogged by oxide particles that chip or flake off from tapes. You can prevent clogging by using quality tapes (labeled "high grade" or "super high grade"), which don't shed oxide easily. Discard tapes after about 100 hours of use, and clean tape heads regularly.

• If the picture is distorted or has tiny white flecks, the tape heads may need cleaning. Use the head cleaning system suggested by your VCR instruction book or the one below.

• If you use a commercial tape head cleaner tape, please follow the directions explicitly. Run the tape for only 10 to 15 seconds or whatever the exact time prescribed on that specific tape. Longer is not better. It will only tend to gum up the tape heads more.

Portable VCRs/Camcorders

• These wonderful rec-tech devices should never be left in intense heat. When used outdoors, they should never be pointed directly at a bright light source. Bright lights can burn pick-up tubes in cameras that have them. Direct light can damage the CCD (charge couple device) in cameras that have them.

• Clean the lens with a soft cloth or brush, and keep the cover on when the camcorder's not in use.

• To protect your camcorder, check out the rain and thermal covers available from equipment stores. If you use your camcorder in cold weather, a thermal cover will protect it for operating at less than 32 degrees Fahrenheit and from condensation when you take it indoors from the cold.

• Keep a plastic bag in your equipment bag so that you can protect your camcorder from moisture damage when it rains.

• Never travel with a portable VCR that's not protected from shock and moisture by a hard case or custom-fitted shock bag. Also, let the camera get adjusted to extreme changes in temperature before you try to operate it.

Here are some trouble-shooting tips.

• Color balance: Check for adequate lighting and proper setting on the color temperature correction switch. Also check to see if the white balance needs adjusting.

• Color rendition: Check scene lighting, if color temperature correction switch is set properly, if color control knob needs adjusting, if the color setting on the TV set or monitor needs adjusting.

• If the fade switch is on, the VCR won't pause immediately when the trigger is squeezed.

Videotaping Tips

• Many of the cassette-taping tips can be useful for videotaping. You can voice your comments and descriptions on the newer video recorders so you don't have "silent movies." In that same vein, when you are videotaping family events, remember that the idea is to film moving people even if you have them standing together. You can use a still camera for "picket fences" of family members frozen in position.

• Like TV reporters, talk while you film with your camrecorder. Record your "Gee whiz!" feelings instead of just descriptions and straight information. If you record impressions "on site," you won't sound like a dull travelogue later and will better capture those special moments.

• Use your camcorder to film antiques and family treasures. Describe them while you are filming them, as someone shows all sides and the manufacturer's marks on the bottom and, if they are gadgets, demonstrates how they work. Add any anecdotes about the treasures.

• Film a party and have guests tell their favorite jokes. Then, years later, you can decide if the jokes are still funny. Or each guest tells a favorite guest-of-honor story.

• Treat your taping sessions as if you were making a TV documentary:

Start your party filming with pre-party cooking and other preparations; finish with the cleanup.

Start wedding films by showing the bride putting her makeup and veil on. If available, you could start a wedding film with some footage of the bride and groom that led to this important occasion. Have the camcorder scan the bridal pictures of the newspaper's wedding and engagement announcements page, leading to the announcement of the engagement or wedding.

Show the "locknut A's" being joined to "toggle bolt Z's" when a child's bike is being assembled and then show the child learning to ride it.

Film a few scenes of the pool's construction and then show your family enjoying the new pool.

• You can also have fun using your imagination and newspaper headlines or book jackets for titles, even if they are only semi-appropriate. For example, *A Tale of Two Cities* or *Europe on $5 a Day* could be the title for your vacation trip film. "Hurricane Gilbert Leaves Path of Destruction" could be the title preceding your after-party shots or a film of children playing after they've totally emptied a toy box. *The Joy of Cooking* could be the title preceding a barbecue scene. "Classified" cut from the want-ad section could be the title for just about any tape.

Audio Cassette Tapes

• Store tapes in their protective plastic cases to prevent dust buildup and damage to the tape surface.

• Cassette tapes should be kept tightly wound. If a tape gets loose, you can tighten it by inserting your finger or a wooden pencil into one of the holes and then turning the hub.

• Try not to touch the tape surface itself when a tape gets unwound, because you can scratch it and lose parts of the recording.

• Tape players need cleaning and demagnetizing occasionally (about every 10 to 30 hours of play) to help eliminate noise on the tapes and maintain the output levels. You can buy tape cleaning and demagnetizing kits.

Here's what they do: The cleaner removes oxides that come off the back of the tape and adhere to the tape heads, capstans, and pinch rollers of your player.

(You can use concentrated isopropyl alcohol and a cotton swab too, but avoid using rubbing alcohol, which could damage the pinch rollers.)

As always, read the manufacturer's instructions for care of your player; they'll tell you which fluids to use.

• When you demagnetize your tape machine, be certain that all recorded tapes are at least one foot away from the player to avoid erasures. The demagnetizer removes residual magnetism from the player. It can also erase parts of the tape. In fact, to avoid accidental erasures, you shouldn't store tapes near any magnetic source, including speakers and television sets.

• One of my resources says that all prerecorded cassettes manufactured after 1984, whether higher-quality chromium dioxide (CrO_2) or standard (ferric), will automatically play back on the "normal" setting (if your deck has an automatic sensing device). If you have manual settings, use "normal" for all post-1984 prerecorded cassettes for optimum playback. Modern technology enables us to play tapes without making all sorts of adjustments.

• Not many people have the seven-inch reel-to-reel type of audiotapes, but collectors of these tapes often find that the old labels and boxes in which they are stored are worn, not to mention covered with notations about what's on the tapes.

If you stick adhesive-backed shelf paper (with simple patterns or solid colors) on the boxes so that you wrap the sticky paper around the front, the hinged part, and the back of the boxes, you not only cover the boxes and make them look nice, you reinforce the hinges. Then you can play the tapes to make sure what's on them and properly label the boxes so that you can index them.

Storing Audio Cassette Tapes

• Audio cassette tapes are about the size of an index card, so if you're lucky enough to find old library card files at antiques or "junque" shops, you'll have a handy, dust-free storage case for audio tapes.

• The "cubby holes" of antique desks can hold tapes and your portable tape recorder too.

• You'll have a handle on carry-out audiotapes if you store audiotapes in a plastic tote (the kind sold to carry household items and cleaners).

• The three- or four-section plastic divided silverware trays usually used in kitchen drawers can be used as a cassette tape tray. And, if you have space, the tray can be put into a drawer and kept clean.

• Computer disk files will hold two rows of cassette tapes if they're standing sideways. Buy them at discount or on sale. They come in various sizes, so you can keep the different types of music and tapes separated for easy finding.

Putting It on Tape

Cassette-Taping Tips

• Take a tip from store-bought tapes: Do mark your tapes with "Side A" or "Side 1" if what you have recorded continues from one side to the other. That way you'll know exactly where the material you taped is located. Add also the date, name, and subject or time span of the information (if you are taping the history of your family as remembered by one of the grand old members!).
 Here are some tips for things you'll have fun taping.

• Living histories: Tape the history of your family at reunions, using the family's patriarchs and matriarchs as speakers. Other generations will thank you.

• Take a portable recorder and two-hour tape to the nursery to record baby's first cries, and then add baby's coos and gurgles, first words and expressions. As your child gets older, record favorite nursery rhymes and songs. You can even record short conversations in which you ask questions and the child answers. Older children can enjoy being "stars" when they record, "This is Betsy, I'm six today, and my favorite color is purple. . . ." With an introduction, you'll automatically be identifying the tape. It's important to record dates, occasions, and baby's name in writing as well as verbally on tape. (Years later all of the children in the same family may sound the same, and you won't know which child said what!) These are keepsakes and "sharesakes," because you can save tapes for yourself and children and also copy them for grandparents who live far away.

• Birthday parties: Tape the "Happy Birthday to You" each year, with a few of the comments at the end from the birthday person (adult or child). You may also want to have the guests record their names and some other pertinent facts.

• Surprises: If you are surprising someone at the office for a special occasion, arrange for someone to tape the "honored" person's reactions. Then give the honoree the tape as a remembrance.

• Grandma books: Have Grandma or Grandpa tape children's books, telling children the page numbers and when to turn the page. With so many families living apart, anything that keeps up awareness is very valuable.

• Letters: Tape (on cassette or videotape) letters from friends, family, or children to grandparents or to people who are blind or visually impaired.

• You can cassette- or video-tape a message to someone who is just too ill to read a letter and add some music or a stand-up TV comic's act from television to spice up your "letter." Don't make it too funny if your friend is recovering from surgery and might pop a few stitches!

• Taped "round-robin" letters can be passed around among friends so that everyone can keep in touch. Each person who receives the tape can add a message and mail it to the next person on the list, which is sent along with the tape. The tape can make a full cycle if each person on the list will be honor-bound to mail it onward.

A second tape can be added if the first is full, and once each person has had the chance to hear everyone on the list, you can start all over again, recording over the first tape, or save for history.

• Tape carefully chosen music or a collection of favorite artists as a gift "concert" for a relative or friend.

• Instead of a letter, tape your favorite music and send it to a friend or relative with a note that says, "Here's what I've been listening to lately. I'll trade it for a tape of your favorites."

• Notes: I've seen many tourists cassette-taping their impressions of what they see on their trips. It's easier than writing notes, and some of the microcassette sets are so small and light they are actually more convenient than a notebook! In foreign countries you can tape the accents, and in many cities here and abroad you can tape street musicians too, for your memory bank.

(Don't forget that you may be expected to tip musicians and, if you are taking pictures or making tapes in third-world countries, you are expected to tip children with coins or gifts such as balloons or candy and some adults with a certain amount. If you are on a guided tour, ask the tour guide what is appropriate.)

• Carry padded envelopes and mail your tapes home if you accumulate too many.

• When you are studying a foreign language, try taping verb conjugations or other exercises. Then you can play the tapes in the car (if they don't put you to sleep) or anywhere else when you need those rote-memory study sessions.

• To make a self quiz on tape when studying for tests: First record questions, then leave a pause of 10 to 20 seconds, and then record the answer. When the tape is played, the recorder becomes the tutor, since there is time to answer the questions after each one, and then the correct answer is given by the tutor-tape.

• You don't have to miss your favorite radio shows if you're gone. If your radio and tape recorder permit it, set them up on a timer so that you can tape radio shows as conveniently as you tape TV shows with your VCR.

• Books on tape make long car trips seem short. You can even "read" those classics you've always wanted to read but never had the time for. Taped books cost about the same as hard-cover books, and you can trade tapes the way you trade novels. Taped books are often on sale at bookstores. Many main-branch libraries have books on tape to borrow too, so you don't have to buy them.

• You can substitute books on tape for music when you wear a headset and catch up on your reading while you jog or walk or just relax in your backyard.

Musical Notes

Compact Discs

Music lovers love compact discs. Even if you have a "tin ear," you know how wonderful the sound is. But these discs are expensive and need care.

• After playing your compact discs, return them to their protective plastic cases. Scratches affect the sound. Be especially protective of the unlabeled side, which is the one the laser reads. Handle your CDs only by the center and edges.

• The correction system of a good player will handle scratches, so you may hear a note indistinctly or hear a split second of "mush" instead of the "tick, tick" that you hear when regular records are scratched.

• Your player will ignore some dust. However, when grease or skin oils from handling fill the tiny pits in compact discs, the laser can become "confused" and reflect the wrong way, which can result in garbled sound.

• To clean a CD, it's best to just wipe it with a dry, soft, lint-free cloth. You can rinse it under running cool water and blot dry with a lint-free towel. When you wipe your CD, always do it in a straight line from the center to the edge. Never clean CDs with solvent or abrasive cleansers. Some sources say that you can use ethyl alcohol as a solvent if necessary, but most say commercial cleaning kits are the safest way to clean CDs.

• Most of the time, the player's error-correction circuits compensate for defective discs, but really bad defects will cause a clicking noise or cause the player to mistrack the disc.

• Occasionally, a disc will have an uneven coating of aluminum, which causes poor reflectance. You can detect poor reflectance by holding a CD up to the light and looking for a mottled or unevenly mirrored surface.

• You can copy CDs onto cassettes for your car, but you may find that very quiet musical passages can be lost and very loud passages may be more than your tape or cassette player can handle.

• See the section below about playing CDs in cars.

• CAUTION: Compact discs are made of polycarbonate plastic, and while it's not easy to warp them, they will soften at 220 degrees Fahrenheit. When you have CD discs in your car, protect them from the sun's heat. The sun will warp them if you leave them on the dashboard or seat.

• Although CDs are considered to be virtually indestructible, they should always be stored away from heat and dust and handled as instructed above to prevent scratches and fingerprints. As this book is being written, there is disagreement among the experts about the life of compact discs. Some are saying they have a life expectancy of eight years, certainly disappointing to collectors. A British firm's research indicates that the shiny reflective layer beneath the disc's surface is made from a substance that chemically self-destructs, making the layer cloudy. Cloudiness makes the laser beam bounce back, spoiling your music. Some firms are considering changing the substance used in manufacturing the reflective layer.

• Although they are only about 4¾" in diameter, and therefore take less storage space than regular records, many of the storage tips for records will be suitable for CDs. If you've invested in many discs, it's probably better to buy commercially made storage cases especially designed to protect them.

• If you carry around your CDs in a portable case (to play in your car or elsewhere), don't tempt thieves by identifying the case's contents with labels.

• Portable cases should fit under a car seat, protect the discs from shock, and have secure handles. Some portable cases have a lift-out plastic liner that can be used for home storage.

Compact Disc Players

• Although a compact disc player doesn't have a stylus, and claims are made that it can be bumped without damage, avoid jolting the compact disc player anyway. Jolts may put the laser off track. One of the main differences between more and less expensive players is that the more expensive players are better able to cope with vibrations and shocks. They are not indestructible!

• Don't turn up the volume as soon as you start up your CD player. It can send a blast of clipped and distorted sound through your audio system, which, in turn, can damage the speakers' tweeters.

• The first thing to check if your player doesn't play when you start up is the disc loading slot or door containing the beam. All CD players are designed so that the lasers won't operate until the slots or doors are properly closed.

• Don't panic if your CD goes off for no reason that you can see. A spark generated by touching your player after walking across a carpet may be the culprit that shut it off. If this happens to you, turn the player off, wait about 30 seconds, then turn the power back on. All should be in order.

• With an adapter, portable CD players can be plugged into a car cigarette lighter and played through a car sound system or cassette player. Foam-padded automotive shock absorber brackets designed especially for CD players and sold at CD dealers will solve the problem of bumpy roads jarring the player.

Record Players/Turntables

• Place your record player or turntable in a stable location to avoid having the stylus bounce and scratch the record surface.

• To get the best sound, cover only one of two opposing surfaces in your "music listening room" with sound-absorbing materials. For example, if you have a carpeted floor, don't use acoustic tiles on the ceiling. If you drape a window, don't drape the opposite wall. Remember that glass reflects sound and upholstered surfaces absorb it.

• When setting up your stereo system, make sure you have followed the instructions for tone arm weight and pitch adjustment to ensure proper playing of your records and to avoid unnecessary damage to them.

• Don't expect your stylus or needle to play on forever. Check the manufacturer's directions for play life. A diamond stylus is good for about 1,000 hours of play. If you don't know how long you've had your stylus, take it to an equipment store to have it checked for wear.

• Some systems allow you to change the stylus yourself. However, if you have a service technician check your stylus for wear, you can, at the same time, have the stylus force adjusted and the tone arm balanced. Keeping the stylus and tone arm in best condition protects your record collection and therefore saves you money in the long run.

• The stylus can collect dust, and commercial stylus cleaners are available in electronics stores.

• CAUTION: Never touch a stylus with your fingers, because even the lightest touch can break or misalign it. If you are dusting a stylus, always brush from back to front, never from front to back or side to side.

• Keep your turntable covered when it's not in use. If the turntable is dusty, you'll get fuzzy, garbled sound. Clean the turntable with a damp, lint-free cloth.

• Before getting your turntable serviced when it's not working properly, check the fuses. You can check and replace fuses yourself with some systems, and instructions for doing so are in the manufacturer's instruction book.

• CAUTION: Always unplug the system before checking or replacing any parts. And never use wrenches or pliers to tighten connections—use fingers only! And, the rule is: If it doesn't fit, don't force it, because you are either doing something wrong or you have poor-quality parts.

• Children often lose the adapters that you need for playing 45-RPM records on their players. If you stick a spool (the kind that holds 325 yards of thread) on the record player post, you'll have an adapter that isn't so easily lost.

Records

• When you buy records, take off the plastic skin wrap and then always store your records in their protective inner sleeve and jacket in a vertical position. If you have a large collection, you may want to store records in categories (jazz, classical, pop) and/or alphabetically by artist's name or album/song titles.
   Some handy record/album storage bins include:

1. The fiberboard cubes available at most large hardware stores, which can be painted to coordinate with the room or, in the case of students, in school colors. Heavy and stackable, these cubes can be "built" into a sturdy place for a turntable and other sound equipment.
2. Plastic milk cartons have become popular for storing and moving records. If you have small children toddling about your house, you can tie straps made from wide elastic across the openings of these crates. You can still get the records out without too much trouble and baby will be discouraged from damaging your record collection.

• Help very young children to learn how to take care of their records. In large print, mark a letter of the alphabet on the upper right-hand corner of the jacket and then the same letter on each side of the record that goes into this jacket. You'll be teaching "ABCs" and neatness at the same time to your preschoolers.

• When the jackets of 45-RPM records get too shabby to protect the records, put the records (and the jackets too, if they are collector records) into a small, zippered plastic bag and they'll stay dust-free. The plus is that you can still read the labels through the plastic bags.

• Children's 45-RPM records can also be stored on an empty, solid deodorizer plastic cartridge. Just pull the top up and off and "spindle" the 45s.

• When you are moving records yourself, you can place a thin foam rubber sheet between albums to prevent damage from bumps and jarring.

• When you pack your possessions into your car, never put your records where the sun will shine on them, even if your car is air-conditioned. Sun shining through the car window can be warm enough to damage records.

• Sometimes warped records can be "unwarped" to a more playable condition if you place the record on a warm, flat surface such as the television set or top of the fridge and then weigh it down with heavy books. Leave the record undisturbed for several days. While this won't work for all records, it's certainly worth a try, because the warped record is useless anyhow.

• If a record is permanently warped beyond use and cannot be salvaged, you can put it over an appropriately sized cake pan or any metal form which is sized so that you get the "border" width you want, and then "bake" it in an oven at 350 degrees Fahrenheit for two or three minutes. You get a cute ruffled tray for holding spice bottles in the kitchen and many other things. You can also melt records over clay flowerpots and then, if you put some waterproof tape (duct tape, layered) over the hole, you'll have a "pot plant saucer" that adds black accents to your pot plant collection.

(If you don't normally do crafts, this is one that's fun, because it doesn't require equipment or cleanup. Also, if it doesn't turn out the size you want, you haven't lost anything, because the record was useless anyhow.)

• If your records have been dampened somehow and have become mildewed, try washing them as follows:

1. Holding the record by the edges, rinse both sides under a stream of cold tap water. After rinsing the record well and while it's still wet, squirt a small amount of mild liquid detergent on your wet fingertips. Rub around the record gently, being certain to rub with grooves and not across them. (No bar soap, just mild liquid detergent, please!)
2. Rinse well, still holding the record by its edges, and give it a few shakes to get most of the water off.

3. Set the record on edge in a safe place to dry. Never use a terry towel or other lint-producing fabric to dry records. Instead, get a cloth sold just for wiping records.

• If you really treasure your records, wear white cotton gloves while handling and cleaning them to prevent leaving smudges, fingerprints, and dust that can damage the records and the stylus.

• To clean records so that they play well and long, use a kit available where sound equipment is sold, which contains an applicator brush and anti-static cleaning fluid. The fluid removes residue and restores anti-static properties to your records. The fluid can also cut down on friction and thereby lengthen your records' life, because it provides lubrication between the stylus and record grooves.

• You can "poof" away dirt and dust from your records with a clean plastic squeeze bottle from eye or nose drops. But be sure it is carefully cleaned and totally dry.

Speakers

With more television shows broadcasting in stereo, speakers are becoming as important to viewing pleasure as they are to listening pleasure.

• You can use an adapter to get stereo sound from an older stereo-adaptable TV set (check model numbers with your dealer). With a non-stereo-adaptable TV set, you'll need a service technician to convert to stereo if your model permits it.

• Most manufacturers say that lower-priced speakers sound better if located off the floor and away from corners. "Ear level" will give the best sound from lower-priced speakers.

• Higher-priced speakers radiate more of their energy to the rear or sides and bounce more of their sound off the walls, producing more of a stereo effect than conventional speakers.

• You can get theaterlike "surround sound" by hooking a surround sound device to your stereo TV set and VCR, tape deck, or CD and spacing four speakers around the room. If the surround sound device is used with non-stereo TV sets or VCRs, it simulates stereo effects.

• When you are buying speakers, make sure that each speaker in the pair sounds the same. Different-sounding speakers could indicate defects or damage. Also, make sure you can return or exchange the speakers if they don't sound right in your "listening room" at home.

Headsets and Stereo Headphones

Headsets make jogging and walking more pleasant and prevent people from inflicting their musical tastes upon others, but CAUTION: Don't play your headphones so loud that you don't hear oncoming traffic. It is illegal in many areas to wear a headset while operating any kind of motorized vehicle.

• Even open-air type of headsets, which are designed to let you hear outside sounds, may be turned up too high to allow hearing them and be a threat to your safety.

• Continuous extended playing of headsets at high volume can damage your ears. If you have a ringing in your ears, either reduce the volume or stop using headsets.

• Whether you are buying a headset or a set of stereo headphones, comfort is the priority. If you can (perhaps by borrowing from a friend), try wearing the model for a half hour or so to comfort-test it. Just putting a set on for a few minutes won't tell you much. If you can't test it for an extended time, find out about the dealer's return/exchange policies.

• Another reason to try out stereo headphones is that if you are new to their use, you may not like the superstereo effect they give to music. Violins sounding as if they are coming in from the far right and music recorded with multiple microphones and other supersound techniques can be very uncomfortable to some people.

• Most stereo headphones come with cords ranging from 7 to about 14 feet. If you need a longer cord than that, get an extension cord from an audio shop. (If you've bought an electrostatic model that uses non-standard cords, you'll need to lengthen the wires to the adapter.) Some newer models are cordless and work well up to about 50 feet away from the source.

• If you like to hear music or watch TV until you fall asleep, you can buy headphones that turn off themselves and the TV set after you nod off.

Audio-Video Furniture

• Check that the wiring holes are where you need them and are convenient for organizing your equipment. Otherwise, you'll be drilling holes for wiring!

• Many antique armoires can be converted into audio-video centers, with the advantage that, in addition to being fine furniture, the armoire doors can be closed to keep dust out when they're not being used.

CAUTION: When you plan audio-video centers, always make certain that the equipment is well ventilated to prevent overheating when in use.

• Don't operate electronic equipment placed on beds or carpet; such soft surfaces can prevent ventilation at the bottom and cause overheating.

When the TV Tube Plays Its Last Picture Show

• One of my readers wrote that her family inserted an aquarium into their old TV cabinet and now watch fish instead of television shows, which, in the case of some shows, may be a whole lot more entertaining!

• Large console chests are often very good pieces of furniture, and too often a seriously burned-out television set can't be repaired, nor can the works be replaced so that they fit properly into the chest. After removing the works, plywood that can be stained, good-quality see-through plexiglass, or stained glass can be inserted into the television tube opening. Then the top can be removed and then replaced so that it's hinged from the back. The console can then be used to store blankets, toys, out-of-season clothing, or any other bulky and not-too-often-used items, such as punch bowls, chafing dishes, or large serving trays.

Where you keep the converted console chest depends upon the room decor and how well your project turned out.

If the console is not too tall, the top can be padded and upholstered, placed in a hall, and used as a bench and for boot and shoe storage.

Recycling is always a good idea, and if you can enjoy being creative, it's an even better idea. It saves money for you and saves the environment for all of us.

Cameras

• There are so many cameras with so many different operating procedures that I can't begin to give tips in this book, but here's one that will save you a trip to the repair shop: If your 35-mm camera won't click and the shutter seems to jam, you may not have a broken camera. Get new batteries! Camera batteries run the whole camera, not just the flash mechanism. (I thought I'd gotten sand in the camera at the beach and sand was jamming the shutter!)

• Take the batteries out when you aren't using your camera (or battery-operated cassette recorder) and they will last longer. A small amount of "juice" is being drained from the batteries as long as they are in place.

• In damp climates, or if you've taken your camera to a damp place, such as the beach, the battery connection point can corrode. You are less likely to have this problem if you remove batteries as a matter of habit when you store your camera for a couple of weeks. If you've been at the beach or fishing, you might want to dab the battery section off with a cotton-tipped swab to dry the area and clean out dirt/sand specks.

• Since most pocket cameras are made to focus with your right eye, vision problems in that eye can also cause picture-taking problems for some people. But, if you turn the camera upside down, you can use your left eye for focusing. The camera and film don't care if the up side is down or vice-versa.

• Here's a tip for you if you've ever "taken pictures" when there isn't any film in the camera. If you put a twistie on the camera strap when you put film into the camera and always remove it when you take film out, you'll always know when your 35-mm camera is "on empty" and you won't miss important photo shots.

• If you are taking instant camera pictures at a special occasion such as a shower or wedding, why not put the pictures into an album (the kind that has lift-up plastic covered pages) and then present the album to the honoree as a remembrance at the end of the party. Honeymooners would enjoy taking the album along so that they can see their wedding pictures before the official ones arrive from the photographer.

• When you move into a furnished apartment, take photos of furniture and carpeting so that you can show how worn they were when you moved in. If you are the landlord, photos will show how new the furnishings were when the tenant moved in. Include a sign with a date to prove when the photos were taken.

• If you own a furnished vacation cottage or home and rent it out, you should store valuables and take photos of each room, major appliance, or furniture piece, and the exterior of the house in case you have to make insurance claims because of damage or theft.

(The above two tips can also be used with your camcorder.)

• Save 35-mm film containers to use as mini-storage for all sorts of things, such as: spices for camping cookery, pill bottles (always label pills), paper clip holders in your purse or briefcase, and many other tiny things.

Carrying Around Audio/Video Equipment

• A backpack may be more useful and comfortable for carrying all your cameras, film, and tapes than some of the traditional bags made for that purpose.

• Lose your camera case? A small padded and zippered cassette tape case with a handle will hold many types of cameras, along with extra film, and cushion it when it's in your suitcase or on the overhead rack of a tour bus. Cassette tape carriers can also cushion cassette players safely in your carry-on bag.

• You can pad a camera case for traveling safely by gluing foam rubber to its inside surfaces.

• A cosmetic bag will hold extra film and a small camera, and the advantage of having the film and camera in a case is that you can quickly take the case out of your carry-on bags and hand it to the security attendant to hold while your bags are X-rayed and you go through the security gate.

• Stick an address label on your camera and each film container so that if you do lose these items, a finder can return them to you.

• Put lens caps in your pocket, camera case, or in some special place each time you take them off, or buy them two at a time, because they'll get lost. Or get a camera that has the lens cap attached with a cord.

• If you do a lot of photography, invest in a photographer's vest available in catalogs and specialty clothing stores, such as outfitter stores. These multi-pocketed canvas vests are useful for fishing, camping, scout troop leading, and a variety of other activities that require you to keep track of bits and pieces. They are sturdy, washable, and sized generally enough to be shared by family members.

• When you are going fishing, don't miss that great fish picture. Take your camera along, but protect it from water by sealing it in a plastic bag and then putting the bagged camera into a coffee can with a lid.

• In hot weather, your car can get to 100 degrees-plus temperatures very easily. Protect your camera and film by keeping them in an insulated foam cooler if you have to leave them in the car. The plus is that potential thieves won't see an expensive, attractive camera, just a cheap, unattractive cooler, and so they aren't as likely to be tempted to break into your car. (Although it's always best to lock things in your trunk, some trucks and hatchbacks don't have good hiding places for valuables.)

• Electronic television video game cartridges fit nicely into eight-track tape carrying cases. Store them free from dust and protected from damage and then tote them to friend's house when you want to.

• Computer disk games that you have copied yourself and that have written instructions as well as disks can be stored and carried around in pocketed loose-leaf paper holders that children usually use for different subjects in school. The printed information sheets are hole-punched and fitted on the grommets, and the disks are stored in the pockets. You can use different colors for each game and, if you feel artistic, draw appropriate pictures on the front of the folder.

Rec-Tech Information Source

Many of the electronic equipment tips in this chapter came from the Electronic Industries Association, Consumer Electronics Group, which offers free care, maintenance, and safety pamphlets from its "Consumers Should Know" series to those who send a stamped, self-addressed envelope to the association.

To request pamphlets, state the subject (television, compact discs, audio products) or pamphlet name when you write and include a No. 10 stamped, self-addressed envelope. A separate envelope is needed for each pamphlet. The address is: Electronic Industries Association (HH), 2001 Eye Street, N.W., Washington, D.C. 20006. You can call to get information on pamphlet subjects and for the names of various pamphlets. The phone number is 202-457-4900.

• Your public library also has numerous books to help you research before you buy.

Help Tech

Answering Machines

We take these machines for granted, but the tapes do wear out and you may be missing your messages due to malfunctions. Most machines have a setting that allows you to check your outgoing message periodically to see if it's working properly.

• Remember that when you replace the tape that receives messages, you need to replace it with a tape made for answering machines. Most regular cassette tapes have a lead segment at the beginning that doesn't record anything. If you put an ordinary tape into an answering machine, you'll miss parts of or most of the first message on the machine. Answering machine tapes have no "empty" lead space and will record immediately.

• These mechanical secretaries need to be cleaned with a head cleaner for audio cassette recorders to keep on taking your messages. See the manual for how often.

• Don't think that the only time you can use an answering machine is when you are out. Teach yourself to let the phone ring and the machine answer when you are busy doing something that just can't be interrupted, when you are taking a nap break, and when you're in the garden, pool, or tub. It may take you awhile to get comfortable doing this; however, you will be amazed at how many times it's simply a wrong number or a salesman.

If you turn up the volume, you can hear the message being given on your machine and then decide if you need to call back immediately.

• If you have a new baby, put a message on the machine that gives the baby's weight and other vital statistics, then say that you and the baby are napping and you'll call back later.

• Use your message for other good news announcements too. Not all messages have to be straightforward and businesslike.

• Some messages can actually be messages, such as "Kevin or Barbara, call Kim at 211-9333 after six P.M. Friday."

• Play background music while you record your message and, if you like humor, try some of the prerecorded messages or tape conversations from humor albums, TV shows, comics' monologues, and so forth. At Halloween you could put horror sounds from scare records on your tape; at Christmas, it could be a carol; Valentine's Day, a silly but short love poem. If you aren't inspired by holidays, let your imagination entertain you and your callers. We've even had Zinfandel, our talking miniature schnauzer, bark a message to our callers.

• Give an alternative number that the caller can use to reach you if there is one.

• Don't ever have your message say that nobody's home; let a prospective burglar guess.

• If you've been having too many telephone sales calls or calls from anyone else that you don't want to talk to, let your machine answer all calls, and then return important calls immediately.

• If you are having a series of obscene or just annoying callers, it's better not to put your name or any other identification on the machine. Just say, "Leave your message at the beep and I'll call you back" until the harassing calls stop. Don't return calls to any name or number that you don't recognize. Most of the time, the caller will hang up. If not, you have a record of what was said if you report the call. Look in your phone book for instructions on what to do about annoying or harassing calls. And don't hesitate to call your local phone company for help with this problem.

Telephone Installation

Installing your own phones with modular plugs and jacks means that you have to know the dos and don'ts. Here are a few from the Electronic Industries Association.

• Don't ever attempt to install telephone wiring if you wear a pacemaker.

• If you take the phone off the hook when you're working on it, you'll reduce the possibility of small electrical shock if the phone rings.

• Don't place phone wire in any conduit or outlet box that contains electrical wiring or water pipes.

• Never place a telephone jack where it would let a person use the phone in the bathtub, shower, swimming pool, or anywhere else near water.

• Four-conductor telephone station wire used for house wiring is very low voltage, so you can safely hide it under carpets, between walls, over basement ceiling joists, up and around doors and windows.

• But don't run any wire through places where it will be damp, excessively hot, pulled out by mistake, or subjected to abrasion. (Worn wires can cause interference.)

Cordless Phones

Most tests show that even though the newer models are much improved over the old ones, these phones don't really deliver the sound quality of regular phones. However, they are useful if you are involved in some outdoor activity and are expecting a call that you don't want the machine to answer.

• Expect a certain amount of "false ringing" with these phones; it comes with the territory.

• Also coming with the territory (literally, with the area in which you live) is a certain amount of interference from power lines and metal (plumbing, chain-link fences, sliding doors, screened porches). Even positioning your body between the base and handset can reduce the calling range.

• Although most models allow use of only one FCC channel, it's really better to spend the money for a multi-channel phone. If your neighbor happens to have a cordless phone on the same channel, you'll suffer party-line syndrome— one phone owner can't call out if the other is on the phone, and you can listen to each other's conversations.

Multi-Function Phones

Use your imagination with the functions of these fun phones.

• What a time-saver programmable phones are! Not only can you program frequently called numbers of friends, relatives, businesses, and emergency aid numbers, you can program pizza delivery, weather, time, and any other useful numbers.

• Speaker phones work better for group phone calls than having several people get on different extensions, which may weaken the signal and make hearing each other difficult. Also, everyone gets to hear what the person on the other end of the line said, so he or she won't have to keep repeating, "I'm fine, thank you" or "It's [snowing, raining, steaming hot, horribly cold] here."

• When using a speaker phone with lots of people, it helps if you say, "It's Jane" or "This is Bob" before you start to talk, so the people on the other end of the line don't have to keep asking, "Who said that?"

• Phones with redial or busy-dial functions will help you win radio phone-in prizes, because it's faster to punch one button than to dial or punch a whole phone number's worth of buttons when you're trying to get through on a very busy line or be the first caller.

• Being able to punch only one button also helps if you are trying to voice your opinion on radio and TV phone-in talk shows, which have super-busy lines.

• When you have any problems with these phones, the first thing to check is if the batteries need replacement—something we didn't need to think about with old-style phones. Some booklets recommend changing batteries every six months or so without waiting for any malfunctions.

Car Phones

Working moms, people who work out of their cars and/or drive deserted roads, and others who need to be contacted at any time are buying car phones in increasing numbers. If you are planning to buy one, here are some of the features you should consider.

• A glass-mounted antenna, which allows the signals to be picked up without having a hole drilled into the car body.

• Easy-to-use controls. Most of these phones have controls on the back of the handset.

• Memory and speed dialing; it avoids a lot of button pushing, which is safer. However, you really should pull over to the side of the road and stop when you are using a car phone if it's possible. Dialing and driving don't mix!

• A speaker and microphone will let you have your hands free for driving and let others in the car participate in the conversation, just as a home phone with a speaker does.

• A portable unit allows you to connect to a battery pack so that you can walk away with the phone and still use it when necessary. And you can remove it from the car so that it won't tempt thieves.

• Call timers are available to help you keep the toll costs down by keeping calls shorter.

Intercom Systems

Although the best system is one installed when a house is built, you can buy equipment to install yourself. Simple systems can be made up of just two speakers and wires that get plugged into an outlet.

Intercoms are safety devices that let you know who's at the front or back door and if you should open it, as well as energy savers, eliminating the need to walk up and down stairs, to and from the garage, or from room to room when you need to talk to someone.

• Use an intercom system in baby's or younger children's rooms, so you know when they are waking up, coughing too much, or, in the case of older children, playing instead of going to sleep. Simple two-speaker setups that are relatively inexpensive can be used to listen in on baby when you don't want the expense of installing a full house system.

• When you are listening to a room with a simple two-speaker intercom, remember to turn up the volume of the "eavesdropping" speaker and turn down the volume of the "listener's" speaker.

TV Shopping Channels and Offers

Being able to order things from TV shopping channels is one of the best help techs for people who just don't have the time to wander through malls or who can't get out to shop. However, it takes some consumer knowledge to shop wisely when a product or item pops up on the screen and tempts you to phone in your credit card number.

Here are some "need-to-knows" about shopping for just about any product, but especially when you are buying from TV shopping shows and special TV offers on merchandise that you can't actually examine hands-on.

• Know the company's refund and cancellation policy.

• Know who pays for shipping charges if merchandise is returned and who is responsible for shipping insurance. What is the company's policy for lost or damaged items?

• Will the company have the right to substitute comparable goods and is there a warranty or guarantee available?

• How long is the shipping time? How do the prices compare with local stores, catalogs, and other local sources?

• As in catalog shopping, keep a record of your order, especially the date you placed it, and the method and amount of payment, including taxes, and shipping and handling costs.

• And, here's a word for the wise shopper: Watch for consumer stories or columns about TV offers and catalog shopping services to find out if any products have been investigated for postal fraud or misrepresentation. The latter is especially a problem, with many weight-loss or medical "miracle" products sold on TV.

• You can find out if complaints have been made about local companies and products and can make complaints by calling or writing your local Better Business Bureau. Check up on nationally sold products and companies by writing or calling the Federal Trade Commission, Complaints and Inquiries, Sixth and M Avenue, N.W., Washington, D.C. 20580. Phone: 202-326-2418.

The Postal Inspector investigates if the United States mail has been used to defraud the public (chain letters, false billing, undelivered merchandise). Write to your Regional Chief Inspector, U.S. Postal Service, if you think you have been the victim of such frauds. You can get the address from your local main post office. The Regional Chief Inspector uses consumer complaints as a basis for investigations.

Comfort Tech

Air-Conditioning

One wonders how people survived in hot climates before air-conditioning made comfort and life as we know it now possible. How our ancestors must have sweltered!

• Since air-conditioning utility costs can be 50 percent of your utility bill in a hot climate, you should choose your air-conditioning system wisely. Buy neither too big nor too small a system. Here's how the Department of Energy says you should calculate to determine air conditioner sizes:

Find out the square footage to be cooled. An air conditioner usually needs 20 Btu for each square foot of living space.
If a room is 20 feet long by 15 feet wide, calculate $15 \times 20 \times 20$ (Btu) = 6,000. The room needs an air conditioner with a 6,000-Btu capacity. Buy a unit within 5 percent of this capacity. (Calculating Btu capacity for central units also has to take a home's individual needs, such as ceiling heights, floor plans, and number of stories, into consideration. Sometimes, more than one central unit is needed in a home.)

• The Btu can be lowered if you have the benefit of trees and shrubs to cool the house; using heat-producing appliances will increase Btu needs.

• Energy efficiency is probably the most important consideration when you are buying an air conditioner, and all air conditioners have yellow "Energy Guide" labels that show their efficiency ratings. Units with a "9" or more are very efficient.

Here are some tips from CARIERS (Conservation Renewable Energy Inquiry and Referral Service) on keeping down those utility bills when you're air-conditioning for comfort in the summer.

• Set the fan speed on high, except in very humid weather. In humid weather, set the speed low. Although you'll get less cooling, more moisture will be taken from the air and this will make you feel cooler.

• When you first turn on the air conditioner, it won't cool faster if you set the thermostat lower than the temperature you want. It will cool to a lower temperature and therefore waste energy and increase your utility bill. Set the temperature that you want and let the thermostat do its job.

• Keeping filters clean can cut your utility bill by 5 to 15 percent. Check filters monthly and clean or replace them as needed.

• If you have acquired a long-haired pet, you'll be surprised at how quickly your filter becomes full of hair! You may have to check it more than once monthly. My service technician told me that if a dirty filter allows pet hairs to get to the AC heating unit's coils, the damage caused is considered "lack of maintenance" and may not be covered by home-owner's appliance insurance. Not keeping the filters clean could be expensive!

• If you place heat-producing appliances near the thermostat, it becomes "confused" and runs longer than necessary.

• The fan motor on outside air conditioners is hard to get at when you try to oil it. Here's how to do it without taking off the cover:

Straighten a wire coat hanger, touch one end to the oil hole, raise the other end, and drip oil onto the wire; the oil will flow down nicely to the oil hole.
(Use this method for any hard-to-get-at oiling place.)

• Most central air-conditioning and heat pump units are placed a distance from the outside wall of your house to help muffle the fan's noise, which means the unit may be deprived of shade from the building. Heat from summer sun increases air-conditioning energy use by about 5 percent. In winter, sun exposure increases the unit's heating capacity.

It's generally recommended that you provide some sort of portable shade for the unit that can be removed in the winter, such as a collapsible lath-covered frame made from two-by-two laths or an awning if the unit is close enough to brace the awning on the house. Awnings can also shade window air-conditioning units in the summertime.

Programmable Thermostats

• If you are gone most of the day, you can save utility bills by using programmable thermostats that will automatically adjust the temperature according to a set of instructions you preset. If your heating needs vary through the day—for example, if you want heat when you wake up, but prefer to save heating bills by keeping your apartment or home cool at night and during the day when you're at work, these thermostats can be a perfect solution. They are sold at electric supply stores and some hardware stores.

Ceiling Fans

There's no question that ceiling fans make air-conditioning and heating units work more efficiently and economically.

• Ceiling fans aren't just for summer cooling. They are especially useful for blowing heat down from cathedral-style ceilings in the winter.

• If you are installing a ceiling fan in a high hallway or in a room with a cathedral ceiling, a remote-control fan can be more convenient, since you won't have to reach for different chains and pulls.

• If you bought ceiling fans when they first became popular and had old-style motors that required regular oiling, you may find that buying new fans is less expensive than repairing your old ones.

Humidifiers

The relative humidity ratio is always given as a percentage at a given temperature. The ideal indoor comfort range, according to my sources, is 40 percent relative humidity with 68 to 70 degrees Fahrenheit, plus or minus 5 percent relative humidity.

• Humidifiers (either freestanding units or those that can be attached to a furnace) prevent electric static in cold climates, your furniture's joints from drying out and getting loose, and your home fabrics from getting brittle and wearing out sooner. They also make your house plants happy. People with respiratory difficulties can benefit from adding moisture to the air, and even people who are normally healthy can get sore throats from too-dry environments.

Also, in cold weather, you feel colder in a dry room; humidifiers generally save about 15 percent of fuel costs in the winter.

• Here's how to test your home or office to find out if the humidity ratio is adequate (and comfortable):

1. Take a glass of water and place three regular-size ice cubes in it.
2. Let it sit, and within five minutes, if your room has adequate moisture in the air, you'll find plenty of condensation—beads of water—forming on the outside of the glass.

If the condensation doesn't happen within 5 to 15 minutes, the room needs humidification.

Of course, if you have static electricity when metal objects are touched and have frequent sore throats and dry skin, you don't need a test for humidity ratios.

• When you are deciding where to put a humidifier, consider that bathrooms and kitchens produce a certain amount of moisture in the air. Therefore it's best to locate a humidifier in an area that's not too close to these rooms.

• In a two-story house, you can put the humidifier at the bottom of a stairwell, but it's really better to have one unit for each floor.

• If you place your humidifier in front of or near a wall heater or radiator, their heat and air movement will increase evaporation.

• Maintenance includes replacement of worn pads, belts, plates, and orifices for solenoid valves, plus cleaners recommended by the manufacturer's manual that dissolve mineral deposits and lime, mold, and algae. Keeping your humidifier clean prevents musty odors, not to mention the possibility of spreading the mold and algae, which can really play havoc with allergies.

Dehumidifiers

In some climates and some tightly constructed homes, high humidity is a problem, especially when many showers, wet towels, drying clothing, cooking, floor washing, and ground moisture add to the situation. Mildewed shoes in closets, musty smells throughout the house, and general physical discomfort for the people in the house are symptoms of too much moisture.

Attic fans can replace warm, moist air with cool, dry outside air, and mechanical dehumidifiers recirculate room air and reduce the relative humidity.

Here are some features to look for when choosing a mechanical dehumidifier.

• An adjustable thermostat regulates the on and off cycles that maintain the selected humidity conditions.

• Exposed air-drying coils let you clean the unit easily and keep it at peak performance, with resulting lower operating costs.

• Catch buckets need to hold at least 10 quarts of water and should be easy to remove and empty without spilling. (Dehumidifiers work by drawing moist air over refrigerated coils. When the air hits the cold surface, moisture condenses and drips off into the collection bucket or to a drain hose connected to a drip tray.)

• An automatic water overflow control shuts the unit off when the water bucket is full to prevent spills.

• Recessed wheels increase stability and mobility. Two recessed wheels are usually enough.

• Maintenance includes cleaning dust and dirt from the refrigeration coils, condenser, and fan units, and, of course, emptying the catch bucket.

Heaters

Room heaters help if you are trying to save energy costs by practicing "zone heating." In zone heating, you close off unused rooms' registers or heating vents, or shut off the furnace and heat only used rooms with room heaters.

• Although room heaters are not as efficient as furnace heat, in some houses room heaters can heat one or two rooms at less expense than a big heater.

• Portable heaters use 110 volts. When selecting a portable heater, you need to check the wattage, because the rule of thumb is that you need one watt per cubic foot of air volume in the room.

Electric Blankets

• Never layer bedding over an electric blanket while it's on. You can cause the wiring to overheat to the point of catching fire.

• If you need a king-size electric blanket and find twin-size ones on sale at a good price, you can tack the edges together and make your own dual-controlled king-size blanket at a cost much less than that of a king-size one.

• If you have a Hollywood-style bed (without a footboard), the electric blanket cord tends to stick out from the foot of the bed and catch your ankle when you are making the bed. Try attaching a cup hook to the underside of the box spring, with the open part of the hook pointing toward the head of the bed. Thread the cord through the hook, and the cord will stay out of your sight and way.

• You can take an electric blanket to a professional cleaner when it needs freshening, or you can launder it yourself, if so indicated on the care label, as follows:

1. First disconnect the electric control and machine wash in warm water with mild detergent. But note that long wash or spin cycles may damage the blanket.
2. When the machine is filled with water, let it agitate a bit so the detergent dissolves if you use powdered detergent, then put the blanket into the water and let it wash three or four minutes at the most.
3. After the water drains, follow with a short spin cycle. Rinse again and spin briefly again so that only part of the water is removed. Press the remaining water out with your hands.
4. Line dry over two parallel lines. Machine drying can damage the wiring.

• NEVER run an electric blanket through a coin-operated dry-cleaning machine; the solvent can damage wiring and cause electric shock when the blanket is used.

• If your electric blanket is old and you don't trust the wiring anymore, you don't have to throw out the blanket. Just snip at the ends of the wires at the head and foot of the blanket and pull out the wires. You'll have a spare blanket at no cost. You can also use the blanket as a filler in a hand-sewn quilt or coverlet.

CHAPTER 11

Pets

I t's no secret that I love animals. As this book is being written, three dogs—
Zinfandel, the miniature schnauzer; Sheba, the keeshond; Willie, the Brit-
tany—and three birds—Rocky the Military Macaw and Fussy and Doley, male
cockatiels—are sharing my home and my life. I have also had ferrets named
Fanny the Ferret and Fred the Ferret.

I can't imagine life without pets, and from my mail I know that many people
share my feelings about them and enjoy reading about my pets when I write
about them in my newspaper and *Good Housekeeping* magazine columns. I get
frequent requests for my schnauzer Zinfandel's "autograph" and photo.

Choosing a Pet

When you decide to get a dog or cat, remember that cute little puppies and
kittens really do grow up. Some little balls of fur become very large dogs who
need fenced-in yards to roam in and long exercise walks. Others become feisty

tomcats that annoy neighbors and even their owners with their fighting and spraying if they aren't neutered.

• Find out how big the breed of dog you choose will be when mature. If you live in a house with a big, fenced-in yard, you can have any dog or pet you choose that is allowed by your city's zoning laws. But if you live in a small apartment, you may want to choose small, quiet pets that don't need as much "elbow" or tail-wagging space.

• Add up the costs of pet ownership before you get one. Pets need immunizations and grooming in addition to food, water, love, and attention. Animals that will not be bred need to be spayed or neutered.

• Make getting a pet a family decision so that everyone feels a sense of responsibility for the pet's care.

• Pets can't be given as gifts the way stuffed animals are given. The experts say that choosing your own pet helps to establish a binding relationship with the animal.

• Children younger than three should never be given any kind of small animal as a pet. Many a puppy, kitten, chick, or gerbil has unintentionally been "loved" (translate that as "mauled") to death by a child that really didn't know any better.

• When you're ready to begin looking, don't forget your local animal shelter. It's sad to think about the numbers of stray animals that have to be euthanatized because nobody wants them.

According to the Humane Society of the United States, an estimated 15 to 18 million animals enter shelters each year, and the Cornell University College of Veterinary Medicine estimates that 13 million shelter animals must be destroyed annually—an average of one animal every three seconds. About one-fourth of these animals are purebreds, so it's not just mutts that people abandon or "throw away."

And my personal theory is that most pets that you adopt from a shelter or who adopt you, as Sheeba, our keeshond, did, seem to know that they are lucky and turn out to be very faithful and lovable animals.

I guess, speaking as one animal lover to another (and you must be one if you are reading this chapter), my best Heloise advice is: If you can't properly care for a pet, don't get one. And if you don't plan to breed your pet, have it spayed or neutered.

General Pet First-Aid and Health Tips

• If you can't afford a private veterinarian, call your local Humane Society to find clinics with less expensive services for neutering, spaying, and immunizations.

• It's a misconception that female animals need to have a litter before spaying and that spayed or neutered animals automatically get fat and lazy. Ask your vet!

• Don't ever leave your pet in a car unattended. You may think that it's not hot when it's only 85 degrees and you're parked in the shade, but even with the windows slightly opened, in less than 30 minutes the temperature inside the car can get as high as 120 degrees, causing heat stroke and possibly death. Please, when you go out, leave your pet home!

• Protect kittens and puppies from their own curiosity. Prevent them from licking electric connections that could electrocute them; from falling into swimming pools, where they can drown; from chewing and swallowing dangerous small objects or eating poisonous plants, such as Dieffenbachia, mistletoe berries, and poinsettia.

• Safeguard pets at night. Cats allowed to roam at night and even dogs trained to heel without being on a leash should wear reflective collars or have reflective tape stuck to their collars to alert motorists.

• When you need pet health advice, see a veterinarian, not a pet store owner, who is in business to sell animals and pet food and isn't likely to know much about nutrition, disease, and pet problems.

• Find a veterinarian by asking your friends for recommendations and then have your pet examined once or twice a year and given immunizations, as the vet suggests. As with people, health problems should be found and treated before they become serious.

• If the vet you choose doesn't have time to talk to you and answer your questions, find one who does.

• Remember that after the initial series of immunizations, booster shots are needed annually.

• Warm weather decreases animals' appetites. The heat may cause some dogs to be less active, and therefore they will eat less. Kittens shouldn't be allowed to fast too long; give them frequent, small feedings on hot days.

• Many animals actually like to graze on grass. It's okay for your dog or cat to eat grass; it's their version of salad.

• Worming medications are dangerous if improperly used. Medicate your animals only with prescription medicines from your veterinarian. And, by the way, worms aren't caused by eating candy, nor can they be cured by feeding your dog garlic.

• Since animals can't talk, you have to be a detective to find out if they are in pain. Some symptoms of pain are lameness, stiff neck, reluctance to get up or lie down, and/or tense abdominal muscles. See the vet!

• Keep puppies away from other dogs' droppings. Infected feces transmit a serious disease called parvovirus, which kills 75 percent of puppies under five months of age who get it. Older dogs are more or less immune. All dogs should be vaccinated to prevent this disease.

• If your dog is nauseated, take away all food and water for 24 hours but give the dog small amounts of water to prevent dehydration by providing ice cubes to lick.

• A dog that can't urinate should be taken to a vet at once. It could die of uremia if it doesn't urinate for 24 hours.

• A dog that shows the signs of shock should be kept warm. His position shouldn't be shifted too suddenly, because sudden movements can cause the shock to go into an irreversible stage.

• Prevent dogs from straining with impacted feces by adding a teaspoon of cooking oil to each food serving. The oil will also put a shine in the dog's fur.

• When the vet requests a stool sample from your dog, try not to include any soil in the sample. Dirt can contain harmless soil worms that may confuse the examiner. A clean margarine tub and a plastic spoon will help you scoop up and transport the sample for the vet.

• To give liquid medications to a frisky, objecting dog, avoid a mess by putting the dog into the bathtub at medication time.

• To pill a dog, insert the pill into its mouth, then close the mouth quickly and tap his nose with your finger or gently blow on the pet's face. This causes the dog to lick and then swallow.

• Stroking a dog's throat will make it swallow a pill.

• You can bury pills in cream cheese, peanut butter, cheese, or liverwurst—whatever your dog thinks is a treat.

• Heartworm pills (which are scored for breaking into quarters) can be broken in four pieces and placed on top of your dog's dry food or poked into canned food if your dog doesn't think these pills are a treat.

• Cats and lap-size dogs can be wrapped and held securely in a towel before pills are popped into their mouths. Towel wrapping also works well if you have to apply ointments to eyes or ears of small pets.

• Pet "pillers," which look like a long, thin syringe with a rubber holder at the end, can be used to poke pills down animals' throats. Again, stroking the throat hastens swallowing after the pill is inserted.

• When you start giving a dog heartworm pills, handle the pill as you do his other treats. Have him do a trick for it and then give him the heartworm pill as a reward. (Just the opposite of the way you medicate children, who should never be taught that medicine is "candy.")

• If all else fails when you are trying to pill a pet, just open the pet's mouth and put the pill way back to the throat, close the mouth, rub the throat, and, if necessary, cover the pet's snout. It will usually swallow the pill with this method.

When we started giving Zinfandel and Sheba their heartworm pills every day, we made it appear as if the pills were a treat, covered with peanut butter for Sheba and a little butter for Zinfandel. They both have to speak for their goodies and now they demand them every morning.

Pet Dental Care

According to veterinarians, 90 percent of all cats and dogs suffer from some type of dental disease by the age of six years.

While pets have good natural defenses against tooth decay, plaque and tartar build up after years of soft food diets. Crisp foods and leather chew sticks help, but they don't clean teeth at the gum line, where tartar and plaque buildup encourage the growth of bacteria that can lead to generalized infection, even heart disease.

For your pet's sake, prevent periodontal disease. Here are the symptoms that should tell you your pet needs to see a veterinarian about dental problems:

1. Persistent bad breath.
2. Tartar formation (creamy-brown spots on teeth).
3. Inflamed gum line.
4. Bleeding or receding gums.
5. Loose, infected, or missing teeth.

A veterinarian will treat periodontal disease by cleaning your pet's teeth to remove tartar and plaque. The veterinarian will then recommend regular brushing, along with periodic checkups.

Fleas

To give you an idea about the magnitude of the flea problem: One female flea can create 800 virtually indestructible eggs in her lifetime, and under good conditions 10 fleas can produce a quarter of a million new fleas within 30 days. And the reason you can't just slap one when you see it is that fleas can accelerate 50 times faster than the space shuttle!

In some parts of the country, "flea season" is a torture for animals and humans. Animals can develop "hot spots" (irritated skin patches that are actually hot to the touch and that are rendered hairless by the animals' efforts to bite the fleas), and humans, too, suffer from itchy bites.

• Vacuum floors, rugs, and furniture at least weekly to collect fleas and their eggs, being especially careful to vacuum in dark corners and crevices. Toss a couple of mothballs into your vacuum cleaner bag to kill the fleas as you pick them up and then throw out the bag.

• CAUTION: When you spray commercial insecticides indoors and out it's imperative to follow directions for the particular brand you use. Some directions say that your pet should not be allowed to walk on carpets or grass sprayed with insecticide until the chemicals are dry. Allowing pets to romp on some wet insecticides could poison them.

• To avoid skin irritations from too-potent flea collars, air out the collar for several days before putting it on your dog or cat. But air the collar where it's safe from people and pets!

• Excessive amounts of flea powder in a pet's coat can be licked off and may make your pet ill. Brush off all excess flea powder within 30 minutes after it's applied to prevent your dog or cat from ingesting the residue.

• Don't use flea preparations formulated for dogs on cats. Cats lick/groom themselves more than dogs do, and cat formulas take that into account when the chemical strengths are determined. Many preparations available at your veterinarian are safe for both dogs and cats. Get advice from your vet!

• If you have a cat or small dog that really resists being powdered or sprayed for fleas, powder or spray a bath towel and then wrap the animal in the towel, holding it wrapped for about 15 minutes so the chemicals can work.

• If you have a water-hating cat or a dog too large to dip for fleas and ticks, thoroughly wet the animal's coat, and then spray the dip (mixed in proportions according to directions) onto the pet with a spray bottle.

• Shampooing your dog more than every 10 to 14 days can dry out its skin. If your flea shampoo and dip aren't effective for the entire interval between bath and dip, you'll need to use sprays or powder in between shampoos.

• It's better to let your pet dry naturally after being dipped. Towel drying will remove some of the dip.

• Flea and tick powders and sprays should never be combined with each other or with a flea collar, because you may overdose your pet with these chemicals. This is especially true of small breed dogs. Please don't take a chance.

• Cedar shavings or pine needles will repel fleas from animal bedding and doghouses. Salt also repels fleas, so washing your dog's doghouse periodically with salt water is a good prevention.

• Fleas are attracted to light. Make a flea trap with a light-colored, shallow pan, and a 25-watt lamp, without shade:

1. Every night for several weeks, fill the pan with soapy water and set it on the floor.
2. Position the lamp next to the pan so that the bulb is a foot or so above the water. (This should be the only source of light in the area.)
   When the light is turned on, fleas will jump toward the heat and fall into the water.
3. Rinse out the pan in the morning.

• To help keep fleas off you, bathe daily with soaps containing green dyes.

• Fleas spend only a short time on your pet; most of the time they are happily breeding in carpets, bedding, and your yard. To prevent reinfestation, you must treat your home and yard as well as your pet.

While each flea control product has its own set of instructions, the basic principles of eliminating fleas from your and your pet's environment are as follows:

1. In the yard, use a commercial spray with a garden hose hook-up.
2. Inside, clean and vacuum the house, and immediately dispose of the vacuum bag. Then use a room fogger and spray hard-to-reach areas with a kennel spray.

• Remove all pets and cover fish tanks and exposed food before you use a fogger.

• Close exterior doors and windows, and turn off the furnace or air conditioner to allow insecticide to disperse.

• Put a fogger in each room and position it in the center of the room on newspapers to protect the floor or carpet from droplets.

• Do not reenter the home for two hours and then when you do, open doors and windows to ventilate for at least 30 minutes.

Traveling with Your Pet

Like some people, some pets are not good travelers and are best left with a sitter or in a boarding kennel. If the trip is short, perhaps a neighbor could look in on your pet while you are gone. Often older pets fare better when kept at home in familiar surroundings instead of in a kennel.

Your vet or local Humane Society can recommend safe, well-run kennels in which to board your pet.

• You will need a veterinarian's exam to get the legal documents needed for transporting animals interstate and internationally. In addition to examining your animal to determine general health, the veterinarian should provide any inoculations your pet requires, such as for rabies, distemper, infectious hepatitis, and leptospirosis.

• A veterinarian can prescribe a sedative or tranquilizer for jittery traveling pets, but you should never give your human medicines to pets. Some human medications can, at the least, make them ill and, at worst, damage the pet's internal organs or be poisonous.

• If you take along familiar food and even water from your hometown supply, stop frequently to give your pets water and exercise, and check ahead to make sure the hotel or motel you've reserved will accept pets, you'll make traveling with them easier.

Legal Requirements for Transporting Pets

Dogs and cats crossing state lines need to be accompanied by a valid health certificate and a certificate of rabies inoculation.

(While state pet travel health restrictions are rarely enforced, having the proper documents avoids the risk of having your pet quarantined or refused entry into a state.)

• Within the United States, pet travel is generally unrestricted, with the exception of travel to Hawaii, where there is an unwaivable 120-day mandatory quarantine for all dogs and cats.

• To enter Canada, cats don't need special documents if they are healthy. Dogs must have a certificate of rabies vaccination issued within the previous 12 months. Also, a definitive description of the traveling dog is required.

• Before taking a pet to Mexico, a health certificate, prepared in duplicate, should be mailed to the Mexican consulate with a fee. The certificate must include a description of your pet, the rabies vaccine used, proof of distemper vaccine, and a veterinarian's statement verifying the animal is free from infectious or contagious diseases. You may proceed with your trip when the certificate has been certified and returned, which can take some time, possibly months.

How to Select a Pet Carrier

• The carrier should have opaque sides, several venting holes on all sides, a grille door, and be durable, with enough space to allow your pet to stand, sit or lie down. A secure door handle is a must. Most domestic airlines sell pet carriers that meet travel standards.

CAUTION: Zinc nuts used to secure some types of dog cages can be toxic to dogs if the dogs swallow the nuts. If the cage you've bought has zinc nuts, substitute stainless steel or nylon nuts, often sold for car license plates in automobile supply stores.

When Your Pet Is a Car Passenger

• Expose your pets to car travel gradually with short trips before you attempt a cross-country journey with a pet.

• Dog harnesses that attach to seat belts are available in pet stores. It's not safe to have pets crawling on your lap or around your feet while driving.

• Cats, because they tend to move erratically, should be in carriers. It saves them from getting injured by closing doors and getting lost if they make a panic leap from the car when you make a rest stop.

• Put two collars with identification on your pet when it is traveling, just in case one falls off. And please include an area code and phone number of someone who can be reached.

Birds

My two cockatiels and Rocky, a Military Macaw, keep everybody who visits me entertained. I keep them in my office so that they can see my staff and visitors all day long.

• All birds need companionship, either with other birds or people. They've been known to pull out their feathers when lonely or bored. Give them toys, bells, and mirrors so that they can keep themselves amused and give them attention, too, just like you do with dogs and cats.

• You really shouldn't keep your bird cage in the kitchen. If a non-stick pan accidentally burns dry, it will give off toxic fumes that can cause polymer-fume fever and that can be fatal, especially to small birds.

• Small birds, such as canaries, finches, and parakeets, have delicate respiratory systems and are sensitive to fumes of all kinds—hair sprays, deodorants, and flea powders and sprays.

• A bird cage should be placed out of drafts, away from air-conditioning or heating ducts, and not near a window where the sun will shine directly on it for long periods of time, especially in the summer. Place the cage where the bird can have plenty of light and circulating air and cover the bird when the sun goes down.

• To teach your bird how to talk, repetition is the key. You can put the word (repeated many times) on cassette tape and then play it for your bird when you don't have time to chat or when you go away on a trip and don't want your bird to forget.

• Birds need exercise and attention. A lonely parakeet can actually get "love-sick" and act strangely. If your bird begins to preen before a mirror or plastic cage toy (some birds may even regurgitate food onto the mirror or toy), it is practicing courting and nesting behavior, which is usually reserved for mates and offspring. The cure for "lovesickness" is to remove the "love object" from the cage for two to three weeks and give your bird more exercise and attention.

• NOTE: Regurgitation by parakeets and other birds can also be a symptom of digestive ailments. If your bird regurgitates frequently but has no other "lovesick" symptoms, check with your vet.

• CAUTION: When you buy an imported pet bird, be sure that it has entered this country legally. Many birds are smuggled in without the benefit of quarantine, a practice that endangers birds in the United States. Outbreaks of exotic Newcastle disease, a devastating bird disease, have occurred in the past because of illegal importation of pet birds.

On a recent trip to a Mexican border town, I saw some parrots, wild cardinals, and other birds offered for sale, and when I asked about a yellow-headed parrot, the salesman offered me a price reduced from $25 to $15 that included taking the birds across the border and delivering them to me. I refused, of course, because not only is such a practice illegal, it's a way of smuggling in bird diseases along with birds.

• Buy a bird only from a reputable dealer. All imported birds must have stainless steel leg bands, which are put on when they enter quarantine.

Cats

Cats are affectionate pets. Who can resist their purrs?

One reason for their increased popularity these days is that cats are such practical pets for apartment dwellers. However, cat owners should know that even if Tabby never goes outdoors, it should be inoculated annually against many diseases.

• Outdoor cats may be better off without a collar, unless the collar is elastic and can slip off if your cat gets caught on something while climbing trees and rooftops. You can still attach a bell and rabies tag on the elastic collar.

Disciplining a Cat

There are ways to train a cat to stay off furniture and out of house plants.

• Spritz the cat with water from a spray bottle each time the cat does something wrong or goes to a place it doesn't belong while you sternly say, "No!"

He'll soon associate it with what he was doing and will eventually stop. You have to be consistent; cats can learn the word "no" just as well as a dog.

• If your cat has decided that water won't deter it from certain places, try this: Each time the cat goes to the forbidden place, dab a cotton ball moistened with vinegar on the cat's lips . . . just a dab, you don't have to rub or hurt the animal. If you are consistent, kitty will learn that going to the forbidden place means touching that nasty vinegar smell and give up. You can leave the saturated cotton ball in the forbidden place as an added deterrent.

• Keep cats out of your plants by covering the soil with wads of nylon net or a layer of pine cones. You can water plants through the net or cones.

• Keep cats out of newly seeded plant beds by laying rolled or crumpled lengths of chicken wire on the beds.

Cat Toys

Cats like to bat around just about anything.

• Put a few pebbles or a tiny bell into a small plastic pill bottle and close it tightly.

• Roll up a sock into a ball.

• Toss your cat a tennis ball, or even a wad of crumpled paper.

• Hang a fishing float on a string from a door knob and watch kitty bat it around.

• CAUTION: Don't give your cat a ball of yarn. He can become entangled and strangle himself while playing.

Cat Scratchers

• Play a game with your cat by getting it to chase a scratchable toy that you dangle from a fishing rod; you can reel in the toy while kitty chases it. Then, use this game to lead kitty to using its scratching post by dangling the toy over and on the post. Soon kitty will play and scratch on the post whenever the mood strikes.

• You don't need to buy a scratching post. Cover a length of log (cat-length high and about six inches in diameter) with carpet and nail its end to a flat board base.

• Some cats—those that are used to scratching the wooden fences they walk on—will be happy scratching on a 2" × 4" wooden wall stud that's about twice the cat's body length. Just saw off a piece and let it lie on the floor. Kitty will stand on it and scratch at the same time.

• Sprinkles of catnip can lure a cat to a scratching post, but don't be surprised if your cat ignores catnip; not all cats like it.

Cat Health

• Cats that look malnourished even though well fed and have frequent loose stools, a lackluster coat, and bloated stomach could have worms. See a vet quickly.

• When a cat's membranous eyelids half-cover its eyes, it's generally a sign of intestinal illness. Consult the vet immediately.

• Constant discharge from a cat's eye can be a symptom of local infection or systemic disease—another case for the vet.

• If a cat stops urinating normally or seems to have trouble urinating, get it to a vet quickly. A cat with urinary problems may stop using the litter pan because it associates the litter pan with pain. Treating the problem will help get the cat to use its litter again. Cats really are clean animals and prefer to use their litter.

• Cats build up tartar on their teeth, and while a little dry food helps prevent tartar buildup, it doesn't replace an annual vet checkup and cleaning.

Neutering and Spaying

• Even a neutered male cat will sometimes "spray" in the house, particularly if it perceives a threat to the status of its environment (such as the appearance of a new baby). Such spraying normally stops after the cat has adjusted to the change. Some cats will spray their own images in the mirror, thinking the image is an enemy. Try the "forbidden place" discipline if your cat is spraying a certain mirror.

• A female cat that hasn't been either spayed or bred will come into heat for two to three weeks twice a year. If you want to avoid living with a cat that periodically acts like she's insane, either have her spayed or let her have kittens. But if you let her have kittens, be sure you can find homes for them. Stray kittens abandoned on the road meet the same sad fate as abandoned dogs.

Cat Litter Boxes

• Pregnant women should avoid changing or handling cat litter boxes. Toxoplasmosis, a disease transmitted from cats to pregnant women, is responsible for about three thousand birth defects annually, according to the March of Dimes Birth Defects Foundation.

This disease, caused by passing of parasites from cats to humans, also causes brain damage and death in people with poor immune systems. About two million people are infected each year. As this book is being written, a vaccine can be administered to cats but not humans and may be years away from general use.

• Wear rubber gloves and wash your hands carefully when you change that litter pan!

• Baking soda sprinkled on the bottom of a litter pan before the litter is added helps deodorize the litter.

• A newspaper section placed on the bottom of the litter pan makes it easier to dump out the litter.

• Avoid mess by putting the whole pan into a large plastic garbage bag before you tip it to empty it. Tap the back of the pan while it's still inside the bag to get any stuck litter off, then hose off the litter tray, and, if you can, leave it in the sun for a while to air.

• Tape newspapers to the wall behind the litter pan with masking tape to protect the wall from flying litter if you have an especially enthusiastic cat.

• For a quickie temporary deodorizer for litter, sprinkle baking soda or carpet or litter freshener powder on top of the litter and give it a bit of a stir with your "pooper scooper." It'll stay reasonably fresh for a few hours until you can change the litter.

• Keeping an air freshener in the room with the litter box helps, but nothing works as well to keep odors down as frequent changing of the litter.

• If you change litter brands, to one with a different texture or odor, your cat might develop "litter phobia." The cat may refuse to use the new litter and actually suffer from urine retention and constipation.

To avoid this, add new litter in increments of one-fourth new litter to three-fourths old brand of litter, increasing the increment of new litter gradually as you change the litter pans so that your cat can get used to the new brand.

• Some cat owners train their cats to use newspaper sections instead of litter in the litter pan. It's easier to lift out a newspaper section than to dump messy litter, and you don't have litter tracked around in the "litter room." However, you have to believe that the cat won't use your newspapers before they get put into the litter pan—you could be forever uninformed about what's going on in the world.

Cat Carriers

With newspapers on the bottom, the following can be used to transport a cat.

• A bird cage will hold a small kitten en route to a new home.

• Two small laundry or storage baskets, one right side up and the other upside down, laced or tied together will serve as an emergency cat carrier in the car.

• A sturdy case from bottled beer, tied shut with rope, will serve as a cat carrier. The handgrip spaces provide air and see-through windows.

Dogs

Bringing a Puppy Home

• On puppy's first night home, if you place a ticking clock wrapped in a soft towel near him in his bed at night, it will help him think he still hears his mother's heartbeat. Being allowed to sleep on a hot water bottle wrapped in a towel will comfort a puppy too.

Housebreaking a Puppy

• To create a bed, cover the bottom of an old plastic wading pool or playpen with a plastic shower curtain or drop cloths and then layers of newspapers. The puppy will soon get used to such a new home and enjoy it until he is too big to confine.

• When you take a puppy outside to "outside-break" it, don't just plop the puppy on your porch, patio, or doorstep—he will use those places to relieve himself. Instead, place him where you prefer to have him perform his duties.

• It helps to take a rag you've used to clean up a mess and place it where you prefer the puppy to relieve itself, and then always take the puppy to that area. A dog's acute sense of smell will tell him that is where he is to do his job.

• Be sure to praise the pup when he performs as you want him to. If your puppy relieves himself in the house, discipline the pup if you catch him in the act; a puppy has a short memory and will not understand why you are scolding him half an hour later.

• It helps if you confine your new puppy to one certain room, especially a room with a wipeable floor, until he is housebroken.

• You can use ready-cut 2' × 4' pegboards as temporary doorway barriers for small puppies. Prop the pegboards in place in the doorway with a chair or other furniture; there's no need to make holes in walls or woodwork. With only a "half door" in place, your puppy won't feel as isolated as he will with the door closed, and if he scratches up the pegboards it won't matter as much as if he scratches up a door.

The pegboards can be used to hang things in your garage after the puppy gets free reign in the house.

Some dogs get the idea that the pegboard means "no admittance," and then you can use the pegboards to bar your dog from any off-limits room (bookcase, chair) at any time by just using a pegboard piece as a "stop" sign.

• Crate-training a dog will also help to housebreak it. Animals don't soil their own environments, and if a crate (or cage) becomes a dog's inside doghouse/bed, he won't urinate or defecate in it.

While some people don't like the idea of a dog in a cage, a crate-trained dog is a happier dog at the vet's when he's ill or in a boarding kennel if you're on a trip. If you don't treat the crate as a "punishing place," the animal will soon look upon it as his secure home and will be content to sleep in it and be put in it when non-dog people are visiting your home.

• While it seems counterproductive to give your dog water while you are crate-training it and housebreaking it at the same time, the dog needs water at all times.

• Some crated dogs will step in and tip over their water bowls. The solution is to buy a "rabbit cage" bottle at the pet store. A rabbit-size bottle holds about a quart and comes with a wire holder that you can attach to the crate.

Heartworm Medication

This deadly disease can be avoided if you take your dog to the veterinarian for annual blood tests and give him the preventive pills. Heartworms are transmitted by mosquitoes and affect only dogs.

• Contrary to what some pet owners think, the preventive pills should be given year-round, whether you live in warm or cold climates, according to the American Heartworm Association. Call your vet for complete information on heartworm disease.

Feeding Your Dog

• If your dog always tips over his outdoor food dish or likes to carry it around, get a sturdy plastic bowl or dishpan, pound a wooden stake (like a tent stake) through its bottom, and anchor the dish to the ground.

• Use heavy old butter crocks (from junque shops) for food and water with small or medium-size dogs who aren't likely to tip them over. I have seen larger dogs carry crocks around.

• A clean plastic garbage can with a lid can be used to store large bags of dry dog food and to protect it from insects and rodents if you store it in a garage.

General Dog Care Tips

• Exercise your dog early in the morning or late at night during the summer. Midday heat can cause heat exhaustion. Remember, dogs are so eager to please they will run and keep going well beyond their capacity to tolerate heat.

• A newly clipped dog shouldn't be walked in the peak sunshine, because its skin could get burned.

• Salt and chemical de-icers can irritate and cause cracks in the skin on a dog's feet in wintery climates. Wash the dog's feet off when you bring him in from a walk.

• If the pads of your dog's feet become dry or cracked, rub a little petroleum jelly into them. Wipe off the excess to protect your carpet. You can also put creamy lotion on them to help healing. This is a special treat for both Zinfandel and me in the wintertime.

• It's best not to keep your dog on a leash in the car. A leash can get caught on door handles and other projections and your dog could be injured.

• Leave your radio on if you have to leave your dog alone at home for several hours. The sound will reassure your pet and make him feel less abandoned. Dogs are pack animals, and since their humans become their pack when they are brought into a family, many dogs panic when left alone.

(A radio that's on also deters would-be housebreakers. They're likely to assume that someone's home.)

• Leave a rag or towel and old bathrobe or shirt that you have used with your dog when you go away, or, in the case of a new puppy, when you go to bed, and your scent will comfort him. Send along something with your scent on it or a rawhide bone that your dog's been chewing on when you board your dog, too, to make him feel at home.

• Wipe away the daily rheum that gathers at the corners of your dog's eyes with a dab of cotton dipped in a boric-acid solution.

• You don't have to get soaked when you wash your dog. Try making a coverall apron for yourself by cutting holes for your heads and arms in a plastic trash bag.

• Some dogs won't stay put when being washed out in the yard with a garden hose but will at least stand in one spot if you have them stand in a child's plastic wading pool or other large low-sided water holder. The advantage is that the dog's feet will be soaked clean while you lather and hose the rest of him.

Tropical Fish

Choosing Tropical Fish

Although fish don't require leash walking, litter changing, and regular trips to the vet for inoculations, they do require care and attention, and saltwater aquariums require even more attention than freshwater ones.

Whether or not hand-feeding many saltwater tank inhabitants, such as invertebrates (sea urchins, anemones), is fun or a chore is one factor to consider when you are choosing between saltwater and freshwater aquariums. The other is that saltwater aquariums require frequent testing to maintain the proper pH and salt concentration in the water, and the inhabitants are more sensitive to temperature changes.

If you just want to watch fish swim, you may prefer a freshwater tank.

An aquarium is a community of fish that functions best if the community is planned. Here's what to do when you are setting up a new aquarium community.

• If you are starting up a new saltwater tank, be aware that the water has to become "seasoned" for several days before you put any living creatures into it. Use your test kit to see if the pH and the salt content are suitable for fish. You will put invertebrates such as sea urchins, anemones, crabs, and starfish into the tank first, wait several days or weeks for the water to be seasoned again, and then add vertebrates—the actual finny fish.

• A fish tank is a "jungle."

1. Buy fish of similar size and maturity to keep them from becoming each other's dinner.
2. Select fish according to their natural characteristics. For example, although they eat their own young, peaceful platy will be compatible with other live-bearers and Mexican tetras. Tetras and barbels like to live in schools, so buy three to five of them at one time. The common angelfish we see in fish stores will live in pairs and with other peaceful species but need to have the cover of seaweed to swim in. However, regal angelfish are very aggressive and territorial; you can have only one in a large tank with other similarly sized fish. A lionfish can be kept in a tank only with fish its own size or larger; it will corner smaller fish and eat them. Tiger fish are so aggressive that they can be kept only with their own species. And so on. . . .
3. Choose the fish according to the aquarium level at which they prefer to live. Observe the fish in the store tanks and get advice from someone knowledgeable. For example, catfish breeds tend to live and feed at the bottom; tetras swim around in schools near the top, and angelfish and gouramies tend to stay around the middle of the aquarium. When fish have their own territories, they are more likely to leave each other alone.

• When you add new fish to an established aquarium community, disorient the "home" fish so that they "forget" which part of the tank they've claimed as their territories. Do this by rearranging the foliage, shells, ceramics, or other tank decorations at the same time that you add the new fish. All the fish will then have a chance to stake out their squatter's rights as if it were a new tank, and you'll have fewer fish fights and harassments.

• Prevent introducing fish diseases into your aquarium by having a "holding tank" for new fish. Quarantine new fish for about a month before putting them in with the rest unless you deal with an aquarium store that quarantines fish before selling them. (Sometimes, they'll have holding tanks in a back room if they quarantine new fish.)

• If your aquarium store has already quarantined the fish, you can add them to the tank from their plastic bags, but don't just dump the fish in, whether it's into the main or holding tank. Allow the bagged fish to float in the tank for about 15 to 20 minutes so that the new fish can become acclimated to your tank's temperature. After the waiting time, open the bag while it's still in the tank and allow the fish to swim into its new home.

Maintaining Aquariums

• A well-balanced aquarium with bottom-feeding and top-feeding fish and a properly functioning filter system needs less maintenance than most people think. In fact, too much fussing and water changing can disturb the pH and the bacteria balance in a tank, not to mention disturbing the fish, which will become disoriented if you change their scenery too often.

• Don't put things into your aquarium for decorations unless they are from an aquarium store. Souvenir shells from the ocean may be contaminated with bacteria or parasites; shells from a dime store could be lacquered, and some decorations could have poisonous paints or other chemicals on them.

• Always dechlorinate water before adding it to a fish tank and always return some of the "seasoned water" to the tank when you clean it. Dechlorinate water by letting it stand for several hours or by using commercial preparations that dechlorinate water with a certain number of drops per gallon.

• A large plastic wastebasket or small plastic garbage can can be used to mix up your salt water or dechlorinated water for the aquarium. If you don't keep a container specifically for this purpose, avoid getting harmful substances into the tank by lining the wastebasket or garbage can with a clean, sturdy plastic garbage bag, which you can use for garbage after you've mixed the water and put it into the tank.

• Move aquarium decorations (shells, ceramic things) with plastic salad tongs instead of contaminating the water with your hands. A plastic "spaghetti grabber" also helps you move things around in the tank.

• Anchor plastic vegetation to the bottom of the tank with the weight of glass marbles.

• A kitchen baster (used only for the fish tank) makes a good vacuum for the bottom of the tank. Just be sure not to wave it around as you remove it or you'll splatter fish gunk everywhere.

• Non-saltwater aquarium water is good for your plants.

• Putting a fish tank in front of a window may seem like a good decorating idea, but sunlight makes algae grow. Note that aquarium stores keep their tanks in the dark and use the tank lights to display fish.

• Leaving your tank light on too many hours during the day also will make algae grow. How many hours depends upon how light or dark your room is naturally—experiment with light and dark to see how many hours your tank can be lit without growing excess algae.

• Allow some of the green algae that form under your tank lid to fall to the bottom and feed invertebrates in a saltwater tank. Then you won't have to buy green algae from the pet store freezer compartment.

• If a lot of algae have turned white coral or other tank decorations murky gray, you don't have to throw these expensive decorations away. Make them white again by soaking them overnight in a solution of one part liquid chlorine bleach to four parts water.

CAUTION: You must remove the bleach before returning the decorations to the tank. Do this by soaking the items in water to which you've added at least five times the normal amount of dechlorinating chemicals. Soak them until you can't smell any chlorine in them at all.

Aquarium Equipment

• Don't buy your aquarium and fish at the same time. Even if you don't have to allow the water to season, as you do for saltwater fish, having the tank set up for a few days gives you a chance to make sure the filters and motors work properly and that the tank doesn't leak. It's no fun to move fish around when you find defects in your aquarium setup, and it can harm the fish.

• Always have a lid on the aquarium to keep things from falling in and to keep fish from jumping out. Yes, even some very small fish are "jumpers" and will land belly-up on the floor!

• When your usually quiet aquarium motor starts to hum loudly, it's probably getting ready to die; better buy a spare.

• Unplug mineral deposits from aquarium tubing with wooden shish kabob sticks. Also, keep extra tubing on hand in case you can't unplug some tubes.

• Make a long-handled cotton swab to clean algae out of a tube by wetting the end of a shish kebab stick and twirling the wet end in an appropriately sized wad of cotton.

• If the room in which you keep your aquarium has a constant temperature, you may not need to heat your aquarium and, in fact, you may tend to overheat the water. Check water temperature frequently with an aquarium thermometer. Most fish live well at 68 to 72 degrees Fahrenheit. Fish are healthier if they aren't submitted to too many changes of water and temperature, and they will be most active at moderate temperatures. Too cold or too warm water makes them sluggish and can encourage growth of harmful bacteria in the tank.

Fish Nutrition

Fish suffering from dietary deficiencies can lose weight, have cloudy eyes, pale color, scoliosis (twisted spine), or a bloated appearance known as ascites.

Although dried commercial fish foods are formulated to be nutritionally balanced, they can lose their nutrients during processing or while sitting on the shelf.

• Boost your fish feedings with this homemade supplement once or twice a week: Mix nine parts of minced, partially cooked beef liver and one part commercial food, plus 400 mg vitamin C, in a blender and process until combined. This mixture can be frozen for future use.

• When you buy fresh shrimp, save a few pieces (raw) for your fish. Cut finely and drop the pieces into the tank, but feed only the amount that can be totally consumed in five minutes. You can buy a fish feeder that holds individual pieces of shrimp or other fish food and lets you hand-feed invertebrates like anemones or sea urchins. Freeze the leftover shrimp for future fish treats.

• Uneaten food can spoil and pollute the tank; that's why you should feed only the amount your fish will consume in a single feeding frenzy, which usually lasts five to ten minutes. Feed enough food so that the top and bottom feeders get their share.

Gerbils, Hamsters, Guinea Pigs

These little animals can be wonderful pets for apartment dwellers. They live in self-contained environments; are clean; odor-free if their cages are kept clean; and don't bark, claw the carpet, or otherwise annoy landlords.

Also, they make especially entertaining pets for children who are bedridden or confined to wheelchairs, because they are always busy exploring, chewing, and climbing.

• A ten-gallon aquarium with a wire screen or mesh cover over it is a perfect home for gerbils and hamsters. (Guinea pigs need a bit more space.) There is no mess from litter coming through, as with a regular cage.

• Many plastic aquarium/tunnel homes can be bought for gerbils and hamsters, and, if you are handy, you can make a habitat from plexiglass panels bolted together (much larger and wider than, but similar to, an "ant farm" container); then, fill it with cedar shavings and other critter bedding so the gerbil or hamster can make its own tunnels and hideaways. If you make your own, don't forget the air holes and a secure place to hold a water bottle.

• Small rodents need to adjust to handling. They should be handled for increasing periods of time to "tame" them. They like to burrow in pockets and sleeves, and if they are gently and frequently handled, they become pleasant, cuddly pets.

• The females will become very restless when they are in heat and if they can, they may find a way to escape from their homes. Always be certain that lids and tunnels are properly fastened, especially during the females' restless periods. Males are generally more docile than females.

• An exercise wheel or ball will help your guinea pig, gerbil, or hamster get rid of excess energy and will entertain you too. Just don't forget that your pet is "at the ball" and leave it without food and water for too long.

• An exercise ball is a good carrier for a gerbil or hamster if you have to return it to the pet store or take it to a new home.

• Small rodents will eat carrots, lettuce, and many other foods in addition to store-bought pet food. They like to take their food from the food dish and hide it as if they were in the wild and had to stock up for the winter. They also eat live insects that might get into their cages.

• Metal jar lids can be used to hold seeds and other food. These small rodent pets will often eat plastic items, so it's best to use judgment about what you put into their cages. Small (nonedible) ceramic food bowls can be bought at pet stores.

- Rodents, and that includes tiny gerbils and hamsters, need to chew, so provide them with chew sticks and carrots to satisfy their needs; otherwise they will chew on their cages.

- Don't try to keep a gerbil, hamster, or guinea pig in a cardboard box "home." Cardboard is just another munchie, and they will chew their way out in no time at all. Many chew holes in the boxes they are put in for transport to their new owners' homes before they get carried through the doorway!

- These animals also are very supple; a grown hamster can squeeze out through a hole the size of a quarter. So inspect their homes often to make sure they can't escape.

- Gerbils don't usually climb straight, smooth sides well, so if you have a number of babies, a deep plastic dishpan will hold them until you can get a covered cage.

- A bird cage will hold a gerbil or hamster, but be sure to tie the lift-up door shut, because they are smart enough to get out through such an escape hatch.

- Although they don't drink much water and they get some of their water needs met by eating lettuce and other vegetables, these animals need to have a supply of fresh water in a stopper bottle at all times.

- Most pet stores have inexpensive booklets on raising gerbils, hamsters, and guinea pigs, and you can get information from the library to help you too.

Wild Animals

- If you find a featherless baby bird that is completely helpless and unable to keep its head up, you should try to help. As in the case of any helpless wild animal, call your Humane Society for help.

Loss of a Pet

Much is written about the love that binds people to their pets, and recent medical research has shown the mental and physical health benefits of having a pet. For most of us, losing a cherished pet is like losing a member of the family—consolation is difficult and mere words can't totally describe the grief. However, here is an excerpt from "The Last Will and Testament of an Extremely Distinguished Dog," written by Eugene O'Neill (published by Yale University Press, 1956, Copyright 1956, Carlotta O'Neill), which I have found to be comforting and which I've sent to others who have lost pets to comfort them:

The dog "writes" of his love for his Master and Mistress, asks them to remember him but tells them not to grieve too long, and then makes one last request:

> One last request I earnestly make. I have heard my Mistress say, "When Blemie dies we must never have another dog. I love him so much I could never love another one." Now I would ask her for love of me, to have another. It would be a poor tribute to my memory never to have a dog again. What I would like to feel is that, having once had me in the family, now she cannot live without a dog! I have never had a narrow jealous spirit. I have always held that most dogs are good . . . some dogs, of course, are better than others.

As I always say about the small zoo at our home, they own us, we don't own them, and I wouldn't have it any other way! A pet is more than a watchdog, attack cat, or alarm bird; they are members of the family. Think about how little they ask for—food, water, a scratch or two behind the ears, and a pat on the head. Isn't it amazing that they usually give love and attention so unconditionally? Boy, I sure wouldn't "speak," or do a flip, or sit up for a dog bone, but we ask them to. Please remember, our animal friends may not be able to talk in human terms, but they sure can speak to us in many other ways, so take the time to listen when they say "I love you."

CHAPTER 12

Entertaining

Having Fun at Your Own Party

Trust me; it's possible to have fun at your own party, even if you are doing all of the cooking yourself.

• Do as much as possible ahead of time and, above all, make a list of things to do and what to serve so that you don't have to clutter your mind with details on the day of the party. Also, if some of your guests are helping you serve, lists enable them to help you more easily.

I've listed some pre-party chores below. As you complete your party preparations, check them off on the list so that you have a feeling of accomplishment.

• It's hard to host and parent at the same time. The best tip to parents of small children who are having a party is to hire a baby-sitter to entertain them, either in your home or at one of your guests' houses. School-age children can sleep over at friends' houses and you can return the favor to their friends' parents when they have a party.

• To avoid possible messes, pretest the capacity of serving pieces by filling them with water measured according to the anticipated recipe amount.

• If you are having your party catered, book the caterer as soon as you know when you're entertaining. Whether you are having the party in your home or elsewhere, don't assume anything. Have all details about food, beverages, and serving them spelled out in the contract so that on party day nobody says, "I assumed you were doing that." This is especially important if you are having food brought into your home.

• Make a detailed list of who will provide:

1. All food on the menu, from entrées to nuts and mints, and if serving dishes for these items will be yours or the caterer's.
2. All beverages, including soft drinks, wine, mixers, coffee, ice, coolers, and glasses or cups in which to serve them.
3. All tableware, including napkins, plates, cups, flatware—disposable or not.
4. Table linens and centerpiece.

Also agree upon in writing:

5. Time the food will be served.
6. Fees for bartending and food service.
7. Price per person and variations of the price if you furnish the wine, a special dessert, or cheeses or whatever else you will take responsibility for.
8. And, are the leftovers yours, or does the caterer get to take them with him or her?

Here's what to do two weeks before a big party if you are doing the cooking:

• Plan your menu and make a two-part shopping list.

1. First list nonperishables to buy ahead of time, such as bottled beverages, canned and bottled food items, spices, and paper plates and napkins if you'll be using them. Buying these things as soon as you know you'll need them eases the last-minute scramble before the party and ensures you're having exactly the products you need.

   It's a good idea to order special cuts of meat ahead of time, too, even if your supermarket "always has that," because Murphy's Law will prevail; the day before your party will be the first day that your supermarket doesn't have those special brands and items.

2. Make a second shopping list, of the perishables to be bought the day before or on the day of the party—such as salad veggies, coffee cream, baked goods.

• Post a copy of your menu on the refrigerator door; it's the best way to make sure you serve everything you've cooked or bought for the party.

• On the day before your party:

1. Review your lists to make sure you have everything.
2. Check out your serving trays and bowls to make sure they are clean and ready for use.
   Make some tentative arrangements on the table and make sure that you have enough trivets and so forth to protect your table from hot dishes and that the centerpiece fits.
3. Check out your table linens to see if they need ironing (or, with some permanent-press, a spin in the dryer with a damp towel) to make them look right.
4. Cut, chop, slice, marinate, cook, and do anything else to the food that can be done the day before.

• On the day of the party:

1. If you haven't bought your perishables, do it in the morning when you are still calm.
2. Cook what needs cooking.
3. Set up what needs setting up.
4. Take a break for yourself.

• Notice that I didn't schedule any housecleaning. That's because we all have different standards for cleaning before a party.

Some people clean every nook and cranny with a toothbrush before a party and even wash their windows for a nighttime event held indoors with all the draperies closed. Others think top cleaning is good enough and focus on the food and fun.
One of the best party givers I ever knew never did heavy cleaning before a party. She just fluffed around with a feather duster, shined the bathroom sinks, and then went through the house on the day of the party replacing all light bulbs with colored or very dim-wattage bulbs on the premise that nobody who matters cares about the house anyway and that the time to clean up is AFTER the party.

• If you can't afford to pay for help with a party, make a trade-off deal with a friend in similar circumstances.

• Date and keep your party lists and menus for reference. If you entertain a lot, it's easy to forget what you've served, how you served it, and to whom. Having a record helps you to remember such things as:

1. What amounts of food you prepared for how many people, and if you ran out or had too many leftovers.
2. How much longer you had to bake four casseroles than it usually takes to bake one in your oven.
3. If you served shrimp to Eunice and then found out that she is so allergic to them that she stops breathing.
   (It's not bad manners to ask a guest, "Do you have any allergies?" when they respond to your invitation.)
4. If Albert is totally wild about your kumquats au gratin you should serve them again.
   (If at all possible, always invite one guest who really loves all food. It's good for your ego.)

Food Planning

• The amounts of food necessary depend upon the occasion, how early the food is served, and which guests you invite.

• A buffet is the easiest way to feed large groups in your home.

• Always offer non-alcoholic beverages when you're serving alcoholic ones so that everyone can have something.

• When you need to cool a lot of canned beverages, use your washing machine as a large cooler. Fill it with cans and dump ice over them. You might want to put a towel in the bottom to prevent chipping enameled washers.

A family-size washing machine holds approximately four cases of soda water plus a few more. Guests can help themselves. The cover opens and closes easily, the cans stay nice and cold, and it sure saves wear and tear on your freezer or bothering with a cooler that never seems to stay shut properly. In the morning, simply take out any remaining cans and spin the water out of the washing machine using the spin cycle.

Here are some tips for estimating amounts of food needed.

• If you are having a "come and go" reception, tea or coffee for adults, plan about three small sandwiches, two small finger foods, and two beverages per person. If you are serving children and teenagers, plan more food, especially cookies.

• A gallon of punch makes about 40 punch cups.

- A pound of coffee brews 50 cups.

- A 20- to 24-ounce loaf of sandwich bread has about 25 slices and will make 52 small, triangular, closed sandwiches.

- One pound of cooked lean meat will provide 32 ½-ounce slices for small sandwiches.

- A ½-ounce slice of cheese is enough for a small sandwich.

- A 3½- to 4-pound chicken will make chicken salad for about 70 small triangular sandwiches.

- A quart of dip, such as crab or broccoli, will make about 150 teaspoon-size servings.

- A 12-ounce can of nuts should serve 20 to 25.

- One-half pound of small candies serves 25.

Using Your Freezer for Parties

- Freeze fruit juice punch in gallon milk jugs or cartons. Remove from freezer several hours ahead of time to thaw to a "mush" and then add cold ginger ale when ready to serve.

(If you can't get the mush out of the plastic milk jug, just take a serrated knife and saw off the top section. Always cut away from yourself, even when you're rushed at a party!)

- When baking cakes ahead of time, layers may be lightly glazed and frozen, leaving the final frosting and decorating until later, or they can be completely decorated and then frozen.

- Pies can be frozen either baked or ready-to-bake.

- Freeze frosted cupcakes for children's parties.

- Such foods as spaghetti sauce, lasagna, chili, or sloppy Joes can be frozen and just reheated for spontaneous parties, especially for teens.

- You can whip and freeze individual "toppers" of sweetened, flavored whipped cream to dress up warm cobblers, puddings, or shortcakes.

- Roll scoops of ice cream in tinted coconut or finely chopped nuts, then serve with fruit, fudge, or caramel sauce or liqueurs.

(Ice-cream balls or scoops can be put into barware cocktail glasses or small, clear or holiday-decorated old-fashioned-style plastic tumblers ready to be topped with fruit, fudge sauce, or liqueurs.)

• Freeze individual fruit salads.

• Cookies, fruit and nut breads, party sandwiches, canapés, some dips, cheese balls, and other appetizers can be frozen and then heated on party day.

• Cream puffs can be filled with ice cream or whipped cream and frozen until needed.

• Meringue shells frozen in airtight containers can be filled with ice cream, sherbet, fresh or frozen fruit, or lemon sauce.

• Freeze coffee cakes, rolls, and muffins for company breakfasts or coffee.

(Layer a store-bought angel food cake with your favorite ice cream so that you have three layers of cake to two layers of ice cream and then keep it in the freezer so that you can top it with appropriate liqueurs or sauces for an easy, always-ready dessert.)

• Make double batches of your favorite recipes; eat one and have one on hand for unexpected guests or expected ones, for that matter.

• Most cookbooks have information on how best to freeze foods. Just remember that fresh, crisp vegetables get limp in frozen sandwiches. Egg whites toughen and become rubbery, so they must be chopped very finely or put through a sieve or food processor if egg salad is to be frozen.

• If such fillings are to be frozen, use salad dressing instead of mayonnaise, and if you must use mayo, use it only sparingly.

The "Good China, Crystal, and Linens"

How you store your china, crystal, good linens, and other items used mainly for special occasions and entertaining has a lot to do with how often and how exhausting it is to use these things.

If your "good things" are stored where they get dusty, you'll be washing and wiping before and after using them.

If they are stored so that you have to move heaven and earth to get at them, the chances are they won't get used at all.

My personal philosophy is that you should use your good china, crystal, silverware, and so forth, as often as possible. Now obviously, if you have small children in your household that are capable of dropping things, I wouldn't use them every day; however, set them on a shelf that you can reach and use them when you fix yourself a sandwich, a glass of tea, or the like. And as my mother used to always say, "If you don't use them, the second or third wife will."

Tableware

Storing China, Crystal, Serving Pieces

• Dishes and serving pieces that are stored in the back of lower kitchen cupboards will be easier to slide in and out if they are in a box, small plastic storage baskets, or dishpans. You won't have to crawl into the cupboard to get them. The other advantage of having them in a box or other covered container is that they will stay clean.

• If you have extra cupboard drawer space, try storing flat baking dishes and platters in drawers instead of on cupboard shelves. You can just pull them out easily when you need them.

• Protect your china from chips and surface scratches by placing cushions between plates, cups, or other stacked pieces. Use coffee filters, napkins (paper or cloth), paper towels, paper plates, cloth remnants cut into handkerchief-size pieces, clean handkerchiefs, clean foam meat trays. If you have some spare time and want to spend some money, buy flannel, felt, or nonwoven interfacing at fabric shops when it's on sale and make custom-size pads to go between china pieces.

• Store the padded stacks of pieces you use only a few times a year in plastic bags or just cover them with plastic bags the way people cover kitchen appliances with ready-made covers.

• Store larger items in plastic bags closed with a twistie or in boxes to keep them clean. Silver items can be wrapped in tarnish-preventing cloth or bags, not with light plastic and rubber bands. However, a heavy plastic bag that you can close is sufficient.

• Instead of wrapping each piece or stack of seldom used china or crystal, you can make a "tarp" or "drapery" of plastic wrap over a whole cupboard shelf of items. The construction of some cupboards will allow you to tape a "window" of plastic wrap over the shelf face. This is especially effective for that top cupboard shelf that seems to attract greasy dust like a magnet.

• If you are moving, you can pad your breakables with clean old clothing or towels.

• If you live alone, you may find that you use only the top one or two plates of a stack, while the bottom ones gather dust. Rotating your dishes occasionally will give them all a turn at being used and washed.

• When you don't have a full dishwasher load, you can fill up the space with seldom-used tableware so that it gets a bath between uses.

• If you've stacked glasses or other similarly shaped items and find that you've got two stuck together, don't reach for a hammer and don't despair: Try filling the top glass or cup with cold water or ice cubes and then put the bottom glass or cup into warm or hot water. The cold water in the top piece should shrink it slightly and the warm water around the bottom piece should expand it just enough to let you separate the two pieces.

Also, dribbling mineral oil around the stuck parts and allowing it to seep through will often do the trick.

Next time, put a pad of something in between pieces or don't stack them!

• You don't have to stack glasses to save shelf space if you put them in rows, alternating one glass right side up and the next upside down. Alternate right side up and upside down with the rows, too, and you'll be surprised at how many more glasses can be put on a shelf. This method works very well with slanted water glasses and many shapes of stemware.

Tableware Tricks

• If your china has dark scratches on it from being stacked, you may be able to remove these marks by rubbing them with baking soda.

• When a favorite dish or plate gets a slight crack, try putting it in a pan of milk, then bring to a boil and simmer for 45 minutes at low heat. In many cases, this method makes the crack disappear and you can use your dish again.

• Old ironstone items that are crazed and stained from food and oven heating can sometimes be reclaimed if you soak them in liquid bleach, diluted by half with water. If you can't submerge an item, such as a platter, in bleach because it's too large, try wrapping paper towels around it before putting it into a plastic bag. Put the bagged item in a bathtub or sink where it will be safe from children or pets and then pour bleach over the paper toweling. The paper will keep the bleach on the platter's surfaces and edges and you'll use less bleach than if you try to submerge a large item. Close up the bag and let the bleach do its job for 24 or more hours. Some badly burned plates can't be recovered, but most stains will come out with this method. You may have to do this in two steps, bleaching the top side of a platter or bowl the first time and then the bottom with the second application.

• In some cases, you can remove stains from china by "painting" the item with liquid dishwasher detergent and waiting several hours or a day.

• A "poultice" of baking soda or powdered dishwasher detergent will also remove some stains.

Here are a few tips on clean-up which are included in Chapter 1, but which bear repeating:

CAUTION: Wear rubber gloves when you work with strong bleach or dishwasher detergent to protect your skin.

• If you spray glass baking dishes with oven cleaner, let them stand for about 30 minutes; you'll get the burned-on grease off and have sparkling clean dishes again. This is especially important if the glass dishes are used with silver holders, where burned-on gunk looks doubly bad.

• Soak dirty dishes in hot, soapy water as you are preparing a meal for family or guests and you won't have as much scraping to do during the final cleanup. Just fill the sink with water and then add utensils and dishes as you work.

CAUTION: Don't bury knives in this dishwater. What you can't see in the suds can hurt you!

• Soak dishes and pans with dried egg or milk on them in cold water. Hot water actually cooks these foods onto their containers and makes cleaning more work.

• Dip washed dishes in vinegar water bath to rinse them clean.

• When you wash fragile china or glass in the sink, line the bottom with a washcloth or small towel to prevent chips and scrapes and a case of nerves, too!

• If you break a glass, let the water drain out and use a paper towel to retrieve it so you don't cut your hand.

• Have an extra sink strainer handy to accommodate the extra dishes you use when you have company. If you have people drying dishes as you wash, you can put one strainer on each side of the sink and ease the traffic congestion in the kitchen. (With two strainers, you can also give the more fragile pieces to the more careful dish dryers, especially if you have children helping you!)

• Make a spare strainer and avoid clutter in your cupboards: Cover several layers of newspapers with a clean towel, and the newspaper will absorb the dripping water and keep it from flowing across your countertops.

• If you are washing stacks of dishes, put the whole stack into the dishwater at one time so that the bottom ones soak while you swish off the top ones. This is much easier than putting a stack of dishes beside the sink and putting dishes one at a time into the dishwater for washing.

• When you are loading the dishwasher after a party, it may be easier to wash a whole load of just saucers and plates of various sizes, and then a load of cups, glasses, and odd-size pieces. Then, if you have to stack cups or odd serving pieces on the plates for storage, the plates will have been washed first and will already be in place in the cupboard and you won't have as much shifting around of heavy china.

• Save TV dinner plates and/or have paper plates (especially those with compartments) handy when you have a party and you can give your guests leftovers to take home. Then, if you are dieting, you won't be tempted to eat "for shame," as in "it's a shame to waste that."

Heating Plates

• If you have a gas stove, you'll find that the pilot light will heat your dishes if you put them into the oven for several minutes before serving.

• Heat plates by running them through the rinse cycle of your dishwasher.

• Your microwave oven will heat plates too, but remember, not all dishes are microwave safe. For a quick test from the Association of Home Appliance Manufacturers that will help you determine whether or not a dish is safe, see Chapter 1, "Saving Time in the Kitchen," page 43.

Linens

Table Setting

• Here's a terrific tip for parents of small children who like to entertain and use tablecloths instead of place mats:

As any toddler parent knows, a dangling tablecloth says, "Pull me" to any toddler. To keep small children from giving the tablecloth a disastrous yank after you've set the table for guests, just open the table's groove, as you would to insert an extra table leaf (about an inch), then crease the tablecloth into the groove and close it up. If you are adding a leaf to the table, insert the tablecloth on either side of the leaf.

A slight line across the table is certainly more attractive than the pile of broken china and crystal that can result when little fingers and curious minds operate in a dining room! And your peace of mind is the bonus!

Linen Laundering

• Protect a lace tablecloth by laundering it in a mesh bag.

• Save yourself a lot of anguish: DON'T launder a crocheted tablecloth with long fringes in the washer, not even in a mesh bag. Believe me, the result is the worst tangle you'll ever cuss at. Hand wash such items!

• Shaping a lace tablecloth after washing it is easy if you just drape it over the protected dining room table to dry. If it's starched, you'll need to pin it in place on a clean bedsheet using nonrust pins. But remember that water is an enemy of tabletops! Protect the table surface with a flannel-backed plastic cloth, a shower curtain, or a painter's drop cloth.

• Here is a way to iron a tablecloth, even a large Irish linen cloth, without really ironing it:

1. Place a large sheet on the floor.
2. Straight pin the wet tablecloth to the sheet with nonrust pins, smoothing out wrinkles as you pin.
3. Let it dry while you read a book or do something else that's more fun than ironing a large tablecloth.

• When ironing tablecloths on an ironing board, reverse the board so that you are ironing on the wider end. Iron curtains on the wider end too. (If you sew and have a padded cutting table, that's the place to iron any large items the easiest way!)

• You can also iron a large tablecloth (and curtains or bed cover) right on the bed.

• Hopelessly stained or yellowed white linen damask cloths can be dyed commercially and given a new life.

• It may be possible to cover up an unremovable coffee stain on a white tablecloth by dyeing the whole cloth with coffee to get a champagne-colored cloth.

Brew a big pot of strong coffee, pour it into a large plastic pail or tub, and then slosh the stained tablecloth around until the color is evenly distributed.
(See the clothing chapter's spot removal chart for tips on removing stains from fabric.)

Repairing Linens

• Small cuts or slits in lacy tablecloths (and sheer or lacy curtains too) can be repaired as follows:

1. Place a piece of wax paper under the cut.
2. Apply a little clear nail polish across the threads.

After the nail polish dries, the mend should be nearly invisible.

Storing Linens

• ALWAYS clean linens before storing them. Spots and stains will set if left in the fabric. With fine linens, you'll be saving money in the long run if you have them professionally cleaned. And tell your dry cleaner what those spots and stains are so that they can be properly treated before cleaning.

• If you store your fine linens in a cedar chest, the fumes from cedar oil may yellow them.

Instead, store them in a dry place where they won't mildew or get musty-smelling. You can prevent yellowing of white linens that will be stored for a long time by wrapping them first in white tissue paper, then in blue tissue paper.

• Hang linens on hangers that you can cover with dry cleaners' bags or garbage bags. Before putting tablecloths on the hangers, fold as described below.

• Here's how to fold a tablecloth so that the creases look as neat as hotel banquet cloths:

1. Make the first fold down the middle with the right side out.
2. Then fold each side back toward and slightly beyond the center.
    When the tablecloth is opened, the side creases will be alike and you won't have a dust streak down the center.

• Having such even folds helps you center the cloth when you are putting it on the table.

• An adjustable tension curtain rod installed in the back of a small closet will also hold table linens neatly and out of your way.

• If you have a round table and several round tablecloths but very little storage space, store all of the tablecloths right on the table—two, three, or four deep. Put a plastic tablecloth under the one currently in use to keep the bottom layers clean. The best bonus of this is that all of your round tablecloths will be stored without wrinkles. You know how difficult it is to fold or hang a round cloth neatly!

Miscellaneous Tips

Not everything has to be used according to its original purpose.

• Use covered bonbon dishes for serving grated cheese or jelly.

• Any stemmed drinking glass can be a holder for a short candle at Christmas time. Turn it upside down so that you have the candle on the bottom of the stem; then you can put an ornament into the glass and then set up rows of pretty Christmas candles. Melted candle wax or floral clay will stick the candles to the glass-stem bottoms.

CAUTION: Don't let candles burn too low; the glasses can get too hot and may crack.

• Serve company salad in a glass punch bowl.

• Ice down wine or champagne in a silver punch bowl.

• Serve coffee to a crowd in glass punch cups.

Most people would rather have coffee in a mug or real cup instead of paper or foam ones, even if the mugs and cups don't match. At a casual buffet, just put the mugs and small paper cocktail napkins beside the coffee urn and let guests serve themselves. I have set out mugs with different sayings on them that were gifts from friends, and guests have enjoyed laughing at the messages and pictures printed on them. Saucers for cups are optional if yours is a casual group. Just make sure there are a lot of coasters distributed throughout the house to protect your furniture.

• Make mulled cider in your party-size coffee percolator. Or heat it in the microwave oven in a heat-safe glass punch bowl (or pitcher) and then serve it in the same container.

• Those long French bread baskets or other appropriately sized ones will hold silverware on a buffet table.

• If your buffet requires only forks, use an appropriately sized vase as a holder. It will save space on a small table.

• Use a clean, new clay flowerpot to hold silverware on a casual buffet table and also in your kitchen as a drain for newly washed silverware and cutlery. In either case, it won't tip.

• An ice bucket is a handy mini-cooler for radishes, carrot and celery sticks, or other crispy raw veggie munchies at your tailgate picnic.

• Ice down your picnic jug of wine in a deep plastic tub.

• Chill canned beverages in your washer or laundry room sink when you're having a party. The melted ice will drain away!

• Sugar cube tongs will pick up tiny pickles and things on a relish tray.

• Use a sentimental silver baby cup for a sugar bowl and baby's spoon for the sugar.

• Small, fringed terry-cloth towels make colorful place mats for casual settings. And for families, terry catches spills before they drip to the floor.

• Washcloths can be super family table napkins, especially when you find them on sale by the dozen!

- A spa-size bath towel can be a picnic table cloth.

- If you sew, twin or double permanent press sheets, depending upon the size of your table, can be cut and trimmed so that you can make a tablecloth and matching napkins. If you don't sew, a twin sheet will fit some tables as is.

- A thin flannel sheet or blanket can be a good table pad.

- Four dinner-size napkins stitched together could cover a card table.

- For a novelty party tablecloth, spread a clear plastic drop cloth or tablecloth over anything flat and colorful, such as fall leaves or dime store paper decorations for Saint Patrick's Day, Valentine's Day, Easter, Christmas, or a birthday. You can even put a plastic cloth over a decorated paper cloth when you have a child's birthday party so that the first spill doesn't totally destroy the whole table decor.

- Spread a solid-color tablecloth or sheet on the table and have everyone at the party autograph it with felt-tip pens or liquid embroidery paint. (Make sure that there's a pad beneath the cloth to protect the table.)

- Your centerpiece need not come from the florist. Pick any greenery from your backyard to serve as a base and add fruit, flowers, peppers, pine cones, candles, figurines, wood carvings, or anything else that looks right to you. Even pot plants set in a pretty bowl can be a centerpiece.

- If you are serving a decorated cake or other pretty dessert or salad, especially fruit, that is the centerpiece.

- No space for a centerpiece? Cut a few strands of any kind of ivy and use as runners down the center length of the table. A fat candle or single flower in a bud vase in the center will be the finishing touch.

- Confetti on the tablecloth at a New Year's party will decorate a small table so that you don't need a centerpiece.

Bridal/Groom Showers and Weddings

Since many newlyweds already have fully equipped apartments and are in enough of a quandary about what to do with "his and hers" everything, personal items or pantry food items may be more appreciated than such traditional shower and wedding gifts as toasters, blenders, and silver. Shower invitations can say that it will be a "kitchen," "pantry," or "personal" shower. Many showers now include the groom, too. Often the bridesmaids pitch in together to buy the bride a negligee or some item for the couple that none of them could afford to buy alone.

Here are a few suggestions for gifts you can make or assemble that may not only save the day but save you some money if you're on a tight budget.

• A personal shower: For the nondomestic bride (and groom), a few trousseau items: negligee, lacy underwear, favorite bath product or cologne, leisure clothing. For the groom: a robe, wallet, pocket knife, or shirt.

• Toys: Games such as word games, banking games, board games, and puzzles. (Remember the saying that "you can tell the age of the boys by the price of their toys"?)

• Books, craft supplies: If the couple has hobbies or special interests, buy books and items related to them. If you buy cookbooks, add some of the spices used in the recipes to the top of the package as a decoration.

• A honeymoon kit: Include headache pills, antacids, adhesive bandages, a small tube of antiseptic or spray that can be used on sunburn if the couple is going to the shore, hand cream, tweezers and clippers for hangnails and splinters, and maybe a couple of granola bars for emergency middle-of-the-night hunger pangs.

• A home-warming kit: Scissors, gauze, tape, cotton, thermometer, heating pad, hot water bottle, upset-stomach remedies, pain relievers, and other accessories for a home first-aid cabinet, including a first-aid book.

• A fix-it kit: Include a hammer, set of screwdrivers, pliers, nails, picture hooks. You can also add a gas can, oil or silicon spray, garden hose, and any other home-aid items.

• A cupboard kit: Grocery staples and boxed mixes such as cake mix, corn bread mix, meat helper mix, pastas, basic spices, flavorings and colorings, and other food items that are nice to keep on hand. You can also include casserole dishes or baking pans and wooden spoons or spatulas to go with the mixes.

• Recipe kit: A recipe box with your favorite recipes, and if you're the mother of the bride or groom, her or his favorite recipes. You can ask each shower guest to bring her favorite recipes to add to the box. Also, if it's a kitchen shower, favorite recipes could be accompanied by nonperishable ingredients and the proper pan (cookie cutter or other utensil) needed to prepare the recipe.

• You could "theme" the kits so that you provide the staples and spices for making Italian, Cajun, Tex-Mex, or other ethnic foods.

Tuck in a few store coupons with food kits.

• A munchies/picnic kit: A picnic cooler filed with disposable plates, cups, napkins, and flatware and some munchies, ranging from bean dip and a six-pack to caviar and champagne, depending upon the taste of the couple.

• A sewing kit: A supply of different-color thread, a sewing box or basket, measuring tape, mending tape (fusible, iron-on), scissors, needles, straight and safety pins, a few assorted buttons, snaps, hooks, fabric glue, pin cushion, and anything else that catches your eye at the store that will help a couple keep themselves and their clothing out of tatters and tears.

(If you like, ask each shower guest to put a spool of colored thread on the gift as a decoration.)

• Happy memory quilt: If the shower guests sew, each can bring a quilt square embroidered with the guest's name, so that all the squares can be sewn together for a treasured keepsake.

• A reality kit: Include a bucket, broom, mop, cleaning supplies, sponges, and other facts of life.

• You can attach small kitchen items (potato peelers, can opener, wooden spoons) to a clothesline and then put them into a laundry basket; as the line is pulled out, so are the utensils.

• A Heloise kit: A copy of this book and some of my favorite "do-alls," such as white vinegar, lemon juice, salt, candles, baking soda, dental floss, and any of the other ordinary items used in my hints to do many extraordinary things.

Shower Memories

• Make a copy of the guest list with names and addresses to help the honoree send out thank-you notes. Leave about three lines of space so that a description of the gift can be noted after the name as the gifts are opened.

• Have each guest write her name, address, and the gift on a slip of paper or index card to be used for a door-prize drawing at the shower and by the honoree for writing thank-you notes after the shower. Index cards can be put into a permanent address file for Christmas cards.

• Have each guest write her name, address, and her hint for a happy, successful marriage on an index card, which can be read by the bride during the shower and, as noted above, kept in a permanent address file. Reviewing friends' hints for a happy marriage in the address file is a cure for the monotony of addressing Christmas cards.

• Take instant pictures during the shower and put them into an album for the honoree.

• Mothers of the bride and groom could assemble photo albums of precious shots from birth to adulthood and present them to the couple, or friends could call the mothers and ask for the photos so that they can assemble them. (This is a good idea for a baby shower, too. Everyone wants to know "who the baby looks like," and so such an album can be a reference after baby is born.)

• Have shower (and wedding) guests sign a guest book, which the couple can use in their home. The custom of guest books comes and goes, but anyone who's been married a long time and has kept one through the years knows how nice it is to remember good times, not to mention how nice it is to be able to find the answer to "What was Harry's first wife's name?"

• Autograph a plain tablecloth with laundry pens or liquid embroidery/fabric paint and give it to the honoree. Or have guests autograph a wooden rolling pin, tray, or cutting board with a felt-tip marker, then shellac it and present it to the couple after the shellac has dried, for a lasting memory.

• Have the wedding invitation matted and framed professionally for a gift or, if the couple have written their own vows or have a special poem or biblical text read at the wedding, have the words done in calligraphy and framed for a keepsake gift. We were lucky enough to receive three of our wedding invitations mounted, matted, and framed, and it's such a delight I have one in each area of the house. There is one exceptionally beautiful one hung in my bathroom, and each morning when I brush my teeth I look at it and smile.

• Cut a hole in the center of a paper plate and, as each gift is opened, poke the ribbons through the hole, leaving the bows on top. By the end of the gift opening, the bride will have a bouquet to save or to throw as she chooses.

Baby Showers

Buying baby gifts is fun, but what do you buy a mother of several children who already has equipment and lots of leftover clothing? Here are some tips that could also be given a first-time mother.

• A baby shower tree: Attach coupons for "Three Hours of Baby-sitting in Your Home or Mine," interspersed with store discount coupons for baby supplies, to a small, squatty end of a tree branch that has been spray painted white and weighted in a flower pot so that it won't tip. Multicolored bows can be attached in between the coupons so that this table centerpiece can be a decoration in baby's room after the shower and after all the coupons have been redeemed and used.

• A hospital kit for Mom: Include toiletries, comb, brush, instant "dry" shampoo, regular shampoo, lotion, mascara, lip gloss, and a bag of change so that Mom can use a pay telephone or vending machines once she's up and about in the hospital or birthing center. A nice bed jacket, robe, or nightgown is a help too. Make sure these open conveniently in the front if Mom plans to breast-feed. Breast pads could be included in this kit if you feel very practical.

• A certificate for a manicure and pedicure to be used during those last months of pregnancy when Mom-to-be can't even see her feet, much less give them a pedicure.

• A certificate for a haircut and/or set by a hairdresser who makes house calls if your city has these services. Very new mothers often need such a boost in the first week or two after baby comes and may have trouble getting out of the house, especially if breast-feeding.

• A frozen casserole shower: Food that's ready to thaw, heat and eat is a blessing to new mothers, especially those with other children at home. Just make sure to put the food in disposable containers so that there's no chore of returning dishes.

• A gift certificate for a cleaning service day, to be used when the mom-to-be gets a frantic "nesting" urge to "have everything nice and clean for the baby" or a couple of weeks after baby is born, when the house has been neglected for more important things—like enjoying the baby.

I especially like these ideas, as it seems to be Mom who has done all the work needs to be pampered.

Other Help for Mom

• If the person who hosts the baby shower buys thank-you notes and envelopes and has each guest address the envelopes, the envelopes can be used to draw for a door prize and by the mom-to-be when she sends out thank-you cards. Some etiquette experts may say this is not proper, but I think it's certainly a help to the mom-to-be.

• Have guests address birth announcements to themselves at the shower and save Mom (or Dad) a lot of energy.

Long-Distance Bridal and Baby Showers

Being separated by miles doesn't necessarily mean families and friends can't have the traditional showers that mean so much to brides and moms-to-be. The shower tradition just needs to be carried out in some untraditional ways. Here's how to hold a shower for someone far from home.

• For a surprise shower: Tell the honoree to call home (or elsewhere) at a specific time and day. When the call comes through, have all the guests shout "surprise" and then take turns wishing the bride or mom-to-be good thoughts and love. If you don't want to make it a surprise shower, just tell the honoree that you will be having a long-distance shower and that you will call her at a certain time on that day.

• While the honoree is on the phone, have each guest describe the gift brought to the shower. These gifts need not be wrapped; just have cards attached to them for identification. The host can just pack up all the gifts and send them to the honoree.

• If you can, photograph, cassette-tape, or videotape the event, including the shower games and some of the guest conversations.

Long-Distance Birthday Party

• College students need love and remembering too. Send photos of the family, including pets, along with gifts, paper plates, napkins, decorations, and money for cake, ice cream, and other refreshments to a responsible roommate so that your student can have a really happy birthday. Make plans to call wherever the party is held so that the family can sing "Happy Birthday" too, and have the roommate take pictures for a remembrance.

• You can mail a whole party to someone. Just enclose non-perishable favorite foods, party paper plates and napkins, and anything else your imagination tells you to include.

Some of the "memories" tips from showers can be used for other party occasions. Here are some tips for a farewell party.

• Put a sheet of paper in some easily accessible place, and then have guests sign their names, addresses, and phone numbers so that the person leaving won't lose touch.

Instead of a list, have them sign an appropriate poster, menu from a favorite restaurant hangout, program from a special event shared by the honoree and guests, an address book, or any other meaningful or sentimental item. Put one of the guests in charge of this list if you're too busy with the party to make sure everyone signs.

• Take instant photos of the party and mount them in an album, leaving space for each guest to write a personal message beside the picture.

General Party Tips

Organizing a Co-Hosted Party

Here's when you really need to make a list and keep all information handy, because these events, often held by church, school, and office groups, are often potluck and cost-sharing.

Usually, in these parties, the co-hosting agreement is that those who bring less expensive foods or those who bring nothing will contribute cash to the party fund for reimbursing those who brought more expensive items and to contribute toward paying other expenses, such as hall rental and entertainment.

• Make a sheet of paper with columns so that each column is headed with certain information and so that you can enter this information as you receive it.

You need to record names, addresses, phone numbers, and descriptions of potluck dishes brought and gifts (to avoid duplications). Record each guest's cost for the potluck foods or beverages (and contributed cash amounts) so that all costs and contributions are in black and white and can easily be prorated.

Keep all receipts for your expenses, too, and note your expenses as contributions.

Where's the Party?

• Whether the party is for adults or children, identify the house with a "you are here" sign, ribbons, or a bunch of inflated balloons tied to a porch, mailbox, or whatever will hold them without breaking them.

• Inside the house, place small signs directing people to bathrooms so that they won't always have to be asking directions. Put a sign on the bathroom door too.

• If your house is the kind that keeps you from hearing the doorbell or if your doorbell rings too softly to be heard above the chatter, either assign a friend to stay near the door to let guests in or put a sign on the door telling them to "walk in" or "go around to the back patio," because "we can't hear the bell." Put up signs with arrows directing guests to the backyard gate.

CAUTION: If you and your guests are all out in your backyard, it's a good idea to lock your front door so that you don't get any unwelcome guests in the house.

Traffic Flow

At a buffet dinner where guests will fill their plates and then seat themselves at different tables, here's how you can have the guests move smoothly to their places without asking where to sit.

• Be traditional and make up place cards.

• If you have seating at two tables in two different rooms and don't want to suggest who is to eat with whom, try this: Use two sets of china and linen colors and designate "blue cornflowers" to the "blue table" and "green bamboo" to the "beige table." Then, set the plates for the table farthest from the buffet service at the top of the plate pile.

Breaking the Ice

Sometimes, when your guests are strangers to each other, you need something to get them comfortable and in a party mood.

- If you can afford to hire a musician who knows how to entertain at your type of party, music really does soothe the savage breast and stranger guest. A guitar player from the church choir can lead Christmas carol singing in your home as well as in church; a restaurant fiddler can serenade guests in a home as well as in a restaurant. Such musicians need not perform more than an hour or so, because your guests can't converse well in a home if music is too loud.

- If you have a lot of musicians in your circle of friends, even amateur ones, ask them all to bring their instruments and jam for about an hour at your party.

- If you have a player piano, provide vaudeville-style straw hats, kazoos, and other noninstruments for guests to wear and play while they are both the entertainers and the entertained.

- If you have a pool table, have a tournament and give silly prizes.

- If you have yard space, and it's a casual party, set up a horseshoe game, badminton net, and/or a croquet set. Again, offer silly prizes to winners.

- If you have a swimming pool party, don't be offended if only a few people actually swim. For reasons that I can't figure out, people tend to stand around and admire pools at pool parties but seldom actually bring their suits and swim.

- Make fortune balloons instead of fortune cookies. On small pieces of paper, write out "fortunes" that pertain to the particular group of people you've invited and then put the papers into balloons before inflating them and tying them securely. Let each person pop a balloon to find a prediction. This could be especially fun at a New Year's Eve party, where you could make predictions for the upcoming year.

- For a Valentine's Day party, cut inexpensive valentines in half with different zigzag cuts for each one, and then have guests find their matching halves to meet each other or to be dinner or bridge partners.

- Cut cartoons from newspapers and use them the same way suggested for valentines.

- One of the best tips I can give for enjoying your own party is to make sure that you get at least 15 to 20 minutes of rest at some point on party day. It's hard to smile when your feet are killing you, you are exhausted, and you are wishing that you had never even thought of having a party.

Entertaining can be as easy and simple as you want it to be or a full-blown black-tie dinner. Do what you're the most comfortable with, and make no excuses. If you don't say that the dessert didn't turn out as good as it usually does, no one will really know, so don't tell on yourself! Take a few minutes to write everything out, do the best that you can, and when someone asks, "May I help?" for heaven's sake say yes if you need someone to pitch in.

CHAPTER 13

Leaving the Home Behind

Work for many people means carrying a suitcase along with a briefcase and accumulating frequent-flyer bonuses.

I travel so much that I don't ever completely unpack my suitcases. My toiletries and the other "security blanket" comfies that make my hotel room my home away from home are always kept replenished and in their places, already packed for the next trip. And I know that I'm not the only working gypsy, because my mail has all sorts of tips from "frequent flyers" and "frequent roadies."

I also know that I'm not the only traveler who carries all my luggage onto the plane. I have to do this because I frequently travel to a different city each day and my luggage, if lost, might never catch up to me. Because I carry it all on, I have to pack very efficiently; *lightweight* and *coordinated* are my buzzwords.

Traveling around the country for business and fun has been a real learning experience for me. I've learned a lot about doing and "making do" when you're on the road, which I've included in this chapter.

Planning Your Trip

Buying Airline Tickets

• With so many discounted fares available, it's time-consuming to call different airlines to get the best fare for your trip. Travel agents have all this information on their computers, at the touch of a finger.

When you are deciding to buy discounted tickets, you need to consider which is more important to you: Price or scheduling? Will you fly at a less convenient time to save $25? Can you change your reservation without a penalty? What will the airline do for you if your flight is canceled?

• Always make reservations several months in advance if you plan to fly on a holiday.

• In large metropolitan areas your fare may vary, depending upon which airport you use.

• Remember, the cost of the ticket is the price in effect when you pay for your ticket, not the price in effect when you make your reservation.

• If you travel a lot, collecting frequent-flyer bonuses is really a bonus. You can use your accumulated business travel benefits to take a vacation—which you'll probably need desperately if you've accumulated lots of bonuses.

• Always phone to confirm your flight a day or so before it's scheduled.

International flights need to be confirmed at least 72 hours before flight time. No confirmation can result in a canceled reservation on international flights.

• If your flight is delayed and you have a full-fare ticket, check with other airlines to find out if there are available seats on flights to your destination. Many airlines honor other airlines' tickets. If the second airline won't honor your ticket, you can request a refund from the first airline. If you have a discounted ticket, however, you may get only a partial refund or no refund at all.

• If you arrive early and find that the airline on which you are booked has available seats on an earlier flight, you may be able to switch to the earlier flight. This is another instance where carrying on your bags comes in handy.

Dealing with Travel Agents

• The best way to find a travel agent is to get recommendations from friends who travel. They'll know if the agent takes time to answer your questions, knows the intricate details about getting you to your destination, is efficient, and has full computer service so that you get the most current information about rates and changes in tours or tickets. A good agent will ask about your trip after you've returned to check on the tour, accommodations, and so forth.

An agent should belong to some professional organizations, such as the American Society of Travel Agents, the International Airlines Travel Agent Network, or the Airlines Reporting Corporation. If your agent displays evidence of membership in the ASTA, IATAN, or ARC, it generally means that the agency meets professional standards. If your agent is not meeting professional standards, you can complain to these professional organizations. You can also complain to your state government's Consumer Protection Division and to the Better Business Bureau in your area.

How to Complain About Poor Travel Service

• Whenever you complain, provide a daytime phone number where you can be called, and when you write to complain, always include a return address. If you don't properly identify yourself, you can't get results!

• Complain about travel agents to ASTA Consumer Affairs Department, 4400 MacArthur Blvd., N.W., Washington, D.C. 20007.

• When you have any type of travel service problem (with airlines, buses, trains), complain to the U.S. Department of Transportation, Consumer Affairs. The phone number is 202-366-2220. Or write to: U.S. Department of Transportation, Office of Community and Consumer Affairs, 400 Seventh St., S.W., Room 10405, Washington, D.C. 20590.

This department will usually contact the airline (bus or train service) to find out if your complaint was properly handled and get back to you. It will also provide information about your rights under federal laws. Consumer complaints are kept in the department's records and used to document the need for changes in consumer protection regulations.

At the time this book was being written, the U.S. Department of Transportation was offering a free booklet entitled "Fly Rights" to those who call and request it.

• The airline needs to know what you want before it can take any action at all, so if you write exactly what you want the airline to do: settle the claim with money, have the rude employees send an apology note, or do something else to compensate for your inconvenience. The airline may offer to settle your claim with a check or other compensation, such as a free trip.

• To complain about safety hazards, write to the Federal Aviation Administration, Community and Consumer Liaison Division, APA-400, Federal Aviation Administration, 800 Independence Avenue, S.W., Washington, D.C. 20591, or call 202-267-3481.

Lost Luggage

• The only real way to preserve valuables is to keep them on your person. Never check anything of great value, such as money, jewelry, cameras, medicine, liquids, glass, negotiable securities, or anything else that is irreplaceable, is very fragile, or has sentimental value.

• Double-check all destination tags put on your checked baggage and always take off old tags before you check the bags to avoid confusion.

• Some airlines have a ceiling of $1,250 on delayed, lost, or damaged bags on domestic flights. If your luggage or contents are worth more than that, you may want to buy "excess valuation" coverage if it is available. On international flights the liability is 250 French gold francs (you need to get current conversion for this to United States dollars) for each kilo (about 2.2 pounds) of checked baggage. Your baggage should be weighed for international flights to ensure your being able to claim the right amount. If your bags aren't weighed, your claim will be based on the assumption that your bag weighed 32 kilos (about 70 pounds).

• Keep records of everyone you speak to about your lost baggage and never throw away any travel documents or receipts for money spent in connection with the baggage loss. If you give your baggage tags to the airline when you fill out a loss form, the form should note that you did give up those claim tags when it was filled out.

• Generally, airlines will pay for a reasonable amount of inconvenience due to the lost bag, but this amount must be negotiated. Some airlines have emergency funds for purchases and will give you cash; others will pay later. Save those receipts! (Delayed luggage is delivered to you at no charge.)

• If your bag is really lost and not just delayed, you may have to fill out a second claim form; check with the airline.

• Airlines usually pay "depreciated," not "replacement," costs. Keep receipts for the clothing and other items as well as for the bags, so that if your luggage is lost, you have a better chance of settling your claim without too much bargaining with the airline.

CAUTION: Don't exaggerate your claim values. The airlines can completely deny claims they believe to be inflated or fraudulent!

Vacation Information Sources

• If you are planning to visit a major city, call that city's tourist or convention office to get information about what's to see and do when you get there. Knowing what you might do helps you plan your time and finances so that you can enjoy as much as you want and can afford.

• If you plan to travel by train, Amtrak sends a free travel planner for traveling in the United States, complete with maps and money-saving hotel and tour packages. Call 1-800-USA-RAIL. This is a very busy line; don't be discouraged if you are on hold for a minute or so. You can also write to Travel Planner, Dept. N, Amtrak Distribution Center, P.O. Box 7717, Itasca, Ill. 60143. It takes about eight days for the packet to reach you if you call for it.

Travel for Handicapped People

• A nonprofit organization, Society for the Advancement of Travel for the Handicapped (SATH), sends information about travel to handicapped people. Send a stamped, self-addressed envelope and $1 for postage and handling for general travel information, or $2 if you also want the "U.S. Welcome for Handicapped Visitors" booklet. It's important to send the postage, because this society receives no funding other than membership fees for its services. Members (dues in 1988 were $40 per year for adults and $25 for students and retired persons) receive a quarterly newsletter and other helpful publications for handicapped travelers. Write to SATH, Penthouse Suite, 26 Court St., Brooklyn, N.Y. 11242.

Deciding on Vacation Ideas

Here's a tip for getting everyone's frank opinion on where to go and what to do.

Write down, on a secret ballot, all the activities that are possible during the vacation, such as: visit the zoo; white-water rafting; charter a fishing boat; sleep all day; and so forth.

Beside each activity, draw a row of boxes in which to rate the activity according to: want to do very much; would like to do; wouldn't mind doing it if everyone else does it; rather not.

Give a ballot to each person going on the trip with instructions not to talk about it until all the ballots are in. The official trip planner can then pick the activities accordingly, so that everyone gets a turn at doing the "want to do very much" activities at least once.

Everyone doesn't have to be together every minute of the vacation time. You may want to split up to cover more activities.

Finding a Place to Stay

• Have a travel agent make all the phone calls. I still meet people who think they have to pay for travel agent services. Travel agents are paid by their travel industry clients and can save you money in phone calls and by finding low travel and accommodations rates, not to mention a lot of time. Often, the agent has been in the area on a "fam tour" (familiarization tour) and can give you tips on time, financial, and wardrobe needs.

• Most hotel chains have 800 numbers, so you can call to find out whether they accept children or pets, and what kind of facilities they offer. To get 800 number information, dial 1-800-555-1212 and then ask for the 800 number for the hotel/motel chain you want to call.

Cruises

If you've been in a high-speed mode at work and need a rest, try a cruise. Most cruise ships offer optional side trips off the ship every other day or so, alternating with days to sleep and relax.

• If you are on a fixed income or budget, a cruise may be the kind of vacation you can enjoy without worrying your wallet and heating up your credit cards. All your meals and lodging are paid for. Extra expenses are for drinks, tours, and souvenirs. Often plane tickets are included in the package.

• Picking the right cabin for your cruise can make you more comfortable physically and financially. The most expensive cabins are on the top decks, but most people prefer to be at the water line of the ship, because that's the most stable level of the ship. Cabins in the center of the ship are more expensive than those at either end, and outside cabins are more expensive than inside ones, but if you need a porthole to prevent claustrophobia, the extra price is worth it.

• If you tend to get motion sickness, see your doctor for some of the newer medications that don't make you sleepy. Also, get a room mid-ship at the water line for best stability and the least rocking and rolling.

• You can save money by traveling off-season. For example, May and June are off-season for Caribbean vacations. Prices drop 25 to 60 percent on air fare, hotels, and rental cars. Even the stores have sales on resort clothing during these off months.

• Travel "standby." Often special tours or cruise ships have cancellations or vacancies, and since they want to have a full roster of clients, they will offer huge discounts to people who can travel with a few days' notice. Check with your travel agent.

• Save all travel brochures until after the trip. They are the proof of what was offered to you, in case you have to take legal action against a travel company for not providing what it advertised.

• Don't forget time-share vacations. For some people, they offer the perfect alternatives.

The American Resorts and Residential Development Association offers general information about time-share accommodations in a booklet entitled "Consumer's Guide to Timesharing." Send $2 and a No. 10 envelope to ARRDA, 1220 L Street, N.W., Suite 510, Washington, D.C. 20005.

Boating

• If you want a sailing vacation but don't own a boat, check with your travel agent about sailing vacations in which you can rent a sailboat (usually with crew), just like renting an RV (recreational vehicle).

• When equipping your own boat, it's safety first!

Many people who die in boating accidents do so because they have no lifesaving gear aboard. The U.S. Coast Guard requires personal flotation devices (PFDs) on all boats. The number, type, and sizes required for each boat depend upon the number of people per boat and size of the craft. Generally, at least one PFD is required per person.

• Be cautious when using inflatable mattresses, toys, and rafts. They aren't true safety flotation devices and shouldn't be used for that purpose. They can take you into deep water, slip away, or develop leaks and leave you in serious trouble far from shore.

• The best safety rule is to learn how to swim and to administer lifesaving techniques just in case.

• If you have too much boat and not enough garage, the trailer tongues and wiring will be exposed to the rain. To keep the wiring from shorting out, put a sandwich bag over the wires and tie it shut with twisties.

• Ever-faithful nylon net helps boaters too. Use it to remove dirt and scum from the bottom and sides of a fiberglass boat. David usually wipes his boat while it's still in the water and then all he has to do when he gets home is to rinse it off with a garden hose.

• You'll never have to worry about losing or getting your keys, driver's license, glasses, makeup, or whatever wet when you're on water in any kind of boat (canoe, raft, whatever) if you put such items in a plastic travel jar or, if you have many items and a big boat, into a cooler. Well-sealed jars will float for a while and so will some coolers; you can retrieve them if they fall overboard. (Do this at the beach, too, to keep sand and water away from cameras and other items.)

• Wide, flat-bottomed coffee cups designed to be set on car dashboards are really useful on boats.

• Most camping, kitchen, and trailer tips apply to boating—using tight-fitting lids on containers and putting them into plastic bags prevent spills, and anything that conserves space is a blessing. (See camping hints later in this chapter.)

Traveling by Car

• If you are driving alone, take a break at least every two hours to prevent dozing off after being mesmerized by the road.

• Get your car tuned up, checked, and serviced before a long trip to prevent trouble on the road. And especially, check those tires and belts! (But you knew that, right?)

• Keep duct tape in your trunk. It will seal and hold many broken car parts together long enough for you to get to a service station.

• Also keep a large towel or blanket in the trunk to lie on in case you have to look under the car, or to place in front of or behind tires for traction in snow or ice.

• A couple of containers of cat litter, gravel, or sand also come in handy for ice emergencies.

• Check out an automobile shop for aerosol tire inflation products, which will fill a leaky (not seriously damaged) tire with enough air to get you to a service station. It's probably a good idea to replace the aerosol product from time to time to make sure it won't be outdated and will work when you have an emergency.

• Don't forget the universal signal for car trouble is a raised hood. It helps, too, to have one of those cardboard sunscreens that has a picture on one side and HELP, CALL POLICE printed on the other side.

• If you are driving in Europe, you are required to put a danger signal on the road or shoulder a short distance behind your car to warn motorists that a stalled car is ahead. Red triangle signs on a stand are sold there for this purpose. (That's what that thing in your rental car trunk was!)

• When you rent a car, before driving off take some time to find out how to turn on the headlights, windshield wipers, flashers, air conditioner, or heater, even if the type of car seems familiar to you. Also check to see if there is a spare tire, jack, and operating manual in the car.

If you should have an auto accident:

1. Get the name, address, phone number, and license number of the other person involved and names, addresses, and phone numbers of any passengers in the other car or of witnesses.
   Make a note if any injuries occurred, to whom, and if everyone was wearing seat belts.
   If possible, while you are still at the scene, make a rough diagram of the street or intersection, positions of the cars and point of impact, including compass points and car colors and makes, so that you won't have to rely on memory when you fill out insurance forms or tape-record a report on the phone, as is required by some companies.
2. Call the police as soon as possible. Some cities have designated off-the-road places to go in case of an accident; in others, you have to wait for the police to arrive before moving. In most cases you can pull off the road to let traffic flow, if your car can be moved.

3. Notify your insurance company. Most larger national companies have an 800 number to call, which you should keep in your wallet. Write your policy number on the note card with the phone number so that you can refer to it when you call. Your insurance company can also advise you if your policy covers a rental car to use while your car is being fixed.

4. If you have an accident while driving a rental car, call the rental office. You'll find the number on your rental contract.

Renting a Car

On the surface, renting a car seems expensive, but according to Tom Brosnahan's book *How to Beat the High Cost of Travel,* no rental fees are carved in stone.

Don't just pay the fee without asking about the many hidden savings, such as discounts for longer rentals, weekend rates, unlimited mileage or number of free miles, free return and delivery, discounts for belonging to certain groups, and frequent-flyer car rental bonuses.

Calculating Expenses of Car Travel

Many people erroneously think traveling by car is the least expensive way. Travel writer Brosnahan says four or more people sharing a car is "budget travel," but one or two people sharing a car is "luxury travel." When you add up the costs realistically, you may find that air or train travel is less expensive.

• When you calculate the cost of travel in your own car, add up fuel, oil, tires, maintenance, wear and tear, insurance, parking and tolls, highway food, and overnight hotel/motel costs.

• When you calculate the cost of rental cars, add up the daily or weekly rental charge, mileage charge (this and fuel are the biggest expenses), plus taxes, fuel, parking and tolls, pickup and delivery charges (if you use those services), and various other stamp taxes, "document fees," or "execution fees."

• If you are staying in the downtown part of a city, it may cost less to use cabs if you don't really need to have a car every moment. You won't need a rental car if most places you'll go are close enough for low taxi fares, if you'll be walking part of the time, or if you can use public transportation.

• If you are older than 21 and have a driver's license and references, you may be able to drive someone else's car from one point to another for a "drive-away firm." These firms arrange for people's cars to be delivered to various parts of the United States. You will have to sign a contract, and pay a deposit and fuel costs, but repairs are paid by the owner. You'll have to meet the car owner's schedule, but some owners may allow you to spend a day in a tourist city en route.

• Often colleges offer driver services that enable you to share driving with a car owner who doesn't want to drive alone on a long trip. Find out by calling the largest university in your area.

Eating Out While on Vacation

• Don't just go to the first restaurant recommended to you. Ask several people for recommendations. If the same name comes up often, you'll know you have a winner.

• You'll save money if you select in-season and regional foods from the menu, such as strawberries in early summer, seafood in coastal cities, and beef in Kansas City or Texas.

• You'll get better meals if you choose the chef's daily specials. This is based on the idea that the chef gets bored with the regular menu and puts more effort into daily specials. Specials are more likely to be made with fresh, perishable ingredients than regular menu items, which may come from the freezer in some restaurants.

• Ask how menu items are prepared and if the appetizer you are ordering goes with the entrée. In a good restaurant, waiters or waitresses should be able to help you order complementary foods and select wines if there is no sommelier.

• Be aware that dining customs in foreign countries or even different parts of the United States may be different from yours, so don't get annoyed if you don't get whatever you are used to having. For example, coffee is served with meals in some Midwestern states, whereas it's served after dinner in other areas. In some foreign countries, coffee drinking is a breakfast and mid-afternoon activity, not always with or after meals.

In Southern states, asking for "tea" will bring iced tea automatically unless you specify "hot tea." And asking for iced tea in early May in Maine will get you a look of horror.

You're not likely to get an automatic glass of water in foreign countries, and in some third-world countries that's good, because the water isn't safe to drink.

Tipping

• When you are on tour in a foreign country, it's best to ask your guide about appropriate tipping.

• On most cruise ships, you will tip at the end of the cruise, and the suggested tip will be noted in the ship's daily newsletter. Most provide special envelopes on the last day for you to use, which are printed to indicate tips for cabin or dining room and bar personnel.

• In a restaurant, read the menu or bill to find out if the tip is added automatically. If so, you can still tip anyone who has given you special service if you wish.

• Generally, 15 percent is the normal tip to waiters and waitresses in a "modest restaurant," and 20 percent of the total bill in an expensive restaurant.

In an expensive restaurant, divide the 20 percent of the total bill into 75 percent to the waiter and 25 percent to the captain of the table (the person who supervises waiters and table busing or attends to special requests).

If you can't figure 15 percent of anything in your head, buy a tip card, sold at greeting card stores, or just compute 10 percent of the total amount, which is easy; add it to one-half of whatever is 10 percent; and you'll get a total of 15 percent.

• Tip the maitre'd $5, $10, or more for a table, depending upon the type of restaurant and the size of the city, and if you are getting special consideration, such as a best-located table.

• Tip the wine steward, or sommelier, $3 to $5 per bottle. In an expensive restaurant, tip 15 percent of the wine bill.

• Bartenders usually get 15 percent or the change, if it's a reasonable amount.

• Ladies' room attendants can be tipped $1 per woman using the facilities.

• Hotel bellhops get $1 or $2 per bag in most cases.

• Tip the doorman who summons a cab or your car $1; the garage attendant who brings your car up front $1 or $2.

• I've learned that if you are going to be staying in a hotel or frequent a restaurant a lot, tip early on, instead of waiting till the very end of your stay, and you will get great service.

• If you are in doubt, ask about local customs and then tip the concierge a dollar or two for providing the information. Ask for restaurant and entertainment recommendations, and for directions while you're at it, and get more info for your tip!

While You Are Gone

• Make arrangements for someone to keep your house looking "lived in." Rather than canceling newspaper subscriptions and having your mail held for you (which alerts a lot of people whom you don't know and tells them exactly how long you'll be gone), ask a reliable friend or relative, or pay someone to house-sit.

• Most major cities have house-sitting services in which bonded people check your house daily; pick up newspapers, flyers, and mail; water your house plants; feed your fish; and take care of your cat and/or dog. The fee you pay is worth it if you get peace of mind. Always ask for references and check them out when you hire a sitter service for anything.

• Set lights on timers so that lights go on and off instead of staying on 24 hours a day (which advertises that somebody is gone and is trying to make the house look occupied).

• If you are going on an extended trip of several months, and you want to rent out your house or condominium apartment, check with your insurance agent about your policy's coverage.

• If you have an automatic garage door, unplug it to avoid having the door opened by someone with an opener on your frequency. Most people who have automatic garage doors report occasional mysterious openings due to others having the same-frequency openers.

Getting Packed

Carry-On Luggage or Checked Luggage

• If you plan to carry on or check unusually shaped or very large items, call the airline ahead of time to make sure it'll permit it. For example, most airlines will provide a box for a bicycle, but you'll probably have to dismantle the bike and pay an extra fee for shipping it. On international flights, a bicycle counts as one of your two free pieces of luggage, so if you already have two pieces of luggage, you'll have to pay a substantial fee for shipping it.

(You'll probably need to furnish your own box for a bike when traveling by bus.)

• Always put your name and address on all your possessions when you travel. Stick-on address labels can be stuck on cameras, binoculars, and anything plastic (they peel off some fabrics).

• Tape business cards inside your bags for identification in case luggage tags get ripped off.

• When you carry on baggage, be among the first to board in your section and you won't be left "holding the bag"—literally—when all the compartments are full.

Travel Wardrobes

Whether you are a woman or a man, the best way to pick out a travel wardrobe is to stick to a basic color scheme. Mine is black, but yours could be navy, brown, or whatever is your favorite basic, neutral color. I plan what I will wear when I go on public-relations tours and actually write up a "menu" of the combinations of separates and accessories I will wear and then tape the menu on one of the hangers.

Here's my favorite on-the-road combination, which could be anyone's menu, with some additions and subtractions. Believe it or not, by mixing and matching and changing accessories, I can and have lived comfortably for as long as two weeks with what's listed here.

• A black suit; a gray skirt in the same fabric as the suit; a topper (blazer, jacket, or vest); three blouses in white, red, gray, or a print that has these three colors (I don't like to travel with busy-printed dresses, because you get tired of them when you have to wear them over and over again—I'd rather save the prints for a blouse or scarves to flash some color); and a sweater for cool weather (turtleneck or pullover).

• Accessories include belts in gold, black, and/or gray or red; a couple of scarves with black, red, gray, and white patterns to dress up blouses, tie up my hair, and use as belts or hat bands; panty hose in black, gray, or white, depending upon the season; a pair of gray shoes and black shoes, including a pair of comfy walking shoes; a handbag that holds everything I need en route.

In addition to the above, I pack the following things for evening wear.

• A pair of black dressy slacks; a black or white overshirt of fabric similar to the dressy slacks that I can wear alone, belted, or over a camisole or tube top; a camisole or tube top to wear under the overshirt or with my black suit, with or without a dressy belt; a pair of dressy sandals and a lightweight evening bag.

Men's Wardrobes Need Coordinating Too

A man's wardrobe for traveling is similar and also depends upon what kinds of business events are connected with the trip.

• Generally, a dark suit, worn with a white shirt and a coordinated tie, will take a man anywhere.

• Add a sport coat and slacks (one or two pairs), and shirts in colors that go with the dark suit and the sport coat and slacks combination, plus ties that are also interchangeable with the suit and sport coat. It helps if the suit pants can also be worn with the sport coat in case of spills or stains.

• Add a sweater or sweater vest for cool weather, and then this wardrobe is versatile. An extra pair of shoes rounds out the male travel wardrobe for business.

General Tips on Selecting Travel Clothes

• In both women's and men's suits, you'll find that year-round fabrics such as lightweight wool, wool blends, and silk and wool blends are the best travelers. If you take a sweater and a lightweight raincoat, you can keep warm by layering and keep cool by unlayering.

• Denim is always a good casual traveling fabric.

• A sweater or sweater vest is a good cover-up if you have a spot on your last clean blouse or shirt and still want to look respectable on the return flight!

• Check out fabric stores. You'll find many new spot removers and wrinkle-removing sprays to help you keep your wardrobe in reasonably good shape while you are traveling.

• If you are going to a resort, or on a tour or cruise, note how the people are dressed in the brochure's photos. Then you'll have a clue whether you'll need casual, dressy, or even formal clothing.

• If you are going on a vacation trip, you'll need play clothes according to what play you've planned and how hard you play! Some folks can play 18 holes of golf in the noonday sun and still look like they just came out of the club-house; others get as rumpled as an unmade bed just walking from the hotel door to the tour bus.

How to Pack

Unless your trip is an emergency, pack more than a couple of hours before you leave so that you have time to organize your wardrobe and accessories. I honestly find that, as my trip progresses, I become a better packer each time I repack. Here are some ways to pack so that you don't crush and smash things.

• Some luggage comes with packing instructions; don't throw these away, especially if you've bought any of the newer hanging, folding, and generally innovative travel gear. Between trips, it's easy to forget the manufacturer's carefully devised "goesintas." (As in: "This goesinta this pocket" and "That goesinta that zipper compartment.")

• Heavy things should be packed at the bottom of your suitcase so they won't squash everything when the suitcase is picked up. And, when I say "bottom of your suitcase," I mean whatever will be the bottom when the case is picked up.

• When you put shoes into a standard suitcase, put them sole to sole with the heel of one shoe touching the toe of the other. Stuff small light things into your shoes to save space and to help keep their shapes. I stuff my shoes with slips, underwear, panty hose (especially if the hose matches that pair of shoes), and even small bags of vitamins or pill bottles.

• Fill empty spaces with softies, such as socks, underwear, T-shirts. Put large clothing items on the top.

• Fold skirts once and keep them flat. You can pad the fold with another garment.

• You can match pants cuff to cuff, then fold in half (over each other if you have several pairs) or roll them.

• This idea of folding clothes over other clothes can be carried out with almost all of your garments if you alternate large garments with smaller ones until everything fits in. For example: You can lay an unfolded pair of trousers horizontally in your suitcase, with the top of the pants placed against the suitcase's edge and the pants' bottom hanging out over the side. Then, place a smaller garment, such as a shirt, vertically in the suitcase, with the top placed at the suitcase's edge and the bottom hanging over the edge. If you alternate garment with garment, each placed in the opposite direction in the suitcase, you can then flip up all the ends of the garments that have been hanging over the edges and close your suitcase. All garments will have padded the others and you'll have fewer wrinkles.

• To pack a dress in a standard suitcase, hold up the dress by its shoulders and lay it in the suitcase so that the top of the dress is in the suitcase and the skirt is draped over the edge. Then fold the sleeves across the front of the dress, and fold the skirt up across the dress top. If the dress has a very full skirt, fold the sides inward first and then fold up the skirt.

• I hate to bring up panty hose again, but here's yet another use for them. If you roll garments for packing, you can make tubes from panty hose legs that have the tops and toes cut off. These tubes will hold your clothing rolls neatly in the suitcase.

• In fact, you can even pack panty hose in panty hose! Use the leg of an old pair to hold all your new ones and then use the "panty hose sausage" you've created to pack folds in folded garments. Rolled-up underwear can also pad sleeves and folded garments and will stay in a roll if you pack it in a panty hose leg.

• Stuff clothing or tissue into folds of clothing to prevent pressing in the creases and button up, zip up, or belt clothing so it stays in shape.

• I use a lightweight hanging-type garment bag so that I don't have to fold up clothing. If you use a heavy-duty bag, you can tuck shoes, hair dryers, and other bulky things into the top two corners above the "shoulders" of your clothing; then you save the pockets for other things.

• If your dress is too long for a garment bag, slit a cardboard tube and put it over the hanger so that you can fold your dress over the tube, in half or at the waist, so that the dress is only half as long and won't get a crumpled hemline.

• If you keep clothing in plastic dry-cleaners' bags and then put them into the hanging bag, they don't get as crushed. I don't know why—they just seem to slip around and stay unwrinkled.

• Hang-up cosmetic bags that have small, clear plastic compartments for your personal items are nice travel aids, because you can hang them on the back of the door of the hotel bathroom and see all of what you need at a glance. I imagine they are a blessing for hotel maids, because your stuff isn't strewn all over the bathroom. They certainly keep you from forgetting personal items when you leave. I've seen these bags in department stores and in some catalogs.

• Find a packing system that works for you. We all have ways of doing things that work for us and not for others. For example, some people don't ever get all the way unpacked when they travel; others, like me, like to get partially unpacked because they feel more "at home" in the hotel when they have their things in view and easier to get at.

Don't Forget Your Comfies

• If you carry on luggage, a collapsible luggage carrier is a real source of comfort.

• If your travel is a series of "one-nighters," it's easy to get disoriented when you wake up in the middle of the night. Carry a small plug-in night-light or keep a pocket flashlight on the nightstand; neither weighs much, and being able to figure out where you are in the middle of the night is worth adding another thing to your travel kit.

• Tea bags and individual packets of instant coffee, cider, cocoa, or whatever beverage makes you happy can be a godsend when you are on the road and don't feel like waiting for room service or if you feel wanton and guilty when you order a $7 cup of coffee.

• There's no rule that says you can't pick up individual juice portions at a convenience store near the hotel, take them up to your room, and pour the juice over ice for a pick-me-up drink. More and more hotels are putting fridge hospitality in their rooms, but many times the markup on the beverages makes room service seem a bargain!

• People with special dietary restrictions can often get special diet foods on meal-serving flights if the airline knows in advance. I always special-order a vegetarian or fruit platter. It seems that everyone who is eating mystery meat or gray roast beef often wonders how I was lucky enough to receive a special meal. All you have to do is call in advance.

• On flights that don't serve food, you may want to bring your favorite nutritious snack to eat on the plane.

• On long flights, consider tossing some "footies" or sport socks into your carry-on bag so that you can slip off your shoes and walk around the plane in comfort.

• You may also want to carry a sleep mask if you're the kind of person who needs absolute darkness before you can nod off.

• Soft foam ear plugs are an absolute must for me; I carry one set in my makeup case in my purse and another in my carry-on travel bag. It makes all the difference in the world when you want to close your eyes and shut out the airplane noise for a few minutes.

Packing the Essentials

I keep my "essentials" packed all the time because I travel so much. The general categories on my mental checklist are: makeup, hair-care items, body-care items, medications, clothing, accessories, and business supplies.

You can make your own mental list by going from head down or from feet up (e.g., shoes, stockings, lingerie, clothes, makeup, jewelry, coat, purse, briefcase.)

• Buy the little sample sizes of shampoo, creme rinse, deodorant, hand lotion, baby oil, and so forth, that you see in the drugstores, just in case the hotel's hospitality corner doesn't have these items. I have even found sample sizes of eye drops and nasal spray.

• Remember that shampoo can double as laundry soap, and creme rinse can double as shaving cream.

Travel Checklist

My checklist may differ from yours, but here it is.

• Makeup and something to remove eye makeup.

• Toothbrush, toothpaste.

(Save the smidgens at the end of a big tube and use that for travel or get the smallest-size tube.)

• Bath powder, deodorant, perfume in small sizes.

• Facial tissues, individual packets of "wipes," a few cotton balls and swabs.

• Shaving equipment, a pair of tweezers, small scissors (folding embroidery scissors are nice 'cause they don't poke holes), safety pins, and a small sewing kit.

• A few adhesive bandages and/or felt adhesive pads in case a shoe rubs you the wrong way and place.

• Eyeglasses and/or contacts (and an extra pair), plus any of the "extras" you need to care for your contacts. You can buy eyeglass-cleaning tissues for plastic or glass lenses, and these can be a real aid to sightseeing.

• Credit cards, traveler's checks, tip change—single dollars or loose change. If you don't have a credit card for phones, you need an assortment of dimes and quarters. And boy, does this loose change come in handy when you want a soft drink, fruit juice, or snack in the middle of the night, and normally you don't have any change.

• Small notebook, pen or pencil, to keep track of phone numbers, expenses, people's names, any other information. Include a few of your address labels in case you need to identify a package. The free suitcase tags from the airport ticket counter can come in handy if you go shopping on your trip and buy something that has to be checked. Tuck a marker, twine, or packaging tape into your luggage if you are a dedicated traveling shopper.

• Something to read.

(In my case, it's usually column or book printouts, but occasionally, I like to read a novel or catch up on my magazine reading.)

• Take your own travel alarm clock, unless you are extremely optimistic and can go to sleep with total trust in whoever at the hotel desk took the message about your wake-up call. I also prefer the sound of MY alarm. It's too much of a jolt to hear different buzzes, beeps, and strange radio stations when you are in the twilight zone in a strange city.

• Here's an important tip from a traveling friend of mine who once got startled out of a sound sleep at 2 A.M. If your hotel has them, check the clocks and clock radios before your turn in for the night to make sure they aren't set and to make sure you know how to turn them off.

• I have cut down on the weight of my "essentials" by calling the 800 number of the hotel where I'll stay to find out if they provide hair dryers, irons and boards, and so on. Some hotels even have curlers and electric razors available on request. Some hotels charge for use of such items and some don't; ask when you call. Don't forget that if you are traveling in Europe, your electric things must work on 220 voltage and have adapter plugs.

Crushed Clothing

• The old "hang it in the bathroom when you take a shower so the steam loosens wrinkles" still is the best tip.

• If you have stubborn creases and don't have a travel iron, you can sometimes "iron" them out by sliding the creases over a well-dusted hot light bulb. Just remember to put the lamp shade back on the lamp when you are finished!

• If you have a travel iron, you can make an ironing board by putting a pile of towels on the floor and ironing away. If the nap of the towels is too thick (meaning you stay at better hotels), put the towel "pad" into a pillowcase. When you are finished, put the pillowcase back on your pillow and dream away. Using makeshift ironing boards on the floor usually works better for me, but you may want to use the bed.

• Some new aerosol de-wrinkle sprays are sold at fabric and other stores; read the labels to make sure these sprays are compatible with your clothing fabrics.

Other Hints

• Tuck in some spring clothespins to clip skirts and slippery fabric garments to hangers and to clip things you've rinsed out to whatever you've hung them on. Most hotels have retractable drying lines in the shower.

• Avoid laundry. Travel with disposables. I know women who make disposable panties by cutting off panties from panty hose that have runs. You can have other disposables, too, such as those bras you've never liked, panty hose that has nailpolish mends in the foot where it doesn't show, any underwear that has semi–stretched-out elastic, or any other garment you want to get rid of anyway. Wear 'em and leave 'em behind!

• Instead of toting around brochures and other papers, mail them to yourself in large, brown self-addressed mailing envelopes. If you are in a foreign country, don't forget that you have to buy the stamps of that country! Which is especially nice if you are a stamp collector or know one.

• If you don't want to carry a folding umbrella, a one-yard square of plastic, like the kind paint drop cloths are made of, folded and kept in a plastic sandwich bag can be your umbrella, rain cap, or coat, and something to sit on when you need a rest. Cut a face-size hole in the middle if you want it to be a hood.

• Zipper-sealed plastic sandwich bags are a must when you travel. I put anything that might leak into bags. The bags also keep your hose from getting snagged, your underwear in easy-to-find clusters, and so forth.

• Some parents, when traveling with children, pack each day's change of clothing in a large bag and then use the bag from fresh clothing to hold the previous day's laundry.

When You Travel Outside the United States

• Always take all medications and hygienic items with you, especially if you travel to third-world countries or the Soviet Union. This includes aspirin, allergy and cold medicines, and those for upset stomach.

• Take along a flat rubber sink stopper if you like to take baths. These stoppers are also handy when you are traveling with children and stopping in camping facilities that have only shower stalls. You can get at least two to four inches of water stopped up in a shower stall to bathe a small child or at least give yours or a child's feet a soothing soak.

• Don't forget soap, washcloth, and small towel; not all guest facilities in other countries provide these things.

• I like to carry a quick-drying sponge instead of a washcloth, when I travel anywhere, and I know a lot of people who like to wash with the soaps their skins are used to instead of those provided in hotels, no matter what designer labels are on them.

• Check with the Centers for Disease Control (CDC) in Atlanta, Foreign Travel Department, to find out which, if any, immunizations are needed for the country you will visit. The number to call is 1-404-639-2572. The main switchboard number for the CDC is 1-404-639-3311. Often local agencies and doctors don't have current information, so it's better to call the CDC.

• It takes several weeks to get a passport. You need proof of citizenship, such as a birth certificate or a voter registration card, and four small pictures from a place that specifies "passport photos." If you have an outdated passport, you can renew by mail. Get your passport forms and instructions at federal or state courthouses or post offices. Passports are good for ten years.

• When you are traveling abroad, remember that some countries have special customs. For example, in the Middle East, a woman needs to be more covered up—no shorts, halters, sleeveless tops, and so forth.

• When you travel, always take your best patience and your sense of humor and remember that you are the guest/visitor/outsider in foreign countries. It's their country and their rules prevail!

As a wise traveler once told a complaining one, if you want everything to be just like you have it at home, stay at home!

Camping and Hiking

The National Park Service has information on campsites and trails, but remember that Park Service campsites and cabins, when they are available, are very popular and therefore booked well in advance. You can't just decide to go to Yellowstone National Park next week and expect to get space if it's the peak of summer travel season.

To get information about the National Park Service facilities, look in the federal government section of your phone book under "Interior, Department of" and then National Park Service Administrative Office.

Hiking

• A small lightweight book on plants makes hiking more fun. It's like going to a party and knowing the other guests' names instead of going to a party where you don't know a soul. And nature's beauty is certainly a party!

• Also, even the clearest streams can contain Giardia and other parasites that will turn your walk into a run when you get gas, diarrhea, and stomach pains. If you are going to an area where you will have to drink from rivers, lakes, streams, and yes, even springs, buy water purification products or devices from stores that sell camping supplies.

• You can purify water by boiling it for at least 15 minutes, or you can use commercial purifiers.

• You can pack oranges in your backpack to quench your thirst. Put the peels into the plastic litter bag you tucked into your backpack. You did take a litter bag, didn't you?

• Raisins and other dried fruit, nuts, and granola all make good snacks on the trail, because they give you energy without being heavy to carry. If you like it, beef jerky is also a lightweight snack.

What to Wear

• Remember that if you go hiking during hunting season, be sure to wear brightly colored clothing or, better yet, wear a bright orange hunter's vest so that you are very obviously not game! Wearing brightly colored clothing is a must for children so that, if they do wander off, they can be seen more easily.

• When you think about comfort in the wilderness, "the right stuff" means the right clothes. Hypothermia, or what used to be called exposure, can happen to anyone while backpacking or camping.

• Bring a set of "sweats" on long hikes or camping trips to put on when you get wet.

• Always bring extras for children, who, bless their little curious hearts, tend to fall into water and mud puddles as naturally as breathing.

Trudging On

• Make sure your shoes fit properly so that their heels don't rub and cause blisters. Wearing cushiony terry or wool socks helps protect your feet. Hiking is supposed to be fun, not pain! If you plan to do serious hiking on rough terrain, you will need hiking shoes that support your ankles and have treaded soles to prevent your slipping down hills. New hiking shoes are as light and are made of the same materials as tennis-type sport shoes.

Insects—Unwelcome Outdoor Companions

• Insect repellent is a must in the great outdoors, and you'll find some repellents in individual packets that can be tucked into a pocket. Insects carry many diseases, so their stings and bites can be more than just annoying and itchy! To be less appealing to the insects don't wear your favorite perfume, scented hand lotion, hair spray, or aftershave cologne, which will only let the little buggers know exactly where you are.

• The traditional way of killing chiggers is still the quickest. Paint their bites with clear nail polish (or red, if you're itchy and that's all you have).

• If the area in which you travel is known to have disease-bearing ticks, wear long pants and long-sleeved shirts, and use insect repellent. Remember it's necessary to remove a tick's head when you remove the tick. If you just pull off the body, you risk infection. The best way to remove a tick is to gently pull it with tweezers until it releases its grasp; then you'll get the whole tick out. Put a pair of tweezers in your first-aid kit and it will be handy for stickers too.

• Treat insect bites with alcohol, witch hazel, or antibiotic preparations.

• Ant bites can be made wet and sprinkled with meat tenderizer to neutralize the venom. The same technique works for many other stinging insects.

• Ammonia or vinegar dabbed on with a cotton ball can also help itchy stings.

• Baking soda mixed in water will help itchy stings as well.

• Remember what Mom told you about scratching bites. Don't! They will leave scars if they get infected from dirty fingers. Cleanse, disinfect, and then keep the area clean until it heals! If you must scratch, scratch on either side of the bite, and it will psychologically help relieve the itching.

Hiking with Pets

• Hiking with your faithful dog companion can be a wonderful experience, but keep him controlled on a leash.

• Carry a small plastic bowl for giving your pet water.

• Don't forget to tick proof and bug proof your pet, and when you check for insects and ticks on yourself, don't forget your faithful little friend.

Sleeping Bags

• If you are cold, sleeping in a sweat/jogging suit is one way to add keep-warm layers. Layers are the key, because they keep more warm air trapped in the bag.

• Most campers prefer man-made fibers for sleeping bag insulation, because they are lighter in weight and when wet still keep you warm. When goose or duck down sleeping bags get wet, they no longer hold air to insulate you.

• Children can sleep in adult bags. Just fold up the empty bottom flat to cover the child or fold it under to make a softer "mattress" for the child.

• Remember that you can freeze from the ground up, so always put a mat, some plastic, or an air mattress under your sleeping bag.

Disposable and Homemade Camping Aids

• A "hand washer" can be made from a gallon jug, which can be hung from a tree limb or tent rope by its handle. Poke a small hole in the bottom and insert a stick or piece of twig for a plug. If you make the hole no bigger than your "pinkie" finger, you won't have a mess under the "hand washer" from excess water. Most of the time you only need a "spritz," not enough to shower or wash your hair!

• Hang a bar of hand-washing soap that is tied in the foot of a panty hose leg nearby, unless you have one of those soaps-on-a-rope that people give as gifts. I guess you could call this camping aid "soap in a sock."

• You can also put a mixture of regular liquid detergent and water into a detergent bottle that has a plug/squirt cap and use it to wash hands, dishes, whatever.

• If you have old terry "footies," use them as camping washcloths; they can be tossed into the dumpster when you're finished with them.

• You can hang a roll of paper towels up on a tree branch if you open one side of a cardboard-tubed pants hanger, slip on the roll of towels, and put the hanger back together again. If the cardboard breaks, you can just bend the wire ends so that they hold the paper towels.

• An inflatable plastic wading pool can be a portable bathtub, and it won't take much space in your camper but will be a blessing if you camp at a site with no bathing facilities. If you need privacy, hook a shower curtain to a plastic hula hoop and balance the curtain between a couple of tree branches or above swing-out camper back doors.

• You can also put a garbage bag inside a clothes basket or clean trash can for a makeshift bathtub/foot soaker when you're camping where there aren't any bathing facilities.

• Tent ropes can be clotheslines; if you have a camper, bring along a folding ironing caddy to hang things on.

• When you set up your camp table, putting its feet into tuna cans filled with water will give each table leg its own moat to trap hungry, pesty ants.

• A painter's drop cloth can be an emergency raincoat, something to sit on so that your "sitter" doesn't get damp from the ground, and something to put under your sleeping bag as a barrier between the damp ground and you.

• If you think it's hard to make the beds of your camper, just use sleeping bags.

• You can make a totable "cushion" for sitting on if you put something flat (newspapers, your towel) into a handled plastic shopping bag, especially the kind that can be snapped shut at the top.

• Get a bunch of super-long, super-strong shoelaces and hang a whistle and your utility "army" knife around your neck. The whistle is a signal in case you get lost and/or injured and need to call for help. Having the "army" folding knife around your neck just makes it easier to find it when you need it.

• To make ice for your cooler, freeze water in quart or gallon jugs; you can drink this water as it thaws.

• Cold-natured campers who want some warmth at night can take a hot rock that was close to the fire and warm up like folks did before central heating was invented. Handling the hot rock with oven mitts, wrap it in a couple of layers of heavy foil, then place it next to your feet. It will generate enough heat to keep your feet warm and cozy.

• If you want to cushion the benches on a picnic table while camping, use foam rubber that's about 1½ to 2 inches thick. Cut it into four strips (10 inches by 4 feet).

Cover each pad with permanent-press denim or any other sturdy fabric. Sew it on the machine, leaving one seam open to hand stitch closed once the foam pad is inserted. When you're finished, you can sew elastic to each side of the pad's end so you can anchor it to the bench.

• When camping and traveling, carry two extra pillowcases for the dirty laundry—one for white clothes only, the other for colors. When the clothes are dirty, into the proper pillowcase they go. Let everyone do their own wash, so the work isn't left to just one person.

• Toss a couple of fabric softener sheets into the soiled clothes bag to keep odors under control and to make dumping them into the wash more pleasant for whoever ends up with this chore.

• This is a hint for campers who use a tent with a center pole: If you will invert a tin funnel over the center pole before inserting it to raise the tent, you won't tear the ring out.

Eating in the Wilderness

The two keys to camp cookery and cook's convenience are: planning to ensure that you have everything you need to cook and clean up, and the scouting motto "KISS" (Keep it simple, stupid).

• If you want to grill hot dogs on a stick, be sure you know what kind of stick you are using if you've cut it from a tree or bush. Oleander is poisonous, for example, so don't cook a hot dog on an oleander branch! You can make disposable hot dog and marshmallow roasting sticks from unbent wire coat hangers.

• Take along a block of frozen chili or stew and use that for your first meal at the campsite.

• You don't need a colander if you cook noodles in a coffeepot that has holes in the spout.

• Wrap diced potatoes, a hot dog cut in one-inch pieces, some sliced carrots, and a dab or two of water, wine, or beer in a heavy-duty foil pouch and cook about 20 minutes on coals. The time on this depends upon how big the food pieces are and how hot your fire is, so 20 minutes is just an estimate. Eat out of the foil to save mess.

• Beer is a good liquid to add to a camp stew pot because it makes a rich sauce without adding a lot of ingredients that aren't likely to be handy when you are camping.

• Measure the spices needed for a favorite camping meal, put them into a plastic bag or envelope, and label it "chicken dish" or "good stew," and then it will be ready to sprinkle on the food when you start cooking at the camp fire.

• When traveling in a camper, put opened milk cartons or juice cans in a plastic bread bag and tie with a twist tie before you put them back into the cooler or camper fridge to prevent spills.

• If you coat the bottoms and sides of pots and pans with liquid detergent or rub with a bar of soap before you set them on the open camp fire, they won't get black from soot and smoke, and cleanup time will be quick and easy.

Camping with Children

Believe it or not, avid camping families say that camping or backpacking with babies younger than one year old is easy. They nap often, are not too heavy to carry on a hike, and don't complain about having "nothing to do." Also, feeding is simple, and a small child can sleep with Mom or Dad in a sleeping bag.

• Even disposable diapers are light, but be sure to carry along a plastic bag to hold used ones until you can dispose of them properly.

• Do cover a child's head with a hat or light blanket and use sunscreen on all of baby's exposed skin. Baby skin is tender and will get redder than you think just from reflected sun, and that includes sun reflected on a cloudy day, too.

• If you are hiking or camping with a toddler, be sure to pack a lot of patience and do some advance planning to deal with children at this active age.

• Camp with other toddler parents. Not only will the children enjoy each other, but you'll have more helping hands and feet to keep up with them. (Many families take along a friend or cousin of older children, too, so that their children will have the company of someone their own age.)

• Taking along favorite toys, or that special blanket or other "life-preserving" necessity, helps a toddler adjust to different surroundings. Many toddlers don't like to have their nap or bedtime routines disrupted and will be difficult all day if they haven't slept well.

• Small children have short attention spans. Scenery doesn't thrill them for long. Bring lightweight, plastic "pretend" camping gear so that a small child can mimic your activities—cooking, chopping wood, and so on.

• Get your toddler a small backpack and use it to carry crayons, paper, scissors, and so forth. When you are settling down to prepare a meal, small children can draw things they've seen on the trail.

• A diary is a good idea for older children, so they can record their feelings and whatever they have seen. Children who can't write can draw in their diaries, which can be simple, lightweight notebooks. Paste a picture from a travel brochure or magazine on the front.

• When you travel with a baby who is still drinking from a bottle, you may want to put the 2 A.M. feeding into an insulated carrier so that it's ready when baby is. It's no fun to stoke up a fire or fiddle around with a camp stove at that hour to heat up formula or juice.

• If you're not sure how good a traveler your baby or child is, you might try some "training sessions."

Camp overnight in your backyard, take a hike in a nearby park, go to the zoo or a botanical center. Let your child "help" with the planning so that it's your child's trip, too, even if it's just deciding what toy to take along.

In addition to conditioning your child to dealing with outdoor trips, these pre-trip events will help you know what sort of food, clothing, and equipment you need.

• If the children go away to camp without you, give them prepaid addressed postcards so they won't have any excuses for not writing home.

• Most send-away camps provide lists of what children should bring with them, and it's best to stick to the list so your child will have the same things the others have and feel more like "one of the guys/gals."

• First-aid kits should include syrup of ipecac to induce vomiting in case a budding gourmet does some forbidden tasting of the flora on the path. If you have space, you might want to carry an "instant ice compress." These light-weight plastic bags of chemical crystals are activated if struck and can be applied to painful sprains and bruises.

The Heloise Survival Kit

Through the years, certain things have become absolutely essential to life in a Heloise Home.

Vinegar, baking soda, and nylon net have had the most press, but there are many others. I've listed them here, from A (ammonia) to V (vinegar). You'll find them used throughout this book, sometimes in unorthodox fashion. For example, in Chapter 3, "In and Around the House," you'll find vinegar used at least 11 times. Here's the Heloise Survival Kit:

Ammonia	Newspapers
Baking Soda	Nylon Net
Bleach	Old Gloves and Socks
Borax	Oven Cleaner
Candles	Panty Hose
Cat Litter	Petroleum Jelly
Clothespins	Plastic Squeeze Bottles
Coffee Cans	Prewash Spray
Coffee Grounds	Rubbing Alcohol
Cornstarch	Salt
Crayons	Sandpaper
Cream of Tartar	Silicon Spray
Dental Floss	Shoeboxes
Dryer Lint	Steel Wool
Fabric Softener Sheets	Tackle Box
Fishing Line	Toothbrushes
Hair Spray	Toothpaste
Innertubes (old, used)	Typewriter Correction Fluid
Nail Polish	Vinegar
Nail Polish Remover	

INDEX

Adult education classes, 130, 277
Aerosol cans, 196
Air conditioners, 31, 255–56, 312–14
Air travel, *see* Flying
Alarm systems, home, 31
Alcoholic beverages, 246, 249, 346
Alfalfa, 161
Allergies, 100, 146, 255–56, 346
Allowances, children's, 207–8
Allspice, 65
Aloe vera plant, 156–57
Aluminum pans, 51
Aluminum screens, 137
American Cancer Society, 252, 254

American Heart Association, 246, 252
American Lung Association, 252
American Resorts and Residential Development Association, 373
Amtrak, 371
Animals, *see* Pets
Animal shelters, 319
Anise, 79
Antibiotics, poisoning by, 262
Antihistamines, 255, 262
Anti-static sprays, 112
Apartments, renting, 266–67, 304
Apples, storage of, 87

Appliance cords, fire safety and, 148
Appliances, 30–48, 283–317
  children's safety and, 197
  electronic, general tips on,
    283–85
  instruction booklets for, 30,
    283–84
  large, polishing, 150
  life expectancies of (table), 30–32
  servicing of, 284–85
  warranties of, 284
  See also specific items
Aquariums, 335–39
Arthritis, 259–61
Ashtrays, 109
Asparagus, 75
Aspirin poisoning, 262
Association of Home Appliance
    Manufacturers, 352
ASTA Consumer Affairs
    Department, 369
Asthma, 256
Audio tapes:
  for answering machines, 306–7
  cassette, 292–95
  reel-to-reel, 292–93
Avocado plants, 155, 156
Avocados, 79

Babies, 180–93
  bathing, 189–91, 193
  bringing home, 181–83
  feeding, 182–87
  high chairs, 187–89
  laundry of, 191–92
  safety rules for, 194, 195
  teething, 193
Baby food, 186–87
  storage of, 88
Baby powder, 191
Baby showers, 361–62
Babysitters, 205–7, 343–44
Bacteria, food and, 64, 82
Bananas, storage of, 88

"Barf bags," 198
Basil, 65, 170
Bathing children, 189–91, 193
Bathrooms, 95–103
  bathtubs, 100
  mirrors, 102–3
  showers, 97, 101–2
  sinks, 51, 98, 100
  storage shelves in, 127
  tiles in, 50, 97–98
  toilet bowls, 99–100
  wall decorations for, 50
Bathtub mats, 100
Batteries:
  camera, 303–4
  car, 151
  telephone, 310
Bay leaves, 66
  growing, 167
Bean sprouts, 161–62
Bedding, storage of, 104–5
Bedmaking, 104
Bedrooms, cleaning, 103–5
Beef, storage of, 88
Beets, 170
Berries, storage of, 88
Better Business Bureau, 312, 369
Bicycles, 154
Bill paying, 242–44
Birds as pets, 327–28
Birthday parties:
  children's, 201–2
  long-distance, 362–63
Bleach, 51, 99, 140, 215, 217, 351
  all-fabric, 191
Bleach spots on carpets, 113–14
Blenders, 48
Blinds, cleaning, 120
Blood stains, 213
Blouses, ironing, 211, 223–25
Boating, 373–74
Bok choy, 81
Bookshelves:
  in closets, 127

to "frame" windows, 126
for home offices, 270 \
Bottle feeding, 44, 182–85
Bouillon cubes, 62
Bouquet garni, 68, 69
Boric acid, 56–57
Brands of canned goods, 81–82
Brass, cleaning, 55–56, 122
Bread, storage of, 88
Breakfasts for toddlers, 188
Breast-feeding, 182, 185
Broccoli, 75, 80
growing, 172–73
Brosnahan, Tom, 376
Budgeting, 267–68
Buffets, 346, 356, 364
Burping babies, 183, 184
Business cards, 240
Butter stains, 215
Butter, storage of, 88
Buttons, replacing, 227
Buying Produce (Murdich), 76

Cabinets, painting, 145
Cables, locations of, 129–30
Caffeine, 61
Cakes:
birthday, 201
frozen, for parties, 347, 348
storage of, 88
Calculators, 31, 74
Camcorders, 290–91, 304
Cameras, 284, 303–4
transporting, 305–6
Camphor, poisoning by, 262
Camping and hiking, 389–96
children and, 390, 394–96
clothing for, 389–90
dealing with insects, 390–91
food for, 389, 393
with pets, 391
Canada, taking pets to, 326
Cancer, colon, 79
Candies, 347

Candle holders, 355
Candle wax stains, 213
Canned goods, 62, 81–82
storage of, 83–84
Can openers, electric, 31, 48
Carambola, 78
Cardamom, 66
Cardiopulmonary resuscitation
(CPR), 177
Carpets, 95, 112–14
stains on, 113–14, 216–17
Carpet sweepers, 48
Car phones, 310
Carrots, 75, 170
Cars:
accidents, 375–76
air conditioners in, 255–56
parking in garage, 152–53
pets in, 320, 326–27, 335
recorded music in, 296, 297
renting, 376
in snow or ice, 176
traveling in, 204–5, 374–77
washing and maintaining, 151–52
Casseroles, 62, 63, 88
Cassette tapes, *see* Audio tapes;
Video cassette tapes
Casters, 110
Cast-iron cookware, 51–53
Cats, 328–32
carriers for, 332
dental care of, 322–23
and dryers, 218
garden fences and, 174
health of, 320–23, 330
litter boxes, 331–32
neutering, 318–19, 330
training, 328–29
traveling with, 326, 327
See also Pets
Catsup stains, 214
Caviar, 89–91
Cayenne pepper(s), 66, 81
Ceiling fans, 314

Celeriac, 80
Celery seed, 66
Centerpieces, 357
Centers for Disease Control, 82,
    388
Cereal(s):
    storage of, 82
    for toddlers, 188
    See also Grains
Cervical collars, 260
Chain saws, 174
Chairs:
    for home offices, 271
    wobbly, 110
Champagne, 91–92
Charcoal grills, 31
Charities, clothing donations to,
    233–34
Checks, mailing, 243–44
Cheeses, 86, 88
Chemicals, safety and, 59, 96, 132,
    162–63
Cherries, storage of, 87
Chervil, 66
Chewing gum stains, 214
Chicken, 64, 68
    quantities of, for parties, 347
    storage of, 88
Children, 194–209
    allowances for, 207–8
    camping and hiking with, 390,
        394–96
    dressing, 199–200
    feeding toddlers, 187–88
    hiring sitters for, 205–6
    at home, alone, 200, 206–7
    intercom systems and, 311
    parties for, 201–2, 343–44
    pets and, 319
    playing with, 202–4
    and records, 299
    safety and, 59, 96, 171, 177,
        194–97, 206–7, 262
    sick, 198
    traveling with, 186, 193, 203–5

    wading pools for, 179
    See also Babies
Children's rooms, 127
Chili, 62
    canned, 82
Chili peppers, 81
Chili powder, 66
China:
    care of, 350–52
    "good," when to use, 348–49
    storing, 349–50
Chinese mustard greens, 80
Chinese okra, 81
Chives, 66, 170
Chocolate stains, 214
Chocolate syrup, 87
Cholesterol, 246–47, 263–64
Chopping-block countertops, 49
Chore assignment, 96
Chrome/chromium, 42, 122, 132
Cigarette burns, 114
Cilantro, 66
Cinnamon, 66
Cleaning-fluid rings, 214
Cleaning kits, 106
Cleaning products:
    abrasive, 42, 50–54, 98, 101
    safe storage of, 96
    toilet-bowl, 100
Cleaning systems, 95–96, 105–6
Cleanup:
    of cooking pots, 67
    after painting, 142–44
Clocks, electric, 31
Closets, 219, 232–36
Clothes, 210–38
    children's, 199–200, 235
    crushed, 386–87
    donating, 233–34
    dry cleaning, 210, 226–27
    for hiking and camping, 389–90
    how to pack, 382–84
    initialing, 219
    ironing, 211, 221–26
    repairing, 227–28

sewing, 228–32
shopping for, 236–38
stain removal from, 211–17
storing, 219, 232–36
for traveling, 380–81
washing, *see* Laundry; Washers,
    Clothes
Clothespins, 69
Cloves, 66
Cobwebs, 120–21
Cockroaches, 56–59
Coconut palms, 156
Coffee, 59–60
    as house plant, 156
    microwave ovens and, 44, 59–61
    for parties, 346, 356
    in restaurants, 265
Coffee makers, drip, 47
Coffee percolators, 32, 47
Cold preparations, poisoning by,
    262
Compact disc players, 297–98
Compact discs (CDs), 284, 296–97
Composting, 165–66
Computer games, 281, 306
Computers, *see* Personal computers
Conservation Renewable Energy
    Inquiry and Referral Service
    (CARIERS), 313
Contact lenses, 258–59
Continuous-cleaning ovens, 39–41
Cooking, 62–67
    camp, 393–94
    herbs and spices in, 65–67
    leftovers, 62–63
    microwave, 65
Cookware, 51–54
    aluminum, 51
    for camping, 394
    cast-iron, 51–53
    cleanup tips for, 67
    enamel, 53–54
    glass, 36, 54
    non-stick, 53, 67
Copper, cleaning, 55–56, 122

Cordless phones, 309
Coriander, 167
Corn, growing, 169
Cornmeal, storage of, 57, 83
Corn poppers, 31
Cosmetics, 214, 256
Coumarins, 61
Countertops, 49–50
Coupons, 71–73
    holders for, 72–73
Crayons, 202
Cream, 247
Credit cards, 244, 386
Cruises, 372–73, 378
Crystal:
    "good," when to use, 348–49
    storing, 349–50
    washing, 36
Cumin, 66
Cupboards, painting, 145
Curry powder, 66
Curtains:
    alternatives to, 126
    ironing, 223
    washing, 120
Custards, 88, 91
Cutoff valves, water, 130
Cutting boards, plastic vs. wooden,
    64
Cuttings, plant, 157

Date palms, 156
Dating:
    of groceries, 73–74
    of leftovers, 63
Daybeds, 105
Decals:
    decorative, 50
    on doors and screens, 137
Defrosters, electric, 38
Defrosting refrigerators/freezers,
    38
Dehumidifiers, 315–16
Demagnetizing audio tape players,
    292

Dental care, 254–55
  for pets, 322–23
Desks for home offices, 269–71
Detergents:
  on cars, 151
  dishwasher, 32, 33
  in Laundromat, 221
  and refrigerators, 37, 38
Diabetes, 79
Diapers, 191–92
Diet(ing), 245–51
  balanced, 245–49
  computers and, 280
  to gain weight, 245
  to lose weight, 249–51
  low-fat, 83
  vegetables and, 78
Dill, 66, 167
Dips, 347
Dishes:
  for frozen meals, 62
  hand washing of, 29, 36–37, 351
  microwave ovens and, 43, 44
  See also Tableware
Dishwashers, 32–35, 352
  cleaning, 34–35
  detergents for, 32, 33
  enamelware and, 53
  life expectancy of, 31
  running, 33–34, 351, 352
  silverware and, 35, 54
  trouble-shooting, 35–36
Dogs, 332–35
  dental care of, 322–23
  feeding, 334
  health of, 320–22, 334, 335
  for security, 147
  training, 332–33
  traveling with, 326, 327
  See also Pets
Door hardware, 137, 145
Door hinges, 147
Doors:
  repairing, 137
  security and, 147

Dowels, glueing, 110
Downspouts, painting, 142
Drain cleaners, 131–32
  garbage disposals and, 46
Drains:
  clogged, 131–32
  "sweetening," 47
Drapes, washing, 120
Drawers:
  organizing, 103, 235
  sticking, 110
Dresses, ironing, 223
Driveways, 175
Drop cloths, 140
Dry cleaning, 210, 226–27
Dryers, clothes, 31, 197, 218, 223
  trouble-shooting, 220
Dust, allergies and, 255, 256
Dust mites, 255

Ear plugs, 385
Eating out, see Restaurants
Eggplant, growing, 167
Egg poachers, 186
Eggs:
  floor stains from, 120
  storage of, 85, 89
Egg slicers, 67
Electric blankets, 31, 317
Electric socket plugs, 197
Electric wiring, location of,
    129–30
Electronic Industries Association,
    284, 306
Emergencies, phone calls in, 57,
    196, 261
Enamel copperware, 53–54
Epsom salts, 261
Exercise, 244–45
Extension cords:
  appliance function and, 47
  as fire hazard, 148
Extension services, 164, 165, 195
Eyeglasses, 256–58
  computers and, 277, 278

Eyes, 256–59
  contact lenses, 258–59
  makeup and, 256

Fabric softener, 218
Family newspapers, 242
Fans:
  ceiling, 314
  electric, 31
Fat, dietary, 246–47
Faucets, 130
Fax machines, 31
Feathers, allergy to, 255
Federal Aviation Administration,
    370
Federal Trade Commission, 312
Fences, 165, 174–75
Fennel, 66
Fertilizer, 160, 164, 165, 171
Fiber, dietary, 78, 245–46, 249,
    250
Fiberboard cubes, 270, 299
Film containers, 305
Finger foods for toddlers, 187
Fingermarks on felt, 214
Fingernails:
  baby's, 193
  broken, 260
Fingerpaints, 202
Fireplaces, nonworking, 127
Fire safety, 148–49, 206
First aid, 177, 196, 206
  for camping trips, 396
  for poisoning, 261
Fish, 247
  refreezing, 90
  storing, 86–88
  tropical, 335–39
  See also Seafood
Fleas, 323–25
Flooding, carpets and, 114
Floor drains, 132
Floor polishers, 31
Floors, 115–20
  bathroom, 97

  dents in, 117, 120
  garage, 153
  hardwood, 116–18
  scrubbing, 119
  squeaky, 117–18
  vinyl, 116, 118–20
  waxing, 116, 119, 120
Floppy disks, 273–75, 277
Flour, storage of, 57, 81, 82
Flower beds, 166–67
Flying, 367–71, 384–85
  buying tickets, 368
  with children, 205
  lost luggage, 370–71
  preparing luggage, 379–80
  protesting poor service, 369–70
  travel agents and, 369
Food and Drug Administration
    (FDA), 82
Food poisoning, 64, 82
Food processors, 48
Food storage, 82–91
  in refrigerator, 38–39, 57–58, 67,
    82, 86–90
  temperature danger zone and, 87
  See also Freezing
Forceps, 68
Foreign languages, tapes and, 295
Formula:
  stains, 191, 213
  See also Bottle feeding
Freezers, 37–39
  cleaning, 37
  defrosting, 38
Freezing:
  of baby food, 186
  dating system for, 63
  of eggs, 85
  to kill weevils, 58, 59, 82
  of leftovers, 62–63
  for parties, 347–48
  refreezing, 90–91
  of seafood, 86, 87
  time limits on, by food, 87–90
  of vegetables, 84–85, 90

Frozen foods, 266
  during defrosting, 38
  foam cooler for, 74
  food processors/slicers and, 48
  thawing, 63
Fruit juices
  refreezing, 90
  stains from, 214
  storage of, 88
Fruit trees, 165
Fruit(s):
  for babies, 186–87
  canned, 84
  growing, 162, 169
  in health diet, 246
  refreezing, 90
  shopping for, 76–79
  storing, 87–88
  See also specific varieties
Frying pans:
  cast-iron skillets, 51–53
  electric, 47
Furnaces, 31
Furniture, 107–12
  audio-video, 302–3
  cleaning and polishing, 107–9
  home-office, 270–71
  refinishing, 111–12
  repairing, 109–11
  upholstered, 114–15
Furniture polish, homemade, 108
Furs, storing, 236
Fuse boxes, 130
Fuzzy dust, 120–21

Garages, 147, 152–54
  parking in, 152–53
  for storage, 153–54
Garbage disposals, 31, 45–46, 83
Gardening, 161–75
  composting, 165–66
  equipment for, 173–74
  herb, 167–68
  indoor, 161–62
  lawns, 171–72

pesticides/insecticides, 162–63, 170–71
  pets and, 329
  planting from seeds, 168–69
  resources for, 164–65
  walls and fences, 174–75
  watering, 172–73
Garlic, 64–66
  for decoration, 127
  growing, 166
Gas burners, cleaning, 42
Gas pipes, locating, 129
Generic products, 81
Gerbils, 339–41
Gifts:
  for baby showers, 361
  for bridal showers, 357–59
Gilt frames, 107
Ginger, 66
Glass cookware, 36, 54, 351
Glasses, see Eyeglasses
Glassware:
  dishwashers and, 33–35, 351
  hand washing, 9, 36, 351
  See also Crystal
Glueing furniture, 110
Glue stains, 214
Gold-trimmed dishes, 35, 43
Gourds, 127
Grains, 247, 248
  storage of, 57, 82–83
Grandparents, 208
Grass:
  allergy and, 255
  ground cover vs., 165, 172
  near pools, 178
  pets' liking for, 321
  stains from, 214
  See also Lawns
Gravy, 89
Grease stains, 214
Greeting cards, 240
Grills, charcoal, 31
Ground cover, 165, 172
Ground meat, 64

Grout, 49–50, 97–98
Guarantees, appliance, 30, 284
Guavas, 76
Guinea pigs, 339–41
Gum disease, 254

Hair:
    plastic lid as clip for, 69
    tangles in, 260
Hair dryers, 31
Hairs, cat and dog, 114
Hall trees, 104
Hammering, 135
Hamsters, 339–41
Handicapped travelers, 371
Hanging pictures, 123–25
Hawaii, taking pets to, 326
Headsets, 302
Heartworm pills for dogs, 322
Heaters:
    room, 316
    water, 32, 33, 134, 135, 148
Heating pads, 186
Hedges, 165
Hemming, 211, 229
Herbs, 65–67
    growing, 167–68
    in microwave cooking, 65
    storing, 83, 168
Herb teas, 61
Hi-fi systems, 31
    See also Stereo equipment
High chairs, 187–89
Hiking, *see* Camping and hiking
Hiking shoes, 390
Home offices, 268–71
Home satellite television, 286–87
Honey facials, 251
Horseradish, 170
Hoses, 174
Hotel reservations, 372
Hot peppers, 81
    for decoration, 127
House plants, 155–60
    from cuttings, 157

drainage of, 159
pest control for, 159–60
watering, 157–58
from pits and seeds, 155–56
Houses, hosing down, 150
How to Beat the High Cost of Travel
    (Brosnahan), 376
Humane societies, 320, 321, 341
Humidifiers, 31, 112, 314–15

Ice removal, 175–76
Ice cream:
    for parties, 347–48
    refreezing, 90
    storage of, 89
Ice-cream makers, 31
Immunization for pets, 320, 326,
    328
Index cards, 240
Ink stains, 213
Insect bites, 390–91
Insecticides, *see* Pesticides
Insect repellent, 390
Insects, *see* Pest control
Instruction booklets, 30, 283–84
Intercom systems, 310–11
Internal Revenue Service (IRS),
    269–70
Ipecac, syrup of, 196, 261, 396
Ironing, 211, 221–26
    linens, 353–54
Ironing boards, 226
Iron preparations, poisoning by, 262
Irons, 31, 221–22
    travel, 387
Ironstone, 350–51
Ivy, 165, 172

Jasmine, 165
Jewelry
    for children, homemade, 202–3
"Job jar," 96

Kale, 80
Ketchup, 88
Keys, spare, hiding, 146

Kitchen appliances, *see* Appliances
Kitchens:
  cleaning, 49–51
  decoration of, 127
  design of, 29–30
  pest control in, 56–59
Kitchen sinks, 50–51
Kitchen utensils, 51–56, 67–69
  for microwave ovens, 43
  storing, 67, 69
  wooden, 64
  See also Cookware; *and specific items*
Kiwis (kiwifruit), 76
Knickknacks, 106, 123
Knob celery, 80
Knobs, loose, 110
Kumquats, 77

Ladders, 141–42
Lamps, cleaning, 106–7
Laundromats, 220–21
Laundry, 211, 217–21
  baby's, 191–92
  linens, 353–54
  See also Dryers, Clothes; Washers, Clothes
Lawn mowers, 31
  storing, 148, 154
Lawns, 171–72
Leases, 266–67
Leather
  storing, 236
  upholstery, 115
Leaves, 165, 166, 171
Leftovers, 38–39, 62–63, 67, 90
Legumes, 247–48
Letters:
  computers and, 281
  taping, 294
  writing, 241–42
Lettuce, 75, 89
  indoor growing of, 161
Lights:
  outdoor, 176
  underwater, 177

Linens, 353–55
  "good," when to use, 348–49
  repairing, 354–55
  storing, 354–55
Linoleum, 118, 119
Lint, 218, 220
Lipstick stains, 215
Litter boxes, 331–32
Locks, 137, 147
Loquats, 77
Luggage
  for air travel, 379–80
  lost, 370–71
  See also Packing

Macaroni necklaces, 202
Mangoes, 77
  growing, 156
Margarine stains, 215
Marigolds, 166
Marjoram, 66, 167
Mattress stains, 217
Mayonnaise, 89
Meat, 247
  for babies, 186–87
  buying, 75
  ground, 64
  kitchen shears and, 68
  quantities of, for parties, 347
  refreezing, 90
  storing, 86–89
Medications:
  for children, 192, 197–98
  disposal of, 262
  poisoning by, 262
Memo books, 239–40
Menu planning, 71
  for parties, 344
Message center, family, 207, 264
Mexico, taking pets to, 326
Microwave ovens, 31, 42–45
  baby's bottle and, 44, 183, 184
  children and, 197
  cleaning, 45
  coffee and, 44, 59–61

cooking with, 65
heating plates with, 352
safety precautions for, 44
tea and, 44, 61
utensils for, 43–44
wattage of, 42–43
Mildew, 215
carpets and, 114
on grouting, 98
painting and, 140
on records, 300–301
Milk, 89, 247
Milk crates, 270, 299
Milk stains, 192, 215
Millipedes, 160
Mint, 67, 167
Mirrors:
bathroom, 97, 102–3
hanging, 125
Modems, 271, 276, 278
Moisturizers, 252
Mold allergies, 255–56
Muffin tins, 187–88
Mulch, 165
Mung bean sprouts, 161
Murdich, Jack, 76
Mushrooms:
poisonous, 196
slicing, 67
Musicians for parties, 365
Mustard greens, 80
Mustard powder, 67

Napkins, 356, 357
National Institute on Alcohol Abuse
and Alcoholism, 249
National Park Service, 389
Neutering (spaying), 318–19, 320,
330
Non-stick cookware, 53, 67
Notebooks, personal, 239–40
Nuts, 347

Obesity, definition of, 250–51
Odors:

carpet, 114
in closets, 236
garbage-disposal, 45–46
refrigerator, 39
Offices, home, 268–71
Oiling furniture, 107–8
Oil paintings, 107, 124
Oils, dietary, 247
Okra, 81
Oleander, 196
O'Neill, Eugene, 341–42
Onions, 64, 84, 166, 170
Organization, personal, 239–44
Orthodontics, 255
Oven cleaner, 36, 40, 41
Oven racks, cleaning, 40
Ovens:
continuous-cleaning and
self-cleaning, 39–41
standard, cleaning, 41
toaster, 48
See also Microwave ovens
Oxalic acid, 170

Packing, 367, 379–80, 382–88
Painting, 138–46
choice of paint, 139
cleanup after, 142–44
closets, 232
color selection, 139
cupboards and cabinets, 145
fences, 174–75
fiberboard, 270
preparing surfaces for, 140–41
spray, 145–46
storing paint, 144–45
using ladders, 141–42
Paintings, 107, 124, 125
Paint stains, 215–16
Palms, 156, 160
Pans, *see* Cookware
Pants:
hemming, 211
ironing, 224
Papayas, 77

Parsley, growing, 161, 167
Parties, 343–66
  audio taping at, 294
  catered, 344
  children's, 201–2, 343–44
  co-hosted, 363–64
  freezing food for, 347–48
  linens and, 353–55
  planning for, 343–47
  swimming-pool, 365
  videotaping, 291
  See also Showers; Weddings
Passion fruit, 77
Passports, 388
Pasta, 89
Patina, 54
Patterns, sewing, 230
Peanut butter, 89
Pegboards, 127, 153
Peppers, 81, 84, 167
Percolators, 32, 47
Periodontal disease, 254
  in pets, 322–23
Persimmons, 77
Personal computers, 271–82
  backing up work, 275, 277
  basic terminology, 278–79
  buying, 276
  disk care, 273–74
  for household tasks, 71, 280–81
  life expectancy of, 32
  phobia about, 276–77
  printers for, 281–82
  screen glare, 277
  surge protectors for, 272–73
  turning off and on, 271–72
  word processing on, 274–76
  work-station arrangements,
    277–78
Personal flotation devices (PFDs),
    373
Perspiration, stains from, 216
Pest control, 56–59, 82, 95
  in gardens, 170–71

  for house plants, 158–60
  roaches, 56–59
  weevils, 57–59
Pesticides/insecticides, 58, 59,
    162–63
Pet carriers, 326
Pets, 207, 318–42
  allergies and, 256
  children and, 319
  choosing, 318–19
  dental care for, 322–23
  first aid and health, 320–22
  fleas and, 323–25
  hiking with, 391
  household chemicals and, 59, 171
  loss of, 341–42
  traveling with, 325–27
  See also specific animals
Pewter, 123
pH factor, 151
Photograph displays, 123
Photographic equipment:
  transporting, 305
  See also Cameras
Picture frames, cleaning, 107
Pictures, 107, 123–25
Pies, 88, 91
Pilling pets, 321–22
Pillows:
  extra, 105
Pineapples, 78
Pipes:
  frozen, 133
  location of, 129–30
  noisy, 132–33
  See also Drains
Pits, planting, 155–56
Plant food, 160
Plants:
  poisonous, 195–96, 320
  See also Gardening;
    House plants
Plaster, patching, 138
Plastic utensils, 64, 67

Plates:
  heating, 352
  See also Dishes
Play clay, 202
Playing with children, 202–4
Plumbing, 130–35
Plungers, 131
Poison Control Center, 196, 261
Poisoning, 194, 261–62
  boric acid, 57
  emergency routine for, 57, 196
  by household products, 59, 96,
    162–63, 261–62
  by medications, 262
  oxalic acid (rhubarb spray), 170
  by plants, 195–96
  See also Food poisoning
Pomegranates, 78
Pools, *see* Swimming pools; Wading
    pools
Porcelain enamelware, 53–54
Porcelain sinks, 51
Pork, 88
Postal fraud, 311–12
Postal scale, 241
Potatoes:
  freezing, 85
  growing, 170
  storing, 89
Potato necklaces, 202–3
Pot roasts, 62
Pots, *see* Cookware
Potted plants, 172, 173
  See also House plants
Poultry, 64, 68, 247, 347
  buying, 75
  refreezing, 90
  storing, 87, 88
Power surge protectors, 272–73,
    284
Pregnancy:
  alcohol and, 249
Pressing hams, 224
Prickly pears, 78

Printers, computer, 281–82
Produce:
  shopping for, 75–81
  See also specific items
Projection televisions, 286
Protein, dietary, 246–48

Quilts, 123

Rabies inoculation, 326
Radishes, 75
Ranges, 39–42
  continuous-cleaning/self-cleaning
    ovens, 39–41
  life expectancy of, 32
  range tops, 41–42
  standard ovens, 41
Record players, 298–99
Records, 284, 299–301
Refreezing, 90–91
Refrigerators, 37–39
  cleaning, 37
  defrosting, 38
  door seals of, 38
  fresheners for, 39
  life expectancy of, 32
  organizing contents of, 38–39
  safety and, 196
Renting apartments, 266–67, 304
Reservations:
  hotel, 372
  restaurant, 265
Restaurants, 265–66
  dieters and, 250
  traveling and, 377, 378
Rewards, 96
Rhubarb leaves, 196
Rhubarb spray, 170
Ribbons, computer-printer, 281
Rice, 82, 89
Roach control, 56–59
Roasters, electric, 47
Room heaters, 316
Root vegetables, 90

Rosemary, 67, 167
Rust:
  on bathtubs, 100
  on iron, 215
  on tin, 55
  on toilet bowls, 99

Safety precautions:
  boating/sailing, 373–74
  chemical products, 59, 96, 132,
      162–63, 171, 177
  for children, 59, 96, 171, 177,
      194–97, 206–7, 262
  fire, 148–49
  pool, 177, 178
  See also Poisoning
Sailing, 373–74
Salad bowls, wooden, 64
Salad dressings, 89, 91
Salmonella, 82
Salt, 246, 248
Sanders, paint removal with, 140
Sanding floors, 116–17
Savings, 268
Scorch marks, 216
Scouring powders, *see* Cleansers,
      abrasive
Scratching posts, 329–30
Screens, window, 136–37
Screwdrivers, 135–36
Seafood, 64
  storage of, 86, 87
  See also Fish
Security, home, 146–47
Seedlings, transplanting, 169
Seeds:
  planting, 155–56, 168–69
  sprouts from, 161–62
Self-cleaning ovens, 39–41
Septic tanks, 130, 134
Sewing, 228–32
Shavers, electric, 32
Shaving, 260
Shears, kitchen, 67, 68

Shellfish:
  refreezing, 90
  storing, 88
Shelves:
  to "frame" windows, 126
  in garage, 153, 154
  space-saving, 127
  See also Bookshelves
Sheets, 104, 105
  storing, 219
Sherbet, 89
Shirts:
  ironing, 211, 224–25
Shoe bags, 128
Shopping, 70–82
  clothes, 236–38
  coupons, 71–73
  lists for, 71–72, 74
  menu planning and, 71
  organizing trips, 73–75
  for parties, 344–45
  for produce, 75–81
  for staples, 81–82
  via television, 311–12
Shopping carts, 74, 75
Shower curtains, 102
Shower stalls, 97, 101–2
Showers, 357–63
  baby, 361–62
  birthday, 362–63
  bridal/groom, 357–60, 362
  long-distance, 362
Shrimp, 86, 87
Shrubs, 165
Silver-trimmed dishes, 43
Silverware, 35, 54–55
Sinks:
  bathroom, 51, 98, 100
  kitchen, 50–51
Sink strainers, 36
Skillets, cast-iron, 51–53
Skin problems, 251–52, 256
Skirts:
  hemming, 211, 229

ironing, 225
quick repairs for, 227, 228
Sleeping bags, 391
Sleeping pills, poisoning by, 262
Smoke detectors, 32, 149
Smoking, 252–54
Snow removal, 175–76
Snow throwers, 32
Society for the Advancement of Travel for the Handicapped (SATH), 371
Sodium, *see* Salt
Soil, 163–64
Soups, 62
canned, 83
storage of, 89
Sour cream substitute, 64–65
Spaghetti grabbers, 68–69
Spaghetti sauce, 59
Sparkling wines, 91–92
Spatulas, 67
Spaying, *see* Neutering
Speakers, 301–2
Spices, 65–67
storage of, 83
Spray painting, 145–46
Sprouts, growing, 161–62
Squash, growing, 172–73
Stainless steel, cleaning, 42, 50–51
Stain removal:
from baby's clothes, 191, 192
from carpets, 113–14, 216–17
from clothes, 211–16
dry cleaning and, 227
from mattresses, 217
spot-treating before washing, 217–18
from upholstery, 115
"Stand by" travel, 373
Staples, shopping for, 81–82
Starch in ironing, 221–23
Star fruit, 78

Static electricity, 112
Steak tartare, 64
Steaming face, 251
Stepping stones, 175
Stereo equipment:
headphones, 302
players/turntables, 298–99
records, 299–301
speakers, 301–2
Sterling silver, 54
Stews, 62, 88
Stinkweed, 196
Storage space, 127–28
for bedding, 104, 105
for clothes, 219, 232–36
drawers, 103, 235
in garages, 153
Stoves, *see* Ranges
Strainers, sink, 36
Strawberries, 169
Styling combs, 32
Styluses, 298
Subleases, 267
Sugar, 90, 246
Sunglasses, 257
Sun tea, 61
Surge suppressors, 272–73, 284
Survival kit, Heloise's, 397
Sweet peppers, 81, 84
Swimming pools, 176–79
cleaning, 178
parties, 365
safety and, 177, 178
Swiss chard, 81

Tablecloths, 353–55, 357
Table setting, 353
Tableware, 348–52
care of, 350–52
"good," when to use, 348–49
storing, 349–50
See also Dishes
Tapes, *see* Audio tapes; Video cassette tapes

Tarnish:
    on copper and brass, 55
    on gilt frames, 107
    on silver, 54–55
Tarps, substitute, 146
Tarragon, 67, 167
Taxes, home office and, 269–70
Tea, 60–61
    herb, 61
    microwave ovens and, 44, 61
Teething, 193
Tele-cine adaptors, 288
Telephone answering machines, 32,
        182, 206, 306–8
Telephones, 147, 308–10
    car, 310
    cleaning, 106
    cordless, 309
    installation of, 308
    location of cables of, 130
    multi-function, 309–10
    next to computers, 274
Television(s), 32, 285–86
    home satellite, 286–87
    old, uses for, 303
    shopping via, 311–12
    stereo, 301, 302
    See also Video cassette recorders
Temperature danger zones, 87
Thermostats, programmable, 314
Thorn apple, 196
Thyme, 67
Tiles:
    bathroom, 50, 97–98
    decals for, 50
    floor, 118, 119
    homemade cleaners for, 97–98
    kitchen countertop, 49–50
Timers, home-security, 146
Time-share vacations, 373
Tin, care of, 55
Tipping:
    in restaurants, 265–66
    on vacation, 295, 377–78
Toaster ovens, 48

Toasters, 32, 47–48
Toilet bowls, 99–100
Toilets, clogged, 133–34
Toilet seats, 97
Toilet tanks, 134
Tomatoes:
    canned, 84
    freezing, 84–85
    growing, 167, 168, 170, 172–73
Tools, 135–36
    gardening, 173–74
    protecting chrome from, 132
Toothbrushes, electric, 32
Toothpaste on sinks, 98
Towels, storing, 105, 219
Toys:
    homemade, 203
    safety of, 194–95
Train, traveling by, 371
Trash compactors, 32
Travel agents, 369, 372, 373
Traveling, 367–96
    abroad, 295, 375, 386, 388–89
    by air, *see* Flying
    with baby, 186, 193
    boating, 373–74
    by car, 374–77
    with children, 186, 193, 203–5
    clothes for, 380–81
    cruises, 372–73
    eating out, 377, 378
    for handicapped, 371
    home arrangements while, 158,
        379
    hotel reservations, 372
    ironing and, 224
    packing, 379–80, 382–88
    with pets, 325–27
    tape recording and, 295
    tipping, 295, 377–78
    by train, 371
    vacation ideas, 371–72
    See also Camping and hiking
Tropical fish, 335–39
Trousers, *see* Pants

Turners, 67
Turntables, 298–99
TV dinners, home frozen, 62
Typewriters, 32

U.S. Coast Guard, 373
U.S. Department of Agriculture, 76,
   82, 87, 164, 245
U.S. Department of Health and
   Human Services, 245
U.S. Department of Transportation,
   369
U.S. Food and Drug Administration
   (FDA), 87, 248
U.S. Surgeon General, 252, 253
Upholstery, 114–15
Urine stains, 216–17
Urine test tablets, 262
Utensils, *see* Kitchen utensils

Vacations, *see* Traveling
Vacuum cleaners, 32, 48
   children and, 197
   emptying, 112
Vaporizers, 158
Variety meats, 89
Varnish, cleaning, 109
Vases, 127
Vegetables:
   for babies, 186–87
   canned, 62, 81–82
   freezing, 84–85
   growing, 161–62, 166–67,
      169–70, 172–73
   in healthy diet, 246
   leftover, 62, 90
   refreezing, 90
   shopping for, 75–76, 79–81
   See also specific varieties
Velvet, water stains on, 217
Veterinarians, 320–25, 328
Video cassette recorders (VCRs),
      32, 208, 283, 287–91
   buying, 287
   care of, 289–90

covers for, 284
portable (camcorders), 290–91,
   304
taping TV shows with, 287–89
Video cassette tapes, 287, 289
converting movies and slides to,
   288
Video games, 306
Vinyl:
   floors, 116, 118–20
   furniture, 115
Vodka, 91
Voltages, outlet, 130

Wading pools, 179–80
Waffle irons, 32, 48
Walkways, 175
Wall coverings:
   cleaning, 121–22
Wall hangings, 123–25
Wallpaper:
   choosing, 126
   cleaning, 121–22
Walls:
   cleaning, 121
   decorations for, 50
   garden, 176
   repairing, 137–38
   shower-stall, 101
Warped boards, 111
Warranties, appliance, 30, 284
Washers, clothes, 197, 218
   life expectancy of, 31
   running, 33
   trouble-shooting, 219–20
   used as coolers, 346
Water:
   for coffee, 47
   conservation of, 134, 158, 172
   contaminated, 82
   hardness of, 33, 34, 47, 100, 134,
      220
Water heaters, 32, 33, 134–35, 148
Watering plants, 157–58, 172–73
Watermelons, 78

Water-pipes, *see* Pipes
Water pressure, 132–33
Water purifiers, 135, 389
Water stains:
  painting and, 140
  on velvet, 217
Waxing:
  cars, 151
  floors, 116, 119, 120
  furniture, 107–8
  large appliances, 150
Wedding gowns, 235
Weddings:
  bridal/groom showers, 357–60,
    362
  instant photography at, 304
  videotaping, 291
Weed killers, 171
Weeds, 171
Weevils, 57–59
Weight:
  definition of obesity, 250–51
  diet and, 245, 249–51
  exercise and, 245
  quitting smoking and, 253
Wheat sprouts, 161

Wicker furniture, 111
Window cleaner, homemade, 97
Windows:
  decorating, 126
  painting and, 141
  repairing, 136
  washing, 150
Window screens, 136–37
Wine, 91–94
  in microwave cooking, 65
Wine racks, 93
Wine stains, 217
Wintergreen, oil of, poisoning by,
    262
Wiring, location of, 130
Wisteria, 196
Wooden utensils, 64
Wood floors, 116–18
Woodwork:
  cleaning, 121
  painting, 141
Work schedules, 269

Yogurt, 65

Zone heating, 316

Heloise ®

from
A to Z

ACKNOWLEDGMENTS

To simply acknowledge is not enough, but to say thanks with a zillion hugs to Marcy Meffert, my always upbeat and reliable assistant/researcher/editor/helper and dear friend. Thanks for making my work life do-able and fun. Eugene Brissie, friend not foe. What a joy to work with a publisher who makes me laugh, not cry! Ted Hannah, Director of Advertising and Public Relations for King Features Syndicate who guides me through the maze of what and how with Southern charm. My office staff who are the worker bees who try to please: Ruth, Joyce, Kelly, Jinny Angie, and Janie; and our office managers, Fussy and Doolie. Never last or least, David, my husband, who is always here for me, even when I am not!

To: Sheba, our sweet, adorable Keeshond, who adopted us many years ago and now is in doggie Valhalla. You always had a ready "smile" and wagging tail for those you loved. You make us smile still. Woof!!

PREFACE

As I travel across the country, readers give me hints of all sorts but, in the past year or so, one hint began to pop up wherever I went. It was a hint to write a book of hints in dictionary form for people who are so busy they don't even have time to look in an index first. So, here it is—a dictionary of hints. You'll find some new hints, some old favorites, and some "new-old" hints—old favorites with a new twist.

Just for fun, I've added the "Letters of Laughter" sent to me by readers who sometimes got unusual results from using Heloise hints. For example, the man who sprinkled cat litter too deeply on his driveway to absorb motor grease and inadvertently created a kitty Valhalla—just about every cat in the neighborhood was happy to find a giant, driveway-size litter box!

Since my last book, *Heloise Hints for a Healthy Planet,* I've gathered more hints for helping to save our environment by recycling and using mild cleaning solutions and homestyle remedies that don't involve harsh chemicals. I've labeled those "Healthy-Planet Hints."

The very first hint in this book is the very first hint in my Heloise office files, ABRASIVE CLEANERS, and, as you've probably guessed, my two favorite non-abrasive cleaners are the same ones my mother recommended, baking soda and vinegar. These two safe and inexpensive household helpers have become synonymous with Heloise.

The last hint in the book is ZZZZ, 7 WAYS TO GET TO SLEEP. So many of us have so much to do that even with Heloise Hints, our activities are as abrasive to our nerves as harsh cleaners are to household fixtures and we lose our sparkle just like household fixtures cleaned with abrasives.

In between ABRASIVE CLEANERS and ZZZZ, you will also find some hints marked "Quick-Fix" which are emergency measures. For example, a "thread tail" of a machine-sewn shirt or blouse button is dangling on the button front; you know that means the button will soon pop off and you are on your way out the door to a meeting. You can avoid the button-pop embarrassment if you dab a drop of clear nail polish on the thread and "tail."

I have also included several "Checklists" of points to consider when you are avoiding allergens, saving energy (and energy dollars) in your home, winterizing cars, running a successful garage sale, avoiding mistakes on your taxes, questions to ask a Realtor before you list your house. Also, shopping to get best value, buying on layaway, and reading the fine print on an insurance policy or a warrantee agreement. The checklists can save money, energy (yours, too), and time for any consumer, but they are even more helpful to inexperienced consumers who too often pay more for less when they don't have enough information to make decisions.

And what Heloise Hints book would be complete without those "that's so simple, why didn't I think of that" hints from readers who have found a better way to do ordinary things? For example, a hint like grabbing a hot light bulb with the corrugated paper "box" from the new bulb instead of burning your fingers. Or, unusual how-to hints on feeding horses, snakes, and turtles, handling your pet salamander and keeping fishing worms from escaping. Look for hints on how to file the hints you clip from columns, too.

We are publishing this book in time to be given to new summer brides and grooms and students going away to school or graduating and moving from home to live on their own for the first time. The latter, for example, will find hints for making decisions at work and getting comfortable at the computer along with the ever popular Heloise Home Hints for cleaning, cooking, and yes, my most requested Spots and Stains Removal section. Believe me, most of the questions I get are about removing spots and stains from clothing, furniture upholstery, and carpets so I've tried to assemble as much information about this as I possibly can. The second most annoying problem seems to be odors—how to get rid of them and how to make rooms and things smell fresh.

I realize that Heloise hints can't solve all the world's problems, but they can help to make each person's individual world and daily life less stressed by the little things that are so aggravating. How often does one more little thing gone wrong become the proverbial straw that breaks the camel's back or the nudge that pushes us over the edge?

I've tried my best to alphabetize the hints according to the words most people would think of when looking them up. I hope you will use this hints dictionary often and as I've suggested in other books, working parents who delegate chores to children can copy sections of the book, such as laundry hints, and tape them up near the washer and dryer, or copy freezing food hints and tack them up inside a kitchen cabinet or near the freezer. The idea is to have the information where it's needed most.

If you have any hints you'd like to share, you can send them to me: Heloise, P.O. Box 795000, San Antonio, TX 78279-5000. Or FAX it: 1-512-HELOISE.

As always, hugs,
Heloise

A

• **ABRASIVE CLEANERS,** *Healthy Planet, Protecting Sinks and Tubs:* Here are some reasons why I recommend cleaning with baking soda and vinegar—two simple, gentle, environmentally safe cleaners. I should note that my mother and I both recommended them because they are cheap and safe, long before I even met my husband, David, a plumbing contractor. David and I joke about having a premarital agreement that if he finds a can of scratchy stuff stashed away anywhere in our new home, it could be justifiable grounds for divorce.

1. Most powdered cleansers on the market will scratch your sinks and tubs and can cut the life of a new fixture by ten to fifteen years. They also scratch kitchen fixtures, plastic-type surfaces like laminated countertops, fiberglass sinks and shower stalls. Once these cleansers scratch surfaces they lose their shine, become dull, porous and more easily stained.

2. If you prefer commercial products to plain, cheap baking soda and vinegar, clean with spray-on, foamy-type bathroom cleaners. Also, powdered dishwasher detergent has enough chlorine bleach in it to clean like powdered cleansers, but protect your hands if they are chlorine-sensitive. Sometimes a squirt of liquid dishwashing detergent and a little extra elbow grease will do the job. *Letters of*

Laughter: I suggested using "elbow grease" in my newspaper column and found out later that many younger readers had never heard of the term. They asked supermarket managers where they could find "that elbow grease Heloise recommended in her column."

• **ACRYLIC PLASTIC DOOR PANES,** *Restoration:* Despite careful cleaning with various commercial products, one reader said that her storm door's acrylic panes stayed dull and cloudy most of the time. Then she applied liquid furniture polish with a soft, lint-free cloth and was amazed at how easily they became sparkling clean and clear.

• **ADDRESS BOOK:** Losing an address book is an incredible inconvenience. I keep a duplicate one in my safe in case of fire—the addresses are as important to me as any other valuable! Write the names in ink and the address and phone number in pencil. Then you can erase when the people move.

• **ADDRESS BOOK/FILE,** *Quick-Fix:* Cut the return address labels from envelopes and tape them to file cards or in address books with transparent tape.

• **ADDRESS CHANGE POSTCARDS,** *Time-Saver:* When you have a large family and circle of friends and move a lot, filling out change of address forms from the post office is a chore. (**Note:** These are FREE at your local post office for the taking, add a postcard stamp.) One reader gets one change of address form from the post office and fills it in appropriately. Then she has a local print shop copy the filled-out address form onto blank, plain 4 × 6 index cards—much faster and easier than writing in the information over and over! Don't forget to mail the cards!

• **ADDRESS FILES:** Instead of an address book, keep track of your mailing list in a 3 × 5 index card file, then you can replace the cards of people who move a lot. Add to the cards notes on birthdays, anniversaries, home and work phone numbers, and other helpful information such as a couple's children's names (if you see them infrequently), their food preferences/allergies, and directions to their homes. (My family was military and I remember how hard it is to keep track of such information when you have a large circle of friends who stay on the move.)

- **ADDRESS LABELS:**

1. Give extra address labels (like those you get from organizations soliciting donations) to your college students or elderly relatives to use when they write to you. (And in the case of students, hope they use them!)
2. Also, if addressing envelopes is a bother, either have labels printed for the people to whom you write most, get labels duplicated at a copy shop (ask for a "master" on which to put addresses), or ask people for their extra labels! Then, don't forget to write!
3. When you move, send a label with your new address to your friends and business contacts so they can just put the new label over your old address. **Hint:** Look for labels that will hold four lines so that the first line can be "We've Moved to:" or "Note New Address" and, if you can get five lines, have your new phone number printed on the label, too. To make sure there's no way not to notice, have them printed on yellow-green or other bright "Day-Glo" paper.
4. Stick one on your note or tablet paper for "custom-printed" stationery. Your address will always be legible.
5. Identification for Joggers/Walkers: Put an address label on the tongue of each walking/jogging shoe so that you will be identified in case of an accident on the road.
6. Halloween Trick or Treats: Stick your address labels on the treats you give away so parents know who gave them and that they are safe.
7. Stick one on your casserole dish and serving utensils when you take them to potluck affairs and you'll always get them back.

- **ADHESIVE BANDAGE,** *Removing Without Pain:* Soak a cotton ball with baby oil and apply it to the sides of the bandage. In about 10 minutes, the adhesive will be softened so much that the bandage will come off automatically and painlessly!

- **AFTER-CHRISTMAS SALES,** *Time-Saver, Saver:* Before you pack away those Christmas cards, wrapping paper, decorations, and all bought during the after-Christmas sales to save money, write down what you bought and make note of what you still need and then attach the list to the November page of your next year's calendar. It's easy to forget what's been bought and it's a chore to unpack early to find out what's needed.

• **ADVENT CALENDARS,** *Reminder:* If your family has the Advent calendar and/or Advent wreath tradition but forgets to get them started on time, pack the Advent things with Thanksgiving decorations as a reminder. Save by buying Advent calendars at post-Christmas half-price sales.

• **AFTERSCHOOL TALK WITH CHILDREN:** When all of the children arrive home from school and want to tell you about their day, feelings get hurt when they interrupt each other and some may feel left out. One mother of seven solves this problem by having the children draw numbers written on slips of paper when they come home from school. Each gets to talk in order from one to seven and they all feel fairly treated. It's easier on the mom, too!

• **AIRLINE TRAVEL,** *Seating:* Many frequent flyers agree that the smoothest ride is in the seats in the middle compartment over the wing's forward part. The quietest ride is in the front. There's more leg room if you get a seat next to the exit or at the bulkhead. A reader wrote that after he quit smoking and no longer had to sit in the back of the plane, he was surprised to find out how much more comfortable every other part of the plane was—one more good reason to quit, he said.

• **ALABASTER,** *Cleaning:* Alabaster is similar to marble (both are very soft) and so you can clean it with some marble-cleaning kits. Read the instructions on the label. You can also wipe alabaster items gently with mild detergent suds, rinse and dry with a clean soft cloth. Use this general cleaning method only occasionally; too frequent cleaning can damage alabaster. Commercial cleaning kits are available, too.

• **ALARM,** *Finding Snooze Button When You're Half-asleep:* Stick a self-gripping fabric dot on the snooze button and you'll find the fuzzy button with your eyes closed and one hand still gripping your pillow.

• **ALBUMS AND SCRAPBOOKS,** *When Old Pages Begin to Crumble:* Place pages between clear plastic protector sheets; protect odd-size page with clear protective covering from hobby shops.

- **ALLERGY,** *Checklist of ABCs for Relief:*
    A—Air-condition your home.
    B—Bathroom mold and mildew can cause allergy symptoms; scrub sinks and fixtures regularly.
    C—Cats and dogs can cause runny eyes and sneezing. Avoid pets or restrict them to certain areas of your home.
    D—Damp-mop hard surface floors at least once weekly.
    E—Enclose your fireplace; stay away from smoke and fumes and don't store wood indoors.
    F—Fluff-dry drapes and small rugs in your dryer to keep them dust-free.
    G—Go see your allergist regularly, on schedule.
    H—High-efficiency, non-electronic, ozone-free air cleaners can remove up to 99 percent of airborn contaminants from circulation. Get one for home or office.
    I —Invest in an efficient kitchen exhaust fan.
    J —Junior's fabric toys can trap dust and other irritants, so stay away from them; keep them clean.
    K—Keep emergency medication handy but out of reach of small children.
    L—Leave trees and plants alone during allergy season. (Or wear a surgical mask to reduce the pollen you inhale.)
    M—Mattresses should be vacuumed regularly and pillows and other bedding should be non-allergenic synthetic fibers.
    N—Notify school nurse and teacher of children's allergies and symptoms. Provide emergency phone numbers if your child has a serious problem.
    O—Outdoor activities should be minimized during allergy season. Stay indoors in an air-conditioned area whenever possible.
    P —Proper relative humidity during the winter furnished by a central humidifier will alleviate itchy skin and skin allergies.
    Q—Quit smoking; it's needless extra irritation for eyes, nose, throat, and lungs.
    R—Replace or clean air cleaner, air conditioner, and furnace filters as needed.

S —Stay away from odorous chemicals and heavy perfumes. Avoid industrial areas and high-traffic areas, too.

T —Tile your kitchen and bathroom floors; rugs trap allergens.

U —Use wood or vinyl furnishing rather than those with heavy upholstery fabrics.

V —Vacuum your whole house every week.

W—Windows and door should be shut and sealed tight.

X—X-tra care is needed during summer months.

Y—Year-round attention is important to allergy relief.

Z—Zip right through the allergy season with symptom relief, using common sense and these preventive tips.

• **ALMONDS,** *Roasting In Microwave:*
1. Toss almonds with oil to coat them lightly. Arrange them in a single layer on a microwave-safe plate.
2. Heat on full power for two minutes. Toss again and let rest one minute. Heat two minutes longer, until almonds are golden brown.
3. Drain and cool on paper towels.

• **ALUMINUM CANS,** *Recycling:* Pick up aluminum cans when you walk; you'll be exercising and helping the environment at the same time. If you don't want to turn the cans in yourself, give them to a church or other fund-raising group.

• **ALUMINUM FOIL,** *Healthy Planet Recycling:* If you line cookie sheets with aluminum foil, use that same foil, unwashed, to cover up the plate of cookies or between layers of cookies if you store them in a tin. **Hint:** If everybody could use every disposable thing at least twice, we'd cut our daily trash output by a half. That's not really realistic, but we can try to use as many disposables as possible at least twice to decrease trash output and save landfill space in our environment!

• **ALUMINUM FOIL,** *Recycling for Reuse:* Clean with a damp sponge, wiping the foil from the center out to the edges—it smooths the foil as it cleans.

• **ANIMAL FOOD,** *Storage:* If you feed your pets outside or feed birds, squirrels, etc., it's convenient to store the food outdoors. Keep uninvited animal guests from eating it by storing it in a self-locking trash can. **Hint** for feeding stray cats and dogs: Unless you plan to adopt the animal permanently, get it neutered and its immunizations, it's really kinder to call your local animal rescue organization. Strays lead a hard life—fighting disease, each other, traffic on dark streets, and they usually lose the fight. Also, the animal you're feeding may be registered as lost with the shelter and its owner may be anxiously waiting for word about it.

• **ANIMAL REPELLENT,** *Keeping Cats and Dogs from Shrubbery and Porches:* Sprinkle mothball flakes on the area that needs protection. Flakes will settle into the grass and last for several days so that you only need apply twice a week or so (only once a week after a while). The animals may eventually avoid that place even if you don't put out flakes anymore. **Caution:** Sprinkle FLAKES not moth balls; children can mistake the balls for candy and they are poisonous; also mothballs don't settle into the grass like flakes do.

• **ANSWERING MACHINE MESSAGE TAPES:** Save the messages from grandparents to grandchildren and vice versa in your fond memories box to enjoy again.

• **ANSWERING MACHINE REMINDER:** When you think of "must do's" at work, call your home answering machine to leave yourself a message—no more lost self-notes!

• **ANTIFREEZE CAUTION:** Animals, especially dogs and cats, love the sweet taste and only two ounces can kill. Once ingested, there is little to be done for the animal. Keep all antifreeze containers away from pets and wipe up all spills thoroughly.

• **ANTS,** *Extermination:* Sprinkle boric acid or borax powder along the ant trails and entrances. Keep crumbs vacuumed and any other ant "treats" wiped up so you don't attract more.

• **ANTS, IN OUTSIDE PET FEEDING DISH:** Make a moat! Partially fill a shallow dish with water and place the pet's food dish in the center of it.

• **APPLES,** *Added to Food:* If you can't bite apple chunks because of dental problems, grate apple for adding to salads or fruit compotes. **Hint:** If you can't chew your food properly, proper nutrition is difficult. See your dentist for help; new techniques diminish pain and restore teeth for better overall health!

• APPLES, *Freezing Excess:* Peel, core, and slice. Sprinkle with lemon juice or ascorbic acid (sold at supermarkets and grocery stores) to keep them from turning brown. Store in freezer containers or plastic freezer bags in specific-use quantities like one-, two- or three-cup packs so they'll be ready for recipes.

• APPLES, *Storage:* Apples give off ethylene gas and will make carrots bitter if stored in the same crisper drawer with them.

• APPLESAUCE, *Healthy Planet, Making Homemade Sauce Rosy Pink:* Leave on the skins of red-skinned apples, such as Cortland or McIntosh, when you cook the apples, then press them through a sieve or run them through a food mill (bought in cookware departments or shops) to mash the sauce and remove skins and seeds.

• APPLIANCES, *Cleaning Coppertone Finishes:* Dampen an old terry towel with a solution of half vinegar and half water to wipe off smudges, smears and finger marks; the appliance will shine.

• APPLIANCE SERVICE CONTRACTS/BOOKLETS: Put them in a large envelope and tape the envelope to the back (or side, if inconspicuous) of the appliance. You'll always know where they are. Or punch holes in them and keep all of them in a large ring binder.

• APPLIANCES, *Unplugging When Not in Use:* This safety warning is often given but seldom heeded as we leave toasters, auto-shut-off irons, sewing machines, hair dryers, etc. plugged in feeling confident that they are not on. Readers have sent me examples of near-disasters caused by leaving appliances plugged in between uses. The "toast" button on the toaster oven accidentally got pushed down and wasn't noticed until the smoke detector went off just in time to prevent an electrical fire. A roll of paper towels fell on a toaster oven; it went on and then the towels overheated to the point of catching fire. A rolled-up rug got placed on the foot treadle of a sewing machine, which was threaded and plugged in. The machine ran for unknown hours with the thread tangled in the bobbin case and caught fire. The family woke up to a smoke-filled house from the burning machine. It only takes a few seconds to unplug an appliance—precious seconds that could save your life or property!

Always unplug unused appliances and check smoke alarms frequently to be sure the batteries are working.

• **APPOINTMENT NOTICES:** Tape or staple doctors, hairdressers or other appointment slips to your calendar as soon as you get home and then you won't forget. If you have to remember (or if you want to remind someone else) that they have an appointment (or errand to run) on the way to or from school or work, tape a note on the car steering wheel.

• **APPLIANCE BOOKLETS,** *When They Are Lost:* Dial information, 1-800-555-1212, to get the manufacturer's customer service or consumer information number. Most have 800 numbers, but if there is none, call your local public library's business information number and get the address and/or phone number to write or call for information and to get a new booklet.

• **APPLIANCES,** *Quick-Fix Touch-Up:* Small scratches on white appliances can be covered with white nail polish or white typewriter correction fluid.

• **AQUARIUM,** *Cleaning:*
1. Because detergents may leave harmful residue, scrub an empty aquarium with non-iodinized salt and a heavy-duty plastic pot scrubber (one without any soap in it).
2. To bleach green algae stains from coral, shells and other aquarium decorations, soak in a mild chlorine bleach solution until white, rinse well under running water, and then soak at least 24 hours (until the bleach smell is totally gone) in a plastic basin or clean waste basket filled with water (enough to cover the decorations) and about one small bottle of aquarium water chlorine remover— the clear liquid (anti-chlor) you add to water to dechlorinate it before it goes into the fish tank.

• **AQUARIUM BACKDROP,** *Homemade $aver:* Instead of buying a plastic backdrop from the store, tape to the back of the aquarium a sheet of wrapping paper in a design that pleases you.

• **AQUARIUM GRAVEL,** *Recycling:* Put in a terrarium or the bottom of flower pots before planting; substitute for florist foam in flower arrangements; pour into ashtrays; layer different colors in an apothecary jar. **Note:** Not all fish tanks require gravel; some newer filter systems are not under gravel. Also, some fish, like African Chiclids dig so much that you're better off with pebbles at the bottom of your aquarium. Ask a knowledgeable person at your local aquarium store for advice and get information from library books and books about the specific type of fish you plan to buy.

• **AQUARIUM WATER,** *Healthy-Planet Water-saver:* When you clean out your fish aquarium (not salt-water tank), water plants with this free non-chemical fertilizer solution.

• **ART,** *Letter of Laughter:* A mother who always taught her children that "God is the greatest artist there is" found out that children really do listen sometimes. After a dark and rainy day, the sun came out and so did a rainbow. When her three-year-old saw it, she said, "I'm so glad God likes to paint!"

• **ASPARAGUS,** *Quick-Fix, Microwave Cooking:* For variety, place asparagus in a shallow microwave-safe dish and pour chicken broth over it. Sprinkle cut-up shallots and a bit of lemon juice on top, then microwave for a few minutes (see your microwave book for times per amount of veggie) until the asparagus is hot.

• **ASPARAGUS,** *Storage:* The fresher asparagus is, the better it tastes, but if you have to store asparagus for a day or so, put the uncooked asparagus stalks in a deep pot, cut ends down, put ice water in the bottom and over with a plastic bag. Keep the pot in the fridge until you're ready to cook.

• **ASSEMBLY,** *Bikes, Furniture, etc.:* Take a long piece of masking tape and press the ends together with the sticky side out. Then attach the tape to work table or the carton in which the pieces came and you can stick to the tape all those bits and pieces of nuts, screws etc. They won't get lost while you try to figure out the "easy assembly" instructions. **Hint:** When assembly is required, don't destroy boxes or containers until you're sure all is well. Keep all extra hardware, instructions, and tags in an envelope or zipper bag labeled to identify contents.

• **AUTO,** *Hot Wheels, Hot Seats:* Summer sun can make the steering wheel and driver's seat hot even with a windshield sunshade. Try covering the driver's seat and wheel with an old flannel-backed plastic tablecloth "tent" draped over the wheel and seat back. Or, to Quick-Fix if your wheel's not leather, rub an ice cube over the steering wheel; it'll cool quickly and you won't have to drive with two fingers!

• AUTO, *Rental Use Agreements:* Don't lend a rental car to anyone because the collision damage waiver agreement can be made invalid if damage is caused by a driver who's not listed on the rental agreement. Other reasons for invalidating the agreement can be an accident that doesn't occur on a highway, or if the rental company believes you were the careless driver in an accident (even if the other driver is clearly at fault). The deductible for most collision damage waivers is $100–$250, to be paid by the auto renter if the car is in an accident.

• AUTO, *Safeguarding Against Theft:* Purses have been stolen from car seats at stoplights when thieves break the passenger window and reach in. Either keep your purse hidden on the floor or, before snapping your lap seat belt in place, run it through your purse handle so that you and your purse are safely belted in. Of course, you do lock your doors, especially when driving in unfamiliar places. Please see AUTO THEFT.

• AUTO, *Summer Driving Care:* Overheated cars can spoil summer travel. When the temperature-warning light flashes or the heat gauge registers in the hot zone, try the following hints.
1. Turn off the air conditioner to give your car's cooling system a rest. Turn on the heater to drain some of the heat away from your engine.
2. If your car continues to be overheated, pull out of traffic to a safe parking place. Put the transmission into neutral and race the engine for a minute or two. This increases the fan speed and moves more air through the engine compartment.
3. If the car still says hot, turn off the ignition, raise the hood, and wait for the engine to cool off. Then get to a repair facility.

• AUTO, *Washing off Road Tar:* Spray spots with an oil-based pre-wash spray, let it set for a few minutes and then scrub with nylon net or a plastic scrubber. Repeat application to stubborn areas. Rinse and buff with soft cloth.

• **AUTO,** *Winterizing Checklist:* The following are potential winter trouble points:

1. Battery: Watch for corrosion on terminals and have a mechanic replace loose or frayed cables.

2. Windshield Wiper Blades: When they screech a lot or don't clean properly in the rain, they won't work in the snow either. Replace them. They are relatively inexpensive.

3. Belts and Hoses: Frays, cracks and bulges are warning signs. When the engine is turned off and cold, check for proper fan-belt tension by pressing down on the middle of the belt. It shouldn't give more than half an inch.

4. Lights and Turn Signals: Replace all bad bulbs.

5. Tires: See owner's manual for recommended cold weather air pressure. (Temperature affects pressure—generally, it's one pound for every 10 degrees of temperature.)

6. Radiator: Clean with a garden hose, spraying from front to back so fins are cleared of grease, dirt, and debris. Radiator caps and thermostats should be replaced after four years or 60,000 miles. Coolant should be changed every two years or after 30,000 miles.

• **AUTO,** *Winter Emergencies:* If you're stranded in a car during a snow storm, stay calm and stay put.

1. Don't leave your car unless you can see another shelter close by.

2. While you wait for help, alert passing vehicles with flares, reflective triangles, or even a brightly colored piece of cloth tied to your car antenna.

3. Keep warm in the car by running the heater once an hour, or every half hour in extreme cold. **Caution:** Be sure the area around your exhaust pipe and outside heater vents is not obstructed by snow or anything else to avoid carbon monoxide poisoning.

• **AUTO,** *Winter Emergency Items Checklist:* Keep the following in your trunk:

Flares or reflective triangles; jumper cables; abrasive material for traction (sand, salt, cat litter stored in recycled, clean, dry, plastic gallon jug); flashlight; sleeping bag or blanket.

• **AUTO ASHTRAY,** *Discouraging Smoking In Your Car:* If you aren't bold enough to put a no smoking sign on the ashtray, fill it with coins for parking meters or with potpourri, which smells nice, too.

- **AUTO EMERGENCIES:**
1. Make it easy to get helped. Place an envelope in your glove compartment marked "In Case of Accident" that contains the name and phone number of a person to notify in case of emergency, doctor's name, blood type and allergies.
2. Keep a "throw-away" camera in your glove compartment so that you can photograph damages, license-plate numbers, street signs and configurations, construction work or other obstacles, and anything else that gives you information for filing and proving an insurance claim if there's been an accident.
3. Keep an old blanket in the truck for picnics, for warmth in case you get stranded in the cold, and to drape over the back of the trunk and the bumper when you are loading or unloading a dirty car and don't want to mess up your clothes.

Letters of Laughter: Have you noticed that when you drive your spouse to work so that you can have the car for the day, you always get the flat tire? One reader, who has trouble remembering which way to turn lug nuts (left to loosen and right to tighten) when changing a tire, offers this rhyme which sounds just silly enough to be remembered: "Lefty Loosey, Righty Tighty."

- **AUTO INSURANCE,** *Checklist for Liability Coverage:* Make sure you get the best rate for the amount of coverage that you need.
1. Newer cars purchased with a car loan are required to have full coverage.
2. Older cars of minimal value can get by with liability coverage alone.

To get a free single copy of a pamphlet titled "Oops," send your request with a stamped, self-addressed, business-size envelope to the Insurance Information Institute Consumer Affairs, 110 William St., New York, NY 10038.

- **AUTO INSURANCE,** *Discounts:* Check your insurance to see if you get a reduction in rate for installing an anti-theft device, for having certain safety features such as anti-lock brakes, and so forth. Don't just pay without questions.

• **AUTO KEYS,** *Leaving Them in the Ignition:* Tie your keys to your purse or briefcase with a long leather boot lace so that when you pick up your purse or briefcase to leave the car, you can't go without removing the keys. The thong also helps prevent rummaging around in the bottom of a purse for keys—just pull the thong.

• **AUTO LITTER BAGS,** *Recycling:* Hook the handles of a plastic grocery bag over a floor-mounted gear shift to keep the litter bag handy. When it's full, just remove, tie the handles shut and discard.

• **AUTO MAINTENANCE,** *Simple Do-It-Yourself Checklist $aver:* Keeping your car in tip-top shape will get you a better price when you trade it in and will made it more pleasant to ride in while you own the car.
1. Keep a small bottle of matching color touch-up paint, bought at auto supply stores or dealers, to cover up small scratches, chips and minor nicks before they become rust spots.
2. If you live where road salts are sprinkled to deter ice, wash your vehicle as often as possible to prevent damage and corrosion.
3. Wash your car only with soap formulated especially for car washing. Dishwashing and other cleaners are too harsh for the finish and will eventually dull it.
4. Protect the paint job by waxing your car at least three times a year. Wax protects against grime and sunlight to keep paint shiny. Remember to always apply wax in a shady area. Car wax applied in full sun gets "baked on" and is very hard to remove.
5. In the interior, protect vinyl with a cleaner/protector to keep it from drying out and cracking; it also helps prevent color fading. Vinyl car tops are especially prone to these problems. Maintain cloth upholstery by removing dirt and dust before it gets ground into the fabric. A quick brush or vacuum will do the trick. Foam upholstery cleaner will remove dirt from cloth seats.

• **AUTO-MATICALLY FINDING YOUR CAR IN A MALL LOT:** Some years ago, my column had a hint to put a plastic flower or bicycle safety flag on your radio antenna to make it easier to find your car in mall parking lots. Afterward, I received lots of *Letters of Laughter* telling me that the best way to find your car in the lot was not to follow the hint—it seems that almost everyone attached something to radio antennae and it was easier to spot an undecorated car in mall parking lots.

• **AUTO SAFETY:** Get the habit of saying "Hands Up" to child passengers before you close the door to avoid hand injuries and make "Hands Up" a rule without "Captain May-I" discussions. *Letter of Laughter:* One member of my editorial staff got so used to saying "Hands Up" to her children during years of carpooling that she still says it to adult passengers even though she hasn't carpooled children in ten years!

• **AUTO SEAT BELTS:** When there are three seat belts in the backseat it's hard to figure out which parts go together—unless you color-code the belts with colored Christmas tape or colored "dots" so that riders can just match buckle parts according to color. *Letter of Laughter:* One kids' carpooling reader awards Seat Belt Olympics gold, silver and bronze medals to wear in the car as an incentive to buckle up their seat belts quickly.

• **AUTO THEFT,** *Prevention Checklist:*
1. Always lock your car, even for short absences.
2. Keep car keys separate from house keys. Don't put your name and address on key chains. Don't leave house keys in your car. If you leave keys with a parking valet, leave only the car key, never house keys, and don't tell when you will return.
3. Park your car as close to a building as possible with the front end toward the street to make it easier to spot anyone tampering with the car. At night, always park in well-lighted areas.
4. When parking, always turn the wheels sharply to the curb; it makes towing difficult. Put the emergency brake on.
5. Install an alarm system that turns on light, car horn, or siren if someone tampers with the car.
6. Install a locking gas cap or fuel switch that cuts off the fuel supply when the car is parked.
7. Buy a "crook lock" or "club lock" which locks the steering column to the brake pedal or which prevents the steering wheel from being turned without breaking the windshield. These devices make stealing a car so difficult that they are excellent deterrents— thieves don't want to bother with them.

• **AUTO TRUNK**, *Checklist for Emergencies:* Flashlight with extra batteries; ice scraper; road salt or cat litter; extra windshield-washer fluid; set of jumper cables; flares or reflective devices, extra container of antifreeze; blanket; sweat shirt or jacket; pair of gloves and hat; sandpaper to clean corroded battery terminals; plastic sheeting or garbage bag to kneel on in case you have to fix a flat on wet ground. In the glove compartment, keep spare change and emergency phone numbers, including one for road services.

• **AVOCADO**, *Rooting Plants from the Pits for a Free Plant:*
1. The usual way is to poke toothpicks in the sides and let the flatter rooting end rest in water until roots form and the plant is about four inches tall; then plant it in dirt.
2. Another method is to remove the outer (brown) skin from the seed, then put it in a zipper-type plastic bag with two tablespoons of water. Place bag in warm place. After about a week, the seed splits; after about two weeks, there's root growth; after about a month, there's enough root to plant in soil.
3. You can start seeds in dirt, too. Plant the seed with the pointed end up in a pot full of dirt; place in a sunny spot with no direct sunlight and keep soil moist.
4. I always trim my plant back to keep it from being spindly tall. When it grows to about six inches tall, I cut it in half and it branches out with new growth. I have several that are 10 to 12 feet tall.

B

- **BABY BATHTUB "PLAYPEN":** When a baby is just learning to sit up, let the baby sit in a little plastic bathtub to play with favorite toys. Of course, even if there's no water in the tub, don't leave baby unattended; accidents do happen.

- **BABY BIB,** *Quick-Fix:* No bib? Place a clean dish towel around baby's neck, and let it hang in the front like a bib, secure in the back with a plastic clip or clothes pin.

- **BABY BLANKET,** *Recycling:* Two baby blankets will equal one twin-size mattress pad on a child's bed.

- **BABY BOOK,** *Shower Gift:* Collect Heloise baby hints, cartoons about parenting, and magazine articles about child-rearing and put them into a book for the parents to read and save.

- **BABY-BOOK TAPE:** One mother who's too busy to write cute baby things in the baby book every time they happen, makes notes by talking on tape and then recording the notes when she has time. She saves the tapes, too.

- **BABY BOTTLE,** *Identifying at Day-care Facilities:* Since even permanent marker tends to wear off plastic bottles after a few washings, try sanding an area on the bottle with fine sandpaper and then writing your child's name on the roughened place with permanent marker and cover with clear nail polish. The marker gets absorbed into the scratched area and lasts for months.

• **BABY BOTTLE,** *Washing Baby-bottle Nipples and Caps:* Place them in a small hosiery bag (made to wash hose in the washing machine) and secure them by tying the bag to the top rack of the dishwasher. The heat from the water and drying cycle will clean them.

• **BABY-BOTTLE BRUSH,** *Recycling, Time-Saver:* The pointed tip and flexibility makes these brushes ideal for cleaning crevices and corners, such as the holes of cheese graters or the space around faucets.

• **BABY/BRIDAL SHOWER,** *Addresses for Thank-you Notes:* Save the guest list and note the gift next to the name as gifts are opened; then the showeree will have all the information she needs when she writes her thank-you notes.

• **BABY CAR SEAT,** *Keeping Cool in Summer:* The metal center of the harness can get very hot; place an old sweatshirt or towel over it for shade while you're out of the car to avoid risking a burn.

• **BABY CEREAL,** *$aver:* If baby decides to refuse baby cereal just after you've bought a supply (and that's usually when), mix some adult cereal with the baby-textured ones to keep breakfast-in-a-bowl from being too runny for a baby-held spoon; then you can use it all up.

• **BABY CLOTHES,** *Storing Outgrown Ones:* Store them in empty disposable diaper boxes—you'll always know at a glance which are baby clothes. Mark the outside with the sizes and descriptions so you don't have to play hide-and-seek.

• **BABY CRIB,** *Changing Sheets in the Middle of the Night:* When making the bed, layer rubber mattress protectors with sheets so that you can just pull the top one off if it's wet—without waking baby.

• **BABY CRIB,** *Substitutes When Traveling:* Toddlers—Pad a bathtub (if you can tape faucets so that toddlers can't turn on the water), a plastic toddler wading pool, or other SAFE container. Or try a mattress on the floor in a safe, protected room. Infants can sleep in a padded dresser drawer (removed from dresser, of course!), suitable clean box, or plastic infant bathtub. **Caution:** When using substitute cribs, always make sure there are no lids or loose padding to suffocate the child!

• **BABY EXPANDABLE GATE,** *Healthy-Planet Recycling:*
1. Expandable doorway gates used to keep children and pets out of rooms can be stretched width-wise across the bathtub for sweater-drying. Be sure the gate is plastic-coated or has no metal parts to put rust marks on the sweaters.
2. When your toddler grows up, nail two wood strips inside a closet to support the tension of the gate and make a "closet dam" to hold out-of-season blankets, comforters, extra pillows and children's sleeping bags for overnight guests.

• **BABY-FOOD JARS,** *Quick-Fix Opening:* Instead of wrestling with vacuum-sealed jar lids, place the end of a spoon handle under the rim of the jar lid and pry it open just enough to break the seal and pop the "safety button." The lid comes off more easily and the bonus is that you make sure the safety button was down on each jar and the food is safe for your precious little one.

• **BABY NIGHT FEEDING:** Instead of dashing up and down stairs to get a new baby's bottle for that 2 A.M. feeding, try putting a few bottles of formula in a small cooler with a frozen reusable ice pack and keeping a bottle warmer in baby's room. Then you can feed the baby without long-distance travel.

• **BABY NIGHT-LIGHT:** Install a dimmer switch for a baby's room overhead light and baby won't be startled when you switch on the lights for that 2 A.M. wake-up call session.

• **BABY PHOTOS:** Take photos each month on baby's birth date and include a sign in the pictures that says "Jane is 3 months old today." You can add information on baby's height and weight to the sign, too. Later you won't be confused about which pictures are of whom and when.

• **BABY POWDER CONTAINER,** *When It's Too Generous:* Cut the amount sprinkled out at one time by putting a piece of tape over a couple of the container's holes.

- **BABY'S COMFORT-BLANKET:** Because her first child suffered so much when her favorite "blankie" was in the washer, one mother made a point of buying two identical "blankies" for her second child so that one could be cuddled while the other was in the wash. Some children are comforted by a cotton gauze diaper, all of which look the same, and then there are lots of comforters and laundry time isn't a time of anxiety.

- **BABY SHOWER,** *For the Baby Whose Mom Has Everything:* If mom-to-be has already had a shower or has lots of hand-me-downs from other children, try a theme shower focusing on the one essential all babies need—diapers. Buy large boxes of diapers and containers of baby wipes, or buy gift certificates for diaper service for several weeks if that's mom's choice. Don't forget to clip diaper coupons to add to the gift cards. This hint is especially good for an office shower when co-workers don't know what the mom-to-be has for baby.

- **BABY SNAP BEADS:** Snap together a circle big enough to frame a clock, mirror, or picture and glue in place for a baby room decoration.

- **BABY SOCKS,** *Recycling Lacy Ones:* After washing outgrown lacy girl's socks, fill them with potpourri and sew the tops closed or tie them shut with a ribbon. Grandma or Godmother especially would enjoy having such sentimental sachets for lingerie drawers.

- **BABY-SITTING SOLUTION:** When an older child is the family sitter and younger siblings give their sib-sitter a hard time, try telling the younger ones that if they don't mind and cause trouble, the sib-sitter's baby-sitting fee will come from THEIR allowances. One mother said this solved her problem quickly and quietly.

- **BABY'S ROOM,** *Keeping Cats Out:* Replace the bedroom door with a light wooden screen door. You can see and hear anything that goes on in the room but the cat can't get in to snooze with baby or on baby's bed.

- **BABY, TAKING TEMPERATURE:** When you take a rectal temperature, let baby watch the egg timer you use to keep track of time. Watching colored sand fall or listening to the ticking can keep a small baby occupied during the process.

- **BABY TOWELETTE CONTAINER,** *Recycling:* Store children's crayons and pens; nails, screws, etc. in the garage; rubber bands and safety pins or other bits and pieces in the kitchen; hold plastic utensils and napkins at campouts or picnics. After removing the label, wash thoroughly; the cover fits tightly and small items don't fall out.

- **BABY TRAVEL,** *Taking Supplies in the Car:* Instead of a diaper bag, put baby's diapers, wipes, food, even toys in a plastic basket on the floorboard. It's easier to get to than a diaper bag when you're on the road.

- **BACK SCRUBBER,** *Homemade:* Get a strip of nylon net the length of a bath towel. Put a bar of soap in the middle, wrap the net around it a few times, then tie a knot at both ends to keep it in place. When showering, pull the net "towel" back and forth across your back as if you were drying it.

- **BACON,** *Storing:* If you don't use up a package quickly, try freezing individual strips; the bacon stays fresh and you can take out as many slices as you need. Place individual slices on a cookie sheet and freeze quickly. Then stack the frozen strips in a freezer-safe container with waxed paper between layers. Recycle: Use the waxed paper from cereal boxes for this.

- **BAGS,** *Healthy-Planet, Recycling Idea:* Carry your own mesh or other bags to the store when shopping to avoid collecting grocery bags at home. Europeans have done it for years; we can do it, too!

- **BAGS,** *Storing Plastic Grocery Bags, Healthy Planet Recycling:* Cut a hole about the size of your fist in the side of a clean plastic one-gallon milk or water jug and stuff bags inside; it'll hold more than you think. Then, you can pull one out at a time.

- **BAGS, PLASTIC DRY CLEANERS:** Knot the "hanger" end and line small wastebaskets with them. The bags will hold light paper trash and can be doubled for extra strength.

- **BAGS FOR PRODUCE:** Instead of wrestling a bulky head of leaf lettuce into a plastic bag, put your hand into the bag as if it were a glove, then with your "bagged" hand, grasp the bottom end of the lettuce and invert the bag up and over the head. No more shop-torn salads!

- **BAKING,** *With Honey, Corn Syrup, Molasses, Other Sticky Things:* Spray cups and spoons with non-stick spray before measuring for easy clean up.

- **BAKING DISHES,** *Measuring Capacity:* When you can't tell if a new dish will hold as much as your old one did, pour water to the level your recipe filled in the old dish and then pour it into the new to test for overflow. Or, if you know the quantity your recipe makes, measure that quantity in water and pour it into the new dish to make sure there'll be no overflow. (For example, a nine-inch pie plate holds four cups of liquid exactly.)

- **BAKING FISH STICKS, POTATO NUGGETS, ETC.,** *Fat-saver, Time-saver:* When baking, place food on a wire rack and the rack on a foil covered cookie sheet so that extra grease drips out while food cooks. The sticks and nuggets will be crisper, too, and there's no need to turn them over.

- **BAKING WITH LESS SUGAR:** Replace half the sugar in the recipe with half heat-stable diet sweetener. It will work in most recipes.

- **BAKING SODA,** *Healthy Planet, Recycling:* Baking soda safely cleans many things around the house. Sprinkle on baking soda, wipe or scrub with a damp sponge, rinse well. Sinks, countertops, you-name-it will sparkle. Keep baking soda in an empty plastic jar with a shaker top, like those that dried herbs come in, for easy access.

- **BALCONY,** *Childproofing:* Buy the widest available heavy plastic webbing (for lawn chairs) and then weave it in and out of the railing bars until all spaces are completely closed. Secure the ends and make sure the webbing is close together and strung tightly. Test by pushing on it. This doesn't replace adult supervision because a determined child can get through any barrier. This method can also help confine pets and give a bit of privacy if you like to sunbathe on your balcony.

- **BANANA BREAD,** *When Someone Throws Out the Bananas You've Saved for It:* Substitute canned peaches or experiment with other fruits.

- **BANANAS,** *Storage:*
1. To hasten ripening, store in plastic bag.
2. Once at the proper state of ripeness, you can place bananas in the fridge. The skins will darken but the fruit will be good for about two weeks.
3. Bananas frozen on a stick or in hunks make delicious and nutritious treats, especially for dieters because they take longer to eat.
4. Overripe bananas are perfect for banana bread or other baked goodies. You can freeze them until you have enough for a recipe. But then, use them, don't save them forever! *Letter of Laughter:* Someone once told me that the road to hell is paved with bananas saved for banana bread!

- **BANANA TREATS,** *Homemade:*
1. Freeze peeled bananas, then dip them in chocolate syrup and refreeze until the syrup hardens.
2. Cut peeled bananas into quarters and put peanut butter on the cut sides, wrap in plastic wrap and freeze.

- **BANDAGES FOR PETS,** *Keeping Them On:* Tape usually won't work, especially for dogs; they pull bandages off their legs and elsewhere.
1. Try slipping an elastic wrist sweatband or an elasticized terry ponytail holder (for a small animal) over the bandage to hold it in place. Be sure it's snug but not too tight.
2. If your dog just won't leave an injured area alone, ask the vet for a plastic collar. The dog won't like it, but the collar will prevent it from reaching a sore place and healing will be faster in the long run.
3. The leg from a child's knit footed sleeper can cover a neck sore. Cut enough sleeper leg on the upper side of the ankle elastic to gather (about 3 or 4 inches) and cut just above the heel on the lower side of the elastic, then place the gathered "leg" on the animal's neck with most gathers toward the animal's shoulders.

- **BANK DEPOSIT SLIPS,** *Recycling Excess:* Unfortunately, most of us don't make bank deposits as often as we write checks so we often have leftover deposit slips. Cut out the square area printed with your name, address and phone number and then glue or tape this "address label" to forms for in-store giveaways, on envelopes for

return address, and on other forms that require this information. You've already paid for them, you may as well use them! Keep some in your wallet, handy when someone you've just met wants your phone number.
Or slip them behind the window of a luggage tag.

• **BARBECUE,** *Identifying Food for Scouts, Others:* Clip plastic bread tabs with the person's initials to their clothing and write initials on each foil dinner with permanent marker so that the leader/cook can distribute cooked dinners with less commotion.

• **BARBECUE AUTO-GRILL,** *Letter of Laughter:* I get lots of barbecue hints but this one's ingenious! On a camping trip to the mountains, a family discovered that they'd forgotten their barbecue grill. They took the hubcap off their spare tire, covered it with foil, punched holes in the foil for grease to run out and used it for a grill. The heavy metal worked so well that now they always use the spare tire hubcap for a camping grill! Perhaps a used hubcap from a wrecker yard would do, too.

• **BARBECUE FIRE STARTER,** *Healthy-Planet Recycling:* Half-fill each section of a cardboard egg carton with dryer lint; pour melted wax over it and allow to harden. Cut apart segments for fire starting. **Caution:** Do not use plastic foam egg cartons; they won't burn away and they give off toxic fumes!

• **BARBECUE GRILL,** *Storage for the Winter:* Before storing your grill, be sure to wash the grate well. An unwashed grate sitting all winter can build up bacteria that can contaminate your food and make you sick when you cook on it in the spring.

• **BARBECUE GRILL FIRE STARTER,** *Healthy Planet, Recycling, Making a "Chimney" to Avoid Using Charcoal Lighter to Start the Fire:*
1. To Make the "Chimney"—Wash and dry a one-gallon paint can with a wire handle. Then, take the triangular end of a can opener and make about a dozen triangular openings around the bottom of the outer side of the paint can. **Note:** That's side, not the flat bottom end! Then cut off the flat bottom with a manual can opener so that both ends are open; now, it's a "chimney."
2. To Light a Fire—Place the can in the bottom of the barbecue pit and ball up about six half-sheets of newspaper; put them at the

bottom of the can. Fill the rest of the can with charcoal. Light the newspaper in several places through the holes in the bottom of the can. Because everything is contained in the can, there will be very little flame, just smoldering paper to light the coals. The chimney effect of the can decreases the fire starting time.

3. Before You Grill—When the coals are good and hot, use metal tongs to lift the can out of the grill by the wire handle. **Caution:** Protect your hands and arms with fireproof barbecue mittens and be very cautious when removing the hot can. The can will cool quickly once removed from the grill; it can be reused many times.

• **BARBECUE GRILLING:** When you grill something that cooks only a short time, like fish, have portions of another meat ready to cook on the coals to use up the heat. You can reheat the second meal in your microwave the next day.

• **BARBECUE GRILL PLANTER,** *Recycling:* Drill a few holes in the bottom of an old barbecue grill, remove rust with wire brush, spray inside and out with rust-retarding paint. After the paint dries, put a layer of stones or broken pot pieces on the bottom, fill with potting soil and peat moss; add plants and you have a nice planter.

• **"BAR-LE-DUC,"** *Recipe, Quick-Fix Breakfast or Snack:* Top three-fourths cup cottage cheese or cream cheese with one or two table-spoons of preserves and serve with toast or crackers.

• **BARRETTES,** *Storage:* When you have long hair, usually the combs, barrettes, etc. are a mess in the bathroom. One reader tacked (horizontally) eight separate lengths of one-inch ribbon with fancy tacks to the back of her bathroom cupboard door. She attaches all combs, barrettes, and other hair accessories to the ribbons and can tell at a glance where each of them is.

• **BASSINET SHEETS,** *Substitute $aver:* Slip the bassinet mattress into an inexpensive king-size pillowcase. The bonus is that after baby is no longer in the bassinet, you have extra pillowcases in your linen closet instead of a bunch of bassinet sheets stored in the attic.

• **BASEBALL CAPS,** *Repairing:* If the plastic adjustable strip on the back breaks, sew a piece of three-fourths-inch elastic on one side, measure for the right fit, and then sew the other end in place. Often these caps are one of a kind and are as precious to their wearers as a blanket or teddy bear is to a toddler so repairing them is an absolute necessity!

• **BASEBALL BAT GIFT BOX:** If you want to disguise a baseball bat so that it's a surprise gift, buy a florist's box normally used for long-stemmed flowers. You won't even have to wrap it.

• **BATH,** *"Kitchen" Remedies for Soaking in the Bath:* A reader suggests that you shower first, then fill the tub with lukewarm water, squeeze juice from sliced lemons into the water and throw the slices in, too. Then soak in refreshing, lemon-scented, natural astringent water. I like to put lemon juice in my hair rinse water. It removes all the soap film and oil and smells great all day. (Also, please see SKIN, "Kitchen" Remedies for Soaking in the Bath and BATH SALTS.)

• **BATH ACCESSORIES,** *Handy Storage:* Hanging a three-tier wire "egg basket" near shower or tub, where you can reach without getting out, gives you a perfect holder for shampoos, conditioners, bath oil, washcloths, and extra soap.

• **BATH MAT,** *Drying:* Instead of leaving a rubber bath mat in the tub after you bathe where it stays wet and is more likely to mildew, push an edge of the mat gently to the wall so it sticks on the tile by its suction cups and water drips into the tub.

• **BATH MAT,** *Washing to Remove Mildew:* Toss in washer with hot, soapy water and bleach, add a couple of bleach-safe towels for "scrubbing action."

• **BATH PILLOW,** *Substitute:* Partially inflate a plastic beach ball.

• **BATHROOM,** *Painless Cleaning Without Bending:* Instead of leaning over to scrub bathtubs and tile walls, put a few inches of soapy water in the tub, add some bleach and scrub all with a sponge mop. After tiles are clean, drain the water and mop the tub.

• **BATHROOM,** *Healthy-Planet, Quick-Fix Cleaning:* Using up toothpaste squished into the sink to clean it and the fixtures is an old favorite hint. An update is to use shampoo which has dribbled in the shower or tub for the same purpose.

- **BATHROOM COUNTER CLUTTER,** *Eliminating:* Attach a wicker hanging basket from the ceiling about 10 inches above the countertop to hold brushes, toothpaste, combs and other bits and pieces. There's no rule against using wire mesh kitchen hanging "egg" baskets either.

- **BATHROOM MIRROR,** *Preventing Fog:*
1. Put a bit of shampoo on a dry cloth and wipe the mirror with it before you bathe.
2. When taking a tub bath, run cold water only for the first inch or so, then add the hot water.
3. To "de-fog" quickly without smears, blow the mirror dry with a hair dryer.

- **BATH SALTS,** *Homestyle:* Pour three cups of Epsom salts into a metal or glass bowl. In a separate cup, mix 1 tablespoon of glycerin (available at drugstores), a few drops of food coloring (optional), and some of your favorite perfume. Blend well and slowly add it to the Epsom salts, stirring until thoroughly mixed. Store in a sealed decorative container and add it to your bath water for a treat.

- **BATH TOWEL,** *Pleasure:* Just before you get out of the tub, ask a nice person to warm your towel in the clothes dryer so that you can jump into a warm "cozy" when you get out. (Check out discount linens for bargains on "bath sheets" to wrap in.)

- **BATHTUB DECAL RESIDUE,** *Homestyle Remedy for Removing:* Apply prewash spray and scrub with nylon scrubber; or, when the tub is dry, sprinkle the residue with dry cornmeal and apply elbow grease with a nylon-net scrubbie. *Letters of Laughter:* I used the term elbow grease in one of my columns and found out later that many younger readers had never heard of the expression. They asked supermarket managers where they could find "that elbow grease Heloise recommended in her column."

- **BATHTUB DRAIN PROTECTOR:** Place a one and one-half-inch diameter kitchen sink strainer cup upside down over your bathtub drain to catch bobby pins and other dropped things that can go into the drain. You can still open and shut the drain.

- **BATHTUB/SHOWER DRAIN,** *Quick-Fix, Cleaning Hair from It:* Hate to stick your fingers into the hairy drain? Whisk it clean with a swish of a cotton swab. You touch only the other end of the swab!

- **BATHTUB OR SINK DRAIN QUICK-FIX STOPPER:** A rubber racquet ball (usually blue) will plug the hole of most non-grated drains.

- **BATHTUB OR SINK STAINS,** *Removing:* Scrub with paste made from cream of tartar and hydrogen peroxide.

- **BATHTUB SAFETY,** *When a Toddler Is in That "Me-do-myself" Phase:* Here's one reader's idea. To avoid scalding with hot water, paint a bright line (with model-car paint or fingernail polish) on the faucet handle and on the wall where the two should line up if the water is at the proper temperature for a bath. Then when your toddler insists upon drawing bathwater, the temperature should be safe. **Caution:** The lines are a guide. Never ever let a child prepare to bathe or bathe without adult supervision.

- **BATTERED WOMEN'S SHELTER,** *Helping:* When you clean out your closets, give women's and children's clothing, bedding and towels to your local battered women's shelter. Same for those mini-shampoos, rinse, lotions, shower caps you accumulate from hotels if you travel a lot like I do. If the phone number is not listed, you can usually get the drop-off location from a local volunteer agency, pastors of churches, your local newspaper, and other sources. Also, the next time you are sale shopping, especially at a discount or close-out store, consider buying up some of those bargains on clothing—often good garments that are off-size, or have missing bows etc. and are marked down to less than $5, an amount that's not too hard on the budget. Eventually, you can accumulate a nice wardrobe to donate to a women's shelter to cheer up one of its residents.

- **BATTERIES,** *Storage:* It's no longer advised to store batteries in the refrigerator. Store in a dry place at room temperature. Exposure to extreme heat, such as in attics or garages, can reduce battery life. If kept loose in a purse, coins or keys could cause them to short out.

- **BEANS,** *Dry, Cooking:* Perplexed about changing cooking times for dry beans? The higher the mineral level in your water, the longer it takes to cook beans. Since the mineral content varies from day to day, your cooking times also vary. Also, the older the beans, the longer the cooking time; that's why it's not a good idea to mix bags of beans. **Hint:** Dried beans are less likely to be "gaseous" if you soak them overnight, then discard the water in which they've soaked and cook with fresh water. Also, adding a pinch of ginger works well to remove "gaseousness" of home cooked or reheated canned beans.

- **BED-BOUND PATIENT,** *Back-Saving Helps for Caregivers:*
1. Rolling Over with Ease—Fold a twin flat sheet lengthwise and tuck it in across the center of the mattress on both sides of the bed. When you need to move a bed patient, untuck one side and roll him to the side of the bed where you want him.
2. Getting out of Bed, off and on a Chair, Getting in and out of the Car—Place a big plastic trash bag under the person so that sliding out of bed, in and out of chairs and car seats is easier on both patient and caregiver.

- **BEDDING,** *Reviving Faded, Making "Designer" Sets for Kids Beds from Hand-Me-Downs:* Tie a strip of old fabric around the center of a bed sheet and keep wrapping it around and around until you get to the outside edges. Fasten it tightly, then dye in the washing machine with fabric dye.

- **BEDDING,** *$aver:* If you can't find matching pillowcases at a sale, or if you want to save some money and sew, one twin flat sheet has enough fabric for at least two king-sized pillowcases and usually costs less than a set. So buy top and bottom-fitted sheets plus one twin.

- **BEDDING,** *Storing Extras:*
1. Store in an unused laundry hamper.
2. Put extra shelves above the ones already in your closet.
3. Put extra pillows in shams or corduroy zipper cases and pile them on unused beds or use them on the sofa. Fold or roll extra blankets and put them in pillow shams.
4. Make up unused beds. Toss a fabric softener sheet under the blanket or bedspread to keep sheets smelling fresh.
5. Fold a blanket so that it fits between a mattress and box spring. Store the mattress pad used on a couch under its pillows.

- **BED-MAKING,** *Time-Saver:* If only one person sleeps in the bed and/or if the bed is against the wall, tuck the sheets and blankets in snugly on the unoccupied side so that bedmaking in the morning is just a pull and a tug.

- **BED ROLLERS,** *Replacing When You Have No Helper:* Hold the bed up with a scissor-type car jack. Put a piece of plywood under the jack to keep it from damaging the floor. Also, be sure you know how to operate the jack safely before attempting this.

- **BED SHEETS,** *Fitted Bottoms That Don't Fit:* Newer mattresses are thicker than many old ones; look for "deep pockets" or those that give the depth in inches on the package. Some queen-size fitted bottoms fit thick double-bed mattresses and suspenders can help, too. Adjust suspenders to fit the bed width, slide them between mattress and box springs about a fourth of the way from each end and clip an end to each side of the sheet. You can also buy elastic "garters" to place on each corner from several catalogs.

- **BED SHEETS,** *Pilling:* Sometimes defects in milling cause pilling on sheets; shaving with a fabric shaver is usually not satisfactory. Best idea is to return the sheets to the store along with the receipt that proves purchase, or contacting the manufacturer of the sheets; readers have reported getting replacements.

- **BED SHEETS,** *Quick-Fix Decorating Uses:*
1. Pre-hemmed curtains and drapes (sew pleating tape at top for drapes, gather on rod for curtains, drape over pole for swags).
2. Super-size tablecloth.
3. Sew two together to make a super-size pillowcase to cover a worn/tired comforter (add self-gripping tape to the open side if you feel ambitious or leave as is).

- **BED SHEETS,** *Recycling Old Ones:* Old sheets can be dust covers for furniture, a tablecloth for picnics, tents for children's rainy day activities and can be made into pillowcases, curtains, or costumes.

- **BED SHEETS,** *Saving Money on Water-bed Sheets:* King-size or queen-size flat sheets will fit on a water-bed mattress if you tie each corner of the flat sheet into a knot and slip it under the mattress corner, tucking in sides securely. If you sew, you can sew corners. Then a second king- or queen-sized flat sheet can be the top sheet.

• **BEDSPREAD,** *Finding the Center:* Sometimes an all-over pattern is hard to center when you are making the bed; try marking the top center with a safety pin or a few stitches in a color that blends into the pattern and you'll save time shifting the spread around.

• **BED TABLE/TRAY,** *Temporary, for Sick-a-bed:* Try an adjustable ironing board placed perpendicular to the bed so that the legs slide under it. Cover with a plastic sheet or bag and a cheery tablecloth for meal serving.

• **BELT TAB,** *Securing:* When a belt is too long and sticks out in front, a single pierced earring will secure the end in place. Coordinate the earring stud with buttons or other decorations on the outfit so it's an extra accessory as well as functional.

• **BEEF JERKY,** *Homemade Without Preservatives:* Jerky is best made with lean beef flank steak and cut easily when partially frozen.
Step 1. Cut off visible fat, then cut into thin strips across the grain, making the strips as thin and uniform as possible for even drying. The steak can be dried as is or marinate it overnight in a shallow baking dish in the fridge. If you marinate it, drain it well before starting the drying process.
Step 2. To dry, lay strips close together but not touching on a cookie-cooling rack and place in the oven. If you have a gas oven, the pilot light will give off enough heat to dry them, but if your oven is electric, turn it on at the lowest setting. Prop the door open for good air circulation. Dry the jerky for twelve to forty-eight hours, testing it every so often. It's done when a piece snaps in half if you bend it.
The drier the jerky, the longer it keeps without refrigeration, but if you don't like it too dry, store it in the freezer until you're ready to eat it.

• **BEREAVEMENT GIFTS,** *Gifts from the Heart:* Sometimes the death of a spouse causes a drop in income that turns things we consider necessities into luxuries. But even if the remaining spouse is not suffering loss of income, a small gift can help knowing there is a special someone who cares. Some helps are a book of stamps in with the sympathy card; gift certificate for a food store in the area, beauty or barber shop, or department store; a check for gas, oil change, or tune-up at a nearby garage (call to find out the cost). And, most of all, an invitation to dinner out which is special because it provides companionship in addition to food. Eating alone is difficult for widowed spouses.

• **BICYCLE,** *Fitting the Right Size to a Child:* Riding a poorly fitted bike can result in an accident.

1. Have your child stand barefooted and measure her/his inseam from crotch to floor.

2. Take this measurement, subtract 10 inches for a boy's bike and 9 inches for a girl's model to get the proper frame size. (Adult bicycles generally measure from 19 to 26 inches.)

3. Buy a bicycle helmet when you buy a bike; consider the helmet and bike as going together like seat belts and autos. Thousands of deaths and head injuries from bike falls could be prevented if bikers wore properly fitted helmets—they should protect without obscuring vision.

• **BICYCLE,** *Checklist for Protection from Thieves:*

1. Most bicycles have serial numbers. Record this number and keep it along with a picture of the bike and the sales receipt in a safe place. This information will help police if your bike is stolen.

2. When you leave your bike at a destination, lock it to a solid object like a telephone pole, and use a heavy-duty bike lock. Light chains, cables, or locks are easily broken by thieves.

3. At home, never leave your bike on the front lawn or porch. Keep it in a safe locked place like your garage. **Hint:** Another reason to store your bike out of sight was given me by a door-to-door salesperson. A house with lots of bikes is a house with lots of children and parents who may be good sales targets for encyclopedias, insurance, and other family-oriented items!

• **BIKE RACK,** *Mind-Saver:* Tripping over children's bikes lying askew on the front lawn? Make a bike rack from a large uniform log. Treat the wood with wood preservative and then dig a shallow ditch and place the log in it. Using a saw, cut equally spaced grooves—one for each bike in the log—and make each groove the proper width to hold the front tire of a bicycle.

• **BIKING,** *Safety:* See JOGGING, Safety at Night for Joggers or Bikers.

• **BIKE SAFETY COLOR:** Hot pink clothing, even if you hate the color, is the safest, most visible color to get you noticed by motorists. You can also sew bands of fluorescent material around sleeves and legs of your biking outfit. Fluorescent bands sewn on hot pink would be double safety! A good idea if you ride in heavy traffic!

• **BILL PAYING,** *Keeping Your Financial Balance:* You don't have to own your own business to have a business account. If your company reimburses you for business expenses that you put on your credit card, such as lunches or trips, deposit your reimbursement checks into a separate account so that the right amount of money is always available when your credit card bills come in. Pocketing the reimbursement money could lead to spending it and being "short" at the month's end! You'll have better records for tax preparation, too.

• **BIRD CAGE,** *Bottom Liner:* Stack seven or eight pages of an old phone book or catalog in the bottom and remove one at a time as they get soiled.

• **BIRD CARE HINTS:**
1. Buy a bird only from a reputable pet store or dealer to make sure the bird has been brought into this country legally. Illegal birds may be diseased. Have pet birds checked by a vet who specializes in birds; many don't offer bird care.
2. Buy a cage large enough for the bird to fly from one perch to another and place it away from air-conditioning and heating ducts, out of drafts, and away from direct sunshine. Keep the cage out of the kitchen and clear of kitchen fumes, which can be deadly to birds. Also, cooking oil and grease settling on birds' feathers can destroy their natural insulation. Birds are sensitive to fumes of any kind, such as insecticides, paint and varnish, deodorants and hair spray.
3. Birds don't need immunization shots like dogs or cats but should have regular checkups and diagnostic exams if they appear ill.
4. A bird will accept a wide variety of food for a balanced healthy diet if it is hungry at feeding time. Don't keep food dishes filled all day. Instead, set up feeding times and give it fewer seeds and more fruit and vegetables. Feeding time is also a special bonding time

with your pet and is also a time to observe changes in eating habits or health.

• **BIRD FEEDER,** *Keeping Squirrels Away:*
1. Hang the bird feeder from a straightened wire coat hanger. It will hang far enough from the tree branch to keep squirrels and other unwanted guests from eating the bird food.
2. Hang the feeder with heavy filament fishing line; squirrels can't climb up or down. **Note:** I keep a separate feeder for squirrels on the same tree with my bird feeder in an attempt to keep all of the critters happy.

• **BIRD FEEDER,** *Pinecone:* Spread a thin layer of peanut butter or honey onto a pinecone, roll it in birdseed and tie it to a tree with a piece of string.

• **BIRD FINDER,** *Letter of Laughter:* A reader wrote that when her neighbor lost her parakeet, she put out a neighborhood flyer describing the bird and telling people to listen carefully because "He will give his phone number." He did; the finder called, and the parakeet was returned to his owner! He sure was no "bird-brain!"

• **BIRDS,** *Scaring Them Away from Fruit Trees:* Readers have said hanging mirrors from old compacts in the trees, suspended with string or rope, work like a scarecrow. Also, hanging a few rubber snakes in a fruit tree scares birds—and sometimes the neighbors, too!

• **BIRD SEED,** *Healthy-Planet Recycling:* If you dry watermelon and cantaloupe seeds during the summer, you can feed them to the birds in the winter. **Hint:** If you begin to feed birds in the winter, they will come to depend upon you and may perish if you stop feeding. So don't start if you don't intend to continue feeding until the weather allows "your birds" to find their own food.

• **BIRD SEED,** *Recycling:* If you have pet birds who don't always eat every seed, when you empty their food dishes, save the leftovers and put them where outdoor birds can sift through and get the seeds missed by your pets.

• **BIRTH ANNOUNCEMENT,** *When Friends Keep Calling to Ask If This Is THE Day:* Tell your friends to watch your mailbox. Put a big white bow on it when you leave for the hospital to deliver and, after the baby arrives, place a pink or blue bow on the box to signify the sex. You can also put the vital statistics on your answering machine and then, after Mom comes home, friends can get information even when Mom and baby are napping and not taking calls. My editor's daughter made a message from baby and Mom that said, "Tell them we are napping (baby coos and gurgles), tell them to leave a number and we'll call back later (baby coos again)," etc. Everyone loved it!

• **BIRTHDAY/ANNIVERSARY,** *Remembering:* Mark them on your calendar at the beginning of the year and if you have colored highlighters handy, color-code birthdays with one color and anniversaries with another. Some people like to address all cards at the beginning of the month and then send them out at intervals so that they arrive in time.

• **BIRTHDAY BOOK GIFT:** When one Heloise reader took birthday cake and decorations to her daughter's day-care center, she also took a book in which she wrote the child's name, birth date, and a brief note saying that the book was a gift from the child to the school on her birthday. Teachers liked the idea; so did other parents, and now birthday children are proud of their books each time they are read in class.

• **BIRTHDAY CARD CENTERPIECE:** To make sure children remember who sent them birthday cards and to get more enjoyment from the cards than just a momentary glance, make a dinner table centerpiece. Lay the cards facedown, side by side, on a flat surface, and tape them together. Then tape the last and first cards together to form a circle. Place the circle in the center of the table and by the end of the week, children will remember who the cards are from and the birthday person will feel honored all week long!

• **BIRTHDAY CELEBRATION,** *For Child Born on Christmas Eve:* Having a birthday during the holidays can make a child feel not-too-special. One reader solves the problem by having a "Half-Birthday" for her Christmas Eve child in late June. She sends all guests an invitation on a half sheet of paper; serves half of a sheet cake and freezes the other half for Christmas Eve; wraps presents with half birthday paper and half Christmas paper. If a gift the child wants is very large, she gets part of it in June and the rest at Christmas. For example, on the "half-day" she got a doll and a few clothes for it, then on Christmas Eve, she received the rest of the doll's clothing and other accessories.

• **BIRTHDAY GIFT,** *For a Friend Who Has Everything:* Give the friend a calendar at the beginning of the year and mark a promised lunch date near the birthday date. Don't forget to mark your own calendar, too!

• **BIRTHDAY PARTY,** *Substitute for Competitive Games for Young to Young Adult Children:* Tape a long piece of white shelf paper over waxed paper and lay it out on a floor or lay out a white poster board and provide lots of crayons. Have all the children at the birthday party write their wishes for the birthday child; they can also draw pictures if they wish. Even very shy children can participate in this activity along with the more outgoing ones. After the party, date the art work, roll it up (the waxed paper prevents smudges on the "art" side of shelf paper), and put it into an empty cardboard wrapping roll for storage. Taking the rolls out after years of collecting them is a fun nostalgia trip for the whole family.

• **BIRTHDAY "POPCORN" CAKE,** *To Mail:* To send a birthday cake to a student or overseas military person, make your favorite popcorn ball recipe and pack it into a well-greased bundt or angel-food pan; let cool. When it's hardened, remove and decorate like a regular cake. Popcorn cakes travel well and stay fresh.

• **BIRTHDAY SURPRISE:** Blow up about twenty or so balloons and decorate the bedroom after the birthday child has fallen asleep so that the special day can start off with the child awakening to a colorful surprise.

• **BIRTHDAY TABLECLOTH,** *Happy Memories:* On a solid color tablecloth, have birthday party guests sign their names with embroidery paint or fabric markers for a "keepsake cloth." Use a different color each year and be sure to include the date and year. The names and dates could be embroidered over the fabric marker, too. **Caution:** Protect the table top from ink "bleeding" through with appropriate padding.

• **BISCUITS:** Brush lightly with butter or margarine as soon as they are removed from the oven to make them look like an ad and taste extra delicious.

• **BLANKET BAGS,** *Recycling Zippered Ones:* Blankets, mattress pads, and bedspreads often come in heavy-duty zippered bags that you can recycle for storing all sorts of linens, clothing, and just plain stuff. One reader keeps old picnic and football game blankets in the zippered bags and hangs them in the garage so that they are handy to grab when the family goes on an outing.

• **BLANKETS,** *Laundering Washable Woolen Ones:* If the care label says the blanket is machine washable, here's how to get a comfy, clean renewed blanket.
1. Fill the washer with warm water, add detergent, and agitate to completely dissolve the detergent. Stop the washer and load the unfolded blanket evenly around the agitator. Soak for 10 to 15 minutes, then agitate on the gentle cycle for one minute. Stop the washer and advance the timer to the drain cycle and spin for about one minute.
2. Rinse by filling the washer with cold water for a deep rinse. Add fabric softener and allow the washer to complete the rest of the cycle automatically.
3. To dry in the dryer, set the temperature selector to the high setting. Place three or four bath towels in the dryer and turn the dryer on for a few minutes. Heated towels help absorb moisture so that the blanket dries more quickly. Place the blanket in the dryer and set the timer control to 20 minutes. Check after 10 minutes and remove the blanket while it's still damp. Overdrying and excessive tumbling may cause shrinkage. Place the blanket on a flat surface or stretch over two lines to complete drying. Gently brush up the nap with a nylon brush. Press the binding with a cool iron if needed.
4. To line dry, hang the blanket over two parallel lines and straighten to shape. As the blanket dries, change the position and straighten. Then brush up the nap gently with a nylon brush.

• **BLANKETS,** *Recycling Electric Ones:*
1. If an electric blanket no longer works, unplug it; feel for the wires at the end of the blanket; make tiny slits there; snip the wires;

pull them through the slits. (You may have to enlarge some slits to remove thermostats.)

2. After removing the wires, sew up the slits, reattach the loosened bindings and you have a usable blanket.

3. If you don't feel like sewing up the slits, put the blanket in a comforter cover that coordinates with the colors in your bedroom. These covers are sold in some linen departments and catalogs and can be used as cover-ups when blankets are moth-eaten, worn, or just don't match anything.

- **BLANKETS,** *Recycling Old and Worn Ones:*
1. Old baby blankets can be sewn together for a memory blanket a young child can cover up with—especially at grandparents' house; it's extra nice to curl up under the blankets which have comforted the child's parent, aunt and/or uncle in the past.
2. Cut rounds or squares from old worn blankets for pads to place between non-stick coated frying pans, china and other stackables that might scratch each other.

- **BLANKET,** *When It Shrinks in the Dryer and Is Too Short:* Sew a strip of matching-color fabric to the bottom of the blanket. You can tuck this section under the foot of the mattress and your bed will still look nice.

- **BLENDER,** *Washing:* Tried and true is to fill the blender about halfway with water, add a couple drops of liquid dishwashing detergent and put the lid on. Blend for a few minutes, rinse and dry.

- **BLOUSE SIZE,** *Letter of Laughter:* A woman wrote that the husband of another secretary in her office called her to ask for his wife's blouse size. When she said "medium" or "size 36," he just couldn't believe it. He said he wore a 33 sleeve and his wife's arms were not "that long." He was relieved to know that women's blouse size 36 doesn't mean sleeve length.

- **BLT WITHOUT THE "B":** Substitute imitation bacon bits for real bacon when you make a bacon, lettuce, and tomato sandwich and you'll get the flavor without the fat calories.

- **BOOK MARKING,** *Passages, Quotes, Recipes You Want to Find Again:* If you can't bear to dog-ear or pencil mark pages of a book, attach a pocket to the inside flap (made from an envelope—bend back the flap and glue the flap to the book cover) and write the page numbers you want to check later or just place a small sheet of paper in the front that lists page numbers and notes subject or names of recipes.

• **BOOKCASE,** *Portable Student "Model":* The traditional brick (or concrete block) and boards student bookcase can be dressed up if you cover the bricks with cloth, felt or wallpaper scraps, or paint the whole thing. If you spray-paint the parts, put them one-by-one inside a box when spraying so that you avoid mess. **Hint:** If the shelves are made from pressed wood, they will absorb lots of spray-paint unless you brush paint them with a primer before painting on the final color.

• **BLINDS,** *Cleaning Mini-blinds and Others:*
1. To dust, put old socks on your hands (inside out terry is good) and spray them with dust attracting spray, then dust each slat separately as noted below for washing.
2. To wash, put old socks on your hands and spray them with window cleaner. Close the blinds and starting at the top, go over them side to side, then do the back side.
3. To wash, take them down and put them flat on a surface you can get wet and soapy (sidewalk, driveway). Wash with a soft brush or nylon net (or old panty hose scrubber) dipped in a solution of mild dishwashing soap and water. Rinse well and dry immediately. **Caution:** Be very careful when you clean blinds; they are easily scratched and mini-blinds can break if handled roughly. **Hint:** Prevent heavy dust buildup by frequent vacuuming; the upholstery attachment works best.

• **BOAT BAILER,** *Recycling:* Cut off the spout of a plastic milk jug, leave the handle on, and you have a good bailer.

• **BOBECHES,** *Substitutes:* Make foil bobeches to catch dripping candle wax. Cut a square 1½-inch piece of heavy foil, then cut a slit in the center. Carefully slip the foil over the tapered candle and flute or turn up the edges so that they catch the wax drips. No more scraping wax from tablecloths!

• **BOOKENDS,** *Substitute, Recycling:* Decorative tins (especially those from fancy gourmet teas) filled with sand will keep books standing at attention in your bookcase.

• **BOOKMARKS,** *Recycling, Time-Saver:* That leftover strip of wrapping paper—too narrow to wrap anything—can be cut into shorter pieces for bookmarks. Take all of the strips and put them into the front of a cookbook so that as you use recipes, you can put a gift-wrap bookmark at the page to make it easier to find the recipe the next time. If you want to get even more organized, mark holiday recipes with appropriate holiday paper or colors. Make note on the bookmark if you changed the recipe in any way with different spices or other additions. **Note:** I have a friend who really needs this hint. She usually forgets which recipe she fixed and often adds other spices and ingredients to change recipes. When one of her innovations turns out to be good, her children say, "Gee, this is good. Too bad we'll never have it again!"

• **BOOKMARK,** *Sentimental:* Press leaves or flowers between two sheets of clear laminated plastic to make a bookmark. Flowers from your wedding in your family Bible or a photo album are a nice sentimental remembrance.

• **BOOK MEMORIAL:** When a dear friend passed away, a reader donated books to the library in her friend's name because she and her friend both enjoyed their local library's selections. The library gave her a list of wanted books and put a memorial sticker to honor the friend in the ones she bought.

• **BOOKS,** *Getting Yours Returned When You Lend Them:*
1. Stick your extra address labels inside each book or cover the book with brown paper (recycle grocery bags) and write on the cover your name and the date you lent the book.
2. In your calender or in a card file make note of who borrowed the book and when. (Ring-bound index card packs sold with school supplies make good small index files for just about any information. Also, you can carry one in purse or briefcase and make notes on cards at business meetings or when traveling. The cards are perforated so that you can remove them and put them in a permanent file (addresses, books, recipes, etc.).

• **BOOKS,** *Packing for Moving or Transporting to a Fund-Raiser Book Sale:* Books are heavy all by themselves; packing in cartons adds more weight. Try sorting books according to subject (or by price for a book sale) and then packing them in paper or plastic grocery sacks. Seal bags with masking tape; mark as to contents for easy sorting at your destination. To move bagged books from one place to another without straining muscles or tempers, stack the bags on a hand truck (dolly) or a sturdy luggage carrier.

• **BOOKS,** *Removing Price Stickers:* Heat the iron to Medium, put a pressing cloth over the book and press the sticker for a couple of seconds. The warmth softens the stickers enough to let them be pulled off easily and shiny covers aren't damaged.

• **BOOSTER CHAIR FOR YOUNG CHILD:** Tape together several catalogs or old telephone books. Or, if you don't want them so permanently joined, place them in a pillowcase, wrapping the "tail" around the stack to hold them together.

• **BOOTS,** *Drying, Storing:* Stuff boots with newspapers to keep their shape while drying and for storage. Newspapers also help absorb odors.

• **BOTTLE STOPPER,** *Unsticking Stuck Ones:* Pour a bit of THIN lubricating oil or mineral oil around the stopper and let it sit for a while (some take a day or two), then gently pull it out. Lubricating oil is thinner than cooking oil and will slide down quicker and more easily.

• **BOTTLES,** *Recycling Baby Food and Sample Jelly Jars:* If you do crafts with beads, sequins, wiggle-eyes, bits of jewelry, tiny bottles are super see-through storage containers. They also hold sorted buttons.

• **BOWL SCRAPER,** *Recycling Plastic Lids:* Cut off the rim about halfway around lids from dips, sour cream, and cottage cheese; leave the rim on the other half-side for a handle. These scrapers clean a bowl in seconds and they are free!

• **BRA SIZE,** *Determining with Measurements:*
1. Bra Band Size—First measure your chest (just under your bust-line); add five inches to this figure and if the total is an odd number, round it off to the next higher number to make it an even number. This is the band size. For example, if your chest measures 32 inches, adding five will give you 37, so round up to 38 for the correct band size.

2. Cup Size—Measure the fullest part of your bust while wearing a bra. This total, compared to the band size, will give you the cup size. For example, if the bust measurement is one inch more than the band size, your cup size will be an A; two inches over the band size is a cup size of B; three inches over the band size is a C; 4 inches over the band size is a D; and so on.

Not all bras in the same size fit the same so it's important to try bras on for a good and comfortable fit.

• **BRASS,** *Cleaning Door and Other Hardware:* Clean hardware on doors, drawers, etc. with a good brass cleaner, then to prevent tarnish, rub on paste wax, let dry, and polish to a shine or spray with a clear lacquer finish. **Note:** Sometimes it's easier to remove the hardware (street numbers, etc.) to clean it without messing up the area with brass polish. Or, knobs can be poked through a slit in cardboard or posterboard so that the door or drawer finish is protected. (This is a good idea when you clean brass buttons, too.)

• **BRA STRAP PAD ON C-CUP SIZES,** *Keeping Them in Place:* If you pin the pads in place, then run a machine stitch across the front and back ends, they will be anchored and won't twist to make bumps under the shoulders of lightweight blouses.

• **BREAD,** *Dough Rising:* To prevent plastic wrap from sticking to rising dough, spray one side of the wrap with non-stick vegetable spray and put that side against the dough. The wrap will peel off easily.

• **BREAD,** *Quick-rising Dryer Method:* A reader tried the dryer method in which you heat the clothes dryer first and then balance the bowl of dough on a cookie sheet inside to quick-start the rising process. But, she forgot to turn the dryer off and so when she closed the door, the drum revolved one full turn before she could stop it. The good news was that it all went so fast that the dough bowl and cookie sheet didn't even move and ended up exactly as they had begun—a real circus act. However, she suggests that an unbreakable stainless steel bowl would be best when using this hint, just in case!

• **BREAD,** *Recycling Stale Slices:* Use the slice for a spoon rest while you cook and then toss it out for the birds to eat.

• **BREAD,** *Setting Dough to Rise:* If the hints readers send me are an indication, getting bread dough to rise is one problem that has as many solutions as there are bread bakers. Here are just a few:

1. Put the rack in your microwave oven, place a pan of very warm water on the bottom of the oven and the dough bowl on the rack. (You don't turn on the microwave for this.) If your microwave has no rack, use a cake-cooling rack.

2. Turn the oven on "warm" for just five minutes, then turn it off, leaving the door closed. Cover the dough and pop it into the oven. The temperature should stay about right if you don't open the door too often.

3. Turn the oven light on and it will usually maintain just enough low heat to work.

4. Place a pan of hot water in the oven on a lower shelf; change the water if it cools off.

5. Heat a slow cooker only to its lowest warm setting; then unplug it, put the dough in and keep the cover on it during rising.

6. Turn the clothes dryer on for a few minutes, turn it off, set the bowl of dough in it and close the door. Be sure to let people know that the dryer is being used for bread raising! See BREAD below.

7. Put the dough where the sun will shine on it, cover the bowl with a black plastic bag and let solar heat do the work. How about this for new-tech solar energy-saving?

• **BREAD,** *Storing When You Don't Eat Much of It:* To prevent bread from getting stale or mouldy, double bag the loaf (with a bag from the previous loaf) and store in the freezer. Close bags with twisties or a spring clothes pin. When you remove a serving, always leave the "heel" plus one or two slices frozen together; they're a "lid" to protect the remaining slices from drying out. To thaw, either toast or zap in the microwave (ten to twenty seconds per one or two slices). Storing bread in the refrigerator may cause it to dry out.

• **BREAD CRUMBS,** *Quick-Fix:* Grate frozen bread if you don't have stale bread; it's easier to get "crummy" than fresh unfrozen bread.

• **BREAD CRUMBS,** *Substitute:* Crush commercially packaged croutons with a potato masher in the bowl you'll use for mixing meatloaf or on the plastic foam meat tray you'll use for dipping meat to be fried, and you'll have a tastier entrée from the flavored crumbs and less mess, too. Substitute unprocessed bran, wheat germ, or dry corn cereal for a flavor change when you bread fish or meats.

• **BREAKFAST FRUIT**, *Heating on Cold Mornings:* If cold grapefruit is an unpleasant shock on cold mornings, heat it. Heat sectioned grapefruit halves in the oven at 350°F for about 10 minutes or in the microwave oven 30 to 45 seconds.

• **BRIDAL SHOWER KITCHEN MAID:** For fun, make a "kitchen maid" gift for a bridal shower. The main part of the "maid" is an ironing board. Tie a pretty apron around the middle of the ironing board to form the waist and put a dishtowel in the apron pocket. Attach a toilet plunger to one side for an arm and a bowl brush to the other side for another arm. A mop, attached to the back with the mop end over the top of the ironing board, will be the hair. For an extra touch, add a colander for a hat. Two scrubbies can be eyes, a small sponge for the nose and a nail brush for the mouth. Add a dustpan for the feet and a few personal final touches and you have the fun favorite "kitchen maid." Also see WEDDING SHOWER, For Couples Who Have Everything.

• **BRIDEGROOM "TROUSSEAU":** Since most brides have a shower and grooms don't, one mother buys each of her sons a "trousseau" when they get married that includes two nice dress shirts, a couple of work shirts, some T-shirts, socks, pajamas, slippers, and a robe.

• **BROCCOLI**, *$aver Saving Stems:* After removing the "flower" ends of broccoli, slice the stems thinly and toss into a green salad or add to stir-fry veggies for an extra crunch and food value.

• **BROOCH**, *Remembering to Remove:* To prevent loss or a brooch ending up in the washer when it's left attached to clothing, try pinning the brooch through a blouse and onto a slip or bra strap. Then, you can't undress until you take it all off.

• **BROOCHES**, *Storage, Recycling, Time-Saver:* Pin brooches on an old T-shirt and hang it in your closet. Then you won't have to dig through your jewelry box in the morning when you're in a rush to get dressed and gone.

• **BROOM,** *Storage:* Screw a magnet into your broom handle about halfway down and you can store it stuck to the refrigerator between fridge and wall.

• **BROWNIES,** *Remedy If You Overbake Them:* Place them in the microwave on "Low" for a few seconds right before eating and they'll get nice and soft.

• **BROWNING DISH (BROWNER), MICROWAVE:** This specially designed dish is treated with a metal coating so that the bottom absorbs energy from the microwave to make the surface hot enough to sear and brown foods. It has a non-stick surface that's easy to clean and can be submerged in water. Some are dishwasher safe. When you buy a browning dish, look for "browner" or "browning" to be printed on it or look for directions that say the dish needs preheating. Always follow directions for use and care.

Generally, the browning dish is preheated on "High" for a period of time that depends upon the food to be cooked. When you sear a piece of meat, the first side may brown more evenly than the second side and second batches may not brown as well as the first batch because the dish cools as food absorbs its heat. Browning dishes work best for one to four servings. Never cut anything with sharp utensils on the dish. **Caution:** The dish gets hot enough to melt plastic and can cause serious burns to your skin. Never touch it without pot holders or insulated gloves protecting your hands. When removing the dish from the microwave, set it only on a heat-proof surface.

• **BROWN SUGAR SUBSTITUTE:** This mixture will not have the same texture as store-bought brown sugar but can be substituted in a pinch. Mix together one cup of granulated sugar with four tablespoons of dark molasses. Mix with a fork to make sure the molasses is evenly distributed. (Molasses is one of the ingredients used in manufacturing brown sugar. The amount added determines light or dark brown sugar. You can substitute dark for light or light for dark in recipes. However, the dark has a stronger flavor due to having more molasses.)

• **BUBBLE FUN,** *Substitute for Store-bought:* Mix half water and half mild dishwashing (not dishwasher) liquid. Dip a ring from a canning jar or leftover ring from commercial bubbles and bubble away. **Note:** This is definitely an outside activity!

• **BUG COLLECTING CAGE:** When children want to study fireflies, grasshoppers, crickets, little lizards, and other "nature pets," place a half-gallon milk carton on its side and cut away two opposite sides leaving two sides intact along with the bottom and top of the carton. Slip an old nylon stocking over the container and tie a knot on the bottom, leaving about 6 inches on top. The top can be opened and closed when the child puts grass, food, or another critter into the container. To close, pull the stocking tight and tie a knot. The critter gets plenty of air and can be seen by your budding biologist, who will, of course, be kind enough to set insect-eating critters free after observing them for a few hours and never keep them overnight.

• **BUG REPELLING,** *Selecting and Experimenting With Healthy-Planet Homestyle Methods, Letter of Laughter:* A cafeteria manager tried cucumber peelings as a repellent for ants; they worked very well when left on the kitchen counter overnight. Then a friend said that watermelon was even better so they chopped some up and left it on the counter overnight. The next morning it was loaded with feasting ants. The manager decided to stick with the proven hint of cucumber peelings!

• **BULBS,** *Selection Checklist:*
1. Get planting instructions from the garden center if you are buying bulk bulbs. Packaged bulbs usually have printed instructions.
2. Select bigger bulbs for bigger blossoms.
3. Don't buy soft, mushy, moldy, or heavily bruised bulbs. But, you can buy bulbs which have loose or torn "tunics" (the outer papery skin like on onions). Loss of the tunic does not damage the bulbs and may actually promote faster rooting after planting.

• **BUMPER STICKER,** *Removal:* Heat the sticker well with a hair blow-dryer, then lift the corner with a sharp knife (be careful not to scratch the bumper!) and peel it off. If you don't get it all, repeat the process. **Hint:** Next time when you put a sticker on, remove only a 2-inch strip of the backing from around the edges and leave the center intact. Then removing it will be easier; just split the center and pull it off.

• **BUNK-BED LADDER,** *Recycling:* When the ladder is no longer needed, paint it to match the room, hang it on the wall and the steps can hold knickknacks.

• **BUNK-BED SPREADS:** For two spreads that fit without hanging over the sides, cut a king-size bedspread in half lengthwise and hem the cut edges.

• **BUNS,** *Leftover Hot Dog and Hamburger Buns:* Butter and add garlic and other spices as usual, broil for a few minutes and you have garlic bread to serve with spaghetti or other meals.

• **BUSINESS CARDS,** *Recycling Old Ones:*
1. Punch a hole in the edge, write a description of clothing placed in a storage bag, and put the card over the top of the hanger outside of the bag. Or, write on the back of the card and tape it to a storage box. No more guessing what's inside.
2. Write a brief description of a recipe on the back of a card's shorter edge and poke it into a cookbook so you don't have to look in the index.

• **BUTTER,** *Storage:* When you are counting fat calories, cut butter sticks into 24 same-sized pats and store in airtight container; you'll know exactly how much you use each "dose."

• **BUTTER (MARGARINE) "PATS":** While the butter/margarine stick is still cold, slice it into individual "pats" with an egg slicer. "Pats" are easier and less messy at the table and if you are dieting, you'll know how many pats to the stick and therefore how many you can take.

• **BUTTER (MARGARINE) STICK MEASURE:** Before you remove the paper from a stick of butter or margarine, score the stick on the measure lines provided then you can still get a measured "dose" when you need it without messing up a measuring utensil.

• **BUTTER WRAPPER,** *Healthy-Planet, Recycling:* When you unwrap a new stick of butter or margarine, fold it butter sides in and store in a zipper bag in the freezer. Then when you need to grease a pan, pull out a wrapper, grease the pan and then toss the wrapper in the trash. Imagine if you could use every disposable thing that comes into your house at least twice instead of once; imagine if everyone did likewise—our landfills would last longer!

• **BUTTON,** *Quick-Fix, Preventing Pop-offs:* Inexpensive blouse and shirt buttons are sewn on by machine; a thread tail usually hangs loose and if you pull it, the button comes off. Try putting a small dab of white glue on each button before wearing the garment. The buttons will stay on longer.

• **BUTTONS,** *Replacing:*
1. Can't find the color you need? Paint buttons with fabric-matching epoxy paint before sewing them on.
2. Sew on buttons with six-strand embroidery floss. It's stronger and matches any color.
3. If you have to sew on a popped white button at the office with colored thread because that's all you have, cover the thread after sewing with typewriter correction fluid.

• **BUTTONS,** *Sorting and Storing, Recycling Time-Saver:* Those extra twist-ties will hold similar buttons together in your button box and you'll save time rummaging through loose ones.

• **BUTTONS,** *Strays, Recycling:* When the container in which you keep stray buttons for emergencies is full, get creative.
1. Decorate sweatshirts and T-shirts or sew different colors of buttons on a white blouse for a designer fashion.
2. Glue buttons flat to thumbtacks to give them bigger heads and to make them "designer," too.
3. String buttons to make jewelry for children, or adults, too. Give them to children for rainy-day stringing of necklaces or bracelets. Two matching strays (or non-matching if you like) can be glued to earring backs for boutique-look earrings to match a certain garment.
4. Toss into the bottom of glass flower pots instead of rocks.
5. Copy boutique ideas—create a "garden" of button flowers on a sweatshirt or one flower on each mitten by sewing one larger button in the center surrounded by smaller ones for "petals." A bow can be the "leaves" beneath the "flower."
6. Sew stray buttons in designs on sweatshirts and down the seams of sweatpant legs to make a boutique workout suit.

C

- **CACTUS,** *Repotting Painlessly:* Repotting cactus when it outgrows it's original container can be a sticky situation unless you have some carpet scraps to handle the plants.

- **CAKE,** *Baking:* Instead of water, substitute the same amount of club soda when making a German chocolate cake from mix; you'll get a delicious moist and tasty cake.

- **CAKE,** *Baking, Heart-Shaped:* If you don't have heart-shaped cake pans, bake a two-layer cake as directed on the package.
1. But, instead of two round layers, bake one 8-inch square layer and one round 8-inch diameter layer.
2. To assemble heart shape, cut the round layer exactly in half across the diameter. Place the square layer on a doily-covered cookie sheet or tray in a position that lets you add the cut diameter-sides of the round layer on either side of the top corner to form a heart.
3. Frost to cover "seams." Decorate with Valentine candies or decorator frostings.

- **CAKE,** *Cutting Unfrosted Layers:* It's easiest to cut cake layers with a long piece of thread or dental floss held taunt than to mess around with a knife.

• **CAKE,** *Dinosaur Decorations:* After frosting a regular cake for a child's birthday, decorate the top with graham cracker dinosaurs, sold by the box.

• **CAKE,** *Dome-Shaped Layers Prevention:* Try baking at 250°F for one hour and 20 minutes; or, from cake-decorating supply stores, buy wrap for around the outside of the pan.

• **CAKE,** *Football-Shaped:* Grease and flour a roaster pan as you would a regular cake pan. After baking, take the pan out of the oven and place it on a wet towel. The cake will slide right out. Color coconut with brown food coloring to cover the cake icing and make "laces" with black licorice.

• **CAKE,** *Freezing:*
1. It's best not to frost and fill cakes before freezing; fillings can make the cake soggy. However, you can frost a cake with confectioners' sugar or fudge frosting (using frosting instead of cream fillings to join layers). Freeze the frosted cake, THEN WRAP, and place in a heavy carton or other protective container.
2. To freeze layers without frosting, wrap cake as soon as it's thoroughly cool, then freeze. Store in carton or other container to prevent crushing; cakes do not freeze solid.
3. To thaw: Thaw in wrapping to prevent moisture from forming on cake surface. Large cakes take two to three hours at room temperature; a cake layer, about one hour; cupcakes, about 30 minutes.
4. Storage time: Unfrosted cakes may be kept frozen up to three months but frosted cakes are best stored only a month or two.

• **CAKE,** *Layer Stuck in Pan:* If you forget and let the cake get completely cooled and then it's stuck in the pan, put the layer into a warm oven briefly to soften the shortening used to grease the pan. When the pan bottom is warmed, remove it from the oven and turn the layer out immediately onto a cooling rack.

• **CAKE,** *Packing Neatly in Lunches:* If you slice a piece of sheet-cake in half (lengthwise) and then "fold" the two pieces so that the icing is in the center (top to center), the icing won't stick to the plastic wrap or lid of a margarine tub or other container.

• **CAKE,** *Preventing White "Flour Dust" on Cake Layer Bottoms:* After greasing the cake pan, sprinkle some of the mixed dry ingredients of the recipe or some dry cake mix on the pan to "flour" it. Return the excess to the mixing bowl and proceed with mixing the cake recipe as usual.

• **CAKE BAKER HELPER,** *Letter of Laughter:* When they were baking a cake, a grandmother told her five-year-old grandaughter that it was time to grease and *flour* the pan. She said, "I'll get the scissors if you will tell me which flowers I need to cut." Now that she's older, they share a joke whenever they bake together about not forgetting to "*flower* the pan."

• **CAKE DECORATING,** *Quick-Draw with Spaghetti:* Drain cooked very thin spaghetti, cut to desired length, let sit in several drops of red or other food coloring while you decorate the rest of a cake. Then, after removing drips of color if there are any, use the colored spaghetti to outline shapes. You can "draw" Easter bunny whiskers and mouths, etc.

• **CAKE FROSTING,** *Getting the Color Black:* Add some blue food coloring to chocolate frosting. Experiment until you get the desired results.

• **CAKE FROSTING,** *Quick-Fix Decorating Bag:* Substitute a plastic sandwich or storage bag. Cut a corner out of the bottom of the bag, slip in the decorating tip and close the bag.

• **CAKE FROSTING,** *Quick-Fix, Time-Saver Substitute for Chocolate Drizzle Icing:* Instead of making drizzle icing, cut a chocolate bar in little pieces and put them on top of the cake while it's still warm.

• **CAKE PAN,** *Recycling, Greasing:* Keep a plastic sandwich bag in the shortening can so that you can insert your hand, grab some shortening and grease pans with the same bag over and over.

• **CAKE PANS,** *Odd-shaped:* If you need to measure the batter capacity of an odd-shaped pan (hearts, lambs, bells, stars, etc.) to equalize the amounts used in different-shaped layers, fill the pan with water and measure the amount of this water. To fill an odd-shaped pan half full of batter, use half that amount of batter.

- **CAKE PAN SUBSTITUTE:** In a pinch, substitute stainless steel mixing bowls for cake pans. See CAKE PANS above.

- **CAKE TESTER:** A long thin piece of uncooked spaghetti will test angel food or other deep cakes for doneness, substitute for a toothpick when you're out of them, or just keep you away from oven heat by letting you test long-distance.

- **CALENDAR,** *Recycling Your Favorite:* If you don't want to part with a special calendar (school band picture, gorgeous scenery) leave it up. Then tear off pages from a freebie calendar to tape over corresponding months on the old calendar.

- **CALENDARS,** *Family Activities Records:* Have each family member post activities with different colored ink so you can tell at a glance who has to be where and when. (You can also color-code—color dot on label and so forth—each member's possessions accordingly so that you can tell quickly whose stuff is lying around the house and who owns which tube-socks, T-shirts, etc.)

- **CALENDARS,** *Healthy-Planet Recycling:* Don't toss out the "days" of desk calendars. Write notes, grocery lists, phone messages, etc. on the backs or send the cartoon "days" to people who might enjoy them.

- **CALENDARS,** *Recycling Linen Ones:* If you don't want to use them for towels, sew them together and turn them into children's quilts or tablecloths. If you crochet, you can crochet them together for children's summer coverlets.

- **CALENDARS,** *What to Do When You Get Too Many Freebies:* One reader tacks a small bookmark-size calendar near the front door to record newspaper payments so she can keep track of which weeks are paid for. Keep a booklet calendar in the car to record mileage if your job involves getting reimbursed per mile or if you need to report work-related travel miles at income tax time.

- **CAMPFIRE HEAT SHIELD:** Stick marshmallow or hot dog roasting sticks through aluminum pie pans to shield your hands from the heat of the fire while the food toasts.

- **CAMPING SHOWER:** With an inflatable pool for the bathtub, and a hose for water, you can balance a hula hoop with shower curtain attached in tree branches above the "tub" and have a private shower anywhere.

• **CAMPOUT COOKING,** *Time/Energy-Saver:* Coat the bottoms of pots and pans with a bar of soap before placing them over the fire. The black soot will wash off easily.

• **CANDIED FRUIT,** *Quick-Fix Mincing:* When a recipe calls for finely minced candied fruit, cut it into small pieces and run through the food processor to mince. No sticky fruit wads to deal with!

• **CANDLE,** *Bathroom Light:* Light a safely contained scented candle in the bathroom when you have a party and guests won't have to fumble for the light switch. Or light it when you are home without guests just to enjoy the scent. **Caution:** Always, for safety's sake, remember to put candles out before retiring for the night!

• **CANDLE HOLDER,** *Avoiding Stuck-on Wax:* Spray the inside of each holder lightly with non-stick vegetable spray before putting the candle in. The wax will pop right out for easy cleaning.

• **CANDLE HOLDER,** *Removing Wax from Metal Holders:* Run under very hot water and wax will rub off.

• **CANDLE LIGHTER:** Light one end of a piece of raw spaghetti and you can light candles, especially on a birthday cake when there are so many to light. Also, please see MATCH HOLDER.

• **CANDLES,** *Quick-Fix When They Wiggle in Holders:*
1. Paper "cups" from boxed chocolates put on the bottom of a candle can help it stay put in its holder.
2. Wrap the bottom of the candle several times with a thin piece of tape to make the bottom a little fatter and, if you wrap the tape sticky-side out, it really holds candles in place.
3. Thin foam sheets used for padding china and giftware can be cut in small squares or circles to put on candle ends before poking them into candlesticks. Cut the foam so that it extends up the sides of the candlestick hole but doesn't show.

• **CANDLES,** *Recycling:*
1. Gather partly used candles and melt them in a coffee can placed on an electric frying pan at low heat or in a double boiler made from a can placed in a pot of water. Remove all wicks with a fork.

2. Dangle a long wick in the center of a mold as you pour in the melted wax.

3. After the wax cools completely, remove from mold and trim the wick if it's too long.

Hints for molds: Easy-to-use molds (because you can cut them away from the candle after the wax hardens) include clean milk cartons and long, narrow potato-chip cans. Just be sure the mold will hold hot melted wax. If you use metal cans, you'll need to place them in hot water for a few seconds to get the candles out. To get translucent effects as the candles burn down, put ice cubes or hunks into large molds (like milk cartons or large shortening cans) and pour the wax over.

• CANDLES, *Recycling Yellowed White Ones:* You might be able to get the yellow off older white candles if you rub the candle with a soft cloth and rubbing alcohol or wash it in warm (not hot to melt), sudsy water, and rub gently. Polish with a pair of old panty hose.

1. If you can't whiten it, try creative "play"—melt colored crayons or old colored candles and let the soft wax drop onto the candle so that each candle has its own unique design. Harden wax by placing the candle overnight in the refrigerator.

2. Or just melt all your candles and make new ones. See CANDLES, Recycling below.

• CANDLESTICKS, *Removing Wax Drips:* Place them in the freezer for at least an hour. The wax will harden and will be easily picked off.

• CANDLE WAX, *Removal from Dishes:* Gently scrape off large pieces, rinse or soak in very hot water. Finish by washing in hot sudsy water and, if necessary, scrub with nylon scrubber. (Skin-buffing pads that have become too rough for your skin are good for removing wax, sticky goo from labels, etc.)

• CANDY, *Freezing Leftover Chocolate:* Should a miracle occur and leave you with uneaten chocolate candy—for example, if you were to get two boxes of Valentine chocolates—freeze the extra pieces in plastic freezer bags. An unopened plastic-wrapped box can go into the freezer as is. Many people freeze chocolates to avoid the temptation to overeat—they take out only the allocated treat allowance for any time period.

- **CANDY,** *Saving for a Rainy Day:* Label a jar "Rainy Day Savings," and have children put all extra candy in it (like from Halloween Trick or Treat or Birthday Party Favors) and then, when they are cooped up in the house during bad weather, they can take out the jar and have a snack. (Not all of it, but some!) You'll be monitoring their candy consumption and teaching them about "delayed gratification" at the same time; they may also learn the advantages of saving money for a rainy day by this example.

- **CANISTER,** *Quick-Fix for Campers or Home Cupboards, Recycling:* Cut off the top half of plastic one-gallon milk jugs, leaving the top of the handle on. Then you can place bags of flour or sugar into the remaining part of the jug—they don't spill and are easy to pull in and out of cabinets.

- **CAN LID,** *Safety Hint:* Drop the lid removed from canned food into the can before disposing and you won't cut yourself if you have to rummage through the trash to find a lost item.

- **CANNED FOOD,** *Size Number Equivalents to Weights:*
  - No. 1 can = 10 to 12 ounces
  - No. 300 can = 14 to 16 ounces
  - No. 1½ or No. 303 can = 1 pound, 17 ounces
  - No. 2 can = 1 pound, 4 ounces or 1 pint, 2 fluid ounces
  - No. 2½ can = 1 pound, 12 ounces to 1 pound, 14 ounces
  - No. 3 can = 3 pounds, 3 ounces or 1 quart, 14 ounces
  - No. 10 can = 6 pounds, 2 ounces or 7 pounds, 5 ounces

- **CANNING CAUTION:** If you want to reduce sugar and salt in your diet, it's not a good idea to reduce the amounts in canning recipes because ingredients such as sugar, salt, lemon juice, and vinegar control spoilage. Instead get the new recipes that allow less sugar and salt while still keeping home-canning safe. To get the new recipes and methods, contact your county home economist. Look in the U.S. Government section of the phone book, under Agriculture Department.

- **CAN OPENER,** *Quick-Fix for Stuck Hand-held Model:* Oil the parts with vegetable oil.

• **CANS,** *Storing Fruits and Vegetables in Them:* The United States Department of Agriculture says it's okay to leave leftover food in the can and store it in the refrigerator for a couple of days. However, don't store acidic foods (such as tomatoes) in cans because they may get a tinny taste. Don't buy dented or otherwise damaged cans or bulging cans; you can get food poisoning.

• **CAR CARD GAME:** Cut out pictures from newspapers and magazines of anything children will see while traveling—cars, trucks, animals, buildings, bridges, etc. Then paste the pictures on index cards. "Deal" the same number of cards to each child when you leave the house. As the children see the objects on their cards, they put the card down in a "seen scene" pile. The child who "sees" all his cards first is the winner.

• **CARE PACKAGE,** *Healthy-Planet Packing Goodies with Goodies:* To send fragile items or food in a "care package" to a student or overseas service person, pack with packages of popcorn or marshmallows or peanuts in the shell—all are edible!

• **CAR KEYS,** *If You Frequently Lock Them Inside the Car:* Make it a habit to lock the car doors only with the keys even if your car can lock automatically.

• **CAR KEYS,** *When Teens Drive and Driveways Become Parking Lots:* It takes organization to avoid stress and confusion in multiple driver families.
1. When teens start driving the family car, give each person a set of car keys so that the teens don't have to borrow the parent's keys.
2. When teens have their own cars, have each person's keys or key chain color-coded so that finding the right one is easy. Have one central place for hanging all the keys so that finding any of the keys is possible. Then, if several cars are in the driveway and someone has to make a quick trip to the store, the rule is that you drive the last car parked in the driveway. You'll know its keys by the color!

• **CARPET,** *Bathroom Carpeting, Making Patterns:*
Method 1: Lay the carpet out and press it against the sink cabinet. Put straight pins all around the area to be cut. Do the same around the commode. Straight pins with large colored heads will be easier to locate, and you'll need a good sharp razor knife and scissors for

cutting. After marking, lay the carpet on a flat surface and cut around the line of the pins. **Note:** Don't think you can put the carpet upside down and draw markings with a marker. You will end up with a reverse pattern of your bathroom floor and, of course, when the carpet is right-side up, it won't fit properly. Few commodes and counters are positioned with identical spaces on either side.

Method 2: Make a paper pattern to fit the entire bathroom floor then you can trace the pattern on the back side of the carpeting. (You can also make all your mistakes on paper before cutting on the carpet and save the pattern for the next time.) **Caution:** Be sure to reverse the pattern when laying it on the backside of the carpeting or it won't fit. See above **Note.**

• **CARPET,** *Protecting Areas Beneath Children's Chairs:* Put a flannel-backed vinyl tablecloth under the chair; it's easy to wipe up and liquids don't soak into the carpet.

• **CARPET,** *Recycling Old Pieces:*
1. Lay runners on garden paths between rows of vegetables to avoid walking in mud.
2. Staple or nail pieces to garage walls and ceiling for free insulation.
3. Wrap carpeting around a post to make a cat scratching post.
4. Cut circles to fit drink coasters (plastic lids from different containers), then the coaster won't be stuck to the bottom of a "sweaty" glass when you pick it up.

• **CARPET,** *Removing Crayon on Acrylic Carpet:* After you've scraped off as much crayon as you can (a spoon works well), place paper towels over the stain and then gently press the towels with an iron on low-medium heat setting. Move the towels to a clean spot as they absorb the crayon and change them as needed. If color remains (and red is very difficult to remove) try a good commercial spot remover specifically made for carpets.

• **CARPET,** *Removing White School Glue:*
1. Working from the outside in, use a damp sponge to wet the area and then blot dry with a paper towel. Continue doing this until you've cleaned the entire stain.

2. If some of the glue remains, wash the area by applying a solution of 1 teaspoon mild dishwashing liquid dissolved in 1 cup of warm water, being careful not to make the rug too wet; blot with a clean cloth. Remove the cleaning solution by rinsing well with a small amount of water, then blot until dry.

• **CARPET BURN HOLE,** *Repair:*
1. Cut patches the size or a tiny bit larger than the burn holes.
2. Clean all the burnt fibers from the carpeting by rubbing with a spoon or cutting with cuticle scissors.
3. Put a bit of transparent or fabric glue on the patches and along the edges, then push each one into a hole, cover with waxed paper and place a heavy book on top.
4. After the patches are dry (about twenty-four hours), brush with an old toothbrush to lift up the fibers.

• **CARPET INDENTATIONS,** *Removing:* When heavy furniture has left indentations in the carpet, put an ice cube in each indentation and let it set overnight. The ice cube will melt slowly into the carpet. In the morning, blot up any moisture with paper towels and fluff up the carpet fibers carefully with the tines of a fork.

• **CARPET PROTECTOR:** Before you decide to protect new carpeting from traffic pattern wear with scraps of the carpeting, check the bottom backing. If the underside is rough, it will wear down the carpet like sandpaper. Only rubber-backed rugs should be placed over carpeting to protect traffic pattern wear and soiling. Also, remove the rugs often to vacuum beneath them so that dirt doesn't get ground into the carpet below.

• **CARPET TAPE,** *Removing Adhesive of Double-faced Tape from Tile Floor:* The Tile Contractors Association of America suggests lighter fluid. Be sure to test an inconspicuous spot first because the fluid could dull some tile finishes. **Caution:** Lighter fluid is highly flammable; be sure to ventilate the area well. Also keep it away from small children and pets.

• **CARPET TEAR,** *Quick-Fix:* Place a strip of carpet tape beneath the tear and press down. A permanent repair is to sew up the tear with a heavy upholstery needle and strong nylon thread and then reinforce the tear with tape. If the tear is in new carpet, it could be a defect; check with the manufacturer or store about replacement or at least professional repair.

• **CARPOOL CODE:** Plan with your carpool that if you can't reach a driver by phone to say that you won't be riding that day, you will put a piece of colored paper in a front window of the house. The driver won't have to waste time stopping or annoy neighbors by honking a horn.

• **CASSEROLES/COVERED DISH,** *Taking to a Potluck:*
1. Prevent spills in the car from casseroles by putting them inside a plastic grocery bag or a plastic bag lined box.
2. If the dish has no lid, place plastic wrap over the top and sides, heat on "High" in the microwave for a couple of minutes and the plastic wrap will have a tight seal that avoids a mess. This hint is useful even if the dish has a lid; some lids leak.
3. To keep hot—Put a folded towel in the bottom of a small foam ice chest; cover the casserole with another folded towel. With the lid on the chest, the casserole will stay hot until serving time, even up to an hour. **Caution:** My sources say food shouldn't stand for more than two hours between preparation and eating and should be kept at 185°F or reheated to that temperature before serving.

• **CASTERS,** *Runaway Wheels on Tables or Chopping Blocks:* Insert wedge-shaped pieces of wood between the wheel and the frame on two wheels, diagonally across from each other. Remove the wedges when you need to move the furniture and reinsert for stability.

• **CASTS,** *Care:* Proper care of your cast will prevent extra doctor's office visits, new casts, and time away from work for unnecessary replacements.
1. Plaster Casts: These harden in five to ten minutes but take two to three days to dry completely and reach full strength. Don't stand on your cast or rest it against hard surfaces for two to three days and wait the same time before letting people write on it. Once a plaster cast contacts water, it gets soft and ineffective and you'll have to get a new one. Protect your cast with plastic bags when bathing. If it gets dirty, you can touch it up with white shoe polish, but don't ever paint it entirely because the cast needs to "breathe."
2. Synthetic casts: They harden and dry immediately and reach maximum strength and can bear weight in about twenty minutes.

They are water resistant and lightweight. But, even if the cast can get wet, your injury may not allow it. Check with your doctor before getting the cast wet. Dry the cast thoroughly to prevent skin problems; if your skin feels damp and clammy under the cast, it's still wet. Wrap the cast in a towel to remove excess water or dry the cast more quickly with a blow-dryer set on "Low." Sorry, you usually can't write on synthetic casts!
3. Don't scratch under casts with hangers or sharp objects. You can try sprinkling baby powder into the end of the cast to relieve itching.
4. Make a "toe warmer" for your cast with an oversized sock or an old knit hat.

• **CAST COVER-UP:** Buy colored knee-hi stockings to match or contrast with your outfit, or plain white to go with an arm cast and man's shirt. Then, cut the toe off and put the stocking on the cast, elastic on top. For an arm cast, cut a small hole for the thumb and tuck edges under the cast.

• **CAT,** *Adopting a Stray:* To save yourself heartache, before you get too attached to a stray cat, take it to a vet for a checkup and testing for feline leukemia. Often the strays of an entire neighborhood have passed the infection around, and it's just a matter of time before the cat dies; sometimes only a couple of weeks. If the cat isn't infected, you'd need to see a vet anyway so that it could get neutered and all of its immunizations, which include vaccination against feline leukemia. If you bring an infected cat into the house, you will have to wait six months before bringing another cat into that area to prevent infection of the new cat.

• **CAT BOX,** *Quick-Fix, No Mess Litter Changing:* Line the cat box with a large plastic garbage bag, using a homemade elastic band to hold the bag in place when the cat digs. Make the band from ½-inch to 1-inch elastic tied into a circle (or use the elastic from old men's undershorts). To clean, just lift up the bag. **Note:** If your cat digs vigorously, put a layer of newspaper in the bottom before adding litter so kitty won't scratch through the bottom of the bag.

• **CAT BOX,** *Remove Odors:* After you discard the used litter, pour in a half-inch or so of white vinegar, or generously dust the bottom with baking soda and add an inch or two of water. Allow to stand for a few hours; then rinse and dry. AVOID future odors by sprinkling a generous layer of baking soda on the bottom of the clean pan and covering it with a newspaper section before adding the litter. Then on the next change, you can easily dump the litter with the newspaper, add water to the baking soda in the bottom, let stand; then rinse, dry, etc.

• **CAT CARRIER,** *Quick-Fix Homemade:* Tie two small plastic mesh laundry baskets together, one upside down over the other. Don't forget to put some newspaper in the bottom basket and place newspaper or an old plastic shower curtain or tablecloth under this or any carrier. Some cats will protest being in carriers in their own certain way!

• **CAT COLLARS:** To bell your cat as a warning to birds and jumpy houseguests, tie a small bell on a homemade or commercial elastic collar. Climbing cats can catch collars quickly (say it fast five times) on tree limbs. Elastic stretches and lets kitty get loose safely.

• **CAT COMPANIONS,** *Adding a Second Cat to Your Family:* A young kitten may be a better choice and less of a threat to an older cat. Try to match sizes so that the older, larger cat doesn't harm the smaller, younger one in play. Also, match personalities so that both are playful or both are tranquil loungers. Some vets suggest getting opposite sexes to lessen territorial battles and recommend neutering both pets to make them more compatible. When you bring the new cat home, put each cat in a separate room, then gradually let them be together for short periods under supervision, extending the time as they get used to each other. Provide each cat with its own litter box, food dish, toys and sleeping place. Be sure to show each equal affection and attention and allow time for them to adjust to each other.

• **CAT COZY:** When you have a cat that just won't stay inside, you can make a warm sleeping box by turning an old foam ice chest upside down, placing it on top of the lid, and cutting a hole in one side just large enough for the cat to get in. Put some newspaper on the bottom and a fluffy towel over the paper. Kitty will be insulated and waterproofed by the foam.

• **CAT FOOD,** *Au Gratin:* If a finicky cat refuses the flavor of cat food you've bought, try sprinkling Parmesan cheese on it. While it's not usually good to give milk products to cats, a little cheese, once in a while, won't hurt and you won't waste the cat food.

• **CAT SAFETY:** If cats in your neighborhood lounge around on cars, you can bet that one can crawl under the hood looking for a warm engine "bed." I've received several letters from people whose cats were severely injured when motorists started their cars and instead of an engine's "purr" they heard the shriek of a cat caught in the machinery. Tap on the hood or toot your horn before you turn the key, wait a few seconds, and any kitty sneaking a cozy nap will be out of harm's way.

• **CAT SCARE,** *Letter of Caution:* A reader whose cat, like many cats, liked to play with string wrote a chilling letter. Normally, when her cat finished playing with a string, the reader would pick up the string and put it away. The one time she forgot, she found her cat with a string in its mouth. Unable to remove the string, she took the cat to the vet who also couldn't remove the string; it had worked its way through the cat's system and was wound throughout its intestines. Emergency surgery revealed 31 inches of string! The cat never gets string to play with anymore!

• **CAT SCRATCHING POST:** Buy one or cover a post with nubby carpeting, or for some cats, cover a piece of garden timber with carpeting and lay it on the floor.
1. Encourage the cat to scratch the post instead of furniture by sprinkling it with catnip or by attaching a small toy to it.
2. Lead the cat to the scratching post by dangling a toy on a fishing pole closer and closer to the post and let kitty catch the toy only when it's on or at the post. This training is fun for you and the cat.

• **CATS,** *Spraying:* Sometimes, even if neutered, a cat will continue to spray, usually in the spring when mating instincts occur or if a new carpet or piece of furniture is brought into the home and the cat decides to "mark it." Check with the veterinarian; prescription pills are available to correct this problem. *Letter of Laughter:* A friend of mine loved this hint because it let her continue to love her two old cats—a neutered tomcat who liked to spray his own image in the dresser mirror, much to the dismay of the person who used that dresser, and a spayed female who periodically sprayed the kitchen range burners to the disgust of the whole family. The positive about this was that nobody dawdled during breakfast to avoid going to school if the cat had sprayed the stove the night before!

• **CAT SPREAD:** If your cat likes to snooze on your bed and the result is cat hair on the spread, substitute a next-size top sheet for the bedspread, in a print that coordinates with your bedroom colors. You can more easily wash it than a heavy spread or quilt. Queen sheets cover double beds; king covers a queen mattress.

• **CAT TRAINING,** *Keeping Kitty Out of Dried-Flower Arrangements:* Spray the arrangement with hair spray and sprinkle with white ground pepper. One taste and kitty won't return to the scene of the crime.

• **CAT TRAINING,** *Keeping Kitty Out of Plants:*
1. Try putting lemon, lime, orange, or grapefruit rinds on the soil of planters; cats don't usually like the smell of citrus.
2. Try making a planter cover from lightweight pliable garden fencing. Cut to the right size with heavy scissors and bend to fit into the planter. The wire will still let air, water, and light in but will keep kitty out.
3. Place a layer of pinecones over the pot plant soil; it's unpleasant for cat walking. The bonus is that pinecones keep moisture in the soil while keeping "cat moisture" out of it and look nice, too.
4. Spritz your cat with water each time it goes near the plant.

• **CAT TRAINING,** *Keeping Away from "Forbidden Places":* When a cat is persistent, each time your cat goes to a "forbidden place" touch its lips with a cotton ball moistened with rubbing alcohol or vinegar. You need not use force, just a light touch—cats hate this. Then leave the scented cotton ball at the forbidden place. Later, you can put an alcohol or vinegar scented cotton ball at the forbidden place whenever kitty is near it. It takes patience, but eventually, the cat will avoid that place.

• **CAT TREAT:** Instead of discarding the liquid that comes in canned salmon, tuna, and sardines, give it to your cat—it's kitty champagne to most of them!

- **CEDAR CHEST,** *Renewing Cedar Scent:* Lightly sand the inside of the chest with fine grade sandpaper. (Wrap sandpaper around a big rectangular sponge so the heat of sanding doesn't bother your hands.) Vacuum up wood particles. You can also add cedar balls or blocks from closet stores if this doesn't renew enough of the scent.

- **CEILING,** *Quick-Fix Repair After Removing Swag Lamp or Planter Hooks:* After unscrewing the hook, plug the hole with a cork pushed flush with the ceiling surface; then paint the cork to match the ceiling. See WALLS, Repairing, for other ideas.

- **CEILING FAN,** *Telling Fan from Light Chains:* Put a large wooden or ceramic macramé bead on the light and a tassel on the fan or vice versa—anything that helps you tell one from the other. Cork or plastic fishing line floats or plastic lime/lemon juice squirters are good quick-fix chain pulls for lights or fans. A yellow lemon on a closet light pull makes it especially easy to find in semi-darkness.

- **CELERY,** *Restoring Limp Stalks:* Put stalks in cold water to crisp up again. They will keep in the fridge for a day or two. When there's too much celery to consume quickly, dice it, cook in a bit of water until just tender and then cool, divide into small amounts for soup or casserole recipes and freeze.

- **CELERY,** *Storing:* To make sure you have celery to munch on even if you have no time to cut it up for sticks, cut off the stalk end when you bring the celery home, rinse off the stalks and place them bottom-side down in water in a large wide-mouth vase (like the freebies in which florists deliver cut flowers). Save the heart of the celery for cooking either in the refrigerator or freezer. To further avoid temptation if you are dieting, put your celery "bouquet" on the table for before-dinner munching. A vase will hold the celery vertically and so it takes very little space in the fridge.

- **CEREAL,** *Keeping It Fresh:* If the cereal isn't in a resealable bag, pour it into gallon-size zip-closing bags and return it to the box. It will stay fresh longer. You can use the cereal-box liner to cover foods cooking in the microwave, to hold scraps when you peel veggies, to line drawers, and more.

- **CEREAL-BOX INNER BAG,** *Recycling Ideas:* Cover dishes when microwaving foods; wrap potatoes for microwave baking; base for rolling cookies and pie crusts; crush crackers or cereal in it for breading; open the bag for a flat surface to hold crumbs and flour for breading and a place to lay coated meat pieces as they dry for 20 minutes before frying. (If you let breaded meats dry, flip the meat so each side is exposed to air 10 minutes or so or place on a rack before deep or pan frying, and the coating will stay on better and be crisper.)

• **CEREAL DRIPS**, *Avoiding Them with Small Children:* When children begin to feed themselves dry cereal, mix it with vanilla or fruited yogurt instead of milk. It sticks to the spoon and the extra nutrition sticks to the ribs, too. Low-fat yogurt and milk are about equal in calories per amount.

• **CEREAL FAST FOOD:** There's no rule that says hot cereal must be served in a bowl. Put it in a cup; add a bit more milk so it's thinner; then, drink it. This idea is especially helpful when small children make a mess eating hot cereal with a spoon. Give them a straw and see them slurp up breakfast! If you get a late start, put the cereal in a lidded, insulated coffee cup, insert a straw in the lid-hole and sip breakfast en route to work or when you get there!

• **CEREAL SUGAR**, *When You Don't Want Sugar To Sink to the Bottom:* I've received hints to avoid this problem like dissolving sugar in the milk before pouring it on the cereal but the easiest idea is to pour milk on the cereal first and then sprinkle on the sugar. The sugar granules will stick to the moist cereal.

• **CEREAL SURPRISE**, *$aver:* Mix the last few ounces of different cereals for a "custom blend" that uses up all the leftovers and tastes good, too. **Hint:** When children prefer to eat cereals that have the nutritional value of a cookie, mix the sweetened favorites with "real food" cereals.

• **CEREAL TREATS**, *Without Sticky Mess:* To press rice cereal treat mixtures into the pan, place clear plastic wrap over the top and press away or use a frozen mug as a "rolling pin" to press the mixture down.

• **CERVICAL COLLAR (NECK BRACE) COVER-UPS:** Wearing a cervical collar can be dreary and after a while, you need to cheer it up.

1. Cover the collar with colored sandal-toe knee-hi stockings (or legs cut off panty hose) that match your clothing. Slip on so that the elastic end is inside the fold-over. The self-gripping fabric tape will hook through the stocking mesh, which is easy to wash, too.
2. Pin a brooch or small silk flower jauntily off center.
3. Wrap a silk or sheer nylon scarf around the brace, and pin ends in place if they slip out.

• **CHAIRS,** *Taking Sags Out of Cane Bottoms:* Wipe the surface of the seat with a cloth which has been dipped in hot water and wrung out. Scrub thoroughly, then place the chair outdoors in the sun to dry.

• **CHAIRS,** *Storing Folding Ones and Extra Table Leaf:* To prevent marring walls where they lean and to keep the chairs or table leaf clean and dust-free, put a pillowcase over each bridge chair or table leaf when storing it.

• **CHAMOIS CLOTH,** *Care to Make It Last:* Wash after each use in mild soapy water, leaving a little soap in the cloth to help keep it pliable between uses. After washing, wring it out gently and pull it to its original shape. Lay out to dry, but not in direct sunlight or near a heat source. Also, never use a chamois with strong chemicals, oil, grease, or as a sponge when washing the car.

• **CHAMPAGNE CORK,** *Catching Identified Flying Objects:* Place an oven mitt over the cork and bottle neck after you take off the foil and wire covering. Then holding the bottle and mitt with one hand, release the cork with the other. Exploding corks will fly into the top of the mitt. It's not very glamorous but beats hitting someone in the eye or taking pot shots at the chandelier!

• **CHANDELIER,** *Moving Within a Room:* Hang a swag hook in the new position for the lamp, add more chain to the lamp and make the fixture look like it was intended to be a swag lamp.

• **CHANDELIER CRYSTAL,** *Repair:* If crystals fall off because wires have broken, replace the wire with a twist-tie. Scrape the paper off the wire and put it through the opening of the crystal; hang it back on the chandelier.

• **CHANGE,** *Loose Change Uses:*
1. Put a large decorative bowl in a catchall spot so that all family members can easily contribute, then when there's enough money, take each other out to a restaurant.
2. Put parking-meter coins in your car ashtray so people won't put ashes in it or think twice before smoking in your car.
3. Collect loose change from laundry pockets until there's enough "pocket money" to buy something for the chief laundry-doer even if it's just an ice-cream treat.
Letter of Laughter: Someone I know calls coins left lying around the house or left in pockets "mad money" because it makes her mad to see her family treat money so carelessly.

• **CHARITY,** *Donations Guide:* When you are asked to give to charities, you want to give to those groups that use your money wisely. One way to check on any charity, national or local, is to call your local Better Business Bureau. BBBs have information on charities and how they meet the BBB standards for money usage, public accountability, fund-raising practices, solicitation, and informational materials (if they are truthful), how they are governed, and if they comply with laws and regulations.

• **CHECKBOOK ACCURACY:** When you write a check while shopping, collect the receipt and note the check number quickly on the receipt; then place it in your checkbook. When you get home, record all of your purchases at one time and balance the amounts. No more mystery checks that you forgot to record and therefore have no idea of the amount!

• **CHECK CHECK:** Place a small bookmark or piece of ribbon at the point in your checkbook where you have only five checks left. Then, you'll be reminded to put your next book of checks into your purse or checkbook case.

• **CHECK PRINTING,** *When Mother Remarries and Children Have Different Names:* Please see NAMES CONFUSION.

• **CHEESE,** *Preventing Mold:* If mold hasn't penetrated too deeply, scrape it off; you can eat the cheese. (But yogurt, cream or cottage cheese which has molded should be discarded.)

1. Moisture can cause cheese to mold. Place a few sugar cubes in a self-sealing plastic bag with the cheese. When the cubes become soggy in a few days, replace them.
2. To keep mold from forming on large hunks of cheese, the traditional way is to wrap the cheese in a cheesecloth (what else?) which has been moistened with vinegar (moistened but not dripping wet). Place wrapped cheese in a plastic bag and into the refrigerator. The vinegar doesn't affect the taste of the cheese, and you may have to sprinkle more vinegar on the cloth every now and then if you are storing the cheese for several weeks.
3. When buying "surface-ripened" cheeses like Camembert or Brie, make sure to "sniff test" if you can. If they have even a hint of ammonia scent, they are past their peak for eating. Don't buy them. It's a cheese-seller's myth that the ammonia scent is okay.
4. If you have a large hunk of cheese, instead of putting the whole thing out, cut off only the amount you expect to eat and allow it to come to room temperature (best for eating). Going back and forth from fridge to table dries out the cheese and speeds up spoilage.

• **CHEESE CUTTER:** Grasp each end of a piece of dental floss and slice away. Dental floss also neatly cuts cake layers horizontally.

• **CHENILLE BEDSPREADS AND ROBES,** *Recycling:* Cut 10 × 10-inch squares and hem them to make dishcloths. The chenille knots are terrific for removing stuck food from dishes and pans.

• **CHILD-PROOFING,** *Kitchen Checklist:*
1. Hang a knife rack on a cabinet door out of children's reach.
2. Put safety covers on electrical outlets.
3. Remove stove knobs if a child can reach them and keep them in a basket on your countertop. You can put a knob on when you turn on the burners.
4. Keep spices and other non-edibles out of reach. Instead of keeping cleaning supplies under the sink, put them in an upper cabinet out of reach.
5. Invest in safety locks for drawers and cupboard doors. A quick-fix is to put a rolled magazine in the cupboard door handles to keep a toddler out; older children will remove the magazine!

- **CHILDREN,** *Calling Them in at Night:*
1. Arrange to signal "time to come in" by flipping the porch lights off and on. It saves your voice for talking to children instead of yelling for them to come in.
2. Cut a plastic bleach bottle in half and use the bottom for plant clippings and the top for a megaphone so you only have to shout softly when you herd your family!

- **CHILDREN,** *Keeping Them Occupied in Doctor's Waiting Rooms:*
1. Put coloring books, crayons, stickers, and small toys in a large, self-sealing plastic bag and give one to each of your children when you arrive.
2. Give children a couple of pipe cleaners to twist and make things like stick people, alphabet letters, and anything else their imaginations can come up with.

- **CHILDREN,** *Safety on Outings:* A child can get lost in just a few seconds at such outings as the zoo or hiking.
1. Carry current photos and descriptions of each child and, if children's friends are guests on the outing, know their parents' names, addresses, phone numbers, and potential medical problems (allergies to stings, etc.) just in case of emergency.
2. Children should be taught to go to a park employee and say their parents' full names and phone number, to go to an easy-to-find meeting place in case of separation, and use the "buddy-system" to stay close together.
- Equip each hiker with a whistle and instructions to blow it if lost, but ONLY if really lost! Tell the story about the boy who cried wolf too many times.

- **CHILDREN,** *School ID:* Plastic pin-on name-tag holders like those we collect at meetings and conventions are handy name-tag holders for kindergartners or first-graders in a new school. Add your name and phone number to the back of the tag, too. Our precious ones can forget important information in the confusion of school buses, new classrooms, and all!
Or, buy a supply of stick-on name tags; you can put them on books, lunch bags, etc. as well as on your children.

- **CHILDREN'S FRIENDS,** *Parent-sanity Saver:* Often when children come to play, they've been told to return home at a certain time, and then they ask the houseparent for the time ALL OF THE TIME! To make life easier for everyone, ask the children when they must go home, then show them that you are setting a kitchen timer for the amount of time they can stay—actually set it for a few minutes earlier so they have time to gather their stuff and help pick up toys. Ah, peace!

• CHILD'S BATH, *Getting a Self-bathing Child To Wash All Parts:* One mother outlined a boy on a sheet of poster paper and colored it using her son's hair and eye colors. Then she wrote numbers with arrows pointing to the different body areas (ears, face, feet, etc.). In one hand she drew a red washcloth with an arrow pointing toward the washcloth and then she printed the word "SCRUB." She put the poster where he could see it as he bathed and even if he was too young to read, he would follow the arrows and then tell his mom what all he washed.

• CHILD'S GARDEN OF BEANS: To show a small child how plants grow, plant beans along the outside of a fishbowl or large jar filled with dirt. They can see roots go down and stems go up. *Letter of Laughter:* This hint came from a mom who thought of it after her preschooler dug up several of her plants "to see how they work."

• CHILD'S LAWN PARTY, *Summer Birthday Idea for Young Children:* On the invitations, make a note to the mothers to bring their children's swimsuits. For the party, hook up the garden hose to a rotating sprinkler and set it in the yard so the children can run through the sprinkler. Place lawn chairs out for the children to sit on. When the children tire of the sprinkler, they can dry off on the chairs while you serve refreshments.

• CHILD'S TABLE AND CHAIRS, *Curbing Childhood Curiosity for Safety:* One reader found a simple way to stop her toddler from dragging chairs from her child's table and chair set into other rooms so she could stand on them to reach forbidden things. Clever Mom tied one leg of each chair to one leg of the table closest to it. The chairs could still be pulled out to sit on but not removed for use as ladders!

• CHINA CABINET LIGHT: Instead of turning on the lights only when you have guests, plug the light cord of a lighted china cabinet into a socket timer and you can enjoy a few glowing hours each night without having to remember to switch them off.

• **CHOCOLATE,** *Dipping:* Place one or two pretzels (crackers, cookies, etc.) on a potato masher; dip in melted chocolate; pull out, and place on plate to cool.

• **CHOCOLATE MELTING,** *Preventing It from Getting Grainy:* If you are melting chocolate for fondue or other uses in a double boiler, don't let the water touch the bottom of the pan. It will scorch the chocolate and make it hard and gritty. Cooking the chocolate too fast or in a too lightweight saucepan can also make it gritty. The best way to cook chocolate is in a heavy saucepan over low heat and stir it often. I stir with a pancake turner so that the whole pan is scraped in a few swishes.

• **CHOCOLATE SYRUP,** *Good to the Last Spoonful:* When all that's left is a bit of chocolate syrup in the bottom of the container, make chocolate milk by adding milk and shaking until it's dissolved.

• **CHOPSTICKS,** *Recycling Disposable Ones from Restaurants:* They make sturdy plant stakes for indoor potted plants.

• **CHRISTMAS GIFTS,** *Extras:* Buy a variety of gifts, such as mugs, calendars, decorative candles, candy, etc. to keep under the tree and you'll have a surprise for unexpected guests. You can code them (for example, red or with bows for females; green or with crinkle tie for males) if you want to be more elaborate, but I just like to buy generic gifts.

• **CHRISTMAS LIGHTS,** *Annual Installation:* Install cup hooks about every 10 inches to the outside eaves of your house and leave them there as permanent anchors for lights. Then, you can cut a notch in the end of a yardstick and poke the lights' wires into place each year without a ladder. If you can't reach the eaves with a yardstick, screw a cup hook into a broom handle—the broom handle will be a useful "grabber" during the rest of the year and have a hanger so that it doesn't have to stand on end squashing its bristles.

• **CHRISTMAS LIGHTS,** *Healthy-Planet Recycling:* Here's how to make "lanterns" for lining your driveway or walkway during the holidays.

1. After spraying plastic jugs green or red, cut an opening in the top, leaving the handle on. Then, fill them with an inch or two of sand and insert a candle.

2. Save large 32-ounce juice cans and then with a nail, pound holes in the sides either in a random pattern or a design. (To keep the cans from bending when you pound nails into the sides, fill them with water, freeze until the water is a solid block, then pound away.) Spray with flat black paint. Pour in a couple of inches of sand and insert candle.

• **CHRISTMAS ORNAMENT HOOKS,** *Substitute:*

1. Unbend the middle "bend" of a paperclip so that you still have a loop on either end; one for the ornament and one for the tree.

2. Put a twist-tie through the loop of the ornament, twist the ends around each other, then make a hook and hang it over the branch, or just put the twist-tie through the decoration loop and wrap the ends around the tree branch and twist the ends together.

Note: My busy research editor has all of her ornaments permanently attached to her artificial tree. After Christmas, she covers the still-decorated tree with a plastic bag sold for disposing real Christmas trees and stores it in a spare room. Then each year, she brings out the tree, already decorated.

• **CHRISTMAS ORNAMENT RECIPE:** Store these from year to year in a tightly sealed container. In some climates, they can attract insects. One reader stores hers wrapped in tissue and placed in a box with a few mothballs or cedar shavings.

CHRISTMAS ORNAMENT DOUGH

> 2 cups baking soda
> 1 cup cornstarch
> 1 ¼ cups cold water

Mix cornstarch and baking soda in a saucepan and add the water. Cook over medium heat, stirring constantly, until the mixture is the consistency of wet mashed potatoes. Turn it out onto a plate, cover it with a damp cloth and let it cool.

When cool, knead it until it's smooth. Seal it in a plastic bag and store in the refrigerator until you're ready to use it.

Shape ornaments by hand or flatten the dough and cut out shapes with cookie cutters. Insert a wire hanger into the soft dough or make a hole in each ornament with a plastic drinking straw so that you can hang the ornament with crinkle-tie or regular ribbon. Let ornaments dry overnight or heat them in a 250°F oven for 15 minutes. If not completely dry, continue to heat, checking at five-minute increments.

Dried pieces can be painted with water colors, poster paints, acrylic paints, or felt-tip pens. Finish the ornaments with a coat or two of clear nail polish or varnish and they'll last for years.

• **CHRISTMAS SOUVENIR ORNAMENTS:** Instead of buying dust-catching knickknacks as souvenirs, buy Christmas ornaments unique to the area you visit on vacation. You'll have a very personalized Christmas tree, wonderful memories of vacations when you decorate it, and not lots of stuff to dust throughout the year.

• **CHRISTMAS STOCKING TREE:** When one reader's family's new home had no fireplace for hanging their traditional Christmas stockings, they substituted a pole planter which had a hook for each stocking.

• **CHRISTMAS TREE,** *No-mess Watering:* Insert into the water pan a long funnel, the type designed for a car transmission, sold at auto parts stores. No more breaking ornaments and knocking things off when you're crawling under the tree to water it!

• **CHRISTMAS WREATHS,** *Hanging One on Each Side of the Door:* If both wreaths are about the same weight, try tying a sturdy ribbon from one to the other and draping it over the door. The weights of the wreaths will balance like a teeter-totter. Apply a heavy-duty tape, like duct tape, across the ribbon on top of the door to keep the ribbon from sliding when the door is opened.

• **CIGARETTE CASE,** *Recycling After You Quit Smoking:*
1. The extra-long snap purses that held cigarette packs and a lighter make good sun or reading glasses cases.
2. They can hold sewing supplies or jewelry when you travel.

• **CLEANING SUPPLIES,** *Carry-Around and Storage:* Leave the handle on, but cut out the top side of a large plastic milk jug and you'll have a container to store bathroom cleaning supplies, sponge, and scrubber.

• **CLOCK,** *Stopping an Annoying Humming Noise:* Try turning the clock upside down and leaving it that way for a day or so; it lets some of the small parts get "re-oiled."

• **CLOSET CALENDAR,** *Memory Jogger:* Mark a one-year calendar with birthdays, anniversaries and special events and then hang it up in your closet so that you will get a reminder each day when you get dressed. The reader who sent in this hint said his wife gave him a calendar like this one and wrote in their anniversary in big red letters. Very, very smart!

• **CLOSET CLUTTER SOLUTION,** *For Hats, Mittens, Gloves:* Attach spring clothespins with heavy duty staples or nails to the coat closet door so that hats, mittens, and gloves can be hung up and therefore found the next day.

• **CLOSET HANG-UPS,** *Healthy-Planet Recycling:*
1. Hang beads, chains, scarfs on a towel rack and hang belts on drapery hooks hooked to the rack.
2. Hang a plastic six-pack cover to a drapery hook or attach it to a hanger with twist-ties to hold scarfs.

• **CLOSET POLE:** Apply floor paste wax to the closet pole and hangers will glide more smoothly.

• **CLOSET ROD COVER,** *Time/Fingernail Saver:* Putting on a plastic closet rod cover is easier if you put a small bottle inside the plastic roll and then push it along in front as you fit the cover onto the rod. No more cut fingers, broken plastic, and broken fingernails!

• **CLOSET RODS:** Cover wooden closet rods with inexpensive (sometimes less than $2) plastic sleeves sold for shower-curtain rods. Hangers will slide smoothly and you can buy colors to match your room or to color-code each person's side of a shared closet.

• **CLOTHES,** *Organizing Work Clothes for the Week:* Instead of last-minute rushing at the ironing board, take 20 to 30 minutes on the weekend to plan your work-week wardrobe. Wash and iron whatever needs it and then hang everything in matching sets in the closet. No more suits without matching their clean and ironed blouses to start your day off with stress.

- **CLOTHES CLOSET SEPARATION,** *Quick-Fix for Family Peace:* When children or even adults share a closet, you can set boundaries for each person's clothing with plastic coffee-can lids. Cut a hole in the middle of each lid large enough to accommodate the wooden clothes rod in your closet and then make a slit from the center hole through the outer rim. Write each person's name on the lid with a permanent felt-tip marker and place on the clothes rod between "territories" to divide (clothing) and conquer (closet complaints).

- **CLOTHES HANGING IN THE CAR FOR TRAVEL:** Instead of a bar extended across the back seat which obscures vision, try placing two large key rings over the clothes hooks on either side of the back seat. The rings let you hang several hangers in each while the car's clothes hooks hold only two or three hangers each.

- **CLOTHESPIN HOLDER,** *Easy Fix:* When hanging a large spread or blanket outdoors on the line, clip clothespins to your shirt bottom and they'll be handy.

- **CLOTHESPINS,** *Recycling Spring-action Pins:*
1. Clamp them on to plastic bread or snack bags.
2. They will hold sheet music in place on a stand, even in the wind.
3. Keep one in the car to clamp on your keys when you switch lights on during the day so that you don't forget to turn them off. Of course, you'll have to remember to clamp on the clothespin when you put the lights on!
4. Clamp scarfs, skirts and other clothing onto a hangar.
5. Plastic-coated metal spring-pins can be attached to recipes, notes, phone messages and hung on a prominent cup hook to keep these things in plain view.
6. Clip together coupons when shopping. Clip a second pin to the cart or your shirt pocket to hold used coupons.
7. Remove mildew from wooden clothespins by soaking them for about an hour in a bucket with water, a bit of laundry detergent and about a cup of bleach. Then rinse and let dry before using.

- **CLOTHING,** *Outfitting School Children:*
1. Take advantage of back-to-school clothing sales, but with teens and pre-teens, it may be better to save some of the budget money for those things "everybody is wearing" that parents never heard of, especially if your child is attending a new school. Children need

not be slaves to fads, but it helps them fit in if they have some "everybody" clothes, backpacks, notebooks, lunch boxes, and so forth.

2. It may help to shop in stores located near the school your child will attend; they'll be catering to the local choices and school requirements.

• **CLOTHING CODING:** Before hanging a garment back in the closet, place a large bangle bracelet on top of the hangers to identify clothing that needs some sort of attention—take to dry cleaners (at the end of the week or after wearing one more time); replace button, fix hem, etc.

• **CLOTHING RECEIPTS,** *Keeping Track of Them:* When you go shopping for clothing, make a shopping list of planned purchases on the front of an envelope. Circle items you buy and insert the receipts. Write down purchases not on the original list. When you return home, put the envelope into a manila folder labeled "receipts" or other file drawer for that purpose only and you'll never have to search for receipts again.

• **CLOTHING SWAP,** *Recycling $aver:* Hold a clothing swap party for your friends to clean out outgrown, no-longer-liked or worn garments. Donate garments that nobody claims to a Women's Shelter or other charity. I'm still wearing a "swap" garment from ten years ago!

• **CLUTTER,** *Eliminating It:* Make it a rule of thumb or, more accurately, rule of hand, that when you leave a room, "don't go empty handed." Always pick up some clutter and take it to where it belongs. **Note:** It's cheating if you just take it to another room where it's still clutter!

• **COCOA,** *Storage:* Some cocoa cans have openings too small for measuring utensils. The solution is to sift the whole 8-ounce can of cocoa into a 2-pound plastic margarine tub with an airtight lid. You can scoop with any measuring utensils and the cocoa won't get lumpy either.

• **COCOA CAN,** *Quick-Fix Opener:* Pry open with a putty knife or clean paint-can lid opener.

• **COFFEE,** *Quick-Fix Flavors:* Add a sprinkle of cinnamon to the ground coffee before brewing. Or, add a drop or two of almond, vanilla or other extract to the ground coffee. For mocha, add chocolate syrup or cocoa mix to brewed coffee.

• **COFFEE CAN,** *Reusing:* When empty, wash and dry and reuse to store staples like pasta, flour, etc. on the pantry shelf. Great for storing items in the workshop, too.

• **COFFEE CREAMER,** *Homemade, Lower-Fat:* Combine non-fat dry milk with low-fat liquid milk; store in fridge and shake before pouring.

• **COFFEE CREAMER SUBSTITUTE:** A spoonful of sweetened condensed milk is both cream and sugar in your coffee.

• **COFFEE FILTER PACKS,** *Homemade:*
1. Place the coffee filter in a large margarine tub, measure coffee, add another filter and continue until the tub is full. Seal with lid to keep coffee fresh.
2. If you grind your own beans but hate the noise in the morning, grind away at night, place the filter in a margarine tub or other sealable container, add coffee, replace lid; then you can wake up and smell the coffee without hearing the noise.

• **COFFEE FILTERS,** *$aver Substitute for One-cup Cones:* To make filters for one-cup cones, fold a regular filter in half, then in half again. Open one side and you have a cone. Ordinary filters cost less than special cone ones.

• **COFFEE-FILTER SACHET:** Pour baking soda into a paper coffee filter, tape it closed (looks like an onion) and toss it into the clothes hamper to keep it odor-free. Replace the "sachet" every few weeks.

• **COFFEE FILTERS,** *Quick-Fixes:*
1. Cover bowl or dish in the microwave.
2. Grab one to clean window, mirror, or polish silver.
3. Place between plates, saucers, and good china or between non-stick cookware pieces to prevent scratches.

4. When serving tacos to children, place the taco in a coffee filter, fill it, and hand it to the child. Less mess!

• **COFFEE FILTERS,** *The Ultimate Way to Separate Filters:* Turn each layer inside out. The struggle is over!

• **COFFEE GROUNDS,** *No-mess Pouring:* To pour coffee into a canister from a can, cut a "spout" hole in the plastic lid and you'll save time not having to wipe up spilled grounds.

• **COFFEE MAKER SAFETY,** *Reminder to Switch It Off:* Is there anyone who has never ever left the pot on for hours and hours? Make it a habit to plug a night-light into the same socket with the coffee pot when you start the coffee and unplug the night-light when you switch off the pot. The extra light can be a reminder, especially if the "on" light of your pot is not very large or bright.

• **COFFEE MAKING,** *$aver for a Tight Budget:* Try making the first pot in a drip coffee maker with the regular amount of ground coffee. Then, for the second pot, leave the grounds in the basket and add half the normal amount of ground coffee on top of them. Brew as usual. For the third pot, throw it all out and start again. It's okay to pinch pennies but don't pinch so hard that Mr. Lincoln says "Ouch" or everyone who tastes the coffee says "Yuck"!

• **COFFEE MUGS,** *Healthy Planet, BYOM:* When your club has a party, have members bring their own coffee cups, marked for identification, and then your group won't need plastic foam cups that don't break down in landfills. You'll save money in the treasury, too. This can also work for casual group parties.

• **COFFEE MUG,** *Heater:* Place your coffee mug on top of the drip coffee-maker when it starts brewing. By the time the coffee is ready, your mug will be warm enough to keep your coffee hot longer as you sip those first eye-openers.

• **COFFEE OLE:** Readers often request this recipe so I'm including it in this dictionary. To a cup of regular coffee, add a little extra skim milk and a tablespoon of powdered skim milk. Add sugar or artificial sweetener to taste. Blend the mixture in the blender until it is foamy. Pour the mixture into a microwaveable coffee mug and heat it on "Warm" for a couple of seconds. Enjoy.

• **COFFEE POT,** *Cleaning Aluminum Percolators:* Fill the coffee pot with water, add a handful of baking soda or two or three teaspoons cream of tartar. Run through the full coffee-making cycle, let cool, then scrub with piece of nylon net. If the pot is badly stained, you may have to repeat this process to get it shiny bright and to get good-tasting coffee again.

• **COFFEE POT,** *Cleaning Burnt Bottoms of Glass Pots:* When you discover that an electric pot has been left on and the pot is burnt, pour table salt into the pot and let it stand for a few minutes. The burnt crust will come loose and you can wash the pot clean. (This hint came from an office worker who used salt because nothing else was handy; that's how most hints come into being!)

• **COFFEE POT,** *Cleaning Mineral Deposits in a Drip Pot:* Follow directions in the booklet that came with your pot. For most types, you can pour a full measure of white vinegar into the water well and run the pot through its cycle. Then run plain water through several cycle to rinse out the vinegar. Heavy deposits may require a repeat of the process. **Hint:** The vinegar can be stored in a jar to clean the coffee pot again. Let the minerals settle to the bottom and use the clear vinegar. Or, clean something with the used vinegar; pour it on weeds or grass in sidewalk cracks, or just pour the remains down the drain to deodorize it.

• **COFFEE THERMOS:**
1. Keep coffee in a thermos instead of on the heater and it will stay hot for a late morning cup without getting stronger.
2. When you have houseguests and need two potfuls quickly, pour the first pot into a thermos as soon as it's brewed so that you can start the second pot immediately.
3. Working people who are slow-starters can make a pot of coffee before retiring and keep it in a thermos so that the first "eye-opener" is ready and waiting. This is an especially good hint that first week of adjusting to daylight saving time or the beginning of the school year!
Hint: Don't forget to rinse out the thermos with hot water to heat it before you pour in hot coffee so that you aren't likely to crack glass inserts and the coffee will stay hot longer.

- **COLD,** *When You Have One:* Avoid putting messy tissues in your pocket or purse. Tuck a small plastic sandwich bag into either one and you can put nose tissues directly into the bag for disposal.

- **COLD-WATER WASHING:** The Association of Home Appliance Manufacturers says that although cold-water washing is energy efficient, detergents do a better job in warmer water. Whites and very dirty clothes wash best in warm to hot water. Also granular detergents don't dissolve well in cold water and so don't clean as well. When washing in cold water, use liquid detergents or dissolve granular ones in water before adding them to the load.

- **COLLEGE RECORDS,** *Storage:* When a child goes off to college provide a metal file and show how to organize files with folders. Then, if the student takes parental advice and files all receipts for tuition and books, dorm information, car expenses, etc. in the file, there'll be no confusion about records. If the student doesn't take advice, well . . . almost everyone grows up eventually! Parents can only do so much!

- **COLLEGE STUDENT HEALTH INSURANCE:** Send with your college student either an extra health-insurance card or copy of the card (both sides) and the student's Social Security number or card. This information is needed for billing in case of an emergency or hospitalization. Without pre-certification, the parent may be responsible for a large portion of a hospital bill.

- **COLOGNE,** *Spraying to Retain Scent:* Step into a walk-in closet when applying spray cologne and the extra fragrance will stay in the closet (to make it smell nice) instead of dissipating in the air. **Caution:** Don't spray on clothing because cologne can stain or damage certain fabrics.

- **COLOR COORDINATING,** *Matching Paint, Fabric, Wallpaper:* Get paint sampler color chips that match sofas, comforters, curtains, rugs, and other "unmoveables" so that you can take the chips shopping for wallpaper, paint, or whatever else you need to buy for redecorating.

- **COMBS AND HAIRBRUSHES,** *Easy Cleaning:*
1. Fill the bathroom sink with hot water and add a couple of squirts of dishwashing liquid or shampoo. Swish everything around

in the soapy water and let soak for 30 minutes or so. Then run the wide end of a comb through the brush bristles to remove hair and hairspray residue, etc. Drain water from the sink and rinse each item thoroughly under hot running water. Place on towel with brushes' bristles-sides down; let drip dry.

2. Put water into the bathroom sink, add a small glug of ammonia and then let combs and brushes soak for a while. Brush combs with brushes and clean both at the same time. Then whisk the brush or a sponge around the sink, let the water run out, and rinse all at the same time.

- **COMICS,** *Recycling:* Amuse children by letting them color black and white daily newspaper comics.

- **COMPACT DISCS,** *Cleaning:* Please see RECORDS, Cleaning.

- **COMPLAINTS WITH CLOUT,** *Checklist for Complaining About Faulty Merchandise or Service:* Be businesslike, not emotional, type the letter if possible and if not, make sure your handwriting is legible. Include all pertinent information, as follows.

1. Your name, address, work and home phone numbers.
2. Date and place of purchase.
3. Serial and model number of merchandise.
4. Name of the person who did the work if it's a service complaint.
5. Make and keep copies of all complaint letters and allow a reasonable amount of time for a response.

Sending complaints by registered letters gives you proof that the company has received your complaint.

- **COMPUTER,** *Checklist for Avoiding Back and Neck Tension on the Job:*

1. Place your terminal so that the top of the screen is at your eye level or just below.
2. Keep your feet flat on the floor.
3. Keep your elbows at 90 degrees—your fingers should just reach the keyboard comfortably.
4. Position your work station so that the screen receives the least amount of glare from windows or indoor lighting.
5. Take short breaks—at the least, stretch your arms for a few minutes each hour.
6. Make sure your chair provides good back support.

- **COMPUTER,** *Insuring a New One:* At time of purchase, check with your insurance company to make sure it's covered by your policy for theft or damage.

- **COMPUTER MONITOR SCREEN,** *Cleaning:* It's best not to clean the screen with wet cloths. You can wipe with a slightly damp cloth. Commercial anti-static cleaning pads are the best choice. Buy them in office supply or computer stores.

- **COMPUTER PAPER,** *Healthy-Planet Recycling:* Shredded office paper and the perforated edges of computer paper can be used for packing materials.
High-tech Hens: One reader uses shredded computer paper on the farm to line chickens' nests instead of hay and says she thinks the hens like it better!

- **COMPUTER-PAPER BOX,** *Recycling:* Many brands of computer paper come in lidded boxes that make perfect file storage.

- **COMPUTER PRINTOUT PAPER,** *Recycling:* You can run those long printouts back through the printer to print on the blank reverse side for a second time around. The quality is acceptable for test runs and informal jobs.

- **CONFECTIONERS' SUGAR SUBSTITUTE:** Mix one cup of granulated sugar and one tablespoon cornstarch in a blender at high speed for several minutes. As with most substitutes, the consistency and texture of the dish may be altered slightly.

- **CONSUMER INFORMATION:** If you can't find a number to call in the manual that comes with your appliance or on a product label, dial 1-800-555-1212 to get the 800 consumer information number of a company. If the company has no 800 number, main libraries of large cities usually have information services you can call to get addresses and phone numbers of national firms.

- **CONTACT LENS,** *Travel Kit:* A plastic soap case will hold all the accessories for cleaning your contacts when you travel.

- **CONTACT LENS CAUTION:** Don't clean contact lenses with generic/ regular hydrogen peroxide. It may contain additives or impurities that can cause soft-lens discoloration or irritate the eyes, even when this peroxide is safe for other uses. Instead, always clean and disinfect contact lenses with the cleaning solutions made especially for them.

• **CONTACT LENSES,** *Wearing Near Water:* Contact lenses let swimmers, snorklers, water skiers, surfers, and divers see better when they're in the water. To avoid losing lenses and the resulting inconvenience and expense of replacing them, here are some hints.
1. Soft contact lenses are less likely than rigid ones to get lost in or around water. Their larger circumference keeps them more stable in the eye.
2. Insert soft lenses at least 30 minutes before entering the water; reduce the risk of lens loss by using one or two drops of saline or, in a pinch, single-dosage containers of sterile distilled water.
3. Close your eyes if you expect a hard entry into the water; at least squint if you expect a splash.
4. Remove excess water in eyes with several fast hard blinks; avoid rubbing the eye.
5. If you get mild eye discomfort after water play, place a clean index finger on the lens and test-move it gently. If the lens slides easily, it can be safely removed, but if it doesn't move, the lens needs to be taken out immediately using sterile saline solution to help it come out more easily. However, it's best to wait 30 minutes after getting out of the water before you remove and disinfect your lens.

• **COOKIE BAKING,** *Time-Saver:* One reader wrote that she makes twenty-five dozen chocolate chip cookies at one baking session and to save time she scoops the cookie dough onto cookie sheets with a large melon ball maker. All the cookies are the same size and are just right for grandchildren and parties. **Note:** Save a teaspoon of chocolate chips when you are mixing the dough. Then when you get down to the last spoonful of batter and, as usual the chips are all gone with the first scoops of dough, you can add the reserved chips to make all of the cookies equally chocolatey!

• **COOKIE BAKING,** *Time-Saver:* Flatten cookies you roll into a ball, like peanut-butter cookies, with a potato masher.

• **COOKIE CRUMBS AND PIECES,** *From the Bottom of the Cookie Jar, Recycling:* Add them to bread pudding for extra Yum! **Note:** It's not true that the calories don't count when you eat broken cookie pieces instead of whole cookies!

- **COOKIE CUTTERS,** *Seasonal Plastic Ones:* Plastic cookie cutters come in many shapes and colors, such as for Christmas, Thanksgiving, Valentine's day, Easter; they can be festive but inexpensive napkin rings.

- **COOKIE DECORATING,** *Avoiding Mess (Especially When Your "Assistant Cook" Is a Small Child):* After preparing the dough and cutting out the cookies, place the cookie cutter around the cut-out cookies before sprinkling on colored sugars or sparkles. The cutter will corral the sprinkles and keep them from being scattered about.

- **COOKIE DOUGH,** *Quick-Fix Homemade Cookies:* When you make a batch of cookies, make double or more amounts and then freeze cylinders of cookie dough to slice and bake when you get an uncontrollable attack of the cookie munchies.

- **COOKIE JAR TRICK:** Fill the cookie jar with low-sugar dry cereal. It's a great snack and helps develop better eating habits!

- **COOKIES,** *Christmas:* This *Letter of Laughter* recipe appeared about twenty years ago in my mother's column and was sent to me by a reader when it was requested by another reader and I couldn't find it in my files. It proves that some recipes are timeless!

CHRISTMAS COOKIES

1. Light oven, get bowl, spoons, and ingredients, grease pan, crack nuts, remove ten blocks, seven toy autos, and one wad of chewing gum from kitchen table.
2. Measure two cups of flour, remove Johnny's hands from flour, wash flour off him, measure one more cup flour to replace flour on floor.
3. Put flour, baking powder, and salt in sifter. Answer doorbell. Return to kitchen. Remove Johnny's hands from bowl. Wash Johnny. Answer phone. Return. Remove quarter-inch salt from greased pans, grease more pans. Look for Johnny. Answer phone.
4. Return to kitchen and find Johnny. Remove his hands from bowl. Wash shortening, etc., etc., off him. Take up greased pan and take out shells from it. Head for Johnny who flees, knocking bowl off table.
5. Wash kitchen floor. Wash table. Wash kitchen walls. Wash dishes. Wash Johnny. Call baker. Lie down!

Perhaps the best way today's working mothers could use this recipe is to update it as follows.

CHRISTMAS COOKIE RECIPE, REVISED

1. Find Johnny, take him to the car and strap him in his car seat, go to the bakery.
2. Return home, sit down with Johnny to read his favorite Christmas story, and then have cookies and milk with him.
3. Lie down while Johnny naps.

Let's face it, some days you just can't do it all so you may as well seize the moment—friends and family have more value than homemade cookies. Make the cookies when Johnny is old enough to really help you!

• **COOKIES,** *Quick-Fix, Homemade, Small Batch:* For one dozen delicious fresh cookies, add to a box of store-bought muffin mix, two eggs and one-half cup oil. Drop by teaspoonfuls on an ungreased cookie sheet and bake. For extra flavor, add optional ingredients such as a spoonful of peanut butter, chopped nuts or raisins.

• **COOKIES,** *Quick-Fix for Peanut-butter Crisscrosses:* Make them with a plastic fork; the batter won't stick.

• **COOKIES,** *Quick-Fix for Too-browned Bottoms:* Rub the brown off with the coarse side of your vegetable slicer/grater.

• **COOKIE SNEAK:** To cut a few calories from chocolate cookies (or at least to feel as if you are trying!), substitute ½ cup of mini-chocolate chips for one cup of regular-size chips. Few cookie munchers will notice the difference.

• **COOKING,** *Substituting Low-fat or Nonfat Yogurt for Sour Cream:* When you do this for cooked foods, it may separate and get watery. Solution: Stir some flour into the yogurt before cooking or, if possible, add it to dishes after removing them from the heat.

• **COOL COOLER:** Instead of buying bagged ice which will just melt and be tossed away, buy frozen orange juice concentrate. Four cans of frozen concentrate will keep two cold six-packs of beverage cool in a small cooler and then you can mix up the juice for breakfast during the week after your picnic.

• **COOLER,** *For Party Beverages:* Ice down canned and bottled beverages for a party by lining the bottom of your clothes washer with a heavy towel and then filling up the machine with ice and cans. When the party is over, remove remaining cans and use the water for a cold water wash that includes the towel.

• **COOLER,** *Storing Without Mildew:* Place a spacer such as a piece of wood or folded cardboard between the lid and rim to prevent the cover from sealing tightly and to let air circulate. Don't forget to sprinkle in baking soda to prevent odors.

• **COPPER & BRASS,** *Quick-Fix, Brightening:* Sprinkle table salt on a wet sponge, rub off tarnish, rinse, and dry. Or, rub darkened places using a half-lemon with or without table salt, rinse, and buff dry.

• **COPY "MACHINE,"** *Quick-Fix with Transparent Tape:* When you are househunting or labeling videotaped movies with the descriptive paragraphs printed in the newspaper, try this:
1. Place a strip of transparent tape over the print area to be copied and rub well with your fingernail, then carefully lift the print from the paper.
2. You can then stick the movie description onto the side of the videotape or stick a house/apartment classified ad onto a sheet of paper or index card. Then, there will be space for writing your comments after seeing the apartment and other information you need to remember when deciding to rent or buy.

• **CORK,** *Removing When It's Been Pushed into a Wine Bottle That You Want to Save:* Pour ammonia into the bottle and leave it somewhere where air circulates. The cork will disintegrate in about a week. Wash the inside well with soap and water and the bottle is ready for display or to root a sprig of ivy in water.

• **CORKS,** *Recycling Those from Wine and Other Bottles:*
1. Use them to protect the points of knives, barbecue forks, ice picks and knitting needles.
2. They will hold safety pins, map pins, thumbtacks, etc.
3. They can be colored for craft projects with fabric or craft dyes.
4. Glue corks into frames of various sizes to make trivets and coasters.
5. Cut lengthwise so that there is one flat side and glue to a backing such as plywood, fiberboard or cardboard. (This project's gluing

phase could keep a vacation-weary child busy for a long time!) OR, glue on the side of a kitchen cabinet to make a message center.
6. Glue on backings for picture frames, Christmas wreaths, refrigerator magnets.
7. Make tiny sailboats with a toothpick-held sail to occupy a child.
8. Place in the bottoms of potted plants to help drainage and place around roots of orchids to stabilize them.

• CORN, *Healthy-Planet Recycling, Avoid Sharing with the Birds:* Cut off the bottoms of used beverage cans and place them on sweet-corn ears a week or so before they're ready to pick. It keeps the birds from eating the corn cobs before you can and doesn't harm the birds.

• CORN-ON-THE-COB-ON-THE-GRILL: After pulling off the corn shucks, boil the corn for about five minutes and then toast it over hot coals in the barbecue pit for several minutes.

• CORN SYRUP SUBSTITUTE: While you can substitute honey for corn syrup in a recipe, the flavor and texture may be altered and honey tastes sweeter. You cannot substitute corn syrup for granulated sugar and vice versa. With one being a liquid and the other a dry ingredient, it's difficult to adjust the recipe ingredients to get the same result.

• COSMETIC CASE, *$aver:* Buy a colorful zipper pencil case sold in school supplies departments of drug or variety stores.

• COSMETICS, *When You Travel in Warm Climates:* Instead of putting your cosmetic case in a hot car trunk, keep it inside the car where it's cooler. Even a thirty to forty-five-minute ride to the airport could damage face creams or melt your lipstick and make a big mess in the case.

• COSTUME, *Quick-Fix with Humor:* They're sold in catalogs but you can make them yourself with a magic marker and a plain over-size T-shirt, any light color or white.
1. Just write on the T-shirt "THIS IS A (Halloween, Tiger, Clown, New Year's Party) COSTUME" and if you can, do a "stickman" or other drawing on the back.
2. Or a T-shirt with, "MY (MOM, DAD) FORGOT TO GO SHOPPING SO THIS IS MY TRICK-OR-TREAT COSTUME" and/or "PLEASE FEED ME"

would surely get the biggest bag of Halloween goodies any child could want from the neighbors!

• **COTTON FROM MEDICINE BOTTLES,** *Healthy-Planet Recycling:* Don't throw this cotton away; it's great for nail-polish remover and cosmetic use. **Hint:** Cotton is placed in pill bottles to keep the pills from bouncing around and breaking in shipment. Once you open the bottle, remove it because it has no purpose anymore.

• **COUNTER SPACE,** *Temporary Cutting Space:* Turn a dish drainer upside down inside a sink and put your chopping board on top. Then you can chop vegetables and fruit with the easiest ever clean up. Just turn on the faucet and send the peelings down the disposal or collect them in the sink by hand and rinse the rest of the mess off.

• **COUNTERTOPS,** *When You Need Extra Work Space:* Open a drawer all the way and put a cookie sheet on it, then close the drawer until the cookie sheet fits tightly. **Hint:** A lower drawer can be an extra "table" for a child if you don't have enough space at the main table. Put a place mat over the cookie sheet after following the extra-space directions.

• **COUPON,** *Storage:* Instead of storing by category (dairy, meats, baking goods), file according to expiration date, leaving an extra envelope for those which have no expiration date. Make "file folders" by cutting sealed ends off used mailing envelopes.

• **COUPONS,** *Storage:* Clip together with a magnetic clip the coupons that correspond to items on your shopping list and keep on your refrigerator beside the shopping list so that both are handy when you go to the store. **Note:** Sometimes, my coupons ARE my shopping list!

• **COUPONS,** *When You Won't Use Them:* Give to charities when you donate clothing and other items; to senior citizen or other community centers; food banks for distribution to needy families and in some communities to coupon exchanges run by churches, libraries, and other social service projects. **Note:** I recently found a coupon taped to a product on the shelf by some generous donor. I don't know if the store manager would like to see flaps of coupons taped to items on all of the shelves, but I appreciated the 50 cents off!

• **COUPONS FOR A CAUSE:** Here's how one reader figured out a way to give several items weekly to her church "care bank" without breaking her budget and without raiding her pantry for donations. Instead of wasting good money-off coupons for foods that she doesn't usually eat but which are good staples, she allocates $1 per week to spend on coupon items to give to the church.

• **COVER,** *Plastic Wrap Tent:* Poke toothpicks strategically into cakes or other foods to be covered with plastic wrap to make a "tent" so that the tops won't get messed up. This works also if you are marinating meat and don't want the meat to touch the wrap.

• **COVERED DISH RECOVERY:** Getting plates and casseroles returned is often difficult and certainly a chore for the event chairperson. Readers have sent in many solutions.
1. Write your name on masking tape and stick it to the bottom of the dish or stick an address label to the bottom.
2. Cover several thicknesses of paper plates with foil or cover sturdy cardboard with foil, cover with a doily and send a cake on a disposable "plate."
3. Buy 12-inch square floor tiles, cover with foil and place cakes on them.
4. Buy casseroles, plates, salad bowls and other serving dishes and utensils at flea markets (sometimes for only 25 cents), run them through the dishwasher a couple of times to make sure they are sanitized and then don't care if they get returned.
5. If the covered dish event is at a friend's house, buy a dish that might match something in her house or a clear glass one and make it a hostess gift.

• **CRACKER CRUMBS:** Readers send in all sorts of shortcuts for crushing graham or soda crackers to crumbs from putting crackers in the blender; putting them in a sealable bag and substituting a glass when you don't have a rolling pin; putting them in a sealable bag and stepping on the bag until the crackers are crumbs. But one reader topped them all—she puts the crackers in a sealable bag and drives over them with her car. I don't think I would want to do this myself, but it makes a good story!

- **CRADLE,** *Recycling Doll or Antique Baby Ones:* Use them to store magazines, display older children's stuffed animals, hold throw pillows from the bed overnight, hold a folded bedspread overnight.

- **CRAFTS,** *Checklist for Selling Crafts in Consignment Shops:* Crafts are cottage industries for many women, who can remain at home but still supplement the family income. Selling in consignment shops in addition to the usual summer craft shows can be year-round income if you make the right connections.

1. Look for a consignment shop that displays a wide price range of varied crafts. Avoid shops that buy most of their products wholesale from other craftspersons or those that also sell lots of import or commercial gift lines. Seasonal orders are placed months in advance. It's probably too late to sell Christmas items in November.

2. If you exhibit at craft fairs, offer to distribute flyers to promote the shop or gallery that handles your work; make sure your retail prices are the same as those of the shop.

3. Keep careful records and get all agreements in writing. If the shop doesn't have a printed consignment form, print some of your own. The agreement should note:

   A. If the shop is insured against theft or other loss such as damage by fire or flood. (You may need your own insurance.)

   B. If you send your crafts by mail, who pays postage and insurance?

   C. The exact percent of commission the shop gets (store mark-ups are typically 100 to 150 percent). Whether payment is monthly or upon sale of a piece should be clearly stated.

   D. Will your crafts be displayed properly or will they be left in a storeroom or worse yet, in a window where they will get faded?

   E. How long will the item be displayed and if it's returned, will it be mailed or do you pick it up? Some agreements say items must be claimed after thirty to sixty days of display or thirty to sixty days after the craftsperson was notified to pick up.

• **CRANBERRY SUBSTITUTE,** *When Your Family Doesn't Eat Cran-berry Sauce for Thanksgiving Dinner:* Please see PEACH SAUCE.

• **CREAM CHEESE,** *Quick-Fix Breakfast Perk:* Sprinkle flavored fruit gelatin on cream cheese after you've spread it on your English muffin or toast.

• **CREASES,** *Removing:*

1. To remove from let-out garment seams/hems, wash the garment first. There may be dirt on the crease that will leave a line if ironed. Apply white vinegar directly to the seam/hem line until it is thoroughly damp. **Caution:** Always test on an inconspicuous place before putting anything on fabric. Place a dry, clean cloth over the line and press with a medium-hot iron. Hang garment up to air; vinegar odors dissipate quickly.

2. To remove creases/wrinkles from wool garments, like those you get in the back of a pants leg, lay the pants (or other garment) out on the ironing board. Dampen a cloth with white vinegar; place it on the wrinkles to be removed. Iron over the cloth and the winkles should come out. Repeat this step if needed, but when repeating, leave more vinegar in the cloth the second time. Continue until wrinkles/creases are out. Then hang the garment in a well ventilated area so the vinegar odor can dissipate.

• **CREDIT CARD,** *When Your Application Is Rejected:*

1. The name of the agency which gave information to your prospective lender that caused your rejection should be included in the denial letter you receive. Write to this bureau and ask for a free copy of your report and the information that caused your application's denial.

2. If you find incorrect or out-of-date information in your file, you can write to the credit bureau and ask them to verify it for you. Also notify the creditor of the problem and try to resolve it yourself. You will need copies of bills, canceled checks and other papers to back your claim; send copies, not originals, to the creditor.

3. If you can't clear up the matter with the creditor, you may have a report of the problem placed in your credit file.

4. It's best to check with your local credit bureau to see if any negative information is in your report before applying. In fact, an

annual check is recommended by some of my sources. Making sure your credit file is up-to-date and accurate avoids problems when you need to borrow money. Credit-reporting firms charge a small fee to review your files; you get a free report only when a credit application is denied.

• **CREDIT CARD PURCHASES,** *Keeping to Your Limits:* Get an extra checkbook register and list your credit cards with the amount you are able to charge for the month on each. When you use a card, immediately write the purchase amount in the appropriate column in the checkbook and subtract it from the total amount you can spend. You will always know your exact balance and when "the well is dry." If you can't get a check book register, a small, lined notebook will do. Check out the spelling-test notebooks sold in school supplies departments; they are good for list making.

• **CREDIT CARDS,** *Safekeeping:*
1. Avoid rubbing the magnetic strips of credit cards against each other in a billfold. The cards can become demagnetized and then useless.
2. Carry cards separately from money clips with magnets, magnetized card keys used to enter buildings, and don't keep them in plastic which also can harm them.
3. Don't scrape ice from a car windshield with a credit card.
4. Leave them behind if you will be in a magnet field such as in an industrial area. The good news is that airport X-ray devices do not harm credit cards.
5. Make copies of all your credit and bank cards on a copy machine so that you have records of all the numbers and expiration dates on one sheet of paper in case you have to report a loss. **CAUTION**—Don't forget to take all of the credit cards out of the copy machine and keep the information in a safe place.

• **CROCHET/KNITTING PLACE:** Keep a pad of self-sticking notes near your chair, then when the phone rings as you are deciphering pattern instructions, you can stick a note on the line you were on when interrupted.

• **CROSSWORD PUZZLES,** *Corrections:* When you do your puzzles in ink, typewriter correction fluid keeps the puzzle neat and readable when you need to correct a mistake. *Crossword Myth Dispelled:* A reader wrote that when crossword fans do puzzles in ink instead of pencil, it's not that they are egotists; it's just easier to read darker pen letters than lighter pencil ones.

• **CUCUMBERS,** *When Your Garden Produces a Bumper Crop:* When you've eaten all the salad, made all the pickles, and cuked all of the friends you possibly can, try cooking cucumbers. Peel, cut into small quarter-sized slices and simmer in chicken broth for about 10 minutes. Drain, add a bit of butter and pepper and you have a tasty veggie dish. If you are cutting calories, cook in skimmed chicken broth and flavor with diet margarine.

• **CUPBOARD DOOR AND DRAWER HANDLES,** *Helping Hands:* People with arthritis often have trouble pulling drawers and doors open with their hands. One reader put fabric loops through her mother's kitchen cabinet handles so that she could open them by slipping her arm through the loop.

• **CUPBOARDS,** *Keeping Closed:* Re-reinforce the closures with self-gripping fabric tape. You can get stick-on dots and strips in neutral colors.

• **CUPCAKES,** *Baking Hints:*
1. Measure cupcake batter into pans with an ice-cream scoop or handled-measuring cup.
2. Pour cupcake batter into the tins with a pitcher.
3. Bake cupcake batter in ice cream cones for children's parties for no-mess eating.

• **CUPCAKE FROSTING,** *Substitute:* Place a small chocolate-covered mint on top of a cupcake, pop it into the microwave for a few seconds, then remove and spread the melted mint just as you would frosting.

• **CURLING IRON,** *Removing Hairspray Build-up:* Cool and unplug iron before cleaning. Then dampen a clean cloth with rubbing alcohol and wipe the wand several times until it's clean. Avoid build-up by cleaning with alcohol about once a month.

• **CURLING-IRON IRONING,** *Quick Fixes:* Run ribbons, dress sashes, some scarfs (depends on fabric), and even seams when you are sewing, through the curling iron.

- **CURTAINS,** *Make Them Crisp and Fresh Without Ironing:* Wash and rinse as usual. Add 1 cup of Epsom salts to a sink filled with water and rinse the laundered curtains in the solution; hang to dry—no need for ironing!

- **CURTAINS,** *Quick-Fix Recycling:* When you switch from window shades to curtains, you can make the curtain casing large enough to accommodate the shade rollers and save yourself the trouble and expense of curtain rods. The bonus is that you don't make more holes in the walls either!

- **CURTAINS,** *Removing Wrinkles Without Ironing:* When you wash sheers or similar fabrics, hang them back up damp and put heavy dinner knives in the hem openings. The added weight helps pull out wrinkles as the curtains dry.

- **CURTAINS,** *When Rods Show Through Colored Sheers:* Spray paint the rods with the appropriate color.

- **CURTAIN TIE BACKS,** *Quick-Fix, Placing the Hooks Exactly Even:* Pull the window shade up to the level where the nails or hooks are to be installed and you'll have a straight line marker for exactly the right place on either side of the window.

- **CUTTER,** *Non-messy for Children:* A pizza cutter will cut pancakes or waffles and other soft, sticky foods neatly.
Pizza cutters also cut homemade noodle dough quickly.

- **CUTTING BOARD HELPER:** Buy a brightly colored plastic dustpan so that after you chop vegetables for the wok, you can push them from the cutting board into the dustpan and from dustpan into wok without "flying veggies" all over the floor. Be sure to mark it "Vegetable Dustpan" so that it doesn't end up collecting dirt on the floor!

D

• **DAY CARE,** *Warm Fuzzy for Young Child:* Sometimes it's difficult for mothers and young children to adjust to the idea of day care. Here's one reader's solution. When her son entered a day-care program that required children to bring their own blankets for nap time, she and her son went to fabric and craft stores to pick out appliqués for the blanket—a Marine emblem because his dad was a Marine, a duck because he liked the story of the Ugly Duckling, and others. One of the final appliqués was a "warm fuzzy," a pink heart with a cotton ball in the middle that Mom sprayed with the perfume she usually wears. Each month when the blanket came home for laundering, Mom resprayed the heart. Mom's fragrance helped the tot take a nap, and Mom felt like she was still "connected."

• **DECANTER,** *Removing Stains and Mineral Deposits:* Fill the decanter with white vinegar and let stand overnight. Then add uncooked rice and shake to remove the stains on the inside that a sponge or brush won't reach. Rinse and dry.

• **DECORATING,** *Accents:* Dresser scarfs can cover "a multitude of sins" such as stains, nicks and scratches on a table-top, buffet or dresser; or substitute placemats or napkins (like the one remaining unstained member of a set), colorful serapes or fringed stoles for traditional dresser scarfs.

• **DECORATING,** *Living/Bedroom Pillow Perks:* Throw pillows always add new color and brighten a room. If you sew, you can make them from fabric remnants and stuff them with recycled panty hose, foam dryer sheets, foam packing materials, or bits of left-over-anything that's soft.
1. If your decor is "eclectic," make large TV-lounging floor pillows by sewing plush corduroy (back) and lightweight Oriental design throw rugs (front) together; stuff with old bedpillows and foam strips cut from carpet backing and other filler.
2. Make children's bedroom throw pillows by sewing shut the necks, sleeves and bottoms of favorite but outgrown T-Shirts and stuffing them. Use larger T-shirts as "decorator" pillow cases.

• **DECORATING,** *Silk Flowers and Plants:* "Dust" with cold air blown from a hair dryer or clean by shaking them in a bag with table salt.

• **DECORATING,** *Table Linen Cover-ups:* Discover a stain on the tablecloth and there's no time to change it? Make it look as if the cover-up is really your purposely placed decoration.
Cover-up with a centerpiece, hotplate-mat or trivet, a wide ribbon/serape/runner down the center, complementary colored napkins (placed diagonally), place mats (one in center or one on either side of the centerpiece) or doilies located so they will be beneath serving dishes or the centerpiece or candle sticks. Scatter holiday flowers or greenery so that spots are covered as part of your decoration scheme. (Cut stems off flowers so they'll lay flat; hold things in place with tape loops.)

• **DECORATING,** *Table Linens:* Colorful fringed "finger-tip" towels bought at white sales can be no-iron inexpensive placemats, especially at the "children's table" for family dinners where they'll also absorb spills.

• **DECORATING,** *Walls:* Group pictures and other hanging mementoes like plaques or plates to dramatize a wall or room area.
1. Avoid making extra nail holes in the wall—spread out a large sheet of wrapping paper or several taped-together newspapers on

the floor and experiment with frame positions. Then outline the frames on the paper, tape the paper to the wall, and drive hooks through the paper into the wall. Then remove the paper and hang the pictures.

2. Make small rooms look larger by installing wall mirrors or mirror tiles from hardware stores; instructions usually come with the products used for this project.

• **DENTAL FLOSS,** *Other Uses:*
1. String beads for necklaces.
2. Sew on buttons with white or new colored flosses; they'll stay on!
3. Faucets with clear plastic covers on the "Hot" and "Cold" knobs can be hard to clean. When you are in the mood to strive for perfection, dental floss cleans not only the nooks and crannies between your teeth but those of covered faucet knobs!
4. Cut cake layers (thread also works better and neater than a knife).
5. Lace up a chicken or turkey for cooking.
6. Household repairs, such as reattaching umbrella material to a spoke.

• **DENTURE CLEANSER,** *Homestyle Method:* Combine 1 teaspoon water softener, 1 teaspoon liquid bleach, and 8 ounces water and soak dentures in the solution for 10 to 15 minutes daily. Scrub with a denture brush and rinse well before replacing them in your mouth. **Caution:** Do not use this or any solution containing bleach if you wear a partial denture that has metal, wire clasps, cast chrome, or gold frame.

• **DENTURES,** *Identification:* Ask the dentist to put the denture owner's name inside the dentures of nursing home residents so that they don't get mixed up with those of other patients. Residents' possessions, including dentures, can easily get misplaced.

• **DENTURE SOAKER,** *Substitute When You Travel:* A resealable plastic bag fits easily in a shaving or cosmetic bag and dentures can soak overnight as easily in the bag as in a hard-sided container.

• **DEODORANT,** *Healthy Planet, Homestyle:* For a non-chemical deodorant, apply dry baking soda to the underarm area, then brush off excess. It's not likely to irritate skin like some commercial preparations affect some people.

• **DESSERTS,** *Keeping Single Servings:* When only one or two people live in a home, desserts can get stale before they are eaten. The solution is to cut all freezable desserts into single-serving sizes and freeze them in plastic freezer-safe bags. A few seconds in the microwave brings them back to freshness.

• **DETERGENT,** *$aver, Time-Saver:* When you empty a plastic squirt bottle of dishwashing detergent, don't throw it away. Instead, fill it with water and shake to dissolve the detergent that remains inside. The resulting diluted detergent is powerful enough to squirt on eyeglasses, your hands or on a sponge to quick-wipe dishes and it will rinse off more easily than when you squirt full-strength detergent on washables. **Hint:** When washing eyeglasses with plastic lenses, remember that paper towels, napkins, and tissues can scratch—dry with a soft cloth.

• **DETERGENT BOTTLE CAPS,** *Recycling:* Caps from liquid laundry detergent can be stacked like building blocks or for sand scoops at the beach (please don't leave them there!) or in a child's sandbox.

• **DIAMONDS,** *Care:*
1. Don't wear while doing housework or gardening. Cleaning products can harm diamonds and gold; a good knock can chip a diamond.
2. Because diamonds can scratch other gem stones, store each piece of diamond jewelry in a separate case or jewelry box section.
3. When you wash your hands, don't take your ring off and leave it near the sink; it can fall down the drain or be forgotten when you leave. I've seen people hold their rings between their lips while washing their hands.
4. Powders, skin oils, soaps and lotions dull diamonds. To clean them, try a squirt of mild liquid detergent in a small bowl of warm water. Let the diamond jewelry soak a few minutes and brush with an old soft toothbrush or eyebrow brush. Rinse well; pat and buff dry.
5. Try dipping each piece in a bit of rubbing alcohol and buff dry. It really makes diamonds sparkle.

- **DIAPERS,** *Laundering Cloth Ones:*
1. Pre-soak diapers in a diaper pail with mild sudsy solution and one tablespoon of bleach for each gallon of water or with borax in water. Rinse and unfold soiled diapers before placing them in the solution.
2. Wash contents (about eighteen diapers per wash load) every two or three days to avoid odors. To wash, dump the solution and diapers into the washing machine and run on the spin cycle. After the spin cycle removes the solution, launder as usual with hot water and cold rinse.
3. Add bleach every two or three washings to keep the diapers white and then run the diapers through a second rinse with one-half cup vinegar added to the rinse water to help remove soap and bleach residues. Fabric softener will make the diapers less absorbent so add it only occasionally, if at all.

- **DIAPERS,** *Recycling Disposable Diaper Boxes:* Store holiday decorations or outgrown baby clothes in them and they'll be easy to spot among the other brown storage boxes in your attic.

- **DIET DINING,** *Avoiding Restaurant-induced Diet Damage:*
1. Call the restaurant in the morning to find out what's on the menu, then if there's no low-cal meal offered, you can either eat somewhere else or eat the main course at home and plan to have a large salad while the others dine. (Ask for salad dressing to be served on the side so the salad isn't swimming in oil.) Good restaurants are happy to prepare a special vegetarian plate if you request it and will leave off fatty sauces, too—you need to ask for such special dietary needs, though. If you're embarrassed to ask at the table (though you shouldn't be), make a trek to the rest room as soon as you arrive and en route, talk to the table server privately.
2. If you know the portion of meat or pasta will be too large for your calorie count, ask for or bring your own "doggie bag" carry-out container so that you can remove the excess before you are tempted to eat it "just because it is there." Don't make a fuss and don't feel self-conscious, just do it; people who care about you want your diet to succeed and remember, good restaurants care about pleasing their customers. (Check out the new microwave safe, tightly sealed plastic ware at supermarkets. You can carry them in your purse.)

3. Order first so that you won't be tempted to change your allowed selections by other people's choices.

• **DIET DIPS:** Substitute blended cottage cheese or yogurt for sour cream or check out the new low-fat or non-fat sour creams.
Dip 1. Mix cottage cheese in the blender with your favorite spices—pepper, paprika, onion/garlic salts, etc. or with low-cal Italian dressing.
Dip 2. Mix 16 ounces low-fat yogurt and a package of regular (not diet) Ranch Dressing mix in the yogurt container. A packet of sweetener is optional as are hotter spices to taste. Let set overnight. (You have to let this set overnight or it won't taste good.)

• **DINNER,** *Family Dinner Planning, Letter of Laughter:* One reader says fast-food has become so much a part of their lives that when she says, "Time to eat," the children all jump into the car.

• **DINNER,** *Quick-Fix When You Don't Want to Cook:*
First Spouse: What's for dinner?
Second Spouse: Fish (or other hated food), but it's not thawed yet.
FS: Oh, let's go out for dinner.
SS: Okay, I'll just put this fish (or whatever) back into the freezer. The reader who sent this hint has used the same package of her husband's hated fish for five years. And he knows it! The package of frozen fish on the kitchen counter has become a signal that she wants to eat out. Now that's communication in marriage!

• **DINNER,** *Quick-Fix When You Forget to Thaw Something, Letter of Laughter:*
First Spouse: What's for dinner?
Second Spouse: Take out.
FS: Take out what?
SS: Take out me!

• **DINNER GUEST,** *File:* List the meals you serve at dinner parties on a 3 × 5 index card along with the names of the guests and keep in a file box. Then you won't serve the same menu over and over to the same people and you can note special likes and allergies, too. You won't serve your famous oyster bisque to someone who stops breathing after eating shell fish—a sure way to make your party memorable, to say the least! **Note:** My research editor once went to a party at which a guest, who didn't know she'd been infected with hepatitis, mixed the salad. The next day all the guests had to go for hepatitis immunizations. People are still talking about the party thirty years later!

• **DIP DISH,** *Healthy-Planet Edible Serving "Dishes":*
1. Cut off the top of a bell pepper carefully and stand it on end in the middle of a veggie platter to hold dip. The pepper can be red, green, or yellow depending upon the color you need to perk up the platter.
2. Put cocktail sauce in a hollowed-out cabbage then skewer a few shrimp on colored toothpicks and stick the opposite ends into the cabbage like antennae on a satellite. Place the rest of the shrimp around the cabbage.

• **DIRECTIONS:** Jot travel directions on pieces of self-sticking notepaper and then stick the note to the car dashboard so you don't have to hold it while driving.

• **DISH DRAINER, DRAINER TRAY, SINK RACK,** *Cleaning Gunk Off:*
1. Fill the kitchen sink with about 2 inches of hot water and add a couple of "glugs" of chlorine bleach. Place items in sink and let soak for about 15 minutes. If you can't put your hands in bleach and have no rubber gloves, after soaking is over, unplug the sink with barbecue tongs and let the bleach water drain away. Rinse items.
2. Best quality dish drainers can be placed upside down in the dishwasher ("Normal" or "Light" setting) for easy cleaning. Just be sure that all moving arms are not blocked by the rack.

• **DISHWASHER,** *Cleaning Hard-water Deposits and Removing Stains:* Citric acid, a main ingredient in powdered lemonade or citrus fruit drink, can be bought in pharmacies. To clean the dishwasher put about a tablespoon of the powder (drink or citric acid) in the detergent dispenser, no detergent, and run a cycle. You can also sprinkle the powder on a stain or blotch before running a cycle. If stains persist you may need to repeat the process.

• **DISHWASHER,** *Recycle Parts:* When a dishwasher can't be repaired, salvage the racks for use as organizers of wrapping paper and ribbons—rolls and ribbon spools fit on the upright progs and flat packages of tissue or gift wrap fit in slots. Also, some old dishwashers have silverware baskets with handles which can carry flatware to the picnic table and be used for informal outdoor buffet serving.

• **DISHWASHER,** *Silverware Basket "Leaks":* Put a piece of nylon net into the bottom of the dishwasher silverware basket if you have small-handled pieces that seem to poke through and possibly interfere with the rotating sprayer in the bottom of the dishwasher.

• **DISHWASHER,** *When Water-force Flips Lightweight Cups:* To stop cups from flipping over and getting filled with water and sediment, line up the cup handles and run a ¼-inch dowel pin through them. Dowel pins are sold in most hardware stores.

• **DISHWASHER DETERGENT,** *Letter of Laughter:* Responding to one of my columns warning not to put regular liquid detergent in a dishwasher, a reader says that while she was in the hospital for surgery, her husband ran their dishwasher with liquid detergent. Her eldest daughter came home to find suds bubbling and flowing from the dishwasher so fast that they had to close all inside doors and open the back one—suds filled the kitchen and rolled out the back door, filling the porch and driveway. Her daughter's comment was "when Dad cleans, he cleans the kitchen and yard, too!" Dad was kidded about it, but he's not the first and I'm sure not the last person to clean the whole kitchen at one time this way!
Another *Letter of Laughter:* This story prompted a reader to tell how her sister decided to make wine and was feeling pretty successful until all the corks started blowing off, one after the other. Instead of a "cleaning mess" she had a real mess. Fortunately, the novice winemaker had a sense of humor and had a good laugh since it reminded her of an *I Love Lucy* episode!

• **DISHWASHER RACK,** *Repair vs. Replacing Rusty Ones $aver:* A commercial liquid plastic product made just for dishwasher rack repair is available from appliance or dishwasher service stores. It comes in several colors to match different brands.

• **DISHWASHING FACTS,** *Healthy-Planet Water and Energy Saving:* An efficient automatic dishwasher, properly used, consumes less hot water and less energy than hand-washing, according to the Texas Energy Extension Service at Texas A&M University.

1. You use a lot of water and energy if you wash dishes and rinse them in running hot water; less if you wash in one pan and rinse in another.

2. New dishwashers have "air dry" or "energy miser" buttons. These features save you money because they turn off heat during drying.

3. Dishwashers with booster heaters allow you to get hotter water for dishes than elsewhere in the house. You won't have to keep your water heater set as high.

4. Look for dishwashers that can dispose of food residue so that you don't have to rinse dishes before putting them into the dishwasher. Just take a used paper napkin or a rubber spatula and wipe off solids and let the machine do its work. **Note:** If your dishwasher consistently leaves residue on your dishes, check for blocked drainage along the line, including your main kitchen drain pipe/sewer line.

• **DISHWASHING SPONGE,** *Keeping Fresh and Clean:* Clip it to the top shelf of the dishwasher at the end of the day so that it won't fall to the bottom and damage the machine while the dishwasher's hot water and detergent deodorizes and cleans it.

• **DOCTOR SELECTION,** *Checklist:* The time to look for a physician or dentist is before you need one in an emergency when there's no time to choose. When you move into a new community inquire with a local medical or dental society or association for reference and ask neighbors, friends, and business associates. It's not easy to choose and remember that you can always change your mind if you don't like your first choice.

1. Check the doctor's background to find out the medical/dental school attended and if the doctor is a board-certified specialist in the area in which you need care.

2. Check the patient scheduling. Look for one that schedules enough time for visits so that you aren't rushed and have time to ask questions. Write down your questions and the answers, too. Also, if you want to avoid waiting, sometimes getting the first appointment of the day helps avoid delays from other patients'

unanticipated problems. **Note:** Also, if you have come to a physician for a cold, don't expect time for a complete all-encompassing physical examination. Different times are scheduled for different patient needs and procedures. (It's like calling the plumber over to replace a faucet washer and then asking for replacement of all the bathroom fixtures.)

3. Does the physician or dental surgeon have privileges in a hospital or surgical center that's close and meets your needs?

4. If you have special beliefs regarding medical care or medical preferences, find a doctor who will work with you. Often state or local laws vary on such subjects and you should put your last wishes in writing as well as tell your physician and relatives and give them copies of your written wishes.

• **DOG,** *Curing Car Sickness:* Common with puppies, car sickness can be outgrown more easily if you take your dog on fifteen-minute trips every other day or so, then increase the time gradually.

• **DOG,** *How to Tell If It's Too Fat:* At ideal weight, you should be able to feel a pet's ribs with your fingers without pressing. Generally, if you can see the pet's ribs, it is underweight. In either case, don't put your dog on a weight-loss or weight-gain diet with prescription foods or other schemes without your vet's advice.

• **DOG,** *Identification, Letter of Laughter:* The parents of a four-year-old son were passed during their walk by a man with a dog. "What kind of a dog is that," the child asked. "A bird dog," the mom replied. "Can it fly, Mommy, can it fly?" the child asked.

• **DOG,** *Introducing It to a New Baby:* Long before baby is born, teach the dog simple controlling commands like "sit" and "stay." While baby is still in the hospital, take home a blanket or article of clothing the baby has worn and let the dog get familiar with the baby's scent. Dogs will be curious about the crying sounds baby makes. It would help to have a tape of a crying baby to let the dog grow accustomed to that sound. **Caution:** Never leave a baby and pet alone. A dog or cat can jump a gate so one favorite hint is to put a screen door on baby's room so you can see and hear, but pets are kept out.

• **DOG BATH,** *Stopping "the Shakes":* Try firmly grasping the dog around his nose. For some dogs, "the shake" starts there—so, if they can't shake their noses, they can't shake anything else either. You'll stay dryer and have less mess.

• **DOG BIRTHING BED:** A child's small plastic swimming pool makes a good puppy-birthing bed. It's easy to clean, has no sharp edges; the dog can step over the side, but tiny puppies will stay in. *Letter of Laughter:* I considered suggesting this bed for mama cats, too, but I've heard so many tales of cats giving birth in peculiar places— dresser drawers, atop a neighbor's roof, under the bed, in a closet shoe-pile, in the backseat of a neighbor's car (he'll never leave windows open again!), I thought the suggestion might be futile!

• **DOG DISH,** *Keeping the Dog from Tipping It Over:*
1. For Outdoor Feeding: Buy a tube baking pan and put it over a stake you've driven into the ground. You can put food or water into the pan and the dog can't tip it.
2. Put dog food or water into heavy-based, widemouthed crocks.

• **DOG DRINK:** When you take your dog in the car, take also a small plastic water bowl or a bowl made by cutting off the bottom of a gallon milk jug and a jug of water. Then, you can "water" the dog when it's thirsty.

• **DOG EARS,** *Keeping Them out of Doggie's Dinner:* A reader wrote that she puts a stretchable headband over her cocker spaniel's head, tucking his ears under it, and he's so interested in eating that he doesn't notice.

• **DOG, HEARTWORM PILLS:** Heartworm pills are now given all year round instead of just summer as was the custom in the past. (Infected mosquitoes, carriers of the disease, have been found indoors when it was 7 degrees below zero outside!) If your dog hates the pill, wrap it in half of a cheese slice. (Wrap the cheese around the pill, then hold the wad in your palm for a minute and you'll have a pill-stuffed cheese ball that fools the dog into eagerly eating it.) Or coat the pill with peanut butter or liverwurst if that's what your dog likes. Pills are available in daily or monthly doses; ask your vet for advice.

• **DOGHOUSE,** *Winterizing:* A reader wrote that the first night's freeze made the leftover carpet placed on the floor of her dog's house wet and frosty—unsuitable for the dog to sleep on. So her husband built a platform about 10 inches high to elevate the house from the cold ground and removed the carpet. Instead, they put tar paper on the floor, covered it with layers of newspaper, then topped it all with a layer of hay. This insulation kept the dog warm and dry.

• **DOG SWEATER,** *Recycling $aver:* For a small dog, recycle an old ski mask so that the dog's front paws go through the eye holes and its head goes through a hole you open in the seam at the mask's top. The dog's tail wags from the neckhole, of course, to thank you for the warmth and kindness!

• **DOG TRAINING:** Praise is the key—pat, hug, and tell your dog "What a good dog!" when it responds properly to training, and reward it immediately with a treat. Hitting only teaches fear to an animal and is not training—it's abuse.

• **DOLL DISPLAY STAND,** *Recycling $aver:* Dolls with small bodies and full skirts can stand up in a widemouthed mayonnaise jar. The bonus is that the jar makes a good skirt hoop.

• **DOLLS,** *Cleaning Adoptable Ones:* **Caution:** While some people wash them in the machine, I must stress that you do it at your own risk and only when the doll is heavily soiled and all other cleaning attempts have failed.
Step 1: Remove all clothing, ribbons, and accessories. Pre-treat heavily soiled areas with pre-wash spray. Put the doll in a pillow-case and close it by tying a knot in the open end.
Step 2: Place the pillowcase in the washing machine, set on a gentle cycle, add warm water and regular laundry detergent. Add a few sheets or towels in with the doll to cushion the bumping.
Step 3: After the washing cycle is complete, remove the pillowcased doll and place it directly into the clothes dryer on low heat for about 10 minutes. After 10 minutes in the dryer, remove the doll from the pillowcase and place it in a well-ventilated area to finish drying overnight.

• **DOLLS,** *Special Clothes for Keepsake Dolls:* Buy a doll from a craft store and make doll clothes that resemble clothing worn for special occasions in the doll collector's life—First Communion, first day of school, etc.

• **DOMINOES CONTAINER,** *Recycling:* Wash and dry a white or colored (just not a see-through plastic) gallon-size plastic jug and cut an opening in the top-half opposite the handle large enough to admit an adult's hand. Then you can keep dominoes in the jug and pass it from player to player to draw from. Passing the jug also speeds up alphabet word games and the jug can also be safe storage so that you don't lose pieces.

• **DOORBELLS,** *For Children and Pets:* Hang a row of small bells on the doorknob so you can hear if children open the door to go out, especially if you have adventuresome toddlers. Also, if your pet scratches the door to go out, it will ring the bells so that you'll always hear the pet's pleas for relief and avoid pet "accidents." *Letter of Laughter:* These bells could be a problem if you have a cockatiel like the one belonging to one of my readers. "Clyde" thinks he's human and answers phone rings with "Hello, hello" and doorbell rings with "Come in." Strangers walk in if the door isn't locked!

• **DOORKNOB GUARD,** *For Toddlers:* Secure an old sock on the doorknob with a rubber band. Adults can open the door but when toddlers try to turn the knob, the sock slides around and prevents a child from getting a good grip on the knob. Or, buy a commercial device that fits over the knob and works the same way.

• **DOOR LOCKS,** *Deadbolt-Lock Checklist:*
1. The bolt should extend at least 1 inch from the edge of the door. (This is called a "1-inch throw.")
2. The connecting screws holding the lock together are on the INSIDE of the door.
3. The strike plate is attached to the door frame with screws that are at least 3 inches long.
4. The cylinder has a steel guard—a ring around the key section. The cylinder guard needs to be tapered or to rotate around the key section when twisted to prevent wrenching.

• **DOOR LOCKS,** *Outside Doors:* Deadbolt locks which need latchkeys inside and out to operate them are the most secure but those which can be opened from the inside without a latchkey are considered safer in case of fire; some communities have safety codes restricting inside/outside latchkey-only deadbolt locks. Check with local building inspectors or other suitable authorities.

• **DOOR LOCKS,** *Quick-Fix:* A lock may not be broken, just stuck. To unstick locks and to keep them working well, squirt the lock mechanism at the door's edge regularly with lubricant.

• **DOOR LOCKS,** *Safety:* Locks provide security only if you use them. Get in the habit of locking doors even if you leave the house for only a few minutes.

• **DOOR LOCKS,** *Types Available and Uses:*
1. Double Cylinder Deadbolt Lock: Placed on doors with glass panels or on all doors, they can be opened only with a key from either side. You can keep the key near the door but make sure it can't be reached from the glass panel; intruders won't be able to break the glass and get the key, but your family can get out in case of fire. Before installing these, check with local law enforcement agencies because some communities restrict use of these locks.
2. Police Lock: For rear and basement entrances and apartments, this is a metal bar bracketed against the inside of the door at an angle; it slides into a small hole on the floor and prevents burglars from jimmying the lock or kicking in the door.
3. Padlocks: Usually used for garages, sheds, and workshops; buy sturdy padlocks that don't release the key until the lock is locked. A padlock should have a rugged laminated case with ⅜-inch shackle so it can resist smashing. A padlock is only as good as its mounting hasp, which should be secured with bolts and mounted on a metal plate. Bolts must be concealed when the padlock is locked.

• **DOOR, LOUVERED PANEL,** *Quick-Fix, No-mess Cleaning:* If the louvered panel on a door to a hot-water heater, furnace, or air-conditioning unit is screwed in place, carefully unscrew the screws, remove the panel and wash it in a sink or tub of warm sudsy water with a soft scrub brush. Rinse, wipe dry, and replace. Trust me, removing the panel for cleaning is much easier than leaving it in place and then making a mess on the floor while you spray on cleaning solution and try to clean the louvers.

• **DOORS,** *Avoiding Frustration and Embarrassment:* Ever feel silly pushing on a door you're supposed to pull open? When you approach an unfamiliar door, scan the frame to see if the hinges are on the inside (PUSH) or outside (PULL).

• **DOORS,** *Recycling Old Ones:* Add legs and paint and you have a desk or table. The height is up to you.

• **DOOR SAFETY,** *Quick-Fix:* Prevent small children from slamming or closing doors on their little fingers—throw a thick folded towel over the tops of doors so they won't close completely.

• **DOORS & DRAWERS,** *Quick-Fix with Hardware:* New hardware gives your kitchen or bathroom a new look. Before you buy do the following.
1. Be sure to measure drawer handle spreads so that you can use the existing holes when attaching the new handles.
2. If you want to switch from handles to knobs, buy backplates to cover the old handle-holes and then drill a new hole in the center for the knob.

• **DOUBLE BOILER:** If you place a small jar lid into the bottom of a double boiler, the rattling sounds will warn you when the water is getting too low. Marbles work, too, but be prepared for quizzical looks if, when someone asks, "What's that noise," and you reply, "I'm boiling my marbles." They may think you've lost your marbles! **Note:** Someone once told me that your mind is like a cartridge and ideas are like marbles. When your cartridge (mind) gets too full with too many marbles (ideas) some of them start to spill out and that's where we get the expression, "losing your marbles." However, I haven't been able to verify this with my usual sources.

• **DOWN-FILLED GARMENTS,** *To Wash or Not to Wash, That Is the Confusion:* The International Fabricare Institute and most garment manufacturers recommend that down-filled garments be dry cleaned. As always consult the care label for exact instructions for your particular garment.

• **DRAFT GUARDS,** *Recycling:* Make draft guards for doorjambs and window sills by filling with sand double- or triple-thicknesses of newspaper bags; tie the open end securely with a twist-tie, and then put the "snake" into a long tube sock.

• **DRAPERY CORDS,** *Quick-Fix Identifying Open and Close:* Either put pieces of colored tape or a dab of colored nail polish on the cord that opens the drapes, or take the letters left over from video-tapes to stick "open" on one cord or "o" and "c" for open and close.

• **DRAPES,** *Easy Way, Removing Dust and Freshening:* When drapes need a good dusting but not actual cleaning, you can toss most washable fabric drapes into the dryer with a fabric-softener sheet. Set the dryer on "Air Fluff."

• **DRAWER KNOBS & PULLS,** *"Decorator" Substitutes:*
1. Toy blocks with holes drilled for the screws can go on a child's dresser. Some craft shops sell these already drilled.
2. Small wooden blocks and large beads used for macrame craft already have holes for screws and make novel pulls.

• **DRAWER ORGANIZERS,** *Quick-Fix When They Slide:* When plastic silverware organizers slide around in a kitchen drawer, keep them in place with double-sided adhesive tape. You can still remove them for cleaning.

• **DRESSES,** *Hanging Those with Spaghetti Straps:* Don't hang by the straps; they aren't strong enough to support the garment's weight, especially if the fabric is extra heavy like velvet or satin.
1. If the manufacturer has not attached long loops of seam binding to the upper side seams for hanging, make some with seam binding or woven hem facing. Be sure to tack them to the side seam allowance.
2. Or, hang over a pants hanger at the waist.
3. Or, clip the bodice to a skirt hanger. Be sure to put foam padding under the clips to prevent crushing or marring velvet, satin, or silk.

• **DRESSER DRAWERS,** *Identifying Which Drawer Holds What for Young Children:* Tape pictures of clothing (cut from catalogs) on the drawers to help young children put their laundry away in the right places. And, sitters can see at a glance where everything is.

• **DRIED FRUIT,** *Baking:* When a recipe requires cutting dried fruit, it's faster and easier to spray scissor blades with non-stick cooking spray and snip fruit into small pieces.

- **DRIVEWAY OIL STAINS,** *Quick-Fix:* Try spraying engine degreaser. Apply; let set about 10 minutes; wash away with a garden hose. Also, please see CAT LITTER.

- **DRY-CLEANER'S BAGS,** *Recycling:*
1. Tie a knot in the end, turn the bag inside out, and it will line a tall trash basket. You can insert a paper grocery bag to prevent things from poking through. Or you can double bag for heavier paper trash.
2. Put bags on clothing to be packed in hanging-type bags when you travel. It helps prevent crushing and helps prevent clothing from getting wet if rain should fall on the zipper area. You can also stuff bags into sleeve arms to prevent crushing.

- **DRYER,** *Quick-Fix, Cleaning the Lint Trap:* A baby-bottle brush sweeps the filter clean with one whisk.

- **DRYER,** *Quick-Fix When Seal Is Broken:* Self-adhesive weather-stripping will replace a broken dryer door seal if you can't get an "official" one from an appliance parts store.

- **DRYING RACK,** *Recycling Idea:* Please see FAN GRATE, Recycling and BABY EXPANDABLE GATE.

- **DUST,** *Removing from Corners and Crevices:* Secure an old sock on a yardstick with rubber bands and poke it into hard-to-reach places like under or behind the fridge. You can also reach cobwebs in corners with it.

- **DUST BRUSH:** An animal hair pastry brush or natural bristle paint-brush removes dust from the inside corners of picture frames, light bulbs and globes, chandelier chains, bric-a-brac, cloth lamp shades, pleated tops of draperies, and other nooks and crannies.

- **DUST MOP,** *Shaking Off Dust:* If the dust from your mop drifts onto your neighbor's porch or apartment balcony, you can help the environment and your neighbor's disposition by tying a paper bag around your mop before shaking it. The bag will collect the "dust bunnies."

- **DUST MOPS:**
1. When synthetic strands of yarn on your dust mop are all tangled from laundering, insert the mop into an old pillow case or make a

large "pocket" from an old towel. (Fold in half and sew up the sides, leaving the ends open.) You can spray the mop "pocket" with a dust magnet product before dusting and then launder it afterward so that you always have a clean mop.

2. To dust walls and remove cobwebs from corners, place an old pillowcase or your "towel case" over a broom or mop head.

• **DUST PREVENTION,** *On Party Crystal and Trays:* Cover them with plastic wrap when you put them away and they'll stay clean between parties. **Note:** This may seem like a waste of disposable wrap but the rule of thumb is that if water is scarce in your area, you use disposables at parties to avoid excess washing water waste. If water is abundant, you avoid disposables to save landfill space.

• **DUST RUFFLES,** *Keeping in Place:* Slipping, sliding dust ruffles can be kept in their place if you sew them on to an old fitted sheet or quilted mattress pad either by machine or hand-tacking. The fitted sheet will hold tight to the box spring.

- **EARRINGS,** *Avoiding Pain from Clip Backs:*
1. Place spongy nose pads sold in optical shops on the clip part and a piece of moleskin on the back of the earring.
2. Cut to fit small moleskin adhesive pads (those made for protecting corns and blisters) and stick them on the offending earring back and the front of the clip so that the pads "sandwich" your poor, suffering earlobe.

- **EARRINGS,** *Holding Them Straight, Recycling:* Cut small circles from plastic lids, such as from coffee cans, and place them behind your ear on the pierced-earring post before you put the back on. You can also buy clear plastic disks for this purpose at costume jewelry stores.

- **EARRINGS,** *Pierced:* Putting a bit of antibiotic ointment on the posts helps earrings go in easier and helps to prevent skin irritation.

- **EARRINGS,** *Prevent Loss:* If you take off your hook-style pierced earrings at the gym or doctor's office, poke them into a plastic foam "packing peanut" so the wires don't get bent or lost. When traveling, poke them through one-half of a washcloth and then fold the other half over them for protection.

• EARRINGS, *Recycling When You Lose One of a Pair:*
1. Poke posts through scarfs or knit ties to hold them in place.
2. A button-style pierced earring can be a stud for a missing button or a small lapel pin.
3. Turn an earring "dangle" into a small pendant and hang it like a charm on a bracelet or necklace.
4. If you have several leftover dangle earrings put them all together on a charm holder (sold at jewelry counters in silver or gold) and then put the holder on a chain or velvet ribbon for a multi-piece "pendant."
5. Poke large earrings through the screen door to prevent people from "walking through it" when it's closed—a special problem with sliding screen doors.
6. Break or cut off posts from the earring back; glue the earring "button" with a hot glue gun to a plain gold or silver ring and you have a new piece of jewelry.

• EARRINGS, *Recycling Single Clip-on:* If you clip a lone clip-on earring to a plain gold or silver chain it's a pendant.

• EARRINGS, *Storage:* Inexpensive, lightweight, clear plastic fishing tackle boxes will store many pairs of pierced earrings for easy selection. Some have twenty or more compartments, each with enough space for several pairs of similar earrings.

• EARRINGS, *Storing Pierced:* Poke them through anything—an old necktie, place mat, fabric belt, greeting card, strips of ribbon from gifts, a not-so perky scarf, a sock, a sentimental baby T-shirt, and on and on. The idea is to avoid losing earrings while recycling.

• EARS, *Cleaning Behind Children's, Letter of Laughter:* A reader whose sons "grow dirt behind their ears," and who complain that it hurts when she tries to rub or scrub them, found a solution. She dots baby fragrance petroleum jelly behind their ears and rubs it in—her sons smell sweet and their ears are spotless the next day.

• EASTER BASKET GRASS, *Substitute:* Instead of plastic/paper grass which seems to get everywhere before it's finally discarded, try a skein of rug yarn. Undo the wrapper, fluff it up, add eggs, bunnies, and other clean items. The bonus is that you can save it for next Easter or crochet or knit with it later in the year. Or, buy only green yarn instead of purple and yellow so that you can tie up Christmas packages with it later on.

• **EASTER BASKETS,** *Healthy-Planet $aver:* Instead of buying baskets which just get broken and thrown away, buy useful items to hold Easter goodies such as bicycle baskets, a football helmet or baseball cap, special milk mugs or cereal bowls, or anything else your imagination conjures up.

• **EASTER BASKETS,** *Substitutes for Adults and Older Children:* Fill a straw or other hat; a small trash can; a mug; collector glass; flying disk; nut bowl. For non-sweets eaters, substitute cheese and crackers, fruit and nuts, travel-size cosmetics, lunch snacks, cassette tapes, or a plant.

• **EASTER BASKETS,** *Using Them Year-round:* Fill with fruit and make a centerpiece; have it hold powder, lotion, and pins in the nursery; clippers, pins, scissors, etc. in the bathroom; spices and other small things on the kitchen counter; the remote control, TV-listing guide and your eyeglasses atop of the TV. Serve hard-boiled eggs in Easter baskets any time of the year.

• **EASTER EGGS,** *Healthy-Planet Dyes:* Boil eggs with onion peels to make them yellow, with spinach or turnip tops to make them green, with a fresh beet to make them red, or add a package of unsweetened powdered drink mix to the pot.

• **EGG,** *Quick-Fix When a Piece of Broken Shell Is in Food or Recipe Ingredients:* Tried and true is to scoop out the piece of shell with one of the larger pieces of the eggshell.

• **EGG,** *Quick-Fix When You Drop One on the Floor:* If you don't have an eager dog or cat to lick it up, pour salt over the broken egg, let it set for about 15 minutes. Cleanup is a cinch!

• **EGG CARTON,** *Recycling:* Place a cardboard or plastic foam egg carton, spread open, into the bottom of a plastic trash bag when you put it into the can. It will prevent the bottom from getting soggy and tearing.

• **EGG SUBSTITUTE IN CAKE:** If a cake recipe calls for two eggs and you discover that you have only one, substitute two tablespoons of mayonnaise for the missing egg.

• **EGGS,** *Cascarones "Confetti Eggs" Decorating:* Popular in my hometown, San Antonio, at Fiesta time, they are easily made.
1. Whenever you use a fresh egg, don't crack the shell in half; instead carefully poke a pin or thumbtack hole in the small end and with a spoon tap out a dime-size hole in the opposite larger end.
2. Hold the egg over a bowl and blow into the pin hole, forcing the egg out the dime-size hole or use a baby bulb syringe to "blow" it out. Gently run water into the empty eggshell to rinse it out, and place it on paper towels to dry.
3. Decorate the eggshells with dye or paint and fill the inside with confetti. After inserting confetti, paste a small piece of tissue paper over the larger opening to hold it in.
4. Have a Fiesta party and pop Cascarones atop the head of some-one for a lot of laughs and a lot of flying confetti. At Fiesta, you know someone really cares when he or she cracks a cascarone over your head! Olé!

• **EGGS,** *Easy Semi-poached, No Broken Yolks:* Spray the pan lightly with non-stick vegetable spray, fry eggs until the whites are barely set, then add about one tablespoon of water. Cover tightly and turn heat down very low. It won't take long at all!

• **EGGS,** *Identifying Cooked:* There's no rule that says you can color eggs only at Easter. Add a few drops of food coloring or onion skins to the water when you cook them and the colored eggs will be the cooked eggs. P.S. Onion skins make a nice mottled marbled look!

• **EGGS,** *Identifying Cooked Ones by Spinning:* Hard-boiled ones spin and raw ones will wobble.

• **EGGS,** *Identifying Fresh:* Just mark the old ones with a pencil when you add new ones to the Fridge. The American Egg Board advises keeping eggs in their original cartons for best preservation and to keep them from absorbing odors.

- **EGGS,** *Rolling Down the Counter:* Stop run-a-way eggs when you are cooking—sprinkle a few grains of salt or sugar on the counter, place the egg on it and it will stay put.

- **EGGS,** *Separating Yolks from Whites:*
Method 1: Hold a funnel over a container and break the egg into it. The white slides into the container and the yolk stays in the funnel.
Method 2: Break the egg into a small bowl, then lift the yolk out with a large slotted spoon.

- **EGGS,** *Substituting Egg Whites for Whole Eggs in Baking:* When two egg whites are substitutes for one whole egg, you need to add one tablespoon of oil and one and one-third tablespoons of liquid in your recipe to make up for the fat in the egg yolk. One reader saves all the yolks she removes from whole eggs in a plastic bag. When the bag is full, she cooks the egg yolks in a greased microwave dish and sets the "egg casserole" out for wild animals to eat. Raccoons, opossums and even foxes feast at her country home.

- **EGGS,** *White vs. Brown for Nutrition and Price:* The American Egg Board has the final word to dispel an "old wives' tale" that's been around as long as the "Which came first, the chicken or the egg" riddle.
    Eggshell and yolk color may vary but color has nothing to do with the quality or nutritive value of an egg. The breed of hen determines the shell color. White breeds lay white eggs; brown or reddish-brown breeds (such as Rhode Island Red, New Hampshire and Plymouth Rock) lay brown eggs. Most Americans want white eggs but in some parts of the country, especially in New England, brown shells are preferred.
    Generally, brown eggs cost more because the breeds that lay them are larger and require more feed, therefore the market price is higher. But why pay more for brown shells when you eat the inside of the egg not the outside?

- **EGGS, DEVILED,** *Expanding Filling:* To make the halves fuller, add about one-third cup of low-fat cottage cheese to six eggs' worth of yolk-filling. Mash all together, add usual seasonings and you'll have enough filling to make a nice mound in each half.

- **EGGS, DOUBLE-YOLK:** The American Egg Board says usually double-yolk egg yolks are smaller than regular yolks and so can be substituted one for the other.

- **ELBOW GREASE,** *Generation Gap Gaff, Letter of Laughter:* After I'd used the term "elbow grease" in a column, a reader shopping in the supermarket overheard a young woman asking the store manager where she could find the "elbow grease" she'd read about in Heloise's column. He thought she was kidding until a second shopper came up and said, "That's what I'm looking for too!" Neither shopper had ever heard the term before and thought it was a new product. When the first Heloise fan explained to them that it was a term meaning a good old-fashioned rubbing and scrubbing, they all had a good laugh, and so did I when I heard about this generation gap gaff. But, wouldn't it be wonderful if somebody would package "elbow grease" so you wouldn't have to use all of your own?

- **ELECTRIC BLANKETS,** *Washing:* If you've lost the instructions that came with the blanket, the following notes are usually safe.
1. Check care label for instructions and unplug the electrical control from the blanket before washing.
2. You CAN wash it in an automatic washer, but NOT in a coin-operated dry-cleaning machine. DO NOT dry in a dryer.
3. Long wash or spin cycles can damage the blanket. First fill the washing machine with warm water and add a mild detergent. Let the machine agitate on a gentle cycle until detergent is dissolved. Add the blanket and let it wash for three or four minutes. After the rinse cycle and the machine drains, set the load for a short spin cycle. Repeat the rinse cycle and a short spin cycle again.
4. Remove the blanket and press any remaining water out with your hands.
5. Lay over a clothesline (or a couple of lines if it is a king- or queen-size blanket) to dry in the fresh air and sun. *Letter of Laughter:* When a couple bought a dual-control electric blanket, they were disappointed because he complained that his side was too hot and she said her side was too cold. For a week they adjusted control knobs, he turning his down and she turning hers up until they decided that the blanket was defective. Then, when changing the sheets—you guessed it—she realized that his control was on her

side of the bed and hers was on his side. She had been "roasting" him and he had been "cooling" her. I'll bet that's not the first time this has happened!

• **ELECTRICAL EXTENSION CORDS,** *Healthy-Planet Recycling Storage:* Instead of rubber bands or twist-ties, bind cords neatly with toilet-paper or paper-towel rolls. Write the length on the roll so you don't have to guess.

• **ELECTRICAL SAFETY:** If you have turned off a circuit breaker to do electrical work at home, tape a sign on the circuit breaker that says, DO NOT TURN ON, to prevent people with good intentions from flipping the switch and causing you harm.

• **ELDER HELPER,** *In Apartments:* In apartment complexes where many elderly people live and watch out for each other, many have the custom of putting a red bandana or other marker on the doorknob at night and then removing it in the morning as a signal that all is well in that apartment. If the bandana is still on the doorknob by midday or afternoon, someone checks on the person who lives in that apartment to see if all is okay.

• **ELDER HELPER,** *When Eyesight Is Poor:* Write letters in large, bold print. Some eye conditions make red felt tip pen easier to see than black. Then include a self-addressed, stamped envelope with the letter so that the elder can write back with less trouble.

• **ELDER HELPER,** *When Fingers Fumble:* When fingers won't button shirts, sew a seam from the second button from the top down to the next-to-last button so that the shirt can be pulled on overhead.

• **EMBROIDERY FLOSS,** *Storing:* You can wrap floss on cardboard spools when it's long enough but, to store shorter strands, buy nine-pocket plastic sheets used to display baseball card collections and you can insert the label with color number along with the leftover pieces of floss. Keep pages in a three-ring binder and just remove the page when you need to take samples to the store for matching or coordinating colors.

• **EMBROIDERY THREAD HOLDER:** Wrap the thread around the post of a permanent wave roller—a separate roller for each color—and clip it in place. It's easy to remove the clip when you need more thread.

• **EMERGENCIES,** *Calling:* When you report an emergency or crime, you'll get faster results if you do the following:
1. If your city does not have a dial 911 emergency system, have the emergency number taped to your phone so it can't be lost or, if you have a programmable phone, program emergency numbers into it and clearly mark the emergency button.
2. When you call, try to remain calm and say "I want to report a (robbery, suspicious person, fire). You will be asked: Where, When, Describe person or situation? Weapons present? Injuries? Which way did the criminal run?
3. Get the number or name of the operator who took the information so that if you call again with more information you can give it to the same person and save time repeating what was originally reported.
4. Do call back if the situation changes or if you get more information. Remember, because of computerized communications systems, a police car can be on the way before you finish your first call; any additional information will be forwarded and can help.
5. Try to remember the description if a car is involved (color, make, any damaged parts) and if you can only get part of a license plate number, the first three numbers are more important than the last three.
6. Install lighting between houses if you live in a city neighborhood.
7. Place your house numbers on the rear of your home if you have a back alley to help police and firefighters identify your house.
8. Cooperate with local Neighborhood Watch organizations or help start one if your city promotes them.
9. If you are victimized, cooperate by going to line-ups and court.
10. Rehearse emergency procedures with your family and emphasize the seriousness of false alarms to children.

• **EMERGENCIES,** *Checklist for Getting Proper Medical Care:* When should we go to an emergency room, urgent care center, call the doctor for an appointment or just wait and see? With the different deductibles on medical insurances, cost of different facilities is as much a worry as the illness itself. The Mayo Clinic Health Letter advises the following.

Seek emergency care when you are ill or in pain if there is:
1. Chest pain or upper abdominal pain or pressure.
2. Sudden, severe pain anywhere in your body or sudden severe headache with no prior history.
3. Dizziness, sudden weakness or sudden change in vision.
4. Severe or persistent vomiting.
5. Difficult breathing or shortness of breath.
6. Fainting or feeling faint.
7. Suicidal or homicidal feelings.
Call your doctor for an appointment if there is:
1. Unexplained weight loss.
2. Lump in your breast.
3. Blood in your urine.
4. Abdominal cramps lasting two weeks.
Wait and see if you have:
1. Vomited once in six hours; no fever, pain or other symptoms.
Note: Age, past medical history, and other conditions change what is "wait and see" for one person as compared to others. Chances are that if you think your symptoms are an emergency, they are and you shouldn't delay getting medical attention. The sooner a doctor treats your illness, the better the chance for a good outcome.

• EMERGENCY, *Personal Affairs Checklist:* In case of an emergency, keep an up-to-date list for your family. Include:
A copy of will and trust agreements; doctor and hospital information; family records (births, marriage, divorce, social security, military service, citizenship); insurance policy information (numbers, agent, beneficiaries); funeral information (preferences, location of cemetery plots, deeds, etc.); safe-deposit box (key and location, person authorized to open it); bank account (number, locations); debts (your own and owed to you); pension plans, IRAs, Keoghs, financial/legal advisors' names and phone numbers, brokerage accounts (with brokers' name and phone number); all business records; all charge accounts. **Note:** Keep irreplaceable documents in a safe-deposit box but keep copies for your home records. Remember

that a safe-deposit box can be sealed when a person dies so that important information may not be available when it's most needed, such as funeral preferences, wills, etc.

• **ENERGY,** *Checklist for Saving on Cooling Costs:*
1. Leaving lights on, especially incandescent bulbs which furnish more heat than light, makes your AC run harder. Please remember to switch them off.
2. Change the AC filter at least monthly, or more often if you have shedding pets, to reduce the load on the AC unit and therefore cut costs.
3. Set your AC thermostat no lower than 78° F and in some climates, shut off the AC and open windows to use cool evening breezes.
4. Close off humidity-producing kitchen, bathroom and laundry areas to keep moisture from the rest of the house. You'll feel cooler in dryer air.
5. When you shower, open the bathroom window or turn on the exhaust vent if you have one to let moisture out.
6. Cover pots on the stove to confine heat and humidity. Covering the pot makes the contents heat up faster, too, so the stove won't be heating the room as long. (But then your mother told you that!) And, to save even more energy, if you turn off the electric stove 3 minutes before you're done cooking, it will stay hot for at least that long.
7. Warm air rises so open second floor and attic windows to let heat escape. In the evening when it's cool, you can let the cooler air into the house and close the windows early in the morning to keep the cool air inside.
8. A large window fan uses one-fourth the energy and costs one-fifth as much as an AC to operate. Placing one in an attic window can push hot air out and draw cooler air in through downstairs windows.
9. When buying an AC unit, bigger is not always better. Look for the Seasonal Energy Efficiency Rating (SEER)—the higher the number, the more cooling efficiency you'll get for electricity costs.
10. AC units work more efficiently when installed on the shady side of your house. Some people shade their units with awnings or trees.

Awnings, of course, also help to keep hot sun from shining into windows.

• **ENERGY,** *Checklist for Saving Cooling Costs for Apartment Dwellers:* For some apartment dwellers, window units are energy and utility bill demons.

1. If your apartment has a room AC unit, check the filter now and clean or replace it. Clogged filters make the unit run longer than needed and operate inefficiently. If you can do it safely, clean the condenser coils and fins (those grills on the outdoor side of the unit).

2. Set the temperature control no lower than 78°F and don't set the control to a cooler temperature at start-up. It won't cool the room faster and you may forget to set the control lower once the room is comfortable, thus wasting energy. Most window units don't have specific degree settings so place a thermometer somewhere in the room away from the AC air flow to get an accurate temperature reading.

3. Remember that lamps, TV sets or other heat sources placed near a window unit can cause it to run longer than necessary.

4. A window fan uses as little as one-tenth the energy of an air conditioner, so buying one to bring cool air into your apartment is good energy economy.

5. If your AC unit has an outside air control to bring in fresh air, you can use it without using the cooling mechanism. The unit's compressor motor guzzles the energy guzzler, not the fan. But remember to close the outside air control when you start cooling again.

• **ENERGY,** *Checklist for Saving on Heating Costs:*

1. Turn down the heat to 60°F in unoccupied rooms. Do this by closing duct covers, turning down radiators or the thermostat if the room has its own.

2. If you have the oven on in the kitchen for a long period of time (baking Christmas cookies, etc.) close off your kitchen hot air duct—you'll get enough heat from the oven.

3. If everyone will be away from home for eight or more hours, turn down the heat at least 8°F. The first one home can turn it back up.

4. When you are snug under a comforter at night, you can have the temperature reduced to 61° to 64°F.

5. If you have a programmable thermostat you can set it so the heat will go off and on when it's needed, resulting in lower heating costs and less fuel waste. Heating costs increase by 5 percent for each degree you set your thermostat above 68°F.

6. Cover all cracks in doors and windows to prevent heat from escaping. Get the children in on this project—they can be "air-leak police." Have them take a six-inch piece of ribbon or strip of paper and hold it near places at windows where air may be escaping, then make a map showing where these drafts are so that the family can stop them.

7. In newer homes, power ventilators cool the attic in the summer. Turn them off in the winter to prevent their drawing warm air up from the house. Such warm moist air can also cause frost buildup and damage in the attic.

8. If you don't like to sleep under an electric blanket or with a heating pad, use them to pre-heat your bed and turn them off when you get in—wearing warm PJs and socks, of course!

• **ENERGY RATING YOUR HOME:** In some cities public utility companies offer free energy-efficiency checks; others charge a minimal fee. If a utility company does an energy check for you, the results will be mailed along with recommendations for improvements, estimates of how much such changes would cost initially and what your long-term savings would be.

1. To be an energy miser, check if your home has adequate insulation in the attic and walls; weatherstripping and caulking in good condition; the proper insulation and temperature setting for your hot-water heater.

2. Check if appliances, heaters and air conditioners are operating efficiently. When you replace these items, look at the energy ratings on their tags before you buy.

Please see energy checklists above.

• **ENGAGEMENT CALENDARS,** *Recycling Pretty-covered Old Ones:* Convert them into specialized recipe collections. Copy recipes in bold print on appropriately sized blank cards and then paste the cards over used pages of past engagements. You can arrange recipes alphabetically or by general subject and put a tab on the first page of each category, if you wish.

• **ENTERTAINING,** *Buffet Table:* Make a long buffet table from two or more card tables placed side-by-side, and keep them from separating by having their "feet" standing, by twos (with a snug fit), in cans.

• **ENTERTAINING,** *Cleaning-up:*
1. Colored bulbs in lamps when you have holiday parties look festive and make dust invisible; they let you spend more time on the food and less on cleaning before the party. You'll have to clean after anyway!
2. Fill the sink with warm soapy water and toss flatware into it as you pick up the plates, etc. so that it will soak clean.
3. Best hint is to say, "Yes, thank you" when guests offer to help bring food or clean up after.
4. Trade "maid-service" with a friend—you "do" her party and she "does" yours.
5. Get a sitter for young children if they aren't included in the party; pay older children as hired help.

• **ENTERTAINING,** *Family Parties:*
1. Place older children in charge of entertaining younger ones; provide board games and other playthings, such as "dress-up" clothing for "pretend" games and plays, in a room out of the food preparation traffic.
2. Offer a reward to older children of a movie or other entertainment for child care and clean-up after family dinner. Adults who remember their teens also recall that they were bored with adult-style visiting after the main feast is over.

• **ENTERTAINING,** *Quick-Fix for Spots and Stains:* Club soda is more than a beverage when you have a party; it can be used on many fresh spots and stains on clothing, carpets and linens, such as wine and foods. See SPOTS AND STAINS on page 398.

• **ENTERTAINING,** *Quick-Fix for Tablecloth Creases:*
1. Toss a tablecloth into the fluff cycle of the dryer with a damp towel; it may get some of the storage fold wrinkles out. After use, store the cloth for the next time on a coat hanger.

2. Prevent a centerfold: Make a lengthwise slit in a cardboard tube from a gift wrap roll (cut to hanger width), then put the tube on the hanger.

• **ENTERTAINING,** *Substitutes for Large Containers:* For family reunions and other large parties, buy new brightly colored plastic dishpans in which to mix and serve potato and pasta salads.

• **ENTERTAINING,** *Tablesetting:* To set the table before the party when you have toddlers, without fear of your child playing "magician" with the tablecloth, open the table as if to insert a leaf, poke about an inch of tablecloth into the crack with your finger, then close the table again. The tablecloth will stay put and your real friends will understand the reason for the crease across the table. Or use place mats.

• **ENVELOPE NOTE:** If the envelope is addressed and ready to go, but not yet, you can write notes to yourself on the upper right-hand corner about when to mail a birthday card, if photos or other items are to be included, when the bill is to be paid, etc. and then cover the note with the stamp at mailing time.

• **ENVELOPES,** *Recycling Junk Mail:* While they make good shopping lists, file holders for bits and pieces, receipts, and other things, DO NOT mail out your bill payments or letters in them. First, it is illegal to use postage-paid envelopes for anything other than the original intended use. Also, many reply envelopes are printed with bar codes that direct them to the intended address no matter what you write on them. Sticking on a label is no assurance of covering up addresses either; a reader wrote me that her label came off so her car payment went to a book club instead and, as a result, she got a late-payment charge on her car loan that would have bought a lot of new envelopes.

• **ENVELOPES,** *Sealing the Unsealable:* Dab the inside flap with a bit of clear fingernail polish and close it up. I use up the decorative stickers and return address labels that I get from various charitable organizations to reinforce the seals, especially on envelopes containing checks.

• **ENVELOPES,** *Steaming Open:* Set your iron on a hot setting, then place a slightly dampened cloth over the envelope seal and press with the hot iron for a second or two. This should open the envelope. To reseal, briefly touch the closed flap with the hot iron. If it doesn't want to stick, try a drop of household glue, tape or nailpolish, as noted above in ENVELOPES, Sealing the Unsealable.

• **ENVELOPES,** *Unsticking the Stuck:* Please see ENVELOPES, Steaming Open above. **Hint:** To avoid this problem in damp climates, place something between the flap and the envelope such as waxed paper, regular paper or just raise the flap of one envelope and place the next envelope under it. Or in really damp climates, don't buy the kind that need licking to seal; instead, buy self-sealers. Sometimes, spending a few pennies more saves a lot of aggravation!

• **EXERCISE,** *Letter of Laughter:* A granny-aged woman wrote that she found a way to keep aerobic and limbering up exercises from getting boring. She closes all the drapes, tunes up the jazziest music she can find on the radio and pretends she's a "go-go dancer" in a room full of panting Romeos. She says it gets her blood circulating!

• **EYE,** *Kitchen-style, Soothing Tired and Puffy Ones:* Working on computers or doing demanding needlework can be a strain.
Soother 1—Put wet used tea bags into the freezer for a few minutes. While they chill, dab olive oil on your eyelids. Place a tea bag on each eye and lie down for 15 minutes or so. Then carefully remove the oil by dabbing lightly with a clean tissue or cotton ball.
Soother 2—Soak a couple of cotton balls in cold milk, apply to closed eyes and lie down for 10 minutes.
Soother 3—Place a slice of cold cucumber on each eye and lie down for 10 to 15 minutes.

• **EYEBROWS,** *Darkening Light Brows:* If eyebrow pencil looks too harsh and fake, stroke a thin flat makeup brush across eye shadow (light brown or grey) and then apply it to your eyebrows. Also, try light upward strokes of mascara to color eyebrows.

• **EYEGLASSES,** *Emergency Repairs:*
1. If you lose the tiny screw from your eyeglasses use a twist-tie without the paper. When the point comes out the other side, cut off the ends you can see.

2. If the screw is just loose and you don't have a tiny screwdriver, try a pencil eraser. It works great, especially on metal-framed eyeglasses that seem to always have a screw loose!

• **EYEGLASSES,** *Removing Paint Spatters:*
1. Rub lenses gently with a soft cloth dipped in soapy water.
2. For glass lenses ONLY (not plastic, plastic coated, or other special coating), carefully apply acetone or mineral spirits with a soft cloth to remove paint. Then wash with soapy water, rinse, and dry.

• **EYE MAKEUP,** *Application:* Shading and color are the keys—dark shading adds depth and light shading comes forward. You can contour your entire face with makeup just like the stars do! **Hint:** If you have trouble putting on eye makeup because your lids twitch, open your mouth to the biggest "O" you can do comfortably and your face will stay put while you apply shadow, liner and mascara to your eyes.

• **EYE MAKEUP,** *Removing Waterproof Mascara, etc.:* Apply mineral oil or petroleum jelly and remove with cotton or a soft, natural sponge. (Note that mineral oil is listed on most commercial makeup remover labels.) Most cosmetologists agree that tissues are too rough on the skin.

• **FABRIC PURCHASE,** *Checklist for Upholstery and Drapery Fabrics:*
There are no returns or exchanges on these usually expensive fabrics so here are some guidelines to prevent costly errors.
1. Always be sure to buy enough fabric to finish the job completely. Dye lots vary; it's better to have excess than to run short. Leftover fabric can be used for repairs or to make pillows, etc.
2. Know the fabric you buy. Check for fiber content, repeating patterns, cleaning instructions, and stain or flame retardancy. These factors affect the amount of fabric needed, durability, and upkeep. Availability is also a factor. If you underestimate, make an error cutting, or decide to have more work done in the same fabric, know that there is more available and it's not a discontinued pattern.
3. Fabric and workmanship are related. Flawed fabrics, irregulars, or seconds will generally affect the outcome of your project. Inspect carefully before buying, especially markdowns. If there is a flaw near the end of a bolt of upholstery fabric, you may be given the remainder to compensate for adjusting the cutting but be sure that you can still cut out the large pieces you need for the project. For example, no extra yardage could compensate for drapery fabric flaws unless they can be concealed in the hems.

4. Get estimates if you are having the work done professionally because costs vary greatly. Ask to see samples of their work or for references.

5. When you go to buy fabric, swatches, paint chips, arm caps, cushions, fabric remnants taken with you are invaluable to selecting a good color match. Taking a tiny sample home is not as effective as seeing your swatches against a large piece in the store.

• **FACE POWDER,** *$aver, When It Hardens in a Compact:* Gently rub a piece of fine sandpaper or an emery board across the powder to loosen it. **Hint:** Makeup and oil from your skin gets on the powder puff and then gets absorbed into the face powder. Avoid caked powder by storing your powder puff upside down in the compact.

• **FACIAL,** *Home Remedy for Oily Skin:*
1. Make a paste of dry oatmeal and water; spread it on your face, being careful not to put it on the delicate eye area skin.
2. Let the mask dry and then splash your face with warm water to remove it or remove it with a washcloth.
3. After all is removed, splash a little cool water on your face for a delicious refreshed feeling. Your face will feel clean and smooth.

• **FAMILY NEWSPAPER,** *Letters to Grandparents:* Have children assemble family news in newspaper style—sports, editorial, world and local issues, advice column—and send a monthly family newspaper to their grandparents.

• **FAMILY WAKE-UP CALL:** *Letter of Laughter*—Tired of repeating children's wake-up calls on school days? One reader gives her children five minutes to get up after being called or she spray-mists them with a spritz water bottle. It took only a few spritzes and now she has no problems.

• **FAN GRATE,** *Recycling:* Save the grate from an electric box fan after the fan is worn out and it will be a good drying rack for sweaters and other garments that need to dry flat.

• **FAT FRYING SPATTERS,** *Quick-Fix, Time-Saver:* Place an inverted metal colander over a skillet. It lets steam escape and the meat brown without splattering fat all over the stove area for you to clean up.

- **FAT SUBSTITUTING,** *For Low-cholesterol Diets:*
1. Substitute vegetable oil for butter or lard in recipes other than bread or baked desserts. You will need one-third less vegetable oil—for example, 2 teaspoons of vegetable oil sub for 1 tablespoon of solid shortening (1 tablespoon = 3 teaspoons). Corn oil stick margarine works also.
2. When you substitute two egg whites per egg in a recipe, you may also add one teaspoon of vegetable oil for each yolk omitted so that the recipe has a better texture.

- **FAST-FOOD CONDIMENTS,** *Recycling:* Buying Fast Food usually means extra plastic-ware, ketchup, mustard, salt and pepper packets. Instead of throwing the extras away, save them for picnics and camping. They take less space in your food basket than whole jars of ketchup, etc. and there's no mess either.

- **FAUCET,** *When the Garden Faucet Is Too Low:* If leaning down to turn on the water is difficult for someone with a back problem or an elderly person, try raising the faucet to a more reachable height. Remove the faucet and put on an elbow fitting. Connect a two-foot length of pipe to the fitting and then attach the faucet to the pipe. Be sure the pipe is attached to the house so that it doesn't break or pop loose if jarred. If you aren't handy, have a plumber do the job.

- **FAX, COVER SHEETS,** *Healthy-Planet Paper-Saving, Time- and $-Savers:*
1. In my office, we made one standard cover sheet for all FAX transmissions. We put it into a clear plastic sleeve (the kind that lets you fax a cover sheet within it), and then write in all pertinent information with a dry erasable marker. When we finish transmitting, we erase the marker with a blackboard eraser and the cover sheet is ready for the next transmission. If several companies are using one FAX machine, each can have its own logo on a master cover sheet and then just change cover sheets in the plastic sleeve for transmission.
2. Have a "header" stored in the computer that has all the information needed to identify the FAX; then "Merge" it on top of correspondence and fill in the information blanks before printing it out.

3. Have a rubber stamp made with all necessary information—name, address, and person to whom the FAX is sent, number of pages, etc. and stamp the info in the margin of the page being FAXed.

4. If you frequently FAX information to one certain person or business, reuse the same cover sheet—just have several lines on which to write the date and subject of each FAX.

• **FEATHERS,** *Cleaning:* When ostrich or peacock feathers get too dusty for just a blowing with cool air from a hair dryer, gently swish them in a cold-water wash or in plain cold water, then gently blow-dry them with a hair dryer set on low cool setting. Hold the dryer at a safe distance from each feather so it dries gently. Don't try to reshape the feathers with your hands; a gentle swishing when dry would be enough to bring back the natural shape.

• **FIBERGLASS SURFACE,** *Cleaning Tubs and Showers:* Fiberglass is easily scratched with harsh abrasives. If you don't have cleaners specially formulated for fiberglass (sold in places that sell tubs and shower stalls), or a cleaner recommended for fiberglass from the supermarket, you can clean this surface with baking soda. Apply with a damp cloth, rub and rinse off residue well. I've also found that cheap shampoo "degunks" soap film on fiberglass.

• **FIBERGLASS TUB AND SHOWER,** *Cleaning:* Readers say they get good results if they wax fiberglass tubs and showers with car or boat wax. Clean with a non-abrasive cleaner and apply wax to the walls and sides and buff with an electric buffer for a super shine. **Caution:** Never wax the shower floor or tub bottom; it makes them too slippery for safety.

• **FILE "CABINETS,"** *Homemade System:* Buy plastic milk-type crates in colors you like, then insert hanging files. The crates can be stacked easily and are lightweight if you need to carry them around.

• **FILE SUBSTITUTE,** *Recycling, For Newspaper Clippings, Coupons, etc.:* Please see JUNK MAIL ENVELOPES, Recycling.

• **FILING IMPORTANT PAPERS IN A WALL SAFE:** To avoid having to unfold each document to see what it is, fold papers so that the letterheads face out. You can just thumb through the files in a hurry.

• **FILM,** *Identification:* To prevent loss when having film developed, print your name and address on letter-size paper and take a picture of it when you start a new roll. If you are traveling, take a picture of a sign printed with the city's (or other location's) name so that you can identify your photos when you get home and your memory is fuzzy.

• **FILM CANISTERS,** *35mm, Healthy-Planet Recycling:* Don't pitch 'em. They can hold jewelry when you're at the gym, address labels and stamps, children's jacks, marbles, lunch/milk money, coins for the laundromat, sewing supplies at work or travel, styling gel in travel kit, and so on.

• **FINGERNAIL,** *Mending Broken or Split One:* A drop of instant glue will repair a split. For a bad tear or split, strengthen it by gluing on small torn bits of white tissue paper.
1. Glue a small piece of torn tissue (facial or toilet tissue or newspaper border, if you have no wrapping tissue) over the tear, then cover it with a larger piece.
2. After the glue dries, gently file the paper with the smoothest side of an emery board.
3. Add several coats of clear nail polish to smooth and, if you wish, colored polish to cover.
This mend will last long enough for a bad tear to grow out and save you a lot of finger pain!

• **FINGERNAIL FILE,** *Quick-Fix Substitute:* When a fingernail breaks and you don't have an emery board or file to smooth the rough edge, try the striking edge of a matchbook. One reader discovered this hint when she assumed that if the striking edge was rough enough to ignite a match it could file a fingernail—creative thinking!

• **FINGERNAIL POLISH,** *Keeping the Bottle from Spilling:* Put a droplet of polish on a scrap of heavy paper or piece of cardboard, then place the bottom of the bottle over it. The bottle will adhere to the paper and tipping is almost impossible. When you are finished with your nails, either remove the bottle from the paper with a drop or so of polish remover or leave it stuck for the next time.

• **FINGERNAIL POLISH,** *Marking Things with Red:*
1. Levels for measuring amounts in cups or buckets;
2. The start of the washer's rinse cycle on the dial;
3. The VCR stop (or other) button that's hard to find;
4. The light switch that's supposed to be left on;
5. Dab different colors (like white pearl and red) on the "On" and "Off" switches of the remote TV control to ID them without glasses.
6. Marking the line-up arrows on child-proof medicine bottles.

• **FINGERNAIL POLISH,** *Opening the Bottle:* Wind a rubber band around the bottle top to get a better grip on it.

• **FINGERNAIL POLISH,** *Repairing Things with Clear:*
1. Stop runs in stockings—an all-time favorite repair. I carry clear polish in my travel kit for this purpose.
2. Glue thread tail on a machine-sewn button so it won't pop off.
3. Spread some polish around the caps of cologne when you travel, replace the caps, and they'll stay firmly in place—no leaks.
4. Mend small holes in a window screen or door screen.
5. Mend a little hole in a window by building up a few layers of polish.
6. Paint on jewelry to keep it from tarnishing where it touches your skin.

• **FINGERNAIL POLISH,** *Thinning:* Add a few drops of enamel solvent (found in drugstores) to dilute thickened nail polish. Nail-polish remover will thin polish but it contains oil and fragrance and so is not recommended. AVOID the problem of buildup, which prevents a tight seal and allows air to dry out the polish, by wiping the neck of the bottle with nail-polish remover on a tissue or cotton ball.

• **FINGERNAIL POLISH BOTTLE,** *Recycling:* After cleaning thoroughly with polish remover, fill the bottle with white latex paint and you have a little touch-up bottle handy when you need to cover nicks in the wall or for correcting mistakes in your checkbook register. (Latex paint can be homemade correction fluid.)

• **FINGERNAIL POLISH REMOVER,** *For Travel or Office:* Insert a small piece of sponge into a small, plastic trial-size bottle and add just enough fingernail-polish remover to be absorbed by the sponge. Then when you need to remove polish, dip a finger into the container. There's no damage from leaky containers and the smaller one takes up less space.

• **FINGERNAILS,** *Quick-Fix, Keeping Clean:* Dig your fingernails into a bar of soap before starting messy chores like potting plants. The dirt will wash right off when you wash your hands.

• **FINGERNAILS,** *Whitening:* Nail polish can stain fingernails yellow. The trick is to apply a base coat of clear polish before adding color. To remove yellow, put your fingernails in a cut lemon half for a few minutes and they'll be white again. Cleaning things with baking soda also bleaches fingernails white, but it may dry some people's skin and nails so apply hand lotion after cleaning sessions.

• **FINGERNAIL SAVERS:** To make fingernails strong, apply white iodine (from drugstores) every day for seven days and then once weekly. Don't overdo or your nails will become brittle. You can polish nails over the iodine. The following hints help you save wear and tear on your fingernails.
1. Pry up the tabs of soft drink cans with the plastic fasteners from bread bags instead of fingernails.
2. Clip a steel-wool pad with a spring clothespin when scrubbing.
3. Wear rubber gloves to protect hands from cleaning solutions. Reinforce new gloves at the fingertips by inserting tips cut from old gloves.

• **FINGERNAIL TALES:** After reading a *Letter of Laughter* about a waitress whose "fake" fingernail caught on fire while she was lighting a restaurant customer's birthday cake candles, a reader sent in the story about her friend, also a waitress, who, after opening a baked potato for a customer, returned to the kitchen and discovered that one of her "fake" nails was missing. Had she driven a nail into the man's potato? He never complained so she still doesn't know!

• **FINGER PAINTS,** *Healthy-Planet, Homemade Non-toxic Formula:* Mix ½ cup cornstarch with two cups cold water in a saucepan.

Bring the mixture to boil and continue to boil until it thickens. Let cool slightly. Pour equal amounts into clean baby-food jars and color each with food coloring.

• **FIRE DRILL,** *Checklist for Family Safety:* Fire is always possible. It's important to have a home evacuation plan and practice it so that everyone knows what to do in case of fire.
1. What is the quickest, safest way out of your home and out of each room in case of fire? Plan an escape route for each room and plan alternate routes depending on the actual fire location.
2. Practice the fire drills so each person knows exactly what to do and where to go, especially children.
3. Instruct the family to feel any door before opening it to see if it is hot; if it is, don't open it. Heat means fire on the other side.
4. Instruct the family to crawl; don't walk upright. Air is safer near the floor. A major fire danger is smoke inhalation or inhalation of chemical vapors formed when man-made fibers and building materials burn.
5. Have a special place for all to meet outside so that you know immediately if someone is missing.
6. Show children a picture of a fire fighter with all his gear on. Very young children especially may be frightened when they see someone in a mask and the other equipment on and then hide. Teach children never to hide but to get to safety as soon as possible.
7. When fire breaks out, get out of the house and call the fire department from a neighbor's house. Time spent on the phone could be the difference between getting out in time or getting trapped.
8. Always remember that human life is more important than possessions. Don't risk your life for things.

• **FIREPLACE,** *Checklist for Maintenance and Winterizing:*
1. Inspection by a professional chimney sweep and cleaning if needed. If you seldom use your fireplace it may not need annual cleaning but frequent use may cause more creosote buildup inside which can ignite and cause fires.
2. If you have a fireplace insert, which is basically a wood stove fitted into a fireplace opening, the fans and blowers should also be serviced by a professional chimney sweep, and older models need to be checked to make sure they meet current safety standards.

• **FIREPLACE,** *Cleaning Soot and Smoke from White Bricks:*
Step 1. **Caution:** Cover the floor and hearth to protect them from bleach; wear gloves and make sure the room is well ventilated.
Step 2. Mix a solution of half laundry bleach and water and put into a spray bottle.
Step 3. Spray bricks with the mixture and scrub gently with a soft-bristled brush to remove soot and smoke stains.
Step 4. Rinse with plain water.

• **FIREPLACE,** *Energy-wise Modifications:* Despite expensive modifications (fireplace inserts can cost about $850 to $1500 and up, depending upon accessories), fireplaces are not considered to be efficient heaters by any of the experts on this subject. About 90 percent of the heat generated by a fireplace goes up the chimney. Glass doors and inserts not only prevent this heat loss, they prevent embers from popping out and starting fires.
1. Glass Doors: Having the doors closed during burning allows for more air control for combustion but cuts your fire's radiant heat output in half.
2. Fan-driven Heat Exchanger System: This can be built in or added to your fireplace to enable the fire to warm the room's air instead of merely radiating heat on objects in the room.
3. Fireplace Inserts: Basically wood stoves designed to fit into fireplace openings, inserts significantly improve heating efficiency and still retain some of the ambiance. These either fit into the fireplace or protrude onto the hearth. Protruding inserts are more efficient. A well-fitted fireplace insert also limits the amount of warm room air that goes up the chimney and the amount of air in the combustion chamber. Fans and blowers improve an insert's efficiency.

• **FIREPLACE,** *Summer Decorating:* Place several large candles in your fireplace and light them for a cheery glow instead of a dark, yawning hole.

• **FIREPLACE ASHES,** *Time-Saver Cleanup:* Take a tip from barbecuing; line the bottom of the fireplace with heavy duty aluminum foil so that the foil covers the bottom and extends a couple of inches up the sides. Then you can just roll the ashes up in the foil and pitch the whole mess.

• **FIREPLACE BRICKS,** *Removing Smoke and Soot:*
1. An art "kneaded" eraser, sold at art supply stores, lifts smoke and soot stains from some porous surfaces such as brick or stone. Knead the eraser until it's pliable, then press it against the smoke-covered bricks. Repeat the procedure until the eraser has removed the stains. When the eraser becomes soiled, knead it again and continue until the bricks are clean.
2. When a fireplace is surrounded by smoother brick or stone surfaces, a kneaded eraser may not work well to remove all of the stain. After cleaning with the eraser, you may need to wash the brick with a solution of one-half cup trisodium phosphate (sold in hardware stores) to a gallon of water. **Caution:** Always wear heavy-duty rubber gloves to protect your skin when cleaning with strong solutions such as trisodium phosphate and follow the box directions exactly.

• **FIREPLACE CAUTION:** Don't burn heavily oiled papers or chemically treated wood products such as railroad ties or outdoor lumber. Dangerous toxins can be released into the air when these woods are burned.

• **FIREPLACE STARTER LOGS:** Roll old newspapers tightly and fit them into empty cardboard paper towel tubes.

• **FIREPLACE TOOLS,** *Quick-Fix Shine:* Wipe with a kerosene dampened cloth. **Caution:** Allow to dry completely before replacing them near the fireplace or using them.

• **FIRE STARTER,** *In Fireplace or Barbecue Grill:* Light a "puff out proof" birthday candle and poke it into the barbecue coals or fireplace kindling. They'll light your fire because they don't go out!

• **FIRST-AID KIT,** *Checklist:* For camper or boat, put the following in a fishing tackle or old lunch box.
Different sizes of adhesive bandages; gauze; medical tape; elastic bandage; antiseptic; rubbing alcohol; cotton; swabs, tweezers; ointments; sunburn pain reliever; sun block; small scissors; eye drops; special items needed by family members; a current first-aid book; a snake bite kit (from camping supply stores) if you are going to the wilderness; emergency ice pack (the kind that activate by tapping

them on a hard surface). Then tape some quarters to the lid so that you have change for emergency phone calls.

• **FIRST AID,** *Time-Saver:* Keep the tube of antibiotic ointment in the box with the adhesive bandages.

• **FIRST APARTMENT SHOWER:** If everyone's on a tight budget, including the person moving into a first apartment, hold a shower in which friends and relatives bring no longer needed household items—pots, pans, dishes, flatware, linens—still usable and in good condition. The organizer of the event can keep track of larger items like mattresses, furniture, etc. so that there aren't duplicates of such things. Any leftovers can be given to charity or sold at a garage sale with the money used for things the person still needs.

• **FISH FEEDING,** *No-mess, Especially for Children:* Transfer small amounts of fish food (small flakes or grains) into a shaker-topped spice jar so that food can be sprinkled in. It helps avoid spilled containers of fish food when children are in charge of their own aquarium.

• **FISH STEAMING:** Before placing fish in a steamer, place it in a coffee filter. Then you can lift out the fish whole instead of in a bazillion crumbled pieces.

• **FLASH CARDS,** *Recycling, Quick-Fix:* To make math flash cards, remove the face cards from a deck of new playing cards or one which has some cards missing or marked. To "play" math, shuffle the cards. Then, deal two cards face up and ask your child to add or subtract the numbers. These homemade flash cards also work for multiplication and division of small numbers. The math game can be played in an airplane, too; ask the flight attendant if cards are available.

• **FLASHLIGHT,** *Finding It in the Dark:* Stick on a strip of glow-in-the-dark tape (or paint a stripe with glow paint from a craft store) around the flashlight head, then you'll be able to find it when the electricity is off. **Note:** This is one of those so very practical hints that it's amazing nobody thought of it sooner—obviously you are most likely to need a flashlight when it's too dark to find one!

• **FLEAS,** *Controlling Them:* Persistence pays off. You need to interrupt the flea cycle because fleas multiply rapidly. Under good conditions (good for them, bad for us), ten fleas can produce 250,000 new fleas in less than thirty days! Flea bombs work; so does spraying; but you need to use these chemicals every couple of weeks in the beginning to kill the flea eggs as well as the fleas. Otherwise the eggs hatch and you're back to square one—or itch one!

1. Bathe pets and apply safe dips that control fleas at intervals according to directions. (If your pet is difficult to dip, mix the dip as directed and spray it on the animal.) Never apply several different insecticides at one time, like powder, dip, spray, etc. Never use dog products on cats unless the product label says it is for both animals. Improper use of insecticides can be toxic to animals. **Hint:** If a small cat or dog resists spraying, spray a towel and wrap the animal in the towel, holding it wrapped for about 15 minutes so the chemicals can work.

2. Vacuum your home frequently. Put a few mothballs in the bag and when you vacuum after spraying or flea-bombing the house, throw the bag away. Keep some mothballs in every bag you put in to kill the fleas vacuumed up.

3. Treat your lawn at the same time as you treat your pet and your house; otherwise the fleas just come back into the house. Follow insecticide directions exactly and do not allow children or pets to walk on the lawn while the insecticide is wet or fresh. Pets, especially, will lick the insecticide from their paws and it could be toxic.

4. Your best resources for ridding your home of fleas is your vet or your county extension agent.

• **FLEAS,** *Healthy-Planet Homestyle Remedies:*

1. Wash doghouses with salt water. Scatter fresh pine needles or cedar shavings under your pet's sleeping pad. Keep bedding clean.

2. Wash your pet and yourself with green soap; fleas supposedly don't like the dye that turns soap green.

3. Make a flea trap. Place a light-colored shallow pan filled with soapy water on the floor next to a 25-watt lamp. Position the bulb about 1 to 2 feet above the water. When the lamp is on, fleas are attracted to light so they will jump toward the lamp and fall into the pan. Rinse out the pan each morning and refill.

4. Fleas can jump as far as 12 inches or more in one leap, and can accelerate fifty times faster than the space shuttle—but you know that if you've ever tried to catch one! Wrap adhesive tape around your fingertips, sticky side out, to form a tape band for dabbing up the fleas when you see them. Fleas stick to the tape and can't escape as they do when you try to capture them with your fingers.

• **FLOPPY DISKS,** *Transporting:* Don't leave disks in the car during the summer, heat can warp them and cause other damage. When transporting floppy disks, put them in an insulated box such as a small cooler to protect them and take them indoors with you if you are making a lengthy stop.

• **FLOUR DUSTER,** *Time-Saver:* Place a brand-new powder puff in your flour canister so that it's handy to dust baking pans. Or, keep flour in a large-holed sugar/salt shaker for dusting pans with flour.

• **FLOWER POTS,** *Covering for Dry Arrangements:* Take a piece of fabric (remnant or one that matches the decor) and cut it a few inches longer and wider than the pot. Sew a casing along the top and bottom sides of the fabric. Insert string or elastic to ensure a snug fit. This won't work for a clay pot with real plants because water seeping through the clay can cause mold on the fabric.

• **FLOWERS,** *Arrangements:* If you've received a fresh flower gift arrangement, after the fresh flowers wilt, remove the dried baby's breath and straw flowers used as "filler" and save for your own arrangements of dried or silk flowers. (Look for seasonal sales on silk flowers at craft stores!)

• **FLOWERS,** *Cleaning Silk Flowers and Foliage:*
1. Silk-type Flowers—Usually made from nylon or polyester with plastic stems, can be washed in a basin with cool water and a few drops of mild detergent. Immerse flowers, gently swish around for a minute or so; rinse and air dry.
2. Most Fabric Flowers—Dust with a blow-dryer on cold-air setting. Or, put ¼ cup table salt in a brown paper bag and place the silk flowers stem-up in the bag. Gather the top shut and shake well; they'll come out cleaner.

- **FLOWERS,** *Cutting Stems:* Cut stems underwater and the flowers will last longer.

- **FLOWERS,** *Dye Carnations TWO Colors:* Popular when dyed in school colors, you can do this at home; it takes about two days.
1. Slit the stem in half lengthwise, about halfway.
2. Using two containers, put a cup of warm water in each and add different food coloring to each one.
3. Set the containers next to each other and put each half of the stem into each one. Leave in water for two days.
4. To dye a flower just one color, make a fresh cut at the bottom of the stem and place in a container of water to which food coloring has been added.

- **FLOWERS,** *Graveside Arrangements:*
1. Fill a coffee can with sand for weight; cut several small slits in the plastic lid and replace on can.
2. Arrange silk or plastic flowers and artificial evergreens by putting the stems through the small slits in the lid.
3. Cover the can with foil and add a ribbon for color.

- **FLOWERS,** *Keeping Cut Flowers Fresh:*
1. When you buy a bouquet, remove all leaves below the water level and cut off one-fourth to one-half inch of the stem. Change the water every other day and recut the stems each time.
2. Many of my readers say adding an aspirin or a teaspoon of sugar to the water prolongs the life of cut flowers.
3. Some say cut flowers stay fresh long if you put the arrangement in the refrigerator overnight when nobody is looking at them anyway.

- **FLOWERS/LEAVES,** *Preserving in Wax:*
1. Carefully melt paraffin wax, cool slightly, then dip each leaf or flower in it. Hold with tweezers or tongs to prevent burning your fingers. After dipping, lay the leaf or flower in the proper place directly on construction paper of a suitable color. No need to glue them, the wax sticks them to the paper.
2. The quick-fix way is to press leaves and flowers between two sheets of waxed paper and seal with a hot iron. Don't forget to put an old towel or cloth on the ironing board to keep the wax from getting melted into it.

- **FLOWERS,** *Preserving by Drying:*
1. Ornamental grasses and grains such as wheat or oats: Cut and hang upside down for a week.
2. Fruited branches like bayberry: Cut and arrange without water.
3. Strawflower, globeflower, thistle, statice, and silver dollar: Cut on long stems and arrange without water.

- **FLOWER SEEDS,** *Gathering Free Ones:* If you have cut flowers that you like, dry the flower and collect the seeds for spring planting. To get the seeds out easily, when the flowers are partially dry, put them into a large paper sack. When they finish drying, shake the bag to get the seeds to fall to the bottom. Then, pour the seeds into a clean dry jar and save for planting. Remember to label the jar so you'll know which seeds are which.

- **FLOWERS, SILK,** *Uses:* Use in flower arrangements to replace dead blooms, replace bed flowers in planters, attach to a comb and wear in your hair, pin on your lapel or blouse, scatter when setting table to cover spots on table linen, attach to a fan for a wall decoration.

- **FOAM MEAT TRAY,** *Recycling:*
1. Make a puzzle for small children—draw a picture and color it with acrylic paints. Then cut into puzzle pieces with a single-edged razor or wood-carving tool.
2. Place as pad between china and non-stick cookware to prevent scratching.
3. Place under iron skillets to prevent grease marks on cupboard shelves.
4. Wash and take on picnics for plates and trays.
5. Pad your knees when you are gardening by holding them on with the elastic top of an old sock.
6. Cover with foil and it's a tray for cookies to take somewhere; it doesn't have to come back. Hold the cookies on the meat tray with plastic wrap and add a bow.

- **FONDUE POT,** *Other Uses:* Melt chocolate in it when you make candy or dip pretzels, strawberries, etc.; the temperature is just right.

- **FOOD,** *Freezing:* You can get specific information on freezing garden surplus from your County Extension Agent or cookbooks, but here are some important rules for best results regardless of what you are freezing:

1. Select only best quality foods for freezing because what comes out will be no better than what you put into the freezer! It's like your computer instructor said, "Garbage in; garbage out!"

2. To control growth of bacteria, yeasts, and molds and to stop the chemical action of enzymes, you need to handle, chill, and freeze foods as quickly and exactly as directed for each food.

3. To keep food from drying out and to preserve its nutritional value, packaging should be moisture/vapor proof. Rigid containers and plastic bags need air-tight seals and wrapped foods should be stored in extra heavy aluminum foil, Pliofilm or polyethylene-lined papers. Use freezer tape around the edges of rigid container lids to ensure a seal. Squeeze air from bags before sealing. ALWAYS label containers with the name of the contents, the date of freezing, and, if you rent food lockers, include the locker number on the package.

4. Freeze fruits and vegetables quickly after packaging. Either put them in the freezer a few packs at a time as they are ready or keep packs in the fridge until all are ready. If you use a locker plant, transfer packs from your home freezer to the locker in an insulated box or bag.

5. Don't freeze too many items at one time; the heat given off by non-frozen foods can raise the freezer temperature. Try to place lukewarm products away from those already frozen to avoid heating up frozen products. (Many upright freezers have a special shelf designated for quick freezing non-frozen foods; see the book that came with the appliance.)

• **FOOD,** *Frozen, Storage Time:* How long you can store food before it deteriorates depends on its handling before freezing, packaging materials, storage temperatures, and the type of food. But, no food can be stored forever. (See chart.)

SUGGESTED STORAGE TIMES FOR FROZEN FOODS

- Beef: 6 to 12 months
- Cooked foods: Varies greatly according to product and preparation.
- Fish: Moderate to high oil content (like mackerel, mullet, croker), 1 to 3 months; Low oil content (like flounder, red snapper, redfish, trout), 3 to 6 months.

- Fruits and vegetables: 1 year or less
- Lamb: 6 to 9 months
- Liver: 1 to 2 months
- Oysters: 1 to 2 months
- Pork, fresh: 3 to 6 months
- Sausage: 1 to 3 months
- Poultry: 6 months
- Shrimp: In shell, 6 to 12 months (remove heads which contain fat that tends to get rancid); Peeled and deveined, 3 to 6 months.

• **FOOD,** *General Storage Guidelines:* Wrap airtight and ALWAYS identify and date purchases and make a list to post near the freezer that shows what's inside so that you save time digging around.

1. Processed meats such as pork sausage, luncheon meats, bacon, and hot dogs keep one to two months.
2. Crab, lobster, and shrimp keep one to two months; fresh fish keep six to nine months.
3. A whole turkey will keep for twelve months, a whole chicken for nine months and chicken or turkey pieces for six months.
4. Fresh pork will keep one to two months, pork chops, fresh hamburger, stew, and organ meats keep three to four months.
5. Roast pork and veal keep four to eight months; beef steaks or roasts, six to twelve months; lamb chops or roasts, six to nine months.
6. Leftover ham, either canned or cured, will keep one month; leftover lamb, beef, fresh ham and pork, two to three months; chicken for four months.

• **FOOD,** *Refreezing:* Fruits, vegetables, and meats which have not completely thawed, or those which have been thawed for a short time and have been refrigerated, can be refrozen but they will have lost quality and flavor. Refrozen vegetables toughen. Refrozen fruits become soft and mushy which makes them suitable for cooking but not for eating uncooked.

Low-acid foods like vegetables and meats spoil rapidly after thawing and reaching 45°F; it's not advisable to refreeze them. Acid foods, like most fruit and fruit products are likely to ferment after thawing and reaching 45°F. Slight fermentation of acid foods may change and spoil flavor but the food is not unsafe to eat.

• **FOOD,** *Storage in Freezer in Case of Power Failure:* A filled freezer will stay frozen for about two days; a half-filled freezer may not stay frozen more than one day. Prevent spoilage by packing the freezer with dry ice. About 50 pounds of dry ice will hold the temperature below freezing in a 20-cubic-foot home freezer for two to three days if you act quickly after the power is lost. **Caution:** Don't handle dry ice with bare hands; it burns.

• **FOOD,** *Storage, Freezer Temperatures:* Make sure your freezer stays at 0°F. Fluctuating temperatures cause frozen foods to lose moisture at a faster rate than normal and results in their becoming rough and dry. A full freezer maintains its temperature better than a half-empty one. **Note:** You can always fill up the freezer with ice if you don't have it full of food. Use bagged ice from the supermarket or recycle clean plastic milk jugs; fill with water and keep frozen. The bonus with the milk jugs (or 2-liter soft-drink bottles) is that you can take them camping or on picnics to ice down foods in your cooler and then as the water thaws, you have drinking water.)

• **FOOD,** *Storage, Recommended Temperatures:*
1. Recommended temperatures for preserving raw foods: 30°F to 50°F, depending upon the product. (Most fruit should be stored at 32° to 35° F; fish should be iced and kept at the same temperature.)
2. After processing or cooking, foods should be cooled quickly to below 60°F. If you can't cool the food immediately, it must be kept at a temperature warmer than 140°F until it can be cooled.

• **FOOD,** *Using Thawed Foods:* Use thawed food immediately after thawing. Not all bacteria are killed by freezing; bacteria become active as food thaws so food not used after thawing will begin to lose its nutritional value and spoil.
Foods which have reached temperatures of 40° or 45°F are not likely to be worth refreezing and may be unsafe to eat as well as deteriorated in quality. See FOOD, Refreezing.

• **FOOD PROCESSOR,** *Time-Saver, $aver:* Do all your grinding and chopping in a single once-a-week session so that you can cook creatively when you're short on time. Making your own bread crumbs and buying hunks rather than grated cheese saves money, too. To avoid lots of processor bowl washing, first chop bread crumbs, then grate Parmesan (or other hard cheese), then grate cheddar cheese (soft cheese), and then chop parsley and onions. You can freeze the chopped ingredients and they will still taste fresher than store-bought processed foods.

- **FOOTBALL BIRTHDAY CAKE:** Please see CAKE, Football Shape.

- **FOOTBALL FAN,** *Letter of Laughter:* A fellow Dallas Cowboys fan wrote me that since her husband isn't one, she usually watches her favorite team alone. She told her husband that she wanted to go to a Cowboy game before she died, and she wrote that so far, he'd taken her to two games. She asked if he was being extra nice of if he just wants her to "kick the bucket!" I think he's just nice!

- **FOOTPRINT FINDER:** One reader who often works at projects in her garage while her child naps has a way to make her child feel secure in case she awakens and "can't find Mommy." Mom cuts "footprints" from colored construction paper and lays them out in a path to where she is working so that her child can "follow the footprints to Mommy." The child thinks it's a "wake-up" game.

- **FOOT THERAPY,** *Reader's Solutions to Aching Feet:*
1. Pour baking soda into a pan, add warm water, and soak your feet. The bonus is that the soak softens rough skin. It also softens cuticles so that you can give yourself a pedicure.
2. Put dry beans in your tennis shoes and walk around to get a foot massage.

- **FORMAL DRESS LENGTHS,** *Which Is Worn When:* Just like reading labels at the supermarket to avoid raising your cholesterol level, you read party invitations to avoid raising eyebrows. Invitations usually give the dress expected for men. Different communities have different interpretations of "formal" and if you're new in town, it's best to ask someone who knows. The following are general "rules."
1. When men wear white tie and tails—women wear long or at least ankle-length dresses.
2. When men wear black-tie tux—the event is called "semi-formal"—women can wear short very dressy dresses. Black-tie/cocktail means women can wear strapless with or without beading and other glitter.

3. Men wear dark suit—women wear cocktail or dressy dinner dresses. A dressy dinner dress is less revealing than a cocktail dress and looks right at a restaurant after the cocktail party.

4. For dinner, theater, or symphony in most communities, women wear less revealing dresses made from rich fabrics such as silk. Revealing strapless dresses are appropriate at black-tie events but not at restaurants or dinner parties in someone's home.

• **FORMS,** *Filling Out on the Typewriter:* When each blank's instructions are under the provided spaces, they are easier to read if you begin typing at the bottom of the form and work your way up to the top.

• **FRAGRANCES,** *When You're Allergy Prone:* One reader solved her problem of sneezing when wearing perfume or cologne by adding a drop or two of her favorite perfume to her bath along with a few drops of mineral oil. She's not bothered by the fragrance when it's diluted by bathwater and still enjoys a bit of the scent when it's left on her skin in the mineral oil (which also softens her skin). **Caution:** When adding any oil to the bath, it can make the tub bottom slippery.

• **FREEZER,** *Quick-fix Defrosting Chest-type:* Turn an all-day job into a one-hour one.

1. Unplug the freezer and empty the food into newspaper-lined laundry baskets, cartons, or picnic coolers.

2. Place several large buckets of very hot water inside and shut the lid. Change the water in fifteen minutes. After a couple of changes, most of the ice and water will have dropped to the bottom. Use a wet/dry vacuum or bathtowels to remove it.

3. When clean, wipe up the residue, plug in the freezer, and load it up.

Caution: Always be careful using electrical appliances near water; never stand in a puddle. Make sure the vacuum is rated "WET." A regular vacuum won't work and is dangerous if used for this purpose.

• **FREEZER BOXES,** *Recycling:* Save cake-mix boxes so that when you put food in a freezer bag, you can put the bag into the cake-mix box; it will freeze in a block that will take less space in the freezer than various lumpy-shaped frozen foods. Either label and date the bags before filling them or remove them from the box when frozen hard and then label/date them. You can reuse the boxes throughout your food-processing season.

• **FREEZER LABELS:** Cut labels from foods and tape them to containers or packages when you freeze leftovers to make identification easier. For example, if you freeze spaghetti sauce, cut those words from the sauce jar label and tape to the leftover before freezing.

• **FREEZER MONITOR,** *While You Are Gone on Vacation:* Place a small clear bag of ice cubes in the top basket or shelf of your deep freeze when you go away, and if you find the ice cubes melted and refrozen into one chunk, you'll know that your freezer has been off for a considerable amount of time and that it may not be safe to eat perishable foods. Also, fill up all empty spaces with bags of ice or frozen water in plastic jugs to help keep your freezer cold in case of power outages. This is a good idea anyway because a full freezer uses less energy going on and off to maintain the right temperature.

• **FREEZER SPACE CONSERVATION:** Freeze soups and casseroles in bread tins or square pans. They will be easier to stack and fit.

• **FRENCH BREAD,** *Saver:* If not eaten the day it's baked, real French bread is nearly a brick the next day but wonderfully edible if you turn it into something else.
1. Do what they do in New Orleans; make bread pudding.
2. Slice it, then bake it until it's brown and hard. Then sprinkle the slices with your favorite grated cheese; let the cheese melt for a few minutes in the oven, then float the crispy, cheesy bread slice in a bowl of any kind of soup.
3. To make croutons for salads, soups, or snacks, bake French-bread cubes in a 275°F oven for thirty to forty-five minutes or until golden brown and crunchy. For flavorful croutons, before baking, drizzle over a spiced butter mixture.
Butter Mixture: For one-half loaf of French bread, simmer together one stick of butter or margarine, one teaspoon of minced basil (fresh is best), and two cloves of minced garlic while you cube the bread. Place the cubes in a roasting pan, drizzle spiced butter mixture over and bake as directed above. Store in a tightly sealed plastic container or jar.

4. For a quick breakfast or light supper, cut stale bread into cubes; mix with beaten eggs and fry in a small amount of butter or margarine as you would French toast. Serve with or without syrup.
5. Make French toast! Sprinkle with powdered sugar before serving.

• **FRENCH TOAST:** Add a dash of vanilla to the batter to perk up the flavor.

• **FRENCH TOAST FOR CHOCOHOLICS:** One reader mixes a bit of chocolate syrup to the egg coating for French toast and then drizzles a syrup of mixed maple and chocolate syrup on it before savoring it.

• **FROZEN JUICE,** *Quick-Fix Frustration Avoiding:* Does mixing frozen orange or other juices in the morning rank equally in your life with untangling wire coathangers? Try these ideas.
1. Break up the frozen juice chunks with a potato masher.
2. At bedtime, dump the frozen juice out of the can into a container, add the required amount of water, and place the container in the fridge. When you take it out in the morning, the juice will be thawed and you need only shake or stir.

• **FROZEN TREAT,** *Recycling, Avoiding Mess with Children (and Some Adults?):* Cut a slit in a clean margarine tub, then poke the stick through the slit so the tub will catch the drips.

• **FROZEN TREATS,** *No-mess Freezing:* Instead of dribbling sticky spills from a frozen treat "ice-pop" tray when you carry it from counter to freezer, fill the tray with a turkey baster.

• **FRUIT,** *Homestyle Candied:*
1. Wash and dice fruit peels to appropriate size. You can collect peels as you eat the fruit. Store them in the freezer until you have about four each of oranges, lemons, and grapefruit.
2. Slowly boil two cups sugar, one cup water, and one-fourth cup corn syrup over low heat for 30 minutes. Add peels and cook for 45 minutes to an hour. It's done when all the syrup is absorbed.
3. Sprinkle sugar on waxed paper, lay peels on it and toss to distribute, then allow to dry for a couple of days.
Keeps indefinitely in the refrigerator.

- **FRUIT, DRIED:** Please see DRIED FRUIT.

- **FRUIT JUICE TREATS,** *Frozen:* Pour the liquid "juice" from canned fruit (light syrup is best) into molds or paper cups, add Popsicle sticks and freeze. Enjoy!

- **FRYING-OIL TEMPERATURE GAUGE:** Drop a kernel of popcorn in it. If the popcorn pops, the oil is hot enough to begin frying the food.

- **FUDGE,** *Quick-Fix, Neat Cutting:* After homemade fudge is hard, cut it with a pizza cutter.

- **FUNNEL,** *For Filling Spice Jars:* Cut one corner of an envelope and you have a funnel for filling spice jars or creating designs with colored sugar on cakes.

- **FURNACE,** *Healthy Planet Maintenance:* Keeping your home furnace in good condition can decrease your fuel consumption by as much as 10 percent, which saves about fifty gallons of oil (multiply by oil costs in your area to get saving) and keeps 1,089 pounds of carbon dioxide emission a year from our air. In addition to keeping your filters changed winter and summer, have regular maintenance inspections and cleanings of your furnace by an authorized company. Often, by contracting for regular service (spring and fall each year) you can save on the overall service fee.

- **FURNITURE,** *Renovating:* You may not need to refinish marred and scarred furniture.
1. Scratches can be covered with colored markers, shoe polish, the meat of a pecan or walnut, or commercially prepared lemon or boiled linseed oil.
2. Renew a piece of furniture by cleaning it with mineral spirits (read container for directions and for surfaces it will not damage) or use my Heloise furniture polish. The recipe for Heloise Furniture Polish is: Mix together one-third cup vinegar, one-third cup turpentine, and one-third cup boiled linseed oil. Moisten a soft cloth with polish and rub over furniture, polish with a clean cloth. **Caution:** Never attempt to boil linseed oil; it's highly flammable. Buy it at the hardware store. **Also:** ALWAYS clearly label homemade cleaning compounds and keep them away from children and pets.

- **FURNITURE,** *Repair:* Cover the damaged top of a dresser, buffet, or coffee table with tiles. Look for tile kits in craft or hardware stores; tile is terrific for surfaces which are likely to be in frequent contact with cosmetics or liquids.

- **FURNITURE BOOTIES,** *Recycling Fabric Softener and Liquid Detergent Caps:* Basement furniture and storage cabinet "feet" can get damp (and even wet, if storms cause water on the floor). Putting on plastic cap "booties" keeps them dry and prevents rust stains on the floor from metal furniture or feet with metal "buttons" on them. Please see PLASTIC CAPS, Recycling for other recycling ideas.

- **FURNITURE FINISH,** *Determining Type:* Dampen a cotton ball with nail-polish remover and rub it across a small inconspicuous area like the underside of a chair.
1. If the finish gets gummy or sticky, it's either clear oil-base varnish, shellac, or lacquer. You can use liquid furniture refinisher.
2. If the finish remains intact with no damage, it's probably a plastic-resin base. It can be removed with paint remover.

- **FURNITURE MOVING:** Get a grip on this chore and the furniture by wearing rubber gloves and place rugs like bath mats (upside down if they have rubberized backing) beneath heavy furniture to make it slide across the floor without scratching the flooring.

- **FURNITURE POLISH,** *Healthy-Planet Homestyle Recipes:* Aerosol sprays, chemicals in personal and home products cause air pollution inside our homes. The following polishes are inexpensive and safer. **Caution:** Always test new polishes on an inconspicuous place.
Polish #1: Add 1 teaspoon lemon oil to 2 cups mineral oil for a lemon-scented oil polish.
Polish #2: Mix 1 teaspoon olive oil with the juice of one lemon, 1 teaspoon brandy or whiskey, and 1 teaspoon water. This must be made fresh each time.
Polish #3: Mix 3 parts olive oil with 1 part white vinegar.
Polish #4: For oak furniture, boil 1 quart of beer with 1 tablespoon sugar and 2 tablespoons beeswax. When cool, wipe mixture on wood, allow to dry and polish with a chamois cloth.

- **FURNITURE POLISH,** *Healthy-Planet Touch-up:* On some finishes, apply mayonnaise, rub in and then wipe off, buff with clean cloth to touch up scratches and/or remove white areas from heat. *Letter of Laughter:* When one reader tried mayonnaise to polish a low wooden chest, she applied too much, so she left the room to get a cloth to wipe off the excess. When she returned, she found her big old tom cat purring happily as he licked it off. She says she sat on the floor and laughed while he finished his snack. So, furniture polishing can be fun sometimes!

- **FURNITURE RENTING INSTEAD OF BUYING,** *Checklist:*
1. Most rentals are made with no down payment, no credit check, and you take the item home quickly. Ideal for a week or two until you can buy an item.
2. It's possible to have a part of the rental fee applied toward a purchase price if you have the item a longer time, but you may end up paying two to five times the true cost you'd have paid on a regular credit purchase plan. It's an expensive way to buy.
3. Terms must be disclosed in your rental agreement. Read all of the print very carefully. Also, don't get caught in the $11-a-month trap—how many months or years?

- **FURNITURE TOUCH-UP,** *On Black-Painted Metal:* Buying office furniture at an office supply store "scratch-and-dent" sale is a real bargain. Cover scratches on black-painted metal file cabinets, bookcases, desks, etc. with permanent wide felt-tip marker. Apply wax over the marker to finish.

- **FURNITURE, WATER "BLEACH" SPOT,** *Homestyle Treatment:* Rub the spot with equal parts of toothpaste (not gel) and baking soda, applied with a soft, damp cloth. Rinse out the cloth and wipe off any residue. When the finish is smooth, buff with a clean soft cloth. Restore color and shine by rubbing the spot with the meat of half a pecan, then buff.

- **FURS,** *Storage:* Never store furs in plastic bags; they need to breathe. Instead, make a protective cover from an old sheet or place a king-size pillowcase over the garment. You'll need about a three-inch deep or wide shoulder cover to keep dust off without crushing the fur.

G

• **GARAGE DOOR,** *Automatic:* Always disconnect your automatic garage-door opener when you go on a trip. One never knows when someone else's opener will have the same frequency.

• **GARAGE DOOR AUTOMATIC OPENER,** *Safety Checklist:* Older units don't have the sensitivity devices newer models have. These devices have an emergency reverse built in the motor that reverses the door when it hits something—when five to twelve pounds of pressure is applied.
1. Have all garage doors checked, adjusted, and reset each year. The clutch can stick if not reversed often or not used for long periods of time; doors can change during the years and get out of line.
2. To check if your garage door reverses immediately, put something solid (like a two-by-four) under the door that will stop it. When it touches the item, the door should lift up immediately.
3. If you have any doubt about your unit, get a garage-door company to inspect and adjust it. Non-functioning or improperly functioning automatic garage doors have caused many deaths and injuries.

• **GARAGE SALE,** *Checklist:* First, consider asking neighbors and friends if they want to join you; sales advertised as "several families" or "neighborhood" attract more buyers.

1. Check with your city to learn if there are any garage sale restrictions in your area, and if you need to get a permit.

2. Advertise in local newspapers, noting several of the best or most unusual items for sale in the ad.

3. Separate clothing by size and hang it up for easy pickings.

4. Mark prices on each item so that people don't have to ask. If you know you will have a sale when you are cleaning closets, stick prices on discards immediately so you won't have so many to price the week before the sale.

5. Price items objectively and reasonably. If several families are participating in the sale, use colored stick-on tags with a different color for each family. Then as you sell an item, remove the tag and stick it in a notebook; each family will know exactly how much it has earned.

6. Place large eye-catching items on the lawn or in the driveway to attract customers.

7. Have boxes, newspaper, and paper or plastic bags to package sold items.

8. Be ready for the "early birds" who show up an hour or two early to get the best bargains.

9. Keep someone at the money box at all times and arrange the tables so that buyers have to pass the "checkout" to get out. Of course, never leave the cash unattended.

10. Don't accept personal checks unless you know the buyer. Also, have plenty of change ready at the beginning of the sale. You can keep coins in muffin tins.

11. Since the object of the sale is to get rid of the stuff, be ready to bargain with buyers. There's no money at all if you give or throw away the items, so why not give discounts?

12. Give leftover items to a charity.

• **GARAGE WINDOWS,** *Security:* If you don't want to put old curtains or draperies on them, you can buy window-frosting paint or apply frosted adhesive-backed plastic for privacy. **Hint:** To apply plastic, hold a piece of the adhesive-backed plastic up to one of the panes and cut with a razor for a perfect fit. Remove the backing and apply carefully, smoothing out wrinkles. If you get a small bubble, let the air out with a tiny pin prick and press down.

• **GARBAGE DISPOSAL,** *Cleaning:* If your dishwasher drains through your garbage disposal, flip the unit on when hot soapy water is running through it so it gets a good cleaning.

• **GARBAGE DISPOSAL,** *How to Distinguish It from the Light Switch:* Is there anyone who has not switched on the disposal and got startling noise instead of the light you expected? Mark disposal switch with red nail polish, a stick on frown-face, a red stick-on dot, or colored tape—anything to stop the grating shock!

• **GARDEN,** *Making Indoor Gardens:*
1. Plant Display: Cover the floor with a heavy-duty plastic bag to protect it from water or soil stains. Cover the bag with ceramic tiles and set your pot plants on the tiles.
2. Indoor Winter Garden: If you have a sunny corner, make a pattern or take measurements to a sheet metal shop and have them make a planter deep enough to hold a ficus or other indoor-growing tree and other plants at the base. Fill the planter with a couple of large rocks for bottom-weight, soil and your favorite plants. If you need more light, install a grow light in the ceiling above.

• **GARDEN,** *Planning, Checklist:* Start small by first planning the area in which you spend the most time, then gather information about your yard before you go to your local nursery to get advice and buy bedding plants or shrubs.
1. Measure the space; draw a picture (graph paper helps you keep to scale) or take a photo that shows the plants already there. Note if a fence is near (for climbing or tall plants).
2. Determine if the area gets morning or afternoon sun and how much sun (shade, partial shade, full or partial sun).
3. Check drainage and type of soil (sandy, rich black earth, clay). Garden centers and your county agent can test soil if you bring them a coffee can full.
4. Consider plants native to your area; they will thrive with less effort than "imports."

- **GARDEN EDGERS/STRING TRIMMERS,** *Checklist of Cautions:*
1. Protect your eyes from flying debris by wearing a mask or goggles and protect your shins with soccer pads or pads made for that purpose.
2. The monofilament lines used to cut grass and weeds can damage shrubs, vines, and young trees by removing part of the bark. If you trim so closely that you remove parts of the bark, you can damage the cambium tissue just beneath it, thus preventing the flow of "food" to the root system.

- **GARDEN HOSE,** *Finding the End:* Use yellow paint to mark about 12 inches at the end of the hose. Then you can always find the end when the hose is tangled up.

- **GARDEN HOSE,** *Repair Leaks, Make Irrigation System:*
1. Repair: Lightly sand the area around the holes with sandpaper. Cut patches from an old rubber tube and sand the patch lightly, too. Apply contact cement to both surfaces, let dry to the touch, and press firmly over the hole. Keep the patch in place by wrapping it with black electrical tape or duct tape.
2. Make a Healthy-Planet Drip Irrigation System: With a large nail or ice pick, poke more holes into the hose at strategic intervals on one side. Then lay the hose between garden rows or in flower beds so that water dribbles through the holes into the ground without evaporating as it would with an ordinary sprinkler.

- **GARDENING,** *Growing Tomatoes in Pots:* Read the tags on bedding plants to find out the plant's mature size; larger plants (30 inches high) will grow in two gallons of soil and smaller ones (12 inches high) in hanging baskets. Get advice on growing conditions and methods in your area from local garden columns and your local Cooperative Extension Agent.

- **GARDENING,** *Herbs:* Herbs can grow in the ground, in hanging baskets, in window boxes, in pots (indoors in a sunny kitchen window or outdoors on patio, porch, or apartment balcony), even in a terrarium made from an old fish tank, large jar, or bowl. Remember, the farther away from the kitchen herbs are planted, the less they are used! Contact your local Cooperative Extension

Agent for best ways to grow herbs in your area. (See HERBS, Growing Your Own Herbal Teas.)

• **GARDENING,** *Plastic Mulch:* You can keep soil temperature and moisture constant by "mulching" plants with black plastic—plants are inserted in holes made in plastic sheeting or plastic sheeting is used to cover soil around them. Or, use organic mulch to reduce soil temperature and moisture fluctuations. (In some areas, heavy rainfall can cause rot when plastic mulch is used; check with your county agent or local botanical center/gardening experts.) Always plant in well-drained soil.

• **GARDENING,** *Pruning:* Spruce up your landscape by pruning trees and shrubs.
1. Cut crossed branches that rub each other; remove one to prevent damage to the other.
2. Remove dead or diseased wood. If a plant has been winter damaged, wait until new growth occurs so that you know what parts are really dead.
3. Prune spring flowering plants after they bloom. This includes climbing roses, which also are pruned after spring blooming. Other roses are pruned (in fall in most parts of the country) after their blooming period to a height of 18 to 24 inches, leaving four to six strong canes for the next year's growth.
4. If you have a tree or shrub that has outgrown its location, you can prune as much as one-third of the total plant. However, it's best to prune and shape plants each year on a schedule to avoid such major cutting.

• **GARDENING,** *Sowing Small Seeds, Healthy-Planet Recycling:* Pour seeds into an old spice shaker, put the lid on, and sprinkle over each garden row to evenly disperse small seeds. Cover seeds lightly with soil, water according to package directions, wait for results.

• **GARDENING,** *Watering Shrubs and Trees:*
1. Newly planted trees and shrubs need watering every five to seven days. When you water, apply a thorough soaking so that enough moisture gets to the roots and helps them become well-established.

But, don't water more often than every five days; roots will suffocate because too much water removes oxygen from the root zone.

2. Consider rainfall when making a watering schedule. Even well established trees and shrubs need water when less than one inch of rain falls during a one-week period. If your area hasn't had rain in 7 to 10 days, you'll need to water to maintain healthy plants.

3. Mulching the soil surface maintains moisture and prevents evaporation of water. It also regulates soil temperatures so that you get better root growth.

- **GARDENING,** *Winterizing Checklist:*

1. Mulches: In cold climates, mulches of straw, salt hay, evergreen boughs, pine needles, and non-packing leaves prevent the alternate freezing and thawing of the soil. In warm climates, mulches prevent soil from drying and crusting and keep it cool during hot weather. Before layering mulch on your garden beds, remove dead or diseased plants to ensure a healthy start in the spring. You can find out about winterizing trees and shrubs in your climate from your Cooperative Extension Agent (county agent), local gardening columns, and local garden centers.

2. Evergreens' Care: Evergreens grow in almost every state and they aren't just pretty shrubs. Planted strategically, they can be windbreaks, privacy screens, hedges, background plants, and foundation plantings. Plant evergreens adapted to your local climate so that you don't need to wrap them for protection against winter winds and freezing temperatures and can continue to enjoy seeing them year-round.

When heavy snow and sleet blankets shrubs in the winter, sweep or shake branches to relieve them of the weight as soon as you can because ice buildup can break branches and cause deformed shapes. Winter winds can dry evergreens and cause browning of needles in certain species; water evergreens right up to the freeze-up if your weather has been dry. Because they don't lose leaves in the fall like deciduous trees, evergreens continue to lose moisture by transpiration (through the green needles) all winter long.

3. Roses: If your area temperatures regularly drop below zero, you need to protect your roses.

A. *Climbers:* Remove canes from the supports and tie them together in several places. Place a round object, such as a plastic bucket, on its side at the base of the plant and then bend the tied canes over it. Keep them pinned to the ground by tying them to a notched stake. Then cover the whole plant with at least 10 inches of soil or soil-mulch mixture.

B. *Bushes:* Prune tops back to 6 inches, using slanted cuts at about ¼ inch above the strong outside buds. You should have three healthy canes remaining after pruning. Apply wound compound to the cuts as directed on product. Make a collar around the base of the plant with builder's felt and then mound soil over the stubs for winter protection. The mound should be 8 to 12 inches deep. In the spring, when new shoots are about ½ inch long, remove the mounds by spraying them with the hose.

4. Grass/Lawn, Fertilizer: Apply fertilizer in the fall to encourage root growth and help it build up nutrient reserves for the winter. Good organic fertilizers include cottonseed meal, castor bean pomace, blood meal, composted cow manure or even compost, if you can sift it fine enough for a top dressing. Before you feed the soil, it's best to have it tested by your county agent or local garden center to determine what it needs and the pH of the soil. Fescues and bent grasses grow best in a range of 6.5 to 7 pH; bluegrass, ryegrass and Bermuda grass like a slightly higher level. Most grass plants absorb nutrients best when the pH is 6.5 to 7 and when the lawn soil has been aerated. To aerate the soil, you punch out small cores of soil 2 to 4 inches deep with an aeration machine, which you can rent.

5. Grass/Lawn, Thatching: Early fall is the best time to have your lawn thatched so that the lawn has a chance to recover before growth slows down for the winter. Thatching means removing the thickly matted organic material such as old, dead roots and runners. If your lawn has a very thick layer of thatch, a rake won't do. It's best to rent a thatching machine from your local gardening-supply store or other source. You can toss the material you remove into your compost pile for next spring's fertilizing.

• **GARDENING CALENDAR:** On a gardening calendar, note what was planted when; when plants sprouted; when they were watered, fertilized, and harvested. Then, you can plan the next year by seeing what grew, produced well, and in how much time.

• **GARDENING TIMER:** Take a kitchen timer outdoors with you so that you won't get so absorbed with gardening that you're late for other activities.

• **GARDENING TRAY:** A rubber garbage-can cover will hold small plants, gardening tools and other necessities so that you can carry them around the garden and avoid back and forth trips.

• **GARDEN SEEDLINGS,** *Planting in Egg Cartons:* When planting seedlings in egg-carton cups, place an eggshell half in the bottom before adding soil; then, it's easy to lift the whole seedling at planting time.

• **GARDEN TIMBERS,** *Healthy-Planet Recycling:* Instead of buying garden timbers to border flower or vegetable beds, tie rolls of old newspapers with wire or old panty hose twine and place them end to end.

• **GARDEN TOOLS,** *Avoiding Loss:* Paint handles of your rake, shovel, and other garden tools bright orange so you can see them at a glance if they are left somewhere in the yard. Also, if you lend the tools to anyone, they'll be identified easily as yours (unless the borrower also has orange-painted garden tools). If you frequently lend tools, it's best to put your name on them! I even put my mailing labels on my books so that they get back to me instead of spending eternity on someone else's shelf.

• **GARDEN TOOLS,** *Storage:* Put rakes, hoes, shovels, etc. into a large garbage can and hang smaller tools on S-hooks around the rim. Then you can drag all of your tools along with you as you work.

• **GAS,** *Keeping the Smell Off Hands at Self-serve Stations:* Either carry a rubber glove or cheap, thin sandwich bags in your car's glove compartment (where else would you keep gloves?). Your hands will stay clean and odor-free.

• **GELATIN,** *Why You Can't Add Fresh Pineapple:* Fresh or frozen pineapple has not been processed and so it still contains the enzyme bromelain which breaks down gelatin and won't let it set. Canned pineapple has been processed so it can be added to gelatin.

- **GELATIN MOLD,** *Unmolding:*
1. Dip the mold in hot water to loosen the gelatin and go around the edge with a thin knife.
2. Place lettuce leaves on top of the gelatin with the leaves folded down around the edges of the mold.
3. Place the serving plate (upside down) on the lettuce.
4. Now, holding the mold and plate firmly, turn the whole thing over so that the mold is on top and the plate is on the bottom. Shake the mold gently in a circular motion while holding the plate and mold in place.

The salad should drop down and be centered on the lettuce.

- **GENEALOGY,** *Tracking Lost Relatives:*
1. Main libraries of most large cities have phone books of most major cities for reference use. Check different city's phone books for names and addresses of people with your family name (bearing in mind that spellings change as people move around), and then send out letters in which you explain what you are doing and what information you seek.
2. Whenever you travel to another city or state, look up your family name in the phone book and send more letters.
3. Get a book on genealogy that tells you how you can trace ancestors through citizenship papers and immigration records.

- **GEOGRAPHY,** *Teaching Children (and Reminding Us Adults):* Put up a world map in the television room and then whenever the news or other program goes on, point to where the action is taking place. Even very young children can learn shapes of countries. International Understanding, *Letter of Laughter:* In some countries overseas, people are taught to cross the number 7. I was taught to do this and so was a reader who helped a friend's child to do math homework. Afterward, her friend called to say that the child was worried about his homework because he thought there was no way it could be right—his mother's friend didn't even know how to write the number 7! *Related Letter of Laughter:* There aren't just differences from one part of the world to another; geography affects viewpoints in different parts of the U.S. A Florida child, who was playing outside when snowflakes started falling—a rare event there—ran indoors excitedly shouting, "Look, Mommy, it's raining grits!" She had never seen snow "in real life" before!

• **GERBIL TREAT,** *Recycling:* Give a gerbil cardboard tubes from paper towels and tissue to chew on and shred for its nest; you recycle, and the gerbil gets something to do. Also give a gerbil scraps from salads such as carrot tops, lettuce, and celery about once a week.

• **GET WELL CARD,** *To Cheer Long-term Hospitalized Person:* Provide one flat sheet (or posterboard) and permanent markers of many colors so that well-wishers can write messages on the sheet along with, if they wish, a drawing of something cheery, or something relating to hobbies or interests. You can write the recovering person's name down one side of the sheet and put an adjective describing him by each letter. The sheet or poster can then be a keepsake to remind the recipient that people do care! **Note:** If you decide on a sheet, put something under it when writing so that the markers don't bleed through to hospital bedding or to the patient's leg!

• **GET WELL CARD,** *Mailing to Hospitalized Person:* Put the patient's own return address on the card. Then, if the patient leaves the hospital before the card arrives, the card will follow the person home via the mails.

• **GIFT,** *Ideas for Long-term Hospital Patients:* A calendar and clock to keep track of days, which seem to get lost when you are confined; a personal radio with ear plugs so the patient can listen without bothering others; change for the telephone. Don't bring food unless you find out if it's allowed. If you bring cut flowers, bring a jar or inexpensive vase to put them in; but, you might check first about allergies before bringing flowers!

• **GIFT,** *Ideas for Nursing Home Residents:* Socks; washable and dryable slippers; toothbrushes; large print books; lap quilt or small afghan; soft candy like gumdrops or mints (ask if they should be sugar-free); cards, paper, or postcards with stamps; powder, perfume, and hand lotion for women; shaving supplies for men; family pictures put in plastic pages; a bulletin board for posting pictures and cards; bib made with hand towel and self-gripping tape; gift certificate for hairdo or cut; ride in the car to change the scenery; one fresh flower (or silk flower) and a visit.

Also, gift certificate for manicure/pedicure; coin purse of change for telephone and vending machines; reading materials, including large print magazines and books, if there's a vision problem, and newspaper subscriptions for long-term care patients; radio or tape player with headphones. (Check first if person will use them, some elderly people don't accept the concept.)

Sweaters are appreciated but all clothing must be machine washable and dryable and it's better to buy a size larger so that stiff limbs don't have to bend so much. Find out about the home's identification system and if the resident has labels to sew on garments to ID them; if so, sew them on securely; otherwise mark all possessions with indelible markers.

- **GIFT GUESSING FUN:** Place some loose, raw macaroni in the box with a gift so that those who like to shake before opening will have a harder time guessing what's inside.

- **GIFT IDEAS:**
1. For elderly person—installation of a second phone in a convenient place
2. For friends or relatives—a photo collage that remembers good times together
3. Person in hospital or nursing home—see above

- **GIFT QUILT,** *Wrapping:* Since it's so large and hard to wrap anyway, put it in an under-bed storage container so the recipient can store the quilt in its own box.

- **GIFTS,** *Mailing:* Protect bows in the mail by placing a clean margarine tub upside down over them before packing. Secure with a bit of tape.

- **GIFT OF THOUGHTS:** A reader whose younger brother was in the hospital recovering from a serious back operation wanted to give him something to show that she was thinking about him even if she couldn't visit him often. Recalling that he said he remembered little of his childhood, she bought a school composition book and wrote stories about things he did, about their family's history and about important people in their lives. After receiving the book in the mail, her brother called to say that if she'd sent him a million dollars he would not have been happier. She had included things he'd always wanted to ask his parents but didn't. I think this gift shows that not all treasures cost money!

• **GIFT WRAP**, *Healthy-Planet Paper-Saving:* Wrap a going-away present in a road map to the recipient's destination. Wrap a baby present in a baby blanket or diaper to which you've pinned a rattle or other toys with diaper pins.

• **GIFT WRAP**, *Recycling:* Foil party balloons, after they deflate, can be gift bags. Cut the little neck off the bottom, and staple or tape it closed. Then cut across the top, either in the shape it is or straight. Then insert tissue paper with the gift and tie it shut with a ribbon.

• **GIFT WRAP**, *$aver:* You'll have wrap handy for all occasions if you keep plain white paper, not glossy, on hand. Then decorate and personalize it with stencils and colored markers or crayons. Top your art work with a matching ribbon or bow.

• **GIFT WRAP**, *Storage:* To keep rolls of wrapping paper from getting mashed or mangled with torn edges, slide the roll into the good leg of old panty hose and hang the "leg" on a small nail inside your closet. I think that if you had several rolls to store, you could leave the panty hose whole, put one roll in each leg, let the legs straddle a hanger, and then put the hanger with three to five panty hose paper rolls in your guest closet. Then wait for comments from surprised guests!

• **GIFT WRAP**, *Substitute:* None in the house? Wrap the gift in aluminum foil, shiny side out, covered by a sheet of colored plastic wrap, then add a ribbon or yarn bow or a flower. The foil holds its shape so you don't even need a box. If you cut the plastic wrap larger than the foil and press both sheets together, you don't even need tape.

• **GIFT WRAP**, *When Item Is Large or Awkwardly Shaped:* Place the item in a colored plastic trash or department store bag and tie it shut. If the item is so large that it requires two bags, join the seam where the two bag open-ends come together and cover the joint with a wide ribbon.

• **GIFT WRAP BOWS,** *Healthy-Planet Recycling:* A curling iron will "iron" crumpled bow loops and make them look new in a few seconds.

• **GIFT WRAPPED IN A BOTTLE,** *Recycling:* When a two-liter soda bottle (with opaque bottom "bowl") is empty, run hot tap water over the outside to remove the colored bottom from the clear part. Then cut a hole in the bottom of the clear part and put a gift inside the bottle. Then stick the colored part of the bottle back on and tie a ribbon around the neck. Then, have fun as people try to figure out how you got the gift into the bottle! **Hint:** This also can be a terrarium for small plants, which can also be a gift!

• **GIFT WRAP RIBBON,** *Substitute:* Forget the ribbon? Cut strips of the remaining wrapping paper, curl them with scissors, and glue them to the package. These curls match better than ribbon!

• **GLASS,** *Quick-Fix Cleaning Up Shards of Shattered Glass:* After carefully picking up large pieces, wet a piece of newspaper and then put the paper on the tiny bits and pieces; lift it up and the glass will cling to the paper. Be sure to "blot" the entire floor—when glass shatters, it's amazing how far the pieces will fly!

• **GLASS CLEANER,** *Homemade:* Mix 2 ounces of rubbing alcohol, 2 ounces of non-sudsing ammonia, and 12 ounces of water and store in a clean spray bottle. **Caution:** Always mark containers of home-made solutions clearly to avoid accidents.

• **GLASS DECANTER,** *Removing Stains from the Inside:* Sometimes stains in antique decanters cannot be removed. Some dealers mix about ¼ cup dishwasher detergent compound with hot water. When the water cools, fill the decanter to the top and let soak for a few hours or overnight. A bottle brush may remove stubborn stains, too, but some may remain. **Note:** Since recent studies show that lead leaches from crystal containers into the contents, you may not want to store liqueurs or wines in the decanters for long term. One of my friends displays her favorite decanters with food-coloring tinted water and it covers up some of the stains.

• **GLASS DOOR ON STEREO SET:** If the stereo components are in a shelved cabinet with a clear, glass-only panel door, place a decal near the top so that people can see when the door is open.

- **GLASSES,** *When Two Stacked Ones Get Stuck Together:*
1. Put cold water in the top glass and dip the bottom one in warm to hot water. Gently pull the glasses apart.
2. Or, pour some baby oil or mineral oil between the glasses, allow to set for a while and then gently pull them apart. Wash in hot soapy water and rinse.

- **GLASSES, WASHING BY HAND,** *Avoiding Water Spots:* Wash with the proper amount of liquid dishwashing detergent and rinse in the hottest water safe for the glasses and your hands, and then dry with a soft, lint-free cloth. **Hint:** Wear rubber gloves to get a good grip and protect your hands from hot water. If your area has hard water, rinse the glasses in water to which a splash (less than a glug but more than a spritz!) of vinegar has been added.

- **GLASSWARE, CRYSTAL,** *Spot Removal:* Dip spotted glassware into water to which a splash of vinegar has been added, dry with lint-free dishcloth. Please see GLASSES, Washing By Hand.

- **GLUE,** *Healthy-Planet Ideas:* To avoid harmful chemicals, use staples or reusable metal paper clips and if glue is a must, use a glue stick (made from petroleum derivatives), white glue (made from polyvinyl acetate plastic) or yellow glue (made from aliphatic plastic resin). When using tape select aluminum or brown paper tape.

- **GLUE,** *Homestyle Healthy-Planet Recipes:* Here are some glues you can make yourself with ingredients from your kitchen and hardware or drug stores:
Glue #1 —*Paper, Glass, or Porcelain Glue:* 6 tablespoons gum arabic; 1 cup water; ½ cup plus 2 tablespoons natural glycerin. Dissolve gum arabic in water, add glycerin, and mix well. Apply to both surfaces with toothpick or tongue depressor, hold together for 5 minutes. You'll need to make a fresh batch each time, this doesn't keep.
Glue #2 —*Paper Glue:* 4 tablespoons wheat flour; 6 tablespoons cold water; 1½ cups boiling water. Blend flour into enough cold water to make a smooth paste, boil 1½ cups water and stir into mixture, stirring until mixture is translucent. Use when cold.
Glue #3 —*Paper Glue:* 3 tablespoons cornstarch; 4 tablespoons cold water; 2 cups boiling water. Blend cornstarch and cold water

to make a smooth paste. Stir paste into boiling water, continue to stir until mixture becomes translucent. Use when cold.

Glue #4 —*Paper Glue:* ¼ cup cornstarch; ¾ cup water; 2 tablespoons light corn syrup; 1 teaspoon white vinegar. Blend all ingredients above in medium saucepan. Cook over medium heat, stirring constantly, until mixture thickens. Remove from heat. In separate bowl, mix until smooth ¼ cup cornstarch and ¾ cup water. Add this to the first heated mixture, stirring constantly. This glue will keep two months in a covered container.

Glue #5 —*Paper Glue:* Blend 4 tablespoons wheat flour and 6 tablespoons cold water to make a smooth paste. Boil 1½ cups water and stir in paste, cooking over very low heat for about 5 minutes. Use when cold.

• **GLUE GUN:** When you use a hot glue gun to glue trim on fabric, press the trim in place with the end of a chop stick (the cheap wooden ones that come in packages) and you won't burn the tip of your finger.

• **GOLD,** *Quick-Fix Polishing:* Wash in lukewarm, soapy water, dry and polish with a chamois cloth.

• **GOLF BALLS,** *Healthy-Planet Recycling Storage:*
1. Egg cartons will hold a collection of golf balls in neat stacks.
2. Rather than have them rolling loose, slip three balls into a tube from a roll of toilet tissue. Mark the outside with the brand of balls inside and then just peel off a portion of the tube to extract a ball.

• **GOURMET COFFEES,** *Quick-Fix Homemade:* The directions for all of them are: Blend ingredients in a blender or food processor until powdered. Substitute appropriate amounts of artificial sweetener for sugar and powdered creamer for powdered milk, if you wish. To serve, put 2 rounded teaspoons of coffee into a cup filled with hot water.
1. Orange Coffee: Blend ½ cup instant coffee, ¾ cup sugar, 1 cup powdered milk, and ½ teaspoon dried orange peel.
2. Mocha Coffee: Just mix ½ cup instant coffee, ½ cup sugar, 1 cup coffee creamer, and 2 tablespoons cocoa.
3. Cinnamon Coffee: Blend ½ cup instant coffee, ⅔ cup sugar, ⅔ cup powdered milk, and ½ teaspoon cinnamon.

- **GRABBER:** Too short? Can't reach? Make a "grabber" for picking up small items, pulling the oven rack in and out, and to hook on other unreachables by attaching a cup hook to one end and a coat hook to the other end of a ½-inch wooden dowel cut to a 3-foot length. (It also reaches that place in the middle of your back that itches!)

- **GRAHAM CRACKER CRUMBS,** *Substitute:* When she had no graham crackers to "crumb" for a dessert bar recipe, one reader substituted 1½ cups crushed ice-cream cone crumbs for one cup of graham cracker crumbs and loved it!

- **GRANDMA/GRANDPA GIFTS TO CHILDREN:** So that very young children who live far away can understand who sent the gift, take a photo of grandma/grandpa holding it and enclose it with the gift.

- **GRANDMA/GRANDPA VISITING:** To keep children occupied while adults talk and visit after dinner at the table, keep a bookcase in a nearby room filled with coloring books, picture books, storybooks, crayons, markers, games, bubble pipes, and plastic building blocks. Adults can excuse the children with some hugs and kisses and continue to talk while the children play. **Hint:** Cut puzzles and games from newspapers and save them for older children to work on. You could even paste them in a scrapbook or spiral notebook to make a puzzle book if you feel ambitious.

- **GRAPES,** *Frosted for Garnish:* Dip fresh seedless grapes in beaten egg white and then sprinkle them with gelatin. Put the gelatin in a salt shaker for easier shaking and use sugar-free gelatin if you are counting calories.

- **GRAPES,** *Frozen Treats:* Buy too many grapes? Freeze grapes in a plastic zipper bag or a well-sealed container for healthy sweet treats. Also, holding a frozen grape in your mouth for a while is a good dieter's trick for fighting an attack of the munchies.

- **GRATING CHEESE OR VEGGIES:** To prevent such "additives" as the tips of your fingers when you grate foods, put a thimble on the finger you usually abuse. For many people, it's the thumb.

- **GRAVY WITH "BLAHS,"** *When Chicken or Turkey Gravy Looks Pale:* Add a tablespoon of low-salt soy sauce or Worchestershire, depending upon your taste. Also, sprinkle paprika into the gravy as it boils to thicken and watch how it gets a nice warm brown color. Paprika doesn't affect the taste unless you add mass quantities of it. **Hint:** Sprinkle in paprika until the color improves, but don't sprinkle directly from the can or jar. Steam rising from gravy or sauces causes powdered spices to cake and loose their zip! Instead, sprinkle some in your hand, then, from hand to pan.

• GRAVY WITHOUT LUMPS: Always add powder to liquid not vice versa. Pour liquid (water, milk, bouillon) into a clean, empty jar with a tight-fitting lid. Add flour or cornstarch, screw on the lid, and shake until all is completely blended. Add mixture to casseroles, soups, gravies, etc.

• GRAVY SERVER: Try a large teapot for no mess gravy pouring at family dinner. It'll stay warmer, too, with a lid and tea cozy on it.

• GREETING CARD DISPLAY: Toss Christmas and other greeting cards into a pretty basket and keep it where it can cheer you up anytime.

• GREETING CARDS, *Having Spares:* When you shop for greeting cards, buy spares so that you have some handy when you can't go shopping. Watch for gift wrap sales, too, and stock up.

• GREETING CARDS, *Healthy-Planet Recycling Used Ones:* If you don't recycle them yourself by cutting off the fronts and using them for gift tags or postcards (draw a dividing line for message and addresses), call your local United Way and ask for information Referral Service (most have one) and they'll try to find a local organization that can use them. Sometimes pre-school or day-care centers and elementary schools can use the cards (and suitable magazines) for arts and crafts projects. **Hint:** If you include a handwritten note in your Christmas card, write the current Christmas message on last year's card fronts and each card you received will be used twice!

• GREETING CARDS, *Time-Saver:* When you buy extra cards, file them in an accordion record file or pattern file box according to "birthday," or "get well," etc. and you won't have to dig through them all when you want one. Toss a perfume sample from a magazine page in with them and they'll smell nice, too.

• **GRILLED CHEESE SANDWICH,** *Quick-Fix, No Mess, Less Fat:* Toast two slices of bread in the toaster, put cheese in between, zap in the microwave for 20 to 30 seconds (depends on type of cheese and your microwave wattage). No frying, less mess and fewer calories! **Hint:** If you like the toast to stay crisp, put the sandwich on a paper plate, which absorbs the moisture, before zapping.

• **GROCERY BAGS,** *Healthy-Planet Recycling for Kindling Wood:*
1. Put kindling wood in paper grocery sacks and then put sack and all into the stove or picnic bonfire as a firestarter.
2. When you buy charcoal for the grill, divide it into paper grocery sacks so that you have a "dose" ready for the fire without having to handle the charcoal again.

• **GROCERY SACKS,** *Easy Lifting:* If the handles of heavily loaded plastic grocery sacks cut into your hands when you carry them into the house, try hooking three to five bags on a boot hook (the kind used to remove cowboy boots). No more pain!

• **GROUT,** *Cleaning:* When bleach won't work, you may have to replace the grout. Oil that gets into grout of ceramic-tiled kitchen floors cannot usually be removed. You have to remove the stained area and regrout. An alternative can be to stain all of the grout, but that's a major project.

To avoid this problem, protect grout from stain, mildew and washing out by spraying a water-seal product on the area. Spray, then wipe excess from tiles while the product is still wet. Seal will remain in the grout and make it look good longer.

• **GUEST ROOM WELCOME:** This cute saying could be embroidered or printed on a plaque to make guests feel at home.
You are welcome here,
Be at your ease,
Go to bed when you're ready,
Get up when you please.

• **HAIR,** *Checklist for Choosing Shampoos:* Each shampoo seems to have some magic ingredient—wheat germ oil, aloe, collagen, jojoba, sheep's placenta, ammonium lauryl sulfate—that also makes the price "magic." I use baby shampoo or any shampoo that's on sale because I've found that the result is the same, no matter what I use. I often dilute my shampoos; they last longer and are easier to rinse off. Now, research reported by the University of California, Berkeley Newsletter confirms that many claims are meaningless and costly ingredients just go down the drain. Here's some help when you read those labels.

1. Washing Oil Out: You can wash your hair with bar soap but it leaves a film. Shampoos have detergent to remove oil and dirt. Oily hair shampoos just have more detergent. Most shampoos have foam boosters because suds make people feel clean.

2. Putting Oil In: After detergents take the oil out, people want conditioners to put it back in. Using a separate conditioner makes hair feel better to the touch. Conditioners include lanolin, balsam, glycerol, propylene glycol, and other oils.

3. Other Additives: Proteins such as keratin or collagen are supposed to make hair look fuller and botanicals like mint, chamomile,

or other "natural" herbals are supposed to add luster. These usually just add price and go down the drain when you rinse. Other additives are scents, colors, and preservatives. Citric acid is added to counteract the alkalinity of shampoos—the "pH"—but makes little or no difference to your hair's look.

4. Dandruff Shampoos: Contain active ingredients like pyrithione zinc, selenium sulfide, a sulfursalicylic compound or coal tar. They remove dandruff if used frequently but so do ordinary shampoos. Everyone has some dandruff; it's natural for the skin to shed its outer layers. If you have severe dandruff that causes crusting, itching or redness, see a dermatologist. The same advice applies to other scalp disease.

5. Hair shafts are dead tissue; the only cure for split or roughened hairs is to cut off damaged parts.

6. Price does not determine shampoo quality and most people can't tell one shampoo from another in blind studies. Try using less. Also, you don't need to lather up twice, especially if you shampoo frequently.

• **HAIR,** *Creme Rinse:* Laundry fabric softener diluted 1 teaspoon to 1 cup of water can be used for creme rinse after you shampoo. I've done it for years and it makes my hair manageable and soft.

• **HAIR,** *Dyes, Healthy-Planet Alternatives:* Many hair dye products contain potentially carcinogenic chemicals. They also contain chemicals which are absorbed through the scalp and which can cause problems for people who are allergic to them or have sensitive skin. These chemicals include coal-tar dyes, ammonia, detergents, hydrogen peroxide, and lead.

1. Henna is the safest commercial hair color product, henna can darken or highlight hair and it washes out gradually over a six-month period. Generally speaking with plant materials like henna, often sold at health food stores, you process the product as directed and then strain and cool before using. Pour the liquid through the hair 15 times, catching it in a basin so that you can rerinse with the same liquid. Then wring out excess, allow to remain in hair for 15 minutes and rinse with clear water.

2. To lighten hair: rinse with mixture of 1 tablespoon lemon juice to 1 gallon warm water.

3. To darken hair: rinse with strong black tea or black coffee.

4. To get red tones: rinse with strong tea of rosehips or cloves, or use strong black coffee.

5. To cover gray, simmer ½ cup of dried sage in 2 cups of water for thirty minutes, then steep for several hours. Apply tea to hair after it cools, allow to dry, then rinse and dry hair again. Apply weekly until you have the shade you want and then monthly to maintain the color.

• **HAIR,** *Healthy-Planet Homestyle Shampoos:*

1. Castile Soap: It's tried and true for shiny hair! Grate castile bar soap and mix it with pure water in a blender or food processor, then blend 1 cup of this liquid with ¼ cup olive, avocado or almond oil and another ½ cup distilled water. Store in properly marked squirt bottle. Use sparingly.

2. Baking Soda: Here's my baking soda again! This time it's a dandruff remedy. Wet your hair, then rub in a handful of dry baking soda, then rinse. This may make your hair seem drier than usual for the first weeks of use but soon your hair's natural oils will make your hair very soft.

(Many commercial shampoos are not as benign as they used to be; some contain ammonia, potentially harmful colors, cresol, detergent, EDTA, ethanol, formaldehyde, fragrance, glycols, nitrates/nitrosamines, plastic (PVP), sulfur compounds and a lot of other ingredients, such as the coal-tar solutions or recorcinol used in anti-dandruff shampoos, which can cause harm to internal organs if swallowed; some can be absorbed through the skin.)

• **HAIR,** *Making Thinning Hair Look Thicker:* After using the following methods, don't brush too much because you'll flatten your poufed hair.

1. Blow-dry in the opposite direction, starting at the roots, from the way you normally style or brush it.

2. Blow-dry your hair while bending forward from the waist.

• **HAIR,** *My Favorite Homestyle Conditioner:* Massage a dollop or two of real mayonnaise (not salad dressing) into your hair before shampooing; wrap your hair with plastic film, and cover all with a bath towel. Leave on for at least thirty minutes; wash hair as usual with warm or cool water, not hot. Rinse very well and enjoy great feeling hair.

• **HAIR,** *Removing Green Resulting from Pool Chlorine:* Try dissolving six to eight aspirins in a glass of warm water; saturate hair strands; leave on for ten to fifteen minutes; rinse thoroughly and shampoo. Also look for special shampoos formulated to remove discoloration caused by chlorine and minerals. They are usually referred to as swimmer's shampoo and can be found in beauty supply stores and some hair-care products sections in supermarkets.

• **HAIR,** *When the Perm Is Too Curly/Wavy:* Speak to the salon about the problem. If nothing can be done, styling with a hair dryer will straighten it out somewhat. Other ways to help the curl relax include applying a conditioner after each shampoo and controlling your hair with mousse or gel.

• **HAIR ACCESSORIES,** *Recycling for Other Uses:* If you cut long hair short, your favorite barrettes, ponytail rings and other hair accessories can be recycled as scarf rings and clips.

• **HAIR CONDITIONER,** *Other Uses:*
1. Smooth on conditioner after bath or shower and it's a nice body lotion.
2. Substitute conditioner for lather when shaving your legs; it won't leave your skin as dry as soap or shaving cream.
3. Put conditioner in warm water for a manicure/pedicure soak.

• **HAIR RIBBONS,** *Quick-Fix:* Iron them with the hair curler!

• **HAIR SHAMPOO/CREME RINSE,** *Slippery Containers:* Wrap a couple of fat rubber bands around your shampoo and creme-rinse bottles and they won't slip out of your hands in the shower.

• **HAIR SPRAY,** *Keeping It Off Earrings and Out of Ears:* Cover your ear on the side you are spraying with the spray-can cap.

• **HALLOWEEN,** *Trick or Treat Non-Sweets:* Instead of candy, buy small party-favor toys, balls, baseball cards, and other inexpensive items and let children pick some from a bowl.

- **HALLOWEEN PUMPKIN,** *Trick and Treat:* After carving, sprinkle the inside of the lid and inside bottom of the pumpkin with a bit of nutmeg and cinnamon. Then when you light a candle, "Jack-O'-Lantern" will look bright and smell nice, too.

- **HAMBONE BROTH:** Place the bone with leftover ham still on it into a large pot and cover with water. Bring to a boil and boil until all meat falls off. Cool and skim off the fat. Place the ham and broth into small individual containers and freeze. Then you can use the broth to season beans, vegetables, and more.

- **HAMSTER CATCHER:** When your hamster escapes, find a box with a lid and line the bottom with a small towel or crumpled newspaper. Make a hole in the lid large enough for the "escapee" to drop through, then lay a paper towel or hanky over the hole and put some food on it to entice the hungry hamster to the trap.

- **HAMSTERS, GERBILS, MICE AS PETS:** Rodent pets (Yes, they are rodents but nice ones!) are low-cost and easy upkeep pets, especially in apartments where dogs and cats aren't allowed.
1. Housing: One or two can live nicely in a ten-gallon aquarium with a wire screen on top or in any metal cage that same size—any "home" that they can't chew their way out of.
2. Needs: Small glass ashtrays make good feeding dishes. Food is usually sold in supermarkets or grocery stores. Treats include carrots or celery and unsalted sunflower seeds. A water bottle is a less messy way to give them water. They love to chew ice-cream sticks. An exercise wheel is important so they can run for health.
3. Maintenance: Cages need cleaning every couple of weeks and they will be almost odor-free. They are nocturnal—they'll do most of their running in the evening so a child can enjoy them after school but they can be noisy if kept in a child's bedroom overnight. Be sure to put some lubricant on the exercise wheel's moving parts!

- **HANDBAGS,** *Recycling Broken/Worn Ones:* They can hold craft items to work on when traveling or visiting, store small items in the closet, hold tools for odd jobs around the house, hold tools and other emergency items kept in a car trunk, organize temporary files, and more.

- **HANDBAG SHOULDER STRAPS,** *Prevent Slipping:* If one strap keeps slipping off your shoulder, join the straps by machine-stitching a

2-inch strip of self-adhesive tape to them; they will automatically stick together and you can still pull them apart when you want to. If the straps are too thick to stitch yourself, you can have a shoe repair shop do it.

• **HANGERS,** *Color-Coding to Organize Closet:* Durable plastic hangers in assorted colors can help you find your clothing quickly. One reader codes blue for blouses, red for slacks, yellow for skirts, white for dresses and so on and can always find blouses if they've been "misfiled" among the skirts or slacks.

• **HANGERS,** *Making Them Non-Slip:* When garments slip off their hangers, punch a hole in the center of a piece of fabric and slip the fabric over the hanger hook so that it hangs over and covers the "shoulders" of the hanger. Some fabrics can be old sheets cut to size, leftover yardage from sewing projects, an old diaper, terry-cloth towel, or just an old T-shirt hung normally.

• **HANGERS,** *When Wooden Ones Snag Clothing:* Sand them smooth with sandpaper then brush on clear shellac.

• **HANGERS,** *Recycling Wire Ones:* If your dry cleaner doesn't take them back, call local thrift stores, preschools, or Scouting organizations; they may be happy to have them for hanging clothes or for crafts.
1. Bend the wire into a circle, cover with old panty hose and you have a small leaf skimmer or paint strainer.
2. Remove the paper tube from pants hangers, bend the wire ends inward and you have a paper towel holder outdoors or when camping.
3. Straighten and hang a bird feeder from it; squirrels can't get to the food.
4. Unhook one end of a pants hanger, put rolls of gift ribbon on it and replace the end. You have a multi-roll dispenser.
5. Bend both "arms" of a wire hanger upward to hold spaghetti-strap garments in the closet or to hang bra straps on for drying indoors.

• **HANGING LIGHTWEIGHT THINGS ON WALLS:** To hang lightweight wall decorations, calendars, etc. without damaging walls, with pliers break the eye off a sewing needle, and use the needle as a nail.

When you need to remove it, just pull it straight out from the wall and close the tiny hole with your fingernail.

• **HEADBANDS,** *Recycling, Storing Neatly:* Empty three-liter soft-drink bottles, washed and dried, will hold headbands neatly and the ones with bows or ruffles won't get crushed.

• **HEATING,** *$aving, Energy-Saving:*
1. Practice "zone heating." Close the registers or heating vents in all unused rooms; heat only the rooms you actually live in.
2. Room heaters are not as efficient as furnaces, but will heat rooms or areas with less energy consumption. They generally plug into a 110-volt socket. Check the label for wattage, too. The rule of thumb is that you need one watt per cubic foot of air volume in the room. Also see ENERGY saving ideas.

• **HEIRLOOMS,** *Passing Them On:* Many people like to pass on family heirlooms before they pass on themselves because they enjoy seeing the heirs using them. For example, a silver service that is seldom used by parents who don't entertain much anymore is a treasure to a daughter who is just beginning to entertain more formally. The trick is to give possessions when the time is right, to the child or children who will really love, use, and appreciate them. A good time is on happy occasions when all the people involved are present so they all share lifetime memories. My father and I "share" certain special family treasures that we trade back and forth.

• **HELPING PEOPLE,** *Checklist, How to Offer Help So That It Can Be Received:*
1. Be specific about what you can do. Say: "I'm going to the dry cleaners on Wednesday. I can stop by and get your cleaning, too." Or: "I'm grocery shopping on Friday. If you make me a list, I'll shop for you." Or, "I'm getting my hair done (or going to the movies, taking a class) Thursday, would you like to go with me?"
2. If you take over a casserole, and this is a wonderful help, especially when there's a new baby in the house or the family cook is sick, take it in a disposable container, and maybe include paper plates, napkins, and cups so there's no clean up or returns.
3. Offer to mail items or buy stamps for shut-ins or to take a shut-in's pet to the vet or groomer.

4. If you have a friend who is disabled, or a friend with a periodically disabling disease like arthritis, offer to change beds, dust, wash windows, clean blinds, rake leaves, sweep sidewalks, do minor repairs, or other everyday chores which are difficult for someone who isn't agile.

5. Offer to host a birthday party for a disabled friend's child or to take the child somewhere where the friend can't go, such as trail hiking or roller-skating. If your friend is having a party, offer to come over an hour early to help in preparations.

6. People who have disabling or chronic illness say they would rather answer questions about their problems than have people wonder about or assume certain things about the illness. And then, after the questions are answered, they would like to move on to lighter conversation and not dwell on illness. Also, a hug is always welcome even if it's awkward to hug someone in bed or in a wheelchair and, if your friend has arthritis, a hug is better than a handshake which can be painful to arthritic fingers.

- **HEMMING,** *Time-Saver:* Instead of threading just one needle, thread two or three before you start to hem a garment. Then when you run out of thread, you can pick up another threaded needle without stopping and breaking your work rhythm.

- **HEMMING-TAPE MISTAKE:** If you put iron-on hemming tape on the wrong side of the fabric, try this:
Place a damp cloth over the tape, hold a warm iron on it for at least ten seconds, then pull off the tape while it's still warm. It may take several tries. If residue remains, hold a steam iron above the area and the residue should disappear into the fabric. Wash as the care label directs.

- **HEMS,** *Repairing Suede or Leather:* These garments are hemmed with acrylic latex glue (water-based and clear-drying) made especially for leather and suede and sold at leather-craft stores.

- **HERBS,** *Growing Your Own Herbal Teas:* There are many herbs which grow indoors as well as outdoors. Grown indoors, herbs can be decorative houseplants as well as tea leaves. **Caution:** Do not experiment with unfamiliar herbs when making homemade tea blends. Some herbs are actually poisonous (like some ferns) and others, like some mints, have medicinal properties that could be harmful to people with certain health conditions. Get information from your county agent or local botanical center. (See GARDENING, Herbs.)

• HERBS, *Preserving for Tea* (See **Caution** above):
1. For herbs that don't dry well, brew a concentrate and freeze it in cubes so that you can thaw one cube for a cup of hot tea or add melted cubes to lemonade. To steep: mash leaves, cover with hot water, allow to steep for a day or so, strain liquid, and freeze in cubes.
2. To make tea "infusion," strip leaves from stems and chop; measure twice as much water as you have chopped leaves; add leaves to water when it boils; boil for 5 minutes; let cool; strain into a jar for storage in the fridge. For a cup of tea, add twice as much boiling water as infusion, sweeten to taste with honey; lemon, optional.
3. To dry herb leaves for tea: Cut branches just as they mature or flower, hang for about a week in an airy, shady place, then crumble dried leaves into airtight jars. To make tea from dried leaves, steep in boiling water. To make one cup of tea, place a few leaves in a cup; pour boiling water over them; add honey and lemon juice to taste.
4. Mint is a common tea herb. To make tea from fresh mint, choose larger leaves or pinch off leaf clusters at the stem end (instant pruning); drop a handful or so into a quart of boiling water; steep 10 minutes; strain and serve. To dry mint leaves for tea, cut branches before blooming, hang in a shady place until dry, then gather dried leaves and store in an airtight jar.

To make frozen concentrate, add about 2 cups coarsely chopped mint leaves and stems to a pint of boiling water; allow water to boil, remove from heat, cover, let cool about 1 hour; strain; freeze in ice-cube trays. For tea, heat a cube with enough water to make 1 cup or add cubes to other teas, punches, or soups. For a special treat, freeze a block of mint concentrate (with a nice sprig or two in the middle for decoration) and let it float in the punch bowl.

• HERBS, *Making Your Own Herbal Vinegars:* Heat vinegar in an enamel pan and pour it into a vinegar bottle; add one or several culinary herbs to taste. Do not let vinegar boil. Let the mixture steep for two weeks before using. Any type of vinegar can be used; it depends upon your preference.

• **HERBS,** *Making Herbal Butters:* To one stick of unsalted butter, add 1 to 3 tablespoons dried herbs or 2 to 6 tablespoons fresh herbs, ½ teaspoon lemon juice, and white pepper to taste. Combine ingredients and mix until fluffy. Pack in covered container and let set at least one hour. Any culinary herbs and spices may be used. (See Herbal Combinations below.)

• **HERBS,** *Making Your Own Herbal Combinations for Cooking:*
1. Fine herbs: Includes parsley, chervil, chives, French tarragon (and sometimes you can add a small amount of basil, fennel, oregano, sage, or saffron).
2. Bouquet garni mixtures: Bay leaf, parsley (two parts), thyme. The herbs may be wrapped in cheesecloth or the parsley can be wrapped around the thyme and bay leaf.
Note: When you cook herbs, bay leaf, whole peppers, etc. in soup or stew, put them in a mesh or perforated metal tea ball so that they are easily removed and nobody bites into a pepper ball or risks choking on a piece of bay leaf.
3. Barbecue blend: Cumin, garlic, hot pepper, oregano
4. Italian blend: Basil, marjoram, oregano, rosemary, sage, savory, thyme
5. Vegetable herbs: Basil, parsley, savory
6. Tomato sauce herbs: Basil (two parts), bay leaf, marjoram, oregano, parsley (optional additions could be celery leaves, cloves)
7. Salad herbs: Basil, lovage, parsley, French tarragon
8. Poultry herbs: Lovage, marjoram (two parts), sage (three parts).
9. Fish herbs: Basil, bay leaf (crumbled), French tarragon, lemon thyme, parsley (options include fennel, sage, savory)
10. Egg herbs: Basil, dill weed (leaves), garlic, parsley

• **HINT, POSTING FOR PROMPT USE:** When you cut out diet or food hints, put them on the fridge door; if you cut out makeup or bathing hints, tape them inside the medicine cabinet. When hints are stored where they'll be used, you're more likely to remember to try them.

• **HOLIDAY DECORATIONS SWITCH:** When holiday decorations replace knickknacks in certain places, solve the problem of where to safely put the knickknacks by storing them in the containers that normally hold the holiday decorations.

• **HOLIDAY DECORATOR LINENS:** Wait for after-holiday sales to buy Christmas Santa, Easter Bunny, Valentine Heart and other fabrics and then make special holiday pillowcases for cheery decorations in children's or adults' rooms.

• **HOLIDAY DESSERT TOPPING:** Add a few drops of food coloring to dessert topping to make it festive. Try orange-colored topping on a Thanksgiving pumpkin pie, red and green for Christmas, red for Valentine's day, green for St. Patrick's day, or a favorite color of the birthday person.

• **HOME BUILDING,** *Photos:* Photograph everything that goes underground like pipes, wires, septic tank, gas lines and then it will be easy to find them when you need repairs—hopefully, with a new home, you won't need repairs too soon!

• **HOME BUYING,** *Checklist:*
1. The general cost formula is that the home price should not exceed two to two and a half times your annual family income or the monthly mortgage, electric, water, and maintenance bills should not exceed 25 percent of your total monthly income.
2. Get a house inspector or construction expert to look for flaws, damage, and possible repair problems in the future before you buy, unless the price is such a bargain that the repair costs are not a factor.
3. To make sure you've chosen the right house, consider distance to schools, availability of bus service, how long it takes family members to get to work or school.
   Are there shopping malls, grocery stores, post office and hospital nearby? How high are area taxes? Are ambulance and fire service available?
   Are any unusual restrictions enforced? Ask area neighbors if they have encountered any unique problems.

• **HOME PERMANENT,** *Catching Drips:* Put on a terry-cloth sport/exercise headband and tuck cotton inside. It will catch drips better than cotton stuck to your skin with petroleum jelly, the usual drip solution.

• **HOME PERMANENT,** *Sectioning Off Hair:* If you don't have hairpins or clips to hold sections in place, try twist-ties. Just make sure no metal wire touches the permanent solution because it might discolor.

• **HOME PERMANENT PAPERS,** *When You Have Leftovers:* Carry in your purse to absorb oil on your face without disturbing your makeup and to blot lipstick. They work so well, you may want to buy the papers for that purpose from a beauty supply house.

• **HOME PERMANENT PAPERS,** *Substitute If You Run Out:* Coffee filters cut to the proper size.

• **HOME SECURITY:** One reader puts a large (size 14), dirty pair of men's work boots outside her front door to dissuade would-be intruders. She occasionally runs a little water over them to make them appear as if they had recently been worn. This may be false security, but if I were an intruder, I'd think twice before risking confrontation with a guy who wears size-14 boots!

• **HONEY,** *Reclaiming Sugared:* If honey gets sugared in storage, place the jar into the microwave for a couple of minutes and it will return to a pourable state. **Caution:** Microwave time will vary according to amount; better to zap it less time than too much. Also, do not place metal containers in the microwave and for extra caution, place the honey jar in a dish you know is microwave safe.

• **HONEY SUBSTITUTE:** Generally corn syrup can substitute for honey in most recipes but since it's not as sweet as honey, the dessert won't be as sweet. As with all substitutions, the texture and flavor can be slightly altered.

• **HORSE BLANKETS,** *Recycling:* Instead of putting saddle pads right on the horse, first put down an old baby blanket. It's soft on the horse's back, keeps the pads clean and is easier to launder in the machine than bulky pads are.

• **HORSES' FEEDING CAUTION: Note:** I'm not sure how many hints books have "horse hints" but I live in Texas where horses are working animals as well as "pets." However, horses graze in fields all over the country where dangers lurk. This warning information was sent to me from the Illinois Animal Poison Information Center. 1. Partial List of Plants Poisonous to Horses—Alsike clover, bladder pod, black locust (strip bark), black walnut, bluebonnet (lupines), buckeye, castor bean, chokecherry (wilted leaves), cock-lebur, coffeebean, corn cockle, death camas, ivy bush, Jerusalem cherry, jimsonweed, Klamath weed, lantana, larkspur, laurel, laurel cherry, locoweed, milkweed, oleander, pigweed, red maple, rhodo-dendron, tobacco, wild jasmine, yellow star thistle, yew, and rayless goldenrod.

2. Ingestion of fresh summer annual forages of Johnson grass, Sudan grass, and common sorghum causes a condition in the south-western U.S. called enzootic equine cystitis and ataxia. This condi-tion is only from eating FRESH Sudan or grazing on the plant in pasture. Clinical signs are straining to urinate, dribbling urine, lack of coordination, and mares who appear to be in constant heat.

3. Fescue grass is a commonly fed pasture forage. There is a cau-tion against allowing brood mares to graze fescue during the last three months of gestation. If mares cannot be removed from fescue pastures, they should be feed good quality alfalfa hay.

4. Check areas near fence rows, ditches, and springs where poison-ous plants flourish. If some plants are seasonal or hard to control, horses may have to be removed from some pastures at certain times of the year.

5. Horse owners can get help from local veterinarians, extension advisers, or local plant stores.

• HOSE $AVER: My readers say that if you put new panty hose into the freezer for twenty-four to forty-eight hours, then allow them to thaw, they don't run nearly as often.

• HOTEL RATES AND VACANCIES: While major hotel/motel chains have 800 numbers to call for reservations, calling the individual hotel, even if it costs a dollar or two, may help you get a discount and, when a special event has filled your destination city's hotels, you may be more likely to get a room since the national reservation office may not be aware of recent cancellations at individual sites. Note: Since larger cities often have several locations of national chain hotels/motels it's best to make sure you're staying on the most convenient side of town. Also, you'll need to tell the airport taxi driver which one to take you to.

• HOT TUB, Recommended Temperatures: My sources say the maxi-mum temperature should be 100°F; heat stroke can occur in some people at temperatures above 104°F. Many people find that 95°F is comfortable. **Caution:** People with certain health problems, such as high blood pressure, diabetes, or epilepsy, shouldn't soak when home alone.

• HOUSE, *Checklist for Making Your House Appeal to Buyers:*
1. Get rid of outside clutter; trim bushes, weed flower beds, and mow grass to give a good first impression. Also repair or remove fences if they are unsightly.
2. Clean doors and windows and sweep the sidewalks and driveway. Remove stains from sidewalks, driveways, and patios.
3. Clean the entire house inside, paying special attention to the kitchen, bathroom, and master bedroom. Make the stove, oven, sinks, and floor shine and fix any drippy faucets.
4. Clean, orderly closets and cabinets appear larger and make the whole house appear less cluttered.

• HOUSE, *Selling Trick:* As close to showing time as possible to allow for cleanup time, bake a batch of cookies to entice buyers with a homey, friendly aroma. (Refrigerator cookies will do, there's less cleanup, too!) Or, simmer a potpourri in your microwave!

• HOUSE, *Selling Yours:* Ask your friendly real-estate broker the following questions before you allow it to be listed.
1. Will you work up a fact sheet and brochure on my house?
2. Where will the sale be advertised and how often?
3. Will my house be placed in the multiple-listing service?
4. Will other brokers be invited to an open-house showing?
5. How will you publicize open houses and who will attend?
Interview at least three brokers and pick the one who best answers your questions. Don't be surprised if the broker says your asking price is too high, most people overevaluate their houses. The broker has to find someone who loves your home as much as you did and is willing to pay the asking or negotiated price for it.

• HOUSEHOLD INFORMATION NOTEBOOK, *Time-Saver:* Record all floor and window dimensions to make buying new curtains and flooring a snap. Record the different paint colors and brands and glue the paint-store samples of paint colors of the different rooms on the page with the description of that room; the same for swatches of wallpaper.

- **HOUSEKEEPING CREED,** *Letter of Laughter:* A reader sent in this Housekeeping Creed which she thought was a good New Year's Resolution.

> *I get into an awful state, just 'cause I procrastinate.*
> *And jobs that I abominate, pile up and accumulate.*
> *This new year I plan to liquidate,*
> *each lousy task immediate!*
> *That is, if doing what I hate,*
> *doesn't make some pleasure wait!*

- **HOUSEPLANT HELPER,** *Letter of Laughter:* My stepson Russell, trying to be helpful, volunteered to mist some avocado plants. He got so enthused that he misted all the plants—then found out that one big green plant was actually artificial!

- **HOUSEPLANTS,** *Safety:* If ingested, many common plants can be harmful to children and pets—philodendron, dieffenbachia, rhododendron, and various anemone species, to name just a few. Even the medicinal aloe vera plant, popularly used for skin irritations, can be harmful if eaten.
1. Keep the name tags on your plants and record their botanical names so that if a curious child or pet tastes any part of it, you can give an accurate description and proper name to your Poison Control Center. Call information to get the number and then keep it by the phone or program it into a programmable phone BEFORE you have an emergency.
2. If you have to rush a child or pet to an emergency facility, take the plant along with you to confirm its identity. If the plant's too large, cut off a twig; if it has flowers, seeds, fruits or exposed bulbs, take them, too.

- **HOUSEPLANTS,** *Watering While on Vacation:* Water plants thoroughly, then set on a small rock- or pebble-filled tray. Fill the tray with water, but don't overfill so that plants are soaked. Place tray with plants in indirect sunlight (direct may be too hot), and they will wait happily for you to return from a short vacation.

- **HOUSEPLANTS,** *Watering Without Mess:* Place a few ice cubes here and there; they'll melt slowly and you'll have no spillovers.

- **HUMIDIFIER,** *Removing Mineral Deposits:* Always check the manufacturer's instructions for details on cleaning your particular room humidifier. If you don't have instructions, the following method works for most humidifiers.

1. Fill the humidifier bowl with white vinegar and soak it for a couple of hours, or overnight for heavy buildup. Pour out the vinegar and rinse with fresh water. If deposits remain, repeat the procedure.

2. To soak an impeller (the little rod that actually sticks down into the water), fill a tall glass or jar with vinegar and immerse the impeller in it. Be careful not to bend the impeller or to get vinegar or water into the motor.

3. Regular soaking will cut down on the amount of buildup and soaking time. Using distilled or mineral-free water will also help prevent buildup. **Note:** Keeping the humidifier clean and deposit-free helps it work better and last longer.

• **HUMIDIFIER ALGAE,** *Avoiding It:* When small humidifiers get algae buildup in the water, frequent thorough cleaning is needed to remove the yucky slime. Add about one tablespoon of household bleach each time you fill the reservoir and the water will stay nice and clean. This small amount of bleach won't give off an unpleasant odor.

I

• **ICE CHESTS,** *Storage, Preventing Odors:* See COOLERS, Storage and COOLERS, Preventing Odors.

• **ICE CREAM,** *Healthy-Planet Freezing Individual Portions:* Save on the cost of individual ice cream portions (vs. quart or gallon sizes) and recycle clean one-cup lidded yogurt containers at the same time. Buy large containers of ice cream and put individual portions in the yogurt cups—there's no mess when children serve themselves and dieters aren't tempted to take larger portions than allowed.

• **ICE CREAM,** *Making Ice for Homemade Ice Cream:* Freeze water in empty quart-sized milk cartons overnight. Then, take a hammer and strike all four sides of the frozen carton a couple of times. Open the top and the crushed ice drops neatly into the ice-cream maker. Five quarts of ice with a layer of rock salt after each one is enough for the average ice-cream machine processing.

• **ICE CREAM,** *Snow-made:*
1. You must have fresh, clean snow. Collect it in a large plastic container as it falls.

2. Season heavy cream with a couple of drops of essence of lemon or maple syrup and powdered sugar.

3. Stir in snow until it's stiff like ice cream. Enjoy!

• **ICE CREAM,** *When It's Hard as a Brick:* Zap a half-gallon of ice cream in the microwave on "Low" for about 30 to 45 seconds depending on the wattage of your microwave—experiment to find the right amount of time. It will be easier to scoop.

• **ICE-CREAM CONE,** *Preventing Drippy Messes:* Place a small marshmallow in the bottom of the cone before you put the ice cream in. Then, if the ice cream melts, the marshmallow keeps it from dripping out of the bottom.

• **ICE-CREAM CONE,** *Quick-Fix, No Mess Serving Cup:* Put children's healthy snacks, such as dry cereal, small crackers, raisins, etc., in an ice-cream cone—no dishes to wash or clean up when the container is edible!

• **ICE-CREAM CRYSTALS,** *Prevention:* Ice cream should be kept at 20 degrees below zero. Crystals form when temperatures fluctuate and can indicate that the freezer is opened and closed too often or that there is a problem with the freezer itself. Keep track of your family's freezer use and if fewer open/close times don't help, the freezer may need servicing.

• **ICE-CREAM STICKS,** *Healthy-Planet Recycling:* Wash and save for stirring coffee; scraping mud or other goo from shoe bottoms; keeping in canisters to level off measuring cups; marking with depth measurements to help you plant seeds, bulbs, etc. and you can write on them for plant markers.

Also, they can spread condiments at picnics; glue, paste, grout or anything else that requires a disposable spreader. They can also stir paint in small containers. Check out craft books and shops for children's "keep-busy" ice-cream stick projects.

• **ICE CUBES GRANDE:** When the weather is hot and you need serious-size ice cubes to keep drinks cool, freeze them in muffin tins. Please see ICE CUBE SURPRISE below.

• **ICE-CUBE SURPRISE:** Freeze a maraschino cherry or a couple of mint leaves in each cube for pretty drink decorations.

- **ICE-CUBE TRAYS,** *Stuck Cubes:* Most ice-cube trays are coated and putting hot water into them melts off that coating; so does washing in hot, soapy dishwater or in the dishwasher. If cubes stick in your ice-cube trays, try spraying the trays with non-stick vegetable spray every now and then.

- **ICED TEA AND COFFEE:** Freeze leftover tea and coffee in ice cube trays to avoid dilution by regular cubes in your iced tea or coffee.

- **ICE PACK,** *Emergency for a Child's Lip Injury:* A frozen juice treat stops the tears and swelling when a child falls, hurts a lip, and needs a distraction as well as an ice pack.

- **ICE PACK,** *Homemade:* Mix one part rubbing alcohol with two parts water and freeze in a zipper plastic bag. It will be pliable enough to conform to a knee or elbow and can be refrozen after each use. Be sure to place a damp cloth between the skin and the ice pack to prevent frostbite.

- **INFLATABLE POOL RAFTS,** *Recycling:* If the raft has two valves—one for the pillow and the other for the body—and the body section is too leaky to patch, cut off the pillow section and save it for car trips, slumber parties, or for a bathtub pillow.

- **INFORMATION,** *Free:* More than 200 booklets with information on just about any subject you can think of are offered free or for reasonable prices by the Consumer Information Center. To get the catalog, send your name and address, requesting a current Consumer Information Catalog, to: R. Woods, Consumer Information Center, Pueblo, CO 81009.

- **INFORMATION,** *Source:* Your local County Extension or Cooperative Agent is an excellent source of free information on just about anything connected to family, home, and garden. This branch of the Department of Agriculture offers advice, booklets, information over the phone, and sometimes tele-information services (you dial to hear information tapes on specific subjects). Look in the government section of your phone book, under United States Government, Agriculture Department of, Extension Service County & Home Economics Agents.

• **INGREDIENTS,** *Keeping Safe from Foragers for Recipes:* If you don't want a family member with a case of the munchies to eat certain ingredients bought especially for a recipe or meal, have a code worked out with your family such as placing a red dot sticker on the container or just stick a warning note on the item. You'll save quick trips to the store and avoid those moments when you've got ingredients all mixed up, and you reach for the last one, and . . . need I say more?

• **INHERITANCE,** *Marking Household Possessions for Heirs, Letter of Laughter:* A reader wrote that she, her children, and grandchildren had a week-long party while she was marking household possessions with the names of the people who would inherit them and attaching notes saying where she got the item, how old it is, etc. She noticed that nobody ever found anything that wasn't wanted by somebody except the tax bill!.

• **INSURANCE,** *Trip Cancellation Insurance Checklist:* Basic travel insurance policies cover such elements as trip cancellation or interruption, baggage loss, emergency evacuation, worldwide telephone assistance, accidents, sickness, or accidental death or dismemberment. Most travel insurance is bought through a travel agent.
1. If you are traveling to just one destination or to just one country, the Insurance Information Institute says extra insurance may not be necessary, but a long trip to many places or special medical conditions could warrant it.
2. Before buying, check your homeowner's and health policies to find out what's already covered while you travel (theft, baggage loss, health problems).
3. Trip cancellation insurance may reimburse you for first-class tickets if you cancel just because you change your mind, but there's no reimbursement on non-refundable discount tickets for that reason. Basic costs are based on number of days away from home and the coverage.

• **INVENTORY:** If you keep a small notebook and write in it the names and locations of seldom used items, you don't have to play the "Lost and Found" game with yourself.

- **INVENTORY,** *For Insurance Purposes:* Whether or not you are moving, having photos of your possessions is proof of ownership, their description, and condition. If you have a lot of jewelry or other valuables, you may want to use an instant camera; then you can immediately write on the back (or on a label to put on the back) the original cost and any other information that will help you make a claim if the item is lost through theft or fire. The photos should be in a safe or safe-deposit box so that they don't get damaged with your possessions in fire or flood.

- **INVITATIONS,** *Checklist:* When sending invitations to weddings or other similar events, include an emergency phone number for out-of-town guests. For example, wedding invitations tell the location of the church and reception, but parents of small children hiring a sitter for the event would want to also provide the phone numbers, just in case of emergency.

- **IRON,** *Starch Buildup:* If the sole plate is stainless steel, remove the brown, gummy film by wiping with a cloth dampened with rubbing alcohol; then buff with extra-fine steel wool, and wipe off any residue. Follow manufacturer's directions for other sole plate finishes. If you've lost the directions, call 1-800-555-1212 to find out if the manufacturer has an 800 customer service/consumer information number.

- **IRONING BOARD,** *Other Uses:* Cover the cloth top with a plastic sheet or old flannel-backed plastic tablecloth and you have an adjustable worktable for crafts, wrapping gifts, etc. that's kind to your back because you can adjust the height.

- **"IRONING" IN A HOTEL:** Tried and true is to hang a garment in the bathroom while you shower to let the steam "iron" it. If the fabric is not very frail, you can "iron" some creases out over a hot light bulb. Remember to put the shade back on the lamp.

- **IRON SKILLET,** *Storing:* Place a paper towel on the inside of the skillet when you put it away to absorb moisture and prevent rust.

J

- **JACKET, IDENTIFYING YOURS IN A CROWD:** If you have a popular-style jacket that looks like everyone else's jacket when hung on a rack at a restaurant, turn one of the sleeves inside out before hanging it up so you can see at a glance which is yours. No more walking out wearing one that's not yours! **Note:** If it will stick to the lining, a self-sticking address label on the inside-out sleeve will help prevent someone from accidentally walking off with your jacket. I stick one in the pocket of my black raincoat because there are so many black raincoats.

- **JAMS/JELLIES/FRUIT SPREADS,** *Definitions:*
1. Jam is fruit (or vegetables like chutney) which has been cooked and pureed into a soft and thick consistency.
2. Jelly is made from fruit juice or clear liquid and syrup or sugar. It's called jelly because the cooked mixture gels.
3. Fruit spreads are usually smooth and thick and made from fruit pulp and spices. Some of the newer ones are sugar-free or have greatly reduced sugar content. You have to read those labels!

- **JAMS/JELLIES FOR GIFTS:** Instead of putting the jelly in jars, divide it into coffee mugs, seal with paraffin, and then add a bow and ribbon when you give it as a gift.

• **JAR LABELS,** *Removing for Special Offers:* Moisten a couple of paper towels or a cloth with hot water and wrap it around the label on the jar. Leave it on for a few minutes and remove. The label should peel off. If not, remoisten the cloth and try again. Or, soak the whole jar in warm water until the label comes off. **Note:** labels tear easily when damp; handle gently.

• **JAR LIDS,** *Tightening Hot Jelly Jar Lids:* Put on a clean pair of gardening gloves when you make jelly to prevent hot hands while stirring and to tighten lids after processing. No more juggling hot wet jars with pot-holder mitts or dish towels.

• **JEANS,** *Prevent Fading:* Before the first washing, help set the color by soaking them in a few gallons of water containing either one box of salt or one gallon vinegar—not both!

• **JELLY,** *$aver, Using It All:* When there's just a bit of jelly or jam left in the jar, add milk and shake vigorously and you'll have a delicious fruity shake.

• **JET LAG,** *Checklist for Prevention:*
1. Give your body time to adjust to changing patterns of sunlight and darkness as you travel by car, train or ship through different time zones.
2. Drink plenty of water, at least one glass per hour. Dry atmosphere in airplanes can cause dehydration. I like to mist my face and put lotion on my hands periodically.
3. Eat lightly. Most airlines offer special menus but you must call ahead. When I reserve my plane space, I always ask for a fruit or vegetarian plate.
4. Wear comfortable shoes and clothes, nothing tight. Stretch periodically and put your feet on a tote bag so your knees are higher than your hips. Try to move about the cabin every now and then and find an out-of-the way place to stretch and keep your circulation moving.

• **JEWELRY,** *Homestyle Cleaner:* Mix sudsy ammonia with an equal amount of water. Soak jewelry for a few minutes, then carefully clean around stones and designs with a soft toothbrush. Rinse well, dry and buff with soft cloth. **Caution:** Don't use this solution on gold electroplate or on jewelry with soft stones such as pearls, opals, or jade.

• **JEWELRY,** *Precautions:* Remove rings and other jewelry before doing housework.
1. Silver jewelry tarnishes when exposed to rubber gloves and ordinary household compounds like mayonnaise, salt, vinegar, eggs, and some cleaners.
2. Gold is damaged by exposure to mercury and some chemicals. Alloys in gold and soldered areas are weakened by chlorine and so it's best to remove jewelry when swimming in a pool or cleaning with bleach solutions.
3. Various precious and semi-precious stones can get scratched by housework or have their surfaces dulled by household compounds. Pearls, opals, and jade are especially at risk.

• **JEWELRY,** *Preventing Green Marks on Skin:* Paint the part that touches your skin (like the inside of a bracelet) with clear fingernail polish or have it coated by a jeweler.

• **JEWELRY,** *Quick-Fix Cleaning:* Rub a bit of toothpaste on the jewelry with your finger, rinse well, and polish with a soft cloth. **Caution:** Don't use this method too often, it could be too abrasive for some jewelry. Also don't use it for soft gems such as pearls, opals, or jade because they could be damaged.

• **JEWELRY,** *Quick-Fix, Safeguarding at the Gym:*
1. Keep a stray athletic sock in your gym bag to hold jewelry that you take off while working out. Stick the sock into your shoe and you won't waste time digging in a gym bag looking for it.
2. Put small earrings, rings, and other valuables in a 35mm film case and then into your shoe or gym bag pocket.
3. Poke hook earrings into a cork or foam packing chip for safe keeping.

• **JEWELRY,** *Recycling Old Costume Jewelry:* Instead of just throwing it away, give it to children to use as prizes when they play games.

• **JEWELRY,** *Rinsing After Cleaning:* Put jewelry in a tea strainer; there's no risk of its going down the drain when you rinse it after cleaning.

• **JOGGING,** *Safety at Night for Joggers or Bikers:* Sew silver reflective tape from major fabric stores around each leg or wrist of your jogging suit and sew ½-inch stripes across the back of a jacket. The tape makes you visible 1,000 feet away!

• **JUMPER CABLES,** *Recycling:* Cut off the alligator clips from a non-working set of battery jumper cables and save them for workshop projects.

• **JUMP STARTING YOUR CAR,** *Checklist for How-To:* Put a copy of these directions in your student driver's glove compartment and maybe in your own, too.

1. Position both cars so they face each other. If your car is against the curb, park the other car next to yours on the battery side. Put both vehicles in "Park;" apply the emergency brake, and turn ignitions off.

2. Important SAFETY measure—remove the cap from the top of each battery.

3. Locate the positive cable (red clips) and the negative cable (black clips) on the jumper cables. Locate the positive and negative terminals on the batteries. (You may need to clean the battery surface around the terminals to find the markings—there should be a " + " or "pos" to denote positive and a " − " or "neg" to denote negative.)

4. Attach one of the red clips to the positive terminal of the dead battery. Attach the other red clip to the positive terminal of the good battery.

5. Then, connect the negative cable to the negative terminal of the good battery and to the engine block of the stalled car, away from the battery, carburetor, fuel line, and any tubing or moving parts. (NOT to the negative terminal of the dead battery.)

6. When the jumper cables are properly hooked up, start the car with the good battery. Then try to start the car with the dead battery; when it begins to run, let it idle with the motor on for a minute or two.

7. To disconnect the cables, remove the black (negative) clip from the engine block first, then the red (positive) clips. To avoid electrical sparks, don't let the positive and negative cables touch each other.

Note: Most newer batteries have vented caps. With these, you must check to make sure they are tight and level before hooking up the battery to be jump-started. If a damp cloth is available, place it over the vent caps to decrease the chance of a spark igniting fumes that might be released from the battery. **Caution:** Serious eye injuries can result from batteries exploding. Exercise caution and wear safety eyewear to protect yourself and NEVER stand over a battery looking down at it when jump-starting it.

- **JUNK-MAIL ENVELOPES,** *Recycling:*
1. Large (9 × 12-inch) envelopes: Cut the envelopes at the edge instead of the top and slip in newspaper articles you want to save. Then turn the envelope over so that the address is facing the back; put a title at the top and file it in a shoebox. This system allows you to file newspaper or magazine recipes with their pictures!
2. Business-size envelopes: Write shopping lists on the backside and put your coupons inside. While shopping, paper clip the used coupons to the outside of the envelope and take the unused ones home in the envelope.

- **JUNK MAIL "GRANNY" TOY,** *Recycling:* Grandma can save all the junk mail and then when grandchildren visit, they can open their personal "mailbox" and play with "important papers" while adults chat. Many mailouts have nice stickers to stick and colored pictures to cut out, too!

- **KEY,** *Safekeeping:* It may be a sign of the times, but readers have begun sending me safety hints in case of mugging or theft. Attach your housekey to the band of your skirt or pants with a large safety pin; then if you are mugged, you can get into your house, and it prevents giving a thief your key along with the address found in your wallet. It's a good idea also to carry concealed change for phone calls or taxi money so that you can get home if you lose your wallet or purse. My mother used to pin my key inside my coat pocket when I was a child.

- **KEYS,** *Avoiding "Mystery Keys":* When you get new keys, trace them on a sheet of paper and keep it in your household files or trace on a sheet of paper in a household information notebook. Then you have a pattern to match when you are trying to solve key "mysteries."

- **KEYS,** *Car Key Reminders:* Put your car keys on anything you need to remember to take or to check; you can't leave home without them. Some examples are listed below.
1. Hang them near the kitchen stove and/or coffee pot and you'll check that the kitchen appliances are off before leaving the house.

2. If you tend to forget if you've unplugged your curling iron or hot rollers, hang car keys there so that you have to check these appliances before you leave.

3. Put them on your "doggy bag" in the refrigerator and when you leave "Mom's" (or some other generous nice person's home) you won't forget the goodies.

• **KEYS,** *Recycling Old Ones:* Attach keys with fishing line to a clothes hanger, piece of tree branch, wooden embroidery hoop, or other hanging device and you'll create a novel wind chime. Old keys can also substitute for missing parts of an existing wind chime.

• **KEYS,** *Safekeeping Spares in Yard:* One reader attaches the spare housekeys to her dogs' collars along with the rest of their ID tags. She says neither dog "takes kindly" to having a stranger mess with its collar but relatives and friends who need the key can easily get it from one of the dogs.

• **KEY-TABS, KEY RINGS,** *Recycling Extras:* Plastic fluorescent key-tabs, often given away as promotional items, make great glow-in-the-dark light pulls in a closet or basement. Others may be attractive enough for ceiling fan pulls.

• **KITCHEN,** *Cleaning Ranges, etc. Letter of Laughter:* One reader sent me a surefire method for keeping a stove clean—Don't use it! This reminded me of an old joke in which a husband says that for their wedding anniversary, he's going to take his wife on a trip to somewhere she's never been—their kitchen! In these days of working couples sharing kitchen chores, a wife might tell the same joke about her husband!

• **KITCHEN TIMER FAMILY PEACEMAKER:**

1. For a very young child who dislikes naps, set the timer and leave it in the child's room to show when nap time is over. **Note:** The ticking lulls some children to sleep!

2. Set a kitchen timer to limit teen phone conversations.

3. Set the timer to limit your own conversations; it'll make the process seem fairer to the teen.

- **KITE FLYING SAFETY,** *Checklist:*
1. Never use any metal in making a kite, including wire or string containing metal fibers.
2. Never fly your kite on rainy or stormy days, and always make sure your kite string is perfectly dry. Wet string conducts electricity.
3. Fly your kite in an open field, away from overhead, electric lines, and public roadways. Never take a chance!
4. If a kite becomes tangled in an electric power line or catches on a utility pole, leave it. It is simply too dangerous to try and retrieve it.
5. Never climb on utility poles, towers, or other utility equipment. Aside from the danger of being electrocuted, you could fall and injure yourself.

- **KITTENS,** *Feeding Abandoned Newborns:* If a mama kitty abandons a litter, you need to keep the kittens warm—a box lined with shredded paper and a soft cloth will do.
1. They need to be kept at about 88 to 92°F when they are a week old; about 80 to 85°F when they get to fourteen days old; about 80°F when they are about a month old. It helps if you have a thermostatically controlled overhead infrared lamp.
2. Keep a pan of water near the box to add humidity since dehydration can be a problem.
3. If you can't get to a vet to buy the proper formula, this emergency formula can substitute. Mix 2 cups of milk, 1 teaspoon corn syrup, the yolk of an egg, and a pinch of salt. Keep the formula in the refrigerator and take out what's needed for each feeding. Feeding should be room temperature and feed only eight to ten drops per tiny kitten.

- **KNICKKNACKS,** *Remembering Arrangements:* When you are dusting shelves that hold figurines, framed photos, or other collection arrangements, snap a picture of the display with an instant camera so that you can put them back as they were when you are finished. This is especially helpful if you're dusting at a relative's or friend's house. Keep the photos for insurance records.

- **KNIFE CASE,** *Carrying a Knife Safely in a Picnic Basket:* Put a paring knife in a toothbrush holder or flatten an empty paper-towel roll and tape the end shut to hold a larger knife.

• **KNIT GARMENT,** *Care Label for Hand-knit Gift:* Enclose a label from a yarn skein so that the person receiving the gift will know what kind of yarn was used and how to care for it.

• **KNITTING NEEDLES:** Knit with two different-colored, same-size needles and you will always know which row you are on—even or odd.

L

- **LABELS,** *Quick-Fix, Removing Gummy Glue:* To soften gummy glue on a glass or plastic jar, put it in the microwave with a damp towel over it; set on Low and check it every 30 seconds or so. The heat softens the glue and you can usually pull the label off easily.

- **LABELS,** *Removing Sticky Residue:* See STICKERS, Removal.

- **LADDER TOOL HOLDER:** Instead of climbing up and down the ladder to get this tool or that, hammer some nails along the right edge of a wooden ladder so that before you start a job, you can assemble all the tools you need and hang them at the height at which you will work. If you hang your tools at your usual work bench with self-gripping fabric tape you can stick self-gripping tape to a metal ladder. Either way, you'll save ladder climbing.

- **LAKES,** *Remembering the Great Lakes Hint:* Think the word "HOMES"—Huron, Ontario, Michigan, Erie, Superior.

- **LAMPSHADE,** *Quick-Fix Dusting:* Blow dust away with a hand-held hair dryer set on cool.

- **LANDSCAPING,** *Hanging Plants:* Make a plain fence or apartment balcony rail into a garden focal point by hanging potted plants from it with S-hooks or, if you are handy, attach shelves for plants to a wood fence.

• **LANDSCAPING,** *Fish Ponds:* If you are installing a fountain outdoors and plan to have fish in it, it should be at least 10 inches deep. If you install the pool at ground level, you can insert into the hole you've dug a fiberglass pool like those used for children's swimming pools or a heavy-duty rubber or plastic liner. Pools made specifically for fountains (fiberglass or copper) can be above ground, but they're more expensive than make-it-yourself models.

• **LANDSCAPING,** *Fountains:* A water fountain in a garden room or outdoors in the yard makes a soothing, therapeutic sound and adds a luxurious touch to the decor. Many need no plumbing at all because they operate with water-recirculating pumps. (Basic pumps cost about $40; good professionally-made fountains cost $300 to $1000 and up.) If you buy the complete fountain "works" from a specialty shop, all you do is fill it with water and plug in the pump; no skills required! **Caution:** Make sure all electrical outlets are grounded.

• **LAUNDRY,** *Bleaching:* Always follow care labels on garments and never allow undiluted chlorine bleach to contact clothing; it can damage color and fabric. If your washer doesn't have a bleach dispenser, dilute bleach with one quart of water and add the solution to the washer after it has filled with water.

• **LAUNDRY,** *Dryer Filter Safety:* Dust and lint buildup in dryer filters and exhaust ducts is a major cause of home fires (about 14,000 a year). Clean the filter after each load and check the exhaust duct regularly. Also check the outside vent tube to make sure excess lint isn't plugging the air exit; this also can be a fire hazard.

• **LAUNDRY,** *Dryer Safety:* We know it's best to remove clothing from the dryer as soon as the cycle is finished to prevent crushing, but did you know that some materials, when left in the heated dryer drum, can spontaneously heat up enough to catch fire?

• **LAUNDRY,** *Getting Dryer-made Wrinkles Out:* Add a large damp bath towel to a load of dryer-crinkled clothing and run the dryer for about 15 minutes. Be sure to remove garments as soon as they are dry!

- **LAUNDRY,** *Getting Help from Children:*
1. Give each child a personal laundry basket. The basket of dirty clothing is to be brought to the laundry room each morning before breakfast. Children then take their clean laundry back to their rooms in the same basket at the end of the day.
2. Teach children to sort laundry when they bring it down. Have a framed cloth hamper for each load—each of a different fabric according to how you sort your laundry. For example, a denim hamper is for jeans, pants and heavy clothes; a sheet fabric hamper holds sheets, towels and whites; a print fabric hamper is for light-weight colored clothing. Even the youngest child or adult with "selective incompetency" can sort laundry when it's coded this way, and it trains children to do their own laundry when they leave home.

- **LAUNDRY,** *Healthy-Planet Energy Saving Checklist:*
1. Match water level to the load size—set lower water levels for smaller loads or delay washing until you have a full (but not over-loaded) large load.
2. Pretreat spots and stains and then set the cycle and wash time to the type of load to avoid rewashing.
3. If your washer has a water return system, when you reuse water you need to start with lightly soiled items first; you may need to add more detergent for additional loads.
4. Wash in hot water only when necessary for heavy or greasy soils, whites, etc. and wash with cold for light soils. Rinse all loads in cold water.
5. Reduce dryer time by using a high spin speed in the washer for highly absorbent fabrics.
6. Dry full (but not overloaded) loads and separate lightweight and heavy weight items for faster, uniform drying.
7. Don't overdry. In addition to wasting energy, it can give a harsh feeling to some fabrics and shrink others. Allowing garments to stay in the dryer after it's shut off causes wrinkles.
8. Use residual heat—reload the dryer while it's still warm from a previous load.
9. Keep lint screens clean—buildup increases drying time and can be a fire hazard.

10. Do laundry during off-peak hours, usually early morning and late evening. Check with your local utility company to find out about off-peak hours.

• **LAUNDRY,** *Ironing:* Dry place mats draped over the side of the bathtub; some may not need ironing if they are "handpressed" against the sides of the tub while they are still wet.

• **LAUNDRY,** *Lint on Clothes:* Today's dryers catch most lint in their filters but some people still have problems with it. Most of the time, poor sorting before washing, overdrying and static electricity cling cause lint to cling to clothing.
1. Sort properly. Don't wash and dry lint-makers like bath towels with lint-collectors like synthetics or permanent press.
2. Remove all papers and tissues from pockets before washing and drying clothes. Tissues seem to expand when laundered.
3. Use fabric softeners to reduce static electricity.
4. Don't overload washers and dryers; they won't work as well as they can.
5. Try to remove clothing when it's still slightly damp. Static electricity builds up in overdried clothing so that lint clings more easily.
6. Clean the dryer lint screen after each load so that it can catch more lint; you'll be saving energy, too, because the machine is working more efficiently.

• **LAUNDRY,** *Soaking Bleachable Stained Items:* Mix ¼ cup chlorine bleach with one gallon of water in a sink or pail and soak for five minutes. **Note:** Chlorine bleach doesn't remove protein-type stains such as egg, grass, or blood; these are best removed with a pre-soak product. Please see SPOTS AND STAINS on page 398.

• **LAUNDRY,** *Sorting, Letter of Laughter:* One mother solved the problem of putting away her teen's laundry. She just put underwear, etc. in the wrong drawers for several weeks and finally, her teens said they preferred to put their own away!

• **LAUNDRY,** *Sweaters:* To handwash, use cool or lukewarm water. With the sweater inside out, immerse it for 5 to 10 minutes turning it over once or twice and squeezing suds through the fabric—gently.

Rinse the same way in basins of water until the water is clear. Air dry flat so you can block the sweater back into shape.

To machine wash (if care label says so), turn sweater inside out (place delicate sweaters in a mesh bag or pillowcase) and use cool or lukewarm water; remove before the spin cycle. Some machine-washable sweaters can be put into the dryer for a short time and then removed while damp so that they can be dried flat and blocked. But some synthetics require tumble drying for the full cycle to be re-blocked into shape; check care labels.

• LAUNDRY, *Test for Colorfastness of Fabric:* Make a solution of 1 tablespoon of bleach and ¼ cup of water. Put a drop or two of this solution on in inconspicuous spot such as an inside seam and check for color loss.

• LAUNDRY, *Turning Socks and Underwear Right-side Out, Letter of Laughter:* After many years of marriage and four children, and many many hours turning socks right side out after they came out of the laundry, one reader decided to tell her family that anyone who had to turn socks inside out when removing them could just turn them for himself before wearing them again. She discovered that she was the only person in the family who cared if socks were right-side out. Everyone just wore them as is. And, one of my staff read this and agreed; she doesn't turn underwear right side out either, she said, "It's not my problem."

Seems to me that a lot of us allow ourselves to get aggravated about chores which are really just unnecessary "busy work" because we're the only ones who care. Anyhow, consider that these families wear their socks and underwear the "right" way 50 percent of the time! Not a bad percentage for anything!

• LAUNDRY, *When Suds Overflow:* Please see SUDS OVERFLOW.

• LAUNDRY, *When Washer and Dryer Are in a Garage or Basement:* If you can't hear the cycle change buzzers, you'll get to the washer and dryer before the wrinkles do if you set a kitchen timer to go off approximately when a cycle will finish and keep it where you are in the house.

• LAUNDRY APPLIANCE SURPRISE: When an appliance service person asked, "Did you check for valuables?" before hauling away her old washer and dryer, a reader opened the fronts of her appliances at his suggestion and found her wedding band, earrings, $7.42, and other odds and ends in the accumulated lint! Check it out before it goes out!

• **LAUNDRY BAG,** *For Travel:* Put a drawstring in the open end of an old pillowcase. It will fit to any shape in your suitcase if traveling by plane; it protects souvenirs on the way home, too. When traveling by car you can toss the laundry bag into the trunk fender well so it's out of the way.

• **LAUNDRY BASKET,** *Safe Carrying:* If you have to carry your laundry down steep steps to a cellar, it may be unsafe to carry a basket which limits your vision and puts you off balance. Instead you can put your laundry in a plastic bag or in pillow cases and just toss it down the steps ahead of you! If it won't hit anything, you could also just let a plastic basket of laundry slide down the steps.
P.S. However you do it, considering how most of us feel about doing laundry, tossing it down the steps any way at all could be a happy, frustration releasing experience!

• **LAUNDRY DETERGENT BOX,** *Quick-Fix:* Open pour-type boxes with a beer can opener to save fingernails and temper.

• **LAUNDRY DETERGENT, LIQUID:** After measuring liquid laundry detergent and pouring the liquid into the washer, toss in the measuring cup so it gets rinsed off automatically.

• **LAUNDRY AND LAUNDROMAT LESSONS,** *For the Novice:*
1. Sort clothing into whites that can be bleached, whites that can't be bleached, light colors, dark colors, heavily soiled items and lint-giving articles. These should be separate loads but most college students dump all together to save a few coins and end up ruining garments that cost dollars. Compromise by making one light/non-fade load and one load of dark jeans and other dark colors.
   (You can always tell a freshman college student—pink socks from mixing white and colored loads are a dead giveaway; upper-class students have only grey shirts, gym socks, and underwear from years of washing light-colored clothing with jeans.)
2. Buy large, light-colored duffel bags and a couple of indelible pens. Write washing instructions on hot-, warm- and cold-water washing on the face of each laundry bag with the pen.

3. Cut a pocket from an old shirt and sew it into the inside of the duffel bag with a little snap for closure. This is a convenient place to put laundry money for the machines. Or toss in a plastic yogurt cup with a lid to hold change.

4. Premeasuring detergent and fabric softener into small margarine tubs, yogurt cups or self-sealing plastic bags is a big help—you don't have to lug around the whole box or bottle.

5. After placing clothes in the washer and shutting the lid, place a large colorful magnet or a stick-on paper dot on the machines you are using so you can find your clothes at a glance.

6. Take hangers with you so that you can hang up clothes from the dryer and avoid ironing them.

• **LAUNDRY POWDER,** *Preventing Lumps In Damp Climates:* Store in a clean plastic gallon milk jug with a tight-fitting lid. It will be easier to handle, too.

• **LAUNDRY PROBLEMS,** *Checklist for Avoiding Them:*
1. Keep jeans and other cotton pants from fading by turning them inside out before washing and drying.

2. Prevent pilling on sweaters and printed T-shirts by laundering them wrongside out.

3. Make it a family rule for each member to spot-treat clothing or at least to warn whomever does the laundry about spots and stains.

4. Do not use chlorine and non-chlorine bleaches together.

5. Check pockets—then you won't wash pens, crayons, tissues or other things that stain or leave lint behind.

6. Close all zippers and fasteners to prevent their snagging other garments.

7. Mend rips and tears; sew on loose buttons—a stitch in time really does save nine or more!

8. Don't add wet garments to a partially dried load in the dryer.

9. Clean lint filters before every load.

10. Select the proper cycle, water temperature, time, and load level recommended by your laundry equipment books. Manufacturers spend a lot of money developing these booklets and since you've paid for the information, you may as well use it!

- **LAUNDRY, TANGLED,** *Sanity-Saving Checklist:*
1. To avoid washing machine cruelty to you and your clothes, make sure all hooks are fastened (especially bras and other undergarments), close all zippers.
2. If shirt or blouse sleeves seem to be the cause, button each sleeve to a buttonhole on the front.
3. Place clothing into the machine piece by piece laying each garment in a circle around the agitator. Make sure you set the appropriate water level and washing time. If you have mostly bras, long-sleeved, soft/silky fabric blouses or shirts, nylon slips, etc. in a load, wash on "Delicate" or "Knit" and set a higher water level than when you had the tangles; more water and less agitation time in the washer-machine may prevent agitation of the washer-person.

- **LAWN FURNITURE,** *Painting:* Get a large cardboard box from a local furniture store; cut out one side. Place lawn furniture into the box and spray paint for no mess or painted grass.

- **LAWN MOWING,** *Safety Checklist:*
1. Wear proper protective clothing—long pants, sturdy shoes, and protective eye wear.
2. First walk the area to be mowed to find and pick up objects that could be thrown by the mower or could damage the mower.
3. Never disconnect safety controls; they are there to protect you.
4. Never refuel the machine while it is running or the engine is still hot—gas fumes are flammable.
5. Don't mow wet grass; it clogs the mower and may damage it.
6. Store the mower in a ventilated area, especially in hot weather, to prevent combustion of the gas remaining in it after you finish.

- **LEFTOVERS,** *Bread:*
1. Stale bread makes good bread pudding. Dried bread can be cubed and oven toasted for croutons or if dry enough, made into bread crumbs. (Take dried bread, put it into a sturdy plastic bag, place it on the floor, and step on it until the bread is crumbs. You can also place it on the counter and use a rolling pin but it won't be as much fun.)
2. Stale, but still soft, sliced bread can be pushed into greased muffin cups, baked until toasty, then used as an egg cup.

3. Use old bread for French toast or cut bread in cubes and mix with egg or egg substitute for "egg cubes."

4. Dip days-old bread slices in sweetened condensed milk, then in flaked coconut and then place on a baking sheet and toast in hot oven until bread is hot and coconut is brown for quickie cookies.

- **LEFTOVERS,** *Cake:*

Recipe 1. Break in pieces and layer with slightly softened ice cream, freeze and slice for a new dessert. (You can drizzle an appropriate liqueur over each serving, such as coffee-flavored liqueur over chocolate ice cream and angel food cake.)

Recipe 2. Prepare one package of cooked chocolate pudding mix as directed, cool. Whip one cup whipping cream with ⅓ cup confectioners' sugar and fold into cooled pudding. Cut up one layer of cake (white, yellow, or chocolate) and place in bottom of an 8-inch-square baking dish. Pour pudding over cake and sprinkle with ½ cup chopped nuts (optional). Chill several hours in fridge before serving. Serves 4 to 6.

- **LEFTOVERS,** *Cheese:* Bits of leftover cheese can be melted with canned skim milk and turned into cheese sauce for veggies or noodles or for cheese dip. The more different kinds of cheese, the better the flavor.

- **LEFTOVERS,** *Disguising for Fun:* When you have accumulated several meals of leftovers, have a family "Buffet Day" to eat them up. One reader makes a joke of her leftover day by posting a menu on the fridge that has the name of a leading restaurant of her city printed on top and a list of the "Choices du Jour."

- **LEFTOVERS,** *Egg Whites or Yolks:* Save egg whites for meringues or fruit whips. Save yolks for custards, sauces or to add to scrambled eggs.

- **LEFTOVERS,** *Fruits:*

1. Too many grapes? Freeze them for snacking later.

2. Too many bananas? Freeze them and use them (sliced in hunks) instead of ice cubes and malt to froth up blender milk shakes.

3. Slightly bruised fruits? Cut off bad parts and make a fruit salad, pie, or add fruit to tuna salad—apples and grapes are delicious!

• **LEFTOVERS,** *General Use:* I like to think of leftovers as pre-cooked convenience foods. To make any leftover taste new, add a fresh ingredient such as browned onions, garlic, vegetables, bouillon or new spices or herbs, or all of the above.

• **LEFTOVERS,** *$aver, Getting Every Smidgen Out of a Container:* When you get to the bottom of the dishwashing liquid, shampoos, conditioner, ketchup, salad oil, salad dressing, hand/body lotion or baby lotion, prop the container upside down for a day or so and you get at least one more "dose" out of it.

Also, add water to a ketchup bottle and flavor noodle, rice or meat dishes with the "puree." Add water to dishwashing detergent and you can squirt a sponge with the mixture to wash odds and ends at the sink. The diluted detergent rinses out faster and is kinder to detergent-sensitive skins.

• **LEFTOVERS,** *Meats:*
1. Any leftover meat can be used as slices in a sandwich or ground up to make sandwich spread (add commercial sandwich spread or mayo and chopped carrots, celery, mushrooms for filler).
2. Heat meat slices in leftover sauce for hot open-faced sandwiches or to serve over leftover rice or noodles.
3. Cubed meats can be mixed with noodles or rice and salad dressings for a luncheon salad.

• **LEFTOVERS,** *Vegetables:*
1. Keep a tightly covered container in your freezer and add all bits of leftover veggies and their cooking water, then, when you have enough, make vegetable soup by adding browned onions, bouillon or stock, and your favorite herbs/spices to the mix. Simmer at least 20 to 30 minutes to blend flavors.
2. Add leftover cooked veggies to any salad—mixed combination salads, sandwich spread, or just on top of your lettuce.
3. Cut up leftover potatoes and add them to scrambled eggs or scrambled egg substitute. Brown the potatoes and add some onion, if you wish, before adding the eggs.
4. Mash leftover starchy vegetables, add egg, leftover egg yolk or egg substitute, crumbs to thicken, and deep fry like hushpuppies for "veggie puppies."

5. Make vegetable hash by cutting up leftover mixed vegetables such as corn, peppers, potatoes, peas and beans, then fry in skillet with onion, garlic and other seasonings of choice.

• **LEMON,** *Aids:*
1. Add a few slices to drinking water to perk it up or to bathwater to perk you up with the fresh scent.
2. Rub your hands with pieces of lemon to remove odors like onions and garlic.
3. Add lemon juice to rinse water for your hair.
4. Put rinds down the garbage disposal to freshen it.
5. Cut in half, remove insides and fill with gelatin.

• **LEMON/LIME JUICE PLASTIC BOTTLES,** *Recycling:* When empty, rinse well and fill with water so that children can carry them for a handy squirt of drinking water.

• **LEMONS,** *Freezing:* Seal them in a sturdy plastic bag and freeze. When you need one, take it out of the bag and microwave it for a few minutes; let stand on counter for 10 more minutes before using.

• **LEMON SQUEEZER,** *Substitute for a Strong Grip:* Place a lemon half in a nutcracker and squeeze away.

• **LETTER WRITING,** *Time-Saver:* Buy carbonless paper which comes in pre-collated two- to six-sheet sets. For example, if you have four people to whom you write regularly, buy four-part carbonless. Then instead of writing four separate total letters you can type or hand write your main body of news only once, add personalized notes, questions and comments and mail the letters off. You'll enjoy writing more often to friends, kids at college, and so forth. Of course if you have a computer or word processor, you can do the same without the carbonless paper, just print out different letters with different headers and personalized notes.

• **LEVEL,** *Substitute:* If you are hanging a shelf and have no level, try filling a tall straight-sided plastic bottle three-quarters full of water. Tightly close the lid so that you can lay the bottle on the shelf on its side. Adjust the shelf until the water is level. Then screw the shelf to the wall.

• **LIBRARY LIST:** Keep a log of books checked out from the library and then you'll not only see how many books your family has read in a month, but you'll have a checklist to help you gather all of the books when it's time to return them. No more forgetting and paying overdue fees!

• **LICKING LABELS AND STAMPS:** Fill a shallow dish with water and place a burned-out light bulb in it. The bulb turns with a touch in the water and you can glide stamps, etc. over it without ever licking yucky stamps, labels or envelopes again.

• **LIGHT BULB,** *Changing Without Burning Fingers:* Take the new bulb out of the corrugated cardboard "box" and place the "box" over the old light bulb to unscrew it. You don't get burned fingers and the bulb ends up inside the "box" ready for disposal!

• **LIGHT BULB,** *Removing a Broken One:* **Caution:** First make sure the switch is turned off. Then insert an old-fashioned clothespin, not spring-type, so that the two prongs are inside the broken socket and carefully unscrew it.

• **LIGHTING,** *Brighten Without Using More Energy:* Lighting accounts for more than 16 percent of our electric bills and most of us overlight our homes. You can brighten and still save.
1. Use 25-watt reflector flood bulbs in high-intensity portable lamps. They'll give about the same light but use less energy than the 40-watt bulbs that usually come with these lamps.
2. If you have "pole" or "spot" directional lamps, try using 50-watt reflector floodlights which give about the same light as standard 100-watt bulbs but with half the wattage.
3. When using night-light bulbs, get 4-watt bulbs with a clear finish instead of the usual 7-watt ones; they'll be almost as bright with half the energy use.
4. Put photocell sensor units or timers on outdoor lights so that they will turn themselves off in daylight.
5. Install dimmer switches or high-low switches when replacing light switches to reduce light intensity and save energy.
6. When buying new lamps, get those with three-way switches so you can use high for reading and low when you don't need bright light.

7. Fluorescent lights give out more lumens (light measurements) so use them whenever you can. New 20-watt deluxe warm white fluorescent can be used in makeup and grooming areas for a warmer light.

8. Keep all lamps and lighting fixtures clean; dirt absorbs light.

9. When decorating, save lighting energy by choosing light-colored walls, rugs, draperies and upholstery which reflects light and so reduces the amount of artificial light needed.

• **LINEN CLOSET,** *Organizing for No Mess Time-Saving:* Linen closets can become a jumbled mess, especially when children make their own beds. Organize bed linens into sets: Fold one flat sheet in the middle, fold it in half and then in half again (both folds the long way). Then fold a fitted sheet the same way, and lay it on top of the folded flat sheet. Add one or two pillowcases, each folded in half the long way also. Then roll them all together into one neat roll. Whoever is making a bed can grab only a roll instead of rummaging around and making a mess.

• **LINT,** *Removing It from Self-Grip Closures on Children's Shoes:* Accumulated lint affects the "grip" in addition to looking unsightly. Remove it with a small crochet hook. Avoid lint accumulation problems by closing the self-grip tapes when children take their shoes off.

• **LINT ON LAUNDRY,** *Avoiding It:* Turn inside-out before washing garments made from fabrics that attract lint, such as corduroy, dark cotton socks, etc.

• **LINT PICKING:** A clean mascara brush will get lint out of hard-to-reach places on clothing like shirt-front plackets, shirt pockets and hems.

• **LIPSTICK,** *Preventing Loss in a Purse:* Put lipstick, a few tissues and other cosmetics in a self-sealing plastic bag. You can move the bag from purse to purse and never have to dig around in the bottom for a lipstick tube. No more rumpled new tissue clutter either!

• **LIPSTICK,** *Using It All Up:* Use up the last smidgeons of lipstick in the tube with a lipstick brush. Or, do as I do: Scoop out those smidgeons with a toothpick or clean frozen treat stick and put several different colors of lipstick in a small compact (one left over from other lipstick, rouge or powder) and then you'll have a color-choice lipstick compact in your travel makeup kit or purse. Be sure to include a lipstick brush for application.

• **LITTER BAGS,** *For the Car:* Save the small plastic bags from frozen foods, card shops and drug stores and keep them in a larger bag in the car so they'll always be handy.

• **LOLLIPOP TREE,** *Gift for Hospitalized Child:* Into a potted plant, stick drinking straws and then poke lollipop sticks into the straws for a "lolli-flower" arrangement. **Caution:** Check first to find out if the child can have regular candy or if the child can have sugar-free lollipops before you tantalize with forbidden foods!

• **LOW-FAT COOKERY:** Frying meat adds fat. When you want to reduce the fat in your diet, try other methods.
1. Roasting—Roast leaner beef and lamb on a rack in a roasting pan. When you cook in the oven by dry heat, the temperature of the meat should be between 135° to 140°F. Cook pork to 160°F; veal to 170°F; a whole chicken to 180°F.
2. Broiling/Barbecuing—Cook quickly and by direct heat in your range broiler or on a barbecue grill. Marinades add flavor and soaking meat in an acid solution tenderizes it. Make a marinade with a base of vinegar, wine or lime juice and your favorite herbs and spices.
3. Poach/no-fat Braise—In a non-stick pan, add a little oil and brown the meat. A regular pan, sprayed very lightly with non-stick vegetable spray can also be used. Cover the meat and let it finish cooking in the simmering liquid until tender. This can be done on top of the range or in a medium oven.
4. Stir-fry—Fry meat, which has been sliced thinly across the grain, uncovered in very little oil (or in a very small amount of bouillon if you want to avoid fat altogether).

• **LUGGAGE,** *Identifying Lost Bags:* Clip a picture of your suitcase, hanging bag, etc. from a catalog or ad and tuck it into your wallet so that if it's lost in transit, you can show exactly what it looks like. ALWAYS keep receipts for luggage and possessions you travel with so that you can establish insurance claims if the luggage is never found.

- **LUGGAGE,** *Preventing Lost Luggage:*
1. Take off old flight tags to avoid confusion about your destination, and check to make sure the correct tag is put on to the exact destination.
2. Place an identification tag on the inside and outside of each piece of luggage. Don't put your home address on the outside; it alerts people in the airport that you are away.
3. Avoid traveling with obviously expensive luggage; it attracts thieves.
4. Claim baggage as soon as possible; the longer it waits, the longer it tempts thieves.
5. Never leave luggage unattended, even for a minute—it can disappear that fast. Also, most airport security now collects unattended bags and the announcements on PA systems in some airports say that security requires destruction of picked-up unattended baggage, so a word to the wise should be sufficient!

- **LUGGAGE,** *Quick-Fix to Identify Yours on a Conveyor:* If your suitcase looks like everyone else's, tie on a piece of colored yarn or ribbon, add a yarn pompon to the handle, or stick on a bumper sticker, bathtub applique, or just a design with colored plastic tape.

- **LUGGAGE,** *Sizes for Carryons:* See TRAVEL, Luggage Sizes for Carryons.

- **LUGGAGE TAG:** One reader's luggage was returned safely to her home when it was lost by the airline; unfortunately, the mishap occurred at the beginning of her trip so all she had was her overnight case. Now she puts the address of her DESTINATION instead of her home base on her luggage tags.

- **LUNCH, BROWN BAGGING IT,** *Fruit:*
1. Juice—Freeze individual containers of juice; they will thaw by lunchtime and keep the other lunch foods cool.
2. Whole fruits—Place softer fruits (like peaches, plums, grapes) in clean yogurt cups or other containers to keep them from getting squashed.

- **LUNCH, BROWN BAGGING IT**, *General Protective Packing:*
1. Place foam meat trays in the bottoms of paper lunch sacks to keep them from getting wet and having their bottoms fall out.
2. Keeping cold foods in clean used food containers prevents them from sweating so much that the bag tears and best of all, follows my Heloise philosophy of trying to reduce garbage output by re-using packaging as often as possible.
3. If you need to send lunch or milk money along with a very young child, poke a hole into the lid of a 35mm film canister, then poke both ends of a cord (that's long enough to go around your child's neck) through the hole. Knot the ends several times so that the cord won't come out of the hole. Put the money in the canister, attach it to the lid and your child will have a safe lunch money "necklace."

- **LUNCH, BROWN BAGGING IT**, *Salad lunch:* Pack a green or chef's salad in a clean 16-ounce yogurt or 12-ounce cottage cheese carton and add a 35mm film canister containing salad dressing. Just before you eat, pour the dressing over salad, replace lid so that you can toss the salad neatly, and enjoy.

- **LUNCH, BROWN BAGGING IT**, *Sandwiches:* Make sandwiches on grocery-buying day, assembly-line style, and freeze them: Each sandwich has two slices of bread lightly spread with margarine—no mayonnaise or mayonnaise-type salad dressing, since it doesn't freeze—two slices of two different lunch meats (usually turkey types to reduce fat) and one slice of cheese. Breads are sliced white, grain, whole wheat or rye. Each sandwich is placed in a plastic sandwich bag and then returned to the original bread bag so that all know what kind of bread was used. Lunchmeats and cheeses are a surprise. Frozen sandwiches will thaw by lunch time and taste fresher than those made daily and they help keep the other foods in the lunchbox cool.

- **LUNCH, BROWN BAGGING IT**, *Veggies:* Toss an ice cube or piece of wet paper towel into the zipper bag (or clean yogurt/margarine container) containing carrot and celery sticks to keep them fresh and moist.

- **LUNCH LEFTOVERS AT THE OFFICE:** One group of men wrote that they all keep lunch leftovers in the office refrigerator and color-code them with a different color of plastic wrap for each day. Then they know which day the food came in and when it should be thrown away. I presume they write the day of the week on the box of wrap so that everyone knows the code!

• **LUNCH MONEY,** *Time-Saver, Keeping It Handy:* See "Workday Survival Hints."

- **MAGAZINE RECYCLING:** One Middle West library grossed $4,800 in one year by offering donated used magazines for sale at 10 cents each. Volunteers sort and group magazines by type and stand them in boxes on a table with a locked coin box nearby. Payment is on the honor system; buyers drop a dime into the box.

- **MAGAZINES,** *Organizing Clippings:* As you read a magazine, tear out the pages you want to keep, then store them in file folder or punch holes and store the pages in a ring-binder. The information you want will be where you can find it and you can pitch the magazine to get rid of clutter.

- **MAGAZINES,** *Renewing or Canceling Subscriptions:* Cut the address label from the last issue of the magazine and paste or tape it to the space for name and address; there won't be any mistakes when you renew or cancel because your subscriber number and other identifying codes will be on that label.

- **MAGAZINE SYSTEM,** *To Avoid Getting Overwhelmed by Saved Stacks:* As soon as a magazine arrives, scan the articles and cut out everything of interest; cut out and file coupons. Save the articles in a "to read" file and discard the rest of the magazine.

• **MAGNET:** Keep one in your sewing kit to help you find and pick up pins and needles quickly. **Note:** The other way to find and pick up dropped pins is to walk around barefooted—you'll never miss one but it sure is the hard way!

• **MAGNIFYING GLASS:** Keep a small magnifying glass in the car to help you read maps. One of my readers wears one of those large magnifying glasses you hang around your neck to do needlework when she travels. She can see a larger area of the map and doesn't get lost on vacation trips anymore.

• **MAILING,** *Checklist:* The U.S. Postal Service handles more than a half billion pieces of mail daily and says properly addressing letters speeds up delivery.
1. Print or type addresses clearly.
2. "Attention" lines should be put above the address not in the lower left corner as is often done.
3. Street address lines should always include directions such as North or South, whether it's an Avenue or Street, and a room or apartment number if applicable.
4. ZIP code is a must and should be next to the city and state; include the extra four numbers if you know them.
5. Always include a return address.
6. When envelopes are included in a bill or correspondence, use them—they are coded to facilitate mail routing.

• **MAIL ORDER:** Write on your check the phone number of the company from which you order. Then, when you have a canceled check but no merchandise, the number to call will be handy.

• **MAIL ORDER,** *Keeping Track of Orders:*
1. Make a note on the calendar of the approximate merchandise arrival date. If delivery is promised in six to eight weeks, make a note to check on the order in week nine.
2. Make copies of the order and keep an "in progress file" for reference if there is a problem.
3. If your checkbook is the kind with stubs, write the name and address of the company and numbers of items ordered on the back of the stub, then, if you have a canceled check but no merchandise, you can write to the company to inquire.

- **MAIL ORDER PROBLEMS:** ALWAYS save copies of your order so that you have dates, check numbers and address of the company so that you have proof in case there is a problem. Sending a complaint that includes all the above information by certified or registered mail will get more attention, too. But if your complaint is ignored, there is help.
1. If your local newspaper has one, contact the consumer-action reporter, they usually get timely responses.
2. Look in your phone book for your state and local consumer protection agencies and contact them.
3. File a complaint with the Better Business Bureau.
4. You can also file a complaint with The Direct Marketing Association (DMA), 6 East 43rd St., New York, NY 10017.

- **MAIL ORDERS,** *Checklist:*
1. Write name and address neatly or attach an address label. Illegible writing makes filling orders properly difficult.
2. Include ALL digits of your credit card number and the expiration date if it's requested. Orders with incomplete credit card numbers must be returned to customers; a delay!
3. Address must include all numbers, street name, apartment number or lot number for mobile-home parks, and zip code or the post office and/or parcel delivery service will not deliver.
Mail order houses receive thousands of orders daily and can only process them promptly if all information is complete.

- **MAKEUP,** *Checklist for Buying Foundation:* When choosing a makeup base, you need to consider skin-type as well as color and manufacturers use various terms to help you.
1. Hypoallergenic—less likely to irritate sensitive skin.
2. Non-comedogenic—helps prevent pores from clogging which results in blackheads; for women with large pores.
3. Hydrophilic—contains hydrophilic ointment; this makeup is combined with water which is recommended by dermatologists.
Caution: Always consult a family physician or dermatologist if skin problems persist; skin or nail conditions can signal certain health problems.

- **MAKEUP,** *Keeping It Off Clothing:*
1. Before slipping a dress or sweater over your head, place a shower cap under your chin and up over your face, then pull the garment on. Carry one in your purse when you go shopping so that you don't leave makeup on garments you try on. Disposable shower caps found in hotels and motels are good for this hint.
2. Instead of a shower cap, drape a large, square, silky scarf over the top of your head and you won't mess your hair or makeup. If you're traveling and don't have a scarf, a slip or nylon panties can substitute.

- **MAKEUP,** *Making It Last Longer:* Cosmetologists say most makeup probably won't last more than six hours, no matter what type or application method.
1. Powder sets makeup and helps it last longer. Apply loose or pressed powder then dab a lightly dampened sponge over it to give your skin a glow. You can also dampen a sponge or cotton ball in astringent lotion instead of water to set the makeup. Hint—the area around your eyes will have a moister look if you don't powder it.
2. Store powder so it keeps dry. Loose powder is easier to shake out from a salt or pepper shaker. Shake it into the palm of your hand, then dip a powder puff or makeup brush into it. Brushes can be old blush brushes or a clean dry shaving brush.

- **MAP,** *Marking:* When you move to a new city or in a city you visit often, mark with red or other color places you've gone. It will jar your memory and help you orient yourself to your new surroundings. If there is a space, you can put a red "X" or dot on 1234 Maple Street and then draw a fine line to the margin (or into a river or lake if there is one on the map) and note "Acme Book Store," or "Smiths."

- **MARBLE,** *Water Stain:* If a water ring is only on the surface, try rubbing with a good marble-polishing powder, usually tin oxide, from a hardware store or marble manufacturing company or funeral monument manufacturer. These companies are a good source for advice on polishing marble. Avoid trouble in the future by trying to convince your family and friends that marble is porous and absorbs moisture. Also, wipe up spills, even plain water, ASAP.

• **MARGARINE SQUEEZE-CONTAINERS,** *Recycling:* Since these containers fit so well in refrigerator door space, wash them well so that they can hold syrups, ketchup, mustard, salad dressings, steak sauces and anything else you want to squirt on your food. Less clutter in the fridge and fewer search missions into the back to find things. Don't forget to write on the outside what's stored on the inside!

• **MATCH HOLDER,** *Safety Idea:* Hold the match with a spring-type wooden clothespin when you light candles, barbecue or fireplace starters. No more singed finger tips!

• **MATERNITY SLACKS,** *Creeping and Slipping Down When You Sit:* Wear suspenders under your blouse or sweater to keep them in place.

• **MATTRESS,** *Anchoring Slippery Ones:* Mattresses quilted with shiny, satiny fabrics often slip off the box springs and can make it difficult to keep sheets neat. Place a thin sheet of foam rubber between the mattress and the box spring, then another thin sheet of foam rubber on top of the mattress before you add pad and sheets. Sometimes, just placing foam on the corners of a mattress will hold the pad and sheets on. (Foam corners are sold in catalogs and elsewhere and some catalogs sell special non-skid sheets to place between mattress and box spring.)

• **MATTRESS,** *Turning Cues:* Turning a mattress every few months makes it last longer and prevents "dips" in the springs. But who can remember which way to flip the thing?
Method 1: Write the date you turn the mattress on some masking tape and tape it to a top corner of the box spring so you'll know at a glance when you should turn it again.
Method 2: Write a code on the corners of the mattress with permanent marker. For example, on one side of the mattress, mark J-M for January-March and on the diagonal corner, mark A-J for April-June. On the other side of the mattress, mark two diagonal corners again with J-S for July and September and O-D for October and December. Then you'll know which corner to turn when.

• **MEAT,** *No Mess Marinating:* Put all the ingredients in a plastic bag large enough to accommodate the meat and seal, forcing out as much air as you can. Then put the bag in the fridge (on a dish if you're afraid of leaks) and then when you need to turn the meat all you turn is the bag.

• MEAT, *Quick-Thawing a Solid Hunk of Ground Meat for Meatloaf or Meatballs:* Unwrap the meat; slice the frozen meat with a sharp knife; place the slivers in a bowl and they will thaw in about an hour. **Note:** Mix beef bouillon powder into ground turkey and you'll have a beefier flavor when you substitute it for beef in your favorite recipes.

• MEATBALLS, *Swedish & Italian, Time-Saver:* Place on shallow baking dish; bake at 374°F. for about 10 minutes (depending on size). You don't even have to turn them!

• MEAT, FLOURING OR BREADING, *Avoiding Mess:* Open the plastic wrap on the meat carefully and lay it on the counter, then you can put flour and/or bread crumbs on the plastic wrap and/or on the foam meat tray. After breading, toss the mess away. **Hint:** Don't forget to let the meat rest on the wrap or foam trays for 10 to 20 minutes after breading or flouring to let the surface dry (turn over once during drying); the coating will stick better during cooking.

• MEATLOAF, *Substitutes for Bread Crumbs:* Try crushed or blender-ground unsweetened dry cereal, dry oatmeal, instant mashed potatoes or crushed soda cracker crumbs when you have no bread or bread crumbs.

• MEAT MARINADE, *Quick-Fix:* Bottled Italian or other vinegar and oil-style salad dressing will give flavor and tenderize meats and chicken.

• MEAT RE-WRAPPING FOR FREEZER: When re-wrapping meats for the freezer, cut the label off the original grocery package and tape it to the newly wrapped one. The label has all the information— type of meat, date of purchase and weight. No more guessing at how much is in the package.

• MEDICINE, *Getting Small Children to Take Bad-tasting Liquid Medicine:* Mary Poppins used a spoonful of sugar to help the medicine go down but here's a non-sugar idea. Have the child suck on an ice cube or frozen fruit treat for a few minutes to numb the taste buds. To avoid choking in very small children, let the child suck on some crushed ice.

• **MEDICINE,** *Identifying Meds in the Cabinet:* Mark containers with the malady for which they were prescribed as soon as you bring them home. For example, for headache, for cough, for allergy, diuretic (water pills), high blood pressure, etc. While you should always take all of the medication as prescribed for an illness and should not have leftovers, some prescriptions are for ongoing problems (like allergy, diuretic, etc.) and you may forget what (tongue-twister chemical-name) is for. **Caution:** If you forget what a certain medicine is for, call your pharmacist who can look it up in computerized records for you and tell you what it's for and how it should be taken—with meals, not with dairy products, not with certain other medications, if the instructions are not printed on the container.

• **MEDICINE,** *Remembering to Take the Next Dose:* Buy a "will be back at" clock from an office supply store. Then when you take medicine, set it for the next time a dose is due. Hang it where you will surely see it and you won't miss a dose.

• **MEDICINE BOTTLE,** *Easier Opening Safety Lids:* When the cap's directions say "Squeeze at arrows while turning" and your fingers don't do that without complaining/paining, put a nutcracker to the cap. The extra pressure and "torque" makes opening safety caps a snap.

• **MEDICINE CABINET,** *Cleaning Checklist:* Make it a habit to clean out your medicine cabinet at least once a year—perhaps on your birthday, or during the Spring Forward or Fall Back switches between standard and daylight saving's time.
1. Check labels for expiration dates; if expired, discard as noted in Medicine, Prescriptions, below. If there is no date, discard any medicine that's two years old.
2. Discard cracked, smashed or discolored tablets or capsules which have become soft and/or stuck together.
3. Discard aspirin tablets that smell of vinegar.
4. Discard any liquid medicine that has separated.

5. If the prescription label has come off, you can't be sure about contents, dosage or age, so discard it.

6. Keep all medicines in a cool, dry place. The warm, steamy bathroom medicine chest is not good for storage and if kept in a closet, don't keep medicines near mothballs or insect repellent whose vapors can be absorbed by medicine.

• **MEDICINE CABINET SAFETY:** Dowel pins (round wooden sticks sold at hardware stores for less than $1) can be placed in the mirror track of sliding-door medicine chests to prevent young children from opening the doors.

• **MEDICINE, PRESCRIPTIONS,** *Using Leftovers:*

1. If the prescription is for a specific illness, such as antibiotics, you won't have leftovers if you take the medicine exactly as it was prescribed.

2. Medicines should not be taken if they are older than the use-by date on the label or older than one year. Old medications deteriorate and can become either ineffective or even dangerous. Call your doctor or pharmacist before taking any leftover medications regardless of age.

3. **Caution!** When you buy Over-the-Counter (OTC) medicines, ask the pharmacist if they are compatible with your prescription medicines; OTCs are real drugs and can react with your prescriptions.

4. **Caution!** Protect curious children and pets. Flush old medications down the toilet, rinse out containers, and replace caps tightly before discarding.

• **MELON,** *Quick Fix, Removing Seeds:* Try an ice cream scoop!

• **MEMORY ALBUM:** When couples celebrate 25th or 50th wedding anniversaries and don't want gifts, friends can write a personal letter to the couple relating a fond memory that they shared, their first meeting or the like. Put all the letters in a scrap book for many happy hours of reminiscing.

• **MENU PLANNING,** *Quick-Fix:* When you just can't decide what to serve, look at frozen dinners to see combinations of meats, starch and vegetables that you can duplicate with your own home-cooking.

- **MERINGUE,** *Checklist for Success:*
1. Beaters and bowls must be sparkling clean and free from all grease and oil. Use only metal or glass bowls. Plastic bowls, even clean ones, may have a greasy film that prevents foaming.
2. Separate eggs carefully. Fat in the egg yolk is the culprit; even a bit of yolk prevents the whites from foaming properly. **Hint:** Separate eggs while they are cold.
3. After separating, let egg whites set for about one-half hour so that they come to room temperature. They will produce greater volume than if beaten when cold. **Note:** Add ⅛ teaspoon cream of tartar for each egg white before beating.
4. Procedure: Beat with rotary beater, whisk or electric mixer at high speed just until foamy. Gradually begin adding sugar, about one tablespoon at a time, beating as you slowly sprinkle the sugar in. **Hints:** Powdered sugar dissolves more easily than granulated. Always move the beaters or the bowl so that all of the egg-sugar mixture reaches the beaters.

Continue to beat at high speed until the sugar is dissolved. **Hint:** Rub a little of the mixture between your fingers to test if all the sugar is dissolved. If you feel grittiness, beat some more. Whites should stand in soft or stiff peaks, depending on the recipe directions.

- **METAL,** *Polishing:* Please see individual metal's listing.

- **MICROWAVE,** *Container Size for Boiling:* Milk or creamy mixtures and some cereals boil up quickly and tend to overflow; allow plenty of headroom. Containers should be two to three times the volume of the ingredients to avoid messy boil-overs.

- **MICROWAVE,** *Cooking Bags:* Twist-ties contain metal and can cause "arcing" sparks that can damage your oven. Tie microwave cooking bags closed with dental floss and ALWAYS open bags AWAY from you to prevent steam burns.

- **MICROWAVE,** *Cooking in Ring Pan:* Because microwaves cook from the outside in, veggies and some other foods are best made in a ring mold or bundt pan. To make one, place a glass ovenware custard cup, microwave-safe water glass or preserving jar in the center of a microwave-safe round casserole which has the proper diameter.

- **MICROWAVE,** *Covering Food While Cooking:* Waxed paper used to cover food containers won't blow off if you crumple the paper slightly.

- **MICROWAVE,** *Identifying Cookware:* Identify your microwave-safe cookware with an indelible mark (use pens for marking glassware, etc.) so that everyone in the family knows which containers are safe. Then, when you place the container in the microwave oven, make it a habit to center the mark at "12 o'clock" so that if you have to give it one-quarter or one-half turns during cooking, you'll know how much of a turn you've made.

- **MICROWAVE,** *Reheating Chicken and Keeping It Crisp:* Pop chicken in the microwave for one minute on "High," then finish in conventional oven at 400°F for 5 minutes. The chicken will be warmed to the bone and be crispy without burning the coating or making the insides rubbery.

- **MICROWAVE,** *Reheating Rolls and Pastries:* Heating too long makes bread products tough and dry; a few seconds—about 15—is usually enough. To prevent soggy bottoms on sweet rolls or pastries place them on a paper towel or paper plate (real paper, not foam); you can use the plate several times.

- **MICROWAVE,** *Reminder to Rotate Foods:* Put a wooden toothpick under the front of the dish, then move it with the dish as you rotate it. For example, start at 6 o'clock; move to 9; then 12, and so on. You can tell at a glance how often the dish was turned.

- **MICROWAVE COOKING,** *Dont's:*
1. Never warm baby bottles; bottles can feel cool to the touch on the outside but the milk or other fluid inside can be hot enough to scald a baby's throat.
2. Stuffing in stuffed birds (turkey, chicken) may not cook completely and could cause food poisoning.
3. Eggs in the shell can explode due to steam buildup and damage the oven.
4. Popcorn should be cooked only in microwave-safe containers or pre-packaged microwave bags. Kernels can scorch and cause a fire inside the oven if improper containers are used. Reheating popcorn in the microwave also is a fire hazard.

5. Canning in the microwave is dangerous because there is no way to tell if harmful organisms are killed.

6. Deep-fat frying in the microwave is a fire hazard.

7. Let steam out of baked potatoes by piercing them with a fork; otherwise they can explode and possibly cause eye injury or burns if they pop when you are opening the door.

8. Never operate a microwave oven when it's empty. To avoid doing this accidentally, leave a water-filled microwave-safe coffee cup in the oven.

• MICROWAVE COOKING, *Packaging:* When you use foods with heat susceptor packaging experts recommend:

1. Don't microwave products any longer than instructed on the package; it increases chances of the temperature going too high.

2. Don't eat foods, such as popcorn, if the package has become very browned or charred—signs that the food may have been over-heated.

3. Don't re-use container with heat susceptors or remove the susceptors for use with other foods.

• MICROWAVE COOKING, *Foil-covered Frozen Foods:* Although many new products packaged in foil are safe for some microwave ovens under certain conditions, you still need to check the cookbook that came with your oven to make sure it is safe for your oven to avoid serious damage. If your care manual doesn't give you the information you need, call the manufacturer's consumer line which should be given in the manual.

• MICROWAVE COOKING, *Seasonings:* Add most seasonings as usual to microwave recipes. However, don't sprinkle salt on food; the crystals reflect the microwaves and cause uneven cooking. Dissolve salt in liquid, mix it into the food or better—add it just before serving. Pepper becomes more intense when microwaved, so use it sparingly and add more after cooking if you wish.

• MICROWAVE DISPOSABLE TRAYS, *Recycling for Workday Lunches When Your Workplace Has a Microwave:* Wash trays and plates well after home use so that you can put leftovers in them to reheat at work on your lunch break. There's no clean-up or toting dirty dishes home.

• **MICROWAVE DISHES,** *Which Are Best:*

1. Check if the material is safe for microwave cooking and if the size and shape are suitable for that particular food or recipe. Don't cook with any dishes trimmed with gold or silver or any made of metal. Microwave safe materials include glass, ceramic, pottery, special microwaveable plastics and paper. Most sold today will indicate suitability for microwaving. Test older dishes as described below.

Test for Microwave Cooking Safety: Place the dish in the microwave and next to it place a glass measuring cup with one cup of water. Heat on full power for one minute, then check the temperature of the dish. If the dish is cool and the water is very warm, the dish is safe. If the dish is slightly warm, it can still be used, but only for very short-term warming. If the dish is hot, it's not for microwave cooking.

2. Food in deep containers cooks more slowly than food in shallow ones and will require more stirring. Shallow containers expose more food surface to microwaves so more food cooks at the same time.

3. Round and oval casseroles give more even results than square or rectangular ones. More energy penetrates the corners so food there is apt to overcook, giving you dried-out corners and underdone centers.

4. Straight-sided dishes and pans are better than slanted-side ones. Straight sides keep food at a more uniform depth and so it cooks more evenly. Sloped dishes let food on the edges get more energy because it's not as deep; it cooks faster and can overcook before the center is done.

5. Ring-shaped pans are best for foods like cakes and muffins that can't be stirred during cooking. The open center allows microwaves to contact the food from all sides as well as top and bottom for more uniform cooking.

• **MICROWAVE POTPOURRI:** To get your house smelling like baking pies, add 2 teaspoons of pumpkin pie spice to 1 cup of water in a microwave-safe dish. Microwave on "High" until it boils, then cook for 3 more minutes. For delicious roast turkey, cook 2 teaspoons of thyme or sage in water the same way. You can use your imagination to create a tempting aroma any time with any spice you like.

• **MILDEW,** *Prevention in Basements, Closets, and Bathrooms:* Air conditioners and dehumidifiers are the best solutions in damp climates. Leaving a light on in the bathroom or closet helps. Commercial products such as silica gel or activated alumina, found in hardware stores, work well in enclosed spaces like closets. These chemicals absorb moisture from the air. Follow package directions exactly and keep away from small children and pets.

• **MILDEW,** *Removing from Plastic-Mesh Outdoor Furniture:*
Method 1: Mix 1 cup of bleach to 1 gallon of water and test solution on an inconspicuous area to make sure there will be no fabric color changes. If it is safe, apply solution to the fabric and scrub with a soft brush or rag. Be sure to rinse well.
Method 2: If the bleach solution is not safe, vinegar may remove the mildew. Wash the furniture with white vinegar and rinse well.
Hint: Always dry furniture completely to help prevent more mildew growth.

• **MILK SUBSTITUTE FOR COOKING:** Mix non-dairy creamer with a little water to complete a recipe in a hurry, when you're out of milk and can't even borrow some from a friendly neighbor.

• **MINI-BLIND DUSTER:** Try a new and clean two-inch paintbrush.

• **MIRROR,** *Removing Hair Spray:* Clean with rubbing alcohol on a soft cloth. Please see GLASS CLEANER, Homemade.

• **MIRRORS,** *Cleaning:* Mix 2 ounces of non-sudsing ammonia, 2 ounces of rubbing alcohol, a couple of drops of blue food coloring (optional) with 12 ounces of water in a spray bottle which has been clearly labeled. The food coloring helps you quickly distinguish window cleaner from other cleaning liquids but you should label the container anyway.

• **MITTENS,** *Decorating for Identification:* Stitch or embroider the owner's initials on them or "R" and "L" for right and left; add favorite-color buttons or bows.

• **MITTENS,** *Recycling an Old Sweater to Make Mittens:* See SWEATER, Recycling.

• **MITTENS,** *Storing:* Hang a sixteen-pocket shoe bag on the closet rod to hold mittens. No matter what height the child and others in the family are, some pocket will be reachable.

• **MITTS,** *Kitchen/Oven:* When the non-stick surface of your ironing board cover wears out, the less-worn parts can be lined with washable fabric padding and sewn into hot mitts and pot holders. Cover one side with the ironing board cover fabric and the other with a print that coordinates with your kitchen. Bind the edges with bias tape.

• **MIX 'N' MASH,** *Quick-Fix:* A pastry blender is a super masher for avocados, bananas or any other slightly soft food. It quick mixes dips, cream cheese or anything too stiff to mix with a blender. It also substitutes for a wire whisk when you beat eggs.

• **MONEY MATTERS,** *Letter of Laughter:* One reader asks, "Have you noticed that with the economy the way it is that life's little pleasures are now considered luxuries?"

• **MOSS,** *Removing from Patio/Walkway Bricks:* Sprinkle a solution of half water and half bleach onto the moss. **Caution:** This should remove moss without discoloring brick but it's always best to test in an inconspicuous place.

• **MOTHERHOOD,** *Letter of Laughter:* When a four-year-old attending a meeting with his mother heard the word "motherhood" mentioned, he turned to his mom and whispered, "She must be Robin Hood's Mother."

• **MOTHER SCRAPBOOK,** *The Way We Were:* Write down young children's cute sayings and add their "quotables" as they get older and you'll end up with a wonderful and funny record of the joys and sorrows of childhood and teens. Keep the original and make a copy for your children as they leave home.

• **MOUSEPROOFING,** *Healthy Planet:* Instead of dangerous poisons, stuff all the cracks around gas and water pipes with steel wool to keep the varmints out.

• **MOVING,** *Getting Information About the New City:* Subscribe to the Sunday or daily newspaper to find out about the area and write to the Chamber of Commerce to find out about special events and happenings. Some chambers of commerce offer newcomer welcome packets or visitor information packets that are useful to "permanent visitors," too.

• **MOVING,** *Healthy-Planet Packing Materials:* Wrap dishes and breakables one at a time in clean towels, washcloths, sheets, pillowcases and clothing. They arrive clean and you've nothing to throw away.

• **MOVING,** *Making It Easier for Children:*
1. Type your new address and phone number in columns with two-inch margins and fold on lines above and below each address segment so that you and the children can tear off new-address segments for friends. Then, at the new location, make stationery, envelopes and stamps available for children to write to their friends. Allow one five-minute long-distance call per month per child (depending on your finances). Each child keeps track of the date and length of call on a calendar placed near the phone and pays for the call with allowance money when the phone bill arrives. Long distance calls will be kept to the minimum and children will be encouraged to write letters to their friends instead and they will also be encouraged to develop a rewarding life-long habit of writing.
2. Christen your new home by tying a big bow on the front door—one for each child. While each child cuts a bow, take a picture to put into your moving-day scrapbook. Later in the evening, have a family party with cookies, punch and talk. Remember that the talk may be more a "refreshment" than the cookies and punch! Moving can be hard for kids.
Also, please see VIDEO MEMORIES.

• **MOVING COSTS:** When contracting with a moving company find out if charges are different for weekday and weekend; if they charge overtime rates and at what hour does overtime begin. It may be better to schedule two days instead of one with overtime.

• **MOVING FURNITURE THAT WILL BE REASSEMBLED,** *Avoiding Loss or Confusion Over Which Hardware Belongs to Which Furniture.*
Instead of putting all of your nuts and bolts in one basket, box or jar, when furniture is disassembled, gather all screws, bolts and brackets in a sturdy envelope or bag and tape it securely to the underside of a part of that bookcase, desk, etc. Or, securely tape the hardware to the undersides of furniture with duct tape so that it's ready when you reassemble the furniture at your destination.

- **MOVING IN:** Protect carpets from dirt with plastic drop cloths which you can save for later use in the garden or for painting; protect varnished or new flooring from scratches with old flannel-backed plastic tablecloths, bedspreads, and rugs but **Caution:** be sure that the floor "protection" is non-skid people-protection too.

- **MOVING INFORMATION:** Contact the phone company in the city to which you are moving to get a phone book. Then, you can call utility and cable companies to find out what information and fees are necessary to get "hooked-up" in your new location and to set the wheels rolling for faster service. You can look up service people to install appliances and find the name of the local newspaper and order a subscription to the Sunday paper that lets you get acquainted with stores, politics, and other facts before you get to the new city. You can check out the chain department stores and know which credit cards will be useful and which to cancel.

  And, take your old phone book with you when you move, just in case you leave a few "loose ends to tie up." And, you'll have your neighbors' street address numbers, too, when you want to send them a Christmas card!

- **MOVING OUT:** Be kind to the next tenant. Leave an envelope with helpful information such as utility companies, cable TV, garbage pickup days, the local pizza or other food delivery number, a roll of toilet tissue, paper towels and soap, and any appliance booklets for the ones you leave behind.

- **MUFFIN,** *Quick-Fix Removal from Tin:* A shoe horn lifts muffins out of the tin without tearing and can go right into the dishwasher. Of course, the shoehorn is for kitchen use only!

- **MUFFIN TIN GREASING,** *No-mess When You're Out of Non-stick Spray:* Pour about a fourth cup of oil in one of the muffin cups, then dip a waded-up paper towel into the oil. Rub the other cups with the towel, re-oiling it as you go.

- **MUSHROOMS,** *Non-slimy Storage:* Don't wash mushrooms before you put them into the fridge, instead, make sure they're dry and then put them into a paper, not plastic, bag. Paper bags let them "breathe" so that they stay fresh longer; plastic bags or wrap makes mushrooms slimy.

- **MUSHROOMS,** *Quick-Slice:* After washing, cut off stems level with the mushroom cap and then place each mushroom in the egg slicer stem side up—all will have equal thickness.

- **MUSTARD SQUIRT BOTTLE,** *Healthy-Planet Recycling:* Wash thoroughly so that it can be a cooking oil dispenser—a help if you buy the large economy size oil and find it awkward to pour.

- **MUTUAL HELP TRADE-OFFS TO SAVE MONEY:**
1. Set up a babysitting co-op in your neighborhood. Each family gets a beginning bonus of hours (2 or so) and then must "sit" for others to put "hours in the bank" which they can withdraw when they need sitters. Different people can be the "banker" for each month so the responsibilities are divided or you can elect a "banker" for a period of time. Naturally you have to set a limit to "credit" hours so that no parent ends up not paying back hours used.
    Also, with so many women (some statistics show it's 20 to 30 percent) caring for sick and elderly parents, trading elder-sitting is an idea whose time has come. One could even trade elder-sitting for baby-sitting to get an exchange of viewpoints—younger vs older.
2. If all you need is a perm in your bangs, and that's all your friend needs, too, you can share one boxed home permanent and roll each other's hair. You'll both get curls for less than the cost of one person's perm. (Some shops charge $5 per curl when you just have bangs done!) While you're at it, make it a beauty day and give each other facials and manicures, too.
3. If you can't afford a maid, share housework chores with a friend. If you like to wax furniture and your friend likes to shine bathrooms, trade your waxing for her shining. Or, work together on each other's houses; four hands work more pleasantly than two and you can treat yourselves to a nice luncheon out after you finish.
4. Trade talents and interests. For example, if your friend likes to hang wallpaper and paint woodwork but doesn't garden, and you are a gardener, trade off wallpapering a room for planting your friend's flower beds planted with annuals.
5. Trade off house chores for free or reduced rent. Many elderly people who live alone need help with minor chores and yard work as well as companionship so that they can maintain their independent lifestyles. Check out classified ads in the newspaper or place an

ad yourself that says, "Will do work around the house in exchange for free rent . . ." Be sure to spell out in writing exactly what chores you will do for what household benefits and rental charge (if any) so that there is no confusion. Many large cities have programs to match renters with people who need such help. There is also a national agency, Shared Housing Resource Center, which will help you find a local agency on aging that has a house-sharing/room-mates for the elderly program; call 215-848-1220.

6. Trade off homes with couples or families you know in other cities or trade with families in other countries through an exchange program to have a vacation without hotel/motel fees. Some church groups have such exchange programs with overseas churches in which couples trade houses for a period of time.

- **NAILS,** *Quick Pickup:* Please see SPEAKERS, Recycling.

- **NAMES CONFUSION,** *Ending Check Payment Confusion:* When Mom remarries and children's names differ from hers, payments to school, Scouts, and other activities may not be recognized as for that child when the mother's new name is printed on the checks. One mother solves the problem by having her children's names printed on the checks beneath her and her husband's names. The bonus is that the children feel as important as the parents in the family and the name association is more recognizable by activity directors.

- **NAPKINS,** *Healthy-Planet Quick-Fix, $aver:* Instead of paper table napkins or cloth ones that need ironing or show food stains, substitute small, cheap washcloths or finger-tip towels for family dining.

- **NAPKIN RINGS:** See COOKIE CUTTERS, Seasonal Plastic Ones.

- **NECKLACE,** *Lengthening:* If clasps are compatible, add a thin metal bracelet to the necklace. The bracelet will be concealed under the collar so your extension won't show.

• **NECKLACES,** *Avoiding Tangles:* Hang necklaces to a mirror with clear suction-cup hooks; to a wall or in the closet on an expanding peg coatrack; from clothes screwed into a closet door or wall; layer them in a drawer on shoebox lids (line lids with a piece of soft scrap fabric to keep them from slipping too much); place lengthwise on felt and roll necklace "sausages" to be placed in a drawer.

• **NECKTIE PROTECTION:** Many men tuck their neckties into their shirts when they eat—especially on airplanes when a bump could ruin a favorite tie.

• **NECKTIES,** *Care:*
1. Undo the tie before removing it; sliding the knot or leaving it ties causes it to lose shape.
2. Take care when using cologne or after-shave; they can fade colors.
3. Hanging keeps ties from wrinkling; try draping them over a dry cleaner's pants hanger—the kind with a paper tube.
4. If you must press a tie, do it on the backside to avoid shine on the fabric.
5. If you get a spot or stain, just blot it off and take the tie to a dry cleaner. Club soda or water can leave water spots, especially on silk ties. Tell the dry cleaner what the stain is so that there's a better chance of getting it removed.

• **NEEDLEWORK,** *Framing:* Larger cities have do-it-yourself (with help) framing shops to help you save money framing needlework and craft art.

• **NEEDLEWORK,** *Framing:* Use an embroidery hoop, painted or unfinished, to frame and hang a needlework project.

• **NEEDLEWORK,** **Hint:** Tie your needle threader and embroidery scissors on a string, yarn, or old shoelace and you won't lose the threader. (If you haven't done needlework for a long time, new threader designs make using thread or yarn easier than you could ever imagine.)

• **NEEDLEWORK,** *Hoops:* Tack, staple, or tape (masking) smaller embroidery work to an old sturdy picture frame if you don't have a hoop or embroidery frame to work on.

• **NEEDLEWORK,** *From Kits:* Read packets before you buy them to find out what's included. Most needlework pattern designs (needle-point, embroidery, cross stitch, long stitch) have instructions for the types of stitches used so you don't have to know how; you can learn from the pictures. Full kits usually include the needles as well as yarn or thread.

• **NEEDLEWORK,** *Learning How:* Most needlework and craft stores offer free advice and demonstrations to help you get started in such hobbies. Ask about classes for adults and children.

• **NEEDLEWORK TRAVEL:** Replace scissors in your needlework travel kit with a pair of fingernail clippers. They'll snip the threads but are smaller and won't poke holes in anything, including you!

• **NEIGHBORHOOD SWAP MEET,** *Recycling, $aver:* Lots of neighbors join for a garage sale, but how about a swap meet for books, records, tapes, even children's clothing if it doesn't disturb the children. Aside from saving money, it's a friendly, get-acquainted thing to do!

• **NEWSPAPER BAGS,** *Recycling:*
1. Store sewing patterns.
2. Store celery, green onions, and other "long" veggies.
3. Wrap several around a wire hanger to pad it.
4. Place on ceiling-fan blades when you paint to keep spatters off.

• **NEWSPAPER BILLS,** *Keeping Track of Paid Weeks:* If you pay in advance, as many people do, highlight the paid-for weeks on your calendar so you can tell when the next bill will be due. A good calendar for this is the bookmark-style ones we get from various businesses at Christmas time.

• **NEWSPAPERS,** *Recycling:*
1. Wet the edge and use as a dustpan, especially for sweeping up glass or messy things. (Used paper plates from dry foods like sand-wiches can be cut in half for the same purpose.)
2. Comics can be gift wrap.
3. Children can make paper airplanes and hats from them.
4. Roll and stuff inside wet boots and shoes to shape them as they dry.

5. Place inside a plastic bag to pad your knees in the garden or your "sitter" at a picnic.

6. Shred for hamster/guinea pig cages or for the garden compost pile.

7. Place under and inside refrigerators/freezers to absorb water during defrosting.

8. Place under pet feeding dishes for absorbent, disposable place mats.

9. Spread over plastic drop cloths while you paint. They absorb spills and prevent tearing the drop cloth which may let paint get on the floor.

• **NEW YEAR'S RESOLUTIONS,** *Making and Keeping Them:* One reader sent in her system which is similar to business goal-setting. Instead of making resolutions and then forgetting about them, she decides what her resolutions are, plans a definite date on which to start them and a definite time in which to accomplish them. For example, what date will she start her diet? If she will plant a garden, what date will she buy seedlings, when might she put them outside, and so on. Then, the most important step is to mark all the dates on the next year's calendar so that she's reminded of what she wants to do and when.

• **NIGHT-LIGHT:** Plug a night-light in at the bathroom vanity level and you won't have to startle your eyes switching on the regular light if you get up at night. Get an automatic, light-sensor type; it remembers to turn itself on!

• **NON-STICK SPRAY CAUTION:** A reader who frequently sprayed pots and pans with non-stick spray wrote that, apparently, the spray built up on her floor so much that one day she slipped and fell. Now instead of holding a dish "in the air" to spray, she places it in the sink.

• **NUTS,** *Easy Cracking:* Freeze Brazil nuts before cracking. If freezing doesn't work for pecans, try placing them in a microwave-safe bowl, add enough water to cover and heat on "High" in the microwave for about three minutes. Take the pecans out of the water and let them cool. The shells should crack easily.

O

• **OATMEAL,** *Flavoring:* Perk up oatmeal by adding chopped fruit (fresh or dried); nuts; chocolate or butterscotch chips; crumbs from the bottom of a dry cereal to make it crunchy, and then the old favorites—brown sugar and cinnamon, raisins or applesauce, honey or molasses.

• **OATMEAL,** *Homestyle "Granola" in Yogurt:* Add dry oatmeal to your fruited yogurt for extra fiber and a fuller feeling. It won't look particularly pretty, but it tastes good, expecially if you add a few chopped nuts.

• **OATMEAL MASK,** *Homestyle Beauty Aid:* Mix a little water with some oatmeal until it's a smooth paste. Spread mixture on your face, keeping it away from the delicate skin around the eyes. Allow it to dry and rinse off with warm water. Your face will be clean, refreshed, and smooth.

• **ODORS,** Please see the special section on odors on page 420.

• **OFFICE DUSTING:** Dust the copy-machine glass with a coffee filter instead of a paper towel or cloth. It leaves no lint and you'll get clearer, neater copies.

- **OIL BOTTLE,** *Avoiding Mess:* Slip a plastic sandwich bag over the bottom of the bottle, leaving the sides open around the bottle to catch drips that run down the sides. You'll have a clean shelf!

- **OIL PAINTING,** *Faking It:* Put a piece of cheesecloth or swatch of nylon net over a picture, taping around the edges to keep it flat and taut. Then brush on a very thin coat of shellac and gently remove the net or cloth and allow the picture to dry completely. When dry, the picture will have a texture similar to an oil on canvas painting.

- **OINTMENT,** *Applying Smelling One Without Smelly Hands:* Keep a supply of plastic disposable gloves in the medicine chest to keep your hands away from ointments. It's more sanitary anyway.

- **OLIVE OIL,** *Storage:* Olive oil keeps longer than other edible oils. Store in a cool, dark place, protected from light. While it doesn't need refrigeration, you can store it there. Refrigeration makes olive oil thick and cloudy, but bringing it back to room temperature will lighten it again.

- **OLIVES,** *Perking Up for Parties:* Drop a clove of garlic into a jar of olives and add a drop or two of olive oil. Let set for a couple of days and the olives will be tasty and shiny.

- **ONION,** *Quick-Fix:* When you want only one slice of onion for a burger or other sandwich, there's no need to peel the whole onion. Slice through the middle of the onion, cut off one slice, put the two parts back together, then wrap or seal in a plastic bag and refrigerate.

- **ONIONS,** *Peeling Without Tears:* Chopping or slicing onions releases a gas that reacts chemically with the water in your eyes to form sulfuric acid. (Saying the name of the gas almost makes you cry, too—propanethiol S-oxide.) Tears are your defense against the acid irritant and some people are innately more irritated by onion gas than others. The good news is that the more onions you cut the greater your tolerance. If you seldom cut onions, you're likely to cry more. Here are some ways to help you avoid crying while dealing with onions.

1. Place in freezer 30 to 45 minutes before slicing. **Caution:** Don't leave them in the freezer too long or they will get mushy; however,

if you should forget and freeze them, you can still cook with them later.

2. If you only cook with onions occasionally, try dried onions found in the spice department of most supermarkets. You can even brown them for casseroles and other recipes that require it, just watch them carefully because once they start to brown, they can burn to black in a few seconds. *Letter of Laughter:* One reader, whose chile sauce recipe requires lots of chopped onion, wrote that since she began wearing her son's scuba mask while chopping them she hasn't shed a tear.

- **ORANGE PEEL,** *Homemade Drying:*
1. Scrape as much of the white off the peel as possible.
2. Cut into small pieces and place on paper towels.
3. Cover with a paper towel to protect from dust.
4. Let sit for four to five days. The top of your refrigerator is a good place to dry things—flower petals, peels, etc.—because it's usually warmer there (unless it's under an AC vent), and the stuff is less likely to be disturbed.
5. Store in fridge or freezer in self-sealing plastic bags. Grate as needed.

- **ORGANIZING,** *Time-saver Filing New Recipes, Cleaning Hints:* Tape that special tuna casserole recipe to the tuna can or that special cleaning hint to the thing that needs cleaning, and they will be handy when and where you need them.

- **OVEN-CLEANING SQUEEGEE:** Scrape oven-cleaner goop from the oven walls with a short-handled window squeegee. When all the goop is on the center bottom of the oven, scoop it onto a piece of newspaper or brown paper bag and then discard in the garbage. Next, wipe down the inside of the oven with a wet rag and you're done. Also, see OVEN CLEANER in the ODORS section on page 420.

- **OVEN-DOOR LOCK:** If you have a self-cleaning oven, you can keep a toddler from opening the oven door while something is baking by locking the door with the lock lever as you would when cleaning the oven.

• **OVEN-DOOR WINDOW,** *Cleaning:* Wipe the glass window with ammonia and let it set for a few minutes. Then, scrape away goop with a plastic ice scraper like those for removing ice from auto windshields.

- **PACKING FOAM "PEANUTS,"** *Healthy-Planet Recycling:*
1. Sprinkle with a favorite perfume and place in potpourri jars to deodorize a room.
2. Stuff into plastic newspaper bags and you have tubes to stuff into clothing for mailing or travel (for arms, put the bag into the suit coat arm and fill with "peanuts").
3. Toss into the bottom of a pot for drainage beneath your plants.

- **PACKING LIST FOR TRAVEL,** *Computerized Checklist:* Compile a packing list to keep from forgetting anything on your trip and save it in the computer. Then you can print it out when you need it. Make two copies—one for your purse and one in the suitcase to be used as a checklist for remembering to take it all home again. Having the list in your purse is very valuable if your luggage is lost or stolen—so would a magazine picture or instant photo of your suitcase; it's sometimes difficult to compare your luggage with the claim-form line-drawings the airline provides to help you identify the type of luggage.

- **PACKING PEANUTS:** Pad "care packages" and other gifts with real peanuts in the shell instead of foam ones; they are edible!

- **PADDING,** *For Pots, Pans, China, etc:* Please see BLANKETS, Recycling.

- **PADDING FOR WORK SPACE:** Buy carpet samples and place them upside down on work surfaces to protect them from damage; this is especially good on a washer or dryer which is a good back-saver height for many chores, including grooming a small pet.

- **PAINT,** *Artist's Oils:* Oil paints on sale may not be a good buy; make sure they aren't so old that they are hard!

- **PAINT,** *Artist's Oils:* Don't throw away expensive oil paints at the end of the day; cover your palette with plastic wrap and aluminum and store it in the freezer overnight for the next day.

- **PAINT,** *Artist's Oils, Tube Cap:* When the caps get lost or don't fit anymore, insert a roofing nail; it's easy to remove and replace.

- **PAINT,** *Color Selection:* Before you paint the whole room, test the color choice by buying a small can of the paint, painting a posterboard, and then holding it up in various places around the room to see how you like it. Also, you can tell how it looks day or night by sun or lamplight.

- **PAINT,** *Homemade, Healthy-Planet Artist's Paint:* Add just enough hot water to instant non-fat dry milk to reconstitute it into a smooth syrup. Add powdered pigment (from art-supply shops) in small amounts until desired shade is reached. Apply to raw wood with a brush or rag while still warm. This homemade paint will dry to a flat finish.

- **PAINT,** *Removing Enamel Paint Drips/Spills:* Instead of turpentine, wipe up spills and drips with a soft wet towel lathered with pumice soap. Remember, the sooner you remove such paint, the better!

- **PAINT,** *Removing from Skin:* Rub with mineral oil; then wash with soap and water.

- **PAINT,** *Storage to Prevent Drying:* Thoroughly clean a plastic container with a tight-fitting screw-on cap. Pour in leftover paint; apply petroleum jelly around the treads; squeeze container until the paint reaches the top and hold it steady until the cap is screwed on tightly. Identify the container by taking the label from the paint can and writing the needed information on the back and then attaching it to the new container with a rubber band. No more "skin" on top of paint to deal with.

• PAINT, *Storing to Prevent Discoloration by Rust from Cans:* Pour leftover paint in empty mayo jars, cover the top with plastic wrap and screw on the lid. You can see the color through the jar and the plastic wrap protects the paint from a rusty lid. Be sure to mark the jar with type of paint, cleanup instructions, and any other important information.

• PAINT, *Touch-Up:* A cotton swab easily touches up chipped paint on woodwork or small scrapes on walls, and the bonus is no brush to clean!

• PAINTBRUSHES: Keep your good paintbrush bristles from getting bent while soaking in thinner: Cut an X for each brush in a plastic lid and then suspend the brushes in the solvent by poking their ends into the Xs.

• PAINTBRUSHES, *Easy Cleaning:* Pour a little solvent into a self-sealing heavy-duty clear plastic bag—enough to cover the bristles. Put the brushes in and squeeze the solvent through the bristles, getting all the paint out. When you are finished, pour the solvent into a container with tight lid. You can reuse it.

• PAINTING, *Easel:* Make an artist's easel for a child with an old chair. Pound in a couple of nails at the front of the chair to keep the art work from sliding off when you prop it against the chair back. An old bar stool with back could make a taller easel.

• PAINTING, *Hand-painting Small Objects:* Keep them in place on cardboard with double-stick carpet tape; you'll keep your fingers clean.

• PAINTING, *Inaccessible Corners:* Places like abutted door frames often can't be reached with a paintbrush. Try a wedge-shaped makeup sponge. Dampen it slightly, dip in paint and poke into hard-to-get-at spots.

• **PAINTING,** *Spraying Small Objects:* Place the objects (craft items, hardware) inside a carton to confine the spray "spritzing" and ALWAYS spray in a well-ventilated area.

• **PAINTING A CHAIN-LINK FENCE:** Pour paint into a paint tray and dip a roller or sponge into it to paint. Wear rubber gloves if you paint with a sponge and speed up the job by having another person sponge painting the other side of the fence. This really gets the job done in a hurry, and the bonus is that you can visit while you work and make time pass even faster!

• **PAINTING CAUTION:** When you paint around a phone jack, do not get paint inside the jack box; it could block a proper phone connection and make a repair by the phone company necessary. Instead, place masking tape around the wall jack before painting to protect it.

• **PAINTING FLOOR MOLDINGS,** *Knees-Ease:* Instead of sitting and sliding across the floor as you paint, sit cross-legged on a skateboard and wheel yourself around the room.

• **PAINTINGS,** *Cleaning:* Valuable oil paintings should be cleaned by professionals. Have your painting appraised if you aren't sure about its value. Remove accumulated dust with a soft, clean paintbrush. Commercial cleaners from art-supply stores will remove residues from grease or smoke. **Caution:** Don't dust paintings with a vacuum, it can pull chips off and rags can catch on raised peaks in the paint and remove paint sections.

• **PAINT SPATTERS,** *Keeping Them Off Yourself:* Everyone spreads drop cloths to keep paint spatters off furniture and floors while painting. Here's how to keep paint off the painter: Cut a hole in the bottom of a large plastic leaf bag that's large enough for your head and cut one hole on each side for your arms. Put the bag on to protect clothing, then put a disposable shower cap on your head to protect your hair. You'll emerge from your painting unspattered!

• **PAJAMA/PANTS,** *Helping a Child Find the Front of Elastic-Waist Garments:* Sew a button on the front so that the child need only look for the "belly button" to know front from back.

- **PALETTE PAPER,** *Substitute:* Tape a piece of waxed paper about 12 inches long to a piece of cardboard. Some people also use aluminum foil over a wood palette or piece of sturdy cardboard.

- **PAN,** *Removing Burned-on Gunk:* When a pot or pan is black from frying, sprinkle a small amount (1 or 2 teaspoons) of automatic dishwasher detergent in the pot with a little water and the put the pot on the stove, let it come to boil, turn the burner off. After it's cool enough to handle, wash and rinse well. Avoid scrubbing frying pans; make it a habit that when you take the food out, you pour in enough warm water (and a few drops of liquid dishwashing detergent, if there's lots of grease) to cover the bottom about an inch. Then, allow the water to boil while the burner cools down on electric stoves or allow to boil a minute or so before you turn off a gas stove. The pan cleans itself and cools while you eat. Wash as usual.

- **PANCAKE FUN:** When you are making pancakes, take a cake-decorating tube (or pour with a spoon if you are handy) and make faces or names on pancakes, then flip them over. Or, instead of pouring one large round pancake, make squiggles, critters (one larger plus one smaller circle, two "ear" dots and a tail), or large initials of the pancake lovers.

- **PANCAKE OR FRENCH TOAST TOPPING:** Heat up some chunky-style applesauce with a teaspoon or two of cinnamon and spoon it on— Yum! And it adds the nutrition of fruit instead of just sugar from syrup!

- **PANCAKES,** *Keeping Warm:* Keep them in a bun warmer until the whole batch is cooked, then you can serve all at once and the pancake-cooker won't end up eating alone!

- **PANCAKES,** *Serving to Small Children:* Avoid sticky messes—cut up the pancakes and add the syrup before serving them and serve in soup bowls instead of plates.

- **PANCAKES, WAFFLES,** *Freezing Leftovers:*
1. Make bigger-than-needed batches and prepare as usual, but cook the extras until almost done; they will finish cooking later.

2. Cool on racks, separate them with waxed paper or cut up cereal-box liner, put in freezer-safe bag or container and pop in freezer.
3. To serve, heat in microwave oven for about a minute and a half. Some folks like to toast leftover waffles. Enjoy!

• **PANCAKE SYRUP,** *Homemade Substitute When You Run Out:* Mix 1 cup of brown sugar and ¾ cup of water in a saucepan. Bring mixture to boil, let simmer for about 15 minutes. (Don't let it boil again or overcook.) Add a teaspoon or so of maple flavoring to suit your taste.

• **PANTS ELASTIC,** *Replacing:* If the waistband elastic of stitched waistband pants gets stretched out before the pants are worn, you can replace it easily.
1. Remove the four lines of stitching through the waistband, cut a small slit at one of the side seams and then pull out the old elastic.
2. Measure your waist and cut a piece of the new non-roll elastic about 2 inches smaller than your waist measurement. Do not pull the elastic tightly while measuring it.
3. Attach a small safety pin to the end of the elastic to feed it through, and insert the new elastic all the way through the waist casing. Then stitch the two ends of elastic together; sew the opening shut. You may want to add a lengthwise stitch to both side seams to keep the elastic in place.

• **PANTS PATCHES:** Save the bottoms cut off when you hem children's pants, and then you can fuse the fabric to wherever you need a patch.

• **PANTY HOSE,** *Recycling:*
Hairbands, Ponytail Holders—Cut across the leg to make rings, roll the rings up, and you have a ponytail holder that won't break and damage your hair like rubber bands will. Cut off the panty and the foot, tie the ends together, and you have a stretchy headband or hairband. Colored panty hose can be coordinated with your clothing.

• **PANTY HOSE SYSTEM:** Before putting the panty hose of the day into the laundry, mark the waistband tag with a check if they have no runs, an X if they have a run but still can be worn under slacks, and turn inside out the ones that can no longer be worn. Old panty hose can be recycled for many uses. I have at least one hundred uses in my files. They can also be donated to a local school or group that does crafts with panty hose.

• **PAPER-TOWEL CORES,** *Recycling:*
1. They will hold extension/appliance cords (write on the outside to identify the cord size or type), Christmas lights, small plastic grocery bags.
2. Flatten, and insert sharp knives to protect points of knives and your fingers.
3. Wrap ribbon around the outside to keep it untangled and neat.
4. Tape two or three together for a boot tree.

• **PAPER-TOWEL PACKING,** *Recycling:* When moving, pack your glassware and other breakables with paper towels. They are clean, won't leave newsprint marks like some newspapers and best of all, can be used again when you clean up the new home.

• **PAPERWORK AT WORK:** Wear plastic or rubber gloves when preparing and/or collating many sheets of paper for mass mailing. You don't have to lick your fingers or use sticky stuff to get a good grip on the paper and you won't get paper cuts!

• **PARAKEET CATCHER:** Here's a *Letter of Laughter* that might also help you catch a fly-away parakeet. A reader, whose parakeet loved to play with a bell in its cage, got outdoors and she thought she'd lost him. She took the bell from his cage, stood outside ringing it, and sure enough, the parakeet flew down from a tree to perch on her shoulder and play with his toy. She quickly walked back into the house and returned him to his cage . . . with bell, of course!

• **PARROT FEEDING:** Instead of leaving dishes of your parrot's favorite foods in the cage, feed twice daily and remove the dish after each feeding. Then, the bird will be hungrier at feeding time and therefore more receptive to the wider variety of foods needed for proper nutrition.

• **PARTY BEVERAGE COOLER:** Please see COOLER, For Party.

• **PARTY CAKE,** *Special Occasion Friendship Cake:* When you send out invitations for a special event such as a Golden Anniversary, ask each guest to bake and frost a small square cake using their favorite recipe. Then as the guests arrive, piece the cakes together to make a large patchwork cake. Don't forget to take pictures!

• **PARTY FAVOR,** *Recycling Rolls from Paper Towels, Toilet Paper:* Cut paper-towel rolls in half for this idea. Cut colored tissue paper 6 inches longer than the tube; wrap paper around the tube with 3 inches on each end. Gather one end and tie with ribbon. Fill the tube with candy or small trinkets, then gather and close the other end with ribbon. One reader made these favors with her children and took them to nursing homes at Christmas time. (If you do this, fill some of the favors with sugar-free candy and mark them, then those who can't have regular sugar will get a treat, too.) The favors are fun for birthday and school parties, too.

• **PASTA FOR CHILDREN:** Spiral macaroni is easier for children to self-feed neatly than long spaghetti.

• **PASTA COOKING,** *Ending Boil-overs and Pasta Stuck to the Bottom:* Grease the pot (or spray with non-stick spray) before putting the water in to boil. **Note:** Also spray the colander so that draining pasta won't stick to it.

• **PASTA COOKING,** *Energy-Saver:* Add a pinch of salt and a bit of olive oil when you first boil the water, then add the pasta. When the water begins to boil again, cover the pot with its lid and turn off the burner, leaving the pan on the same burner for the recommended cooking time without the heat. After the cooking time has passed, remove the lid and drain the pasta. You'll save energy and keep from heating up the kitchen at the same time!

• **PASTRY BRUSH,** *Getting All the Oil Out:* Most of my readers write that they don't wash pastry brushes. After using a brush, they wrap it in foil or put it in a resealable plastic bag and keep it in the freezer. It only takes a few minutes to thaw when you need it again. However, if you want to wash the brush, soak it in hot water and dishwashing soap immediately after it's used, rinse well and dry before storing it. Some brushes can be run through the dishwasher cycle.

• **PATCHES, MILITARY, SCOUT,** *Easy Sewing on Straight:* Instead of pinning them before sewing, keep them in place with cellophane tape. Tape three sides of the patch to the fabric and start sewing on the remaining fourth side, untaping one side at a time as you go.

• **PATCHING,** *With Labels:* Cut the designer/manufacturer's tag from the neck of a garment and sew it over small tears or holes on that garment or any other. You mend and designer-decorate clothing at the same time!

• **PEACH SAUCE, JELLED,** *Substitute for Holiday Cranberry Sauce:*
    1 large can of peaches
    ½ cup of sugar
    ½ teaspoon of nutmeg
    1 box lemon gelatin
    Drain canned peaches saving the syrup. Puree the peaches in the blender. To the drained peach syrup, add enough water to make one cup of liquid. Pour into a saucepan and add sugar and nutmeg. Bring mixture to boil and let boil for about one minute.
    Empty the box of gelatin into a bowl and stir in the hot liquid mixture until the gelatin is dissolved. Add pureed peaches and pour into a mold. Chill until set.
Note: If you are limiting your sugar intake, substitute diet gelatin and peaches in light syrup or omit the sugar.

• **PEANUT BUTTER,** *Softening Natural-style Types:* When you buy natural peanut butter, the oil is usually separated and floating. Place the jar on its side for a day or so; it will be easier and less messy to mix in the oil if it's not all on top. (If you remove the oil to save fat or calories, you'll end up with very hard and dry, nearly inedible peanut butter so it's better to leave the oil in and count the calories into your daily total. Peanut oil is one of the "good" oils anyway!) Store this peanut butter in the fridge to keep the oil mixed in. If the peanut butter should become hard, put the portion you'll use in a microwave-safe dish and zap it for a few seconds to make it spreadable again.

• **PEANUT BUTTER/JELLY SANDWICH,** *Preventing Soggy Bread:* Spread the peanut butter on both pieces of bread and put the jelly in the middle so that it can't soak through and mess up a lunch sandwich. Substitute a banana or raisins for the jelly to get a change in flavor.

• **PENCIL ERASER,** *Quick-Fix, When It Smudges:* Rub the eraser with a few strokes of an emery board or fingernail file and it won't smudge your paper anymore.

• **PENCIL HOLDER,** *Recycling:* Magnetic plastic flashlight cases will stick to the inside of a school locker door and hold pencils and pens so there's no more hunting for them in the bottom of the locker. The cases can also hold pencils in truck cabs.

• **PENCILS,** *Healthy-Planet, Recycling Short "Leftovers":* Donate them to your church or any other organization; then it's no loss when they "walk away" after people fill out forms.

• **PEN HOLDER,** *For People with Arthritis or Other Finger Problems:* To get a better grip, poke the pen through a tubed foam hair curler or through a small rubber ball.

• **PERFUME,** *Shelf Life:* It's only about twelve to fourteen months. Heat makes a fragrance evaporate and the more alcohol in the product the shorter its shelf life. Storing perfume and cologne in the fridge will give you a refreshing cool splash in the summer or anytime and helps it last longer, too.

• **PERFUME BOTTLE,** *Removing Scent to Recycle the Bottle:* If baking soda or vinegar don't work, try washing the bottle with soap and water, then fill it with rubbing alcohol. Let stand overnight or longer if needed. Rinse again with clear water.

• **PERSONAL AFFAIRS,** *Checklists for Updating:*
1. For tax filing:
All 1099 forms (dividends and interest income) and W-2 forms; cancelled checks and checkbook registers; receipts for charitable contributions; deductible expenses receipts; property-tax receipts; and records of mortgage interest paid, brokerage confirmations and statements.
If you're self-employed, you need a bookkeeping system that records your expenses and stores your receipts according to the various tax-deduction categories (income, repairs, travel, dues and

publications, meals and entertainment, etc.) as listed on the tax form to save time in tax preparation.

2. Here's a list that should be kept up-to-date for emergencies: Copy of will and trust agreements; doctor and hospital information; family records (births, marriage, divorce, social security, military service, citizenship); insurance-policy information (numbers, agent, beneficiaries); funeral information (preferences, location of cemetery plots, deeds, etc.); safe-deposit box (key and location, person authorized to open it); bank account (number, locations); debts (your own and owed to you); all pension/retirement plans; financial/legal advisors' names and phone numbers; brokerage accounts (with brokers' name and phone number); all business records; and all charge accounts.

3. Keep irreplaceable documents in a safe-deposit box but keep copies for your home records. Remember that a safe-deposit box can be sealed when a person dies so that important information may not be available when it's most needed, such as funeral preferences, wills, etc.

- **PERSONAL FILES,** *How Long to Keep Them:*

1. Most canceled checks over six years old can be tossed. Statements and canceled checks from utility, telephone, and water companies should be saved for at least six months unless you need them for a specific reason or just want to keep them to compare costs from year to year. Save checks for home improvements and other deductible costs.

2. Bank statements should be kept for at least a year. (I pare them down to checks I might need for the Internal Revenue Service (IRS) or other reasons and bunch all statements together and keep them for three years, just in case the IRS calls.)

3. Keep all paperwork on major purchases and any investments.

4. The IRS usually has three years to audit tax returns, but in some circumstances can go back further. Be sure to keep copies of the tax returns as well as all receipts, canceled checks, and other necessary tax records.

- **PET,** *Finding Lost Ones, Checklist:*

1. Contact local veterinarians and animal organizations, especially shelters, and give them flyers describing your pet. It helps to have

photos of the pet and to be able to show its distinguishing scars or marks.

2. Tell your neighbors about the loss and post signs in the neighborhood describing your pet and giving a phone number to call.

3. Put signs on both sides of your car describing your pet and giving your phone number.

• **PET,** *Shipping by Air Checklist:* Airlines have specific requirements and some states have immunizations requirements, so check this out long before you have to ship your pet.

1. Generally, the cage should be large enough for the pet to stand, sit, and turn around and should have a water dish attached to the inside to prevent spills during flight.

2. Be absolutely sure that both the pet and the cage have clear identification.

3. Check with your vet to determine if your pet is fit to travel by air and if prescription tranquilizers are appropriate. A week or so before the flight have the vet give your pet a checkup and make sure all immunization shots are up-to-date. You need to have a record of shots with you and if the animal is being shipped by someone else to you at a later time, a copy of shot records may be needed to attach to the cage so that the animal can enter the new state. Also, your vet knows your pet and can advise you about any precautions to take about pre-travel feeding or including pet toys in the cage.

4. Try to book a non-stop or direct flight so there is less chance of anything going amiss and for the quickest trip with least trauma for your pet.

5. Some dogs are comforted (when being boarded) by familiar owner's scents like an old towel or sock that you slept on the night before the trip; ask your vet if this is a good idea for a travel "security blanket" for your pet.

• **PET FEEDING,** *Recycling, No-mess:* Shallow carton-bottoms from canned goods serve as tray place mats for pet-food dishes. Cat-food can "trays," for example, can be renewed each week as you buy your supply. If you don't want to toss out the "tray" each week, you can cover it with adhesive plastic; it is easily wiped and looks nice.

- **PET FIRST AID:**

1. NEVER give a pet medicines of any kind unless prescribed by a vet. "People" medicines can be poisonous to animals.

2. Keep your vet's or your local animal emergency-facility's number handy at the phone and know the emergency-facility location so you can easily find it even when you may be unnerved by the animal's distress.

3. Heatstroke is the greatest danger in summer. If your pet is staggering, vomiting, panting loudly, and looking bleary-eyed, put it in a shady place, sponge him with cool water or even submerse him and cool him down as quickly as possible, especially his head. Then call the vet for further instructions. NEVER leave a pet in a car; it can become an oven in just a few minutes.

4. Minor cuts and scratches (that don't bleed a lot and don't need stitches) need cleaning with soap and water or hydrogen peroxide, followed by mild antiseptic and a bandage. If the wound swells or shows other signs of infection, call your vet; antibiotics may be needed. **Note:** Some pets won't leave a bandage alone and may need a special collar to prevent their reaching a bandage with their mouths. Consult your vet.

5. Cuts that bleed a lot may need vet care. Press a clean rag or gauze over the wound, hold it firmly to slow the bleeding until you can get to the vet. Tourniquets can cause damage to tissues; don't attempt to use one.

6. If you suspect a broken bone, you may be able to put a splint on a limb. A small animal can be placed on a board or large, firm section of cardboard carton. Or, you can wrap a pet in a blanket or large towel.

Caution: Even the gentlest pet may snap at anyone when it is in pain. You may want to make a muzzle by lightly tying the pet's jaws closed with a soft rag or old panty-hose leg.

- **PET-FOOD DISHES:** If your cat or dog leaves a few morsels of moist food in the dish and you find them "cemented" to the bottom of the bowl at the end of the day, try spraying food dishes with vegetable oil spray. The food washes off easily and the pets get some extra oil for their coats. They may even lick off the food bits if they like the spray taste, like butter-flavored spray!

• **PET HAIR,** *Quick-Fix Removal:* Try a damp sponge, a damp hand, transparent tape wrapped around your hand with sticky side out on clothing, rugs, or furniture.

1. Keep a child's broom and mop handy for gathering tuffts of pet hair between vacuuming.
2. Keep tape or a clothes brush in your car so you can do a last minute de-fuzz before going to a party.
3. Check air conditioner/furnace filters frequently during shedding season; hair blocks them and can also go through to the mechanism causing damage.
4. Comb and brush a shedding pet often to remove loose hair.
5. Love your shedding pet anyway! It doesn't really mean to drive you batty!

• **PET HAIR,** *Removal from Furniture:* Rub "hairy" area with a clean sneaker that has a ribbed bottom.

• **PET HAIR,** *Removing from Bedding:* If you have trouble getting all the pet hair off in the laundry, try spinning bedding in the dryer on the fluff (no heat) cycle to remove the pet hair before you launder it. Sometimes, you may not even need to launder it after the hair is off!

• **PET HAIR,** *Shedding Problems:* In addition to regular seasonal shedding, some pets have "stress shedding" and it can result from changes in routine, visits to the vet or boarding kennel, new visitors in the house, etc. If the condition persists for a long time after the stressful situation has gone, have the pet examined by a vet to make sure it's just stress, not disease.

• **PET HELPER,** *Letter of Laughter:* A beauty operator and owner of a "weenie dog" attached a magnet to the low-slung dog's collar, so that as the dog walked around the shop hairpins were neatly collected. She said the dog was down on the floor anyway so it could earn its keep and save its owner the chore of bending down and crawling around to pick up hairpins. What a great and hilarious idea! Most of us have dogs that just go around gathering dust in the house and twigs in their hair when they roam the outdoors!

• **PET IDENTIFICATION:** If your pet has no identifying marks (all black or all white cats, for example), dab on some colored paint or nail polish or snip out a patch of fur on its back or leg so that your pet won't get mixed up with a "twin" when left at the vet or boarding kennel. Collars can slip off and mix-ups can occur even when people are careful. Be sure to point out to the vet or kennel person that you have marked your pet. Some cities have facilities to tattoo an owner's social security number on a pet. Inquire at your vet.

• **PET PEN,** *Puppy Housebreaking with Indoor Pen:* If you have an old playpen or can get one at a garage sale, put an old plastic shower curtain or drop cloth on the floor of the pen; cover it with lots of newspaper. You can put paper on one side and a small blanket on the other. When you start taking the puppy outside, take some soiled paper and put it in the area you'd like your puppy to use and he'll get the hint from the scent. It takes a while but time and patience is rewarded.

• **PET PILLOW/BEAN-BAG CHAIR,** *Stuffing Recycling:* As the plastic pellet stuffing gets mashed and you receive mail with plastic foam "peanut" fillers, just add the "peanuts" to the pet pillow or bean-bag chair.

• **PET PING-PONG,** *Letter of Laughter:* One cat owner wrote that his twelve-year-old Ping-Pong–playing cat always jumps into the game to swat the ball when anyone plays. Everytime they have company, he's the hit of the party!

• **PETS,** *Checklist for Boarding:*
1. If you plan to board the pet, costs usually relate to the pet's size and type of facility. Don't shop by phone and don't use a facility that discourages you from visiting it.
2. When you visit a boarding facility, boarding areas should be clean, well-lit, and free from strong odors. The facility should require current booster immunizations and have policies for emergencies. Observe the people who care for the pets—do they seem friendly and comfortable with animals?
3. Some pets are happier left in their own homes even if they are alone part of the time. If you can't get a friend or relative to pet-sit, a bonded-pet sitting service may be the answer. They will charge by the day or by the visit (three or four per day for a dog; one or two for a cat). Leave the pet-sitter the same information you would

leave a baby-sitter: emergency vet number; information on how to reach you or a local person in case of emergency; written advice on your pet's medications, eating and living habits.

• **PETS,** *Ticks on Dogs or Cats:* It's especially important to protect your animals from ticks in areas of the country where Lyme disease (spread by ticks) is prevalent.
1. For short-haired dogs and cats, try using a lint removal roller, the kind made from sticky masking tape. It will pick up nymphal ticks that are no larger than a tiny speck.
2. If you find a tick on your pet, remove it with tweezers as soon as possible and then flush it down the toilet without touching it.

• **PETS,** *Water:* Drop a few ice cubes in your pet's water dish on hot days to keep it fresh and cool.

• **PETS,** *When They Are Sick and Vomiting:* Vomiting may or may not be a danger signal. When you have two dogs or two cats the dominant one may eat so fast that it may vomit. Especially if the animal exercises a lot after eating. Cats frequently vomit due to hair balls. Get a laxative from the vet to alleviate this problem.

If there are no other signs of illness, home treatment for vomiting includes stopping all food and water until the vomiting stops. However, a small amount of chicken or beef broth given every few hours can help prevent dehydration. Strained meat baby food can be added. Also, a bland diet of boiled rice and well-cooked drained hamburger meat may be good. If the pet does well, it can go back to its regular diet after a few days. **Caution:** If the illness persists, take the pet to the veterinarian. Vomiting can be a symptom of such diseases as kidney failure in dogs and feline distemper in cats. Very young pets that don't respond within a day or two should be taken to the vet.

• **PET SAFETY,** *Puppies, Cats, Ferrets, Gerbils, Hamsters, etc.:* Many kinds of pets like to burrow and so you must always be cautious around folding/recliner chairs, clothes dryers and washers, and any other place they might wander into. Cats and puppies have been killed in recliner chairs when their owners didn't check before operating them. On the lighter side, burrowing animals can surprise you!

I used to have a very curious ferret named Freddie, whom I'd let loose in my office every now and then, and who will never be forgotten by my secretary, Joyce. Freddie ran up her slacks' leg and, for a moment, she didn't know if she should just scream or scream while pulling her slacks off. The happy ending is that Joyce, an animal lover and cat owner, was able to coax Freddie out of her slacks in a few minutes without any harm to either one of them.

• **PET VACCINATION TAGS,** *Dealing with S-clips:* S-clips on vaccination tags are hard to pry open when you want to replace old tags with new ones. Instead, bend the S-clips and slip them onto round metal key rings, then put the key rings on the collar and next year's change will be easier. Use the smallest possible key ring to prevent it from getting caught on fences if your dog is a jumper or if it's on a cat. **Note:** Be careful not to lose the tags if you remove the collar to bathe or flea-spray the pet.

• **PHONE,** *Hearing It Ring While Outdoors:* If you have one, place a child's amplifier near the phone when you go outdoors for an "intercom-outercom."

• **PHONE,** *Ringing, Letter of Laughter:* Have you noticed that the phone is always ringing as you are fumbling with the door keys and that it stops just as you fall over the cat and pick up the receiver!

• **PHONE BOOK,** *Healthy-Planet Recycling:*
1. Recycle old phone books by using pages to hold potato peels and other vegetable scraps for discarding or tossing into your garden compost pile. (Paper is compost, too.)
2. Also, layer seven or eight pages in the bottom of the bird cage so that you can just remove them one at a time as they get soiled.
3. Stack two or three old phone books and join them with duct tape or a fabric cover to make a child's booster seat. If you need to use the books again, join them with lots of rubber bands.
4. Keep the current phone book(s) under your desk for a footrest.
5. Use pages for packing material.
6. Give to relatives and friends who live near but not in your city so that they can refer to businesses they need.
7. Keep one in the car trunk to check addresses or phone numbers.

• **PHONE BOOK,** *Storing Out-of-the-way:* If you have a closet near the phone, slip a couple of wire coat hangers into the middle of the book(s) and hang in the closet.

• **PHONE CORD,** *Quick Fix No-mess Cleaning:* Put a coiled telephone cord on a long wooden spoon handle, pushing the coils close together; wash them with household cleaner on a cloth or sponge and rinse with a clean sponge.

• **PHONE NUMBERS,** *Emergency and Others for Children Who Can't Yet Read:* On a piece of posterboard placed near the phone, put a picture of people to be called with the phone number and address next to it. Pictures of police or firefighters can be placed by the 911 or other community emergency number. To practice dialing, unplug the phone. **Caution:** Teach children the importance of not playing with the phone and that emergency calls are serious business.

• **PHONE NUMBERS:** Write the out-of-town numbers you call on the phone book page where you would normally find them if they were local numbers; they'll be easy to find.

• **PHONE NUMBERS:** Either highlight or make a red check mark by the phone numbers you have used so that it's easier to find them the next time you look.

• **PHOTOS,** *Proper Care:*
1. Don't write on the face; to identify them, write either on the page of the album or on the back with a soft-lead pencil or felt-tip pen—lightly. Ballpoint pens can leave indentations.
2. Handle photos and negatives by the edges to avoid fingerprints.
3. Store negatives in a dark, dry place separately from the pictures in case of accidents. Special storage envelopes that help keep out humidity are available.
4. I always mark the envelopes (Christmas '90, Summer '89, etc.) so that I can easily find the ones I need.
5. Photos are best mounted in a photo album with acid-free archival paper, held in place with triangle photo corners, not tape, glue, or rubber cement. Magnetic or self-adhesive page albums are not considered good storage for photos.

• **PHOTOS,** *Copying:* I get lots of questions about restoring old photographs. To get copies of one-of-a-kind photos, especially very old ones that you're afraid to let anyone work on, take them to a professional photo shop that makes copies with a color-laser copier. The results are great!

• **PHOTOS,** *Mailing:* To safeguard against loss in case the envelope opens or tears, stick mailing-address labels on the backs of precious family photos before mailing them.

• **PHOTOS, NEGATIVES, STORAGE:** To organize negatives, starting with each roll of film you have developed, write a number (for example, 1) on the back of each of the photographs. Put all the negatives from the film role in an envelope and number it "1" as well. The next roll of film developed would be number 2; repeat the same steps. Be sure to add the date of the photos and names of the people in them.

• **PIANO KEYS,** *Yellowed Ivory:* Clean ivory with a mixture of mild soap and water, wiping the keys with a slightly damp cloth—take care not to soak them, just wipe. Rinse well with a damp, clean cloth and dry thoroughly. Never use wax or abrasive cleaners on ivory. **Hint:** Ivory yellows naturally over time but some say leaving the lid open so that the keys get daylight will slow down the process. It is possible to replace the keyboard with new plastic keys without affecting the quality of the sound but if your piano is an antique, plastic keys will devalue it for some collectors. It may be a better idea to sell an antique piano with yellow keys to someone who loves it "as is" and use the money to get a new one with white keys if that's important to you.

• **PICKLES,** *Leftover:* When life gives you too many leftover jars of pickles, make pickle relish. Take the one or two pickles left in each jar and put them through a food processor, and you'll have relish for hot dogs and hamburgers. Add some of the flavored vinegar to salad dressing for a zingy new taste.

• **PICNIC COOLER,** *Child's Camp Trunk:* Pack a child's clothing in a large picnic cooler. The shelf holds small articles, the handles make carrying it easy, and it's waterproof storage at camp as well as a cabin "bench."

• **PICNIC TRAYS,** *Healthy-Planet Recycling:* Cut cardboard box bottoms about 2 inches deep. A cardboard tray holds your drink and plate, keeps plates from sliding, and keeps bread, chips, and other food from falling to the ground, especially for children.

• **PICTURES,** *Displaying Family Photos:* Make a memory wall of family happenings and milestones (first day of school, weddings, etc.). When there are several children, make composite "collages" for each one in a larger frame instead of a frame for each.

• **PIECES,** *Picking Up Small Ones:* Wrap small pieces of double-stick transparent tape around one or two fingers and dab away at bobby pins, paper clips, jigsaw puzzle pieces, stuck pages of a book, and more. This is an especially good hint if your fingers are a bit fumbly due to a physical handicap of some sort.

• **PIE COVER,** *Recycling, Quick-Fix:* Don't throw away the plastic cover from store-bought pie crusts; instead save it to cover the pie!

• **PIE-CRUST EDGE,** *When It's Browning Too Fast:* Cover the edge of the crust with an aluminum foil strip while it bakes. Or make a reusable crust cover by cutting out the center of a foil pie pan to within an inch or so of the edge, leaving the rim of the pan; this is a time- and aluminum-foil saver and a recycling idea especially if you bake a lot of pies.

• **PILL,** *Easy Swallowing:* While most pills and capsules have slick coatings that help you swallow them, some are uncoated. If you have trouble swallowing such a pill, roll it in a bit of butter or margarine; just enough to help it slip down when you swallow. **Caution:** Check with your doctor or pharmacist to make sure the butter/margarine won't interfere with your body's absorption of that medicine. Also, do not cut pills or capsules to make them smaller unless your pharmacist or doctor approves; some are made for "time-release" and you could be changing the way they work.

• **PILL BOX:** Small plastic containers that breath mints come in can hold aspirin (or other pills) for a purse or briefcase. **Caution:** Always label containers when you switch contents and keep these away from children who might mistake the pills for candy.

• **PILLOWS,** *Freshen, Fluff:* Place bed pillows in the dryer with a fabric-softener sheet and tumble on the air cycle for 20 minutes to fluff them up and give them a fresh, clean smell.

- **PILLOW SHAM,** *Stuffing Decorative Ones:* Use the shams to store extra bed pillows or rolled-up blankets/quilts. Or stuff them with saved-up foam dryer softener sheets, leftover foam rug backing, pillow stuffing, shredded old panty hose, and other soft materials, then stitch them shut.

- **PINECONES,** *Burning in Fireplaces:* You can burn pinecones in the fireplace; but **Caution,** they pop and send out sprays of sparks, so keep the fireplace screen in place and never leave the fire unattended while pinecones are burning in it.

- **PINS,** *Storage:* Place a magnetic strip in the bottom of your pin box and even if you drop it, you won't be stepping on pins and needles.

- **PIZZA CUTTER,** *Other Than Pizza Uses:* Cuts brownies or pan cookies, slices dough for noodles, cookies, pastry.

- **PIZZA DOUGH,** *Prevent Sticking to Pan:* After spraying the pan with non-stick spray, sprinkle a tablespoon of cornmeal on the pan before placing dough on it.

- **PLACE MATS,** *Removing Spaghetti Stains from Vinyl:* Soak place mats in an enzyme stain-remover bleach mixed with a little detergent and warm water. Follow the box directions for amounts. After soaking, scrub the spots with a brush and rinse thoroughly. If stains still remain, put the place mats outside on a hot, sunny day and let the sun bleach them out.

- **PLACE MATS,** *Renewing Limp Straw Ones:* Wet placemats, lay them on a flat surface. Push down and flatten all edges, then liberally spray them with spray starch. When they dry, they should look good as new.

- **PLANT POTS,** *Reusing:* Always clean before reuse to avoid spread of plant diseases. Wash pots in hot water with a squirt or two of regular dishwashing detergent, let them soak for several hours in a solution of one part chlorine bleach to eight parts water. Rinse well and dry, then reuse.

- **PLANTS,** *Maintenance:* Sometimes, people who don't have a green thumb find it easier to maintain big plants than small ones because they don't need as frequent watering or repotting.

• **PLANTS,** *Propping, Healthy-Planet Recycling:* Prop drooping plants with balloon sticks, plastic forks, the name-card holders from florist's arrangements, or "trellises" made by bending wire coat hangers into a round loop and burying the hook-end.

• **PLANTS, WATERING:** Wick Method for Vacation Watering: Plants will draw their own water from buckets with this method.
1. Place a couple of bath towels in the bottom of the bathtub. Place the plant pots and one large or several small buckets of water on the towels. Be sure the water buckets sit higher than the plant pots.
2. Snip cotton string lengths to reach from the inside bottom of the water bucket to the top of the plant pot soil. Gently push one string end into the soil to hold it in place and put the other end at the bottom of the water bucket. Fill the buckets with water. And that's all that's to it.

• **PLANT TERRARIUM,** *When You Go Away:* Water the plants well, then cover the entire pot with a plastic bag, tucking it around the bottom. It should stay moist for at least a week. Very delicate plants may need TLC from a neighbor or friend while you are gone, but most plants will last a week or two without their owners.

• **PLASTIC,** *Remove Melted Plastic from Pots and Pans:* Try heating the pan in a warm oven, then scraping the plastic off before washing in hot soapy water. Is there anyone with an old-style toaster who hasn't melted a plastic bread bag onto the toaster? Love the new, cool-sided appliances!

• **PLASTIC BAG STORAGE:**
1. Hold empty plastic bags together with a terry-cloth elastic wristband, the kind tennis players wear.
2. Bend the ends of a hanger all the way up and hang it on a hook, then slip the handles of plastic bags on the hanger ends for neat and orderly storage.
3. Separate different types of plastic bags to save time digging through a pile—put grocery bags in a grocery bag; newspaper bags in a newspaper bag, and so on.

• **PLASTIC CAPS,** *Recycling Those from Fabric Softener or Liquid Detergent:*

1. Keep at kitchen sink to hold soap scraps and a small sponge ready to scrub anything.
2. On the dresser, one lid holds five tubes of lipstick, also makeup brushes, and other small items.
3. At the workbench they help sort screws and nuts; are handy for mixing small amounts of paint for crafts.

• **PLASTIC "FLATS" FROM NURSERY PLANTS**, *Recycling:* Wash, rinse, dry, and they are "IN/OUT" baskets for your home office.

• **PLASTIC FOOD CONTAINERS**, *Cleaning Them When Greasy:* Leftovers can make plastic ware greasy, sticky and just plain yucky. Spray them with laundry pre-wash spray, let stand awhile, scrub with a brush and full-strength dishwashing liquid. Rinse thoroughly and enjoy using again.

• **PLASTIC-LID COASTERS**, *Recycling:* Any size lid that fits under a glass makes a good coaster and my readers have decorated them in many creative ways.
1. Punch holes around the perimeter with a paper hole-punch and then crochet a "frame" linking the "frame" to the holes; or instead of crochet, just make a yarn overcast stitch border in colors that match the room.
2. Cut out colorful pictures and cover the paper with clear adhesive-backed plastic, then push the picture into the lid.
3. Cut plastic needlepoint mesh or buy mesh rounds, then needlepoint designs or solid colors and push the rounds into plastic lids for really absorbent coasters.
4. Cut rounds of leftover fabric, carpet, felt, and push them into the lids.

• **PLASTIC MESH BAGS**, *Recycling:* Tie in a ball and use to scrub pots, pans, car windshields, bathtubs, etc. Or, use them to dry and store plant bulbs, pool and tub toys, picnic supplies such as plastic ware.

• **PLASTIC PICNIC WARE**, *Recycling:* Instead of throwing away plastic "silverware," put it in a mesh bag and secure it to the top rack of the dishwasher. It will come out clean and ready to use again.

- **PLASTIC SIX-PACK RINGS,** *Healthy-Planet Recycling:*
Caution: These rings can become nooses around the necks of large and small birds, squirrels, turtles, and other small animals who then strangle as they try to escape. Cut the circles and loops apart before discarding even if they are going into a trash bag. Many birds and small animals feed at landfills! Instead, recycle.
1. Fold in half to make three "holes," then hook one over a sturdy hanger in your closet. Then hang four or more clothes hangers in each hole to make more closet space.
2. If you crochet, cut them into separate rings, then crochet around them with cotton yarn to make coasters from individual rings or hot mats by combining several rings.
3. Dip in bubble solution to make giant soap bubbles.
4. Cut into individual circles and make hangers for tools such as hammers.
5. Join a couple of them with twist-ties or heavy yarn to make a beach bag.

- **PLASTIC STRAWBERRY BASKETS,** *Healthy-Planet Recycling:*
1. Playpen for small dolls.
2. Candy baskets for holidays. Weave ribbon through the holes, and attach other decorations with appropriate glue.
3. Hold soap and scouring pads in the kitchen.
4. Store perfume, nail-polish bottles, sample cosmetics, small medicine containers.
5. Place over damp area in carpet so it can dry without being stepped on.
6. Hold packets of sauce mix, spices, etc. in cupboard. (Double them to make them stronger.)

- **PLASTIC STRAWS,** *Recycling:* Put several together and secure them to a dinner knife with a rubber band, then wash in the dishwasher. They'll come out clean and can be reused many times. Soaking straws used for milk in cold water helps get them clean.

- **PLASTIC WARE,** *Keeping It Stain-free:* Spaghetti sauce or chili stains plastic containers. To prevent this, line them with plastic wrap before pouring in the food after it has cooled.

- **PLASTIC WRAP,** *Keep It from Tangling:* Store in freezer or fridge.

• **PLASTIC WRAP,** *Prying Film from a Roll:* Wrap stuck to the roll? Apply a piece of transparent tape vertically at the edge of the wrap; lift. You'll pull the wrap free.

• **PLAYPEN MESH,** *Remove Mildew:* Place playpen outside and protect the bottom (if it's cardboard,) with a plastic shower curtain or other waterproof cover. Mix half water and half chlorine bleach in a spray bottle and spray it on the mesh from both sides. To rinse, spray with clear water from a spray bottle. To remove lingering bleach smell, mix 2 capfuls of fabric softener and 2 cups of water in a spray bottle and spray on mesh. Rinse very well and let sit in sunshine for a day or two.

• **POCKETS,** *Making Them Secure:* Sew strips or dots of self-gripping fabric tape on the inside edges of pants or jacket pockets so that wallets or checkbooks won't fall out.

• **POISON IVY:** A tall climbing vine clinging to trees and fences, it's leaves are composed of three leaflets which vary in shape. Leaves are red in the spring but turn to shiny green later.
1. To Get Rid of It—WEARING RUBBER GLOVES, pull up small vines; seal in plastic bags and discard. Wash gloves in soap and water afterward. Kill larger vines with herbicide on foliage and by cutting plants at ground level. **Caution:** Protect "good guys" foliage with a sheet of plastic when you spray. **Hint:** Don't cover good foliage in the hottest part of the day; heat buildup under plastic sheets could burn the good plants.
2. First Aid—You have about 10 minutes after exposure to avoid a skin reaction. Wash affected area thoroughly under running water. Some sources say wash WITHOUT SOAP; that soap removes the natural protective oils of your skin and can increase the penetration of the irritant. Other sources say with soap. They do agree on washing thoroughly and quickly.

• **POOL COVER,** *Healthy-Planet Recycling:* If you cover your pool for the winter, hold the cover in place with large plastic jugs filled with water. **Caution:** Children and pets may mistake a pool cover for a walking surface and can drown if they slip under the cover and get trapped. If you have children and pets, it may be safer not to cover the pool.

- **POOL COVER:** Keep leaves from falling into a small plastic child's pool by covering it with a large piece of nylon net when it's not being used. Either secure the net to the pool's side with clothes pins or weigh down the edges of the cover with gallon jugs filled with sand or water.

- **POPCORN,** *Extra Flavoring:* Try sprinkling with seasoned salts; salt-free herb blends; dry salad-dressing mixes; taco or chili seasoning mixes; grated hard cheeses like Parmesan or Romano or the powdered cheese from macaroni-and-cheese dinners.

- **POPCORN,** *Popping in the Microwave:* Regular paper bags can catch fire at the temperature needed to pop corn and regular bowls and casseroles aren't shaped properly to concentrate the heat needed for kernels to pop. Microwave corn poppers are cone-shaped to concentrate the heat and will give you best results. You can also buy corn in microwave-safe bags if the directions for your microwave say it's okay, however these "kits" usually have added salt and fat.

- **POPCORN BALLS,** *No-mess Serving at Children's Parties:* Form the popcorn balls around lollipops. No more sticky-fingered party guests! Be sure to tell the children there's a surprise in the center so that they don't bite too enthusiastically on the hard core and chip a tooth!

- **POPCORN CUPS:** For edible party munchy holders, shape popcorn-ball mix over the bottoms and side of glasses well-greased with margarine. After mixture hardens, remove "cups" and fill with nuts or other treats. Please see CAKE, POPCORN.

- **POPCORN TOOTH-SAVER,** *Removing Unpopped Kernels:* Popcorn is a good low-cal snack. When you make a batch at night, save some for workday or school lunches. Put the cooled popcorn in a large resealable plastic bag and cut a small hole in the corner of the bag. Give the bag a good shake and all the unpopped kernels will fall out of the hole. Then, when you or a child grabs a handful of popcorn, you're not likely to break a tooth on an unpopped kernel.

- **POSTCARDS,** *For the Letter-phobic:* If you never get around to writing letters, remember that it's the thought that counts and friends would enjoy knowing you think of them even if you don't have time to write the "minutes" of your life since your last meeting with them. Keep postcards on hand so you can send off quick notes, comments to politicians, and even "hints" to Heloise. P.S. You can also FAX hints to me: 1-512-HELOISE.

• **POSTCARDS,** *Making Your Own:* Cut them to size from poster-board or shirt cardboards. You can place colorful stickers on the shiny side of the paper and write on the dull side just as if it's a regular postcard. Draw a line down the middle with address on the right and message on the left. Just remember that a postcard should not exceed 4¼″ by 6″ to be sent by the lower postcard postage rate.

• **POSTCARDS, GREETING CARDS,** *Recycling Pretty Pictures and Pleasant Memories:* Old greeting cards, postcards and even photos can be page markers in recipe books. Each time you open the book you'll get pleasant thoughts!

• **POSTAGE STAMP ROLL,** *Unsticking:* If dampness sticks the whole role of postage stamps together, try placing the stamps in the freezer for about an hour. When you remove them, they should separate. If not, you can return the stamps to the post office for replacement.

• **POSTAGE STAMPS,** *Easy Licking If You Hate the Taste of the Glue:*
1. Lick the envelope's corner instead of the stamp.
2. Put an ice cube in a small bowl or on a dry washcloth and pass the glue side of the stamps over the ice cube.
3. Put water into a clean roll-on deodorant applicator and roll moisture over the stamps.
4. And, tried and true, run stamps over a wet sponge set in a saucer.
5. Avoid moisture altogether—buy a glue stick and just glue stamps and envelope flaps in place.
6. *Letter of Laughter:* Or, train your dog like the Heloise fan whose Rottweiler sits, eyes above table level, nose handy to moisten stamps. After each stamp, he licks his nose so it's ready for the next—he likes the glue!

• **POSTERS,** *Hanging Without Damaging Walls:* Apply pieces of double-stick tape to the backs of posters, pull away the liners and attach the posters to the walls. If there is any residue left on the wall when the posters are removed, you can wipe it away with your finger.

• **POTATO,** *Baking in Microwave:*
1. Check your microwave manual for suggested time; it varies according to wattage and other factors.
2. Poke several holes in the potato with a fork or ice pick to let moisture out.
3. To cook one, place it in the center of the oven in a double-layer of paper towels. To cook more than one, place them in a circle with the smaller ends of the potatoes toward the center.
4. Halfway through the baking time, turn the potato over to help it cook more evenly.
5. Wait about 5 minutes before testing for doneness; potatoes continue to cook after removal from the oven.
6. Top with your favorite topping. I like low-fat yogurt and some parsley.

Or you could make a spread with ½ cup butter or margarine, 2 teaspoons salt, ¼ teaspoon black pepper, and 2 teaspoons finely chopped fresh chives.

Or, when you tire of sour cream, chives, bacon bits, or yogurt, try spaghetti sauce, a sprinkle of oregano, grated mozzarella cheese or Parmesan for a potato-meal.

• **POTATO,** *Baking in Microwave, Techniques:* To avoid rubbery, hockey puck potatoes when baking in the microwave try the following:
1. Place potatoes on a large microwave-safe dinner plate (the plate you'll eat from if it's dinner for one) and slice each twice to allow moisture to escape. Put a little water on the plate, cover with microwave-safe bowl; microwave on "High" for about 4 to 7 minutes per potato (depends on size and your oven wattage) or as directed by your oven's directions.
2. Wrap potatoes in cereal-box liner; bake in microwave about 4 minutes or as directed by your oven's directions.

• **POTATO BUYING AND COOKING,** *Which to Buy for What Purpose:* Pick potatoes that aren't soft, bruised, cracked, wrinkled, sprouting "eyes," or greenish-looking. Potatoes retain more vitamins if cooked whole with skins on. They are high in vitamin C and potassium, low in sodium, and a good source of fiber and complex carbohydrates. A medium-sized potato has only about 100 calories. It's the stuff you pile on top that breaks the diet.

1. Russet Burbank potatoes are large, oblong, with dark, rough skin. They cook up fluffy and make great mashed potatoes and french fries. Idaho Russets are baking favorites.

2. California and White Rose are all-purpose long, oblong potatoes, with thin, smooth skin. They're best for roasting, boiling, steaming, and pan frying.

3. Round reds or whites are sold immediately after harvesting and without being stored. They are called "new potatoes."

• **POTATO-CHIP CAN,** *Recycling:*

1. Make a Cover-up: Cover with adhesive paper or paint to match your bathroom or bedroom decor and then slip them over hair spray, room deodorizer, and other un-aesthetics on the vanity.

2. Mail cookies or other fragile things in them.

3. Store fireplace matches, craft pieces, knitting/crochet needles, spaghetti, etc. in them.

• **POTATO PEELER,** *Other Uses:* Pit cherries and still leave them whole; hull strawberries; grate cheese.

• **POTATO SCRUBBER:** Instead of wasting the vitamins in potato skins by peeling them, scrub with a plastic pot scrubber.

• **POTATO STORAGE:** Keep in a dark, dry place that's relatively cool, about 40 to 50 degrees. Don't put them in the fridge; the cold makes the starch change to sugar and changes the taste and texture. Also, don't store potatoes with onions; moisture from potatoes can cause onions to sprout.

• **POTATOES,** *Leftover Mashed:* Add grated cheese to leftover mashed potatoes and then fry them in margarine for breakfast or other meals.

• **POTATOES,** *Quick-Fix When You Over-cooked:* Wash three or four potatoes, poke with holes and pop into the microwave. Then, peel them; add to the "mushed potatoes," and whip up briefly to make "mashed potatoes." The alternative is to turn the mush into potato soup (add a bit of canned skim milk or dry powder skim milk—only the powder, not mixed with water, and your favorite flavorings like a dash of Worcestershire). Sprinkle a few croutons on top and pretend it's what you planned to serve in the first place!

• **POT HOLDERS,** *Healthy-Planet Recycling:* Cut circles or squares from old towels and blue jean legs (leftover when you turn jeans into shorts) and sew them together for sturdy, heat-protecting pot holders.

• **POT PLANTS,** *Preventing Wind from Blowing Them Off a Balcony Rail:* This works best for clay pots with a large single drain hole. Hammer a large (three-inch) nail into the railing where each pot belongs. Then place each pot over a nail so that it fits through the drain hole. This idea might also work on a wood deck to prevent pots from being nudged over by passing pets.

• **POTS/PANS,** *Cleaning Aluminum:* Put about 3 tablespoons of cream of tartar and about 1 quart of water in the gunky pot. Bring the mixture to a boil and let it continue to boil for about 10 minutes. Wash and rinse the pot well.

• **POTS & PANS,** *Cleaning Burned Gunk Off Stainless Steel:* **Caution:** This method is only for stainless-steel pots and pans, NOT for aluminum pots or pans.
1. Place the pot in the oven to slightly warm it.
2. Spread a plastic trash bag over some newspaper on the counter and place the pot in it.
3. Generously spray the pot or pan with oven cleaner and allow to set for 5 to 10 minutes.
4. Rinse off oven cleaner; wash in hot, soapy water; rinse well.
5. Very stubborn gunk may take more than one application.

• **POUND-CAKE TOPPING,** *Quick-Fix:* Heat about ¼ cup of preserves and 1 tablespoon of flavored liqueur in a small saucepan and dribble it over a slice of pound cake for a yummy dessert.

• **PRESCRIPTIONS,** *Recycling Containers:* If your pharmacist allows, take your prescription bottles for refills instead of getting a new bottle each time. Less plastic in landfills!

• **PRE-WASH SPRAY,** *Homemade:* **Caution:** When you apply this solution, wash the clothing immediately. Allowing it to set for any period of time may create a difficult stain to remove. Mix equal parts of water, ammonia, and dishwashing (not dishwasher) liquid (read the label to be sure it doesn't contain bleach). Put it into a clean spray bottle and label it as pre-wash spray. Please see SPOTS & STAINS on page 398.

- **PRICE STICKERS, LABEL RESIDUE:**
Method 1, Household Items: Apply pre-wash spray or liquid, scrub with nylon scrubber.
Method 2, Household Items: Saturate with vegetable, baby, or mineral oil before removing with nylon scrubber.
Please see STICKY RESIDUE.

- **PRINT WHITE ON DARK PAPER:** For special effects on notes, letters, or invitations, print with typewriter correction tape (the kind that prints, not the one that lifts print off) on dark paper.

- **PROOF-OF-PURCHASE LABELS,** *Removing for Mail-ins:*
1. Soak the container in water until the edge of the label starts to peel. Remove it from the water and blot with a paper towel.
2. Put a strip of transparent tape over the label, covering it completely and rub over it. Cut around the taped area with a single-edge razor; gently raise the lengthwise edge of the tape and pull it off.

A very thin layer will come off in one piece. To recycle the container, remove residue with a plastic scrubber and either a paste of baking soda and water or pre-wash spray.

- **PUMP-SPRAY BOTTLES,** *Recycling:* Wash thoroughly, allow to dry and ALWAYS label with contents.
1. Put pre-electric shave liquid in it. This is especially helpful for someone whose hands or fingers are disabled so that pouring liquids is difficult.
2. Store homemade cleaning solutions, such as vinegar and water, ammonia and water.
3. If the pump spray is from an edible or is a new bottle and so is safe for food, you can put oil in it to spray on pots and pans and also on your breaded chops before turning them over (they don't stick as easily). Or spray oil on a salad for diet portions. You can also spray flavored vinegars on salads to avoid dribbling too much.
4. Take a spray bottle of plain water with you to the zoo or other hot place and spritz yourself and companions when needed. If

you're on a picnic and have a cooler, keep the spritzing bottle in the cooler and really get refreshed!

• **PUNCH,** *Ice:* When you're using punch or store-bought eggnog, pour half into ice-cube trays and freeze so that you can cool the rest of it at serving time without watering it down.

• **PUPPY,** *Checklist for Selecting One:*
1. Shyness usually occurs when pups live with their litter for more than twelve weeks, or when a timid pup gets trampled into a subordinate position. Shy dogs hold back while the others bark and run around, and may be afraid of noise or people. Such a dog may become frightened and attack a person. Also, some owners cause shyness in an otherwise lovable pup by excessively authoritative training or abuse.
2. Look for a curious and somewhat assertive puppy who is not afraid of strangers. Pups need to be handled properly at an early age by humans so that they won't be frightened.
3. If you have a shy adult dog, try giving it loving gentle care; talk to it in a soothing way. In time it may grow out of its fear and be as good a pet as any other.

• **PUPPY,** *Protecting Carpets:* Until a puppy is well housebroken, keep it in an old baby playpen with newspapers layered over an old shower curtain or other waterproof mat. Then puppy can stay in the room with you without causing "accidents" on the carpet.
   Letter of Laughter: One reader tried this hint and wrote that it was not for Springer Spaniels. As soon as he learned to "spring" he would spring up and down like a yo-yo, landing with a reverberating crash on the playpen floor. It was hilarious to watch but definitely wearing on the nerves after a while!

• **PURSES,** *Changing Without Forgetting Essentials:*
1. Keep a drawer or box just for your purse items and dump them in when you come home. Then you won't have to search through several purses looking for scattered bits and pieces when you're in the A.M. rush.
2. Keep all of your bits and pieces (cosmetics, pen, pins, sewing kit, medications, etc.) in a plastic zipper pencil case (the kind you can put into ring binders) or just a plastic zipper bag. They'll be in one place when you switch purses.

- **QUICHE,** *Variations:*
1. Add grated cheese, chopped almonds, or ground pecans to the crust recipe.
2. If you aren't eating bacon, substitute imitation bacon bits for flavor.

- **QUILT,** *Recycling:* Worn parts of quilts can be cut off and the remaining good parts can be finished with a new border to make lap robes, child-size bedcovers, hot-dish holders, or, if the design is suitable, even a vest or skirt.

- **QUILT,** *Repair:* Repair old quilts with fabric from old clothing so that the patch won't be so obvious, as it can be if you make the repair with fabric that's not faded like the rest of the quilt.

- **QUILT MAKING,** *Recycling:* Traditionally quilts have been made from scraps of fabric left over from sewing projects and from the unworn parts of old clothing in addition to making them from new fabric. You can back a quilt with a sheet that matches the decor of your home and pad the inside with a blanket that is too washed-out to look nice on the bed.

- **QUILTS,** *American Art on the Wall:* To make a colorful wall hanging, attach wooden rings to a quilt or attach matching cloth "tabs" and hang it from a wide wooden rod. Or just drape the quilt over a bracketed wall-hung rod.

- **QUILT SHOWER:** Revive the "quilting bee" (the tradition of relatives of the bride getting together to make quilts for her "hope chest"). If the bride and groom's friends and relatives sew, ask each to make a square (perhaps with a special appliqué or embroidered design that recalls special times of their lives) and join the squares for a keepsake wedding present.

- **QUINCE,** *Uses:* When cooked, it's a dessert. It can also be a fruit jelly. But in Victorian times, before chemical air fresheners were invented, quince—like lavender—used to be placed in clothes closets and dresser drawers to prevent musty odors.

- **RABBITS,** *As Pets:* Rabbits are cute, trainable pets, but should never be given to very young children as an "Easter Surprise" to be discarded when children tire of them or when injured. Remember, they are domestic animals, unable to fend for themselves; they won't live if they are just dropped off in the wild. If you buy a rabbit from a reliable pet shop, get books on its care.
1. Rabbits can be trained to use a litter box and so are good, quiet apartment pets.
2. They need a cage large enough to be comfortable and they need to be played with to get enough exercise. They are affectionate; stroke them on the head and back like you do a cat.
3. NEVER pick a rabbit up by the ears or scruff of the neck; don't pull its tail. When carrying a rabbit, support its back by holding it by the hind legs; rabbits have been known to injure their spinal cords or even break legs when kicking and squirming.
4. As with all animals, do not allow small children to handle them without supervision and consult a veterinarian if you think the animal has been injured or is ill.

- **RAIN GAUGE,** *Marking for Easy Reading:* Mark with red nail polish or red tape the one-, two-, three-inch levels on your garden rain gauge so that you can see them more easily and possibly check how much you have watered from a hose or how much nature has watered from the sky by looking out of your window. Put a drop of red food coloring into the gauge whenever it's emptied to help see the levels from your window without going outside. *Note of Laughter:* In one family I know, the children were assigned chores to help their mother when their father went out of town. When the children heard that Dad was coming home that night, the youngest one looked out of the window at the garden and said, "Oh boy, somebody is going to be in big trouble. Somebody forgot to fill Dad's rain gauge."

• **RAINY-DAY GAME FOR CHILDREN,** *Go Fishing:*
1. Cut various shapes from cardboard and write different numbers on each one. Then put a metal paper clip on the edge of each shape and put all into an empty bucket.
2. Attach a large magnet to a broom handle or fish pole and let children "fish" for shapes. Different numbers represent point values for "catching" each shape.

• **RAISINS,** *Preventing Them from Sinking in Baked Goods:*
1. Mix the raisins with the dry ingredients before both are added to the wet ingredients mixture. The flour will help suspend them.
2. Or, cut each raisin in half with a pair of kitchen shears so that they are lighter in weight and won't sink. The bonus here is that the flavor is spread better throughout the batter.

• **REBATES,** *Recycling:* Recycle manufacturer's coupon rebates to help others and feel good yourself. Save all your rebate money and donate it to charity at the end of the year.

• **RECIPE CARDS,** *Holding Them at Eye Level While You Cook:* Tape or tack photo pages with clear plastic pockets to the inside of your kitchen cabinet doors. When you plan a guest menu, insert the cards into the pockets and they'll be easy to see.

• **RECIPE FOR FAMILY LIFE:** I've had to reprint this popular recipe which was sent to me by Francesca Ugolini, a young girl from Corpus Christi.
LOVING FAMILY LIFE RECIPE
   2 or more people
   2½ cups of love

¼ cup of peace
9 tablespoons of faith
6 tablespoons of trust
1¼ cup of caring
7 tablespoons of forgiveness
5 teaspoons of sharing

Mix all ingredients together gently. The result is a happy family full of love, peace, faith, trust, caring, forgiveness, and sharing. **Note:** My editor says there's a part of the directions missing. It's "Don't ever put any of these ingredients in hot water!"

• **RECIPE INGREDIENTS:** To make sure roommates or family don't eat specially bought ingredients before you get a chance to prepare the recipe, have a code such as marking the package with a red X or writing a note on it. Then everyone knows which foods are off limits.

• **RECIPES,** *Family Favorites:* Either clearly write favorite family recipes in notebooks (or type them and make duplicates to be pasted in notebooks) and then give the collection of old favorites to children and grandchildren. P.S. If giving them to grandchildren, you could leave enough space so that both parents' childhood favorites could be placed in the notebook.

• **RECIPES,** *Finding Favorites in Cookbooks:* Note on an index card the name and page of the cookbook in which you can find favorite recipes then file in the recipe box under the appropriate category. You'll save time paging through a whole cookbook collection to find the recipe you want.

• **RECIPES,** *Interpretation, Letter of Laughter:* Told to "add a small glug of butter flavor and a larger glug of vanilla," by his mom when he was making cookies, a teen paused for a while and said, "Mom, I always goof up on the glugs . . . can I just use a spoon instead?" And then, Mom had to try to figure out just exactly how much a glug was when you used a measuring spoon. I also cook with a pinch of this, a smidgen of that, and dollop of this and a blob of that. Now let's see, is a "glug" a pinch or a smidgen? I'll bet it's less than a dollop or a blob . . .

- **RECIPES,** *Recording Those Given on TV:* It's easy to miss some of the ingredients or instructions for recipes given on TV even when you're not interrupted by a phone call. Keep a tape in the VCR and tape the recipe presentation; you can copy it at your leisure and make notes on "how-to."

- **RECIPES,** *Storage:*
1. Instead of piles of clippings, buy an inexpensive binder and polypropylene "sheet protectors" (from office supply stores) or a binder-style photo album with magnetic pages and tabbed dividers to separate recipe categories (breads, meats, leftover uses, low-cal foods, sugarless desserts, vegetarian dishes, Italian, etc.). They'll even hold the pictures with newspaper/magazine recipes. As you collect more, add more refill pages. And, if you keep the binder near your reading chair, you can file each recipe as you clip it—no more messy piles of clippings! These books make nice gifts, too.
2. Tape recipes with non-yellowing transparent tape to index cards and file the cards in a loaf-size plastic bread container which holds more than ordinary file boxes.

- **RECLINER SAFETY WARNING: Caution:** If you have one of these chairs and a small cat or dog, be cautious when you change positions. I've received many letters from people who have crushed their kittens, puppies, or adult pets in recliners.

- **RECORDS,** *Cleaning:*
1. Removing Mildew from Old 45s, 78s, LPs—Hold the record by the edges, wet it well under cold running tap water. Then squirt a little mild liquid soap on your fingers and rub along the grooves in the record, not across them. Once both sides are thoroughly cleaned, rinse again under cold water. Dry placed on end in a safe location or dry with a cloth sold at record stores made especially for drying records.
2. Compact Discs: It's best to use commercial cleaning kits. You can dust them with a clean, lint-free, soft, dry cloth but instead of the circular motion used with analog records noted above, with CDs, you use straight strokes out from the center of the disc to the edge, like spokes of a wheel.

- **RECORDS,** *Recycling Old Ones:* Make flower pots from old 78 rpm records by melting them into shape over clay pots in the oven. To keep the melted shape symmetrical, make a plug out of aluminum foil and force it though the hole in the record and the hole in the clay pot below.

• **RECORDS,** *"Unwarping":* Sometimes, when old records get warped, you can place them on top of a television set where it's warm and dry, and then weight them down with several books. Leave them there for a few days. You may not be able to salvage all of them but this does work for some records and so it's worth a try.

• **RECYCLABLES & NONRECYCLABLES,** *Lists:* The following items are generally recycled.
1. Paper: Newsprint, corrugated cardboard, computer paper and office stationery.
2. Plastic: One and two-liter soda bottles, milk jugs, vinyl siding, antifreeze containers, motor oil and other auto fluids in hard plastic, hard plastic dish and laundry detergent bottles, ketchup and condiment bottles in hard plastic, shampoo bottles, baby wipes containers, Clorox and other bleach bottles, salad oil bottles, and most hard plastic containers.
3. Glass: Clear, brown or green glass bottles and containers. No need to remove labels.
4. Metals: Aluminum and tin cans, clean aluminum foil, clean aluminum food trays, aluminum siding.
   Non-recyclables at this time include:
1. Paper: Colored newspaper inserts, funny papers, cereal boxes, food boxes, detergent boxes, magazines, phone books, junk mail, wax and wax-coated cellophane.
2. Plastic: Cottage cheese and margarine tubs, plastic bags, foam plastic containers (some are beginning to be recycled but not everywhere in the U.S.).
3. Glass: Windows, plates, light bulbs, casserole dishes.
4. Metals: Bottle caps or metals mixed with paper or plastic such as frozen fruit juice containers.

• **RECYCLABLES,** *Magazines, Office Paper, Computer Sheets, Greeting Cards, Boxes, Jars, Paper Rolls, Sewing Scraps, etc.:* Call local pre-schools, day care centers, nursing homes, handicapped persons' craft centers to find out if they can use such things. I get letters from pre-school and other teachers telling me that with budget cutbacks, school art classes can use many items for their projects.

• **RECYCLING,** *Getting General Information:* The Plastics Industry introduced a coding system in 1988 in which a three-sided triangular arrow with a number from one to seven is stamped on the bottom of most plastic containers shows how to separate plastics for community recycling programs. Look under "solid waste" or "waste management" in the white or blue pages of the phone book for the phone number of your state, city, or county recycling agency then call to find out what kinds of plastics, etc. are recycled in your community.

If you want to do your part to keep beverage bottles and cans out of landfills but your city has no recycling program, call the Environmental Defense Fund's toll-free hotline to get information about recycling programs in your area. The number is 800-CALL-EDF.

• **REFRIGERATOR GASKET,** *Cleaning, Removing Mildew:* Wash with mild soap and hot water. Do not wash with bleach; it can cause the gasket to become brittle and crack. The trick is to keep it clean with frequent washing. Badly mildewed gaskets may have to be replaced.

• **REFRIGERATOR GASKET,** *When to Replace:* A brittle or torn gasket won't provide the seal needed for proper refrigerator temperature. Close a dollar bill in the door; if it slips out easily, you probably need a new refrigerator gasket.

• **REFRIGERATOR NOISE,** *Letter of Laughter:* A reader found that her refrigerator made loud vibrating noises because it was "hungry." She lives alone, therefore the fridge was mostly empty. She stopped the shelves from vibrating by "feeding them" several water-filled plastic jugs!

• **REFRIGERATOR TOP,** *Avoid Cleaning Greasy Residue:* Cover the top of the fridge with plastic wrap; clean by removing wrap and replacing it with clean wrap.

• **REMINDER,** *Answering Machine:* Please see ANSWERING MACHINE.

• **REMOTE CONTROLS,** *When They're So Remote You Can't Ever Find Them:* These days, some people have as many as three remote controls—stereo, VCR, TV. Find a suitably sized board, sand it smooth, and then put all your controls on one holder with strips of self-gripping fabric tape. Attach the fuzzy strips to the board and the hooked ones to the controls—then the controls will be unpleasant to carry around and will more likely be left on the board.

• **RHUBARB:** Eat only the stalk; the leaves are poisonous. Because rhubarb is bitter, it is cooked with sugar—either poached, stewed, or baked.

1. To stew: Cut up one pound of rhubarb into small pieces and place in a heavy pot with a couple of tablespoons of water and one-half to one cup of sugar. Simmer for about 20 minutes.

2. Adding strawberries in the last few minutes of cooking makes rhubarb delicious. Remove from heat; cool, then chill.

3. Serve it plain or with ice cream on it. *Note of Laughter:* Since rhubarb doesn't grow in Texas where I live, I got this recipe from our local County Extension Agent for a reader who found it growing in the yard of her new house and asked me what to do with it. When one of my editors saw the recipe in my column, she said in her family, rhubarb was usually liked by adults and hated by children, who were forced to eat it, and, when the reader asked what to do with the rhubarb, I should have responded, "Pour weed killer on it." I'd guess my editor hated it, wouldn't you?

• **RICE-CAKE TOPPINGS,** *When You Think They Are Too Bland:*

1. Spread on margarine and sprinkle with cinnamon and sugar; spread on peanut butter and jelly.

2. Make 'em Mexican—spread on refried beans, some sour cream, and top with grated cheese and then put it in the oven for a couple of minutes.

• **ROACHES,** *Heloise's Boric Acid Mixture:* No Heloise book is complete without the recipe that brings thousands of requests each year. Ingredients: Eight ounces of powdered boric acid, one-half cup flour, one-eighth cup sugar, one-half of a small onion (chopped), one-fourth cup shortening or bacon drippings and enough water to form a soft dough.

1. Mix boric acid, flour and onion. Next, cream shortening and sugar and add flour mixture to this. Blend well and then add enough water to form a soft dough.

2. Shape into small balls and put around the house in areas prone to roaches. If you place balls in open sandwich bags, they'll keep longer without drying out. When dough balls become hard, replace them with fresh ones.
Caution: Keep out of reach of children and pets; large amounts of boric acid can be toxic.

• **ROAMING ROCKING CHAIRS:** Glue velvet ribbon on the bottoms of the rockers along the entire length. Trim off excess. Allow glue to dry completely before turning the chair right side up. You can rock without roaming.

• **ROAST, GRINDING LEFTOVERS,** *Quick-Fix, Time-Saver;* To get the last bits of meat out of the grinder, grind a slice of bread last to push the meat out. You can wash away the remaining bread.

• **ROASTING RACK,** *Quick-Fix, Healthy Planet, Substitute an Edible Rack for a Metal One:* Place three or four whole stems of washed celery across the bottom of a roasting pan and place a roast or whole chicken on top. At serving time, garnish the meat with the celery.

• **RODENT PREVENTION:** These unwelcome guests are difficult to control. Rats and mice can live unseen for months, foraging through pantries, closets and cupboards for cereals, crackers and pet food. Mice can enter your home through a hole as small as one-half inch in diameter, climb almost any wall or pole and drop 50 feet to the ground and land on their feet. Rats can chew their way into your home, too.
1. Make sure all food is stored in covered containers, especially bulk pet food. Garbage should be kept in sturdy cans with tight-fitting lids.
2. To prevent mice and rats from squeezing their way in, be sure all possible entrances to your home are sealed with steel wool, which they can't chew through.
3. Cardboard boxes and cartons are favorite mouse nesting areas. Remove as many boxes as possible from closets and other storage areas.
4. Even with protective measures, you may still find signs of rodents in your home or hear them "go bump in the night." Rodenti-

cides are effective but some can cause the rodents to die slowly within your walls where they will decompose and smell until the remains mummify. If your problem is greater than just an occasional mouse passing through, you may need to call in a professional exterminator.

• **ROOF,** *Inspecting Yours, Checklist:* Early spring and late fall are the best times to inspect your roof so that all is ready for seasonal changes.
1. If you have a shingle roof, look for loose shingles or shakes for curling, fraying and tears at the edges.
2. With tile or slate roofs, look for missing or cracked pieces.
3. Check the flashings around chimneys, vents, skylights and other roof penetrations. They should be tight and in good condition. Call a professional contractor for a more thorough inspection if you have doubts.
4. Clean gutters and downspouts of leaves, sticks and other debris. **Caution:** Stay off the roof; walking on its surface can do a lot of damage. If you must get up on the roof to inspect, climb only on a firmly braced or tied-off ladder with rubber safety feet.

• **ROOM DEODORIZER,** *Recycling:* If the container can be opened, place potpourri in it for permanent air freshener. You can add a few drops of your favorite perfume to renew scents.

• **ROSES,** *Defensive Cutting:* Hold stems with a spring clothespin to keep prickly thorns from sticking you.

• **ROSES AND ROSEBUSHES:** A reader, whose husband always brought her roses when they were dating, wrote that after they were married and had more responsibilities, they couldn't afford them anymore. But, still romantic, her husband planted a rosebush for her on each major holiday so that now she has a yard with many different shades of roses and a heart with lots of happy holiday memories.

• **RUBBER BANDS,** *Storage:* To keep rubber bands from being tangled in a drawer (if you don't use the time-honored method of looping them over a doorknob) loop them into a ball. The ball grows each day if your newspaper comes with a rubber band. The bonus for grandparents is that this ball can be a toy when the grandchildren come to visit.

• **RUBBER GLOVES,** *Healthy Planet, Recycling Old Ones:* Cut good finger tips off and put them into new gloves to reinforce fingertips; cut cuffs and parts of fingers in strips for rubber bands; cut ends of fingers and use them to protect opened spools of thread; use the palm/back for traction when opening jars.

• **RUBBER GLOVES TREATMENT:** Slather lotion or oil on your hands before putting them into rubber gloves for washing dishes or general cleaning. The gloves will slide on and off more easily and your hands will get a good moisturizing treatment, especially if they'll be in hot water.

• **RUGS,** *Making Them Non-Skid:* Either buy rubber-mesh pads for this purpose and place them under the rug, or tack a piece of old rubber-backed drapes (or other flat rubber sheet) to the backside.

• **RUGS,** *Stop Slipping Ones in the Bathroom:* Put a rubber tub mat under the rug.

• **RUGS AND CARPETS,** *Brightening:* Dull colors may not be faded, just dirty. One home remedy is to vacuum to remove dust, then, taking care not to saturate the backing, sponge the rug with a wet rag which has been dipped in a mixture of 1 quart white vinegar and 3 quarts boiling water. Allow to dry completely, then rub surface with warm bread crumbs and vacuum.

• **RUGS AND CARPETS,** *Buying New Carpets:* You can save on carpet if you get top quality thick padding but when considering the overall cost, remember that installation and padding may or may not be included in the price.

• **RUGS AND CARPETS,** *Checklist Care for Oriental Carpets:*
1. Don't use steam cleaners; they remove the wool's natural oils and prematurely age the rug.
2. Blot; don't rub spills. Get a professional cleaner for dried stains. You can dilute the spill with cool water, continuing to blot until the rug seems clean. Don't ever soak unstained parts and always dry the rug thoroughly using absorbent towels on top and underneath the stain.

3. Never put house plants on rugs; moisture will condense beneath the pot causing mildew damage to the rug.

4. Old-fashioned beating is mean; it breaks the foundation of the carpet.

5. Sweep fringes with a broom instead of vacuuming, which can tear them. Broom-sweeping brings out the wool's sheen as well as removing dirt.

6. Vacuum in the direction of the nap. Find the nap by running your hand over the surface.

7. Padding reduces wear and prevents slipping. You can get special pads to prevent slippage of Oriental rugs placed over carpeting.

8. Turn rugs annually to prevent wear paths and equalize light exposure.

• **RUGS AND CARPETS,** *Identifying Hand-Loomed Orientals:* When you see an Oriental rug that appears to fade gradually toward one end and both ends are not finished/fringed exactly the same way, it's likely to be hand-loomed the traditional way. Fringes/threads at the "top" of the loom are tied differently from those at the "bottom" and, because the yarn is dyed in hanks with natural dyes, the first yarn used (from the outside layers of the hank) will be darker hued than the inner layers; the "top" of the rug (woven first) will be darker than the "bottom" edge.

• **RUGS AND CARPETS,** *Repair:* For wear or burnholes, cut out burned section of fibers. I like to use cuticle scissors. Gather strands of fuzz or fiber from an out-of-the-way spot and glue them in the hole with fabric glue. Place a piece of waxed paper over the repair, weight it with a book, and allow it to dry for at least twenty-four hours. Large burns in rugs or upholstery may need professional repair.

• **RUGS AND CARPETS,** *Repairs:* To cover worn areas, buy waterproof colored markers to match the worn spots and just color the carpet backing that's showing through. This works especially well with dark-colored patterned carpets like Orientals.

• **RUG WASH,** *When Washable Rugs Don't Fit Into the Washer:* Take a washable area rug to a do-it-yourself car wash that has high-pressure hoses, dispenses soap in one wash and rinse water in the other. No scrubbing is necessary. After washing and rinsing, roll up wet rugs, place in a large plastic garbage bag and take them home to dry over a fence or a couple of sturdy clotheslines.

• **RUST RINGS FROM SHAVING CREAM, HAIR SPRAY, ETC. CANS:**
1. To prevent them on bathtub or shower surfaces, place shaving cream can in a 3 ½-inch round plastic beverage holder, the kind that holds soft drinks on car doors. You can hold the can in the ring to the hand-rail of a shower door.
2. To prevent rust rings from shaving cream, hair spray or other cans put them in styrofoam or foam rubber soft drink can insulators, fit plastic lids from containers like potato chip tubes to the bottoms, or just place on any plastic lid large enough to hold the can.

• **RUST SPOTS ON STAINLESS STEEL,** *Removing from Flatware and Pots:* Sorry, there's no permanent solution to this but you can remove little spots with a silver or stainless-steel cleaner. Corrosion occurs when acids, salt and even normal use removes the protective coating put on stainless steel items. Avoid rust spots by always rinsing all food residue from flatware so that it doesn't have time to corrode. If you aren't planning to run your dishwasher for a day or two, it's best to wash stainless flatware by hand. I rinse mine before putting into the dishwasher even if it will be run that day.

S

- **SACHETS,** *Free:* Take the perfumed sample paper inserts from magazines and tuck them into your lingerie drawers, clothing or linen closets, and with your stationery and greeting cards for free sachets.

- **SACHETS,** *Soap:* Store scented soaps (unwrapped or even wrapped, if the scent permeates the wrapper) tucked amid the towels in your linen closet. The towels will smell nice and after the scent becomes faint, use the soap for your bath where getting it wet will reactivate some of the scent. The bonus is that soap dries when stored unwrapped and then dissolves more slowly when wet so it lasts longer.

- **SAFETY PINS:** So useful to hold up a torn hem, close up a blouse with a popped button, hold the temple of your glasses to the frame when the screw falls out! My dry cleaner pins tags to the garments and so when I remove the tag, I pin the safety pin to the hem of that garment so that I always have a safety pin handy for emergencies.

- **ST. PATRICK'S DAY GREENS:** Start the day or end it with green food-colored pancakes! Surprise children by putting a few drops of green coloring in milk. Serve green gelatin, green mashed potatoes, green vegetables and salad, too. And don't forget to wear some green to avoid getting pinched!

• SALAD, *Preparing in Advance:* To prevent soggy salad, put the desired dressing in the bottom of the salad bowl, layer in tomatoes and vegetables. Last, add the lettuce or spinach leaves. Place the prepared salad in the refrigerator and toss just before serving.

• SALAD BAR, *To Encourage Family Salad-eating:* Since your objective is to get the family to enjoy eating healthy, nutritious fare, accept the reality that not everyone likes the same ingredients in a salad. Make salads more inviting by offering a family salad bar. Offer sliced mushrooms, carrots, beets, celery; chopped green onions, olives; garbanzo beans, kidney beans, sprouts, radishes, etc. in the cups of muffin tins, served beside a large bowl of greens and several salad dressings. Let family members customize their salads; you'll be surprised at how youngsters will try new things if other siblings seem to be enjoying them. Cover the muffin tins with plastic wrap after dinner to store leftovers in the refrigerator for the next day or two. Food like celery, radishes, carrot shreds will keep fresher for the next day if you put a wet, not drippy, paper towel on top before the wrap.

• SALAD GREENS: Many new greens are sold in grocery stores and you can combine them for delicious salads. Just remember that you don't usually wash and store lettuce in the refrigerator. Just rinse what you will use immediately.
1. Boston lettuce has green outer leaves with yellow-green inner leaves. Its buttery flavor is best enhanced by a mild salad dressing.
2. Bibb lettuce has soft, green broad leaves. Its delicate taste is also best enhanced by a mild dressing.
3. Red-leaf lettuce is usually a large head of frilly green leaves with reddish tips. It also has a delicate taste and is best with a subtle dressing.
4. Curly endive is a chicory and has a somewhat bitter flavor. Its leaves are large, lacy and fringed. The outer leaves are darker in color and have a stronger taste. Mix with some milder greens and a strong-flavored salad dressing.

5. Watercress leaves are small, dark green and have crisp stems. Its strong peppery taste is good when teamed with other pungent greens.

6. Belgian endive has a long, small, firm head. Its leaves are creamy white and have a hint of yellow at the tips. It's crisp, has a pleasantly bitter taste and is best mixed with stronger flavored greens.

• **SALAD-OIL STOPPER:** To prevent bottled salad oil from gushing out too fast, instead of removing the entire seal when you first remove the cap, cut a slit or punch a hole in the seal. It will be easier to measure or sprinkle. **Note:** When you tear up romaine lettuce for a large company salad, wash and put it in a large clean pillowcase and then spin it dry in the washer spin cycle. You won't bruise the romaine and it's fast and neat! Plus, it will entertain your friends, too!

• **SALAD TOSS,** *Quick-Fix:* Tear greens into a large plastic bowl with a tight-fitting lid; add dressing, give it a few shakes and no more tossing and "bruising" the lettuce.

• **SALAMANDERS,** *Feeding:* Salamanders will eat a diet of strained or pureed fruits and vegetables like baby food, insects and, only once or twice a week, canned cat or dog food.

• **SALT,** *Avoiding Lumps:* If you don't want to keep rice or crushed crackers inside the salt shaker to keep it free-flowing in humid weather, up-end a small clear jelly glass over the shaker. The jelly glass "dome" will keep the salt dry and ready to shake.

• **SALT,** *Removing Excess Salt from Soup or Other Heated Liquids:* Add sliced raw potato to absorb the salt. Remove slices when they begin to soften if you don't want to eat them.

• **SALT (SODIUM),** *Reducing in Canned Foods:* Discarding the liquid that vegetables are canned in will lower the sodium content by one-third; rinsing will decrease it even more. This hint is good also for canned tuna and shrimp (rinse shrimp very gently to prevent breakage).

• **SALT SUBSTITUTE,** *Homemade:* Mix 5 teaspoons onion powder; 1 tablespoon each of garlic powder, paprika, dry mustard; 1 teaspoon thyme; ½ teaspoon white pepper; ½ teaspoon celery seed. Combine, store in clean, empty spice jar in cool, dry place.

• **SANDBOX,** *Indoors for Child's Play:* Take a large plastic tray (like those used for busing dishes or mixing cement) and pour a five-pound bag of cornmeal into it. This "sand" is clean, light and safer than real sand if it accidentally gets into the mouth of a youngster. Clean-up is even easier if you place a plastic shower curtain or drop cloth under the play area!

• **SAP,** *Dripped from Trees:*
1. On a wooden patio, carefully scrape off as much sap as you can with a paint scraper and remove remaining residue with turpentine, which will also remove any paint or water sealer from the patio, too, so you'll have to redo the wood.
2. If the sap is on your car, you may be able to get it off chrome parts with turpentine but for painted surfaces, contact your car dealer's service department for advice. Service departments have specific products that work with different auto paint finishes.

• **SAVING MONEY,** *Getting Into the Habit:* One reader who found it hard to save any money at all decided that after she finished paying off a loan, she would put the amount of the loan payment into her savings account. She pretends that she is still paying on the loan and is building up a nice nest egg so that she can handle the next financial emergency without a loan. The big bonus is that she is receiving interest on her money instead of having the possibility of paying interest on an emergency loan!

• **SAW BLADE,** *Storage, Recycling Idea:* An old record rack will hold saw blades safely and protects the cutting edges from damage.

• **SCALE,** *Recovering a Worn One:* Replace dirty, curly-edged covering on a scale with adhesive-backed floor tile. You can trim the edges and cut out the area for the dial and then make an adjustment for the extra weight. If you have such tile in your bathroom, you can make your scale match the floor and be less conspicuous. **Note:** And we want scales to be inconspicuous, especially on those days when the munchies grab us!

- **SCARF HANGER,** *Keeping Scarfs Free of Fold Lines:*
1. Hang them over a pants hanger—the kind designed to hold several pairs on different rods.
2. Crafty Idea: Tack plastic rings about the size of a silver dollar from craft shops across the bottom of quilted or crochet-covered hangers (about three inches apart) and hang scarfs from the rings.

- **SCARF RINGS,** *Recycling Jewelry:* When rings don't fit or even if they still do, they can be scarf rings if you slip the ends of a scarf into the ring, pull up and secure.

- **SCHOOL BUS REMINDER:** Here's a solution from a part-time working mom to remind her young child of which days she will be picked up by her mom in the car and which days she should come home on the school bus. Buy two brightly colored plastic buttons. On one paint or draw a school bus and on the other a car. Attach a safety pin to the buttons with quick-drying glue and then pin the buttons to the child's clothing each day. It eases the child's apprehension and helps the teacher get the child to the proper waiting area after school.

- **SCHOOL-DAZE SURVIVAL (ALSO SEE WORK DAY SURVIVAL):** To avoid having children dart around gathering books, jackets, caps, backpacks and other things in the morning, place a bookcase near the door so that they can put all their school things on a single shelf ready for the next day. Each child gets a personal shelf. Or, keep small laundry baskets near the door for each child's possessions.

- **SCOOPS,** *Recycling Plastic Coffee Scoops:*
1. Put your daily vitamin dosage in them or use them to store small objects like tacks in a drawer.
2. Use to measure household cleaners.
3. Place one in each kitchen canister.
4. Make a stool for a doll house.

- **SCRAPBOOK,** *Quick-Fix for Newspaper Clippings:* Cut out columns, recipes, stories, and then tape or glue with rubber cement to pages of a school composition book. Highlight the line that tells you the subject of the clipping at a glance.

- **SCREEN,** *Repairing Wire Ones:* Cut a piece of wire mesh from an old screen and sew it over the hole with some fishing line or plastic thread. Also look for screen-repair kits in hardware stores. Small holes can sometimes be sealed with clear fingernail polish.

• **SCREENS,** *Cleaning Window and Door Aluminum Screens:* Remove screens from doors or windows; place up against a tree or fence. Scrub with a mixture of one cup ammonia to one gallon of water. After scrubbing, rinse well with water and dry in sunshine.

• **SCREENS,** *Removing Crayon "Kid-art" from a Window/Door Screen:* Put a couple of sheets of paper toweling behind the screen and spray the area with pre-wash stain remover. Scrub with a stiff brush and rinse well. If crayon remains, repeat the process.

• **SCREWDRIVER,** *Substitute for Phillips Screwdriver:* Try a metal potato peeler. *Letter of Laughter:* A friend, who likes to innovate, told me about her daughter pounding a nail into the wall with the handle of a screwdriver and having her husband, a fanatic about his tools, get horrified. "Where did you ever learn that," he gasped. "My mother taught me; she can do it with the side of pliers, too. Anybody can pound a nail in the wall with a hammer," the daughter replied. The next weekend, she was given a tool set of her own for the kitchen, which is a very good idea—include screwdrivers (Phillips and regular), pliers—and also a hammer, if you're conventional about nail pounding!

• **SEARCH FOR LOST FRIENDS OR RELATIVES:** Main public libraries and some universities have telephone directories from major cities; look in them for names of lost friends or relatives. Or, from the library's information service, get the telephone number and address of the county courthouse. Call or write to them for family records, like birth, death, or marriage certificates. Remember that whenever you send a request for information, include a stamped, self-addressed business-size envelope and it usually gets a faster response.

• **SEASHELLS,** *Don't Throw Away Beach Souvenirs:*
1. Put them into a large clear jar and use as a paperweight, door stop, or, if you are handy, make a large shell-filled vase into a lamp.
2. Cover soil of pot plants to hold in moisture and make it less attractive to digging pets.
3. Larger flat shells make good soap dishes.

4. Glue them on an old picture frame and then frame a picture or mirror with it. Boutiques at the seashore sell seashell-framed shiny mirrors! (Say that fast, ten times!)

• **SEAT CUSHIONS,** *Stop Them from Slipping:* Try putting a thin sheet of foam rubber, a rubber sink or bathtub mat, between the sofa or chair cushion and the springs.

• **SEEDLINGS,** *Growing Your Own, Recycling:* It's easy to get seedlings out of their containers whole and undamaged at planting time.
1. If you start your seedlings in paper cups, you can tear away the cup at planting time.
2. If you cut both ends out of juice cans, set them on a tray and plant seeds in them, at planting time, you just gently push all the dirt and roots out at the same time.
3. Start seedlings in egg cartons, but place a section of eggshell in the bottom of each cup so removal is a snap.

• **SEEDS, STORAGE:** If you buy tub margarine, the butter compartment of your refrigerator is unused and just right for storing seed packages. Seeds will keep and still germinate several years after the date shown on the package if they are kept in the refrigerator.

• **SEEDS,** *Testing for Germination:* If you find old seeds in packages, try sprinkling a few between two damp paper towels. If they're still fresh enough, they'll sprout in a couple of days and you can plant the sprouts as well as the seed. Some seeds, such as tomato, cabbage, cucumber, lettuce and squash, will stay fresh for several years and others should be bought each year. Many gardeners keep seeds, sealed in zipper bags, in the refrigerator for many seasons.

• **SENIOR CITIZEN,** *Definition, Letter of Laughter:* When a grandmother took her four-year-old granddaughter to a Senior Citizen meeting, the child leaned over and asked Grandma what the meeting was about. When Grandma explained that it was mostly for old people, the child whispered loudly, "Aren't there any new ones?" Grandma hugged her and told her grandchild that she was the only one there that was close to being new.

• **SEWING,** *For Toddlers:* If your child squirms so much that you're afraid you'll stick him with a pin, mark hems and buttonholes with masking tape.

• **SEWING,** *Hand-sewing Hints:*

1. Keeping your thread shorter than 20 inches avoids knots and tangles.
2. Use a larger-holed needle if your thread keeps fraying.
3. If fabric puckers or gets pulls, your needle might be bent, dull or point-damaged. Get a new needle.
4. If you cut thread on an angle instead of breaking it, needle-threading is easier.
5. You won't save time or money by using old thread from wooden spools because it's likely to break. Wooden spools haven't been used for years and have become collector's items.

• **SEWING,** *Mending:* Embroidery floss is a good substitute for regular thread when you are mending. You can more easily match colors with it and it's stronger, too.

• **SEWING,** *Using Fabric Glues:* **Caution!** If you use those wonderful timesavers like glue stick, liquid seam sealant and basting tape, be aware that they can damage your sewing machine and cause expensive repair bills if you don't follow directions exactly. One important rule is: Always let glues dry completely before stitching over them.

• **SEWING MACHINE,** *Maintenance, Letter of Laughter:* When the sewing machine clatters for six months begging for oil and you finally "feed" it, it's a good idea to sew on mending or other old stuff just in case some oil leaks out. But one reader wants to know why, after you finish with the old stuff, and then start on some pretty new material does the "blamed thing disgorge its last excess drips that you were sure weren't there?" Why? It's another of those "irony of life rules."

• **SEWING MACHINE,** *Quick-Fix Cleaning, Recycling:* A well-washed and dried mascara brush will clean bobbin and shuttle carriers in the sewing machine. It fits into those tight places and you can twist it around to pick up lint.

• **SEWING NEEDLES,** *Letter of Laughter:* A seamstress wrote that when the only needle in her pin cushion was too big for the job at hand, she began kneading the pin cushion because she thought she spied a tiny golden one peeping up. To her surprise, she found thirty-seven needles buried inside her pincushion. Her question was, "Do you think they might have been in there breeding?" I didn't know, but I sure advised her to keep an eye on the situation!

- **SEWING NEEDLES,** *Threading:* Can't thread the needle? Dab a tiny bit of clear nail polish on the tip of the thread, allow to dry, and it's no problem.

- **SEWING NEEDLES,** *Sticky:* Your needle will glide through fabric more easily if you stick it through a fabric-softener sheet a few times. Thread the needle and knot the thread BEFORE doing this.

- **SHAKERS,** *Flour and Sugar:* Keep large shakers of flour and sugar on the kitchen counter to avoid hauling out canisters when you need just a teaspoon or so of either one.

- **SHALLOTS,** *Substitutes in Recipes:* Shallots are members of the onion family but their flavor is somewhere between onion and garlic. Substituting regular onions for shallots won't give you the same flavor in a recipe and can change the taste. **Note:** Shallots become bitter when overcooked so they are usually minced and browned quickly.

- **SHEEPSKIN RUGS,** *Cleaning:* Since it's almost impossible to know what type of tanning process was used on these skins, it's best to take them to a reputable dry cleaner where special cleaning processes and chemicals can be used. **Note:** White sheepskins tend to yellow after they are cleaned.

- **SHELF,** *Level Installation:* Measuring from the floor up to the height for installation and marking both ends may not make the shelf level due to imperfections in construction. Instead, measure to the height on one end and then use the level to mark the shelf line on the wall, making sure that the bubble is in the center before you extend the line.

- **SHELF COVERING,** *Shelves with Pots and Pans:* Shelf paper usually tears in this situation but vinyl floor tiles are easy to install—cut to fit and peel off the backing—and easier yet to maintain by wiping clean.

- **SHELF PAPER,** *$aver:* Buy wallpaper remnants and cut to fit.

- **SHELF PAPER,** *When It's Too Wide:* Cut off the excess through the whole roll with a handsaw.

- **SHELVES,** *Better Storage Capacity:*
1. Rectangular plastic dish pans, new or clean used ones, can double your shelf storage capacity if you fill and stack them. Print contents on tape or labels instead of directly on the dish pans just in case you want to change the contents. They're easier to remove and replace than stacks of items.
2. Small plastic mesh baskets can serve the same purpose and a rectangular plastic laundry basket can hold shoes on the closet floor.

- **SHIRT COLLAR,** *Quick-Fix, Prevention of Frayed Ones:* Apply a commercial product sold in fabric stores to stop or prevent fraying to the collar points when the shirt is new. Reapply periodically.

- **SHIRTS,** *Ironing:*
1. Do cuffs, collar and sleeves first.
2. Using the rounded end of the ironing board, start with the back of the shirt, ironing on the inside instead of outside for a nicer finish, especially on dark fabrics.
3. Begin at the corner where shoulder and armhole meet and work your way down and to the middle. Do the front using the same method.
4. Turn shirt right-side-out and do any touching-up.

- **SHOE BAGS,** *Compartmentalized Hanging Ones:* Yes, they organize shoes when hanging on the closet door, wall or attached to a sturdy hanger, but they also hold socks and undies, school supplies, knitting/crocheting supplies; toys; rolled T-shirts and polo shirts, pantyhose and tights; and just about anything that takes up drawer space or makes it jumbled. You'll want more than one in a closet!

- **SHOEBOX,** *Recycling:* A child's shoebox makes a handy cupboard-file for sauce and gravy mixes.

- **SHOEHORN,** *Substitute:* The tongue end of a man's belt can be an emergency shoehorn.

- **SHOEHORN SUBSTITUTE:** Cut a plastic margarine tub lid to the right shape and it will bend around your heel better than a "real" shoe horn.

- **SHOELACES,** *Keeping Them in Children's Shoes:* Stop laces from pulling through the eyelets when children remove their shoes by tying a knot at each shoelace tip after the first lace-up—makes kid's shoes almost kid-proof.

- **SHOELACES,** *When Toddlers Pull Them Out and Lose Them:* When you lace a toddler's shoes for the first time, knot the laces after putting them through the first two holes. The toddler can still take the laces out of the first couple of holes but not all the way out. No more lost laces!

- **SHOES,** *Checklist for Leather-shoe Care:* The gloss sprayed on new shoes does not protect like polish so polish new shoes before wearing them.
1. Use a sponge and saddle soap at least once monthly to remove dust and grime. Follow with good quality paste or cream to moisturize the leather; never use liquid polish on leather.
2. Use a soft cloth to apply polish, allow to dry; buff with brush in long easy strokes; finish shine with buffing in circular motion with soft cloth to remove excess polish and deepen shine. Clean or get new brushes and shine cloths every six months.
3. Strip off polish build-up every eight shines with leather balm to prevent cracking.
4. Dress the heel edge with black dressing product to lock out moisture which leads to cracks.

- **SHOES,** *Cleaning Heel Marks Off White and Colored Ones:* If the shoes are just marked and the finish is not ruined, pre-wash spray will remove heel-kick marks. It may take a bit of scrubbing but it works.

- **SHOES,** *Coordinating with Wardrobe:* Replace plain white laces in white tennis shoes with colored ribbon or cord.

- **SHOES,** *Drying:*
1. Stuff wet shoes with old pantyhose to help keep their shape while they dry.

2. If you can't toss them into the clothes dryer, put them on the floor next to the hot-air exhaust of the refrigerator to hasten drying. **Hint,** Healthy-Planet Recycling: If children want to go back outdoors and their shoes are still wet, put their feet into bread bags and then into shoes and their feet will be dry even if their shoes are not.

• **SHOES,** *Fixing Driving-Damaged Heels:* A good cleaning and polishing may remove scuff marks. To remove scrapes, heat a curling iron to warm and gently press it against the scraped area. The "ironing" will remove wrinkles so that you can smooth the leather and glue it back into place. **Hint:** Avoid the problem by keeping a pair of slip-on shoes in the car to wear while driving.

• **SHOES,** *Quick-Fix Cover-up for Brightly Colored Shoes:* Fix up little scrapes and scratches on pink, purple, and non-neutral colored shoes with colored felt-tip markers. They come in many shades to match almost any color.

• **SHOES,** *Quick-Fix to Stop Squeaks, Preventing Squeaks:* Moisture in the soles is the usual cause of squeaky shoes.
1. Try shaking some talcum powder in the shoes before and after each wearing.
2. Turn each shoe over and nail a couple of short tacks in the bottom of the sole on either side of the metal arch support. Do not push the tacks all the way through the sole or they will stick your foot.
3. If the above fail, take the shoe to a shoe-repair shop for advice.

• **SHOES,** *Recycling Energy, Quiet-Drying Tennis Shoes:* If the clanging of your shoes drying in the dryer is annoying, place them under the dryer vent so that the warm air flows into them to dry them while you dry other loads.

• **SHOES,** *Suede-shoe Care:* Brush weekly with stiff-bristled brush to remove dirt. Gum eraser can remove light stains; heavier stains need cleaning professionally. Apply water and stain-preventing spray after cleaning and brushing.

• **SHOES,** *TLC Checklist to Make Them Last Longer:*
1. When putting them on, untie, unbuckle and use a shoehorn to avoid ruining the shoe's "mouth." Shoe trees help shoes keep their shape.

2. Let shoes rest in ventilated areas between wearings to dry out; don't store in their original boxes.
3. Clean and polish them regularly. Don't wait until they are scuffed and shabby. See Above.

• **SHOES, REPAIRS:** Replace heels when one-fourth of the heel is worn off. At winter's end, before I store my good leather boots, I like to have them professionally cleaned and shined at my shoe repair shop.

• **SHOES, SCUFF MARKS,** *Removing from White Shoes or Sneakers:* Spray with prewash spray, let set a few minutes and wipe off. Remove hard or stubborn stains by scrubbing with a brush. Washable sneakers can then go into the machine. **Caution:** Although this method has been used on rubber, plastic and cloth parts of sneakers and on other white shoes, it's still best to test all cleaning methods on an inconspicuous place to make sure no harm will be done.

• **SHOE STRAPS THAT SLIP:** Put a piece of moleskin on the inside of the heel strap where it hits your heel or try sticking a piece of thin foam rubber weather stripping. Either material can be trimmed to fit a heel strap and should help keep it in place.

• **SHOPPING,** *Credit Cards:* Compare grace periods, annual fees, and interest rates. If you have a lot of cards, protecting them by joining a credit card protection service may be a good idea, but if you have only one or two cards, you can easily report loss or theft yourself. **Caution:** Never sign up with a registry by phone; there are fraudulent protection services that ask for your card numbers but instead of protecting you they make unauthorized charges on your card.

• **SHOPPING,** *For a Fitness Center:*
1. Ask for a one-day pass so that you can sample the facility. Be sure to visit it during the hours you plan to use it so that, if you plan to go after work, you'll know if it's so busy then that you'll spend all your time waiting for equipment or have overcrowded classes. When you try out classes, make sure the instructors are encouraging and that they note the different ability levels of participants. Talk to members to find out if they are satisfied.

2. Does the facility offer what you want to do? Some high-tech facilities offer sophisticated weight machines and aerobics classes. Others offer ballroom dancing, karate, cardio-fitness classes and other programs.

3. What about the equipment? Is it up-to-date and well-maintained or are there several broken machines, as is common in many facilities? Studios and workout rooms should be spacious, clean, well lit, and ventilated, and have floors of appropriate materials to avoid injury. (Springy wood floors for dance/exercise, resilient surfaces for weight training areas.) Class sizes should allow for enough space for safe, comfortable movement and for individual attention from instructors. Staff should be supervising all areas at all times and there should be enough equipment so several people can work out simultaneously. Are showers, dressing rooms, saunas, pools and steam rooms clean? Are lockers secure?

4. Does the club require a stress test before you start a new program? If you are over forty-five, overweight, at risk for heart disease, disabled or have other health problems, you should have a doctor's exam before starting any new exercise program even if the club doesn't require it. (Be leery of clubs that claim their diet, exercise or fitness programs are better than those suggested by recognized medical sources.)

5. Ask about the qualifications of the staff. Certification is not the law but staff can be certified by the American College of Sports Medicine, International Dance Exercise Association, Aerobics and Fitness Association of America, and the Institute for Aerobics Research. Find out if the club requires its teachers to take in-house training. For example, the YMCA has its own instructor training program. It's best if instructors have degrees in exercise-related fields, such as exercise physiology, kinesiology, or physical education. Instructors and staff should be trained in first aid and CPR and the club also should offer CPR training to members.

6. If you decide to join: Avoid "today-only" sale prices; you should be able to take a couple of days to make your decision. (Most states mandate "cooling-off" periods of three days so that you can change your mind.) Read contracts very carefully. You should be able to take a short-term membership before committing to a year or more and you should be able to freeze your membership temporarily in case of illness, injury or travel.

• **SHOPPING,** *Forming Co-ops to Save Money:*
1. If your city has vegetable or farmer's markets where you can save money by buying produce in bulk, get together with five or six friends and buy bulk produce weekly, dividing purchases and their cost for substantial savings. You'll get a taste of veggies that you might not otherwise have tried, too. In some co-ops, each person takes a turn each week to shop and divide the produce; in others they make it a fun, get-together day for several of the co-op people to shop together.
2. Organize your neighbors, bridge club, etc. if several people are shopping for stereo equipment at the same time and try to buy as a group. Some group members research audio magazines in the library to find out which brands are best quality and how to combine the various components—speakers, CD player, receiver, etc., and others scout local stores to compare prices. Then, all go to a dealer together and try to negotiate a "group discount." Even if you don't get a discount, you'll surely get the best researched buy on your equipment.

• **SHOPPING,** *Gas for Your Car:* Contrary to popular belief, premium gas is not a must for all cars. More than 90 percent of cars run well on mid-level or regular octanes. Experts say that if your car's manual doesn't specify using high-octane, you may not need it. Lower octanes are a bonus for the environment because more expensive premium gas is a pollution source; it doesn't burn as cleanly as lower octanes. And, the engine cleaners advertised as "musts" aren't necessary either. So, you can save money and our air at the same time!

• **SHOPPING,** *Insurance:* Read all policies carefully to make sure you are not paying for duplicate coverage with several policies. (This is especially prevalent with Medicare supplements. Also, people often buy extra insurance on rental cars when their own auto insurance policies already provide the needed coverage.)

• **SHOPPING,** *Layaway Checklist:* Super prices on sale clothing, especially on last year's winter clothing, makes buying on layaway a tempting idea—you don't use credit or pay full price immediately, the store holds the garments and you'll probably be finished paying for the garments by the time you'll need to wear them. **Caution:** If you don't understand the store's layaway policy, you could have problems.

1. Terms: Know how much time you have to pay, when payments are due, what minimum payment is required, and what charges, if any, are added to the purchase price. Some sellers charge a service fee; some charge a penalty for late payments.

2. Refunds: If you decide you don't want the item, some stores may give all of your money back, some may give you credit to apply to other purchases. This information should be in writing.

3. Availability of Layaway Items: Some items are immediately available and others are on display to be ordered upon request. If you buy an item on layaway, find out if it will remain on display (the possibility of getting shopworn) or be stored in a separate area of the stockroom until you get it. If the item must be ordered, find out how far in advance you need to order it so you can get it when you finish paying. To make sure you are getting exactly what you placed on layaway, the receipt should say, for example: "One (1) red 2-piece dress, Size 12, (NAME) Manufacturer, Style No. 678."

4. Pitfalls: If the store goes bankrupt while you are still paying, you may lose your money and the merchandise. Consider the store's reputation before you buy; check with the local Better Business Bureau before buying an expensive item on layaway.

5. Records: ALWAYS keep good records of payments so that you have them in case of disputes.

• SHOPPING, *Long Distance Phone Service:* If you make only a few long distance calls each month costing less than $10, the major long distance phone services cost about the same. Compare the following before you decide on a long distance service: monthly service fee, minimum charges, if and how easily will you get credit if you get wrong numbers, bad connections or disconnected calls.

• SHOPPING, *Sales:* Learn to spot a real sale. Sale items are those which will return to their previous higher prices after the sale is over. "Clearance Sales" are on items substantially reduced. "Promotional Sales" usually are on items not always in the store's regular stock; they are specially priced but not necessarily great savings. "Going Out of Business Sales" can go on all year-round at some unscrupulous dealerships; this is especially prevalent in Oriental rug and furniture stores.

• **SHOPPING,** *Supermarkets:* Stores are designed to promote impulse buying. That's why the most expensive items are placed on shelves at eye level. To avoid impulse buying, don't shop hungry, shop from a list, make your list according to planned menus, and, if you can, leave the children at home. Otherwise, let each child pick one thing only. Coupons save money if you use them to buy things you actually use.

• **SHOPPING,** *Supermarkets, Ways to Cut Spending:*
1. Plan meals from your cupboard using ingredients you already have on hand so that you can use up these foods and free up money to spend on this month's sale items.
2. Before you decide on your menu, check grocery ads to see what's on sale.
3. Plan all three meals for the day, but don't feel bound by tradition—if you like pancakes for supper or lunch and soup or sandwiches for breakfast, it's okay.
4. Change your eating habits. The U.S. Government studies show that nutritious foods are less expensive than junk foods.
5. Experiment with substitutes in recipes: If green beans are on special and the recipe calls for peas, use the beans, both are green. Rice and noodles can be interchangeable and so on. Chicken or turkey can substitute for beef in some recipes; you can doctor them up with seasonings or beef bouillon or French onion soup mix.
6. Avoid convenience foods when you can. They cost more and many are over-packaged, adding to our over-trashed landfills. Also, many are high in fat and salt content.
7. Be creative with leftovers and plan them. For example, if you cook enough rice or noodles for two meals, you can use the leftovers in a casserole another day. Bake double the number of potatoes you need for one day and use the leftovers for stuffed baked potatoes another day, saving baking energy.
8. Be flexible—change your menu to accommodate specials and remember that sometimes buying after the promotion of specialty foods can be a good buy, especially in January when overstocked gourmet foods and condiments get marked down.

9. Avoid too many shopping trips where you "pop into the store to pick up a few things." This encourages impulse buying.

10. Make budget-stretching a game not a burdensome chore. See if you can shop more economically each week and make notes of your savings so that you can take pride in your efforts.

• **SHOPPING,** *Travel Clubs:* Travel clubs can make vacation trips fun and less expensive but beware if you are asked to prepay for a trip before your reservations are confirmed in writing, or if you are required to buy something as a condition of membership that has no relationship to the trip.

• **SHOPPING,** *Warranties and Service Contracts:* Always read the fine print and if you are trying to decide between two similar items, take the one with the most extensive warranty. If you decide to buy a service contract, find out how long the contract will be valid, will repairs be done in your home or a service center, who will do repairs (dealer or repair center), and, if repairs are done by a third party service center, will your contract be honored if the third party goes out of business. Also, will the contracts still be valid if you buy the item under your name and give it away as a gift?

• **SHOPPING WITH CHILDREN,** *Mother-Saver:* If your child gets cranky while you shop, promise that when you finish your shopping, you both will go to the child's favorite store or other place. There's a fine line between bribery and rewarding a child for good behavior but when you're shopping with a child, there's no point in even looking for that line! Whatever works is good!

• **SHOPPING FOR GROCERIES WITH SMALL CHILDREN,** *Keeping Them Busy, Recycling:* Cut out pictures of food and grocery items from magazines, food ads and newspapers. Glue several on a heavy piece of cardboard (like a cereal box side) to resemble a bingo card. When you leave for the store, give each child one of the cards and a crayon. As you shop, the children mark off the items they see. If you want to make it a competitive game, the first child to mark off all of the items gets to pick a special treat. If you don't want it to be competition, each child that marks off all items on the card gets a treat at the end.

• **SHOPPING LIST:** Avoid repeated shuffling through your cou-pons—note on the list which items have coupons and also the best-buy "amount off" with brand name.

• **SHOPPING LIST:** For short lists, write your needs on a self-stick note, attach it to the fridge. When you go shopping, you can stick it on your dashboard or a junkmail envelope holding your coupons and then, you can stick your list on the handlebar of the shopping cart so that your hands are free. *Letter of Laughter:* A funny thing happened to a Heloise fan on the way to the grocery store—she apparently sat on one of the many stick-on notes she writes to herself as reminders. While she was shopping, someone tapped her on the shoulder and said, "Something is on the seat of your slacks." Was she embarrassed! The note printed in large letters read, "LARD." Of all the notes to get stuck there! She's switched from stick-on lists to regular paper.

• **SHOPPING LIST,** *Computerized:* After you've listed every possible thing you could or would buy at the supermarket, save the list in your computer and make a printout when needed. You'll never have to waste time making up a new shopping list again. Keep the list on your fridge door and highlight items to be bought.

• **SHORTENING,** *Measuring and Substitution:* An easy way to mea-sure solid shortening or lard is to use the displacement method. For instance, if you need ½ cup of shortening, fill a one-cup measuring cup with ½ cup of water, then add solid shortening until water level reaches one cup. Drain off water and shortening comes right out without scraping.

When you substitute vegetable oil for butter or lard in recipes other than baking bread and desserts, you may need to experiment with your recipes—as a rule you use one-third less oil. For example, two teaspoons of vegetable oil replaces one tablespoon of solid shortening. Remember that while a good vegetable oil may be low in cholesterol, it's still fat.

• **SHOULDER PADS,** *Quick-Fix:* Tuck shoulder pads under bra straps when you don't have time to sew them in. If you have the "teeth" section of self-gripping fabric tape and the pads are of a soft fabric, you may be able to secure the pads in place by putting a strip of the tape over strap and shoulder pad.

• **SHOULDER PADS,** *Quick-Fix Placement:* If you don't like self-gripping fabric tape or pin-ons, try sticking the double-sided tape safe for walls on the pads and inserting them. The tape is good for emergency hem repair, too.

• **SHOULDER PADS,** *Recycling:* Stuff pillows or children's toy animals or soft-sculpture crafts; make knee pads for gardening or cleaning by holding them on your knees with the tops of old socks or, if you feel ambitious, sew them into work pants knees; insert in bras for "push-up pads" or "enhancers."

• **SHOWER CAPS,** *New Uses for Hotel "Freebies":*
1. Cover leftover food in bowls.
2. Cover round 35mm slide carousels to keep them dust free and to keep the slides in place. Place an identifying index card under the cap so you know what's inside.

• **SHOWER CURTAIN (PLASTIC),** *Laundering:*
1. To remove Water Spots—Spray full-strength vinegar to both sides of the curtain, leave on for at least 30 minutes. Scrub persistent spots with a brush.
2. To remove Mildew—Launder in machine with warm water and ½ to 1 cup liquid chlorine bleach, regular detergent and a couple of white bath towels. Run through a whole cycle. Toss in the dryer for a few minutes to remove wrinkles and re-hang immediately after removing from the dryer.

• **SHOWER CURTAIN,** *Quick-Fix Repair:*
1. When the hanging holes tear, take a hand-held hole puncher and punch a hole about a half-inch from the torn one.
2. For a more permanent mend—if you have clear plastic mending tape handy, it helps to reinforce the area with it before you punch the hole either in the same place or a half-inch from the torn place. Fold the tape over the top so it reinforces on both sides.

• **SHOWER CURTAINS,** *Clear Plastic with Water Spots:* Either get a second shower rod and curtain as a splash guard for a clear plastic one or put a thin film of lemon-oil furniture polish on to prevent the "gunk" from sticking.

• **SHOWER CURTAINS,** *Quick Cleaning:* Pour full-strength vinegar on the shower curtain to remove soap film and mildew.

• **SHOWER CURTAIN SLIDE,** *Quick-Fix:* If your family (Not you, of course, because you are more careful!) tears the shower curtain because it doesn't slide shut easily, it could be due to the rings sticking on the curtain rod. Grease them with petroleum jelly.

• **SHOWER CURTAIN TIE-BACK:** When the adhesive hook that comes with some shower curtains won't stick to the tile, substitute a rubber suction cup to hold the tie-back. It's easy to remove and replace when you clean the tiles.

• **SHOWER DOOR,** *Keeping It Clean:* Install an adjustable shower rod inside the shower next to the door and hang a neutral shower curtain on the rod. The doors stay dry and you can toss the curtain into the washer when it's spotted.

• **SHOWER DOORS AND TILES,** *Removing Water Spots:*
1. Shower doors—Rub with lemon-oil furniture polish to soften gunk. Leave on a few minutes and scrub with nylon net or scrubber. Remove stubborn lime deposits from glass with a single-edged razor taking care not to scratch the glass. **Caution!** Don't get oil on the shower floor; it could be dangerously slippery. After the shower door is clean, apply another coat of oil to prevent water spots.
2. Shower tiles—Remove soap and hard water buildup with tile cleaner. Then apply a good paste wax and buff with dry cloth to deter future water spots.
3. Leave a large sponge or a window squeegie in the shower so that walls can be wiped down after each use to save time for more pleasant things than cleaning showers!

• **SHOWER-DOOR TRACK,** *Cleaning:* Pour full-strength vinegar into the track, let soak for a few minutes, rinse the gunk and vinegar right off.

• **SHOWER SHOCK,** *Avoiding It:* Store your favorite body lotion within the tub or stall area, then after bathing, towel dry yourself lightly and apply the moisturizer before opening the shower curtain or doors. The oil will keep you warm when you do open the door and you'll benefit more because moisturizers capture and retain water for the skin.

• **SHOWER STALL,** *Easy Rinsing Walls:* After scrubbing, rinse with the flow from a long, skinny-nosed plant watering can.

• **SHOWER WALLS,** *Minimizing Cleaning and Children's "Shower Stalling" at the Same Time:* Make a rule that each day, the last person to take a shower wipes down the shower walls and door when they finish. Water spots will be minimal and children seldom ignore parents when they say, "Who's going to shower first?"

• **SICK-IN-BED:** When an elderly, incapacitated or young person is bed-ridden at home and has lost interest in daily life, place a bird bath near a large window where it can be watched from inside the home. Nature perks interest like few other happenings! **Note:** If the bird bath is plastic, fill the base with water, soil or stones for more stability.

• **SIDING,** *Cleaning Aluminum House Siding:* Mix ⅓ cup of ordinary, mild, non-abrasive laundry detergent to each gallon of water used. To clean, apply detergent solution with a soft bristle brush and rub gently. (Rubbing too hard will take the shine off.) Reduce streaking by washing the house from the bottom up and rinsing as you go. To remove stubborn stains, contact the siding manufacturer or a local siding installer for instructions. (To find out if the manufacturer has a toll-free number, dial 1-800-555-1212 and ask the operator.)

• **SILVER,** *Polish:* Rub with paste of baking soda and water.

• **SILVER,** *Storage Cautions:*
1. Never store silver in plastic wrap or thin plastic bags. Thin plastic can melt in the heat of an attic and adhere to the silver.
2. Also, instant silver polish and the instant cleaning method of detergent water in an aluminum foil-lined pan is not safe for antique silver; it can remove all the oxidation that fills darkened parts of the design and make the silver look too white to be old.

• **SILVERWARE,** *Quick-Fix, Cleanup:* Sometimes, if tarnish isn't too bad, you can wash enough of it off for respectability with regular liquid hand-dishwashing detergent squirted full-strength on a sponge. Rinse well and shine with a soft towel.

• **SINK,** *Mending Chipped Areas of a Colored One:* If you can't find the right color in touch-up enamel at paint or hardware stores, check out the automotive department for car touch-up paint. You might find a match, or at least a color close to matching.

• **SINK,** *Shining Dull or Scratched Stainless Steel:*
1. Replace the luster with stainless-steel polish, sold at most grocery stores.
2. Clean regularly with mild detergent, rinsing well and buffing dry with a clean, soft cloth. This avoids water-spot build-up.
3. Wipe with vinegar or a touch of oil on a cloth to make the sink sparkle.

• **SINK DRAIN,** *Avoiding Clogs:* Before draining foods in the sink, place a paper towel (preferably reuse one which has already dried your hands) over the drain; after the liquid drains through it, remove the towel and food bits and toss. No bits down the drain!

• **SINK, PEDESTAL:** When your bathroom has a pedestal sink there's no countertop to put cosmetics, hair curlers, etc. Place a clear acrylic cutting board or an appropriately sized tray of a coordinating bathroom color across the basin—you get a wide, sturdy temporary counter and you can lift away everything on it at once when you need to use the sink.

• **SIX-PACK CARRIER,** *Recycling:* Store and tote baby bottles to day care or cleaning supplies around the house in cardboard carriers.

• **SIX-PACK RINGS,** *Recycling:* Please see PLASTIC SIX-PACK RINGS.

• **SKILLET,** *Care of Iron Ones:*
1. To season cast iron, wash in hot, sudsy water, rinse, dry immediately. Then cover inside of the skillet with vegetable cooking oil and place in a 300°F oven for about two hours. **Caution:** Be careful when removing the skillet; it will be hot. Wipe out excess oil with paper towels. Re-season when necessary.
2. Never let cast iron pots and skillets soak in water or sit with food in them. Always scrub with hot water and a nylon scrubbie (never steel wool), and then rinse and dry quickly to prevent rust.

• **SKIN FRESHENER/SOOTHER,** *Healthy Planet:* Add pulp-free aloe vera juice to water in a spray bottle and spritz your arms, legs, back and face for a quick cool-off and moisturizer. This feels especially good at the beach!

• **SKIN,** *Freshener:* Witch hazel, the old-fashioned barbershop aftershave, is an inexpensive and effective skin freshener, and it's especially nice in the summer if it's been refrigerated. Apply with cotton ball and allow to dry before applying makeup.

• **SKIN,** *Healthy-Planet Cleansing:* Using a washcloth to wash off makeup and skin remedies instead of cotton balls or other throwaway pads is one way to decrease your trash output! Every little bit counts!

• **SKIN,** *Moisturizers, Makeup Remover:* Baby oil or just plain mineral oil cost less than expensive lotions and potions and can be applied harmlessly to soften skin or remove makeup. The oils are especially useful if you react to food dyes, lanolin, perfumes and other ingredients found in many commercial creams. These oils can also be put into your bath water when you soak, but **Caution:** They can make the tub slippery.

• **SKIN,** *Home Skin Test for Sensitivity:*
1. Apply a small dot of the test material, about the size of a match head, to a half-inch square or circle of unmedicated gauze adhesive bandage. Mix dry materials like herbs with a couple of drops of water or mineral oil. Mineral oil is good because it doesn't evaporate.
2. Place the patch on a hair-free area of the skin like the inside of your arm or elbow, or your back. Leave it there for forty-eight hours without getting it wet.
3. If the test area burns, itches, aches or feels even a little bit irritated, remove the patch immediately and flush the area with water. If the irritation continues, get a non-prescription cortisone ointment from your pharmacist or see your doctor. If you are sensitive to the material, you will probably have a reaction in two to forty-eight hours after putting the patch in place and if you have no reaction, such as redness, swelling, pimples, blisters or itching, the material is safe for you.

This test may seem like a lot of trouble, but think about how you'd feel if you soaked in an herbal bath and your whole body reacted to an allergen! I have an allergy-prone friend who spent three days itching from an expensive spa herbal bath. It was anything but a relaxing experience!

• **SKIN,** *"Kitchen" Remedies for Soaking in the Bath:*
1. Milk: Swirl a package of powdered nonfat dry milk or pour a quart of regular low-fat milk into a tubful of warm water and soak. (This also sooths sunburn.)
2. Sea Salt: Add a half pound of sea salt to warm water for a super skin-cleansing bath.
3. Scent-senses: Add leftover perfume, perfume samples or rinse out an "empty" perfume bottle in your bath water and add some coconut, almond, baby or other oil before soaking. **Caution:** Oil and water don't mix and can be slippery in the tub!
4. Cider Soother: Add about two cupfuls of apple cider vinegar to a tub of warm water to sooth sunburned, itchy skin. Some people prefer to splash the cider on their bodies before sitting down in the water; others just add it to the water before soaking.
5. Oatmeal Skin Soother: Dangle a cloth bag of oatmeal (two cups or so) on the faucet as the tub fills and then rub your skin with the bag after it's moistened by the water flow. Or, just add oatmeal to the water, then soak in it. This also is a sunburn or itchy skin soother.
6. Herbal Bath: Many herbs, alone or combined, can be put into a cloth or net bag, tossed into the tub or hung on the faucet as the tub fills so that you can have a soothing herbal bath, with herbs from your garden. They include: rosemary, chamomile, any mint variety, comfrey, rose petals, lavender, yarrow or camphor. About ½ cup of dry or fresh herbs is the usual amount, depending upon how much "flavoring" you want. **Caution:** If you have allergies to plants, do a skin test before soaking your whole body in herbs or herbal combinations.

• **SKIN,** *"Kitchen" Remedies for Sun/Heat Irritation:*
Remedy 1: Rub dry, irritated skin gently with juices from peach or cucumber at night.
Remedy 2: Apply mashed avocado to skin, leave on for a few minutes and rinse off gently to clean and condition it.
Remedy 3: Apply buttermilk as a soothing lotion to cleanse and soften.
Remedy 4: Add one-half cup baking soda to tepid water for a soothing soak for dry, irritated skin.
Remedy 5: Apply cornstarch to prickly heat rash.

Remedy 6: A paste of baking soda and water, vinegar or yogurt can sooth minor sunburn. **Caution:** If your skin is very red or blistered, see a doctor.

• **SKIN MOISTURIZING:** Heating systems dry out the air and can make our skins feel tight and dry even when we apply lotions and oils. You don't need to buy an expensive humidifier to put moisture into the air of your home.

1. Simmer an 8-quart pot of water on the stove for a few hours. Add some potpourri or spices and put a pleasant fragrance in the house, too. Place pretty containers of water around the house to evaporate moisture into the air, but remember to keep them filled!

2. Plants help rehydrate air. Ferns, bamboo, begonias, zebra plants and coleus are among those liking lots of moisture and they grow fast, too. Put the pots in a shallow tray filled with pebbles or moss and water to help keep moisture in the plants and in the air. Keep plants well watered and mist them frequently.

3. Mist your face with a spritz from a spray bottle several times a day. If you can't spritz, dab on water with a cotton ball or makeup square. It's refreshing as well as moisturizing for your face.

4. Let dishes air dry in the dishwasher to save energy and put moisture into the air. Stop the dishwasher after the final rinse and open the door. Hold your face where it will be moistened by escaping steam, but **caution:** not where the steam is hot; it can burn.

5. Avoid overheating; keeping the house a few degrees cooler saves on utility bills and energy use and also prevents the air from becoming too dry.

6. Moisturize skin from within. Drink five or six or more glasses of water daily. Keep a pretty glass on your desk, counter or wherever you'll most likely see it as a reminder to drink water.

• **SLEEPING BAGS,** *Cleaning:* ALWAYS check care labels for cleaning instructions. Most can be laundered or dry-cleaned and should be repaired before cleaning.

1. Home Laundering—Set the washer on slow speed and high water level. A suds cycle should remove heavy soil and a second rinse should thoroughly remove detergent from the filling. Tumble dry to fluff up batting. Fluff down-filled bags by throwing in a clean pair of sneakers or tennis balls.

2. Before dry cleaning repair tears, broken stitching and point out heavy stains or other problems to the cleaner.

• **SLEEPING BAGS,** *Arranging Them to Please All:* Often at slumber parties, cousin or grandma visits, when children bunk on the floor in sleeping bags, nobody wants to sleep on the "outside" and everyone wants to sleep in the middle or next to one child or other. The solution is simple—place the sleeping bags in a circle with all the pillows in the center so that the children and their sleeping bags are spokes on a wheel. Everyone is sleeping next to a "buddy" and can hear all conversations and all have plenty of foot room.

• **SLEEVE LENGTHS,** *For Men's Clothing:* Shirtsleeves should reach to the end of the wristbone. Jacket and coat sleeves should cover the tops of the wristbone.

• **SLIDES,** *Videotaping:* See VIDEOTAPING SLIDES.

• **SLIDING GLASS DOORS,** *Safety Marking:* If you are lucky enough to have a family that keeps these doors so clean people can't tell if they are open or closed, the Quick-Fix way to signal they're closed is to place a stick-on note at eye level. Permanent markers can be decals, stickers, auto window decals, or tub safety decals.

• **SLIP,** *Full-length Colored Slips $aver:* When you need a full-length slip to match a formal gown, buy a full-length nightie in the matching color, cut it off at the right length and hem. Nylon nighties are less costly than full-length colored slips.

• **SLIP,** *Storage:* If you hang slips on a skirt or trouser hanger, they won't be wrinkled and it's easier to tell the length when you have several of the same color.

• **SNAKE,** *Feeding:* If you can't stand to feed your pet snake live mice and other rodents, one reader says you can trick a snake into eating other meat if you get a little mouse, keep it in a separate cage, let it sniff and scramble all over the meat you'll feed the snake. The mouse scent gets on the meat and the snake will swallow it.

• **SNAPS,** *Repairing Those on Baby Clothes:* When they begin to pop open easily, hammer the point part of the snap once LIGHTLY. You'll flatten the snap enough to hold tightly to the other half.

- **SNEEZE STOPPER,** *Letter of Laughter:* A reader sent this rhyme she says helps her to stifle sneezes in crowded company:

    When you feel that warning tickle,
    And your nose begins to prickle—
    Open your mouth and take
    Two or three quick breaths to make
    That sneezy feeling disappear.
    I hope it works for you, my dear.
    But if you find it's not your day,
    That sneeze will come out anyway!

- **SOAP DISH:** Flat seashells make good soap dishes.

- **SOAP DISH,** *Avoiding Mess and Goo:* Put three rubber bands around the soap dish lengthwise. Rest the soap on the rubber bands and it will dry without the messy goo.

- **SOAPS,** *Decorative, Letters to Think About:* When a reader wrote for advice on preventing guests from using decorative soaps and towels, an overwhelming 94 percent of the responses from other readers agreed with my advice to just use them; they recalled cleaning out attic-fulls of new, "too good to use" things after loved ones had died. My mother also always advised using your decorative or "good" china, silver, linens (and fancy guest towels and soap), etc. She always said that if you don't use your "good" things, somebody else will after you're gone; you may as well enjoy them. One reader, who lost everything in a house fire now enjoys using everything and never cares if they get broken or "used up." Best Advice: "Carpe Diem" (Seize the Day)!

- **SOAP SLIVERS,** *$aver, Recycling to Make a Bar:* Tried and true is to moisten sliver and the new bar until they are sticky and press together, blending the edges. Let dry and you have a bigger new bar.

- **SOAP SLIVERS,** *Recycling to Make Liquid Soap:* Separate hand from deodorant soap; they don't mix well for this project.
1. Cut into slivers and soak overnight to soften (optional step).
2. Place all soap slivers into a blender with some hot water. Blend on "Grate" setting. Add more water to thin out the liquid to the consistency you prefer, and blend a bit more.

3. Pour the liquid into a pump-style soap bottle for bathroom or kitchen.

Note: The plus is that your blender gets a good washing, too!

• **SOCIAL SECURITY,** *Checking on Amounts Deposited:* Request a Statement of Earnings (Form SSA-7004) at any Social Security office or by calling 1-800-325-0778. Fill out the form, mail as directed, and in a few weeks you will receive a statement of the total wages or self-employment income credited to your earning record. If your records don't match theirs, contact your local Social Security office to get them corrected.

• **SOCKS,** *Making Non-skid Slipper Socks:* Draw stripes (or designs, or names of sock-owners) on the bottom of socks with a craft pen used to decorate T-shirts. The raised design will keep you off the skids. **Note,** Healthy Planet $aver: Don't waste paper. Buy red socks and substitute them for Christmas Wrap, then write gift recipient's name on the sock bottoms and insert the gift. (If there is just one gift, put the second sock inside with the gift.) Tie the sock shut with yarn or crinkle-tie.

• **SOCKS,** *Preventing Loss in Laundry:* Agitating socks sometimes flip over the edge of the basket and may be found between the drum and washer basket. Some find their way into the drain, believe it or not. Pin them together as they are removed so they will stay together through washer and dryer. *Letter of Laughter:* Here's an ode to socks you can give to family members as a reminder to pin 'em up or lose 'em.

> *Do your socks disappear when you wash 'em out clean?*
> *Does it seem that they're eaten by the washing machine?*
> *Then pin 'em together and this simple chore*
> *Will keep your socks mated forevermore.*
> *So from this day forth, no need to despair;*
> *Just reach in the drawer and pull out a pair.*

And, here's an odd socks story that's truly odd:

Annoyed at her youngest son's habit of tossing dirty socks under his bed and the number of odd socks in that day's wash, one mother marched angrily into her son's room, thrust her arm under his bed to feel around for the odd socks and . . . gasp! Her hand touched something definitely "odd." To her amazement and near heart failure, when her hand came out from under the bed it was holding the biggest black snake she'd ever seen! For a moment, her life passed before her eyes. Then, her eyes focused and she saw that the snake was plastic! Now when she has a load of odd socks, she just puts them into the drawer to wait for their mates.

- **SOCKS,** *Recycling Lonely Ones:*
1. Slip your glass of iced tea or canned beverage in a sock, roll the top down and you'll have dry hands and no puddles under the glass.
2. Keep an old sock in the car to wipe fog from your windshield, sticky fingers, an oily dip stick, and tie it to the steering wheel when fuel is low to remind you to get gas on the next trip.
3. Slip an old sock over a yardstick or ruler so that you can clean crevices such as beneath the fridge, washer or dryer.

- **SOCKS,** *Separating for Color-blind Men:* Men's navy blue, black, and dark brown socks tend to look all the same in a drawer even if you're not color-blind. It helps if you buy small plastic baskets and then put navy socks in a light blue basket, dark brown socks in a tan one, and black socks in a white one.

- **SOCK SORTING,** *Time-Saver:* Black and dark-navy sock colors and styles can look the same when you're matching them. Instead of pinning them in pairs or holding them together with a plastic hook, buy paint pens at a craft store. Match up the socks and label each pair of black socks with a letter and each pair of navy socks with a number. You'll find mates at a glance. If several family members have similar socks, write with different pen colors.

- **SOCK TOPS,** *Recycling:* Cut off the foot and use the cuffs.
1. To cover a crawling baby's knees. They add protection even when baby's wearing long pants.
2. To cover a gardener's knees, or to close up the opening at pants or sleeves cuffs so insects don't get in as easily.
3. Wear for leg or knee warmers.
4. Slip on cool drinks to keep your hands dry.
5. Sew on to child's jacket sleeve to lengthen it.
6. Put on over mitten tops and jacket sleeve bottoms to keep snow out of children's jacket sleeves.

- **SODA-POP FIZZ,** *Maintaining It in Two-Liter Bottles:* Put the cap on loosely, then squeeze the plastic bottle until the remaining liquid comes right up to the neck or as close as possible. Then, while holding it there, tighten the cap. With almost no air in the bottle the contents keep more of their fizz. This works except for the last few ounces.

- **SODA WATER,** *When Two- or Three-liter Bottles Go Flat, $aver:* Instead of discarding flat soda, pour it into ice cube trays and you'll have flavored cubes for your drinks that don't dilute!

- **SOFA,** *Shopping:* Measure the space for the sofa to make sure it will fit AND measure doorways that the sofa will go through. One couple had to return a sofa that just wouldn't fit through the doorway!

- **SOFA,** *Straying Sectionals:*
1. Hook sections together by attaching screen-door hooks to the underside frames. Attach the eye of the hook on the outside frame of one section and the hook on the outside frame of the adjoining section and then hook 'em up so you won't lose friends in the cracks.
2. Keep your sectional sofa from coming apart by using large metal hose clamps around the sections' legs.

- **SOFT-DRINK RATIONING FOR CHILDREN:** When children like bubbly soft drinks, provide nutrition by mixing fruit juice with club soda.

- **SOUP,** *Getting the Fat Out:* Instead of just storing the soup in the fridge so that the fat rises to the top and hardens so it's easier to lift off, put the soup in a container with a tight lid and turn it upside down when you put it in the fridge, then you can just pour the broth off the top.

- **SOUP,** *Quick-Fix When It's Too Hot (Especially for Children):* Put an ice cube in each bowl of soup and tell children to stir until it melts. The soup will cool and they will have something to do while they are waiting. (Children often lack patience when you interrupt their play for something so "irrelevant" as eating lunch!)

• **SOUP,** *Thickening:* Add instant mashed potatoes. Potatoes tend to take salt from dishes so check to see if more is needed after they are added.

• **SOUP CRACKERS (OYSTER CRACKERS):** Pour the tiny crackers into a well-washed and dried plastic quart- or gallon-size jug and put the lid on. You'll have airtight storage for retaining freshness and a handy pouring container, too.

• **SOUP STOCK SEASONING:** Make your own soup stock from left-over necks and backs of poultry (or bones cut off steaks and chops) and lots of herbs and seasonings. Then freeze the stock in cubes, store the cubes in a sealed bag, and you can toss a cube of stock into dishes you want to season. The bonus is that you can make it salt-free, low-fat if you have special diet needs.

• **SPACE-AGE SCHOOL DAZE,** *Letter of Laughter:* When a mother of a young son was explaining that he would ride the big kids' school bus when he went to his new school, the youngster said, "Mommy, I'll have to get up at six o'clock!"
"Why so early?" Mom asked.
"Because it takes a long time to get into those space suits!"

• **SPILLS,** *Quick-Fix Wipe-up, Healthy-Planet Recycling:* Place newspapers over spills and let them absorb the mess in a few minutes.

• **SPILLED MILK,** *Letter of Laughter:* A reader reminded me that when people used to say, "Don't cry over spilled milk," it didn't cost $2 a gallon.

• **SPAGHETTI STRAPS,** *Keeping Them on Hangers:* Cut foam padding which has adhesive on one side into narrow strips about two inches long. Stick the strips on the ends of the hanger where the straps would normally be placed. No more dresses on the closet floor!

• **SPEAKERS,** *Recycling:* Old stereo speakers are great magnets. When you finish a task that involves nails, you can drag them around and they will pick up what you've dropped. This is especially good when you've been nailing outdoors where nails in the grass could ruin a lawn mower blade.

• **SPECIAL OFFER PROOF OF PURCHASE:** Cut out the "proof of purchase" (UPC symbol, bar code) from empty food packages before throwing them out. Then write the name of the product on the back and save them in an envelope so you'll have them when special offers are made.

• **SPICE BOTTLES,** *Recycling Empty Ones:*
1. Fill with cinnamon sugar for toast.
2. Fill with dusting powder for a shaker.
3. Use as a toothpick holder.
4. Store glitter for crafts in it.
5. Put embroidery thread in it and feed through holes to prevent tangling.
6. Keep embroidery/needlepoint needles in it.
7. Fill with flour to sprinkle on meats before frying.

• **SPICES,** *Storage & Determining Age/Usefulness:* Spices don't spoil but they do lose potency over time. If they don't have full aroma, toss them out.
1. Store in cupboard or rack away from stove, oven, and sunny windows.
2. When adding to food, avoid allowing the upside down spice container to absorb heat and moisture from cooking food—measure into a spoon or your hand. Spice cans won't get messy, hard-to-close powder-caked tops with this method.

• **SPLINTER REMOVAL,** *Quick-Fix:* Apply a thin layer of white glue over the splinter, spread it around the area and let it dry. Then peel off the glue and out comes the splinter.

• **SPOON REST NEAR A RANGE,** *Recycling:* I get lots of hints for spoon rests but since you can put a spoon on anything, why not avoid counter clutter and rest a stirring spoon on the dishwashing sponge or cloth, or a paper towel that's only wiped one pair of clean hands?

• **SPOTS AND STAINS,** Please see the special section on page 398.

• **SPRAY CLEANERS,** *Using It All:* Get out the last two inches in the spray bottle by dropping in some marbles to raise the liquid level back to where the spray pump works.

• **SPRAY NOZZLES,** *Preventing Clogs:* After using hair spray, spray starch, or other aerosol cans or pump-spray containers, remove the sprayer and run clear water through it so that it's clog-free and ready when you need it the next time.

• **SPRAY SCENTS,** *Letter of Laughter:* A young reader wrote that her grandmother came home from the hairdresser with a new permanent and then went into the bathroom to spray her hair to keep it neat. Then she noticed a funny smell in the bathroom. As she reached to pick up the hair spray to return it to the cupboard she noticed it was pine air freshener. She smelled like piney woods all day!

• **SQUASH, SUMMER,** *Selection and Storage:* Summer squash is harvested before full maturity and while the rind and seeds are still tender and edible and its flesh is tender and string-free. Select smaller and firm squashes; if either end is soft or if the squash is rubbery, it's old; don't buy it. The most popular summer squashes are green zucchini, straight- and crook-neck yellows and flat, discus-shaped white squash. Store in the refrigerator.

• **SQUASH, WINTER,** *Selection and Storage:* Most winter squash have hard rinds (avoid those with soft spots on the rind) and may be kept for three to six months in a cool dry place, but not in the refrigerator unless cut. The most common winter squashes are: acorn (dark green or orange and green and shaped like an acorn—what else?); buttercup (oval and dark green with whitish stripes); turban (brightly colored with rounded lumps on one end); butternut (long, tubular and creamy brown in color); hubbard, one of the largest squashes, (bumpy all over and in various colors); spaghetti (smooth yellow outside and stringy spaghetti-textured inside).

• **SQUEAKS,** *Stopping:* Petroleum jelly applied to moving parts may help. It's safe around pets so you can use it on that squeaky exercise wheel in your hamster or gerbil cage.

• **STAINLESS STEEL,** *Removing Water Spots:* Rub area with clean, soft cloth dampened with white vinegar. Wipe dry to avoid spots.

• **STARCH,** *Homestyle Sugar Starch:* When regular spray starch won't hold up frail fabrics, try the old-fashioned method great-grandma used for her lacy doilies.

1. Mix ¼ cup water and ¾ cup sugar in a small pan. Stir the mixture over low heat (don't boil) until clear, not sugary. Shut off and let cool.

2. Wet the collar and cuffs of a blouse (or lacy doily); roll in a towel to remove excess moisture and dip it into the mixture. Squeeze out excess starch, then shape the collar and cuffs. (People used to dry small round crocheted lace doilies over a bowl after starching this way; you get a lace-bowl.)

3. Allow to dry and iron on a warm setting. (Lace doilies don't need ironing when you use this starch, just smooth out and shape while wet on a clean flat surface.)

• **STARCHING IN A WASHER:** Although this sounds like a good idea, my sources tell me that few people have enough items to warrant filling a machine to starch them and it's no longer advised. The main problem is that you can't mix colors or colors with whites in a machine starch load because even garments with colorfast labels tend to "bleed" in a starch load. Most people use spray starch these days.

• **STATIC CLING,** *Quick-Fix:* When your slip and skirt have a life of their own and it's embarrassing you, rub a little hand lotion on your hands and then rub your hands over your slip.

• **STEAM IRON CLOGS,** *Homestyle Remedy:* Commercial cleaners are available but you can try white vinegar. Fill the iron with white vinegar, let it steam about five minutes, then disconnect the iron and let it sit for a while. Empty the vinegar and rinse the iron well several times. You may need to poke a toothpick in the steam holes to get gunk out of a badly clogged iron. **Hint:** To avoid the problem, clean your iron regularly and always pour out non-purified water when you finish ironing.

• **STICKER FUN FOR CHILDREN:** Have children put stickers on waxed paper then they can be repositioned many times before the child decides how to stick them permanently in a scrap book.

• **STICKERS,** *Removal:*
1. Remove stickers and sticky residue from wood paneling by rubbing with mineral oil on a cloth or paper towel. Let oil set a while and repeat if necessary.

2. Remove sticky residue from labels with pre-wash spray. Apply, let set, rub off with nylon scrubber.
3. Remove bumper stickers with spray lubricant, following the instructions in Method 2.

• **STICKY RESIDUE,** *General Hints for Removal:* Gummed labels or price tags, children's stickers, bathtub appliques, and similar things often leave a stubborn residue. The remedy is to remove what you can and spray with petroleum-based pre-wash spray or you can spray some labels with the spray without removing any pieces. Allow spray to remain for a while to soften and then scrub off with a plastic scrubber. You can use this on most surfaces, including appliances. **Note:** Acetone (or acetone-based fingernail polish) will remove sticky residue from glass and some surfaces but may also damage some other surfaces and fabrics—it'll also take your nail polish off!

• **STORAGE,** *Finding Space in a Small Apartment:*
1. Store seldom used items in empty suitcases.
2. Stash boxes under the bed.
3. Fold winter blankets and store them between the mattress and box spring.
4. Buy a large plastic garbage can, fill it with stored items, invert the lid and top it off with a round piece of plywood. Cover with a tablecloth and you have a lamp table/storage unit for any room.
5. Put shoes in shoe bags to free the closet floor for other things.
6. Stack storage boxes or add shelves to closet shelves.
7. Have a system of making a proper place for everything and to put everything back in its place; clutter takes up space.

• **STORAGE,** *Organizing:* If you just can't throw it out, store it so that you can get at it when you will use it—whatever it is! Check out closet/storage shops, hardware and discount stores, department store home furnishing sections; you'll find an infinite number of easy-to-install shelves, rods, etc. that will make storage more convenient without major expensive building-in. Many install without tools; others need only a screwdriver, pliers and minimum skill.

• **STORAGE,** *Time-Saver:* Color-code books, records, video tapes with colored stick-on dots according to categories so that you don't have to shuffle through them each time you search for something.

Books can be coded according to fiction, biography, etc.; records according to jazz, country and western, etc.; video tapes according to comedy, drama, homemade family films, home-taped favorite shows or movies.

• **STORYTIME,** *When Mom and Dad Have No Time:* Record children's favorite stories on cassette tapes, using a cooking-timer bell as the chime telling them to turn to the next page. They may not have Mom's or Dad's lap, but they will have the familiar voice reading to them.

• **STOVE,** *Keeping Kitchen Stoves Clean, Letter of Laughter:* A Heloise fan sent this hint for keeping a stove clean: Just don't use it! I like that!

• **STOVE STORY,** *Letter of Laughter:* A reader who always removed all stove knobs when her young grandchild came to visit as a safety measure wrote that one day, when she forgot to do it her grandson went straight to the stove, pulled all the knobs off and brought them to her, saying "Memaw, you forgot to take the knobs off."

• **STRAWBERRIES,** *Quick-Fix Slicing:* After pinching off the green "hat" of the strawberry with a metal gadget made for this purpose, slice it with an egg slicer. No stains on your fingers and uniform slices, too!

• **STREET-MAP DIRECTIONS,** *For Out-of-Town or Other Guests:* Copy your neighborhood's section of your city map or the page of a street map book that has your area. (These books can often be found in the public library.) Then highlight the best routes to your house. If the map print is very small, you can enlarge the section around your house with some copy machines to make it easier to see.

• **STUFFED ANIMALS,** *Washing:* First of all, keep labels and tags so you'll have complete care instructions.
1. If the animal is washable but the stuffing is not, make a small opening in a seam and remove filler before washing by hand if the animal is irreplaceable or by machine if you can risk it. Dry on regular cycle or fluff in dryer before air-drying. Then restuff and sew up the seam.

2. If the animal is not washable, sprinkle liberally with cornstarch; brush with good stiff brush to remove dirt.

• **STUFFED PEPPERS,** *Keeping the Stuffing in While They Cook:* Bake them in a well-greased muffin tin; the peppers stay upright and look more appetizing when served.

• **STUFFING,** *Removing from Turkey, Chicken; Time-saver:* Before stuffing the bird, line the cavity (also the breast cavity of a turkey) with cheesecloth, being careful to leave a generous amount outside to be tucked in after the dressing is inside. Pack dressing loosely; it swells during cooking. You can then remove a sack of stuffing, with none left behind and the flavor remains the same.

• **SUDS OVERFLOW IN LAUNDRY:** Sprinkle salt on soap suds so suds swells subside. (Then say that sentence fast five times before you scold the person who put too much detergent in the machine . . . even if the culprit is you.)

• **SUGAR,** *Coloring:* Add a few drops of food coloring to a cup of granulated sugar in a glass bowl. Mix well until the coloring is distributed evenly. Darken color by adding a drop or two more of the food coloring. Let dry and store in a sprinkle-top bottle for decorating cookies and cakes.

• **SUGAR,** *Softening Brown Sugar:*
1. In a microwave safe container, microwave for a minute or so to soften.
2. Place a slice of fresh bread or piece of fresh apple into the sugar canister or box, seal, and it will soften after a while. *Letter of Laughter:* A reader wrote that when she told a young bride to "put the sugar in a container with a tight-fitting lid and put a slice of bread on top," the bride said it didn't work. When the reader visited the bride, she saw why. The sugar was in the canister and a piece of bread was lying on top of the tightly closed jar.
It's not only what you say, it's how you say it!

• **SUGAR,** *Storage, Recycling:* An empty, clean, plastic milk jug keeps sugar from attracting bugs, from getting hard and lumpy, is easier to handle than a bag, lets you see how much is left, and, best of all, is free for the recycling!

• **SUN-BLOCK FORMULA:** For best protection, you need a good sun block with a sun-protection factor (SPF) suitable for your skin. SPF numbers are based on the time it takes unprotected skin to turn pink. The highest number is the greatest protection. Read labels for your type of skin.

• **SUN-BLOCK LOTION,** *Applying When Nobody Nice Can Help You:* Apply to your back or other unreachable spots with a sponge-type dishwashing mop having a long handle.

• **SUPERMARKET,** *Product-Dating Terms:* Check dates on all items to get the most for your money.
1. Expiration Date—The last day the item should be used or eaten.
2. Freshness Date—Stamped on the item by the manufacturer to tell how long freshness is guaranteed; if the item is stale before that date, manufacturers usually refund your money.
3. Pack Date—Date the product was packaged or processed by the manufacturer. It does not tell how long the food will stay good, but only when it was processed.
4. Sell or Pull Date—The last day an item should be sold; after this date it should be removed from the grocery shelf.

• **SUPERMARKET PRICE MARKING,** *When Your Market Has Scanners:* Who can remember the price of each item? As you put away groceries at home, find each item's price on the register tape and mark it on the container. Then you'll have some way to compare regular prices to weekly specials advertised in the newspaper. It may be too much trouble to do this with everything but would help on frequently purchased foods.

• **SUPERMARKET SHOPPING,** *Healthy-Planet Style:*
1. Avoid products with excess packaging and look for those in recyclable packaging.
2. Take a few minutes to mail wasteful packages back to the manufacturer with a note explaining that as much as you like the product, you will quit buying it if it continues to be over-packaged. Manufacturers listen when money talks.
3. Do recycle all packaging materials that you can. Many supermarkets collect plastic and paper bags, bottles, etc. and many cities

have recycling programs but nobody can come into a consumer's home to get recyclables! You have to sort and deliver!

4. If you don't know what's being recycled in your area, look under "recycling" in the Yellow Pages or call your state's recycling coordinator or the Environmental Defense Fund, 800-225-5333.

5. Take your own bag to the supermarket to reduce the number of bags you take home. Or, collect supermarket bags and take them to the store for reuse with your food.

6. Recycle grocery bags you do take home so that you don't have to actually buy bags. Plastic bags are good for garbage, storage, and all sorts of uses. Paper bags hold newspapers for recycling, absorb grease from fried foods, can be "racks" for cooling cookies, and on and on.

7. As this book is being written, the new "degradable" plastics are considered a waste of money and the Center for Science in the Public Interest is calling for a boycott. Degradable plastic usually ends up in landfills anyway where the landfill's design minimizes the rate at which they degrade. Also, degradable plastics have hindered plastic recycling because some recyclers have quit recycling bags; they say degradable bags get mixed in with the others and cause problems.

8. Wrap your lunch in a reusable container with a lid to avoid disposable products altogether. Reuse yogurt and margarine containers for soft foods. Margarine tubs, which are made from high-density polyethylene, are being recycled in some parts of the country but nobody recycles yogurt containers which are polystyrene or polypropylene.

9. Although aluminum foil is the only sandwich wrap that's recyclable, if you are just going to use the foil once and throw it out, it's better to use something else. The process by which we make aluminum is harmful to the environment.

10. Use a thermos for lunch juices instead of aseptic containers which are made from multi-layers of paper and other products and can't be recycled.

11. Buy canned juice concentrate instead of juice in polyethylene jugs which just use a lot of packaging for extra water that you can add to concentrate at home in a pitcher.

12. If you recycle the jugs, it's better to buy milk in polyethylene jugs than in cartons which are made of paperboard coated with

polyethylene; it's too costly to separate the coating from the carton paper and so these are not recycled.

13. When buying vegetables, look for the most food in the least packaging: A pound of peas in a plastic bag generates less waste than two 8-oz. boxes of peas that have paper wrappers since both types of packaging will end up in a landfill. Buy canned vegetables if you can recycle the cans and don't mind the extra sodium and fewer vitamins in canned veggies.

14. Avoid packaged microwaveable foods in which special bags or separate trays or dishes are used for cooking; these are just marketing gimmicks. If you use these quickie products, look for those where you can serve right out of the package.

15. When you buy eggs, instead of polystyrene cartons, look for molded pulp cartons which are usually made from 100-percent recycled paper.

16. Recycled paper cereal and other boxes are usually grey or tan inside and some have the "Recycled" logo on the outside; non-recycled boxes are white inside.

• SWEATERS, *"Pills":* Gently and carefully remove "pills" with a tiny scissors or a commercial sweater shaver. Always brush or shave gently to avoid damaging the area around the "pill."

• SWEATERS, *Recycling:*
1. Make mittens by tracing an old one on paper or putting it on the bottom of an old sweater. The bottom is a ready-made cuff. Cut and sew around the "hand" shape, double-stitching for extra security.
2. Make leg warmers from sweater sleeves.
3. Save buttons from cardigan sweaters for recycling.

• SWEATERS, *Shrinkage:* Before buying a sweater, check the label for shrinkage potential and if there is no such information, assume the sweater will shrink at least one size. Threads get stretched during the knitting process and that's why knit clothes shrink more than woven ones. Even some synthetics shrink one size like cotton, wool and rayon do.

• SWEATERS, *Snags:* Never cut or tug snags. Try to pull the snag to the underside with a large sewing needle or crochet hook working from the inside of the garment. If the yarn is broken, try to fasten the broken ends on the inside of the sweater with a needle and transparent thread, which you can also use to close up a hole from the inside.

• **SWEATERS,** *Storage:* Most knits are best folded for flat storage because hanging on hangers stretches them out of shape. If you wish to hang them, drape them over a cardboard tube-type hanger, like those cleaners use for pants, or slit a tube from gift wrap to cover the hanger; you'll avoid creases. (If the cardboard tube is slippery, you can wrap it with old panty hose to provide some friction.)

• **SWEET SUBSTITUTES:**
1. You can't substitute corn syrup or honey for baking because sugar is a dry ingredient—it adds bulk as well as sweetness.
2. If you substitute corn syrup for honey, you'll need to add a bit more because it isn't as sweet as honey.
3. If you have to limit your sugar intake, try to substitute other flavorings instead of adding sugar. For example, add cinnamon, vanilla, or other extracts to your coffee; add vanilla or fruit (dried or fresh) to plain non-fat yogurt; sprinkle cinnamon on baked apple or in applesauce; sprinkle pumpkin pie spice mixture on sweet potatoes with a sprinkle of butter substitute; add chopped dried fruit to your cereal.

• **SWIMMER'S EAR:** Getting too much water in the ear canal can make ears susceptible to infection. To avoid spoiling summer fun and vacations with ear infection pain, never swim in polluted lakes or rivers and, if you swim frequently, very gently dry the outer areas of the ear. Use one or two drops of rubbing alcohol and vinegar mixed together in the ear to help dry the canal. **Caution:** Don't scratch inside the ear and, if you should get an infection, ask your doctor for advice on how to protect your ear while bathing or showering until the infection is cleared up.

T

- **TABLECLOTH,** *Keeping It on Outdoor Tables by Weighting Corners:* Sew pockets on the corners to hold small rocks or just knot a rock into each corner.

- **TABLECLOTH,** *Padding Beneath:* The good section of an old mattress pad makes good padding and protection but you'll still need to put a hot mat beneath oven dishes.

- **TABLECLOTH,** *Preventing Stains:* When the cloth is clean or brand new, spray it several times with soil-repellent spray—tough stains won't set in.

- **TABLECLOTH,** *Removing Wrinkles from a Flannel-Backed Vinyl:*
1. Put the tablecloth in the dryer with a couple of damp towels, set dryer on the lowest setting. Then check the tablecloth frequently until all wrinkles are removed. Allow to lay flat for cooling to avoid more wrinkles.
2. You can remove wrinkles by ironing at a warm setting with a steam iron on the flannel side—never the vinyl side.

- **TABLECLOTH,** *Securing When a Toddler Is in the House:*
1. Even a flannel-backed tablecloth will slip when a toddler pulls on it. Crisscross a pair of suspenders under the table and secure

them to the underside edges of the tablecloth. Make the tablecloth fit snugly by adjusting the tabs on the suspenders.

2. If the table separates to allow leaf insertion, pull apart, tuck the tablecloth into the crevice, close and the cloth is secure. Anyone who understands life with a toddler will excuse the crease across the tablecloth!

• **TABLECLOTH,** *Warning About Plastic or Foam-Backed Plastic:* Laying plain plastic or foam-backed plastic tablecloths directly on a wood-finish table can result in the plastic or foam sticking to the finish and the only solution may be to refinish the furniture. You can try removing stuck-on foam with a plastic scrubbie or nylon net and vegetable oil. Picking up plastic sheeting that has been on the table for a while can just pull up sections of varnish on some pieces.

• **TABLECLOTH STORAGE,** *Time-Saver:* Whether you hang your tablecloths on a hanger or fold them and store in a linen closet, save yourself aggravation—safety-pin a small piece of paper to each cloth giving its dimensions and the size of table it fits (one or two leaves or none).

• **TABLE EXTENSION,** *When You Need More Space:* Place a thick pad on the table and then on top, place a piece of plywood, four feet by eight feet long; pad again and cover with a tablecloth. You will be able to seat 10 or more people. Store the plywood under the bed in between dinner parties.

• **TAXES,** *Checklist of Six Common Mistakes to Avoid:*
1. Overwitholding: If you claim fewer exemptions on your Form W-4 than you're entitled to, you'll get a tax refund but, according to the experts, you will have been giving the IRS an interest-free loan of money that could have been in YOUR account earning YOU interest.
2. Underwitholding: If you claim too many exemptions on your Form W-4 or fail to pay estimated taxes, the IRS will impose a penalty. If you think you'll have income increases in 1991, recalculate your W-4 or estimated tax payments.
3. Not Keeping an Eye on Your Tax Bracket: There's a big gap between the rates of 15 and 28 percent so you must be alert when dealing with your investments. For example, if your joint taxable income in 1991 will be $32,450, the tax rate is 15 percent, but if you

sell investments which have increased in value by $5,000, that amount of gain will be taxed at 28 percent or $1,400. If the gain is taxed only at 15 percent, the amount would be only $750.

4. Not timing capital losses/gains. If you think you will take a capital gain, then you need to consider selling a losing investment to offset the gain. You can use as much as $3,000 in capital losses to offset ordinary income and if the loss is greater than $3,000, the excess can be carried forward to future years.

5. Incorrectly calculating mutual funds gains: Keep all customer confirmation and account records because when you sell shares, part of the profit may include dividends and distributions you have already paid taxes on.

6. Mixing deductible and non-deductible IRAs: To avoid paying taxes on the same money twice, you must keep careful records of deductible and non-deductible IRA contributions. Then, when you begin to withdraw the money, you can prove to the IRS what percentage of your savings comes from non-deductible contributions.

• **TAX FILING,** *Checklist:* Brokerage confirmations and statements, cancelled checks and checkbook registers, receipts for charitable contributions and deductible expenses receipt, property-tax receipts and records of interest paid on your mortgage, 1099 forms (dividends and interest income) and W-2 forms.

• **TEA,** *Brewing in Coffee Maker:*
1. For a Mug: Drop a tea bag into the basket and add 2 cups of water, then brew like coffee.
2. For a Pot: Measure the amount of water needed into the coffee-maker tank, put the appropriate number of tea bags in the carafe, turn it on, and presto—hot tea. You can make iced tea with the leftovers. **Note:** Let the bags steep for at least 3 to 5 minutes for fullest flavor.
3. For a Pot: If you prefer loose tea, sprinkle tea leaves into a coffee filter in the brewing basket as you would ground coffee. Try the same amount of cut tea leaves that you would brew in a tea pot or experiment to get the perfect amount for strength and flavor.

• **TEA,** *Spicing-up Iced Tea:* Mix one-half teaspoon ground cinnamon and one cup of orange juice. Pour the liquid into an ice cube tray and freeze. Add a cube to your glass of iced tea. Delicious!

• **TEA,** *Zinger:* Stir your tea, herbal or other, with a cinnamon stick. It can be reused for numerous cups of yummy lightly spiced tea.

• **TEA BAG,** *Avoid "Fishing" in Hot Tea:*
1. Wrap the tag around the pot or cup handle.
2. Cut an L-shaped slit in the tag, starting at the bottom edge and then when you make a cup of tea, open the slit and hook the tag on the cup lip.

• **TEA BALL:** Put peppercorns, bay leaf and other whole spices in a tea ball so that you don't have to fish them out of soup or stew to avoid biting into them. **Caution:** Bay leaf (whole or in pieces) is a special hazard because it can cause choking if it gets stuck in the throat.

• **TEACHER'S AIDE:** One teacher/reader carries her own supplies, such as pens, pencils and scissors, from one class room to another in a spoon caddy instead of relying on each room's desk to be fully equipped with whatever she needs.

• **TEAPOT,** *Healthy Planet, Removing Mineral Deposits:* Fill the teapot with full-strength vinegar, let it boil a few minutes and let the pot sit overnight. If the mineral deposit film is very thick, you may need to soak it for a couple of nights. In the morning, wash and rinse the pot. Avoid excess hard-water buildup with regular cleanings.

• **TELEPHONE, CELLULAR,** *Checklist for Safety Features to Look for When You Buy and Safe Use:* The safest phone is one with the fewest distractions when dialing, talking or answering. Buy one that lets you keep both hands on the wheel and your eyes on the road without having to hold on to a receiver or tuck it between your head and shoulder.
1. A speakerphone with voice command that can be programmed to recognize two voices and up to ten commands per voice is a best choice. A push of a button and a simple voice command will have the phone automatically access the cellular network and dial the correct phone number.

2. Speed dialing means only having to push a one- or two-digit code to have the cellular phone automatically dial a complete, pre-entered phone number.

3. Get a demonstration from the sales representative and become familiar with all the phone's features before you buy.

4. The safest time to dial a phone number on your car phone is when you are completely stopped at a red light or stop sign.

5. If you don't have a speakerphone and you must talk and drive at the same time, move into the far right-hand lane so that you can pull off the road if need be to complete a call.

• **TELEPHONE DIRECTORY,** *Lighten It Up:* Sometimes people with arthritis or hand disabilities have problems handling big thick phone books when their cities don't separate white and yellow pages into two books.

1. Carefully cut apart the white and yellow pages with a sharp knife. Reinforce the spines of both sections with heavy duty plastic tape like that used to seal cartons.

2. Either tape the back and front pages from last year's directory to the coverless sides of the new half-books or make covers from halves of a manila folder.

• **TELEPHONE DIRECTORY,** *Time-Saver:* When you find the number you've searched for in the phone book, highlight it so that it's easier to spot the next time you need it.

• **TELEPHONE MOUTHPIECE,** *Yuck Removal:* A moist towelette will wipe an earpiece and mouthpiece clean with a whisk.

• **TELEPHONE NUMBERS,** *Directory for People with Limited Vision:* Big push button phones help elderly or visually impaired people dial phones, but phone books are a challenge. Make a phone book with a looseleaf notebook filled with unlined note paper. Turn the pages sideways and, with a broad, black (or red for some people) marker pen, print names in large block letters with numbers beneath.

• **TELEPHONE PAD AND PENCIL,** *Time-Saver:* Stick a pen or pencil to the side of your telephone with self-gripping "dots"; remove several stick-on notes from the pad and stick them on the front of the phone (just a few, too many will be too heavy to stick). You'll always have paper and pencil ready for messages and recording information.

• **TELEVISION,** *Before You Call for Service:* Some newer sets have a "reset button" which should be checked if the TV has gone out due to a circuit breaker being tripped by a current surge. If pressing the button twice doesn't get the set on, then call for service. As with all appliances, always refer to the troubleshooting section of your manual before calling for service.

• **TELEVISION CHANNEL SELECTION:** When cable brings you forty or so selections and it's a bother to remember all the numbers, clip the list of stations and channels from your cable guide and tape it to the back of the remote control. You'll always have the right numbers in hand!

• **TELEVISION REMOTE CONTROL:** Prevent it from getting gooey or spilled on by keeping it sealed in a plastic zipper bag.

• **TELEVISION VIEWING CONTROL,** *Letter of Laughter:* A reader of my "Just For Kids" Sunday hints columns found a way to get her thirteen-year-old brother out of the TV room so that she could get to watch shows she wanted. Her hint: Get something good to eat and tell him he will have to get his own. As soon as he leaves, switch on your show. All I can say is "Out of the mouths of babes . . ."

• **TERMITES,** *Prevention:* Termites build little dirt tunnels to travel from one place to another and are always looking for water. If you find termites or their tunnels, destroy the tunnels.
1. Shrubs, fences, trellises, stacked firewood, wooden decks that touch the house and the ground at the same time all provide traveling routes for termites from the ground to your house.
2. Because termites seek water, keep water away from the house. Make sure all gutters drain away from the foundation and repair all plumbing leaks right away. Don't place wooden planters against the house. They are a double invitation to the termites—wood and water!
3. If you see any evidence of termites such as their tunnels, damaged wood steps, porches or decks (Other insects eat wood, too!), or fine powder beneath wood furniture, holes along stud lines of

your walls, or the termites themselves, call a professional exterminator. You won't save money ignoring them and their damage can
be very serious, especially if they eat their way into the supporting
structure of your house.

• **TERRARIUM,** *Watering:* An ordinary basting bulb syringe will
help you get the right amount of water into a terrarium, especially
a bottle-necked one, without disturbing plants or messing up the
sides.

• **TERRY-CLOTH TOWELS,** *Recycling:*
1. When the middles are worn and the ends still thick, make potholders from the ends either by cutting circles and sewing them
together or making long rectangular "casserole" potholders.
2. Make baby bibs from the good parts.
3. Roll lengthwise and place on windowsills, door thresholds to
block drafts and blot condensed moisture.
4. Old terry cloth is great for polishing engraved or patterned silver
or brass. Put the polish on with an old sock and buff with an old
towel, then pitch it all if you don't want to wash rags.

• **TISSUE BOXES,** *Recycling for One More Time:*
1. Place an empty tissue box near the dryer to hold used dryer
sheets and then toss box and all away when it's full. (But don't
throw away used foam dryer sheets; they can stuff pillows, children's plush toys and cloth dolls, craft soft sculptures, etc.)
2. Square designer tissue boxes make good holders for cotton balls
near your makeup area.
3. Store knee-hi stockings in a square designer tissue box—just put
singles of the same color together and you have a dispenser!

• **TISSUES,** *Keeping Facial Tissues Dry on Bathroom Vanity Counters:* When you buy a new box, turn it upside down and stick a
bulletin-board push pin in each bottom corner so that it has "feet"
to keep it above water spills.

• **TISSUE-TOWELS,** *Healthy-Planet $aver:* Attach a toilet-paper
holder to the inside of a kitchen cabinet under the sink and buy the
least expensive tissue to hang there. Then you can save your paper
towels for major wipe-ups and blot up most spills with less expensive, more environmentally kind paper. It's handy for nose-wiping,
too—why waste a whole tissue for each sniffle?

- **THANKSGIVING TREE:** If your family can get together at Thanksgiving but not for Christmas, have a Thanksgiving tree. "Plant" a medium size tree branch in a coffee can weighted with rocks and sand and then put the can into a nice basket. Decorate the tree with bows, fall leaves and other Thanksgiving motif ornaments. Put presents under the tree and have Christmas in November!

- **THANK-YOU NOTES:** Include a picture of the item in use, or the clothing being worn, for a personal touch when you send thank-you notes. I like to send pictures of flowers sent to me by friends so that they can see how they look.

- **THERMOMETER,** *Letter of Laughter:* Families that laugh together make life fun. Young children like silly talk and it helps them develop a sense of humor as they grow up.
Child (who has just come home from school): The nurse took my temperature.
Mom: Did you tell the principal and get it back?

- **THIMBLE,** *Substitute:* Cut a finger off a rubber glove the length of your finger; the end of your finger won't get sore when you do needlework or hand-sewing and you'll have a better grip on the needle if it gets stuck in thick fabric.

- **THREAD SPOOLS,** *Recycling:*
1. String them on a cord for a young child's "necklace" toy.
2. Press cookie-dough balls with the ends of clean, empty spools to imprint a nice pattern.

- **THROW,** *Quick-Fix Comfy:* When you need a throw to keep cozy while napping, try snuggling under your robe if it's full length—but switch ends so that the "shoulders" are covering your feet and the lower robe portion is over your upper body where you need more "snuggle."

- **THUNDER,** *Fear of:* Help a fearful child or pet get used to the sound of thunder: Get a recording of thunder sounds from a record store and play it every other day or so, starting first with very low volume and gradually increasing the volume a little at a time. With a very small child, explain that the noise won't hurt and is far, far away and explain thunder to older children at their learning level. Books about thunder will help.

• **TIRES,** *Recycling Old Ones:* You can paint them or not.
1. Fill with sand to make a small child's sandbox or, if you can get a tractor tire, a larger sandbox.
2. Fill with potting soil for a planter. If you have four, build a pyramid planter with three on the bottom and one top and center. (Place pegboard piece inside the top tire to keep soil in.)
3. Stand at the back of the garage to be a "bumper" for your car.
4. Fill with cement and insert a pipe in the center to hold a pole for tether ball, basket ball, a mailbox stand, temporary small flag pole, etc.
5. Collect them from friends and neighbors and they can be steps on a sloping hillside. Dig into the hillside far enough to lay the tires flat, slightly overlapping each one. Fill them with sand and soil and plant native plants in them. Not only will the hillside look pretty, you'll keep the soil from running off in the rain.

• **TODDLER,** *Recognizing Sounds, Letter of Laughter:* A young mother wrote to say, "Did you know that to a mommy of a one-year-old, dry cat food being poured all over the floor sounds just like a play necklace being shaken in a play coffeepot?"

• **TODDLER TUNNEL,** *Homemade, Recycling:* Tear off the flaps of four large cardboard boxes and duct tape the boxes together to form a tunnel. Let the children decorate the outside with brightly colored paints and designs and use their imaginations playing games in their tunnel.

• **TOILET, LIME DEPOSITS,** *Healthy-Planet Removing:* Pour full-strength white vinegar in the bowl, let sit for several hours and brush away. If that doesn't work, pour a bucket of water quickly into the bowl to empty it, then cover the lime marks with paper towels soaked in vinegar. Let stand for several hours and scrub with sturdy brush or plastic scrubbie. **Caution:** Don't flush the paper towels down the toilet; toss them in the trash. Towel-strength paper can clog sewer or septic tank lines.

• **TOILET TANK,** *Healthy-Planet Water Conservation:* Raise the water level in the tank to use less water per flush with a quart-jar or plastic bag filled with water. Be sure that the water-savers are placed so that they don't interfere with the flush mechanism. **Note:**

People used to recommend a brick for this hint but bricks tend to crumble and damage the toilet's working mechanism.

• **TOILET TANK,** *Test for Leaks:* My husband, who is a plumber, recommends this test: Add some food coloring to the commode tank—green or blue is best. Do not flush the commode for an hour, then check to see if any coloring has seeped into the toilet bowl. If so, you need to replace the tank ball.

• **TOILET TISSUE,** *Tricking an Enthused Toddler:* Sometimes a newly pottie-trained toddler will unfurl most of a roll just for fun. One mom found the solution—after placing the roll on the roller, squeeze it until the inner cardboard roll is bent. This prevents a child from unrolling the whole roll at once.

• **TOMATO SAUCE,** *Substitute:* Add your favorite spices to undiluted canned tomato soup and go on with the recipe.

• **TOOLS,** *Recycling, Rust-proof Storage:* Mix some used motor oil with sand in a pail and then poke garden tools into the pail when they aren't being used. The bonus is that the sand automatically cleans them while the oil protects against rust, and you'll have all your tools in one bucket.

• **TOOTHBRUSH HOLDERS,** *for Travel:* Keep lipstick, eye shadow and eye- or lip-liner pencils in plastic travel toothbrush holders and you won't loose them when you travel or keep them in your purse for repairs. Get different colored holders for eye pencils and lip pencils so you don't have to open them each time.

• **TOOTHBRUSHES,** *Identifying Your Own in a Large Family:* A mother of seven children wrote that she solved the confusion by giving each of the boys different colored brushes (always the same color); all of the girls get the same color brush but personalize their brushes with leftover-lonely pierced earrings attached at the end hole.

• **TOOTHBRUSHES,** *Recycling Old Ones:* Bacteria can multiply in old toothbrushes and if bristles are bent or scraggly they don't clean properly and may cut your gums. Change toothbrushes about every three to six months. After a good rinse, old toothbrushes will clean nooks and crevices in furniture and appliances; apply shoe polish;

scrub stains on laundry before washing; clean a garlic press, graters, and other kitchen utensils; clean jewelry.

• **TOOTHBRUSHING SERENADE,** *When Children Rush and Brush:* One parent made a game of toothbrushing by putting a music box on the bathroom counter and having her child brush until the music stopped. Instead of rushing, the child enjoyed brushing.

• **TOOTH FAIRY TALES,** *Letter of Laughter:* When his six-year-old son lost his tooth while brushing and it went down the drain, dad consoled him and assured him that the Tooth Fairy was "magic," would find the tooth, and would still leave him something even if he didn't put the tooth under his pillow that night. The next morning, the boy came down to breakfast downcast and said, "Well, the tooth fairy did find the tooth but I told you she was going to be mad because she had to hunt for it. The last time I lost a tooth, she left me a dollar bill. Last night she only left fifty cents!"

• **TOOTH FAIRY MAGIC COIN:** Make a magic quarter for the tooth fairy to leave for a child who's lost a tooth. Spray the coin with hair spray and sprinkle it with gold glitter.

• **TOOTHPASTE TUBES,** *Keeping Plastic Ones Rolled-up:* Try holding the roll with a snack bag clip, a clothespin or clothespin-type hair barrette.

• **TOWELS,** *Identifying Houseguest's Towels:* When you have a hide-away cabin, your friends and relatives usually end up hiding away with you. Keeping track of whose towel is whose gets to be a problem, especially if swimming is involved. Write the names of guests on wooden spring clothespins with a pencil and ask them to clip the pins to their washcloths and towels. They can hang their towels outdoors to dry between swims with the same ID clothes-pins. You can erase the names after they leave so that there's space for the next arrivals' names. If you feel "crafty" you can decorate the clothespins with flowers and bows, too.

• **TOWELS,** *Removing Stiffness:* Usually it's due to detergent buildup or overloading the washer. Avoid the problem by using less detergent, hotter water and fewer towels per wash load. Remove detergent buildup by washing towels in very hot water with baking soda, borax or washing soda, then add a cup or so of vinegar to the rinse water. Repeat the "treatment" periodically to keep towels soft and fluffy.

• **TOYS,** *Games to Make:* Some families make up games with rules so silly that nobody can win, but that's the fun of it! For the following games, you can make gameboards or recycle old ones that no longer have their accessories.
1. Make an "opoly" game using streets in your neighborhood and city.
2. Make a war game pitting the football teams of two local high schools against each other.
3. Make up a Family History "pursuit" game listing relatives names, family happenings, etc. on the question cards.
4. Design a whole new game mixing up rules from previous "bought game" or card game favorites. It's your game, your rules! The sillier the better for more fun!
5. Make outdoor games like croquette or horseshoes more complicated by adding "Captain May I" to get permission to take one's turn.

• **TOYS,** *Storage:*
1. After birthday or Christmas, divide very young children's toys into groups (perhaps a bag for each day of the week) and then bring out and put away a "set" each day; young children will feel as if they have "new" toys daily.
2. Keep toys in an old toddler swimming pool; you can slide the whole mess under the bed at night.
3. Keep older children's stuffed animals off the floor hanging in a hammock made from decorator fish net from specialty stores or from Heloise's nylon net. **Caution:** Don't hang mesh net in a baby or toddler's reach.
4. Buy a new brightly colored plastic trash can or clean up an old one. Decorate by painting the child's name on the lid and side or with stickers or decals so that the child can tell the toy box from the real trash can.

• **TOYS,** *Pickup:*
1. Make "pickup" a game: Red things first, then blue; or soft things then hard things; toss unbreakables into a suitable container; play

who's the fastest picker-upper—Mom/Dad or child; choo-choo toy boxes or bags into the closet; whatever works, including, "We'll have more time to read (child's favorite book) if we get the toys picked up faster."

2. If everyone is tired, don't bother to pick-up. Even little children need a day off, just like Mom and Dad.

• **TOY "SANDBOX":** To confine children's building blocks and other small toys so they aren't stepped on or vacuumed up, either use a small plastic wading pool or build an indoor sandbox with four 3-foot or longer 1′ × 6′ boards. Nail or screw them together to form a square with the floor as the bottom. Children can build cities and cabins but all of the pieces stay in the toy "sandbox."

• **TRASH BAG STORAGE:** Toss the whole roll of plastic bags into the bottom of your trash can after it's been cleaned. Draw up the first bag, leaving it attached to the roll, open it and drape it around the top rim. Hold it in place with the elastic from pantyhose or men's shorts. When the bag is full, tie it shut, lift it up and tear the plastic bag off the roll as you grab the next bag. Then drape the new bag over the rim as before.

• **TRASH CAN GARTER,** *Recycling:* Cut off the elastic from men's shorts or old panty hose and use it to hold plastic garbage bags in place in trash cans. Just put the bag in so that several inches go over the lip of the trash can and put the elastic over the bag like a garter. You can also tie together pieces of elastic from your sewing supplies.

• **TRASH CONTAINER,** *Recycling, Mini-trash Can:* When there's no space for a small waste basket, like near a dressing table, vanity or clothes dryer, substitute a designer square tissue box. You can pitch the box out when it's full of used tissues, makeup pads, dryer lint, or any other small trash. And, it's free! Plastic-lined woven-tray baskets that come on florist-delivered plant or floral arrangements make good small bathroom or bedroom wastebaskets; line with small plastic bags from the stores.

• **TRAVEL,** *Checklist, Dealing with Fear of Flying:* Some people feel safer if they take a few special precautions.

1. Pay attention to the flight attendant's emergency instructions and read the safety materials provided.
2. Make note of all exits and how the doors operate. If you are seated at an emergency exit and think you couldn't open the door, ask to be relocated.
3. When you board the plane, notice which other passengers might become obstacles if you have to get out quickly.
4. Avoid alcoholic beverages so that you will be alert in case of an emergency. You'll feel better anyway; alcohol and caffeine can make you feel uncomfortable even when there is no emergency.
5. Don't sleep during takeoffs and landings.
6. Keep your seatbelt fastened even when the light is off.
7. When traveling, dress comfortably with natural fabrics (less of a fire hazard). Don't wear spiked heels that prevent you from walking steadily and quickly. Carry a handkerchief or cotton scarf to cover your nose and mouth in case of choking fumes.
8. If there should be an accident, unfasten your seatbelt immediately and go to the nearest exit. If the fuselage is damaged, go toward the nearest source of light and, like exiting in case of fire anywhere, try to stay low so you avoid inhaling smoke and noxious fumes.

• TRAVEL, *Cruises:* Some cruise lines will put families in larger quarters at no extra cost if they book a certain number of months in advance. Some lines will let people who can travel on short notice fill empty rooms at lower costs. Check with your travel agent or individual cruise lines.

• TRAVEL, *Free Admission and Shopping Discounts:* If you belong to a local museum, zoo or arboretum "friends" association, your group may be offering tours at reasonable prices. Sometimes, these memberships are tax deductible and having a membership card in one association gives you free admission and/or discount shopping opportunities in other cities' facilities. For example, members of the World-Wide Reciprocal Admission Program for Arboretums can get free general admission to eighty-one arboretums and public gardens in the U.S. and abroad. For information on this program, contact the Dallas Arboretum & Botanical Garden, Dept. NC, 8525 Garland Road, Dallas, TX 75218; 214-327-8263.

• **TRAVEL,** *Handling Your Money Checklist:*
1. Find out if your bank is tied to an Automatic Teller Network (ATM) and where the outlets are in your destination city. You may be able to use your ATM credit line and/or get cash amounts from $100 to $500 a day.
2. Don't leave your personal checks at home; many tourist places accept them.
3. Don't put all of your traveler's checks and receipts in the same place; you could lose both at the same time.
4. Traveling couples shouldn't carry duplicate credit cards. Divide them up so you'll still have some to use if one person has a wallet lost or stolen.

• **TRAVEL,** *Home Swaps:* Home Swapping with a family or couple is a relatively inexpensive way to see life as a neighbor instead of just as a tourist. Among the organizations that specialize in matches between house-swappers are: INTERVAC U.S. in San Francisco (415-435-3497); Better Homes and Travel in New York (212-689-6608); Vacation Exchange Club, Youngstown, Arizona (602-972-2186).

• **TRAVEL,** *Hotel-Motel Information:* Most hotels and motels have 800-numbers to call for reservations and information on whether or not pets are accepted or facilities for pets are available nearby. But you can also ask if the facility offers pool and spa services, hairdryers, ironing equipment, or anything else that will make your stay more pleasant and let you travel lighter without your own "electronics." Also, you'll know if you need to pack spa clothing/robes, etc. And, don't forget to ask if you can get room discounts for membership in fraternal, business, insurance or other organizations at some national chain hotels.

• **TRAVEL,** *Luggage Sizes for Carryons:* Airlines differ on the sizes, weight and number of pieces you can carry on but here are general guidelines from the Air Transport Association to help you buy the right size:
1. Underseat bags: Should be 9 × 14 × 22 inches, with total dimensions of 45 inches.

2. Garment bags: 4 × 23 × 45 inches, total of 72 inches.
3. Overhead bags: 10 × 14 × 36 inches, total of 60 inches.

• TRAVEL, *With Pets:* It may be better to leave your pet at home if it is old, in poor health or is just not a good traveler. See PETS, Checklist for Boarding.

• TRAVEL, *Protecting Your Home While You're Away Checklist:* It's most important to make sure that your home doesn't look empty.
1. Set a timer that automatically turns lights on and off in several rooms at various hours. A timer can also turn a radio off and on.
2. Park your car halfway up the driveway to prevent thieves from parking vans or trucks near the house.
3. Be sure to have a neighbor pick up your newspaper, mail and other deliveries. (It's safer to have these things picked up than canceled, I'm told by the police. Canceling tells a lot of strangers that you'll be gone and for how long.)
4. Have someone take your trash out on pick-up day and have your lawn mowed or snow shoveled to maintain an "occupied look." (Check out bonded and insured house-sitting services in your city. Some of these services are nationally franchised and provide people to water plants, care for pets in addition to keeping your home looking occupied. The cost varies but is certainly worth it to keep you from worrying during your fun-time vacation.)

• TRAVEL, *Quick-Fixes for Clothing Problems (Also See Spots and Stains Chart):*
1. Wine or Coffee Spills: Blot the fresh spill with a cloth soaked with tried and true club soda.
2. Oil (Like Salad Dressing) Stain: Rub white chalk into the stain before laundering. Chalk's easy to carry in a purse or bag.
3. Laundering in Hotels & Restaurants: Rub stain with bar soap and wash/rinse. Or, use hotel shampoo on the stain and for washing garments.
4. Some liquid handsoaps in restaurants can be used to quick-clean a spill. (If you want to conceal the wet spot, you can always hold your purse or a stole over it until it dries.)
5. Mud: Allow to dry, then brush off excess dirt and spot clean with detergent or shampoo.

6. Ballpoint Ink: Usually hair spray or rubbing alcohol will remove ballpoint ink from washable fabrics. Don't spray directly on the stain; lightly spot clean it with a cloth dampened with either solution; launder as usual.

7. "Ironing" in a hotel: Tried and true is to hang a garment in the bathroom while you shower to let the steam "iron" it. If the fabric is not very frail, you can "iron" some creases out over a hot lightbulb. Remember to put the shade back on the lamp!

• **TRAVEL,** *Rental Car Insurance:* Check with your insurance adjuster; your rental car may be covered by your policy and you don't need to pay for more. Also, some credit card users have coverage on rental cars if the fees are paid with that card.

• **TRAVEL:** *Renting an RV (recreational vehicle) Checklist:* If you are planning to rent a recreational vehicle (RV) it's more complicated than just renting a car.

1. Get information from local and national rental companies to compare seasonal rates and determine which model best suits your needs. Usually, the longer the time rented, the greater the discount offered.

2. Mileage is often packaged to include a maximum number of miles and the price is usually quoted as a combined total with the RV rental. Ask for the cost of additional miles beyond the package limit. The price quoted may not include prep charges, insurance, mileage, generator fees, linens or kitchenware and may not be in effect indefinitely. Since you pay for the gas, ask about average fuel consumption.

3. Most companies offer basic comprehensive insurance coverage for damage to the RV but check to see if your auto insurance policy provides coverage. If you use your own policy, the RV lessor may ask for a substantial deposit, refundable within thirty days if you return the RV undamaged.

4. Some people like to have trip interruption coverage. These policies vary greatly; read all the fine print carefully!

• **TRAVEL,** *Safeguarding Documents:* Make copies of such things as airline tickets, hotel reservations, rail passes and vouchers, credit card and passport numbers, and keep them in a place other than the originals so that if you lose your documents, you have proof for claims.

• **TRAVEL,** *Speaking "Travelese" When Booking a Tour:* You may need a second language even if you aren't leaving the United States. Here are some of the most frequently used package-tour terms to help you budget for your trip:

1. Add-on Fare: Cost of air travel to the city from which the tour originates.

2. All-Inclusive: The tour package price includes all land arrangements as well as round-trip air fare.

3. Force Majeure: Anything that happens that cannot be reasonably controlled or anticipated by the tour operator.

4. Fly-Drive Holiday: Independent tour that includes a rental car in its package fee.

• **TRAVEL,** *Staying Well Checklist:*

1. Rock and Roll: Don't spoil your cruise with motion sickness. See your doctor for a prescribed adhesive patch worn behind the ear, which will time-release the anti-motion-sickness drug scopolamine; or, buy over-the-counter preparations.

2. High Altitudes: Going to the mountains? Your body needs time to adapt to low oxygen pressure at high altitudes. Give it a chance to adjust for a few days before doing strenuous activities and avoid alcoholic beverages during the adaptation time.

3. Sun Protection: Ultra-violet light is more intense in the tropics than in temperate zones and it also increases by 4 percent for every 1,000 feet above sea level. Cover your skin with appropriate clothing and use maximum sunscreen protection and re-apply protection after swimming or perspiring. If you snorkle, protect your back with sunscreen and an opaque T-shirt.

When boating, especially protect your eyes and lips from water-reflected sun. (Sunglass labels should say they meet or exceed "ANSI Z80.3" which is the newest American National Standards Institute rating adopted by the Sunglass Association of America in cooperation with the FDA.

4. Walking on the Beach: Invest in protective beach shoes for walking on the sand. Avoid insect bites by lying on a blanket or beach chair instead of directly on the sand; use insect repellent and

avoid highly scented colognes or after-shave. Highly colored clothing also attracts insects.

5. Seeing the Sights: Losing your glasses or a contact lens sure can spoil your vacation. Take along extras and a copy of your prescription to make sure you can see the sights you paid to see.

6. Medications: Take all medicines you usually need, copies of essential prescriptions and your personal doctors' phone numbers, just in case of emergency.

• **TRAVEL,** *Tickets:* Help speed up the boarding process. Have your boarding pass out and I try to fold it where it's supposed to be torn so that the ticket taker can tear it more easily.

• **TRAVEL,** *Tourist Information Sources:* If you are traveling out of state or even within your own state, call 1-800-555-1212 to find out if your destination state has an 800-number for its tourist bureau or traveler's and visitor's information department. Most states offer free brochures on what to see and do and often you'll find lists of free tours of special factories or museums, etc. to help your budget as well as how to contact visitor information sources in specific cities that you plan to visit. **Note:** Also, check out travel books, guidebooks and video tapes from your library for travel information. If you are driving, buying a road atlas will give you a lot of good travel information.

• **TRAVEL,** *Travel-agent Services Checklist:* Travel agents are paid by the tourist industry, but you may be charged for some long-distance phone calls, international telexes, visa and tourist card fees and extensive tailor-made itineraries. The following is a checklist of what a travel agent needs to know to give you the best service.

1. Your total travel budget;

2. If you have flexible travel times so that you can use special promotions;

3. What you've liked or not liked on past vacations;

4. Special diet or medical requirements, if any;

5. Your preferred travel companies and arrangements like non-smoking accommodations;

6. Names of frequent flier/frequent traveler programs to which your miles can be credited.

- **TRAVEL,** *Trip Cancellation Insurance:* Before deciding on trip cancellation or any extra health insurance when you travel, check your homeowner's and health policies to find out what's covered while you are traveling—theft, baggage loss, health problems. You may not need any extra and can save that money to spend on your trip.
1. Trip cancellation insurance can reimburse you for first class tickets if you cancel just because you change your mind, but there's not reimbursement on non-refundable discount tickets for that reason.
2. Costs for basic travel insurance policies are based on the number of days away from home and cover such factors as trip cancellation or interruption, baggage loss, emergency evacuation, world-wide telephone assistance, accidents, sickness, accidental death or dismemberment.
3. Typical costs are $20 per person to get reimbursed for 50 percent of the trip cost up to $200 if you cancel for any reason. At least two companies offer trip cancellation or interruption insurance separately from basic travel insurance policies for $5.50 per $100 with reimbursement up to $5,000.
4. Most of this type of insurance is bought from travel agents (who can then compute the cost since they know your trip cost).

- **TRAVEL ASSISTANCE SERVICES:** You can buy services that refer you to reliable medical care, replace medication and conduct medical consultations with attending physicians if you become ill when traveling out of the country. Some services arrange transportation back to the U.S. and others offer pre-trip information on destination cities, can relay urgent messages to and from friends and family and advance cash in emergencies.

- **TRAVEL CRAFT-SNACK,** *To Keep Children Occupied on Long Car Trips:* Place colored cereal rings and licorice stings into separate self-sealing plastic bags. When it's craft time (translation—when children get bored), tie a piece of cereal to the end of a licorice string and give the children more cereal to string on the licorice. After they tire of the necklaces and bracelets, they can eat their creations.

- **TRAVEL GAME,** *Car Trip Word Game:* Most states have three letters plus three digits on their car license plates. Score this game by adding the letter values according to the popular commercial word game plus the numbers of licenses sighted on the road. But please! No accidents by drivers getting too involved in the game!

• **TRAVEL GIFT,** *When a Child Leaves Home on a Cross-country Car Trip to College or a Job, Checklist:*
1. TLC Kit: Road atlas; state road map; change for toll roads; small container of snacks, hard candy and gum; small box of tissues; cassette tapes of music or favorite books; two index cards for the glove compartment—one with parents' name, address and phone number so that they can be contacted in an emergency and the second with the child's destination and name of the contact person there.
2. Road Kit: Can of propellant tire sealer; flashlight; couple of flares; extra set of car keys; jumper cables; book with step-by-step instructions for changing a flat tire and jump-starting a car.

• **TRUCK,** *Driving for the First Time:* If you've rented a truck to save money on a cross-country move, you'll need to adjust some of your driving habits, especially if it's your first time driving a loaded truck.
1. Remember that you're driving a vehicle that's taller and wider than what you're used to; be careful to clear overhead and roadside signs.
2. Trucks need greater stopping distance and a loaded truck doesn't accelerate as rapidly as a car so be especially cautious when following other cars and passing.
3. As always, map out your route before you start so that you don't drive beyond your energy level, especially since you'll be "working" harder driving an unfamiliar vehicle.

• **TUBES,** *Getting All the Toothpaste or Salve:* When no more will come out of the top, cut off the bottom to get every smidgeon out.

• **TUB TOYS:** Put a child's bathtub toys in a tiered plastic hanging basket. You can pull the drip tray off the bottom for drainage and hang the pot from the shower head.

• **TURKEY,** *Avoiding Leftovers:* During the holidays when turkeys are cheapest, have your butcher cut them in half from neck to feet, then freeze them. You can serve half a turkey with dressing, all the trimmings and give thanks all year round for having saved money on main dish meat.

- **TURKEY FOR CASSEROLES:** Divide leftover cut-up meat into two-cup portions (or other frequently needed amount) and freeze in separate freezer-safe bags so that you can just grab a bag of ready-to-use turkey (or chicken, beef) when you're cooking. If you have leftover gravy, freeze it in one- or two-cup portions to go with the meat.

- **TURNING OVER FRYING FOODS,** *Safety Hint:* Place one pancake turner on top and another on the bottom when you flip over fried patties, etc. and you won't spatter grease by plopping the patty into the pan.

- **TURTLES,** *Feeding:* Turtles are very messy eaters. One reader keeps the tank clean by feeding them in another tank. The turtles live in a beautiful tank, designed with rocks and plants, then are picked up and placed in their feeding tank at mealtime.

- **TV-TRAY LEGS,** *Recycling:* Make holders for plastic trash bags for collecting leaves/trash in the yard, storing cans for recycling and for any other time you need to have a bag held open. Fold the top of a plastic trash bag over the top of the tray legs and fasten with spring clothespins.

- **TWINS,** *Telling Them Apart, Letter of Laughter:* When her grand-daughter told her about the twin girls in her class, Grandma asked how she could tell them apart. "Well, one wears blue sneakers and the other wears red," the child replied. When asked if that was the only way, the child added, "Well, if I call Elizabeth and she comes, that's Elizabeth." Surely another "out of the mouths of babes" story. Aren't children smart?

- **TWIST-TIES,** *Recycling Leftovers:* Temporarily mend eyeglasses, tie plants to stakes, make hooks for Christmas ornaments, organize loose keys, hold stitches when knitting, tie up stored extension cords.

U

- **UMBRELLA,** *Cleaning Mildewed Plastic Patio Umbrella:* A reader wrote that she just put hers into the swimming pool, left it there a day or two and all the mildew disappeared. **Caution:** This "swim" treatment is not for canvas umbrellas; canvas shouldn't be bleached. Also, be sure the pool has plenty of chlorine or you could cause an algae buildup in it.

- **UMBRELLA,** *What to Do with a Wet One When Shopping:* This is one of those "Why didn't I think of this before" hints: Tuck a plastic grocery bag in your purse or briefcase before leaving home so that you can put your drippy umbrella into the bag, slip the handles over your arm and proceed to wherever you are going without messing up your clothing or leaving your umbrella someplace where it will "walk off."

- **UMBRELLA REPAIR:** When material comes loose from an umbrella spoke, reattach it with dental floss—it's stronger than thread and waterproof.

- **UPHOLSTERY CAUTIONS:** Always keep cleaning instructions in a safe place so that you can clean upholstery properly.

1. If there is no care label on your upholstered furniture, you may have to rely on professional advice when it gets soiled or stained. Care depends on the type of fabric and if the fabric has coating materials on its reverse side.
2. Don't assume that when an upholstered item has zippered cushion covers that the covers can be removed for cleaning. For example, Haitian cotton is a common upholstery material; but while other fabrics can be hand washed, wrung out and air dried, Haitian cotton is uncleanable. If soiled the fabric does not respond well to water, leaving yellow rings that can't be removed. A good rule of thumb is never remove cushion covers for separate cleaning.
3. Any tumble cleaning method can destroy the backing, shrink or otherwise damage upholstery fabric. If no care instructions are attached to the furniture when you buy it, ask for some. If you have doubts about care and can't get advice it may be a good idea to choose furniture brands that offer care advice—unless the price is so low that the furniture is "disposable" if soiled which is very rare these days!

• **UPHOLSTERY FABRIC,** *Cleaning:* Vacuum pieces regularly to keep dirt and dust from getting ground in. Clean washable fabrics after first testing for color fastness.
1. Mix ¼ cup high-suds laundry detergent with one quart of warm water in a blender.
2. Apply just the suds with a medium-bristled brush. Work lather in small circles, overlapping as you go.
3. Wring out a towel in clean water and go over the entire upholstered surface.
4. When dry, vacuum the furniture to remove any remaining residue.

• **UPHOLSTERY,** LEATHER, *Cleaning and Care:* Always keep the instruction tags that come with leather upholstery; different finishes require different care methods. Generally, you need to dust and vacuum often and clean spots or surface soil with a weak solution of only a few drops of mild dishwashing liquid and water in a gallon of water. **Caution:** Never soak leather! After cleaning, rinse and dry well. Apply saddle soap or an oil made especially for leather if the manufacturer advises it to protect the leather from scratches or getting brittle.

- **UTENSIL BOARD,** *Organizing Kitchen Clutter:* Install on the wall a pegboard painted to match your kitchen and then you can hang on its pegs slotted spoons, skimmers, whisks, strainers and other utensils too large or bulky for kitchen drawers. It makes the kitchen look like it's inhabited by a professional chef, too!

- **VACUUM MIT:** If your upright vacuum cleaner gives you a blister on the palm of your hand when you push and pull it, wear an oven mitt—the padding keeps your hand safe.

- **VALANCE, POOF-STYLE,** *Recycling, Stuffing:* While the directions tell you to stuff the "poof" of valances or Austrian-style shades with tissue paper, when the sun shines through some fabrics, the tissue shows up as a shadow. Try stuffing the valances with clear plastic dry-cleaning bags to get fullness without shadows.

- **VALENTINE CAKE,** *When You Don't Have a Heart-shaped Pan:*
Step 1. Bake two layers—one in a round pan and one in a square cake pan with the same diameter (length across the middle) of the round one.
Step 2. Pour half of the cake batter into each pan, bake as directed.
Step 3. When layers are cool, place the square layer on a large serving platter in a "diamond" position. Cut the round layer in half to make two half-circles, and place the cut sides of each half against the top sides of the diamond. There's the heart.
Step 4. Frost with your favorite frosting, building up the joint where cake pieces meet to smooth the top. Decorate with red candy hearts or cinnamon candies or decorative frosting.

• **VALENTINE MAIL,** *Have a LOVEly Valentine:* To get your Valentine cards postmarked "Valentines," bundle up all of the cards, making sure they are properly addressed and each has the correct postage, and put them in a large envelope along with a note to the postmaster requesting the special postmark. Mail to Postmaster of Valentines, Valentines, VA 23887-9998. Don't forget to include a Valentine addressed to yourself so that you'll know what the postmark looks like.

• **VAPORIZER/HUMIDIFIER/DEODORIZER:** Fill a vaporizer-humidifier to the full line with water, add a little potpourri and as you mist the air, you'll also put a fragrance in it.

• **VASE,** *Cleaning:*
1. Remove lime deposits by filling vase with hot water and then drop in a couple of denture tablets. Let soak a few hours and then scrub with bottle brush, rinse well and let dry.
2. Remove lime deposits by allowing to soak with vinegar for several hours; rinse and dry. **Note:** Save vinegar for other cleaning; it's still good.

• **VASES,** *Avoiding Accumulation of Cloudy Residue:* Use only distilled water for floral arrangements; then washing them is easy. By the way, if you use distilled water to make coffee, it will taste better and cleaning hard water deposits from the pot is a chore of the past.

• **VCRS,** *Cleaning Heads:* Always check directions to find out what type of commercial cleaner kit should be used—wet method or dry method. An alternate method for cleaning a VCR if you have no cleaning kit handy is to record on a new tape for about 30 minutes, then play the recorded part of the tape back several times to let the heads rub against it so that they clean themselves. The next time you clean the heads repeat the process starting at the point where the tape is new and unused. After you have used all parts of this tape for cleaning, throw the tape away.

• **VEGETABLE CRISPER:** A dry sponge placed in the refrigerator vegetable crisper will absorb excess moisture and help keep veggies fresh.

• **VEGETABLES,** *Storage:* Don't wash until they will be used; the extra moisture causes spoilage. Use a container with a lid or a self-seal plastic bag; add a couple of sheets of paper toweling to absorb moisture and keep veggies from getting soggy and then replace the towels as they get damp. This method is especially good for lettuce, cucumbers and mushrooms.

• **VEGETABLE SPRAY:** To keep sticky ingredients like honey, corn syrup or molasses from making a mess in a measuring utensil, spray it before measuring to make clean up easy.

• **VEGETABLES, WASHING,** *Healthy-Planet Recycling:* Save the water for plants indoors or out, especially if you live in a drought area.

• **VIDEO CASSETTES,** *Care:* Videotapes are very fragile, thin plastic film which tends to stretch, wrinkle and break when improperly handled. Video rental stores ask you to rewind the tapes because inserting a cassette that has tape on BOTH reels can cause the tape to misfeed and get mangled. (Some stores charge an extra fee to your account if you don't rewind!)

This applies to your home recording tapes, too. Rewind them and then fast-forward when you add to the tape. Storing tapes without rewinding them allows the tapes to stretch and sag, then misfeed when played.

• **VIDEO MEMORIES:** One family wrote to say that when they moved, they felt sad about leaving their home and neighbors. So they decided to take their fond memories with them by making a film of their home, inside and out, and of their neighbors talking to their children. It made the move easier for the children, too.

• **VIDEO MESSAGES:** When one reader's mother was in the hospital for several weeks, and children weren't allowed in to visit, she made a videotape of her children for their grandmother—they talked to granny, told her stories, sang songs, drew pictures and cards for her and held them up to the camera. Granny was gratefully teary-eyed and the children were happy to do something nice for their grandmother. The bonus is that the tape is a treasured family keepsake.

• **VIDEO-MOVIE LOG FOR RENTAL TAPES:** By the time movies are available in video rental stores, you've usually forgotten what they were about. So, when the movie ads and reviews first appear in newspapers, cut them out, and file the clippings in a file box or envelope. (You can paste them to an index card if you feel ambitious.) Then you can take your file to the rental store to jog your memory when you make your rental selections.

• **VIDEOTAPE LOG:** Keep a small notebook near the VCR. When you tape a show, write the name of the show in the notebook, one per page, as well as on the jacket. After the previous week's TV guide has expired, cut out the description of the show and tape it in the notebook. Then, you have all the information about the show where it won't get lost. If you decide to erase the tape, just tear out the page from the notebook—it's easier than tearing taped information off the jacket.

• **VIDEOTAPES,** *Identification:* When you tape shows to be "keepers," cut out from your newspaper TV guide the tiny paragraph describing the show and use transparent tape to stick it to the "outer" edge of the tape (not the edge that goes into the machine). Each tape edge will hold three or four of these descriptions.

• **VIDEOTAPES,** *Identification:* When you've taped a show that several family members want to view, place a stick-on note on the outside of the jacket with each viewer's name on it so that as the tape is viewed, people can check off their names and nobody can complain about missing the show.

• **VIDEOTAPES,** *Keepers:* You won't accidentally tape over or erase a favorite VCR tape if you remember to remove the tab found on the left side of the tape cartridge edge. (The manufacturer puts it there for you!) If you change your mind and want to record over the tape, just place a piece of masking tape or several layers of transparent tape over the recessed area. You can also buy a small plastic gadget to put over the recessed area when you want to tape over.

• **VIDEOTAPES,** *Re-taping:* Since the recommended life of a tape is about 100 hours, you could get the most out of each tape if you tape daily programs on a tape for several viewings and then tape a movie or documentary "keeper" on that tape which won't be viewed frequently. **Hint:** VCR tapes don't last forever. If you have a favorite tape that is several years old, you should copy it to a new tape before it deteriorates too badly.

• **VIODETAPES,** *When to Discard:* Discard tapes used for daily recording after about 100 hours of playing and recording to prevent clogging of your VCR by oxide particles. (Oxide particles flake off tapes as they play. Using good quality tapes—"high grade" or "super high grade"—helps but you still need to clean your VCR periodically.)

• **VIDEOTAPING SLIDES:** You can have slides, photos, 8mm or 15mm film put on videotape for easy viewing. The process is called video or tape transfer and you can find stores that do it under Photo Finishing or Video Transfer in the phone book. **Hint:** Use good-quality slides; copying causes some quality deterioration; put the slides in order and number them; and be prepared to wait about a week or so. This would be an nice gift for a friend or relative.

• **VIDEOTAPING SLIDES YOURSELF:**
Step 1. Set the video camera on a tripod and project the slides onto a good screen. (Experiment until you get the distance just right.)
Step 2. Working with another person, have one show and focus the slides while the other operates the video camera and says when it's okay. The video operator turns on the camera and counts to four, then turns the camera off while the slides are being changed. One of them can even explain the photo.
Note: This takes a little practice and it helps if your video camera has a freeze-frame feature. There are machines that transfer photos or slides onto videotape, too. Check out photo-equipment stores.

• **VINEGAR,** *Cleaning with:* Keep vinegar in a clean squirt bottle so it's handy for pre-treating stains before laundering, cleaning bathrooms, etc.

• **VINEGAR,** *Homemade Fruit:* Combine a bottle of white wine vinegar with ½ cup fresh, washed and stemmed strawberries. Cover the mixture and let it sit at room temperature for one week. You can remove the fruit or leave it in, but if you leave it, the vinegar will continue to mellow and become stronger. Use in recipes calling for fruit vinegars.

• **VISITORS,** *Letter of Laughter:* A reader reminded us about one of life's ironic rules—that nobody every drops in to visit you when you've just cleaned up your home or apartment and someone always drops by when the place is a wreck!

• **VITAMINS & OTHER SUPPLEMENTS:** The Center for Science in the Public Interest has reported on research that shows more than half of the calcium supplements we buy in the marketplace don't disintegrate soon enough to get into our bloodstreams, which means we are wasting money on supplements if they just pass through our bodies undissolved. This is true of many other supplements, such as the large doses of niacin many people take to lower their cholesterol. Although you can't have yourself X-rayed regularly to find out if your tablets are dissolving in your body, you have some recourse.
1. Ask the manufacturer for laboratory results that show if the supplement you want to take has been tested for potency, stability, and ability to dissolve. (Get the phone number from the package or ask your pharmacist.)
2. If you take niacin to lower your cholesterol, take several smaller doses instead of a sustained-release preparation.
3. Check calcium labels (or call companies) to see if they meet USP (US Pharmacopeial Convention) dissolving tests.
4. Buy only supplements that have expiration dates. This is no guarantee, but it's better than nothing. (Time causes some supplements to decompose or become too hard to dissolve.)
5. You are more likely to get a poorer quality supplement when you buy less-expensive versions of name brands.

• **VOTING TOOL:** The little tool provided for punching out your choices on an absentee ballot need not be returned with the ballot and that's good. It's perfect for setting most digital watches.

- **WAITING GAME WITH CHILDREN:** In places like physician or dentist offices, send them on a scavenger hunt. Give them a list of items and a magazine and ask them to find pictures of the items. When they do, they should write the page number by each item. Such games make a wait more pleasant for parent and child.

- **WAFFLE IRON,** *Stop Sticking:* To temper a waffle iron, clean the surface well. Then take a slice of bread and grease both sides with unsalted fat (never salted fat). Lay the bread in the waffle iron and close the lid. As the bread browns, it greases all the small square surfaces. For a double waffle iron, temper with two pieces of bread. After removing the bread, crumple it and feed it to the birds.

- **WAKE-UP BELL:** When small children get up before their parents to start "exploring" the house, parents need a warning signal—put inexpensive or Christmas jingle bells on the tops of children's bedroom doors. Then, as soon as they touch their doors, the jingling will alert you!

- **WALKER BASKET,** *Handicapped Person Help:* Hang a child's bike basket on the front of a hand walker to carry light items. **Caution:** Carry only lightweight things to avoid getting off balance.

• **WALKING DIARY:** Keep a walking record of hours or miles as an incentive to get your exercise. You can tally up the totals at the end of the month or year to see how far you've gone on the road to good health. For fun, compare mileage totals to distances between cities on a map.

• **WALL DECORATING,** *Hanging Collections Without Damage:* When you are grouping wall decorations with different shapes and sizes, trace an outline of the objects (pictures, mirrors, etc.) on newspapers and cut them out. Tape them on the wall in arrangements until you get one you like, then, place the nails in the wall through the paper; remove paper and hang the real thing. This is a good hint even for one painting or mirror; you can tape the paper to the wall and step back to see if you have it at the right level and place.

• **WALLPAPER,** *Cleaning:*
1. Most washable wall coverings can be cleaned with mild liquid soap and cool water. Work from the bottom up, using as little water as possible. Work on small areas and overlap as you wash. Rinse with clear water and blot dry.
2. Non-washable wall coverings can sometimes be cleaned by rubbing gently with kneaded eraser, fresh white bread, or doughy wallpaper cleaners from hardware stores. If you use the commercial doughy cleaner, be sure to knead and turn it often so you use clean surfaces on the wall.
3. Spot-clean wallpaper before spots set by blotting grease spots with paper towels or facial tissue while you press lightly with a warm iron over the towels or tissue. **Caution:** If possible, always get manufacturer's directions for cleaning your particular kind of wallpaper. And, always test cleaning methods on an inconspicuous place before doing a whole wall or conspicuous place like the areas around light switches.

• **WALLPAPER,** *Leftover Uses:* Cover books or shelves, wrap gifts, make decals for sliding glass doors, cut and laminate for placemats, cut pictures out and frame them.

• **WALLPAPER,** *$aver for Making Borders:* Buy a double roll of striped wallpaper that matches your wall colors and then cut the stripes individually into border strips. You can make wider borders by combining strips. You'll save even more if you catch a wallpaper remnant sale. Whenever you buy wallpaper, remember to consider that you have to match patterns and to get all you need because remnants can be of discontinued patterns and different batches of wallpaper can have slight color variances.

• **WALLPAPER,** *Painting Over:* Before attempting to paint over wall paper, you need to apply a product that primes the paper before painting. It's sold at most paint stores. Painting over paper is easier than removing existing paper and repairing the walls. Also, painting over heavily textured paper is very attractive since the texture shows through the paper.

• **WALLPAPER,** *Removing Grease Spots:* **Caution:** This method is only for washable wallpaper.
1. Make a paste of baking soda and water. Apply the thick paste to the grease stain and let it dry.
2. Brush the residue off with a soft brush or cloth.
Hint: Avoid grease on special places such as behind the stove or beside the trash can, by putting clear adhesive plastic over the "grease magnet" area.

• **WALLPAPER,** *Replacing:* Cost may determine your selection so here's a quick way to estimate it.
1. Multiply Wall Width × Wall Height = Square Feet. Then add the total square feet for all four walls.
2. A single roll of American wallpaper usually covers 30 square feet depending upon the pattern. (You need to allow extra for pattern matching.) A single roll of European wallpaper usually covers 23 square feet.
3. If you are doing only one wall of a room, you may be able to take advantage of remnant sales, but be aware that sale wallpaper may be a closeout and if you underestimate your needs, you may not be able to buy more.

• **WALLPAPER,** *Selection:* Wallpaper is expensive to replace but may last longer than paint in some rooms, but may last too long if the pattern is too busy; less-busy designs stay pleasing longer.

• **WALLPAPER BORDER,** *Substitute:* When you can't find just the right wallpaper border or the right color, try buying heavy ribbon at a fabric store and putting it up with tacky glue.

• **WALLPAPER BORDERS,** *Easy Stick-up:* When putting a wallpaper border around a room at the ceiling, you can save climbing up and down a ladder and constant repositioning of the ladder if you line up all your chairs along the wall and cover them well with old sheets or drop cloths. Then you can step from one chair to the next as you work. If two people work on this project, one can walk in front of the other holding the wet strip of border while the second person applies the other end.

• **WALLPAPER MISTAKE,** *Quick-Fix, Cover-up:* When her dark blue print wallpaper dried, a reader was dismayed to see a strip of white in between each sheet where the paper strips had pulled away from each other. She solved the problem by painting right down the seam with a small brush and some stencil paint that matched the wallpaper. She did about five inches at a time and wiped excess paint from the wallpaper with a damp cloth as she worked. Stencil paint comes in many different shades so you can match just about any color when you need to make a quick repair.

• **WALLS,** *Painting:* When selecting paint colors, remember that blue, green and violet have a tranquilizing effect; use the cool colors in rooms where you want to relax. Warm colors like yellow, orange and red will energize.

• **WALLS,** *Painting Technique:* Sponging one paint color over a neutral color is a popular decorating scheme. Water-based paints dry faster, you won't have to wait as long to dab on the second layer of paint. Oil-based paints dry more slowly; you won't have to work as fast and you'll have time to correct mistakes.

• **WALLS,** *Quick-Fixes:* Quick patching is essential when you move or change wall art arrangements.
1. Patch nail holes in white walls with white toothpaste or moistened crushed aspirin pushed into the hole.
2. On colored walls, dab matching watercolor paints over the mend if you don't have leftover paint. Colored typewriter correction fluid also covers small patches.
3. Fill tack or pin holes with white or appropriately colored soap or toothpaste.

• **WASHCLOTHS,** *For Traveling:* Disposable cleaning cloths cut in half are just the right size for travel washcloths, especially in Europe where washcloths aren't usually provided in smaller hotels. They dry quickly and, if left behind, are no loss. Put a wet one in a zipper bag when traveling with children.

• **WASHER SUDS OVERFLOW:** Please see SUDS OVERFLOW.

• **WATCH,** *Checklist for Buying One:*
1. Whether it's a designer watch or a $15 special, consider it's guarantee of accuracy and the cost of upkeep, such as batteries, and not the price tag alone.
2. The two types are battery-powered by a mainspring. Battery-powered watches usually need a new battery, costing $5 to $10 about once a year. Before you buy, find out what type of battery is needed and how easily it's replaced and if stores in your area carry the batteries and if you can replace them yourself. Some mainspring watches need cleaning and oiling annually.
3. Check the range of overall costs of possible repairs and if they can be done locally. Watches powered by a mainspring and some battery-powered watches can be repaired by local watch-repair shops; but some battery-powered watches must be returned to the manufacturer.
4. Water-resistant means that the watch can be submerged in fresh water to 80 feet and in salt water to 75 feet without leakage or loss of accuracy. Some watches are no longer water-resistant after cases are opened for battery replacement.
5. "Shock resistant" means that a watch can be dropped from three feet onto a hard wood surface without being damaged.
6. "Anti-magnetic" means that the inside working parts of the watch are made from metals that will not magnetically attract each other and therefore work independently.
7. "Jewels" refers to the usually synthetic gemstones that serve as bearings inside a mechanical watch.
8. Watches need to be cleaned regularly to maintain accuracy and many antique watches need regular oiling to keep parts from wearing out or breaking. It can be very expensive to have special parts made for antique watches. A friend paid over $200 to have a mainspring made for a family heirloom watch.

• **WATCH,** *When You Are Allergic to the Metal:* Either paint the back side of the watch with clear nail polish or cut corn pads to fit the back side and stick them on to protect your skin.

• **WATER BED SPREAD,** *$aver:* A twin-size bedspread costs less than king-size and fits most king-size water beds if you tuck it in all around the edges.

• **WATER,** *Buying Bottled Water Checklist:*
1. Natural Sparkling and Sparkling Waters—water that is bubbly because carbon dioxide (but no other chemicals) has been added to it. The word "natural," according to the FDA, has not been defined, so products labeled "natural" may not be different from other brands.
2. Spring Water—comes from a spring and has no minerals added or removed.
3. Drinking Water—comes from a water well and has no minerals added or removed.
4. Purified Water—has all minerals and chemicals removed. Generally not consumed as drinking water unless ordered by a doctor.
5. Distilled Water—recommended to prevent mineral build-up in some appliances such as steam irons. It still contains a minute amount of minerals.

• **WATER,** *Recycling:*
1. When basement de-humidifiers collect water, save it in old plastic jugs and use it to water plants and in your simmering potpourri pots.
2. Place 30-gallon plastic garbage cans at the end of rain gutters so they collect water for watering house and garden plants.
3. Have the water drainpipe from your air conditioner drain water into a flower bed. (You may need to check periodically to make sure the end of the pipe doesn't get clogged with mud or vines; if clogged, the water will back up to its source!)

• **WATER,** *Reminder to Drink Eight to Ten Glasses Daily:* Put eight to ten pennies on the kitchen counter and remove one each time you drink a glass of water.

- **WATER,** *When Pipes Are Frozen in the Morning:* Melt ice cubes in the microwave to get enough water to brush your teeth and for a cup of tea or coffee.

- **WATER CONSERVATION,** *Healthy-Planet $aver:*
1. Shower instead of taking a tub bath.
2. Wash hands, clothing, anything else, with cold water whenever you can to conserve energy.
3. When brushing your teeth, turn the water off until it's time to rinse instead of letting it just run away down the drain.
4. Keep a container of cold water in the fridge to avoid wasting tap water by running it until it feels cool.
5. Wash only full dishwasher loads.
6. Either wait until you have a full load to run the washer or adjust the water level to avoid waste.

- **WATER PURIFICATION SYSTEMS:** As this book is being written, many of these systems are scams and don't do what they claim. Before buying any system, have your water tested by a laboratory to determine if you actually need one. You can get current information about water testing and purification systems from your Cooperative Extension Agent. Look in the government section of your phone book, under "United States Government, Agriculture Department Of, Extension Service County & Home Economics Agents."

- **WATER STAINS,** *Covering Up:* Water stains on ceilings will come back through paint. You need to seal the area first with a special sealant sold in paint stores for that purpose or with clear varnish. Make sure varnish dries before painting over it.

- **WATERING SYSTEM FOR PLANTS,** *Recycling Healthy-Planet Homemade Drip Irrigation:*
1. Pierce a tiny hole in the bottom of a gallon plastic milk jug and put it next to a young tree or shrub and fill it with water. The water will drip out slowly and seep down to the roots. Fill the jugs early in the morning and at night, during dry spells, and you won't waste water through evaporation.
2. A smaller plastic bottle could help you drip-irrigate houseplants without spilling over.

3. For slow drip watering/feeding of houseplants, mix plant food and water in a plastic jug; freeze it; then poke three or four holes in the bottom of the bottle and set it on the pot's soil.

• WAX, *Dripped on a Wooden Dining Table:* First scrape off as much of the wax as possible with a plastic credit card or the dull side of a knife. Clean with a good quality wood cleaner. If the stain doesn't go away, it has probably penetrated the wood and the entire table will need refinishing.

• WAX BUILDUP ON FLOORS, *Removal:* If you don't own one, rent a floor scrubber.
1. Boost the power of heavy-duty general-purpose household cleaner with 1 cup of non-sudsing ammonia.
2. Working a small area at a time, pour a small amount of the cleaning solution on the floor, let it set for a few minutes and go over it with the floor scrubber. After the entire floor has been scrubbed, go back over it with a damp mop.
3. After the floor is dry, apply a fresh coat of wax.
Caution: If you have no-wax flooring, you absolutely need to follow the manufacturer's guidelines for cleaning. It's not the same as traditional flooring. If you have lost the directions, either call a flooring company (which might sell the products you need) or call the manufacturer's consumer or customer service/information line. Most manufacturers have 800 numbers for this; get the number by dialing 800 information: 1-800-555-1212.

• WAXED PAPER, *Liners from Cereal Boxes, Healthy-Planet Recycling:* Cut in squares for dividing hamburger patties prepared for freezing. Store in a cut bottom of a cereal box.

• WEATHERIZING YOUR HOME, INDOOR AIR POLUTION: When you install storm windows, weather stripping, caulking, wall insulation, indoor pollutants (household and personal products, formaldehyde or asbestos in building materials, lead, pesticides, tobacco smoke, radon, molds, gasses from heaters) can become concentrated because less outdoor air is entering your home. Some weatherizers such as caulk can emit some pollutants, too.
Therefore, before you weatherize, you should also take steps to minimize pollution from sources inside your home due to inade-

quate air flow, stuffy air, moisture condensation on cold surfaces, mold and mildew growth. The good news is that sometimes, when you seal up your home to prevent heat loss, you can also reduce indoor pollutant levels. For example, sealing foundation cracks can prevent radon gas from getting into your home.

• **WEDDING ANNIVERSARY REMINDER:** When you buy a wedding gift, also buy a first-anniversary card. Then, when you get home make it ready to mail at the appropriate time. Write the name on the envelope and pencil the date it should be mailed on the corner where the stamp will go. **Note:** It's better not to write the address on the envelope because the couple might move.

• **WEDDING SHOWER GIFT,** *For the Couple Who Has Everything:* A fire extinguisher!

• **WEDDING SHOWER IDEA,** *For Couples Who Have Everything:* One reader had each of twelve guests draw slips of paper printed with the months of the year. Guests would bring gifts useful during certain months and marked the gift for that month. For example, March gifts were spring-cleaning needs; April included Easter goodies; May was vegetable seeds and gardening tools; October included Halloween goodies and a leaf rake. Another reader included a sample list of the couple's likes and dislikes in hobbies and home-entertainment choices when she sent the invitations. Guests had fun picking out such shower gifts as adult board games, craft and hobby kits, and gave gift certificates for videotape rentals, local home delivery restaurants, videotaping of the wedding ceremony, and other "couple" instead of "bridal" shower gifts.

• **WEDDING VIDEO:** Make a copy of the wedding ceremony's video-tape and send it via "chain letter" to all those who couldn't come to the wedding in person. Include a list of names and addresses to send with the tape that begins with the first person who received it and ends with the bridal couple; also include instructions to send the tape to the next person on the list. When the tape returns to the bridal couple, they'll know everyone has seen it.

• **WEDDING OR WEDDING SHOWER GIFTS,** *For Couples Who Already Have Furnishings:* Buy decorated recipe cards and send them to all of the couple's friends asking for their favorite recipes. Then assemble the cards in a file and add a gift certificate to their favorite grocery store or to a gourmet store.

- **WEED-CUTTER SPRINGS,** *Quick-Fix Finding:* One reader solved a problem he had with lost springs from his string weed edger. When the cotter pin dislodged, the cover would come off and the spring inside would fly into the grass. He'd have to stop work until he got another spring. Now he buys spares and paints them bright colors so they can be more easily seen in the grass.

- **WEEVILS,** *Keeping Them Out of Cupboards:* To eliminate weevils from grain products, place all grain products in a zero-degree freezer for seven days when you bring them home from the store; or place the product in the oven at 130°F for 30 minutes. In addition, many people keep grain products in recycled glass jars with tight lids after "treatment." They cut off labels and directions and put them into the jar, too.

- **WEIGHT-LOSS EASES HUNGER:** For each pound that you lose on your diet, buy a pound of dried beans or other non-perishable staple food. When you have lost all the weight you needed to, give the food to your local food charity pantry. Helping the truly hungry will be an added incentive for you to stay on your diet plan. Just lifting the weight will help you remember how cumbersome it was carrying all those extra pounds around, too, so you'll try harder not to gain it all back!

- **WHIPPED CREAM/TOPPING:** Add a sprinkle of allspice, cinnamon, or nutmeg and a drop of vanilla extract to whipped cream or topping to make it extra special. Also: Please see HOLIDAY DESSERT TOPPING.

- **WHIPPED TOPPING,** *Low-calorie, No-cholesterol Substitute:* Whip a couple of egg whites until stiff, add a drop of vanilla and sugar to taste, and whip until foamy and then dollop onto desserts.

- **WHIPPING CREAM/TOPPINGS:** The mixing bowl won't slip and slide across the counter if you place a damp washcloth under it before turning on the mixer.

- **WICKER,** *Washing:*
1. Brush dust out of all cracks with an old toothbrush or scrub brush, or vacuum with brush attachment.

2. With a soft brush, scrub wicker with a solution of 2 pints cool water and 1 tablespoon of salt. Rinse with damp sponge. After furniture dries, rub with furniture polish and soft cloth. **Caution:** Wipe excess polish off chairs with a second cloth to prevent damage to clothing of "sitters."

• WINDOW, *Framing:* Instead of curtains or to accent curtains, frame a window with fabric.
1. Buy wood molding which is 4 or 5 inches wide and ½-inch thick and cut it to fit the length and width of your window.
2. Cover the frame with foam padding and then tack a fabric to the back of it and attach to the wall.

• WINDOW DECALS/STICKERS, *Removing:* Some will come off if you paint a few coats of vinegar on, let soak for a few minutes, and wash right off. Others come off after applying petroleum-based pre-wash spray as you would the vinegar. Still others, like bumper stickers, come off if you heat them with a hair dryer before peeling them off.

• WINDOWPANES, *No-mess Painting:* Dip an old rag (old socks are nice) in petroleum jelly and smear it around the edge of the glass closest to the window frame. After you finish painting, paint smears wipe right off. After the paint is completely dry, you can easily remove the remaining petroleum jelly film with a glass cleaner containing ammonia.

• WINDOWS, *Homestyle Quick-Fix for Wet, Drippy Condensation in the Winter:* Wipe the moisture off the windows and be sure they are dry. With a couple of tissues, apply undiluted hair shampoo to the windowpanes. They may look cloudy at first but should clear up. **Hint:** The best solution is to try to vent extra moisture from your home with kitchen and bath exhaust fans. Too much moisture for too long can cause wood framing to rot or warp and can make paint peel.

• WINDOWS, *Quick-Fix If Stuck:* Try to wedge a putty knife around all sides of the window so that you can spray furniture polish into the space. "Shake" the window to get as much furniture polish as possible down the sides. When it gives a bit, move the window up and down until you can open it all the way. Spray more furniture polish on the inside of the frame to get it lubricated well.

- **WINDOWS,** *Securing Wooden Frames:* Drill a hole about four to six inches above each bottom window section in the inside framework. Insert a bolt into each hole. The windows can be opened only four to six inches, not enough space for a burglar, and you can remove the bolts when you want to fully open the windows.

- **WINDOW SCREENS,** *Cleaning:* See SCREENS, Cleaning.

- **WINDOW SHADES,** *Cleaning:*
1. If the shades are washable, take them down, unroll and lay them on a flat surface. Dust with a clean cloth, wash with mild detergent suds and warm water. Rinse well, wipe dry and hang immediately.
2. If the shades are not washable, they should be cleaned by a professional cleaner; a clothing dry cleaner can recommend someone for you. Or, you can buy a dough-type wall cleaner at paint or wall-covering stores and follow the directions carefully. Always test cleaners on an inconspicuous place before doing a whole project.

- **WINDOW SHADES,** *Healthy-Planet Recycling:* Cut up old window shades for shelf and drawer liners; they are sturdy and free!

- **WINDOW WASHING,** *Homestyle Cleaner:* Add one-fourth cup non-sudsing ammonia to a gallon of water and wash away grime. **Hint:** Minimize streaking by waiting until the time of day when the sun isn't shining directly on the windows; heat causes windows to dry too quickly, leaving streaks behind. Also, you'll get less streaking if you wipe off surface dirt and dust with a damp cloth before washing.

- **WINDOW WASHING,** *Removing Water Spots:* To dissolve hard-water deposits on windows, spray full-strength white vinegar on the window, let it set, then wipe. Heavy deposits may require two or three applications and scrubbing with a stiff brush.

- **WINDSHIELD,** *Cleaning:* Fill a spray bottle with equal parts of rubbing alcohol and water; spritz, and wipe clean with soft cloth or paper towels.

- **WINE,** *Miscellaneous Information:* When you see tiny crystal-looking particles on the bottom of a wine cork, don't panic and think it's broken glass. Usually, these bits are malic acid crystals which have solidified and are evidence of an inferior, but not un-wholesome, wine-making process.

• **WINE,** *Selection:* The rule of white wine with white meat and red wine with red meat may help you select wines for food but this rule isn't the final word because the characteristics of both recipes and wines differ greatly. For example, the heartier flavor in a poultry roast might be better enhanced by a dry, light-bodied red wine instead of the traditional white. Vinegar, citrus juice, and egg yolks (sulfur) can give wine an off-taste. Artichokes, asparagus, onions, pineapples, also can have an unpleasant effect on certain wine flavors.

• **WINE,** *Storage:* Wine that doesn't require aging or that will be consumed soon can be stored standing up for a short time, but wine to be aged should be stored lying down to keep the cork damp and prevent air from reaching the wine. If you buy a case of wine for a party, just place the case on its side in a cool basement or other cool dark place. (Wine rests better in the dark.)

• **WINE,** *Storage, General Hints:* Wine can "breathe" through the cork, so it can absorb cellar odors. Also, keep stored wine away from laundry or other vibrating equipment; aged wines especially don't like vibrations.

• **WINE,** *Storage, Humidity:* The best humidity level for wine storage is 75 percent. (Humidity keeps the corks from drying out and allowing wine to evaporate and spoil.)

• **WINE,** *Storage of Open Bottles:* Don't just cork a half-empty bottle of wine leftover from a meal and put it into the fridge. Pour it into a clean, empty half-sized bottle that you keep for this purpose, then cork and store. Leaving air space between the cork and the wine speeds up deterioration of the wine. (This air space is called "ullage" if you're a Scrabble player or just like to astound your guests!)

• **WINE,** *Storage, Temperatures:* Most wine experts say the ideal temperature for a wine cellar should be 55° to 60°F, with 45 to 70 degrees as the outer limits. Keeping the temperature constant is even more important than the exact temperature.

• **WINE BOX PLASTIC BAGS,** *Recycling:* Remove the plastic bag from the wine box, fill half to three-quarters full of water and freeze so that you have a non-drippy, square ice block for your picnic cooler. You can drink the water as it melts. Then, after it's empty, inflate the bag with air and you have a pillow to make snoozing in the car on the way home more comfortable. But not if you're the driver, of course!

• **WINDSHIELD,** *Quick-Fix Cleaning the Inside of It on the Road:* Squirt washer fluid from the automatic windshield washer on a paper towel or disposable towel and then wipe the inside of the windshield. If you can't reach the window cleaning mechanism while holding the paper towel, just lay the towel on the windshield before operating the cleaner; it should get enough of a squirt to do the job. **Note:** The car should be stopped to do this, but then you knew that.

• **WINDSHIELD FILM,** *Removing with Homestyle Cleaner:* Mix one part vinegar or one part non-sudsy ammonia (not both) to three parts water and clean the windshield with it.

• **WINDSHIELD WASHER FLUID,** *When It Gets Too Frozen to Flow in Winter Weather:* Carry a small spray bottle filled with windshield-washer fluid. Then you can spray the windshield while the wipers are running to clean it off before you drive.

• **WINDSHIELD WIPER BLADES,** *Stopping "Fingernail-on-the-blackboard" Squeaks:* If blades are worn down they will squeak and even scratch the windshield; replace them. If blades are in good condition, tree sap or road tar can cause squeaks and washing with a good commercial cleaner should solve the problem.

• **WIPES,** *Homemade $aver for Baby or Cosmetics:* Fill an old baby wipes container (or other container with a tight lid) with paper napkins to the top. In a separate bowl, mix thoroughly ½ cup of water, 1 tablespoon of baby oil, and 1 tablespoon of baby lotion. Pour the mixture over the napkins and cover tightly. You'll have fresh-scented wipes for baby or makeup removing.

• **WIRE HANGERS,** *Recycling:* Do they really breed in dark closets as one of my readers suggested? If you don't like wire hangers because you think they are too flimsy, tape several together with masking tape for sturdier hangers; add plastic clothespins to some for skirt and pants hangers.

• **WISHBONE, TURKEY OR CHICKEN,** *Quick-Fix Drying:* Microwave a roast turkey or chicken wishbone for a few seconds to dry it immediately for those whose wishes can't wait.

• **WOODEN BREAD BOXES,** *Odors and Recycling:* I've had many letters about "woody" odors in these boxes that even get into the bread stored in them. We've tried every conceivable method to remove the wood-smell without any luck at all. We use our box to store letters and I'm sure there are other uses. The alternative is to return it to the store for refund.

• **WOODEN SPOONS,** *Reseasoning:* After washing spoons in hot sudsy water, scrub if needed and rinse well. Wipe dry and allow to air-dry completely. Then heat some mineral oil (not vegetable oil which can get rancid in wood) over medium heat and dip the spoons in it until they are completely coated. Drain on paper towels (save towels, place one layer of towels over newspapers) until they are cool enough to handle. Wipe them off and they are ready to use.

• **WOOD FLOORS,** *Homestyle Cleaning:* It's always a good idea to check with a flooring specialist for information on cleaning wood floors because certain treated flooring requires specific cleaning methods. But one general wood-floor cleaner is a solution of ½ cup of apple-cider vinegar in 1 gallon of warm water. With a soft cloth or sponge mop with most of the moisture squeezed out, wipe the floor without getting it really wet. Then buff after cleaning to bring out the luster.

• **WOOD STOVE,** *Maintenance Checklist:* If you have a wood stove in your vacation cabin or home, it needs an annual tune-up that includes the following:
1. Chimney cleaning.
2. Thorough cleaning of the stove, including cleaning the secondary air chamber.
3. Install new door gaskets to keep the stove airtight.
4. Adjust the door latch, the thermostat and polish the griddle.

Hint: This chore can be done by a certified wood stove professional or with a tune-up kit sold by stove manufacturers.

- **WOOD STOVE WINDOWS,** *Removing Creosote from Glass:*
1. In an old bowl, put some wood ashes and add enough vinegar to get the consistency of a light paste. Apply it to the window and allow to soak.
2. With a wet cloth, remove the paste and the creosote should be gone.

- **WORKDAY,** *Letter of Laughter:* A dress department store clerk says her job is like working in a comedy club. One day as identical twins tried on dresses, one said to the other, "That looks terrific on you. I wish I could wear it, but the color looks awful on me." Proof that we all see ourselves differently than others do.

- **WORKDAY SURVIVAL HINTS:** Readers with jobs, children, gardens, and who also participate in community activities, offered their hints for organizing their lives.
1. Put in a laundry load before leaving for work and put it in the dryer when you return, or have a rule that the first person home loads the dryer.
2. Put children's jobs on a list with space at the bottom for "add-on" jobs. The list eliminates the need to nag, and children check off jobs as they are completed, thus getting the satisfaction of seeing what they've accomplished.
3. Teach children to make their own lunches and breakfasts. On weekends, make meals so that there are leftovers for Monday and Tuesday and nobody has to cook. Have each family member list their favorite foods and make each person's favorite at least once every other week or so to keep everyone happy and cooperative.
4. After dinner dishes are done, set the breakfast table and include any foods that don't require refrigeration (like cereals) to get a few steps ahead in the morning.
5. To keep lunch, bus, or milk money handy and to save time and tempers on hectic mornings, many families keep a change bowl by the door. They drop all change into the bowl each night and take what's needed in the morning.
6. Realize that few people can really "do it all." Hire someone such as a teenager to vacuum and dust once a week or hire a profes-

sional cleaning service to do the whole house thoroughly every few weeks.

• **WORKING,** *Hints for Success:*
1. Make decisions between 7 and 11 A.M.; depression and anxiety are lowest at this time. Worst time is between 2 and 8 P.M. when depression and anxiety are highest.
2. Do complex tasks midday or late afternoon when body temperature reaches its normal high point.
3. Ask for a raise over lunch when people are most agreeable. A three-year study by Johns Hopkins researchers found that more business contracts are signed over "power" lunches than at any other time.

• **WORKSHOP ORGANIZER,** *Recycling:* Cut about one-third off an aluminum pie plate and tack it to the wall with the bottom side out and you have a handy holder for sandpaper sheets, especially disks for your sander.

• **WORMS,** *For Fishing:* Keep them in a plastic hanging basket filled with good soil. The planter can hang outside, has good drainage, and the worms can't escape but stay buried until you can go fishing.

• **WRAPPING PAPER,** *Recycling Storage:* Roll on paper-towel tubes and put two or so rolls in a newspaper bag.

• **WREATHS,** *Hanging When You Can't Make Holes with Nails:* When metal doors and some landlords don't let you hang holiday wreaths and other door decorations, try a clear suction-cup hook. It will work better than you think, unless the wreath is very heavy.

• **WRINKLE-REMOVING FROM POLYESTER CLOTHING:** Try this. Dampen the garments, put them in a plastic bag and place them in the freezer for a few hours. Then, press with a steam iron while they're still frozen. Use a pressing cloth to avoid making the fabric shiny.

• **WRIST WARMERS,** *Children or Adults:* Exercise wristbands put over jacket sleeve and mitten/glove tops will keep sleeves and mittens together so that your arms and hands stay warm and dry for winter play or sports.

- **XYLOPHONE,** *Child's Toy:* When a child's xylophone makes a tinny noise that keeps your eardrums vibrating, replace the wooden sticks. Instead make new sticks by attaching a small rubber ball, like the kind on paddle-ball sets or from jacks, to a pencil or piece of doweling. You won't have a musical treat but the sound will still be muted enough to avoid a really bad headache. **Note:** This reminds me of a joking "curse" a friend of mine used to place on people who annoyed her. It's "May all your children get drums for Christmas (or Chanukah)."

- **YARN HOLDER:** Plastic six-pack rings will hold looped yarn strands or partial skeins of yarn so that they can be stored or carried neatly.

- **YARN SCRAPS,** *Recycling:* Save small lengths of yarn from needlework and craft projects so that you can loop the yarn on gift tags and tie them on package ribbons. Don't forget to make the gift tags from the fronts of old greeting cards for total recycling!

- **YOGURT,** *Flavoring Plain/Low-fat:* Add fruit, jam, vanilla, or other flavoring (about a ½ teaspoon per cup according to your taste). Vanilla yogurt is a delicious low-cal and nutritious dressing for sliced fruit. I have a dieting friend who adds plain cocoa, vanilla, and sweetener to non-fat yogurt when she has an attack of the munchies and finds that she's consumed all but her allocated calories of milk for that day. It's not ice cream or pudding, but it stops the cravings!

- **YOGURT "CREAM CHEESE,"** *Easy-Fix:* Place a coffee filter in a strainer and empty a container of low-fat or non-fat yogurt into the filter. Place the strainer over a bowl and refrigerate overnight. By morning the liquid will have separated from the solids. Mix with fruit, honey, wheat germ, vanilla, or a bit of sugar for flavoring; then, spread on whole-grain toast or bagel for a nutritious and tasty, low-cholesterol breakfast.

• **YOGURT CUPS,** *Recycling:*
1. Store small bits and pieces like paper clips, thumbtacks, rubber bands, nails, screws, and pins.
2. Save lids and cups, wash well and use for children's or dieter's individual ice-cream portions to avoid mess from large cartons and tempting the dieter to take more than allowed.
3. They are free drinking cups for kids at picnics and in bathrooms (personalize cups for reuse by family members until the cup gets yucky; then dispose of it).
4. Small yogurt cups can be ½- or 1-cup measuring cups; quart-size could be a measure for a dog's daily "dose" of dry food.
5. When packing lunches, they will hold chips, small cookies, grapes, and other fruits (no more squashed plums) and goodies that get crushed in a lunch bag.

Z

- **ZIPPER,** *Quick-Fix, Freeing One Stuck in a Boot Flap:* When this happened to me, I cut a small slit in the leather just above the zipper, then slid the zipper to the top to free it and back to the bottom.

- **ZIPPER,** *Quick-Fix for Stuck One:* Rub the teeth with dry bar soap or candle and zip!

- **ZIPPER PULL,** *Quick-Fixes Emergency Replacement:* If the movable zipper part has a hole on either side, a small paper clip or safety pin can replace the pull tab.

- **ZIPPER PULLS,** *Recycling:* When luggage, handbag, or other zippers are hard to grasp, attach a key chain (especially those brightly colored promotional key chains that accumulate in desk drawers); the remaining "dangles" of unmated earrings; other pieces of costume jewelry; charms; or even a loop made from a piece of leather thong or shoelace.

- **ZUCCHINI,** *Freezing the Inevitable Surplus:* Grate zucchini in a food processor and pack the pulp in freezer bags in portions for making zucchini bread or other recipes later in the year.

• **zzzz,** *Seven Things to Do When You Can't Sleep:*
1. Keep regular hours and bedtime routines.
2. Avoid caffeinated beverages for six to eight hours before bedtime. If you smoke, be aware that nicotine is an even stronger stimulant than caffeine. Alcoholic beverages can hamper your falling asleep easily and sleeping soundly, once you doze off.
3. Afternoon naps and sleeping too many hours at night can interfere with falling asleep.
4. If worries and distractions keep you awake, make "to-do" lists for the next day so that you don't worry about forgetting something as you try to nod off.
5. Keep a note pad and pen next to the bed so that you can jot down last minute thoughts on paper instead of keeping them inside your head where they keep you awake.
6. Starving or stuffing yourself can keep you awake. You can't settle down if a too empty digestive system is rumbling and a too full one is stressed.
7. Mother was right! A glass of warm milk at bedtime really does help—unless, of course, you are lactose-intolerant and can't drink it because it won't digest! Then, a nice hot cup of herbal or spiced tea—a tea without caffeine, of course—can sooth some people as much as the traditional warm milk.

SPOTS AND STAINS

Since spots and stains have a way of showing up when we don't always have exactly the right stuff needed to deal with them, I'm including as many ways to remove each type of spot or stain as I have in my files; some are Quick-Fix and some methods take several steps. Some methods allow full-strength applications of alcohol, vinegar, ammonia, non-iodized salt, etc., and others require diluting them. Let the fabric's sturdiness or delicacy be your guide.

Caution: With all spot removal techniques, ALWAYS test on an inconspicuous place to make sure the method won't harm fabric or fade colors. Of course, if a garment is useless unless a stubborn spot is removed, it won't hurt to try a variety of homemade remedies. However, when in doubt with your better garments, take them to a professional laundry/dry cleaner for advice and help.

- **PROBLEMS A DRY CLEANER CAN'T SOLVE:**
1. Some stains can't be removed without ruining the garment.
2. Some colors bleed even in dry cleaning. "Bleeding" occurs when manufacturers don't thoroughly test dyes.
3. Some fabrics may shrink during dry cleaning because some manufacturers don't pre-shrink materials used in making the garment.

4. Holes or tears can appear after the dry-cleaning process if the fabric has been damaged by insects or acid spills. While they don't show up prior to cleaning, weakened fibers fray or come apart during the cleaning process.

5. Excess shine caused by home ironing can't be removed by dry cleaning. Place a cloth over such fabrics or iron on the wrong side, which is a good idea for all dark colors no matter what the fabric type.

6. When working on spots, blot instead of rubbing which spreads the stain and may damage the fabric, especially silk.

- **GENERAL STAIN REMOVAL RULES:**

1. Fresh stains are easier to remove; old and set stains may not come out at all.

2. Before treating a stain, find out what kind of stain it is, the type of fabric and if it is colorfast (see label), and how old the stain is. Ordinary machine washing and drying will set some stains permanently.

3. Generally, you start with cold or warm water; hot water sets some stains.

4. When bleach is recommended, use a bleach appropriate to that fabric. Chlorine bleaches must be diluted for stain treatment.

5. Test stain removers on an inside seam or hidden area to make sure the fabric won't be damaged or the color won't fade.

6. Putting the stained area facedown on a paper towel or white cloth and then applying the stain remover to the BACK of the stain can force the stain off the fabric instead of into it.

7. Protein stains are easier to remove if you break them down with meat tenderizer or enzyme pre-soaks.

8. Always use dry-cleaning solvents in well-ventilated rooms.

- **ACNE MEDICATIONS WITH BENZOYL PEROXIDE:** Benzoyl peroxide can destroy fabric dyes permanently. To avoid damage to T-shirts, towels, and other garments (even wall paint when you grope for a towel!): after applying the medication, rinse off carefully and wash hands thoroughly to remove any residue before you handle or touch fabrics. **Hint:** Dry face and hands with white towels and switch to white bedding during application periods so that colored towels and sheets don't get ruined. It only takes a bit of this medication to bleach fabrics.

• **ALCOHOLIC BEVERAGES:**
Method 1, Washable Fabrics: Soak or sponge stain promptly with cool water; sponge with white household vinegar and rinse. If stain remains, rub in liquid laundry detergent, rinse, and launder as usual. See BEER, and WINE, SOFT DRINKS.

• **ANTIPERSPIRANT/DEODORANT:** Ironing may set these stains.
Method 1, Light Stains: Rub in undiluted liquid detergent and then launder with hottest water safe for fabric.
Method 2, Heavy Stains: Place stain facedown on a paper towel and sponge the back of the stain (on outside of garment) with dry-cleaning solvent, let dry, rinse. Rub in undiluted liquid detergent and launder with hottest water safe for fabric.
Method 3, Fresh Perspiration Stains: Apply diluted ammonia to the stains and rinse with water. For old stains, try applying white vinegar and rinse with water or launder.
Method 4: Before washing the garment, rinse the area with plain water, then wash with the rest of your laundry in either warm or hot water with good suds.
Method 5: Soak in warm water with enzyme pre-soak product. Wash in hottest water safe for fabric. If stain remains, dampen and sprinkle stain with meat tenderizer. Let stand 30 minutes to an hour. Launder again.
Method 6: If stain remains after Method 5, treat with non-flammable dry-cleaning solvent, then rub detergent into the stain, and launder.
Hint 1: Avoid buildup by washing garments in hottest water safe for fabric every third or fourth time.
Hint 2: If you allow your deodorant to dry completely before you dress, it may help to prevent stains from some brands.
Hint 3: If you want to use a non-staining natural deodorant, try dabbing/dusting your underarm area with plain baking soda.
Note: Also, please see PERSPIRATION in this section.

• **ARTIST'S OILS ON CLOTHING:** Turpentine removes oil paint but can discolor some fabrics. Try removing artist's oil paint with bar face soap. **Note:** You can even clean your brushes with bar soap. Put the soap and brush under warm running water and rub the brush into the soap from side to side, making sure the soap goes all the way up the bristles. Gently rub the soap through the bristles with your fingers until all the paint is removed. Rinse with clear warm water, squeezing out the excess soap.

- **BALLPOINT INK:**
Method 1, Washable Fabrics: Hair spray or rubbing alcohol will usually remove ballpoint ink from washable fabrics. Don't spray directly on the stain; lightly spot clean it with a cloth dampened with either solution. Keep paper towels under the stain and change them frequently because the ink bleeds when in contact with alcohol. Rub liquid laundry detergent directly into remaining stain and launder as usual.
Method 2, Washable Fabrics: Apply hair spray until wet or sponge stain with rubbing alcohol as in Method 1. Flush with solution of 1 teaspoon detergent to 1 quart warm water; rinse in cool water; launder as usual. Apply glycerine to tough stains before washing.
Method 3, Dry-cleanable Fabrics: To home treat, place a blotter under the stained area; drip a compatible dry-cleaning fluid through it; reapply if needed. As always, be sure to tell the dry cleaner what caused the stain and how you treated it if you attempted to remove it yourself.

- **BEER:** Apply hydrogen peroxide to dried stains on white cotton; sponge stains on colored fabrics with white vinegar.

- **BLOOD ON FABRIC:** Getting to this stain ASAP (as soon as possible or sooner than possible is the key). Always avoid hot water; heat sets blood stains.
Method 1, Washable Fabrics: Apply pre-wash stain remover. Or, soak in cold water for one-half hour. If stain is stubborn, rub with detergent and rinse. Really stubborn stains can sometimes be removed with a mixture of 1 tablespoon ammonia and 1 cup water applied to stain. Rinse well before washing with chlorine bleach. Avoid hot water, it sets the stain.
Method 2, Dry-cleanable Fabrics: If you can't get the garment to the dry cleaner immediately, try treating the stain with a solution of 1 ounce table salt to 1 quart cold water. The salt may help prevent color bleeding. Rinse areas and blot with towel. Warm water and

hydrogen peroxide may remove final traces of the stain on some white fabrics.

Method 3: Soak stain in cold water immediately. If stain remains, pour 3 percent hydrogen peroxide over stained area. Test first, peroxide removes color.

Method 4: Dampen stained area with cold water; sprinkle with unseasoned meat tenderizer and let set. You may need to repeat the method until all traces of the stain are removed; then wash as usual.

Method 5: If fabric is bleachable, douse with hydrogen peroxide or diluted ammonia before rinsing in cool water.

• **BRASS/COPPER TARNISH:** Rub into the stain a paste made as follows: Mix together equal parts salt and flour, then add white vinegar to make a paste. You may have to repeat applications.

• **BUBBLE GUM,** *Removing:* While bubble gum is not really a stain, it certainly is a blemish when it's stuck to clothing, hair, furniture, etc. Tried and true is to rub with a small amount of peanut butter and the gum slides off. However, the surface should be washable for this method. **Note:** Please see CHEWING GUM.

• **BUTTER, MARGARINE:** Please see GREASY STAINS and OIL STAINS.

• **CANDLE WAX AND CRAYONS:**

Method 1, Washable Fabrics: Remove surface wax with dull knife; place stain between paper towels and press with warm iron, replacing towels frequently to absorb more wax. Then place stain face-down on clean paper towels and sponge the back of the stain with dry-cleaning solvent. Let dry, then launder. If traces of color remain, wash again with chlorine bleach, if fabric is bleach safe. Otherwise soak in enzyme detergent or an oxygen bleach in hottest water safe for fabric; then launder.

Method 2, Washable Fabric: Rub with ice cube to harden wax before scraping it off with a blunt knife. Place stained area between paper towels or brown paper bags and iron, changing absorbent papers and repeating until all wax is melted off. Sponge away remaining stains with dry-cleaning fluid.

Method 3, Dry-cleanable Fabric: Same as above for washable items. Please see CRAYON entries for more crayon stain removal methods.

- **CANVAS SHOES,** *Stain Prevention:* Spray with stain-resistant fabric spray before the first wearing. They'll be easier to clean. Repeat spraying if they are washed.

- **CARBON PAPER:** Dampen area and rub liquid laundry detergent into the stain. Hand wash garment in warm, soapy water, rinse, and repeat steps if needed until stain is removed, then launder as usual.

- **CATSUP/TOMATO SAUCE:** Dab off excess and soak garment in cold water for 30 minutes. Rub liquid laundry detergent or white bar soap into remaining stain while still wet. Then launder in warm water and detergent.

- **CHEWING GUM:**
Method 1, Washable Fabrics: Rub with ice cube to harden gum before scraping it off with a blunt knife. Place fabric facedown on paper towels and sponge remaining stain with dry-cleaning fluid or treat with pre-wash spray, and then launder.
Method 2, Dry-cleanable Fabrics: Same as for washable items, except don't launder.
Method 3: Rub area with ice until gum hardens and can be removed as in Method 1, then place waxed paper over excess gum and iron lightly over paper; changing paper as gum sticks to it.

- **CHOCOLATE:**
Method 1: Soak garment for at least 30 minutes in cold water. Rub liquid laundry detergent into the stain while still wet. Rinse. If a greasy stain remains, sponge area with cleaning fluid, then rinse and launder in warm water. Bleach will remove some stubborn chocolate stains, but use only with colorfast clothing.
Method 2: Soak in warm or cold water. Brush area with a paste of detergent and hot water. Remove remaining grease stains with non-flammable dry-cleaning solvent.

- **CLEANING FLUID RINGS:** Sometimes, these can be steamed out if the garment is held over a tea kettle. **Caution:** Steam can burn; put the garment, not your hands, over the steam spout!

- **COFFEE OR TEA:**
Method 1, Washable Fabrics: Sponge with cold water. Simple washing will usually remove black coffee or tea stains. You can also

sponge the stain with dry-cleaning fluid if you've used cream in your coffee or tea.

Method 2, Dry-cleanable Fabrics: Treat the same as washables.

Method 3: Immediately rinse area well in cold water. Treat stain with pre-wash spray and launder in warm water and detergent. Allow garment to drip-dry to make sure all traces of stain are gone. (Dryer heat will set stains.) If necessary, repeat all steps.

Method 4: Wipe clean with a paste made from baking soda and water or non-iodized salt and white vinegar.

• **COFFEE STAINS ON FABRIC,** *When They Reappear:* Because they contain tannin, coffee and tea may cause a stain that seems to disappear after washing but returns later. When these stains set too long, they may be impossible to remove. It's best to take the garment to a dry cleaner and point out the stain so that a professional can treat it with special chemicals.

• **COLORED GARMENTS,** *Brightening Dull Colors:*
1. Black Clothing and Stockings: Rinse in clear water to which a couple of glugs of vinegar have been added.
2. Colored Fabrics and Embroidery Cottons: Set colors by soaking washables in a strong salt water before first laundering.
3. Avoid dulling Colors: Wash fluorescent colors separately and same colored clothing together. And always follow care directions for water temperature and bleach use or non-use.

• **COSMETICS:**
Method 1, Washable Fabrics: Dampen stain with detergent until outline is gone, and rinse well. If safe for the fabric, a few drops of ammonia, followed by a good rinse may work on stubborn stains.

Method 2, Dry-cleanable Fabrics: Sponge dry-cleanables with dry-cleaning fluid.

Method 3, General Spot Removal: Wet stain and rub bar soap into it. If the stain remains, use regular liquid detergent. Gently work it into the stain and then wash the garment as usual.

• **CRAYON,** *When Clothing Has Gone Through the Dryer:* Spray liberally both sides of the stain with petroleum-based pre-wash stain remover, and rub it into the fabric with your fingers. Let stand for a while and wash as usual. You may have to repeat the process two or three times. If stains remain on bleach-safe fabric, follow directions on the bottle or box for the amount to use for removing stains from that fabric. If there is any wax on the dryer drum, dampen a small cloth with the spray and wipe out the drum.

• **CRAYON/CANDLE WAX,** *General Stain Removal:* Scrape off excess wax with dull knife; sponge with non-flammable dry cleaning solvent; launder.

• **CRAYON STAINS,** *When a Crayon Has Gone Through the Wash Cycles in a Pocket:* Try this: Rub all crayon stains with waterless hand cleaner, then wash the garment in cold water with detergent but after the wash cycle, stop the machine and let the garment soak overnight. In the morning complete the wash cycle. If some spots still remain, repeat scrubbing the spots with waterless hand cleaner and a scrub brush.

• **CRAYON STAINS,** *Whole Load of Clothes:* First wash with hot water and laundry soap, such as mild baby-clothes soap, and 1 cup baking soda. If color remains, launder with chlorine bleach if fabrics are bleach safe. Otherwise soak in enzyme detergent or oxygen bleach in hottest water that's safe for fabric and then launder.

• **CREAM, MILK, ICE CREAM:** Sponge with non-flammable dry-cleaning solvent.

• **DEODORANTS,** Please see ANTIPERSPIRANT/DEODORANT and PERSPIRATION.

• **DYE TRANSFER:**
Method 1, Whites: Fabric color remover, used according to directions, may remove dye that has "bled" on white fabrics. Launder after treatment. If dye remains, launder again using chlorine bleach if safe for fabric.
Method 2, Colored Fabrics, Non-Bleachable Whites: Soak in enzyme detergent or an oxygen bleach, then launder.

• **DYE TRANSFER,** *On White Collar of Colored Sweater:* You can try a color remover just on the color but if it doesn't work, return the garment for replacement or refund.

• **FABRIC SOFTENER SHEETS,** *On Polyester Silk-Look Garments:* Wet the area, then rub stain with white bar soap or liquid laundry detergent. Rinse well, let air-dry. If necessary, repeat cleaning steps and launder in hottest water safe from fabric. Make sure all the stains are gone before placing the garment in the dryer because dryer heat can set them permanently. It's better to air-dry the garment to avoid having the dryer heat set the stain permanently. **Note:** Too few or too many clothes in the dryer can cause these stains, as well as too high a heat setting. If you are only drying one or two garments in the dryer with a fabric softener sheet, add some lightweight bath towels. **Hint:** Certain polyester fabrics seem especially prone to this problem. Try saving old softener sheets and using the old sheets instead of new sheets with fabrics you think might absorb the softener. Or, just avoid the dryer altogether!

• **FRUITS, FRUIT JUICES, BERRIES: Caution:** don't use soap to treat fruit stains; it sets them.

Method 1: Soak immediately for about 30 minutes in cold water. Rub some detergent into the stain while it's still wet. Wash as usual. If this treatment doesn't work, apply hydrogen peroxide if the garment is bleach-safe, then rinse well.

Method 2, Washable Fabric: Soak. If stain remains, apply white vinegar and rinse; stubborn stains may need application of hydrogen peroxide.

Method 3, Dry-cleanable Fabric: Apply a small amount of detergent on the stain and rinse if the fabric allows, or sponge with dry-cleaning fluid.

Method 4: Soak immediately in cool water; wash. If stain remains, cover area with a paste made from oxygen-type bleach, a few drops of hot water and a few drops of ammonia; wait 15 to 30 minutes; wash.

• **GENERAL STAINS IN HOTELS AND RESTAURANTS:**

Quick-Fix 1: Rub stain with bar soap and wash/rinse. Or, use hotel shampoo on the stain and for washing garments.

Quick-Fix 2: Some liquid hand soaps in restaurants can be used to quick clean a spill. (Spots are one reason to always carry a purse. If you want to conceal the wet spot, you can always hold your purse or a stole over it until it dries.)

Quick-Fix 3: Apply tried-and-true club soda, especially to wine stains. At home clean as usual for that fabric.

- **GRASS, FLOWERS, FOLIAGE STAINS:**

Method 1, Washable Fabrics: If you have no pre-wash stain remover, work detergent into the stain and rinse; then launder in hottest water safe for fabric.

Method 2, Washable Fabrics: Try sponging the stain with one part alcohol to two parts water and rinse. If stain persists try applying hydrogen peroxide.

Method 3: Apply rubbing alcohol liberally to stained areas before laundering as usual.

Method 4, Dry-cleanable Fabrics: If the garment is dry-cleanable only, you probably shouldn't be wearing it gardening but if you did, it may be safe to apply alcohol or sponge with dry-cleaning fluid.

Method 5, Acetate Fabrics: Sponge with non-flammable dry-cleaning solvent.

- **GREASE ON TABLECLOTH:** Sprinkle talcum powder or cornstarch over the stain. As the grease is absorbed, add more powder until no more grease is absorbed; brush it off. Treat the remaining stain with pre-wash spray and wash in the hottest water safe for the fabric. Before putting the cloth in the dryer, check the spot to make sure it doesn't need a second treatment.

- **GREASY STAINS** (Car Grease or Oil, Butter, Margarine, Lard, Salad Dressings, Cooking Oils):

Method 1: Pre-treat with heavy-duty liquid laundry detergent or pre-wash spray or liquid. Launder.

Method 2, Heavy Stains: Place stained areas facedown on paper towels. Apply dry-cleaning solvent to back side of stain, replacing towels frequently. Allow to dry, then rub in liquid detergent or dampen stain area with water, and rub with bar soap or detergent paste. Rinse and launder.

Method 3: Gently rub in talcum powder, cornmeal, or cornstarch and let set. Later, brush or sponge powder away. Please see OIL ON FABRIC.

- **GUM:** Please see CHEWING GUM.

- **ICE CREAM:** Soak garment in cold water; hand wash in warm soapy water and rinse. If a greasy stain remains or if the ice cream was chocolate, sponge the stain with cleaning fluid. After all traces of stain are gone, launder as usual.

- **INKS: Caution:** Regular laundering removes some types of ink but sets others. If you have doubts, take a good garment to a professional. Also, some inks require a color remover and some permanent inks can't be removed.
Method 1: Pre-treat first by placing stain facedown on paper towels and then sponging the back of stain with alcohol or dry-cleaning solvent. If some ink remains, rub with bar soap; rinse; launder.
Method 2: Dampen stain with water and rub with bar soap. Rinse. Soak in enzyme detergent or oxygen bleach in hottest water safe for fabric; launder. If stain remains, launder again with chlorine bleach if safe for fabric.
Method 3, Dried Ink Stains: Rub non-iodized table salt in and dribble lemon juice over the salt. Launder after stain is gone.
Method 4, Old Wives' Tale That Works on Some Fabrics: Soak ink spots in warm milk before they can dry. Then launder as usual.

- **IODINE:** Rinse from underside of stain with cool water. Soak in solution of color remover, rinse, and launder.

- **IRON RUST:** Moisten the stain with water, apply lemon juice, then rinse. You may have to repeat the treatment several times to get the stain out. Hanging a lemon-juice treated item out in bright sun sometimes makes the lemon juice work better. **Caution:** Lemon juice will lighten certain colors. Test the juice on an inconspicuous place on the garment before using it. Of course, if you can't wear the garment with the rust stain, a bleach spot isn't going to matter much.

- **LIPSTICK:**
Method 1: Place stain facedown on paper towels. Sponge back of stain with dry-cleaning solvent, replacing the paper towel underneath frequently so that color can be absorbed. Dampen stain with water and rub with bar soap, rinse, and launder.
Method 2: Immediately, place stained area over absorbent towel and saturate with rubbing alcohol, then rub area with cloth dipped in rubbing alcohol. (Test for color-fastness before using alcohol.) Rinse and launder after all traces of stain are removed.
Method 3: Try pre-wash spray before laundering as usual.
Method 4: Sponge with non-flammable dry-cleaning solvent; launder white fabrics with diluted chlorine bleach or launder colored fabrics with oxygen-type bleach.

- **MAKEUP/FOUNDATION:**

Method 1, Powdered or Water-based Makeup: It's non-greasy and so can be removed by dampening the area and rubbing stain with white bar soap. Rinse and launder.

Method 2, Oily Makeup: Treat with pre-wash spray, then dampen the area and rub to work stain out. After all stain is gone, rinse and launder in hottest water safe for fabric.

- **MASCARA:**

1. Oil-based Mascara: Apply pre-wash spray or stick directly to the stain and machine wash.
2. Water-based Mascara: Try liquid detergent or dampen the area and rub with a bar of soap until suds form. When the outline of the stain has disappeared, rinse thoroughly. You may have to repeat the process.
3. Waterproof Mascara: Some waterproof mascara is impossible to remove.

- **MATTRESS "ACCIDENT,"** *Removing Urine Stain:*

1. Immediately (before the area dries) try to absorb as much of the urine as possible with dry towels. Sponge the stained area with a solution of half vinegar and half water to clean the stain. Again, remove as much of the moisture as possible with dry towels, or dry with hair dryer on "Low" or "Cool."
2. If the stained area has dried, try to keep it from getting larger by rubbing the stain from the outside in toward the center with upholstery shampoo. If the outer ring is still present, repeat the process.
3. After the mattress has dried, spray it with an air freshener made for fabrics to help prevent a musty or urine odor. If you can, place the mattress outside in the fresh air and sunshine to air it out.
4. As with all stains, immediate treatment gets the best results. **Note:** If you fail to remove the stain but are able to remove the odor so that the mattress is still sleepable, cover the mattress with a zippered fabric mattress cover available in many catalogs.

- **MEAT-JUICE, EGG:** Soak in cold or warm water with enzyme presoak. Treat grease stains with non-flammable dry-cleaning solvent. Then wash.

- **MILDEW:** Old mildew stains are almost impossible to remove and mildew fungus can destroy or weaken fabrics. **Hint:** When brushing mildew off garments or items, take them outdoors to prevent the spores from becoming airborne and setting up housekeeping elsewhere in the house.

Method 1: Launder with chlorine bleach if it's safe for the fabric, if not, soak in oxygen bleach for 15 to 30 minutes, and then launder.

Method 2, Bleachable Fabrics: Brush with a stiff brush to remove mold spores and soak in solution of 1 tablespoon of chlorine bleach to 1 quart water for 15 minutes. Rinse and launder, adding ½ cup chlorine bleach to wash cycle.

Method 3, Non-bleachable Fabrics: Brush with stiff brush to remove mold spores. Flush the stain with solution of ½ cup lemon juice and 1 tablespoon of salt. Dry garment in the sun. After stain is removed, launder as usual.

Method 4, Walls and Floors: Scrub with a brush dipped in borax and water.

Method 5, Books and Papers: Dust with talcum powder, cornmeal, or cornstarch; let set two days; brush off.

• **MILK:** Albumin, a protein in milk, is the culprit.

Method 1, Fresh Stains: Soak clothing for several hours in water to which detergent containing enzymes has been added. Launder as usual.

Method 2, Milk, Baby Formula: Soak garment in cold water. Rub liquid laundry detergent into stain and then launder in hottest water safe for fabric with enzyme detergent. If a greasy stain remains, sponge area with cleaning fluid and launder again before drying in clothes dryer. **Hint:** When you have a baby, it's handy to keep a diaper pail for soaking stained clothing. Then you can use a no-hands approach—empty the pail into the washer, put it on "Spin" to remove excess water, then run the wash cycle as usual.

• **MUD:** Allow to dry, then brush off excess dirt and spot clean with detergent or shampoo, and launder in cold water.

• **MUSTARD:**

Method 1: Dampen area and rub liquid laundry detergent into stain. Rinse, then soak in hot water and detergent for several hours. Launder with enzyme detergent.

Method 2: Apply pre-wash spray or liquid, or dampen stain with water and rub with bar soap. Rinse and launder with chlorine bleach if safe for fabric. If not, soak in enzyme detergent or oxygen bleach in hottest water safe for fabric; then launder. You may have to repeat the process.

Method 3: Soak stained area with diluted ammonia before laundering.

Method 4: Immediately rinse in cold water. Wash with hot soapy water with chlorine bleach if fabric is bleachable. Use oxygen-type bleach for laundering colored fabrics.

- **MYSTERY STAINS:** Flush with cold water; apply pre-wash spray and rub into stain. After all traces of stain are removed, launder as usual. These stains are usually water soluble if caught in time.

- **NAIL POLISH:**

Method 1: Test garment for color-fastness and fabric safety for acetone use. If it's okay, sponge stain with pure acetone. After removing entire stain, launder. **Caution:** Acetone will dissolve acetate and triacetate in fabrics. Amyl acetate is safe for acetate fabrics.

Method 2: Place stain facedown on paper towels. Sponge back with nail-polish remover, frequently replacing the towels beneath the stain. Repeat sponging until stain is gone. Launder. **Caution:** Do not use nail-polish remover on acetate or Arnel fabrics. Send them to the dry cleaner.

- **OIL ON FABRIC:**

Method 1, Quick-Fix for Fresh Spots: Salad oil dribble on your shirt or blouse? Apply baby powder to the spots, wipe it off, apply more, and let it set a while. Wipe powder away before laundering.

Method 2, Oil on Washable Fabric, Quick-Fix When Away from Home: In an emergency, toothpaste will remove oil on polyester, cotton and blends but you must apply it carefully because too much rubbing can damage fabric or color. **Caution:** Don't try this on silks or dry-cleanables.

Method 3, Quick-Fix: Rub white chalk into the stain before laundering. Chalk's easy to carry in a purse or bag. **Note:** Please see GREASY STAINS.

- **PAINT:** Check label on the can for instructions.

Method 1, Oil Base: Generally, you can remove oil-base paint with a bit of turpentine or paint thinner if the fabric is color safe; rinse well. Then rub with detergent paste and wash as usual.

Method 2, Oil-base Paint, Varnish: Apply solvent recommended on the paint container. If container is not available, apply turpentine. Rinse, then rub with bar soap. Rinse again, then launder.

Method 3, Paint Thinned with Solvents: Dab solvent onto the stained area. After wetting stain with solvent, work liquid laundry detergent into the area and soak the garment in hot water. Launder as usual.

Method 4, Oil-base Paint: Scrape off fresh paint. Sponge with non-flammable dry-cleaning solvent. Launder.

Method 5, Water-base Paint: If treated immediately, water-base paints may wash out with soap and water. After it has set and dried, water-base paint cannot be removed. Rinse the stain well in warm water to flush out paint, and then launder as usual.

• **PENCIL LEAD:** Try to gently erase as much of the lead as possible with a pencil eraser. Then rub liquid laundry detergent into remaining stain and launder as usual.

• **PERFUME:** Please see ALCOHOLIC BEVERAGES and use the same instructions.

• **PERSPIRATION:** The International Fabricare Institute says that these stains result when you apply a large amount of deodorant and then wash the garment with cold "hard" water (high-mineral, low-alkaline water). Many deodorants and antiperspirants contain aluminum salts. When combined with laundry detergent and cold water, the salts cannot be easily dissolved and so they remain on the fabric. Please see ANTIPERSPIRANT/DEODORANT for removal instructions.

• **PET STAINS:**
Method 1: Soak stained area in warm soapy water. If stains remain after soaking, sponge with solution of equal parts water and white household vinegar which will also help to neutralize remaining odors. Rinse well and launder as usual.

Method 2: Dampen area with equal parts of white vinegar and water; blot dry.

• **PLAY PUTTY:** Remove putty by rubbing liquid detergent into the spot from the underside of the fabric; scrub well. While this should remove the putty, a stain may remain. Try sponging diluted hydrogen peroxide onto the area. Always test in an inconspicuous spot first because peroxide can remove color.

• **REDDISH-TINGED AREA ON GARMENT:** This can be an acid color change, usually due to perspiration or deodorants, fruit juices, and some beverages. These areas are not noticeable immediately; instead they develop gradually when the staining substance remains on the fabric. Clothing should be washed or dry-cleaned often to avoid this problem. Depending upon how long the stain has been on the fabric, a dry cleaner may be able to minimize or neutralize the discoloration. As with all stains, removal is more likely to occur if the garment is cleaned immediately.

• **RING AROUND THE COLLAR:** Rub ring with hair shampoo, prewash spray or liquid laundry detergent. Let set for 30 minutes and launder as usual. You may need hottest water safe for the fabric to remove collar rings. AVOID the problem—it helps if you wipe your neck with astringent (or rubbing alcohol) before dressing, especially if you are in a big city where the air is polluted from traffic and industry.

• **RUST ON LAUNDRY,** *When You Frequently Find Rust Spots on Whole Loads of Laundry:*
1. Sometimes laundry soap has a chemical reaction with certain local water supplies—usually due to iron or manganese in the water. Dirt and soil are washed out but a new substance—the detergent and the soil—is redeposited into the garment; it looks like rust spots. Change laundry detergent. When iron is in your water supply, use extra detergent plus a non-precipitating water conditioner. Dissolve the detergent and water conditioner in warm water before adding it to the washer to get best results. You may also want to consider installing a water softener, chemical feeder, or special filters to remove iron and manganese from the water supply. Also, avoid overloading the washer—clothes should move freely with enough water to rinse away all deposits.
2. Rust stains can also be caused by a rusty water heater or rusty water lines. **Note:** Your local water company or a water-quality company can test your lines for iron or manganese (rust) content.

- **RUST SPOTS,** *Removing:* **Caution:** Do not use chlorine bleach on rust; it spreads the stain and sets it. Commercial rust removers for fabric use are available in the fabric dye sections of the supermarket. But, never use rust remover inside a washer and be careful not to spill any on a washer; it removes the glossy finish on porcelain outside or inside the machine.
Method 1, Few Spots: Apply commercial rust-stain remover; rinse and launder.
Method 2: Dampen stain with lemon juice and sprinkle on non-iodized table salt. Lay garment in the sunshine and continue to dampen area with lemon juice until the stain is gone. Then launder.
Method 3, Rusty Discoloration on White Load: Wash in phosphate detergent, if available, with 1 cup enzyme detergent or an oxygen bleach. If stains remain, dissolve 1 ounce oxalic acid crystals per gallon of water in a plastic container. Soak clothes in this solution for 10 to 15 minutes. Rinse and launder.

- **SALAD DRESSINGS:** Please see GREASY STAINS.

- **SCORCH MARKS: Note:** Severe scorch marks cannot be removed.
Method 1: Launder with chlorine bleach if safe for fabric.
Method 2, Non-bleachable Fabrics: Soak in strong solution of enzyme detergent or oxygen bleach in hottest water safe for fabric; then launder.
Method 3, Color-fast Fabrics: 3 percent hydrogen peroxide fades light scorch marks. After testing fabric for color-fastness, dab 3 percent hydrogen peroxide on scorched area with clean white cloth. Apply until scorch mark fades.
Method 4: Alternate rubbing the area with a lemon slice, then wiping with a dampened sponge until the stain disappears.
Method 5, Delicate Fabrics: Rub scorch marks lightly with a clean white cloth dampened with white vinegar. Wipe the area (don't rub) with a clean, dry cloth. Press if needed.

- **SHOE DYE/POLISH ON OFF-WHITE HOSE:** Soak the discolored section of the hose in rubbing alcohol and wash as usual. You may need to use a color-remover; if so, treat the entire pair because it may change the overall appearance. **Hint:** To keep dye from bleeding onto hose, spray the inside of the shoes several times with a fabric-protector spray; re-spray occasionally.

- **SHOE POLISH: Note:** Some shoe polishes won't come out. Try dampening the stain with cleaning fluid, then wash in warm water and detergent.

- **SILK FABRIC STAINS: Caution:** Do not attempt to remove spill-stains from silk by rubbing the area with a damp cloth. Silk fibers break easily when wet; blot instead of rubbing.
1. Beverage spills may disappear when the fabric dries but sugar in some beverages may cause a yellow stain that appears later. To avoid problems, take silk garments to the dry cleaner as soon as possible and tell what was spilled where.
2. Perspiration and body oils are silk's worst enemies; wear dress shields or spray the underarm areas with fabric protector spray to prevent stains and maintain all silk garments with regular dry cleaning or hand washing.
3. If there is a chafed area that has lost its color or luster, point this out to the dry cleaner who may be able to then give the item a special restoration bath.

- **STICKY RESIDUE,** *From Gummed Name Stickers, etc.:* Carefully dab with rubbing alcohol, petroleum based pre-wash spray, or cleaning fluid—whichever is suitable for the fabric.

- **SUGARED BEVERAGES, COFFEE, FRUIT JUICE, TEA:** Must be treated when fresh because they become more difficult to remove as they age and almost impossible to remove when they are completely set. These stains often show up as brown or yellow spots after clothing is washed; I call them "mystery stains."

- **SWIMSUIT,** *Prevent Fading/Fabric Damage from Pool-Water Chlorine:* From a pet store, buy chlorine remover for aquarium water. Rinse your bathing suit after each swim in a solution of 1 drop anti-chlorine formula to 1 gallon water.

- **TENNIS SHOES, WHITE RUBBER:** Clean stains off with whitewall tire cleaner. Follow directions on the container.

- **TIES,** *Preventing Serious Stains:* Before ever wearing a new tie, spray it with fabric stain repellent; spills won't always become stains. This is a favorite hint for frequent flyers! And, why do airline edibles leap onto your clothing anyway?

- **TOBACCO:** Dampen stain and rub with bar soap. Rinse. Soak in enzyme detergent or oxygen bleach and then launder. If stain remains, launder again with chlorine bleach if it's safe for that fabric.

- **TOOTHPASTE ON FABRIC: Caution:** This method is not for silk or other delicate fabrics because the rubbing motion can break the fibers. Place a cloth underneath the fabric, then work with a damp cloth to remove toothpaste. After removing the toothpaste, blow-dry with a hair dryer. **Note:** Avoid the problem by getting dressed after brushing your teeth or by putting a hand towel "bib" over the front of your clothing to protect it.

- **TYPEWRITER CORRECTION FLUID:** Soap and water will not remove paint-based correction fluid. Most are latex-based and must be treated like a paint stain. Take the garment to a dry cleaner and be sure to point it out and tell the cleaner what it is.

- **URINE, VOMIT, MUCUS:** Remove solid residue from fabric. Then, soak with enzyme detergent and warm water. Launder with chlorine bleach if safe for fabric. If not, launder with oxygen bleach and detergent or all-fabric bleach and detergent.

- **WHITE FABRICS TURNED GREY:** Dissolve 1 tablespoon of borax in hot water and add the solution to the final rinse to make whites get white again.

- **WINE OR COFFEE SPILLS,** *Quick-Fix:* Blot the fresh spill with a cloth soaked with tried and true club soda. Or, apply club soda liberally, then sponge up soda and wine.

- **WINE, SOFT DRINKS,** *Washable Fabrics:* Soak with enzyme detergent or oxygen bleach with hottest water safe for fabric and then launder. If stain remains, launder with chlorine bleach if safe for fabric.

- **YELLOWING** (White Nylon, Polyester, Durable Press, Etc.) Soak overnight with enzyme detergent or oxygen bleach and then launder in hottest water safe for fabric with detergent and bleach safe for these fabrics. Or launder with enzyme detergent/oxygen bleach added to regular detergent and hottest water safe for fabric. **Hint:** Modern fabrics contain fluorescent brighteners which react to the sun; instead of bleaching them, sunlight may cause them to become permanently yellowed. Avoid yellowing by drying white fabrics away from natural sunlight.

- **YELLOWING OF STONE-WASHED JEANS:** When the residue from the stone-washing process has not been rinsed completely from the fabric, yellowing can result when the fabric is in contact with some chemicals and even sunshine. Although it's usually permanent, the yellowing can sometimes be removed by commercial laundering.

- **LAST-DITCH STAIN REMOVER FORMULA**
Here is my favorite last-ditch stain remover for white and bleachable clothes (no silk, rayon, etc.). I use it when all else has failed and I can't wear the garment anyway with the spot on it.

    1 gallon of hot water
    1 cup of powdered dishwasher detergent
    ¼ cup of household liquid chlorine bleach

Mix well in a plastic, enamel, or stainless steel container. (This solution should not be used in an aluminum container or come in contact with aluminum because it will discolor it.)

When a garment has an impossible-to-remove stain, let it soak in this solution for 5 to 10 minutes. If any stain remains, soak longer, then wash as usual.

- **OTHER LAST-DITCH SPOT REMOVERS:**
Note: Applying strong bleach to spots can weaken fabrics where they are applied and those areas can deteriorate with each washing, but again, if you can't wear the garment with the stain, and a professional cleaner can't get it out, a last-ditch method is an alternative to throwing the garment out or sewing an appliqué over the stain. Also, note that these two methods may bleach colors out with the stain.
1. Wet the stain and sprinkle powdered dishwasher detergent powder on it. Work the powder into the stain and let the garment set until the stain is gone. Don't scrub too hard, the fabric may get "pills." Rinse, then launder with whites.
2. Squirt full-strength liquid dishwasher detergent on the spot, and work into the fabric. Again, don't scrub too hard or the fabric will "pill." Let set until the spot is gone. Rinse, then launder as usual with whites.

- **CARE-LABELS HINTS:** Keep a file of hang-labels from your clothing and home furnishings so that if sewn-in ones get lost, you have a record of their proper care needs. Keep price tags, too, in case a restaurant has to replace a garment one of its employees has damaged with a spill or if you have to make an insurance claim for a guest's damage to home furnishings. This is what care-label terms mean:

1. Machine Wash, Warm—Use washing machine, warm setting; hot water should not be used.
2. Hand Wash, Cold—Wash only by hand in cold water. Machine washing with warm or hot water shouldn't be used.
3. Bleach When Needed—All commercially available bleaches are safe for regular use.
4. Only Non-chlorine Bleach When Needed—Non-chlorine bleach is safe for use. Regular use of chlorine bleach could harm the garment.
5. Tumble Dry—Hot, medium, or low dryer temperature settings are safe for use.
6. Tumble Dry, Medium—Medium or low dryer temperatures settings are safe for use. Don't use hot setting.
7. Warm Iron—Iron on medium-temperature setting. The higher setting should not be used.
8. Dry Clean—Item can be dry-cleaned by any commercial method that uses any of the available dry-cleaning solvents.
9. Professionally Dry Clean, Perchloroethylene—Item can be dry-cleaned by any commercial establishment using perchloroethylene. Petroleum or fluorocarbon solvents should not be used.
10. Machine Wash, Separately—This warning must be given if the garment could cause harm to another product being washed with it.
11. A garment with detachable pieces will have separate care labels for each piece if each needs different care but one label for all if all can have identical care.
12. Care labels include all parts of the garment, such as lining, trim, buttons, and zippers, and should note if special care is needed for some parts, such as a warning to "remove trim before cleaning."
13. When the label says to clean separately, it means that the garment has limited colorfastness and some dye-bleeding may

occur the first few times it's washed. This can cause fading as well as dye transfer onto other garments washed with it.

14. International symbols for care meet requirements of other countries, but garments sold in the U.S. must also provide written instructions.

• **LAUNDRY WATER TEMPERATURES:** As most couples who play "thermostat Ping-Pong" during air-conditioning season know, the difference between "hot," "warm," and "cold" is a very individual and personal opinion. Not so with laundry, where terms can be translated into temperatures.

1. HOT—130°F or above; for white and colorfast fabrics, heavily soiled loads, diapers.

2. WARM—90°F to 110°F; for noncolorfast fabrics, moderately soiled loads, man-made fibers, and permanent-press fabrics, knits, silks, and woolens. (Heavily soiled, colorfast, sturdy man-made fibers and permanent-press fabrics can be washed in hot water if you use a permanent-press cycle.)

3. COLD—80°F or colder; for dark or bright colors that bleed, lightly soiled loads.

ODORS

I get a lot of mail about annoying or unpleasant odors and a lot of good solutions from readers. I do believe that odors are second only to spots and stains on the list of "little things" that drive us balmy and add stress to our already stressful days. Baking soda is, of course, one of the best odor-removers of all time and it's environmentally safe, too. Lemon juice and vinegar are also safe and effective odor-removers. So is charcoal. However, my resourceful readers have found other remedies that will work in a pinch and some, like mouthwash or toothpaste for removing onion odors from your hands, are in the "of course, why didn't I think of that" category.

REMOVING ODORS AND/OR ADDING PLEASANT SCENTS

• **AIR FRESHENER,** *Controlling Output of Commercial Products:* If you tear back the foil halfway on small plastic air fresheners, the scent will last longer and won't be overpowering in a small room.

• **AIR FRESHENER IN A JAR:** Soak a cotton ball with peppermint oil and put it in a small jar with a lid. When you need to scent or "de-scent" a room, remove the lid. Peppermint oil works well in smoke-filled rooms and leaves them pleasantly fresh. Keep out of reach of children.

- **AIR FRESHENER IN A VACUUM:** Toss a handful of spiced tea into the vacuum bag and each time you vacuum, the house will smell spicy and nice.

- **AIR FRESHENERS:** Also see ROOM DEODORIZERS.

- **ASHTRAY:** If you still smoke, put a little deodorized cat-box filler in ashtrays. It keeps odor down and cigarettes will be immediately extinguished when poked in.

- **BABY BOTTLE,** *Sour Odors:* Boil bottles in a solution of baking soda and water for a few minutes to rid them of the sour milk smell. Take care with glass bottles so that they don't bump each other and crack. A bottle sterilizer or canner might help. You may need to repeat the process weekly.
Note: To avoid odors, right after baby finishes the bottle, rinse it with cold water, then put about a teaspoon or so of baking soda in the bottle, fill with water and allow to soak until you need the bottle again. (Yes, it's untidy to have a row of soaking bottles in the sink but babies are precious and only need bottles for a relatively short period of time compared to the eighteen or so years they spend with you.)

- **BASEMENT,** *Removing Stale, Musty Odors:* Hang a nylon net bag or a bag from onions or potatoes with some charcoal in a convenient place.

- **BED SHEETS, PILLOWCASES,** *Quick-Fix When Taking Musty Guest Linens from Storage:* Toss bedding into the dryer with a fabric softener sheet or two for ten minutes. Or, put a fabric softener sheet in with the guest linens on the shelf a few days before they arrive.

- **BOOKS,** *Preventing Musty Odors When They Are in Storage:* Store books in a dry place and put charcoal in an old sock and place the sock in the book boxes.

- **BREAD-BOX WOOD SMELL:** No washing or cleaning can remove this smell from some boxes and so many people either return them for refund or use them for non-edibles' storage.

- **CARPET DEODORIZER:** With a flour sifter, sprinkle baking soda over the entire carpet and let sit for 20 minutes or longer, then vacuum. Rub cornstarch into lightly soiled spots before vacuuming and you'll clean your carpet while freshening it.

- **CARPET DEODORIZER,** *Stretching Commercial Brands:* Mix equal parts of baking soda and commercial carpet deodorizer to double the volume and still get equal fragrance.

- **CARS,** *Musty:* A problem, especially in damp climates.
1. Clean upholstery with a "dry"-type upholstery cleaner found in most grocery or discount stores. Follow instructions on the container.
2. If floor mats are removable, scrub them with a solution of half vinegar and half water, rinse well, dry in sun if possible.
3. Shampoo or clean carpeting with a spray-type carpet cleaner, making sure not to let the backing get wet.
4. Spray the ceiling and trunk with a good commercial spray deodorizer.

- **CAT ACCIDENT ON CARPET,** *Quick-Fix:* Company coming and kitty did it again in the dining room? Use a thick towel to blot up as much of the liquid as possible and heavily sprinkle the area with either scented carpet freshener or baking soda. Vacuum up when ready.

- **CIGARETTE SMELLS IN MATTRESS:** Try an aerosol spray from supermarkets made for fabric and upholstery odor removal and then lay the mattress and box spring out in the fresh air and sunshine all day if you can. If odor persists, you may need to thoroughly clean the mattress or box spring with a rented cleaning machine—follow use instructions with the machine.

- **CLOSET DEODORIZER:** Put a tablespoon or two of fresh unused ground coffee in one or two old socks and place them in the closet to prevent musty odors.

- **CLOSET MILDEW ODOR,** *Healthy Planet:* Fill a one-pound coffee can or other container with charcoal of the type used in aquariums and put it in the corner of a closet.

- **CLOSET SCENT:** A walk-in closet will smell nice if you step into it when you spray yourself with cologne. **Caution:** Take care not to spray cologne on clothing; it can stain or damage some fabrics.

- **COOLER,** *Preventing Musty Odors When Stored:* Sprinkle some baking soda into it before closing it up. Then, when you get the cooler out for a picnic, dump the soda into the kitchen sink, run water and it will freshen the drain.

- **CORNED BEEF AND CABBAGE COOKING:** Add a bit of vinegar to the water while boiling it.

- **DOGGIE DEODORANT:** In between baths, dust your dog with baking soda, leave it on 10 minutes or so, brush it out and enjoy a sweet-smelling dog.

- **DOWN/FEATHER-FILLED COMFORTERS, PILLOWS, ETC. MUSTY ODOR:** If tossing them in the dryer for a few minutes with a tennis ball and a dryer sheet using air but no heat doesn't work, find a professional cleaner who has the proper equipment to clean feather pillows and comforters. Not all do, so call first.

- **FIREPLACE ODORS:** Causes include creosote deposit buildup, soot, moisture, or animals caught in the flue and can also be due to the type of wood burned. Have a professional chimney sweep inspect and clean the chimney to determine the cause and solution.

- **FIREPLACE SMOKY ODOR:** If cleaning out all the ash from the fireplace doesn't remove the odor, shampoo carpeting; wash or dry-clean draperies/curtains; change filters in the furnace or air conditioner; and spray furniture with a fabric deodorant.

- **FISHY SMELL ON HANDS:**
1. At Home—Spritz hands with lemon or lime juice and wash.
2. On a Fishing Trip—Soak small hand towels in a mixture of lemon juice and water, put the wet towels in plastic self-sealing bags (two per bag) and store the bags in the freezer. Take as many bags as you think you'll need and put them in a cooler when you go fishing. At the end of the fishing day, the towels are thawed and ready to wipe away fish odors from hands and freshen your face, too.

- **FLOOR SAFE,** *Getting Rid of Musty Odors:* If keeping an open box of baking soda doesn't prevent musty odors, try silica gel available at craft stores, which are installed in cement floors.

- **FOOT ODOR,** *Prevention:*
1. Scrub feet with soap and water at least once daily and dry well. Follow washing with antiperspirant foot spray or powder.
2. Buy shoes made from either canvas or leather so that feet can "breathe" and perspiration is absorbed. And/or try wearing sandals.
3. During the day when feet feel hot and tired, spray with a little cologne. They will feel refreshed. If you have no cologne handy, wipe your feet with a packaged moist towelette. You can do this with panty hose still on.

- **GARBAGE DISPOSAL,** *Deodorizing:*
1. If it's a sturdy model, freeze vinegar and water into ice cubes and run cubes through the disposal.
2. Run a handful of lemon or lime peels followed by lots of cold water. My favorite!
3. Pour leftover drops of peppermint or other extracts down the disposal. **Note:** Please see KITCHEN SINK.

- **GARBAGE PAILS:** Place a fabric-softener sheet in the bottom of the pail before putting in the plastic garbage bag.

- **HANDS,** *Onions and Other Odors:* Rinse hands with mouthwash or scrub with toothpaste. And, next time, wear rubber gloves to avoid the problem.

- **KITCHEN GARBAGE CAN:** Sprinkle floral-scented carpet deodorizer in the bottom of the indoor kitchen garbage can to control odors.

- **KITCHEN SINK,** *Persistent Odor Even After Cleaning in and Under It:*
1. Buildup of bacteria in the drain can make the sink area smell. Pour some bleach down the sink and let sit for several hours to kill any bacteria that may be thriving there. Then run hot water for at least 60 seconds.
2. If you have a garbage disposal, unplug the unit and remove the rubber splash guard located in the sink drain. Wash it thoroughly,

especially the underside. Then run a lemon or orange rind through the disposal for a sweet-smelling sink.

3. Sink stoppers and splash guards are inexpensive and you may want to buy new ones; sometimes the rubber in old ones gets very grungy and harbors musty odors.

• **LAUNDRY,** *Getting a Fresh Fragrance:* Add 1 cup of vinegar to the final rinse water and laundry will be soft and fluffy as well has have a fresh, clean fragrance.

• **LUGGAGE, MUSTY ODOR FROM STORAGE:** Place a shallow box filled with cat-box litter deodorizer in the suitcase, close the lid, and wait twenty-four hours or longer. The litter should absorb the musty odor. You may want to also let the luggage sit outside, opened so that Mom Nature can finish the job for you. **Hint:** Avoid the problem by stuffing the suitcase with newspaper and a handful of fabric softener sheets before storing it and don't store luggage in damp places like basements or garages.

• **LUNCH BOX:** Dampen a piece of paper towel or stale bread with vinegar and put it in the lunch box overnight. Wash in the morning and it will smell fresh.

• **MATTRESS "ACCIDENT,"** *Removing Urine Odor:* Please see MATTRESS "ACCIDENT" in the Spots and Stains section.

• **MICROWAVE:** To remove cooking odors like those from fish, put 1 cup water, 6 whole cloves and half a lemon into a microwave-safe dish. Cook on "High" for about 3 to 5 minutes.

• **MOTHBALL ODOR,** *Removing from an Antique Dresser:* Try spraying evergreen-scented spray left over from Christmas into drawers; take them outdoors and leave in the fresh air for a day.

• **MOTHBALLS,** *Removing Odor:*
1. From Clothing—Allow to air outdoors if possible but don't hang non-colorfast garments or fabrics in the bright sun.
2. From Furniture—Place the chest or its drawers outside in the sun for several days to dissipate the odor. If that doesn't work, clean the inside with a wood cleaner found in hardware or home-improvement stores. Make sure wood is dry before you replace clothing.

3. From the House: Send draperies, bedding, and carpets to professional cleaners. Mattresses, upholstered items, suitcases, and other movable items can be placed outside in the sun to air. Leave doors and windows open; ceiling and oscillating fans may help push the odor out. Air fresheners throughout the house can mask the odor until it goes away but no matter what you do, expect the airing to take a long time.

• NATURAL GAS ODOR, *Checklist for Safety When You Smell a Leaky Gas Source:*
1. Check for the source—such as pilot lights of stove, water heater, whatever runs on gas.
2. Turn off the gas supply and open all windows to allow some of the gas to escape. **Caution:** Do not attempt to light a pilot light without letting gas escape. One of my secretaries didn't ventilate the room enough when she re-lit the pilot on her oven; there was enough gas still present to flare up and singe her bangs, eyebrows, and eyelashes!
3. If the gas odor is strong and you can't find the source, shut off the main gas valve; open windows and doors to ventilate the area; leave the house and call the gas company from a neighbor's house. Do not use light switches, electrical appliances, or even the doorbell—even a slight electric charge could cause a gas explosion. Certainly don't light matches, lighters, or candles to look for the leak! Gas leaks are extremely dangerous and it's best to have a professional deal with them.

• OIL ODOR IN CAR, *Quick-Fix:* Tuck a fabric-softener sheet under one of the front seats. This is not a permanent solution but will work for a while for dirty oil and some other odors. Try having the upholstery cleaned and keeping a sockful of charcoal in the car.

• ONION ODOR, *Avoiding It on Hands:* When you grate onions, put your onion-holder hand into a plastic bag and then when you are finished grating, put the bag around the onion without touching it. The onion is ready to cook and leftovers ready to refrigerate and your hands don't smell!

• ONIONS, *Removing Odor from Hands:* After peeling of slicing onions, sprinkle a bit of salt on your damp hands, work it over and rinse.

- **OVEN-CLEANER ODOR,** *Removing/Preventing:* Here's how to remove all of the oven-cleaner residue so that you don't get a terrible whiff of it the first time you heat up the clean oven.
1. After cleaning an oven with oven cleaner, spread a thick layer of newspapers on the oven floor.
2. With a spray bottle, spray warm water on the top and sides of the oven wall.
3. Dry the inside of the oven with a clean cloth then roll up the newspaper carefully and discard it.

- **OVEN SPILLS,** *Eliminating Burnt Odors and Smoke:* When food baking in the oven boils over, sprinkle a little salt on the burned goo. In addition to killing odor and smoke, it will be easier to wipe up the mess when you have finished baking. **Hint:** Avoid mess by placing a cookie sheet or foil piece under foods that are likely to spill over.

- **PET DEODORANT,** *Homemade "Doggie Spritzer":* Mix 32 ounces of water with two capfuls of your favorite fragrant bath oil and put the mixture into a spray bottle. Spray on pet's coat between baths and rub it in. **Caution:** Always clearly label bottles of homemade solutions.

- **PILLOWS,** *Freshening:* Toss bed pillows in the dryer air cycle with a fabric softener sheet for about 20 minutes to fluff and freshen them.

- **POTPOURRI,** *Expensive vs. Bargain Brands:* While room fresheners mask unpleasant odors, potpourri's function is to add pleasant fragrance to a room. Generally, the more expensive potpourri is made only from botanicals—dried flowers, leaves, pods, seeds, and other plant parts. Less expensive potpourri can be a combination of pine cones, acorns, sweet gumballs from a woods, dyed wood chips and sawdust, with added fragrances, cinnamon, dried orange and lemon peels and or scented wax chips. If all you want is the scent and don't care where it comes from, you'll wonder why you should pay $10 for a bag of scented wood chips in a boutique when you can get a bag of scented wood chips for $3.95 at a discount store. Like everything else, you need to read labels to get your money's worth. And, like so many "designer" luxuries, you can make homestyle substitutes for pennies.

1. To the water in your potpourri, you can add the remaining drops of your favorite perfume (rinse out the bottle with alcohol and pour into potpourri water).
2. Or mix up combinations of orange or lemon peels, cinnamon sticks, allspice (or simmer some poultry seasoning for a Thanksgiving fragrance) according to "taste."

• **POTPOURRI**, *Heloise Formula for Wet Potpourri:* Gather 2 cups of rose petals, 2 cups of rosemary, 2 cups of mint, four cinnamon sticks, ½ cup of whole allspice, and two whole cloves. Place all ingredients in a large jar and cover with heated white vinegar. Let the jar sit for about a week, then place some of the potpourri in a simmering pot. **Hint:** Experiment with different mixtures to find your favorite fragrance.

• **POTPOURRI**, *Substitute "Cookers":*
1. Put potpourri in the portable vaporizer/humidifier water compartment.
2. Simmer potpourri in a mug or old gift cheese crock placed on a coffee-cup warmer.
3. Nuke a bowl of water and potpourri in the microwave.

• **REFRIGERATOR DEODORIZER:**
1. Keep a tried-and-true box of baking soda in the fridge and every few months, replace it. Pour the used baking soda down the sink to freshen it or put the baking soda into the bottom of a cat litter box.
2. When you move or put a refrigerator or freezer in storage even for a short time, place a sock filled with dry coffee grounds or charcoal to prevent musty odors.

• **REFRIGERATOR ODOR FROM SPOILED MEAT:** If washing the inside with baking soda doesn't work, put dry coffee grounds on a couple of paper plates and set them on different shelves. The odor should go away in two or three days.

• **ROOM DEODORIZER MUSHROOMS**, *Recycling by Renewing the Scent:* Put a few drops of a liquid deodorizer or your favorite perfume on top of the "mushroom."

• **ROOM DEODORIZER VACUUMING:** Place a scented fabric softener sheet between the inner and outer vacuum bags or into the bag of an upright vacuum cleaner to put a pleasant scent of fresh laundry in the room when you vacuum. The scented softener sheet can be used for several weeks.

• **ROOM FRAGRANCE FROM FIREPLACE:** Sprinkle herbs—fresh or dried—cinnamon sticks, or spices on a small, gently burning fireplace fire to make a room smell festive. Or you can buy bags of scented chips in hardware stores to make the house smell spicy and sweet.

• **RUBBER GLOVES,** *To Prevent Odors:* If you don't like to sprinkle talcum powder or baking soda inside, try this: After you've finished a chore, dry your rubber gloves (outside surface) while they are still on, then pull them off so they turn inside out. The fingers usually stay stuck in, so cuff the end of the glove and blow it up like a balloon. Hang the inside-out gloves on a towel rack to air-dry. To wear, "cuff and puff" again to blow them right-side-out.

• **RUBBER GLOVES,** *Sweet Smelling:* Sprinkle a bit of baking soda or talcum powder into rubber gloves to help them glide on and off and smell better.

• **SHOES:** Sprinkle a little baking soda in shoes at night after removing them and let it set overnight. In the morning, sprinkle the soda into the bathroom sink or commode to recycle this wonderful deodorizer.

• **SLEEPING BAGS:** To prevent musty odors in sleeping bags, lay fabric softener sheets on the bag and roll them up with the bag for storage.

• **TOBACCO SMOKE,** *Stale Room Odor:* Put about a capful of ammonia in a bowl of water and leave it out overnight (out of reach of children and pets) and the stale smoke odor will be gone in the morning.

• **VACUUM-CLEANER BAG,** *Healthy-Planet Air Freshener:* Add to the bag any of the following fresheners to prevent that stale musty odor that can come from the vacuum cleaner "exhaust"—a few whole cloves, carpet freshener or baking soda, a cotton ball sprayed with your favorite perfume or dabbed with peppermint or almond extract.

- **WATER BED:** If the plastic is the problem, try washing the "mattress" with baking soda and water. Bacteria growth in the water inside the mattress also can cause odors; ask at a water-bed shop for a commercial product to cure odors.

Heloise's column "Hints from Heloise" is syndicated in over five hundred newspapers internationally; in addition, she writes a monthly column for *Good Housekeeping*.